CALENDAR OF WILLS

ON FILE AND RECORDED IN THE OFFICES OF THE CLERK OF THE COURT OF APPEALS, OF THE COUNTY CLERK AT ALBANY, AND OF THE SECRETARY OF STATE : : : : : :

1626–1836

(? I don't see any before 1664 & maybe not before 1674.

COMPILED AND EDITED BY

BERTHOLD FERNOW

LATE STATE ARCHIVIST OF NEW YORK

7/2002

UNDER THE AUSPICES OF THE COLONIAL DAMES OF THE STATE OF NEW YORK, AND PUBLISHED BY THE SOCIETY : : : :

CLEARFIELD

Originally Published
New York, 1896

Reprinted
Genealogical Publishing Company
Baltimore, 1967

Reprinted for
Clearfield Company, Inc. by
Genealogical Publishing Co., Inc.
Baltimore, Maryland
1991, 1999

Library of Congress Catalogue Card Number 67-28621
International Standard Book Number: 0-8063-0110-4

Made in the United States of America

PREFACE.

THE manner in which the intentions of deceased persons, expressed in their last wills, are carried out, or rather in which these intentions are legalized, is *sui generis* in the State of New York, which as a Colony was first governed under Roman-Dutch law, and it seems appropriate that a volume which gives abstracts of wills, made in Colonial days, as well as after the organization of the State, should have a history of the legal proceedings to which last wills were and are subjected as

INTRODUCTION.

According to "The Roman Law of Testaments, Codicils," etc., by Moses A. Dropsie, the form, "last will and testament," almost universally used, and the term "will" for "testament," are incorrect, because the Roman Law, from which testamentary disposition of property was embodied into the common law, only knew the term *testamentum*, and never employed the words *ultima voluntas* or *voluntas*.

It is not intended to take issue on this question here, but simply to tell what was done at different phases of the history of New York, to give legal force to the last wishes of a deceased person concerning his or her property.

New York having first been settled by the Dutch, the Roman-Dutch law regulated the making of testamentary disposition of property. It allowed such dispositions to be made in two ways, *i. e.*, orally or in writing. A party made a last will orally, or by word of mouth ("which kind of last will is mostly in use among us," says van Leeuwen in his *Roman-Dutch Law*), by telling two members of the local Court, respectively an Alderman and the Secretary, or a notary before two witnesses, how the property, owned by the testator, was to be divided among the heirs; the notary reduced these intentions to writing, put the notes into proper shape, and having read the same over to the testator and witnesses, asked the former, in the presence of the latter, whether he or she understood the nature of the document and whether what was taken down was the testator's wish and last will. In confirmation of it the testator, the witnesses, and the notary then subscribed the writing, of which the notary made a record in his official minutes, so that, if required, he could give a copy of it. Wills were made in this way for many years after the Colony was governed by English laws, as No. 1 (A 1) shows, which at the same time was proved according to the Duke's Laws.

A will in writing, also called a *close* will, was one whereby the testator had expressed his intentions in writing, and, having subscribed and sealed it, had handed the same so closed to a notary in the presence of two witnesses, declaring at the same time that the writing contained his or her testament. The document was then endorsed by the notary as "The testament of N. N.," an official minute of the transaction was made, and the testator and witnesses subscribed it. This latter way of making a last will seems to have been the custom during the Dutch period of the Colony of New York, for in no other way can we account for the small number of wills, antedating the year 1664, found in the official records of the Courts and of the various notaries of Dutch times.

Both kinds of testaments, oral as well as close, being invariably made before judicial officers, did not require proof and probate, which came in with the English occupation in 1664.

The English conquerors brought with them

the Code of Laws, called the "Duke's Laws," which say, under the article *Administration*: "Vpon the Death of Any P^r^son the Constable with two Overseers of the Parish shall repare to the House of the Deceased Party to Enquire after the manner of his Death and of his Will and Testament. . . . That noe Administracon be granted until the Second Sessions after the Party's Decease, (except) to the Widdow or Child, Brother or Sister, to whom it may be imediately granted. The said Widdow, Child, Brother or Sister bringing sufficient Security for the p^r^forming of all things the Law requires. . . . If any Executors nominated in the Will and knoweing there of shall not prove the same at the Next Court of Sessions which shall bee about thirty Days after the Decease of the P^r^ty or shall not cause the same to be Recorded by the recorder or Clerke of that Court . . . Every such P^r^son . . . shall be liable to be sued. . . . That the Clerke of the Sessions, when he Carryes the Probates or Commissions of Admicon to be Signed Doe then also certifie into the Recorder's Office att New Yorke the name of the Testator or the Party Deceased. . . . Wills to be proved and Admicon granted in Sessions if the Estate be vnder the Value of one hundered pounds shall pay one shilling, if hundered pounds five shillings, and soe Propotionable five shillings for Each hundered pounds towards the Defraying of Court Charges."

This law distinctly says, a will was to be proved in the Court of Sessions, but the minutes of the Court of Assizes, then not only the highest Court of the Colony, but also vested with legislative authority, tell, under November 2, 1667: "This day the will of William Ludlam was proved in court;" on November 4, 1667, the same Court granted letters of administration on the estate of Samuel Andrews, lying in Oysterbay and Horseneck, L. I., to John Richbell, of Momoronock, "on behalf of Johanna, the widow of Nicholas Davison, and Richard Russell, of Charles Towne, Mass." We further read in the minutes of this Court for its session of October 7, 1668: "Capt. Thomas Exton's will was proved and ye Exect^{rs} allowed of," "Charles Morgan, his will was proved and the Executrix allowed of," "William How, his will was formerly proved in the Mayors Court, the Executors allowed of," "Letters of Administration granted to Mary, the widow and Relict of Robert Seely."

It seems evident, that at that time no distinction was made between the terms of *proving* and *probating* * a testament, although the latter was exercised, as the above quoted reference to the will of William How shows, by the highest Court, which then performed the duties of the later established Prerogative Court. This Prerogative Court had its beginning, as far as the Province of New York was concerned, in the following section of the Instructions given to Governour Dongan, May 29, 1686: "§ 35. And to the End the Ecclesiastical Jurisdiction † of the said Archbishop of Canterbury may take place in that Our Province as farr as conveniently may bee We doe think fitt that you give all Countenance and encouragement in y[e] exercise of the same; excepting only the Collating of Benefices, granting licenses for Marriage and Probat of Wills, which we have reserved to you Our Governour & to y[e] Commander-in-chief for the time being." The same instructions were given to the succeeding Governours, but it is evident from a letter, written by Governour

* According to Abbott's *Law Dictionary*, to *probate* meant the approval of the sufficiency of the will by the proper Court, *i.e.*, in English times the Prerogative Court, while to *prove* a will was to establish by evidence or submit a will with testimony of witnesses as to execution to a Court of proper jurisdiction.

† In England, prior to 1857, probate jurisdiction was in the ecclesiastical court of the Archbishop of Canterbury, and hence the Bishop's Mitre in the seal.

Lord Bellomont to the Lords of Trade and Plantations, May 15, 1699, that the fees from this source of revenue were not large, for he says: "In thirteen months that I have been here, I have got but £83. 6/ N. Y. money (\$208,$\frac{25}{00}$) from the Secretary for passes for Ships, Licenses for Marriages and Probats of Wills and all other things, wherein the Seal of the Province was used."

In the meantime, the first General Assembly of the Province had on the 11th of November, 1692, passed a law regulating the proving of wills, that is the verification by the witnesses of the testator's signature and their own. This law directed that wills relating to estates in Orange, Richmond, Westchester, and Kings Counties be proved in New York. In the other Counties the Court of the Common Pleas, or if the Court was not in session, the Judge of the Court, assisted by two Justices of the Peace, was to examine the witnesses and certify the examinations to the Secretary's office, whereupon the Governour, sitting as Judge of the Prerogative Court, granted his *Probat*. The Common Pleas, consisting of the Judge and Justices of the Peace, were, however, authorized to grant the *probat* where estates were less than £50. This law was amended November 24, 1750, in so far that the

Judges, Justices, and Clerk of Common Pleas for Orange Co. were also empowered "to take the probate of wills and grant letters of administration." The Prerogative Court had also been established, as an "Account of all Establishments of Jurisdictions in New York Province"* tells us: "The Governour discharges the place of Ordinary in granting administracons and proveing Wills and the Secretary is Register. The Governour is about to appoint Delegates in the remoter parts of the government with Supervisors looking after intestates estates and provideing for Orphans."

The Governours went further than appointing "Delegates for the remoter parts of the government," they appointed the Secretary and his Deputy, Surrogates, or Deputy Judges of the Prerogative Court. The result is described as follows in a letter from Governour, Sir Henry Moore, to the Lords of Trade, June 12, 1766: "The Secretary of this Province and his Deputy have been frequently appointed by the Governour's Surrogates, so that the whole business of the office has been in their hands. Upon this they have taken upon themselves an Authority wh[ch] they are not vested with without being appointed Surrogates and have

* *N. Y. Col. History*, iv., 28.

granted probates upon Wills sent up out of the Country, which were proved there, without consulting the Governour or making him acquainted with any such transactions, by which means they would wrest from him the power expressly given by his Maj[y] in his Instructions." Sir Henry appointed Philipp Livingston, Junior, as principal Surrogate and Register of the Prerogative Court, but thereby also involved himself in a quarrel with the Secretary of the Province, which continued for several years after his death in September, 1769, and was not settled until the last Royal Governour, Tryon, could report in 1774, "The Prerogative Court concerns itself only in the Probate of Wills, in matters relating to the administration of Intestates' Estates and granting Marriage Licenses. The Governour is properly the Judge of this Court, but usually acts by Deligate." This procedure continued in the parts of the Province, held by the English, until 1783, while the new Constitution of the State of New York, adopted in 1777, recognized a Judge of the Court of Probates, and the law, passed March 16, 1778,* directed: "The Judge of the Court of Probates of this State shall be vested with all and singular the powers and authorities and have the like jurisdiction in

* *Greenleaf*, chap. XII.

testamentary matters, which, while the State, as the Colony of New York, was subject to the Crown of Great Britain, the Governour or the Commander-in-Chief of the Colony for the time being had and exercised as Judge of the Prerogative Court: Except as to the nomination and appointment of Surrogates in the several Counties, who shall be nominated and appointed by the Council of appointment and commissioned under the Great Seal: And that all letters of administration to be granted by the said Judge . . . shall be tested in the name of the Judge of the said Court."

"From this date," says Judge Charles P. Daly,* "to 1789 this new tribunal, the Court of Probates, continued to exercise the same jurisdiction as the Prerogative Court formerly had done. The proofs of wills, where the deceased had effects in more than one County, were taken before the Judge of this Court, and before the Surrogate, where the effects were exclusively in one County; and in both cases the proof of the will was 'approved and allowed' in the name of the people before the Court of Probates, where it was recorded."

The law of February 20, 1787, "for set-

Nature, Extent and History of the Jurisdiction of the Surrogates Courts.

tling intestate estates, proving wills, etc.," had in the meantime curtailed the powers of this Court, by taking away from it the granting of probates and letters of administration, which, except in certain specified cases, was conferred upon the Surrogates of the different Counties. The Constitution of 1821 provided for the election of officers to perform the duties of Surrogate in Counties having a population of more than forty thousand; and in keeping with this mandate of the Constitution the Legislature of 1823 abolished the Court of Probates altogether,* and granted its powers to the Surrogates of the different Counties, who were to be appointed by the Governour like other judicial officers.

The Revised Statutes† define the powers of the Surrogate as follows: Art. I., § 7, "When any real estate shall be devised by will, any executor or devisee named therein . . . may have such will proved before the Surrogate of the County to whom the probate of the will of the testator would belong"; and Art. II., § 23, says: "The Surrogate of each County shall have sole and exclusive power, within the County, for which he may have been appointed (or, as now, elected), to take proofs of last wills and

* Chapter LXX. of 1823.

† First Edition, 1829, chap. VI., title 1.

testaments so far as the same relates to personal property of all deceased persons."

A law "for the more speedy recovery of legacies," passed by the General Assembly of the Province in 1743, authorized any person, entitled to a legacy under a will, to bring action against the executor or administrator, after it became due, etc., in the Supreme Court, and in this way, whatever powers were not conferred upon Surrogates, devolved upon the Supreme Court, until the Statutes were revised in 1829. The wills, marked as recorded in Volumes IV. and V., are proved in the Supreme Courts at Albany and Utica.

Although the Legislature ordered in 1799, that all wills, on file in the State Court of Probates, and relating to property in what was then called the Southern Senatorial District, should be transferred to New York City, that law, it will be seen, was only carelessly carried out, for this Calendar brings to light many wills of New York City, Westchester County, and Long Island.

In making these abstracts of wills the editor has been obliged to follow the arrangement of the files of wills in the office of the Clerk of the Court of Appeals, which is by the letters of the alphabet and chronological, but, as it will be seen, neither strictly alphabetical nor strictly chronological. To facilitate the finding of an original will the letter and number of each file is given with the date of execution and of proof.

The original spelling of names has been scrupulously adhered to, and whatever oddities and variations may be found in this regard are not the fault of

THE EDITOR.

CALENDAR OF WILLS.

---

1 (A 1) 1679 June 30 Novbr. 4 Dutch

AERTSEN, Rutt, of Albany, shoemaker, born at Twent te Denekamp, Brother Jan Scholten, sisters Gebbeke and Aeltie Aertsen, children of deceased brothers Lambert and Aleph Aertsen, all of Twent. Personal property. Executor Adriaen Gerritsen van Papendorp. Witnesses Andries Teller, Johannes Provoost, Magistrates and Adriaen van Ilpendam, Notary. Also in Albany Co. Records, Notarial Papers, II, p. 97, and Proceedings of Magistrates 1676–80, p. 475.

2 (A 2) 1683 July 27

ADRIANS, Joost, of Bushwick, L. I. Wife Mary Hay sole heiress. No executor named. Will not signed nor proved.

3 (A 3) 1701 May 5

AIGRON, Claudius, mariner of the brigantine Ann of New York, Michael Basset, Captain. Samuel Bourdet of N. Y., mariner, Mr. Garnier of London, instrumentmaker, Daniel Robert of London, mariner, and Pour Perot of London, robbmaker. Personal property. Executor Daniel Robert. Witnesses I. Rolland and Michael Bassett. Last paragraph in French. No evidence of proof.

4 (A 4) 1710 June 26 1711 March 31

ABEEL, John, of Albany. Wife Catharina, children Christopher, Catharina, Neeltie and David. Real and personal estate. Executors the wife with Gerardus Beeckman, Gerrit Duyckingh, Evert Banker and Myndert Schuyler, who shall continue to act as executors after the wife's remarriage. Witnesses David Jamison, Wm. Huddlestone, Ino. Macdenan. Proved before Governour Hunter.

5 (A 5) 1745 Nov. 25 **ABLIN, John,** of ? Wife Elizabeth heiress and executrix of real and personal property. Witnesses Jacob Dempe, Grace Beekman, who at the proving of the will before G. Banyar, Dep. Secretary of the Province on October 10, 1757, has become the wife of Jacob Dempe, and Henry de Foreest.

6 (A 6) 1748 April 20 **ALLISON, Richard,** of Haverstraw, Orange Co., yeoman. " Hannah Hubbs, the daughter of Phebe Hubbs the wife of Robert Hubbs and likewise the child of the wife of Robert Hubbs she is now big with." Executors brother John Allison and Joshua Taylor, who with Hannah Taylor are also witnesses. See No. 7.

7 (A 7) 1749 Jany. 9 1750 Aug. 9 **ALLISON, Richard,** of Haverstraw, Orange Co., Doctor (?), leaves all his real estate to his father, legacies to Phebe Hubs, her daughter Hannah and son Richard, to brothers Benjamin, John, William, Joseph, Elizabeth Cuyper, Deborah Janson, Mary Degroat and Hannah Taylor. Executors John Allison, father and John Allison, brother. Contest over will shows testator to have been dead January 28, 1750. Witnesses Nicolas Kupper junior, Elizabeth Hutchings, Cornelius Cuyper.

8 (A 8) 1750 Decbr. 29 1764 Septbr. 18 **ARNOLD, Henry,** of New York, mariner. Wife Sarah and child or children, which she may bear to testator are heirs of all personal estate. Executors the wife and Thomas Duncan of New York, merchant. Witnesses Rebeker Shourt, Jane Deky and James Emott. Codicil dated September 4, 1764, directs executors to sell farms in Dutchess Co., N. Y., and at Shrewsbury, N. J., and gives legacies to nephew Henry Arnold, son of brother John, to children of sister Susannah Marsh and to sister-in-law Hilah Dekay, wife Sarah to be residuary legatee. Executors the wife and James Sacket. Witnesses Mary Ludlow, Margt. Parks and Cary Ludlow.

9 (A 9) 1752 Octbr. 17. 1755 Decbr. 15

ALLISON, Joseph, of Goshen, Orange Co. Sons Isaac and William are bequeathed 50 acres of Seder (sic) Swamp in the Drowned Lands Wawayanda Patent and £200 New York Currency, daughters Elizabeth, Sarah and Pheby receive personal property, sons Benjamin and Cornelius the remaining land in Cedar Swamp, Wawayanda Patent, eldest son Joseph a walking cane, son Richardson two *armed* chairs and with Thomas wearing apparel, grandson Nathan £25 New York Currency, to go, if he should die before coming of age to Ann Thomson and Margret Bradner, granddaughter Mary Horton is given £8. Executors sons Joseph and Richard. Witnesses Michael Jackson, Samuel Wickham and Francis Drack. Proved before William ffinn, Surrogate of Orange County, vide No. 7.

10 (A 10) 1753 Jany. 14 Decbr. 18

ALBERTSON, Richard, of Ulster County. Wife Sarah, sons Steven, Richard and William, daughters Susannah, Mary, Sarah, Elizabeth and Deborah. Real and personal estate. Executors Alexander Colden and Samuel Fowler. Witnesses Michal Demot, Sarah Demot and Jno. Bickerton. Proved before the Deputy Secretary.

11 (A 11) 1754 June 6 Octbr. 21

ALLISON, John, of Haverstraw, Orange Co. Son Benjamin is bequeathed one third of a meadow and 100 acres on Kaciot Road, adjoining Widow Conklin on the south, also 100 acres near Lewis van Ditmash on Menesalongo Brook; son John, having received his share in land before, is given six shillings; son Joseph receives the farm testator lives on, purchased from Albert Minard and others, bounded north and east by Hudsons River, out of which he is to pay to his brother William and William's son Edward £150 in four years; daughters Elizabeth Cooper, Deborah Johnson, Hannah Taylor and Mary Degrough receive money; Phebe Hubbs, her daughter Hannah and Presila and Presila's unborn child are legatees; son William to have all rights, title and interest to and in lands on Long Island. Executors John Palmer, John Johnson and John Peaterson Smith. Witnesses Joshua Seaman, Cornelius Seaman and Isaac Davis.

12 (A 12) 1754 March 16 1764 Decbr. 28 **ADRIANSEN, Abraham**, of Rombouts Precinct, Dutchess Co., yeoman. Wife Femmetje, son John, children by first wife, viz., son Ram and daughter Femmetje. Real and personal property. Executors the wife and brother Ellebert and Jores Adriansen. Witnesses Henry, Johannes and Jacob Wiltse. Proved in the Court of Common Pleas for Dutchess Co.

13 (A 13) 1757 Aug. 20 1762 Decbr. 30 **AMORY, John,** of New York, mariner and part owner of the ship King William III. Wife Mary, son John, Hester Rynders, daughter of wife by former husband. Personal and real estate, including a house on the Fly Market and 2000 acres, bought from Lawrence van Kleck and wife Jaepie. Executors the wife, Hester Rynders, brother-in-law John Cuyler and James van Cortlandt. Witnesses Whitehead Hicks, Balthaz Kip, Samuel Dodge.

14 (A 14) 1757 Novbr. 8 Decbr. 5 **ALLISON, Thomas,** of Orange Co. Wife ——, children George, Richard, Mary and Thomas. Real and personal property. Executors brothers Joseph and Richard. Witnesses John Allison, Richard Westcott, William Denn.

15 (A 15) 1758 Aug. 5 Novbr. 21 **ADRIANCE, Jores,** of Rombouts Precinct, Dutchess Co., yeoman. Wife Phebe, sons Ellebert, Cornelius, Jores, Theodorus and daughter Sarah. Eldest son Ellebert to have family bible and *sarm*-book of mother's. Real and personal estate. Executors brothers Abraham and Isaac Adriance and brothers-in-law Richard van Wyck and Cornelius van Wyck. Witnesses Pouwel van der Woort, Gerrit Storm and Isaac Lent.

16 (A 16) 1762 Aug. 22 Octbr. 30 **ADAMS, James,** of Albany City, carman. Wife Margaret, sons William, Lambertus, daughter Margaret. Personal and real estate. Executors the wife, Lambertus Beecker and John Johannes Lansing. Witnesses Jakobis Hylton, Johannes van Sante jun., Ja. Stevenson.

17 (A 17) 1762 May 27 Octbr. 23 **ASHE, Dudley,** Lieutenant Royal or First Regiment of Foot. Leaves all his effects in the West Indies to Ensign Thomas Keating, later Lieutenant, 42d Regiment. No executors named. Witnesses Charles Forbes (Captain 42d Regiment) and Robert Cooke. The whole will contains with signatures only 43 words.

18 (A 18) 1763 Septbr. 12 1764 June 18 **ALLISON, John,** of Floraday, Goshen Precinct, Orange Co., husbandman. Sons John, Henry and Richard, daughters Keziah, Elizabeth and Bridget. Real and personal property. Executors brother Richard Allison and John Wisner. Witnesses John Sutton and Caleb Wyley.

19 (A 19) 1763 Decbr. 22 1770 Octbr. 15 **ALLISON, Richardson,** of Goshen Precinct. Wife Ann, son James, and daughter Phebe. Real and personal property. Executors brother Richard Allison and James Howell. Witnesses Michael Jackson, Joseph Allison and Cornelius Allison.

20 (A 20) 1764 Decbr. 3 1765 April 1 **ARDEN, James,** of New York City, tallow-chandler. Children Elizabeth, Samuel and Mary receive all property, except £10 going to Thomas Yarrel, Minister of the Breathren Church (Unitas fratrum, or Moravian). Brother John Arden to be guardian of the children, brother Thomas Arden and Elizabeth Arden to be executors. Witnesses Elizabeth Arden and Samuel Arden. Handwriting sworn to by Jacob Arden of New York, butcher, brother of testator.

21 (A 21) 1764 May 29 July 9 **AYRES, Enos,** of Blooming Grove, Orange Co. Leaves to wife Martha, daughters Martha and Mary his farm and some land on Southside of Wawayanda Road as well as personal estate with remainder in case of death before the daughters are of age or are married to Martin Ayres of New Jersey, son of brother David, and sons of brother Daniel. Executors Hezekiah Howell and Jesse Woodhull. Witnesses Michael Jackson, John Smith and Silas Youngs.

22 (A 22) 1764 March 20 June 10 **ARNOUT, Peter,** of Goshen, Orange Co., gives to his son Cornelius lot No. 5 West Division of Goshen, to sons Jacob, Peter, Cornelius and John lot No. 6, to son William 2 acres of bog meadow on northwest corner of lot 6, to son-in-law Gilbert Veal a house and land for seven years, to wife Lena and daughters Mary, Deborah, Hannah and Lydia personal property. Executors the wife and son William. Witnesses Daniel Hulse, Mary Hulse and Wm. Denn.

23 (A 23) 1765 Septbr. 18 **ABEEL, David,** junior, and wife Neeltie, of the Bacoven, Albany County, give to sons Anthony and Gerret, daughters Annatie and another born on the date hereof all right, title, etc., at the Backoven, formerly occupied by Nicolas Brandow, Peter Sax and Wilhelmus Osterhout, lot on north side of the Cattskil Creek, opposite Benjamin Dubois and right, title, etc., in the Patent of Femmenhoek, in the Patent of Cattskil, as devised by Gerret van Bergen to his children, the share of any of testators children dying to go to Deborah, daughter of Wilhelmus van Bergen deceased, Catharina, daughter of William van Bergen and John, the son of John Persen, provided they pay £30 to Rev. John Schuneman for the use of the Reformed Church at Cattskil. Executors and guardians of the children William van Bergen and Henry Oothout. Witnesses Wilhelmus Osterhout, Anna Maria Schuneman, Metje Osterhout and Annatie van Bergen. No certificate of proof.

24 (A 24) 1766 Decbr. 1 1767 May 6

AUSTEN, Jonathan, of Philipps Patent, Dutchess Co., yeoman. Wife ——, and children Isaac, Jonathan, Silas, Smith, Phebe, Job, Ann, Robert and Rebecker. Real and personal estate. Executors brother John Austen and William Nelson. Witnesses William Youmans, Samuel Haight and Francis Barger.

25 (A 25) 1767 Octbr. 23 Novbr. 10

ALLISON, Richard, of Goshen Precinct, Orange Co., yeoman. Wife Martha, sons Joseph, John and William, daughters Elizabeth, Martha and Margret. Lands on Chambers Ditch. Executors brother-in-law John Wells and son-in-law Samuel Carpenter. Witnesses James Carpenter, James Ryan and Timothy Owen.

26 (A 26) 1768 May 20 1769 March 1

ACKERMAN, Nicolas, of Orange Town, Orange Co. Wife Elcia, sons Johannes, William, David, daughters Maria, wife of Ellebert Onderdonk and Annatie inherit all real and personal property. Executors John Haring and David Benceman (?) Demarest. Witnesses Arie Koonyn (of Orange Co., wheelwright), Abraham Kip and Abraham Haring.

27 (A 27) 1772 June 20 1773 Novbr. 11

ALLEN, William, of Charlotte Precinct, Dutchess Co., yeoman, leaves to wife Mary, daughters Sarah Aursyonche, wife of Benjamin Height, Hester, Elizabeth and Hannah personal property, to son John 100 acres, being one third of all my lands, described only by lines, to son Joseph another third and to son William the remaining 100 acres, adjoining Wm. Bedell. Richard Dogg is bequeathed the rest and residue of my personal estate, not given away before. Executors the wife, son John and Zacheus Newcomb. Witnesses Peter Germond, Benjn. de la Vergne, Zacharias Flagler.

28 (A 28) 1772 June 6 July 2

ALLISON, Joseph, of Goshen Precinct, Orange Co., leaves to son Richard home farm of 50 acres and a lot of 32 acres adjoining John and William Allison, to son Joseph 118 acres adjoining son Richard's, to both a lot of cedar swamp; to wife Abigale and daughters Deborah and Mary personal property. Executors brother Nathaniel Roe and cousin James Sawyer. Witnesses John Conner, William Allison, John Allison.

29 (A 29) 1775 April 2 May 23 **ALDRICH, Peter,** of Southold, Suffolk Co., leaves all real and personal property to wife Phebe, sons Garshem and Enos and grandson Peter. Witnesses David Terry, David Terry junior, of Suffolk Co., yeomen, and David Wells. Letters testamentary granted to widow Phebe Aldrich, Aug. 3, 1775.

30 (A 30) 1776 May 20 1779 Jany. 22 **ACKERMAN, David,** of Poughkeepsie Precinct, Dutchess Co., bequeaths to wife Sarah, daughters Carrebrach and Magdalen personal property, to son Andrees a farm in Hackinsack, Bergen Co., N. J., to daughter Magdalon 30 acres of the homefarm in Dutchess Co., on Great Wappinger Creek, to daughter Annatje 30 acres adjoining Magdalen's, to son David all the remainder of the farm. The wife is made sole executrix. Witnesses Joseph Theal, Cornelius Bower, James Wills.

31 (A 31) 1776 March 12 Aug. 31 **ALLEN, Asa,** of Charlotte Precinct, Dutchess Co. Wife Anna, daughters Rhoda and Anna, sons Ezra, Abraham, James, Asa. Real and personal estate. Executors the wife and son Asa. Witnesses Elijah Tenny, Jonah Tallmedge, Enos Tallmadge.

32 (A 32) 1777 April 11 1782 Jan. 11 **AKIN, Elisha,** of Paulings Precinct, Dutchess Co., gives to wife Sarah, sons Abraham and Murray, daughters Ruth Sheldon, Sarah Briggs, Margaret Akin and Olive Akin, personal property and to sons Thomas, Timothy and James real estate. The right to lands in the New Hampshire grants to be equally divided between all children. Executors "my friends" Jonathan Akin and Timithy Akin. Witnesses Edward Briggs, Wilber (Wilhem ?) Wood, Murray Lester.

33 (A 33) 1778 April 15 1781 Aug. 21 **ARDEN, Jacob,** *at present* of Kakeat, State of N. Y., butcher. Wife Catharine, son Jacob, daughters Abijah, wife of George Wilt, Elizabeth wife of George Leaycraft, and Catharine. Real and personal estate. Executors the wife and kinsman Thomas Arden. Witnesses Jonah Hallsted, Viner Leaycraft, John Leaycraft.

34 (A 34) 1779 Octbr. 1 1782 Novbr. 7 **ALLISON, John.** Wife Amey, children John, Elizabeth, Thomas, Richard, Margaret, William, Joseph, Issac, Jeremiah and Benjamin. "All my estate." Executor John Robart. Witnesses John Dunscomb jr., William Sloo, Charity Sloo. Proved in Dutchess Co.

35 (A 35) 1781 Septbr. 1 1783 Feb. 25 **ARMSTRONG, Francis,** of Orange Co. Wife Martha, sons William, Francis, David, Archibald, John, grandsons Francis, David's son, Robert, William's son, daughters Elcey, Mary and Elizabeth, and the six children of deceased son Robert. Real and personal estate. Executors sons William and Francis. Witnesses Thomas Jackson, Samuel Newman, William Carr.

36 (A 36) 1781 (?) July 5 1784 July 5 **ALWORTH, William,** of Nobeltown, Albany Co. Sister Sarah Alworth and son Thomas. Real and personal property. Executors Seth Pettit, Peter Stulp and Matthew Krum. Witnesses Jonathan Rude, Mary Bigsby, Sarah Alworth.

37 (A 37) 1783 July 16 1784 Jany. 9 **ALEXANDER, James,** of New Perth, Charlotte Co., N. Y. Wife Catharine, son James and daughter Jenny, grandson Joseph Alexander, negro slave Ebenezer Place, manumitted. Real and personal estate. Executors John Gray senior, and Edward Savage. Witnesses Matthew McWhorter, James McWhorter, Zurishadhai Doty.

38 (A 38) 1785 May 12 1786 Aug. 23 **ALWORTH, James,** of Amenia, Dutchess Co. Wife Mary, sons James, William and Thomas, daughters Sarah wife of Barnabas Cole, Rebecca, wife of Matthew

Stephens, children of Mary, wife of Seth Class, and Martha Alworth, children of daughter Alice deceased, viz., William, James, Mary, Joseph and Alice Conner. Lands in lot No. 36 Great Nine Partners and in New Marlborough, Berkshire Co., Mass. Executor son James. Witnesses Silas Roe, of Dutchess Co., farmer, Obed Harvey junior, and Barnabas Payen.

38a 1635 June 12 Dutch

ADRIAENSEN, Annegen Jans, widow of Hendrick, of Laeckervelt, assisted by Schout Roeloff Dirkxen Stout, of Laeckervelt. Son Adrian Hendricksen, da. Maeycken Hendricx. Land at Scherpenwyck, District of Laeckervelt, personal property. Witnesses Roeloff Stout, Adriaen Cornelissen and Adriaen Jansen Brouwer, Schepens. Extract or copy made September 7, 1647. Albany Co. Records, Notarial Papers, I., p. 423.

39 1775 April 22 1785 Aug. 3

ACKLEY, Anthony, of New York City, cooper. Wife Hannah, sons John, Anthony, Daniel, daughters Elizabeth, Catharine and Hannah. House and lot on Crown Street, lease of house and lot in the West Ward on Barclay Street being part of Church Farm, and personal property. Executors the wife, Benjamin Huggit of New York City, bolter, and Stephen Terhane of New York City, painter. Witnesses David Brown, James Shaw, John Young. Recorded in Wills and Probates, I., 131.

40 1792 April 14 1793 April 2

ABRAHAMS, Isaac, of New York City, baker, going to the South Seas on board the brigantine Minerva, Captain Williams. Widow Dorothy Johnson sole heiress and executrix. Real and personal estate. Witnesses Abraham Brevoort, Francis Childs, Francis Childs junior. Recorded ut supra, p. 392.

41 1794 Aug. 27 1795 Septbr. 9, at London

AXTELL, William, of Cherssey Parish, County of Surry, England, gentleman. Daughter Mary by Susannah Nicholl of Watford, Hertfordshire; Cecilia, daughter of William and Susanna Watson, now nine years old; William Watson, Elizabeth, daughter of Rebecca

Shipton; Elizabeth Lewis, waiting maid; Mary Ann, daughter of Mary Morgan, now nine years old; Henry Matthews, my servant lad; Rebecca Gorring, my servant maid. Real estate in England and Island of Jamaica, personal property. Mary Nicholl sole executrix. Witnesses James Goldhawk, John Giles, Wm. Souch. Recorded ut supra, II., p. 162.

42 1812 May 24 1823 Octbr. 21 **ARCHER, George,** of Albany. Wife Mary, sons John, Edward, William, James, George and Michael, daughter Jane. House, store and lots on Pine Street, corner Eagle, Albany, yellow store and three lots on Eagle Street, binding on Lutheran, lot corner Eagle and Steuben Streets. Executors the wife and John Ervin. Witnesses Ebenezer Smith, Christopher Monk, David Johnson. Recorded ut supra, p. 318.

43 1814 May 21 Septbr. 8 **APPLEGATE, Joseph,** of New Jersey. Father and mother, brothers Davison Applegate, Richard, William, sisters Mary, wife of James Davis, and Elizabeth, wife of John Disbrey, nephew Joseph, son of brother Davison. Executor brother-in-law James Davison. Witnesses John V. L. Burhans, J. Lansing junior, Robert Dunbar junior. Recorded ut supra, p. 321.

44 1768 June 1 Septbr. 15 **ALGEO, David,** of New York City, merchant. Wife Margaret, grandsons John, David and William, sons of son David Algeo. Real and personal estate. Executors Garret Rapalje, merchant, and Samuel Johnson, silversmith, both of New York. Witnesses Samuel Janes, Robert Sharp, George Lindsay. Recorded vol. III., p. 105.

45 1809 July 7. 1822 Jany. 10 **ALEXANDER, Alexander,** of Schenectady. Wife Maria, children Stephen and Harriet, brother William Alexander, sister Anna, wife of William Hurry. House and lot in Galway, other real and personal estate. Executors the wife, brother William and Matthew Trotter of Albany. Witnesses Catherine Theresa Beck, Judith van Guysling, Joseph Shurtleff. Recorded vol. IV., 119.

45a 1798 Septbr. 20 Octobr. 25 **ALLISON, James,** born at North Shields, Northumberland, baker. Bartholomew Dillon of New York, cordwainer, property at Germantown, N. Ca. Executors Bartholomew Dillon and Michael Ryan. Witnesses Michael Ryan, Joseph Hoban, John Thomson. Recorded ut supra, vol. II., 87.

45b 1678 Decbr. 4 1681 Septbr. 6 Dutch **ABEEL, Stoffel Jansen,** of New Albany, and wife Neeltje. Children Magdalena, 17 years old and married, Maria, 14 years, Johannes, 11 years, and Elizabeth. Real and personal estate. Executors and guardians the survivor with brothers-in-law Teunis Cornelissen van der Poel and Adriaen Gerritsen Papendorp. Witnesses Jan Verbeeck, Leendert Philippsen and Adriaen van Ilpendam, Notary Public. Albany Co. Records, Court Minutes, 1680–5, p. 169.

45c 1806 Nov. 21 1823 Septbr. 10 **APPLE, Henry,** of Guilderland, Albany Co. Wife Eve, daughter Nancy, wife of David Ogsbury who has daughter Eve, Margaret, wife of Volkert Jacobson, Susanah, wife of Henry Shaven, Eve, wife of Henry Jacobson, nephew Henry Ogsbury. Real and personal estate. Executors the wife, Volkert Jacobson and James Henderson. Witnesses Michael Frederick junior, Chas. Davie. Albany Co. Records, Wills, I., part 2, p. 107.

46 (B 1) 1673 **BETTS, William,** of the Younghers Plantation in the jurisdiction of . . . Orange so-called. Wife Alice, sons Samuel, Hopestr . . . John, daughter Hittabell Tibbot; John, son of Samuel Barret, 20 acres of upland near Eastchester. Personal property. Will incomplete and much worn.

47 (B 2) 1684 **BUDD, John.** Only the last part of this will is extant, appointing neighbours John Tuthill and Issaack Arnold as executors. The will is proved in the Court of Oyer and Terminer for Suffolk Co., N. Y., November 12, 1684.

48 (B 3) Jany. 22 1691-2

BERKHOVEN, Adam Brower, of Bruckland. Wife Magdalena, children of sons Peter and Jacob, and of daughter Aeltje, who are cut off with a shilling for disobedience, and own children, viz., Mathys, William, Adam, Abraham, Nicolas, Mary, Fytie, Helena, Anna, Sarah and Rachel, William's son Adolphus, Mathys' daughter Magdalen, Mary's daughter Magdalen, and Fytie's daughter Magdalen, inherit everything. Peter's daughters Magdalen and Vroutie are to receive each one piece of $\frac{8}{8}$ (\$1$\frac{0}{0}\frac{0}{0}$), besides their share in the estate. Executors Barent van Tielburg and William Nazareth. Witnesses Henry Sleght, Cornelius Siebring and John Fredricks. No certificate of proof.

49 (B 4) 1702 Aug. 14

BRUGHMAN, Hermanus, of New York City, merchant, leaves to eldest son Hendrick and to second son Cornelius all property in the Province of New York and in Holland. Executors Joannis Outman and Gysbert van Imburgh of New York City, merchants. Witnesses Andres Myer, Benjamin Wynkoop, Abraham Gouverneur. Codicil of same date gives the property to the Dutch Reformed Church in New York City in case the sons die without issue. Same witnesses. No certificate of proof.

50 (B 5) 1702 Decbr. 16 1723 Octobr. 22 at Boston

BRIDON, Francis, of Boston, New England. Wife Susannah sole heiress and executrix of all real and personal estate. Witnesses Robert Fitzhugh, Isaac Biscon, Francis Gyles.

51 (B 6) 1706 Decbr. 12 1710 June 8 Dutch

BROWER, Hendrick, of Schenectady, N. Y. Wife and children mentioned, but not named, except son John and stepson Benjamin. Property not described. No executors named. Witnesses Philipp Schuyler, Marten van Benthuysen, Jesse d'Graef. Letters of administration granted to Maritie, widow of Hendrick Brower, May 11, 1711.

52 (B 7) 1706-7 Jany. 29 1727-8 Febry. 10

BURGES, Jeremiah, of Hamilton Tribe, Island of Bermuda. *Cousins* Thomas and Jeremiah, sons of brother John, deceased, cousin Mary, daughter of brother John, cousins Elizabeth, Richard, Samuel, John, William and Jeremiah, children of sister Miriam Peniston, cousin Elizabeth Stovell, Anthony, John, Mary, Sarah Johnson, daughter and sons of sister Sarah Stovell, cousin Martha Dunscomb of Pembroke Tribe, spinster, and her brother Samuel Dunscomb, cousin Ruth Pitcher of St. George's Parish, friends Captain William Stone and Thomas Bostock of Devon Tribe, and the poor of the Parish in Hamilton Tribe are given legacies. Cousin Jeremiah Burges and sister Mary are residuary legatees. Executors Capt. Wm. Stone and Jeremiah Burges. Witnesses Perient Trott (at the Crawl), Nathaniel Dunscomb, Thomas Bostock.

53 (B 8) 1711 May 2 1719 June 8

BOGARDUS, Cornelius, about to go with his brother Ephraim to North Carolina, leaves everything to brother-in-law Johannis van Vechten of Rensselærwyck Manor. No executor named. Witnesses Robert Livingston junior, Hend. Hansen, Kowraet ten Eyck. Johannis van Vechten makes over to Ephraim Bogardus of Kingston all the estate October 3, 1719.

54 (B 9) 1716 April 27 1724 June 17

BICKLEY, May (Attorney General of the Province of New York, 1705). Wife Elizabeth and adopted daughter Elizabeth White to have all real estate. Legacy of manuscripts and law-books left to friend William Sharpas, a ring and silver snuff-box is left to Mrs. Elizabeth Sharpas. Lands in New Jersey called New Brittain and in Kayaderosseras Patent. Witnesses Tho. George, Joseph Waldron, James Adam. The widow, George Clarke and Peter Fauconnier executors. Wishes to be buried without pipes and tobacco, as is usual.

55 (B 10) 1717 April 13 Octbr. 24

BOGARDUS, Evert, of Kingstown, Ulster Co., mariner. Wife Tatie, sons Peter, Evert, Nicolas, daughters Mary and Anaka, heirs to all real and personal property. Executors Hendrik Pruyn and Nicolas Hofman. Witnesses Johannis Wynkoop, A. Gaasbeeck Chambers, Ino. Crooke jun.

56 (B 11) Missing.

57 (B 12) 1721 June 2 1721-2 Jany. 9 **BOUQUET, Jacob,** of New York City, mariner. Wife Margaret sole heiress and executrix. Witnesses Barent Barheyt, Thomas Jennings, Abraham Gouverneur.

58 (B 13) 1725 Novb. 6 1726 Septbr. 24 **BRASIER, Thomas,** of Apperfield, Ulster Co., mariner. Wife Lydia sole heiress and executrix of all real and personal estate with a legacy of £100 to brother Richard Brasier. Witnesses Jacobus Bruyn, John Bayard, R. Bradley.

59 (B 14) 1725-6 Mar. 20 1726-7 March 11 **BEATTY, Charles,** of Marbletown, Ulster Co. Wife Janetie and only child Bata sole heiresses. Executors father-in-law Thomas Jansen and brother Robert Beatty. Witnesses Ysaac le Fevre, Samuel Cock, Nicolas Schoonhoven, Wm. Nottingham.

60 (B 15) 1727 Decb. 27 1728 May 20 **BARBERIE, John,** of New York City, leaves to grandson John, son of Peter Barberie, deceased, one half of the land at Romopock, Bergen Co., N. J., to go to testator's son John in case of grandson's John death without issue; to granddaughter Frances Barberie 2000 acres called Peters Land on Palls Creek, Ulster Co., to go to son John as above; to granddaughter Elizabeth, daughter of son Peter, deceased, 2000 acres at Youfrowshook, Ulster Co., also to go to son John as above; son John residuary legatee and executor. Legacy of six silver teaspoons and tongs, a silver salver and silver teapot to Mrs. Frances Moore and her daughter Frances, wife and daughter of John Moore of New York City, merchant. Witnesses Benj. Ayshford Hole, John Moore junior, Peter Vallete.

61 (B 16) 1721 Nov. 24 1727–8 March 20 Dutch

BROWER, Thomas, of Schonhechtadee, minister of the Reformed Church. His church, Symon, Cornelis, Engettie, Helena, children of Gerrit Symonsen Veeder, Elizabeth, wife of Capt. Evert Banker, Annatie, wife of William Banker, receive personal property, brothers Rev. Theodoris Brower of Dalphin, Overyssel, and Rev. Gerardus Brower of Swoll remainder men. Executors Evert Banker, Gerrit Symonsen Veeder and Rutger Bleecker. Witnesses Stevanus Groesbeck, Abraham Mabie, Cornelius van Dyck.

62 (B 17) 1728 Decb. 16 1732 Decbr. 2

BEEKMAN, Johannes, of Albany City, yeoman. Wife Eva, sons Johannis, Jacob, Martin, Johannis Jansen and Henry, daughters Susannah, Helena, Maritie, Johanna, Alida, Neeltie. Land in Kayaderosseras Patent. Wife sole executrix and after her death the five sons. Witnesses Thomas Williams, Hendrick Mendertsen Roseboom, Daniel Hogan.

63 (B 18)

Same will as preceding.

64 (B 19) 1728 May 8 1733 Octbr. 3

BECK, Caleb, of Schenectady, gentleman. Wife Anna, sons Caleb, daughter Angeltie, son-in-law John Fairly named as heirs of all real and personal property. Executors the wife, Thomas Williams of Albany, gentleman, and Lieutenant Helmas Vedder of Schanectady. Witnesses Robert Yets, Abraham Meebie, Robert Freeman.

65 (B 20) 1731 March 26 1751 June 15

BLAWVELT, Abraham, of Tapan, Orange Co., yeoman. Wife Grietie, sons Isaac, Abraham, Jacob and Johamus, daughters Amarence, wife of John Harring, Marritie, wife of Tunis Kooper, Elizabeth, wife of Peter Dupuy and Gretie, wife of Tunis Helling named. Land on Rears Mountains. No executors named. Witnesses Frederick Wortendyck, Gerret Henneon, David Demarest.

66 (B 21) 1731 July 9 1742-3 Jany. 28 **BEECKMAN, Johannis,** junior, of Albany City, trader. Leaves to wife Hester, only son Johannis and daughters Arjantie and Jannetie all real and personal estate. Executors the wife, brother-in-law Harmanus Wendell, brother Jacob Beeckman, Evert Wendell and Henry Holland junior. Witnesses Johannes de Garremo, Guileyn Verplaenck, Zacharias Sickels.

67 (B 22) 1728 Octbr. 19 1732 May 11 Dutch **BURHANS, Helena,** widow of Jan Burhans of Brabant, Kingston, Ulster Co. Sons David, Barent, Willem, Abraham, Isaac, Samuel, daughters Hilletje, wife of Edward Whitaker, Jannetie, wife of Peter Dubois, Elizabeth, wife of Jan Ploegh and children of deceased son Johan heirs of her personal property. Executors sons Barent and Willem. Witnesses Jan Pietersen Oosterhout, Willem Traphagen junior, Ger. van Wagenen.

68 (B 23) 1732 March 13 1733 Aug. 2 **BANKS, James,** of Albany, gentleman, leaves legacies to Mary, widow of John Price, to son-in-law James Carrell alias Banks of Newark, N. J., the remainder, viz., personal property and a lot of 1½ acres at Elizabethtown, N. J., 3 acres of ground at Newark, N. J., a house and lot near the Fort at Schenectady in trust to John Hansen and Rutt Blaker executors for nephews Edward, son of brother William Banks, of Youthel, Ireland, and John, son of brother Abraham Banks, of the same place. £20 to the Church Wardens of ? to buy a piece of plate or a bell. Witnesses John Allwood, Hugh Othway, Walter Jones.

69 (B 24) 1733 May 27 1739 Novbr. 26 **BLAWFELT, Joseph,** of Orange Co., yeoman, gives all real and personal estate to wife Elizabeth, to go to the eldest son Honnes, when wife dies or remarries. Sons Hendrick, Frederick, Garret, daughters Martha, Anatia, Altha receive money, son Abraham one half of the farm on Demores Kil. Executors the wife and brother Garret Blawfelt. Witnesses Gabriel Ludlow junior, Cornelis Niker (?), Daniel Blawfelt.

70 (B 25) 1733 June 10 1739 Novbr. 26

BLAWFELT, Garret, of Orange Co., yeoman. Wife Marithe is given all real and personal estate. After her death eldest son Isaac is to have the homefarm, daughter Lena 163 acres in Tapan Precinct. Land at Haverstraw to be sold. Executors the wife and brother-in-law Guysbert Crom. Witnesses Ino. McEvers, Gabriel Ludlow junior, Minder Hogencamp.

71 (B 26) 1734 March 30 July 31

BANCKER, Evert, of Rensselaerswyck Manor, leaves all his real and personal estate to children Elisabeth, wife of Gerrit Lansing, Christoffel, Willem, Jannetie, wife of Harmanus Schuyler, Adriaen, Gerardus and Johannis. Executors sons Christoffel, Willem, Adriaen and Gerardus. Witnesses Antony Bogardus, John de Peyster, Rutger Bleecker.

72 (B 27) 1738 Decbr. 22 1746 June 12

BEECKMAN, Jacob, of Albany, blacksmith. Wife Debora, sons Hendrick and Johannis, daughters Maghtel, Efei, and Deborah. House and lot in 2d Ward, Albany, two lots on Vossenkil, Albany, one twelfth of one thirteenth lot at Caniadarosira (Cayaderosseras ?). Executors the wife, son Hendrick and brother (in-law ?) Hans Hansen. Witnesses Abraham Lansing, Abraham Lansing junior, Juryan Hogan.

73 (B 28) 1740 Nov. 17 1762 June 19

BOGART, Marten, of Marbletown, Ulster Co., farmer. Wife Janaka, sons Johannes, Cornelius, daughters Sarah and Rebecca receive all real and personal property. Executors the wife, son-in-law Guysbert Krom, son Johannis and Johannes Thomassen. Witnesses Thomas Jansen, Hendrikus Jansen, John Crooke junior.

74 (B 29) 1742 Decbr. 14 1743 Aug. 16

BENNETT, Robert, of New York City, ship-wright. Sons William and Henery, daughters Johanna and Abigail. Executor son William. Witnesses Haeseuwel van Keuren, John Dally, Isaac Taneau.

75 (B 30) 1743 May 9 July 25 **BLANCHARD, John,** of New York City, distiller. Wife Elizabeth (had first husband Ichabod Loutit), sons John, Francis, daughters Elizabeth, Elenor, Mehitobell, heirs to all real and personal property, including plate. Executors the wife and brother Hezekiah Blanchard of Boston, distiller. Witnesses William Beck, Mary Wessells, Lanc. Green.

76 (B 31) 1744 Septbr. 11 1752 Octbr. 31 **BERKENMEYER, William Christoph,** of Loonenburg, Albany Co., Lutheran Minister. Wife Benigna Sibylla, sole heiress of personal property, including plate. Books to go to Trustees of Lutheran Churchland, Arent van Schayk, Jacob Halenbeck and Jan Hannessen van Hoesen. Executors the wife, with Rev. Peter Nicholas Sommer of the Lutheran Church at Schoharie, Johannes Curts of Queensberry, merchant, Matthys van Loon of Loonenburg (now Athens) and William Halenbeck of the Flats, Albany Co., as overseers. Witnesses Jacob Evertsen, Johs. Mynders, Jacobus Lagranse, Johannis Evertsen. Codicil (in German) dated August 17, 1751, directs burial in Lutheran Church at Loonenburg, revokes the paying of £10 to the consistory for his burial, asks Rev. Mr. Knoll to preach the funeral sermon and appoints Mattheus van Loon, William Hallen Bok and Johannes Kurtz executors. Witnesses Albert van Loon, Jan Caspersen Halenbeeck, Frantz van Husen, Johannes Klaw.

77 (B 32) —— 1747 May 15 **BYFIELD, William,** ——. Wife Elizabeth sole heiress and executrix. Jonathan Hazard to receive one fourth of testators share in all prizes and captures made by the sloop *Dolphin*. Witnesses Antho. Ham, John van Gelder, Joshua Slidell. Will incomplete. Probated in New York.

78 (B 33) 1741 Aug. 15 1744 Nov. 27 **BLAIN, Thomas,** of Orange Co., yeoman. Wife Cathrenah, children Ann, Margret, William, Elizabeth, John, heirs of all property. Executors David Mackamley and William Thomson of Orange Co. Witnesses Richard Edsall, Joseph Perry, Thomas Wright.

79 (B 34) 1746 May 10 1750 May 31 **BOGARDUS, Evert,** of Kingston, Ulster Co. Wife Geertruy to have all real and personal property for life; nephew Evert, son of brother Nicholas, receives house and barn in Kingston; nephew John, son of brother-in-law Petrus Edmundus Elmendorph, land on the road from Kingston to the Gran Kil; brother Nicholas Bogardus, nephew Evert, son of brother Petrus, brother-in-law Charles Crook, sisters Anaka Decker, Maria Decker, Maria Wynkoop, are to have money and other personal property. Executors the wife, brothers-in-law John Wynkoop and Petrus Edmundus Elmendorph. Witnesses Thomas Beekman, John Beekman junior, Charles Clinton.

80 (B 35) 1748 March 6 1756 Febr. 13 **BENNET, Richard,** of Dartmouth, County Devon, mariner. Wife Mary sole heiress and executrix. Witnesses Mary Lampen, John Lampen.

81 (B 36) 1751 May 18 1759 Aug. 31 **BLAUFELDT, Jacobus,** of Tappan, Orange Co. Wife Elesebedt, sons Johannes, Jacobus, daughters Catrena, Elesebedt, Marregretie, Annatie, Sarah and Maria inherit all real and personal estate. Executors friends David Blaufeldt and Abraham Smith. Witnesses Daneel Blaufeldt, Jacob Blaufeldt, Abraham Haring.

82 (B 37) 1751 April 3 1765 Octbr. 1 **BRAS, Adolph,** of New York City, shoemaker. Wife Maritie, children Adolph, Gerret, Catherine, Mary, Jannetie and Gertie. Real and personal estate. Executors brother Hendrick Brass and son Adolph, when of age. Witnesses Amos Pain, John Vredenburgh, Lambt. Moore.

83 (B 38) 1751 Octbr. 29 1752 June 4 **BARNES, William,** of Rombout Precinct, Dutchess Co. Wife not named, sons Anthony, William, Jeams, daughters Sarey and Margit inherit all real and personal estate. Executors the wife and Capt. Henry ter Bos. Witnesses Jacobus ter Boss junior, Issac Heptonstall, Jacobus ter Boss.

84 (B 39) 1753 Jany. 31 **BAYARD, Stephen,** of Bergen Co., N. J., yeoman. Sons William, and Robert, daughter Margaret. Farm, called Hooboken in Bergen Co., to go to son William, farm, called Weehaken, Bergen Co., to son Robert; all other real estate, derived from testators father Samuel Bayard, mother Margaret Bayard or patented to be equally divided among the children. Plate, marked with her mother's name, goes to daughter, other plate, etc., to sons. Executors son William, brother Nicholas Bayard, brother-in-law Peter Schuyler with son Robert and daughter Margaret, when they come to age. Witnesses John McEvers, Nat. Johnson, Archd. Kennedy. Codicil, dated Decbr. 17, 1753, gives all undivided lands to son William. Witnesses Henry Brockholls, John van Cortlandt, Nathl. Fish junior. Only relatives, cousins german, to be invited to funeral.

85 (B 40) 1753 April 3 1759 April 17 **BEVIER, Samuel,** of New Paltz, Ulster Co. Wife Esther, children Philipp, Isaac, Abraham, Louis, Johannis, Margriet, wife of Mathew Lefever, Marie, wife of Abraham Lefever, and Esther. Lands in New Paltz Patent. Executors sons Abraham, Johannes, sons-in-law Mathew and Abraham Lefever and daughter Esther. Witnesses Louis Bevier, Jacob Hasbrouck junior, J. Hasbrouck.

86 (B 41) 1754 Jany. 17 May 8 **BAYLES, Joseph,** of Florada, Orange Co. Wife Phebe, sons Joseph, Daniel, Justus, Elias, daughters Catherine, May and Phebe. Real and personal property. Executors the wife and brother Daniel Bayles. Witnesses George Wood, farmer, William Finn, physician, John Bears.

87 (B 42) 1755 Octbr. 1 **BEEKMAN, Johannes,** Probate of Will of, of Albany, proved before Myndert Schuyler December 2, 1732, with letters testamentary to Eva Beekman, sole executrix during her life.

88 (B 43) 1755 May 22 1761 April 20 **BOGARD, Cornelis,** of Albany, shipwright. Wife Doraty, son Hendrick, daughters Catharina, Jannetie, wife of Johannis Volkertsen Douw, Ragel, wife of Volkert Ans. Douw. House and lot in 3d Ward, Albany, and other real estate. Executors the wife and son-in-law Johannis Volkertsen Douw. Witnesses Harmen Hun, Hendrick G. van Ness, Adryeyen Qakenbos.

89 (B 44) 1755 Febry. 20 1756 June 19 **BULL, William,** of Goshen, Orange Co., mason. Wife Sarah, daughters Mary, Margaret, Catherine, Anne, Elinor, sons John, William, Thomas, Isaac, Richard. House and 100 acres on the road to Goshen, farms on the Wallkil, land adjoining Evans Patent. Executors the wife and son William. Witnesses Thomas Stewart, Philipp de Finx, Derrick Scot.

90 (B 45) 1755 Jany. 4 **BROWN, Benjamin,** of Rye, Westchester Co. Sons Benjamin, Joseph, Daniel and William. Real and personal estate. Executors brothers Thomas and Hacheliah Brown. Witnesses Zebediah Brown, Jonathan Carhartt, John Hill. Copy.

91 (B 46) 1755 June 4 1756 April 22 **BROMLEY, Catharine,** of New York City. Daughter Catharine Godwin. Real and personal property. Executor brother John van Dyck. Witnesses Edward Man, Jean Helme, Richard R. Smith.

92 (B 47) 1756 Aug. 19 **BRUSH, Joseph,** of Huntington, L. I., cordwainer. Wife Rebecca, sons Edward and Joseph, daughters Esther, Jemima and Elisabeth. Real estate, seven acres, called Old Hollow, bought from Daniel Whitman, and undivided lands in the Baiting Place Purchase. Incomplete copy.

93 (B 48) 1756 May 20 1759 Octbr. 15 **BEEKMAN, Johannis,** of Albany, merchant. Wife Deborah, sons John, Jacob, daughters Catrina and Eva. Undivided share in Caniadarosseras or Queensborough Patent, house and lot in Albany, personal prop-

erty. Executors the wife, brother Henry Beekman, brothers-in-law Nicolaes Cuyler and Jacob van Schaick. Witnesses Jacob C. ten Eyck, John Marselius jun., John R. Bleecker.

94 (B 49) 1756 Jany. 16 Septbr. 27 **BLEECKER, Rutger,** of Albany. Sons Johannis R. and Jacobus, daughter Maragrita, widow of Edward Collins, grandsons Rutger, son of Johannis, and Rutger, son of Jacobus. Pictures of himself and wife, silverplate and other personal property, real estate partly inherited from brother Nicolaes Bleecker. Executors the two sons and brother Hendrick Bleecker. Witnesses Isack Verplank, Daved Groesbeeck jun., Williem Verplanck.

95 (B 50) 1751 April 30 1757 Octbr. 24 Dutch **BRINCK, Jacob,** of Sondersorgh (*without Care*), near Kingston, Ulster Co. Wife Anna Marijtje, sons Jan, Cornelis and Jacob, daughters but not named. Executors Jan Eltinge and Christoffel Kierstede. Witnesses Anthonie Hofman, Counraedt Ja. Elmendorph, Willem Eltinge.

96 (B 51) 1757 Novbr. 17 1759 Octbr. 10 **BAYLES, Nathaniel,** of Floredy, Orange Co. Wife Sarah, children Samuel, Tabitha, Nathaniel, Sarah, David, Elias and Mary. Apparently only personal property. Executors David Shepard and William Denn, both of Goshen. The three youngest sons to be apprenticed to trades on Long Island. Witnesses John Bears, James Miller, Martha Whitman.

97 (B 52) 1757 Decbr. 20 1761 April 10 Dutch **BEEKMAN, Thomas,** of Kingston, Ulster Co. Wife Marritie, sons Johannes, Cornelis, daughters Judike, wife of Daniel Whitaker, Alida, Catherine, Elisabeth, wife of Tunis Hooghteyling, and Mally, wife of Cornelis Swart. Personal property, lands, the Island Orchard, woodland, the farm of the poor in Kingston jurisdiction, a house and lot in Kingston. Executors the wife and sons. Witnesses Petrus Bogardus, Christoffel Kierstede, Jan Elting.

98 (B 53) 1758 Febry. 25 Decbr. 13

BRAKIN, Mathew, of New York City, lansman. Loving friends Jeams Brakin and Meary Farroll of N. Y. City sole heirs and executors of all real and personal estate, including prize money coming from ship *Rial George.* Witnesses Robert Harper carpenter, Samuel Crosby. John Haines of Rye, Westchester Co., weaver and principal creditor of deceased, granted letters of administration, Mary Farrol having died and James Braken being absent beyond sea.

99 (B 54) 1758 May 1 Octbr. 20

BRINCKERHOFF, Jacob, of Fishkil, Dutchess Co., yeoman. Wife Elizabeth, children Anna, Catherina and Dirck. Real and personal property. Executors brothers Colonel John Brinckerhoff, Isaac Brinckerhoff, John Brinckerhoff, shoemaker, and Isaac Lent. Witnesses Cor. Osborn, Matthias Horton, Thos. Porter.

100 (B 55) 1758 Septbr. 4 1761 April 4

BORGHARD, Gerrit, of Kinderhook, tailor. Wife Antje, nephew Lambert, son of brother Hendrick Borghard of Sheffield, New England, niece Geesje, daughter of sister Eytje Moor, cousin Abraham, son of Jurreje van Hoesen of Kinderhook, sister Feytje, wife of Andris Kittel. Land South of Kinderhook Patent, derived from father Jan Borghardt. The wife sole executrix. Witnesses Cornelis van Alen, Ellibirtie Goes, Arent van Dyck.

101 (B 56) 1759 April 26 1761 April 15

BROADHEAD, Daniel, of Marbletown, Ulster Co. Wife Maritje, sons Daniel and Samuel. Real and personal estate. Executors brother Charles Broadhead, brother-in-law Johannes Dewitt and nephew Charle Dewitt. Witnesses Louis Bevier, Nathan Smedis, Gysbert Scrom.

102 (B 57) 1759 May 3 1765 June 3

BEDELL, David, of Hempstead, Queens Co. Sons David and Elias, daughters Phebe de Mott, Elizabeth Alburtus, Hannah Hall, Anne Pine and Mary, grandson Jacob Bedell, granddaughters Margaret and

Elisabeth Bedell, daughter-in-law Hannah, widow of Jacob Bedell. Home farm, land at Hungry Harbour and patent rights in Hempstead Township. Executors the two sons. Witnesses Peter Fowler, James Burtis jun., David Batty.

103 (B 58) 1759 July 26 Septbr. 17 **BRADNER, Christian,** of Goshen, Orange Co. Sons Colvil, John, Gilbert and Benoni, daughters Susanna, Mary, Sarah and Elizabeth. Real and personal property (land at Newborough, Ulster Co.). Executors sons Colvil and John. Witnesses Daniel Smith Wood, Abner Wood, William Denn.

104 (B 59) 1759 Septbr. 8 Septbr. 25 **BUTLER, Thomas,** of Albany. Brothers John and Walter, sisters Mary, wife of John van der Heyden, and Ann, daughters Mary and Deborah of bro. Walter and three sons, not named, of bro. John. Farm, called New Land, 1200 acres, bought from widow Scot and her son John M. Scot. Executors Albert Rightman and Peter Canine of the Mohawks Country. Witnesses William Corry, Jacob van Schayck, Martin Myndersen.

105 (B 60) 1759 March 6 1764 April 10 **BEVIER, Samuel,** of Rochester, Ulster Co., farmer. Wife ——, children Andrew, Mary, Abraham, Mathew, Rachel, Elisabeth and Cornelia. Real and personal estate. Executors "my son" and brothers Andrew Johannis Bevier and Jacob Bevier. Witnesses William Dewitt, John Dewitt, Stephen Dewitt.

106 (B 61) 1759 Aug. 10 1760 Octbr. 10 **BRUYN, Severyn,** of Kingston, Ulster Co. Wife Cathrina, sons Jacobus and Johannis, a child about to be born. House and lot in Kingston, land in Harrison Patent of 1720, orchard and lot, bought from the estate of Hendrick Pruyn; personal estate includes twelve silver spoons. Executors three brothers-in-law Abraham Hasbrook, Petrus ten Brook, Benjamin ten Brook and friend Abraham Low. Witnesses Ephraim Low, Benjamin Louw and Cornelius Elmendorph junior.

107 (B 62) 1759 Jany. 16 **BISHOP, Thomas,** of Eastchester, Westchester Co. Wife Mary, daughter Martha Butler, grandson Bishop Hadley, granddaughter Magdalen Hadley. House and lot in the Out Ward, N. Y. City, do. at Eastchester, and a house in New York. Executors the wife and Gilbert Taylor. Witnesses John Ryder, Edward Burling, Philipp Fowler. Copy made June 1, 1764.

108 (B 63) 1759 March 18 June 5 **BUTLER, James,** of Richmond Co. Sons James and Mathias, daughter Elizabeth, wife of Charles Laforge, Mary and Nelly. Real and personal estate. Executors brother-in-law Lewis Dubois and son-in-law Charles Laforge both, of Richmond Co. Witnesses Benjn. Seaman, James Seguin jun, John Segaing.

109 (B 64) 1760 March 13 1763 Febry. 3 **BUTLER, Walter,** of Schenectady, Lieut. Independent Companies. Wife Deborah, son John, daughters Maria van der Heyden and Anna, grandchildren Maria and Deborah, daughters of son Walter dec'd. Land in Coghonawago Patent and personal property. Executors Joseph Yates jun. and son John Butler, both of Schenectady. Witnesses John van Sise, Jno. Brown, Fanny Burrowes.

110 (B 65) 1761 June 1 July 1 **BURHANS, David,** jun, of Brabant, Kingston, Ulster Co. Brothers Jacob, Wilhelmus, Johannis (decd.), sister Helena, wife of Philipp Vielen, Marytie, wife of Samuel Dubois, Cathrena, wife of Samuel Whitaker, Elisabeth, widow of Johannis van Wagenen, nephew Barent, son of sister Catherine Whitaker, and Barent, son of brother Wilhelmus, niece Elisabeth, daughter of sister Marytie Dubois. Real and personal estate. Executors brothers Jacob Burhans and James Hamilton. Witnesses James Whitaker, Philipp Meller, Edward Whitaker jun.

111 (B 66) 1760 Febry. 25 1784 July 4 **BYVANCK, Anthony,** of New York City. Wife Catherine, sons Anthony and John, daughter Catherine. Real and personal estate. Executors the wife and Mary Burnsides. Witnesses Francis Cooley, Geo. Gordon, Michael Saitz.

112 (B 67) 1760 April 18 1761 May 8 **BLAUVELT, David,** of Orange Town, Orange Co. Wife Maria, sons Johannes, Abraham, Jacobus, Cornelius, Teunis and David, daughters Catharina, Maria and Elizabeth. Real and personal property. Executors Peter Haring, John Perry jun., Johannes D. Blauvelt. Witnesses Johannis Haring, Johannis van Houten, John Haring.

113 (B 68) 1760 Febry. 16 Septbr. 8 **BRAT, Johannes Arentsen,** of Schenectady. Wife Maria, sisters Maragreta van Dyck, Catrena Wimpel and Harjaentie van Petten dec'd, sisters Helena, daughter Jannetie Schermerhorn, cousin Jannetie, daughter of brother-in-law John Truax dec'd, four daughters of dec'd brother Andres Brat, viz: Catlintie, wife of John Butler, Jannetie, Helena and Harjaentie, father Arent Brat, brother Harmanus, nephews Arent Andressen Brat and John Andressen Brat, maid servant Maragret Carel. Lands West of and near to Schenectady, on Nistagijoene (Niskayuna) Road, house and lot in Schenectady, and personal property. Executors Simon Johnsen Veeder, Isaac Vrooman and brother Harmanus Brat. Witnesses John Veeder, Henry Roseboom, Johannes van der Heyden junr, Dirck van Ingen.

114 (B 69) 1761 Jany. 12 Febry. 27 **BRUNDAGE, Benjamin,** of Philipps Upper Patent, Dutchess Co., yeoman. Wife Elizabeth, sons Daniel, Nathaniel, James and Nathan, daughter Judah Jenkins. Real and personal property. Executors Moses Travis and James Philipps. Witnesses John Laurance of Dutchess Co. farmer, Elisha Travis of West Chester Co. farmer, Ann Palmer.

115 (B 70) 1762 April 20 Septbr. 28 **BARTON, Joseph,** of Charlotte Precinct, Dutchess Co. Wife ——, sons Benjamin, Eligey, William, Joseph, Lewes, Caleb, Roger, daughters Millisan, Sarah, Rachel, grandson Joseph, son of Benjamin. Real and personal estate. Executors sons Lewis and Caleb. Witnesses Nathaniel Marshall, Ephraim Palmer, Wm. Doughty.

116 (B 71) 1762 Decbr. 6 1768 June 1

BAYLES, Richard, of Floredy, Orange Co. Wife Deborah, sons Richard, and Jonathan, daughters Jean Holly, Lurania, Ruhemis and Sarah. Real and personal estate. Executors Doctor Nathaniel Elmer and George Wood, both of Floredy. Witnesses Henry Case, Margery Case, Wm. Denn.

117 (B 72) 1763 Aug. 12 1766 May 25

BARCLAY, Andrew, of N. Y. City, merchant. Wife Helena, sons Thomas, James, Andrew, Henry and John, daughters Ann Dorothy, wife of Theophilact Bache, Catherine, Sarah, Ann, Margaret, Helena and Charlotte Amelia. Real and personal property. Executors the wife, father-in-law Jacobus Roosevelt, brother Rev. Henry Barclay, brother-in-law Jacobus Roosevelt, son-in-law Theophilact Bache, sons Thomas, James and Andrew. Witnesses Nicholas Bayard jun., John Glover, Ino. Roosevelt.

118 (B 73) 1763 May 13 1771 June 7

BEVIER, Abraham, of New Paltz, Ulster Co. Wife Margrietje, sons Solomon and Abraham, daughters Magdalena, Sarah, Jacomyntje, Cathrintie and Maria. Real and personal property. Executors the wife and brothers-in-law Noah Eltinge of New Paltz and Matthew Lefever of Hurly, Ulster Co. Witnesses Jacob Hasbrouck jun., R. Josias Eltinge, Joseph Coddington.

119 (B 74) 1763 Decbr. 16 1767 June 17

BRAT, Dirck, of Rensselaers Wyk Colony, blacksmith. Wife Cornelia, son Peter Drs., daughter Trintie, wife of Jacob Deforrest, grandsons Jesse Deforrest and Dirk Deforrest, children of dec'd daughter Engeltie. Real and personal property. Executors the wife, the son and Staats van Santvoort. Witnesses Ryckert van Vranken, Symon Johs. Veeder, John H. Lydius.

120 (B 75) 1863 Decbr. 13 1764 Mach 14

BRETT, Catherine, of Fishkil, Dutchess Co., widow. Sons Francis and Robert, children of son Robert, viz: Matthew, Francis, Rombout, Sarah and Robert. Real estate a number of farms and personal property.

Executors son Francis, Colonel John Brinkerhoff, Capts. Eleazar Dubois and Peter Dubois of Rombout Precinct. Witnesses Obadeiah Cooper, John Bailey jun., Catharine Bogardus.

121 (B 76) 1764 March 30 Octbr. 1 **BORGHART, Jan,** of Kinderhook, yeoman. Son Hendrick, grandsons Jan Borghart, Lambert, sons of Hendrick, daughters Eytje, widow of John Moor of Claverack, Feytje, wife of Andres Kittel, Anna, daughter of son Hendrick, children of dec'd daughter Maria, wife of Jurje van Hoesen, grandson Jan Kittel. Land at Sheffield, East side of Housatonic River, or Great Barrington, at Kinderhook, at Petannock, and personal property. Executors Grandsons Jan and Lambert Borghart and Peter B. Vosburgh. Witnesses Louris Goes, John van Alstyne, Laurens van Dyck.

122 (B 77) 1764 Novbr. 8 1765 Jany. 2 **BRINKERHOFF, Johannis,** of Rumbouts Precinct, Dutchess Co., yeoman. Wife Sarah, son Hendrick. Real and personal estate. Executors father Hendrick Brinkerhoff and father-in-law Abraham Brinkerhoff. Witnesses Andrs. Breested, John Cooke, Abrm. Lent.

123 (B 78) 1764 Novbr. 21 1768 June 20 **BELLINGER, Frederick,** of Canajoharie, Albany Co., yeoman. Wife ——, son Thomas, daughter Elisabeth, wife of Jacob Klock. Personal estate. Executors Jacob Klock and Hendrick Frey. Witnesses Peter Eigenbrodt, Johannis Eigenbrodt, Philipp Helmer.

124 (B 79) 1765 Aug. 13 1767 Decbr. 3 **BROWER, Cornelius,** of Schenectady, yeoman. Wife Cornelia, son Hendrick, daughter Mary, wife of John Monroe of Albany, merchant, grandsons Cornelius Rickey and Gerrit van Antwerp. Real and personal property. Executor the wife. Witnesses Lancaster Conner, Tunis van Vleck, Mathew Lyñe.

125 (B 80) 1767 June 4 1775 Septbr. 25 **BOGARDUS, Petrus,** of Kingston, Ulster Co. Wife Rebecca, sons Evert, Jacob, Petrus, daughters Gerritje, Marytje, wife of Benj. Low, and Catherine. Share in Anneke Jans property, other real and personal estate. Executors son Jacob, sons-in-law Benjamin Low and Coenraedt Corns. Elmendorph. Witnesses Coenraadt Elmendorph, Johannis Wynkoop jun., Ch. D. Witt.

126 (B 81) 1767 June 13 1768 April 2 **BURROUGHS, Benjamin,** of Dutchess Co. Children Thomas, Deborah, Elizabeth, Benjamin, James, William, Joseph, Nathan. Real and personal estate. Executors son Thomas, son-in-law Caleb Carman jun., Francis Way and William van Wyck, all of Dutchess Co. Witnesses Theod. van Wyck jun., of Rumbouts Precinct, physician, Aeltje van Wyck, James Peck.

127 (B 82) 1768 March 22 March 28 **BARNES, John,** of Cornwall Precinct, physician. Wife Sarah, son John. Whole estate. Executors John Hill, physician and Israel Sealy. Witnesses Nathl. Jayne, Thos. Coleman, Lewis Donnovan.

128 (B 83) 1768 May 30 Septbr. 12 **BITYER, Adam,** of Rhinebeck Precinct, Dutchess Co., yeoman. Wife Maritje, daughters Catharine, Elizabeth, Geertie. Farm and real property. Executors father-in-law Johannis Righter, brother Wm. Bitsier and John van Ness. Witnesses Jacob Hermanse, Jacob Minkelaer, Anthy Hoffman jun., Zacharias Hoffman, jun.

129 (B 84) 1769 Jany. 11 1784 May 29 **BOCKEE, Abraham,** of Amenia Precinct, Dutchess Co. Wife Mary, son Jacob, daughters Mary Salkeld and Annitie Bockee. Lands in Charlotte Precinct, *i. e.* part of lot No. 17, Second Division, Great 9 Partners, lot in first water lot, First Division, lot in No. 16, Second Division, lot in No. 7, Third Division. Executors the wife, daughter Annitie and the son, when of age. Witnesses Thos. Fish, Joshua Fish, Elijah Browning, John Fish. Codicil, dated January 19, 1776, authorizes executors to sell land in lot No. 27, Second Division, Great 9 Partners. Witnesses Thomas Fish, Isaac Smith, Matths. B. Miller.

130 (B 85) 1769 Aug. 21 1772 June 4 **BROWN, Duncan,** of Wallkil Precinct, Ulster Co. Sons John, Gilbert and Archibald, daughter Christian McLachlin, grandsons Daniel and John, sons of dec'd son Daniel. Homefarm, a town lot, land in Arguile Township, Albany Co. and personal property. Executors son John and Daniel Gillespy. Witnesses Neal McLaughlin, Archibald Brown, Patience McLaughlin.

131 (B 86) 1770 Aug. 20 1771 Febry. 11 **BOCKHOUT, Johannis,** of Rombouts Precinct, Dutchess Co. Sons Pieter, John, Jacobus, Abraham, daughters Hester, Mary, Margriet and Nansie. Real and personal estate. Executors John Cock, merchant, and Joseph Tosten (Thurston), yeoman, both of Rombouts Prect. Witnesses Thomis John and Samuel Barker.

132 (B 87) 1770 Febry. 23 **BURNSIDE, Mary,** of N. Y. City, widow. Brother Peter Peterson, sisters Tuentie Waldron, Catherine Wessels, Gertie, daughter of Dirck Peterson dec'd, James, son of James Wessels of N. Y., inn-keeper. Personal property including a silver tankard. Executors sister Tuentie Waldron and Henry van Vleeck of N. Y. City, merchant. Not signed or witnessed.

133 (B 88) 1770 April 2 1771 March 29 **BLOOM, Phemmetie,** of Rumbouts Precinct, Dutchess Co., widow. Sons Dirck Brinckerhoff, John A. Brinckerhoff, daughters Elizabeth, wife of Abraham Brinckerhoff, Antie, wife of Abraham Lent, grandsons Abraham, son of son John A., Abraham Lent, jun., granddaughters Aeltie, da. of Rudolphus Swartwout, Phemmetie, wife of Thomas Langdon, Phemmetie, daughter of son John A., Phemmetie, da. of son Dirck, the heirs of dec'd da. Altie, wife of Abraham Adriance, the heirs of dec'd daughter Dinah, wife of Rudolphus Swartwout. Personal property. Executors son John A. Brinckerhoff, Gysbert Schenk and Jacobus Swartwout. Witnesses Isaac Brinckerhoff, Altje Swartwout, Roeloff Schenk.

134 (B 89) 1770 July 30 1772 April 15 **BOOTH, Charles,** of the Wallkil, Ulster Co. Sons Charles, George, John, Benjamin, daughter Anna Wilkins, grandchildren William Booth and Lydy Booth, children of dec'd daughter Mary Haines viz: Susanna, Mary, Mehitebel, Charles and Anna, children of da. Anna Wilkins viz: Moses, Mary, James and Charles. Real and personal property. Executors sons George and Benjamin. Witnesses Thomas Bull, Stephen Harlow, Thomas Rhodes.

135 (B 90) 1770 Jany. 4 **BEEKMAN, William,** of N. Y. City, physician. Children Magdalen, Catherine, Gerardus, Mary, William, Abraham, James, Cornelia, widow of Wm. Walton and Elisabeth, wife of Robert Rutgers, children of daughter Elisabeth viz: Harmen, Catherine, Anthony, Robert and Gerard, cousin Abraham, son of Abraham de Lanoy, vintner. Real estate, residence and lot on van Brugh Str., lots in the Fly between John Bogert and Benjamin Moore, together with water lots and wharf, house and lot in Beekman Str., opposite St. George's Chapel, No. 67, lot No. 194 Beekman Str., farm in the Out Ward, house and lot in Maiden Lane; personal property includes plate. Executors sons Gerardus, William, Abraham and James. Witnesses Peter Marsalis, Anthony King and Abraham de Lanoy jun. Official copy.

136 (B 91) 1770 April 21 1781 Septbr. 9 **BLANCHAN, Mattheus,** of Bloomendal, Hurly Precinct, Ulster Co., yeoman. Sons Johannis, Jacob, Mattheus, daughters Annatie, Catherine and Brackey. Real and personal estate. Executors the three sons and son-in-law Simon Frere. Witnesses Samuel Lefevre, Jacob Lefevre, Gab. Ellison, John Cantine.

137 (B 92) 1772 June 9 July 16 **BANKER, Nathaniel,** of Rumbouts Precinct, Dutchess Co., farmer. Wife Annatie, sons Stephen, Adolph, daughters Sarah, Elizabeth and Magdalene. Real and personal property. Executors Johannes Dewitt jun., Samuel Somes and John Jewell. Witnesses John Wilde, Henry Clapp, Stephen Thorn.

138 (B 93) 1772 April 29 1762 (*sic.*) May 10 **BALY, Jonathan,** of Floredy, Orange Co. Wife Elizabeth, sons Richard, Jonathan, Benjamin, Asa. Real and personal property. Executor brother Richard Baly and Nathaniel Elmore. Witnesses Isaac Nicoll, Ananias Whitman, Donal Curwin.

139 (B 94) 1772 Decbr. 30 1773 April 16 **BROOKS, Jonathan,** of Rumbouts Precinct, Dutchess Co. Wife Elisabeth, son Jonathan, daughter Elisabeth. Real and personal property. Executors Joseph Thurston, John Miers jun. and John Low. Witnesses John Kip, William Brooks, John Langdon.

140 (B 95) 1772 July 25 1773 Octbr. 13 **BRETT, Rumbout,** of Dutchess Co. Sister Sarah, wife of Abraham Brinckerhoff, nephew Robert Brett the third, niece Catharine Brett, both children of Matthew Brett dec'd, brother Robert Brett, father Robert Brett sen. Real and personal estate. Executors Abraham Brinckerhoff and Robert, son of Robert Brett sen. Witnesses Henry Ludinton, Abraham Hyatt, John Porter.

141 (B 96) 1772 Aug. 17 Octbr. 1 **BUDD, Nicholas,** of Rumbouts Precinct, Dutchess Co. Wife Phebe, daughters Cloe, Ann, Tamer and Femme. Real and personal estate. Executors Elisha Covet and Joseph Strang, both of van Cortlandt Manor. Witnesses Ebenezer White, Joshua Hyatt, John Furden.

142 (B 97) 1772 10th Day 2d Mth. 1774 Novbr. 19 **BUTT, Samuel,** of Charlotte Precinct, Dutchess Co. Wife Else, brothers John, Gershom, Moses, Aaron and Thomas, nephew Samuel, son of Gershom, sisters Ruth Brownell, Susannah Wellar and Sarah Barns. Homefarm, land in Amenia Precinct or in lot No. 6, Subdivision of Nine Partners. Executors Tripp Mosher and Gilbert Titus, both of Charlotte Precinct. Witnesses Aaron Vail, Phebe Haight, Joshua Haight.

143 (B 98) 1773 Decbr. 9 1774 Jany. 4 **BELL, Deliverance,** of Charlotte Prect., Dutchess Co. Sons Benjamin, Robert, William, daughters Deliverance Finny, Bridget Horskins, Anna Bell and Abigail Bell, grandaughter Dinah Northrup. Real and personal

estate. Executors Joseph Fowler and Ephraim Paine. Witnesses Solomon Finch, Stephen Manchester, Henry Knap.

144 (B 99) 1773 Novbr. 10 1778 Oct. 15 **BREWSTER, John,** of Cornwall Precinct, Orange Co., yeoman. Wife Charity, sons John, Francis, Edward, Isaac, daughter Ruth. Homefarm on the Warwick—New Windsor road, personal property includes silver table spoons and tea spoons. Executors sons John and Francis Brewster. Witnesses Nathan Strong, Samuel Moffat jun., Thomas Moffat.

145 (B 100) 1774 Novbr. 25 1783 Octbr. 10 **BRINCKERHOFF, John A.,** of Rumbouts Prect., Dutchess Co., yeoman. Wife Elizabeth, sons Abraham, George, Isaac and Dirck, daughters Phemmetje and Elisabeth. Real and personal estate. Executors brother Dirck Brinckerhoff, brothers-in-law Stephen Brinckerhoff and George Brinckerhoff, and Jacobus Swartwout. Witnesses Cornelius Wiltse, John Smith, William Alger.

146 (B 101) 1774 July 30 Septbr. 26 **BRODHEAD, Wessel,** of Marbletown, Ulster Co. Wife Catherine, sons Charles, Lewis, daughters Rachel, wife of Jacob van Wagenen, Mary, wife of John Cantine, Catherine, wife of Lewis Dubois, Elizabeth, wife of Dirck Romeyn and Geertruy, wife of Johannis Schoonmaker. Houses and land in Marbletown and Rochester; in the Great Patent, inherited from brother Charles Brodhead. Executors the wife, the two sons, sons-in-law Jacobus van Wagenen and John Cantine. Witnesses Benjamin Alliger, Frederick Rosekranz, Ch. D. Witt.

147 (B 102) 1774 Aug. 5 1781 Febry. 7 **BOSH, Johannis,** senior, of near Fishkil, Dutchess Co., farmer. Wife ——, sons Daniel, Honnes, Peter, Zakarius, daughters Margret, Nostront, Maritie. Real and personal estate. Executors Stephen Brinckerhoff, Ralph Phillips and son Honnes Bosh. Witnesses Isaac Adriance, Peter FitzSimons, Jacob Horton.

148 (B 103) 1774 April 17 Aug. 20

BRODHEAD, Charles, of the Green Kil, Ulster Co. Wife Marritie Hardenberg, brother Wessel Brodhead, nephew Charles Dewitt, two sons of brother Daniel Brodhead dec'd, *i.e.*, Daniel and Samuel, two children of sister Mary dec'd, *i.e.*, Andris Dewitt and Anne, wife of Corns. Newkerk. Lands at the Green Kil, in Hurly, in Kingston and in the Great or Hardenberg Patent. Nephew Charles Dewitt sole Executor. Witnesses Hendricus van Steenbergh, Gerret Freer, John Freer.

149 (B 104) 1774 March 9 1785 Novbr. 23

BEATTY, Arthur, of Little Britain, Ulster Co., weaver. Wife Lilly, sons John, Archibald, Alexander, William and Joseph, daughters Mary and Lilly, brother-in-law Joseph McMichael. Real and personal property. Executors sons John, Archibald and Alexander and Samuel Sly. Witnesses Patrick Barber, John Young, Chas. Clinton.

150 (B 105) 1774 April 30 May 3

BORDEN, William, of Albany Co. Children of the two uncles Nathaniel Hyatt and Jekiel Hyatt. Real and personal property. The aforesaid two uncles executors. Witnesses Benjamin Hicks, Joseph Doty, William Green.

151 (B 106) 1774 Decbr. 17 1779 April 23

BLAUVELT, Jacob, of Orange Town, Orange Co., yeoman. Sons Johannes and Peter, daughters Elisabeth, wife of Peter Perrie, grandchildren, children of son Abraham dec'd, viz: Jacobis, Abraham, Cornelia, wife of George Ramsen, Ann, wife of John Jersey, Elizabeth, wife of Stephen Voorhis and Mary; children of son Jacob dec'd, viz: John, Jacob, Margaret, wife of Captain Abraham Haring, Ranshye, wife of Jacob Terneur jun. and Elizabeth; childn. of son Isaac dec'd, viz: Mary, the wife of Douwe Tallon jun., and Catharine, wife of Claus R. van Houten, great-grandchildren Isaac and Ann, children of grandson Jacob Isaac Blauvelt dec'd. Real estate at Tappan or Orange Town, personal property. Executors son Peter Blauvelt and John Haring. Witnesses Cornelis Cor Smith, Matthew Light, David Bogert.

152 (B 107) 1774 Febry. 18 April 19

BEVIER, Jacobus, of New Paltz, Ulster Co. Wife Antje, sons Samuel, Jacob and Elias, daughters Antje, wife of Samuel Neely, Magdalena, wife of Jonas Freer jun., Sarah, Maria and Jannetje. Real and personal estate. Executors the three sons. Witnesses Gerrit Freer jun., Petrus Hasbrouck, Joseph Coddington.

153 (B 108) 1775 June 19 Octbr. 25

BEADELL, William, of Charlotte Prect. Dutchess Co. Wife Sarah, sons William, John, Jose and Daniel, daughters Elizabeth, Hannah, Eleanor, Mary, wife of Jacobus van de Water, and Sarah, w. of Daniel Doughty; brother Daniel Beadell of Queens Co., L. I. Real and personal estate. Executors the wife and Jacob Smith. Witnesses James Miller, John Hunt, Reuben Hopkins.

154 (B 109) 1775 March 7 March 25

BREWSTER, Edward, of Cornwall Prect., Orange Co., yeoman. Wife Experience, sons Daniel and John. Real and personal property. Executors brother John Brewster jun. and brother-in-law Samuel Strong. Witnesses Francis Brewster, Samuel Taylor, Thomas Moffat.

155 (B 110) 1775 June 24 1779 Jany. 27

BUCK, Jonathan, of Amenia Precinct, Dutchess Co., cooper. Wife Betty, son Zadock, grandson Jonathan Buck, of Bennington, Albany Co., daughters Betty Dewey, Zurriah Spencer and Annah Bennet. Land in Amenia Precinct, Great Nine Partners. Executors the wife and Roswell Hopkins. Witnesses: Barnabas Paine, Noah Brown, Martha Paine.

156 (B 111) 1775 April 24 July 10

BUCHANNAN, William, of Ulster Co. Nephews Alexander, son of brother Robert Buchannan, and Lambert, son of brother-in-law William Crawford. Personal property. Executor brother-in-law William Crawford. Witnesses Thomas Gregory, Peter Welling of Little Britain, Margaret Crawford.

157 (B 112) 1776 Septbr. 10 1779 Novbr. 27 **BRINCKERHOFF, Stephen,** of Rumbouts Prect., Dutchess Co. Wife ——, son John, daughters Meritay and Altje. Real and personal property. Executors Richard van Wyck and George Brinckerhoff. Witnesses John Luyster, Zachariah Bush, William Barkens.

158 (B 113) 1776 May 20 1782 Decbr. 21 **BRUYN, Cornelius,** of Shawangunk Prect., Ulster Co., yeoman. Wife Ida, sons Zacharias and Abraham, daughters Tryntie, wife of John Graham jun., and Geertruyd, wife of Methusalem Dubois. Land on E. side of Shawangunk River opposite to Pacanasink, at Pacanasink on N. side of said river, personal property. Executors the wife, son Zacharias and son-in-law Meth. Dubois. Witnesses Severyn I. Bruyn, Jacobus van der Lyn, Johs. Bruyn.

159 (B 114) 1776 July 30 1779 May 18 **BEATTY, Robert,** of Newburgh Precinct, Ulster Co. Wife Mary, sons Thomas, John, Robert and Francis, daughters Elizabeth, Ann and Mary. Real and personal estate. Executors brother Thomas Beatty and son Robert. Witnesses John Waugh, James Waugh, Cadwallader C. Colden.

160 (B 115) 1776 Febry. 20 1779 June 15 **BEECKMAN, Geertruyd,** widow of Henry Beeckman of Dutchess Co. Nephew Pierre van Cortlandt and his sons Gilbert and Philipp, sons of nephew Stephen van Cortlandt dec'd, viz: Philipp and William Ricketts, sons of brother Stephen van Cortlandt dec'd, viz: Stephen, Samuel, John and Philipp; sons of John van Cortlandt viz: Stephen, Nicholas Bayard and John; children of Andrew Johnston of Perth Amboy N. J. dec'd, William Tyrrell; daughters of brother Stephen v. C., Geertruy, the daughter of sister Cornelia Schuyler dec'd; daughters of sister Catharine Johnstone dec'd, son of niece Ann Tyrrell dec'd; daughters of sister Mary Miln; lame niece Rebecca, daughter of Samuel Bayard, nieces Mrs. Margaret Cockroft, Mrs. Margaret

Gage and Mrs. Margaret Watts. Lands: Front lot No. 10, including Anthony's Nose and other lots in van Cortlandt Manor; personal property includes plate. Executors nephews Pierre and John van Cortlandt. Witnesses Isaac Kip, William Radcliff, George Bull.

161 (B 116) 1777 Septbr. 12 1779 May 10

BROWNE, James, of Moyne, County Galway, Ireland, late of the Island of Jamaica, now of Philadelphia. Natural daughter Elizabeth Browne alias Brady by Betty Brady; brothers Dillon Browne and Valentine Browne of Moyne, sister Frances, wife of Walter Jordan, Ann and Mary Browne. Apparently only personal property. Executors Mathias Hanly, late of the Isld. of Jamaica, now of Philadelphia, Michael Dillon, of Guanaboa, physician, and Edmond Betagh of St. Johns Parish, Jamaica. Witnesses Alfred Clifton, John Lynch. Proved in N. Y. City.

162 (B 117) 1777 Aug. 9 1778 May 28

BELKNAP, Thomas, of New Burgh Precinct, Ulster Co., yeoman. Wife Sarah, sons Thomas, Joseph, Jonathan and John; daughter Sarah, wife of Isaac Belknap. Real and personal property. Executors the four sons. Witnesses Cornelius Wood, Moses Hunt, John Nathn. Hutchins.

163 (B 118) 1777 Febry. 10 1782 June 6

BRINK, Cornelius L., of Shawangunk Precinct, Ulster Co., yeoman. Wife Hester, children Cornelius, Solomon, John, Petrus, Catharina, Elshie, Lena and Rachel. Real and personal property. Executors the wife and the four sons. Witnesses Benjamin van Keuren, Elisabeth Rosekranz, Cornelius C. Schoonmaker.

164 (B 119) 1777 Septbr. 3 1778 May 27

BARNUM, Joshua, of Dutchess Co. Wife Em, sons Joshua, Azor, Eliahim, Jonah, Noah, daughters Em and Hannah. Real and personal estate. Executors son Azor and Benajah Tubbs. Witnesses Joseph Crane, Nathl. Foster of Dutchess Co. yeoman, Allen Ball.

165 (B 120) 1777 Septbr. 17 Novbr. 15 **BROWER, Nicholas,** of Albany City, yeoman. Wife Sarah, sons Nicholas, David, William, Jeremiah, Jacob, daughters Jane, wife of William Concklin, Mary, Sarah, Lene and Catherine, one unborn child. Land in Poughkeepsing Precinct, on Wappin's Creek, on N. side of Mohawk R., 9 miles above Schenectady, lots in Albany, personal estate. Executors the wife, son Nicholas and Henry I. Bogert. Witnesses John David, George Enax, John Roorbach.

166 (B 121) 1777 May 12 1778 July 6 **BARKER, William,** of Goshen, Orange Co. Wife Susannah, sons John and William. Land near Elizabeth Town, N. J., 16 acres, and in Orange Co. Executors the wife and son John. Witnesses James Denton, Wm. Thompson, Anthony Carpenter.

167 (B 122) 1778 April 28 1780 June 7 **BURHANS, Wilhelmus,** of Sagerties, Ulster Co., carpenter (son of Barnet Burhans). Wife Hilletie, sons Barnet, Jerrick, John, daughters Margaret Brink and Maretie Sperling. Land at Sagerties and at Braband (Kingston), personal property (great bible). Executors Henry Schoonmaker, John Brink and Christopher Kierstede. Witnesses Cornelius L. Swart of Sagerties, yeoman, Thark Schoonmaker jun.

168 (B 123) 1778 Aug. 1 1781 Septbr. 14 **BERKENMYER, Benigna Sibylla,** widow, of Albany Co. Thomas Hicks, son of niece Charlotte Hicks, other children of said Charlotte Hicks, and grandchildren of sister Susannah Hurtin dec'd. Personal estate. Executors Coenradt Flake, Francis Hardieck, Johannes van Loon junior and Henry van Hoesen. Witnesses John van Loon jun., Harmanus Bout, Coenradt Flaake.

169 (B 124) 1778 March 3 1786 Aug. 25 **BROWNSON, John,** of Amenia, Dutchess Co. Son Amos, grandson Brownson Foot (if he returns from the army), daughters Rody Graves, Hannah Foot, Mary Foot and Coay Barkar. Land at Waterbury, N. J. and

Sharon, Connt., personal property. Executor Aaron Foot. Witnesses Jonathan Shepherd, Bezaleel Rudd.

170 (B 125) 1779 Novbr. 4 **BARKER, John,** memorandum undated and unsigned of the last will of, proved in Dutchess Co., executors Benj. Gale and Coe Gale sworn in in Orange Co. January 9, 1779. Mentions mother Susannah Barker, daughters Jane and Suky, brother William. Land in Orange Co, six silver tablespoons, a dozen of silver teaspoons, one silver tea tongs, gold sleeve buttons, gold lockets, gold rings, silver buckles. Proved without being witnessed by the testimony of William Thompson of Orange Co., schoolmaster, who swore, that on the 2d of May, 1778 he had been called to write the foregoing mem. and that before he could copy it and "reduce it to Form," John Barker expired.

171 (B 126) 1779 May 10 1782 May 24 **BITCHER, William,** of Rynebeck, Dutchess Co. Wife Margree, daughters Catharine, Greetie, Jenny and Cartie, son John. Real and personal estate. Executors William Bitcher, Jacob Schermerhorn and Ryer Heermance. Witnesses Patt Hogan, Cornelius Schermerhorn, Jacob Stall.

172 (B 127) 1779 Decbr. 13 1780 Jany. 20 **BORLAND, William,** of Ulster Co. Wife Tabitha, sons Thomas, Charles, John and William, daughters Mary Bradner, Jean Armstrong, Patience McLaughlin, Tabitha Smith, Rebecca, Isabel and Phebe Borland. Lands in Ulster and Orange Co., personal estate includes a "large Bible" for son William. Executors the wife and sons Thomas and Charles. Witnesses Wm. Bodle, John McNeal, Wm. Denn.

173 (B 128) 1779 Febry. 13 1784 April 27 **BEATY, Francis,** of Rumbouts Prect., Dutchess Co. Nephew Francis, son of Samuel Beaty of Garg Water, County Terone, Ireland, and nephew Francis, son of Edly Brown, of the same place. Personal estate.

Executors Benjamin Snidar and John Halstead of Rumbouts Precinct. Witnesses John Donnelly, Solomon Sackrider, Henry Baker.

174 (B 129) 1779 Jany. 30 1783 June 20 **BARCLAY, John,** Mayor of Albany. Wife Margaret (second wife); Charlotte, wife of David McCarty, children of John Jonas Bronck, viz: Charlotte, Peter and Jonas; Charlotte, wife of Coenraedt ten Eyck and Peter, son of Andries ten Eyck, children of brother Andrew Barclay dec'd, and of brother Henry Barclay dec'd. Real estate, gold sleeve buttons, two gold rings, a silver tankard, silver mustard pot, two silver salt cellars, a silver tea canister among the personal property. Executors the wife, Peter Gansevoort and John M. Beeckman. Witnesses Henry R. Lansing, Robt. Wendell, Mat. Visscher.

175 (B 130) 1779 Novbr. 6 1784 May 7 **BOOTH, Benjamin,** late of Wallkil Prect., Ulster Co., now of Long Island. Wife Mary, daughters and sons, not named. Real and personal property. Executors the wife, Thomas Bull and Thomas Curtis, both of Ulster Co. Witnesses Thos. Colden, John Colden, Jane Colden.

176 (B 131) 1780 Jany. 21 1784 March 29 **BEEKMAN, John,** late of New York City, now of Goshen Precinct, Orange Co. Wife Christan, son Samuel, uncle Virdine Elsworth, brothers Theophilus and Thomas. Apparently only personal property. Executors Theophilus Beekman and Samuel Gale. Witnesses George Burling, Henry Gale, of New Jersey, physician, and John Shelts. Codicil of Aug. 18, 1780, adds David Matthews as executor.

177 (B 132) 1780 Jany. 11 May 29 **BACKER, Christian,** of Rynebeck Prect., Dutchess Co. Wife Anna, sons Wilhelmus, Petrus, and other children. Real and personal property. Executors Georg Sharp, Wilhelmus Backer and Wm. Seemon. Witnesses George Sharp, William Seemon, Jacob Levey.

178 (B 133) 1781 April 21 Aug. 16

BRUYN, Jacobus, (son of Jacobus Bruyn) of Bruynswyck, Shawangunk Precinct, Ulster Co. Sons Severyn ten Hout, Jacobus, Johannis, Cornelius, daughters Geertruyd, wife of Cornelius du Bois jun. and Mary, wife of Nicholas Hardenbergh. Lands in Shawangunk Prect., on the Klyne Kil, in Rochester Township, at Lower Smithfield, Penna.; personal property includes a silver tankard, silver table and teaspoons, silver milkpot. Executors sons Severyn, Johannis and Cornelius. Witnesses Benjamin Smedes of Shawangunk, Esqre. Abraham Smedes of the same place, farmer, and James G. Graham.

179 (B 134) 1781 Aug. 3 1783 May 6

BARTHOLFF, Jacobus, of Goshen Precinct, Orange Co. .Wife ——, sons Peter, Henry, Criness and Guliam, daughters Matinechee and Hannah, wife of Jacobus Lereau, granddaughter Rachel van Gelder. Farm near Sugarloaf, Goshen Prect., homefarm, personal property. Executors sons Peter and Henry. Witnesses Wm. Wickham, Samuel Bertholf, Stephen Bartholf.

180 (B 135) 1781 May 2 1786 April 18

BOYD, Robert, of New Windsor Precinct, Ulster Co., yeoman. Wife Jennet, son Robert, grandchildren Jennet, Elizabeth, Agnes, Jane, Elinor and Susannah, das. of son-in-law George Harris, Samuel, John, Jennet, Agnes and Robert, children of son Robert Boyd, Mebbe, Jennet and David, children of son-in-law Robert Andrews. Apparently only personal estate. Executors William Scott of New Windsor, cooper, and Thomas Moffat of Orange Co., Esqre. Witnesses John Herron, James Boyd, Hugh Turner.

181 (B 136) 1781 July 24 1782 Novbr. 12

BLAUVELT, Petrus, of Haverstraw Precinct, Orange Co., yeoman. Wife Margreetie, sons Johannis, Petrus, Abraham, daughters Petertie, widow of Claus van Houten, Catherine, wife of Steven Stevensen and two children of dec'd son Jacob. Real and personal property, including a "great Bible" for Johannis. Executors the three sons and brother Johanias Blauvelt. Witnesses David Pye, Resolvert van Houten and Jacob Brouwer.

182 (B 137) 1781 March 24 1784 Aug. 23 **BOGARDUS, Peter,** senior, of Fishkil Landing, Dutchess Co., cordwainer. Wife Elizabeth, children Peter, Egbert, Shiboleth, Cornelius, William, Hannah, Elisabeth, Mary and Deborah, Catharine Schoonhoven, wife's daughter by first husband. Real and personal property. Executors the wife, cousin Francis Bogardus, of Wappings Creek, cordwainer, and Duncan Graham of Poughkeepsie, yeoman. Witnesses John Young, John Phillips, Daniel van Voorhees.

183 (B 138) 1782 April 5. 1783 Jany. 22 **BRIGGS, Thomas,** of Dutchess Co. Wife Elizabeth, sons Nathaniel, William, Thomas, daughter Comfort Gay, granddaughter Amy, da. of son William. Real and personal property. Executor son Thomas. Witnesses Henry Tibbits, Charity Scranton, Jonathan Akin.

184 (B 139) 1782 Septbr. 4 1785 Decbr. 16 **BROWER, William,** of Rumbouts Prest., Dutchess Co., farmer. Wife Mattya, sons Jeremiah, Garret, William and Cornelius, daughter Letty. Real and personal estate. Executors the wife, sons Garret and William, and Abraham Hogland. Witnesses Francis Bogardus, John Ackarman, James Wills.

185 (B 140) 1782 Febry. 20 1787 Febry. 27 **BLAUVELT, Isaac Isaac,** of Orange Town, Orange Co., yeoman. Wife ——, sons Isaac, Abraham, daughters Bridget and Elisabeth. Land in Orange Town and in Haverstraw Precinct, personal property. Executors brother Cornelius Blauvelt and nephew Gerret Smith. Witnesses John B. Sebring, Harman Taulman, John Hering.

186 (B 141) 1782 May 1 1784 May 26 **BUSSING, Aaron,** late of the Out Ward, New York or New Harlem, now Rombouts Precinct, Dutchess Co. Daughters Polly Sickels and Catherine Storm, grandchildren John and Polly Waldron, Aaron and Susannah

Bussing. Real estate at Harlem, personal property. Executors John Sickels sen., Adolf Myers, John Myers. Witnesses Zacharias Sickels, William Delamarter, P. van Steenbergh of New York City, schoolmaster.

187 (B 142) 1782 Septbr. 18 1784 June 11 **BENSON, Johannes,** of Haverstraw, Orange Co. Mother Cornelia, widow of Cornelius Benson, brother Carel. Real and personal estate (one Dutch testament). Executors the mother and Abraham Pew. Witnesses William Campbell, William Campbell jun., Daniel Gero.

188 (B 143) 1782 Octbr. 1 1802 Decbr. 16 **BARCLAY, Margaret,** widow of John, late Mayor of Albany. Heirs of dec'd sister Gerritie, wife of Peter Gansevoort, niece Elizabeth, widow of Thomas Peebles of the Half Moon, brothers Jacob C., Anthony, Barent, Tobias and Andries ten Eyck. Real and personal property. Executors brother Tobias ten Eyck, nephew Conrad Gansevoort and niece Elizabeth Peebles. Witnesses Jas. Livingston, Coenrad Scharp, Abraham A. Lansing. Copy.

189 (B 144) 1786 Febry. 1 **BRADSTREET, Mary,** Probate of Will of widow, late of Boston, then of the Parish of St. Mary le Bone, Middlesex Co., England, by John, Archbishop of Canterbury, Primate of All England and Metropolitan. Will, dated March 23, 1782, bequeathes real and personal property to daughter Elizabeth, wife of Peter Livins, Chief Justice of Quebec, and a legacy to Sir Charles Gould, Knight, who is to be executor. Witnesses Jane Dumeny, John Scot, Sarah Nicholas. Parchment.

190 (B 145) 1783 June 21 1785 Jany. 18 **BICE, Arry,** of Charlotte Precinct, Dutchess Co. Wife Margaret, "reputed" sons and daughters, Henry, John, Arry, Charity, wife of Cornelius Osterhout, Catherine, wife of Benjamin North, Elisabeth, wife of Abl. Ostrander, Margaret, wife of Peter Simson, Cornelia Bice, 5 children of dec'd daughter Magdalene, wife of Frederick Hauver, John Pitcher, son of wife by former

husband. Real and personal estate. Executors John Pitcher, Peter Simson and Arry Bice. Witnesses Wm. Stewart, Benj. Thorn, Benj. Westfall jun.

191 (B 146) 1783 Novbr. 24 1784 Octbr. 12 **BAIN, James,** of Livingston Manor. Wife ———, sons Casparus, Philipp, William, James and John. Real and personal property. Executors John McNeill, Duncan McArthur, Kathren Ban and son Casparus. Witnesses Casparus Schutt, Wellem Fritz, Alexr. Monson. Proved in Washington Co.

192 (B 147) 1783 March 10 April 22 **BANGS, John,** of Fredericksburgh Precinct, Dutchess Co. Wife Lydia, daughters Hannah, Bethia and Mary, son Abner. Real and personal property. Executors Nathanel Foster and Theodorus Crosby. Witnesses Jehabad Lewis, Jeremiah Burges, James Foster.

193 (B 148) 1783 May 16 June 1 **BEEBE, Martin,** of Kings District, Albany Co., yeoman. Wife Dorcas, sons David, Martin, Russel, Daniel, son-in-law Ezra Parks, daughters Ann, Rhode, Mary, Sarah-Silva, Triphena and Lorania. Real and personal estate. Executors the wife, brother John Beebe and Asa Waterman. Witnesses John Stevens, Saml. Curtis, Pat. Hamilton.

194 (B 149) 1784 Decbr. 29 1785 March 31 **BRINCKERHOFF, John,** (son of Dirk Brinckerhoff) of Rumbout Precinct, Dutchess Co. Wife Jannetje, grandsons Adrian Brinckerhoff, John Brinckerhoff van Wyck; children of dec'd daughter Altje, late wife of Dr. Theodorus van Wyck, viz: Elizabeth, Altje, Theodorus, Yanetje, William, Dirk and Abraham. Land in Rumbout Precinct, at Middlebush, derived from father-in-law Johannis van Voorhis, in Birlin Township, a mountain farm, farm on Hopewell-Fishkil Road, in Philipps Precinct, mines at Trent, Connt. Executors the wife, son-in-law Dr. Theod. van Wyck, Jacobus Swartwout and Jacob Griffin. Witnesses Abm. Brinckerhoff, Albert Adriance, Daniel Ledew.

195 (B 150) 1784 Decbr. 6 1785 March 22 German

BASELER, Frederich, of Biver (Beaver) dam, Albany Co. Wife Anna, daughters Maria, Elisabeth, Margaretha, Anna. Real and personal property. Witnesses Christian Sand, Wilhelm Schneider, Christian Spilner. Anna, the wife, appointed administratrix, bond signed by Hendrick Baslaer, farmer, and Peter Fetterly, blacksmith.

196 (B 151) 1785 Jany. 24 1786 Decbr. 20

BOND, Elijah, of Northampton, Burlington Co., N. J. Nephew John Gardner, Mary, widow of John Barnes of Trenton, daughters of Rachel Stille, late of Trenton, viz: Elizabeth Hooton, Mary Hooton, Ruth Hooton and Sarah Hooton, son of Rachel Stille, viz: Pontius Delan Stille, St. Michael's Church, Trenton, Patience Fagan, Hannah, widow of Neel Livingston, late of Trenton, Major Frederick Vernon. Real and personal estate. Executors Isaac D. Cow of Trenton and John Lawrence of Burlington. Witnesses George Ely, Js. Barnes, John Emerson. Probated in N. J. Copy.

197 (B 152) 1785 Septbr. 16 1787 March 21

BLATTNER, Jacob, of Livingston Manor, miller. Wife Maria Sibilla, sons Christopher, Marcus, Hendrick and Johan Thys, daughter Magdalen, wife of Samuel Miller, Isaac, son of dec'd son Frederick, children of son Christopher, viz: Jacob and Maria Sibilla, children of da. Magdalen, viz: Jacob and Maria Sibilla, Philipp, son of son Marcus, Jacob and Maria Sibilla, children of son Henry, Jacob and Maria Sibilla, children of son Johan Theis. Real and personal property. Executors John Kortz, Herman Best and son Christopher Blattner. Witnesses John Cook, Zacharias Voland, Garret Kisselbrech.

198 (B 153) 1786 Decbr. 30 1787 April 5

BEEKMAN, Thomas, of Ulster Co., gentleman. Nephew Thomas Beekman, children Fletcher M. Beekman, Verdine Elsworth Beekman, Henry W. Beekman and Sarah Beekman. Real and personal property (gold sleeve buttons, marked T. B.) Executors brothers James and Theophilus Beekman, both of N. Y. City. Witnesses Henry Am. Williams, Cathalina Mathews, Fletcher Mathews of Wallkil Precinct.

199 (B 154) 1786 Novbr. 10 Decbr. 20 **BURTIS, Stephen,** of Beekmans Precinct, Dutchess Co., wheelwright. Wife Amy, son Isaac. Real and personal estate. Executors the wife, her brother Robert Brush and cousin David Burtis. Witnesses John Burtis, Andrew Skidmore, Samuel Crandel.

200 (B 155) 1786 Febry. 20 April 19 **BELDEN, Silas,** sen., of Charlotte Prect., Dutchess Co. Wife Janetie, sons Silas, Lowrans, daughters Mary, Jane and Elizabeth, heirs of da. Abegal, and Katrine. Land in Charlotte Prect., in Salisbury, Vermont, and in Canaan Township, Albany Co.; personal property. Executors the wife, son Lowrans and son-in-law Christopher Dutcher. Witnesses Daniel Moon, Math. van Dusen, David Rose.

201 (B 156) 1786 Septbr. 4 Octbr. 12 **BARKLEY, John,** of Montgomery Prect., Ulster Co., yeoman. Sons William and Nathan, daughter Jean. Real and personal estate. Executors James McCurdy and Samuel Barkley. Witnesses Samuel, David and Joshua Crawford.

202 (B 157) 1786 Jany. 11 April 26 **BRANDOW, Johannis,** of Cocksakie District, Albany Co., yeoman. Wife Janatie, son William and his sons Arent and William, daughters Elizabeth, Maria and Margaret. Land in Catskil Patent on John Broncks Lake, at Stick Oak in Albany Co., lots in Loonenburgh Patent; personal property. Executors son William, sons-in-law Johannis Conine and Wilhelmus Brandow. Witnesses Saml. van Vechten, Garrit Persen, Jas. Barker.

203 (B 158) 1787 Aug. 11 1800 Febry. 26 **BRADT, Albert,** of Bethlehem, Albany Co., farmer. Wife Elisabeth, sons Storm, Adrian, Francis, Peter and Edward, daughters Magdalene, Hannah and Claura. Real and personal estate. Executors the wife, John Merkle and John Erwin. Witnesses John Erwin, John Merkle, George Thompson.

204 (B 159) 1800 April 19 1801 Febry. 17 **BEARMAN (BOREMAN), William,** of Stephentown, Rensselaer Co. Wife Margaret, grandsons William and John Dixson. Real and personal property. Executors Andrew Hunter of Canaan, Columbia Co., and Hosea Moffit of Stephentown. Witnesses Salmon Bates, Andrew Stephenson, Polly Hunter.

205 (B 160) 1800 June 2 July 10 **BALL, Samuel,** of Albany. Mother Jane Ball. Executors Michael Cox and Isaac Mark. Witnesses David Buck and Christian Loss.

206 (B 161) 1786 April 15 Bond of Margaret, widow of **William BELL** of New Paltz, Ulster Co., boatman, as administratrix of her late husband's estate.

207 (B 162) No date, and incomplete **BREVOORT, Elias,** of N. Y. City, tinman. Wife Lea, sons Henry and John, daughters Jacomintie and Lea. Real and personal estate. Executors brother Henry Brevoort and kinsman Philipp Mint Horn.

208 1779 Decbr. 31 1787 Jany. 10 **BENJAMIN, Jonathan,** of Coromm, Brookhaven Township, Suffolk Co., yeoman. Wife Elisabeth, daughters Phebe, Hannah, Bethia, Sarah and Rachel. Real and personal estate. Executors the wife, son-in-law Benjamin Ovirton, and John Bellos. Witnesses Elijah Davis, David Dayton, John Leek. Recorded in Wills and Probates, vol. I., p. 20.

209 1786 May 3 1787 March 29 **BRUCE, Robert,** of Salem, Westchester Co. Amos, son of Abraham Purdy of Salem, sole heir of real and personal estate, his father executor. Witnesses Deliverance Purdy, Ebenezer Ward, Cornelius van Scoy. Recorded ut supra, p. 87.

210 1784 Aug. 25 1786 Febry. 14 **BLAIR, Frances** (da. of Lawrence van Hook of N. J.), widow of Rev. Samuel Blair, of Londonderry Township, Chester Co., Penna. Granddaughters Frances, daughter of Rev. David Rice of Virginia, Frances, daugh-

ter of son Rev. Samuel Blair, Frances, daughter of Rev. John Carmichael, Mary van Hook Foster, daughter of daughter Hannah Foster, daughters Frances Moore, Martha Edmiston, Susannah Sanderson, son William Lawrence Blair, granddaughters Martha Blair Foster, Hannah Susannah Foster and Elizabeth Foster; Ellinor Elliot and a daughter of Agnes Evans, formerly Haggarty. Real and personal property (a silver tankard). Executors sons Rev. Samuel Blair and William Lawrence Blair and William Hestel. Witnesses Thomas Whan, Samuel Love, East Caln. Recorded ut supra, p. 186.

211 1783 April — 1789 Jany. 2 **BLANCHARD, Francis,** late of N. Y. City, now of Trenton, N. J. Son James. Land in U. S. and in France, personal estate. The son James executor. Witnesses Jacob Remsen jun., of Staten Island, R. Stockton, A. Marroquire. Recorded ut supra, p. 204.

212 1788 Febry. 15 April 24 **BARTON, Joseph,** of Digby, Annapolis County, Nova Scotia. Wife Elizabeth, sons Benjamin, Henry, James, Barrent, daughter Anna. Lands derived from father-in-law Doctor William Brown John in the State of New York, lots at Digby, land in Province of New Brunswick, personal property. Executors the wife, Thomas Milledge and Rev. Roger Veets. Witnesses Christian Tobias, John Grigg, James Wilmot. Codicil of Febry. 16, 1788, directs sale of land on St. Mary's Bay. Same witnesses. Recorded ut supra, p. 205.

213 1774 June 9 1779 Febry. 4 Dutch **BEREWOUT, Frederik,** late Scheepen of Amsterdam, Holland. Wife Mary du Peyrou, daughter Jacoba, late widow of Andries Becker and now wife of Paul Hurgronze of the Admiralty Court, grandson Jan Trip, son of dec'd daughter Maria Catharina and Jacobus Trip Jansen, Secretary of the City, daughter Aaghie, son Jan Frederik Berewout, Director W. I. Comp., daughter

Margaretha Clara, late widow of Heerman van de Poll, now wife of Jan Backer. Real and personal estate. Executors son Jan Frederick Berewout, and son-in-law Jan Backer. Witnesses the Notary I. de Bruyn, Johannis Arnold Lette and Jan van der Spek. Recorded ut supra, p. 218.

214 1781 Septbr. 19 1791 July 29 **BEEKMAN, Gerrard W.,** late of N. Y. City, now of Philadelphia, merchant. Wife Mary, daughters Catharine, wife of Isaac Cox, Johanna, Margarit, Magdalin and Elizabeth. Real and personal estate. Executors the wife, brothers William, Abraham and James Beekman, brother-in-law Gerrard Duyckinck. Witnesses Francis Lewis, Francis Lewis jun., Mordecai Lewis. Recorded ut supra, p. 320.

215 1792 Aug. 7 Novbr. 12 **BANCKER, Adrian,** of Castletown, Richmond Co. Sons Christopher, Abraham, Adrian, daughter Ann Elizabeth, wife of Peter De Groot. Real and personal estate. Executors brother Evert Bancker, kinsman Henry Rutgers and son Abraham. Witnesses Peter De Groot, Peter Haughwoort, Samuel Parker. Recorded ut supra, p. 371.

216 1794 April 3 May 30 French **BORNICARD, Jean Louis,** late of S[to.] Domingo, now of N. Y. City. Wife Charlotte, son Pierre. House and lot in Ann Str., personal property. Thomas Bazen of N. Y. City, merchant, Joseph de la Croix of N. Y. C., Captain Pierre Valliant and the wife appointed guardians of the son. Executor Thomas Bazen. Witnesses Tryacinthe Garein, Wm. Alexander, R. J. van den Broek. Recorded ut supra, p. 416.

217 1794 June 1 1795 Febry. 14 **BRICKMAN, Henry,** of N. Y. City, wheelwright. Wife Catherine. Apparently only personal estate. Witnessed by Peter van Alen, Ludwig Cox, Saml. Cox. Recorded ut supra, p. 462.

218
1795
July 30
Novbr. 2

BEERS, Oliver, of New Town, Fairfield Co., Connt. Wife Catherine, son Cyrenius, daughters Lucretia, wife of Donald Grant Tousey (?), Amy Beers and Catherine Maria Beers. Real and personal property. Executors the wife, brother Andrew Beers of Stamford, Ulster Co., N. Y., cousin Samuel Beers of New Town, Connt., hatter. Witnesses Abraham Beers, John Sterling Beers, Rachel Beers. Recorded ut supra, p. 549.

219
1796
Septbr. 26
on board the
"Mary" of
Baltimore
1797
June 5

BOS, Tryntie, widow of William de Raadt. Cornelis Corns. van der Wal, husband of dec'd husband's sister, of Zequaart, Holland, Jannetie Bos, widow of Hendrick Lafalze, Peter Jacobus de Raadt, Gerret de Groot of Soctermer, Holland, sister Adriana Bos, widow of Ary van der Post, brother-in-law Adrianus de Raadt, "my travelling companion." Real estate in Holland and personal property. Executors Cornelis Corns. van der Wall and Cornelis Maas Kant. Witnesses the Captain, the Mate and two cabin passengers, viz: Daniel Nize, Hansen Conrod, Sybert Frederick, Willem Walters. Recorded ut supra, vol. II., p. 38.

220
1798
June 30
July 5
French

LA BORDE, Jean Alexander, late of Port-au-Prince, Island of St. Domingo, now of New York City. Sisters, Sophie, Emilie and Susette and another, the eldest, whose baptismal name he does not remember, Marie Olive Pierron and her children Valmont and Julie, Jean Alexis Robert. Coffee plantation and other land on the Isld. of St. Domingo, farm at New Marlborough, N. Y. Executor Jean Alexis Robert. Witnesses the N. Y. Notary R. J. van den Broeck, I. Magnac, P. Lertage, Brez. Recorded ut supra, p. 79.

221
1795
Jany. 23
1799
May 22

BARD, John, senior, of N. Y. City, physician. Daughter Dinah Magdalen Muierson, sons John and his wife Mary, Doctor Samuel and wife Mary, son-in-law Nathl. Pendleton and wife Susannah, and daughter Anna Pierce. Land in Minisinck Patent, personal property.

Daughter Dinah Magdalen Muierson sole executrix. Witnesses David Stewart Craig, Spael de Vaux, Marselis M. van Gieson. Recorded ut supra, p. 193.

222 1796 July 5 1800 Jany. 14 **BLOODGOOD, James,** of Albany City. Wife ——, sons William, Francis, James, daughter Eve. House and lot on Market Str. (now Broadway) Albany, personal property. Executors the wife, son Francis, da. Eve and Simeon de Witt. Witnesses Wm. P. Beers, Richard Lush, Peter Edmd. Elmendorf. Recorded ut supra p. 211.

223 1806 Aug. 18 1872 April 3 **BACON, Jabez,** of Woodbury, Litchfield Co., Connt. Wife Lidia, sons Asahel, John, Nathaniel, Daniel, daughters Lavena Tomlingson and Lydia Benedict, children of dec'd son Jabez, of son Garry and of dec'd daughter Jemima. Real and personal property. Executors son Nathaniel and son-in-law David Tomlinson. Witnesses James Moody, Elizur Castle, Abner Deming. Recorded ut supra, p. 305.

224 1783 June 14 Aug. 4 **BROWNEJOHN, William,** senior, of N. Y. City, druggist. Wife Mary, sons William and Samuel, daughters Elisabeth, wife of Joseph Bartow, Mary, wife of Timothy Hurst, Catherine, wife of Oliver Templeton, and Rachel, wife of John Price, children of son Thomas dec'd, viz: William, Elizabeth, Mary and Catherine. House and lot on Hanover Square, lot on Jews' Alley, personal property. Executors the wife, Gabriel William Ludlow, Cornelius Clopper, James Beekman and Henry Remsen. Witnesses Hugh Gaine, Eleazer Miller jun., Danl. McCormick. Recorded ut supra, vol. III., p. 3.

225 1780 Octbr. 30 Letters of administration, granted by James Robertson, Captain General &c. of the Province of New York to Margaret, widow of **John BECK,** late of N. Y. City, butcher and of the Commissary's Dept. at Charlestown. Vol. III., p. 77.

226 1791 March 5 Letters of administration to John Ball of N. Y. City, merchant, brother of **James BALL** of Charleston, S. Ca., merchant. Vol. III., p. 125.

227 1761 Septbr. 12 1766 July 5 **BROCKHOLST, Mary,** of N. Y. City, spinster. Sister Johanna Philipps, nieces Ann, wife of David van Horne, Susannah, wife of William Livingston, Elizabeth, wife of David Clarkson; children of dec'd sister Susannah, wife of Philipp French, children of dec'd niece Mary, wife of Honble. William Brown of Beverly, New England, who was also da. of sister Susannah French, nephews Frederick and Philipp Philipps, nieces Susannah, wife of Beverly Robertson, and Mary, wife of Roger Morris, both daughters of sister Johanna, late wife of Colonel Frederick Philipps. Real and personal estate. Executors David van Horne, Beverly Robertson, William Livingston and David Clarkson. Witnesses Jos. Forman of N. Y. City, merchant, Catharine Wynkoop and G. Jones. Recorded ut supra, p. 132.

228 1792 March 12 1803 Jany. 28 **BLEECKER, John R.,** of Albany City. Wife Elisabeth, sons Jacobus, Barent, John, grandchildren John R. Bleecker jun., Peter Edmonds Bleecker, Elisabeth Bleecker, Maria Bleecker, Blandina Bleecker and Sarah Bleecker; dec'd son Rutger. House and lot in Green Str., Albany, land in Saratoga Patent, at Otsquage, Montgomery Co., in Otsego Co., in Albany Co., on the Schoharie River, house and lot in 2d Ward, Albany City, land in Herkimer Co. Executors the wife and friend Jacob Bleecker jun. Witnesses Gerardus Lansing, Jacob Bleecker, Casparus Pruyn. Recorded ut supra, vol. IV., p. 14.

229 1775 Octbr. 23 1803 Jany. 28 **BEEKMAN, Henry,** of N. Y. City. Wife Gertruyd, daughter Margaret, wife of Robert R. Livingston, godson Henry, son of Wm. Beekman jun. Lots in the angle of Beekman and Cliff Streets, N. Y., house and lot in N. Y. and at Rhynebeck, farm, in Dutchess Co. Exe-

cutors the wife, daughter Margaret and husband, and William Smith. Witnesses John White jun., Johannis George Miller, John Haase. Recorded ut supra, p. 19.

230 1814 March 3 Aug. 13 **BLEECKER, Sybrant,** of Albany City, counsellor at law. Wife Sarah. House and lot in van Schaick Str., lot on Hare Str., Albany, land in Westmoreland Township, Oneida Co., other real and personal estate. Executors the wife, Samuel S. Lush of Albany, counsellor at law, and John S. Roff of the Town of Colonie, merchant. Witnesses Bernard O'Conner, Simpson Hatch, John Hamlin (the last had gone to live in Philadelphia, when the will was proved). Recorded ut supra, p. 80.

231 1805 April 20 1823 Novbr. 3 **BIRD, John,** of Troy, counsellor at law. Wife ——, sons John Hampden and Clarence. Real and personal property. Colonel Albert Pawling, Ebenezer Wilson and Benjamin Smith guardians of the sons and executors. Witnesses Theods. Drake, Isaiah Marble, Howard Moulton. Recorded ut supra, p. 150.

232 1829 Jany. 16 Febry. 2' **BASSETT, David,** of Kirkland, Oneida Co., marshall of the county. Wife Lillis, sons William, Nathan, George, Thomas, Hiram and Otis, daughters Laura, Cinthia, Annis wife, of Osiah Sweetzer, Mary, Eliza and Laura. Real and personal property. Executor Samuel Burgess. Witnesses Joshua White, Simon Hubbard, Marilla White. Recorded ut supra, vol. V., 85.

233 1825 Jany. 24 1829 Aug. 13 **BARLOW, Ebenezer,** of Florence, Oneida Co. Wife Abigail, sons Benoni, Ebenezer and Rowland all of Florence, daughters Abigail, wife of Ezra Gatchet and Anna, wife of Isaac H. Scott, both of Alleghany Co. Real and personal property. Executors son Ebenezer, Shepherd Marvin and Phineas Castle. Witnesses Shepherd Marvin, Joseph Bennett, Philipp H. Cody. Recorded ut supra, p. 92.

234 1642 Jany. — Dutch

BARTRAM, Jan, of Manhatans Island, born at the Gravenhage. Present wife Catrina Lysinck from Coetsvelt. Real and personal estate. Will much torn and parts missing. Witnesses Sibel Claessen, Hendrick Pietersen van Wesoe (?) and Cornelis van Tienhoven, secretary. N. Y. Col. MSS. II., p. 3.

235 1643 Novbr. 9 Dutch

BRONCK, Pieter, of Manhatans Island. Engeltie Maus, father, mother and other kindred. Real and personal estate. Witness Cornelis van Hoykens, fiscal. N. Y. Col. MSS. II., 88.

236 1649 Aug. 19 Dutch

BOUT, Jan Evertsen, from Barrevelt, and wife Tryntie Symons de Witt. The survivor inherits all property. Witnesses Willem Turck, Willem Tomassen and Jacob Kip, clerk. N. Y. Col. MSS. III., p. 58.

237 1663 Jany. 29 Dutch

BOGARDUS, Anneke Jans, first widow of Roeloff Jansen of Masterlant, then widow of Rev. Everhardus Bogardus, living at Beverwyck. Children Sara Roeloffs, wife of Mr. Hans Kierstede, Catrina Roeloffs, wife of Johannes van Brugh, Jan Roeloffs, Willem Bogardus, Cornelis Bogardus, Jonas Bogardus, Pieter Bogardus, children of dec'd da. Sytge Roeloffs, late wife of Pieter Hartgers, vizt: Jannetie and Rachel Hartgers, grandson Roelof Kierstede, grandda. Annatie van Brugh. Farm along the North R. on Manhattan Island, house and lot in Beverwyck (Albany), personal property (four silver cups,) Witnesses Rutger Jacobsen, Evert Jansen Wendel, Dirck van Schelluyne, Notary. Albany Co. Records, Notarial Papers, I., p. 296.

238 1727 Jany. 16 1759 June 1

BRATT, Dirck, of Kanistagiroene (Niskayuna), Albany Co. Wife Maria, children Johannis, Andries, Elisabeth, Cathalyntie, wife of William Barritt, Maria, wife of Ryckert van Francken, and Annatje. Real and personal estate. Executors the wife, Aarent Bratt and Hendrick ten Eyck. Witnesses Hendrick ten Eyck of

Albany City, merchant, Nicolaes Bleecker and Rutger Bleecker. Albany Co. Records, Wills, I., p. 248.

239 1756 Octbr. 14 1762 Decbr. 30 **BOGARDUS, Peter,** of Albany City, mariner. Brothers Shiboleth and Jacob Bogardus, sisters Wyntie, Cornelia and Catherine. Real and personal estate. Executor bro. Jacob. Witnesses Joseph Webb, Jacob de Garmo, shoemaker, and John de Garmo, yeoman. Albany Co. Records, Wills, I., p. 272.

240 1762 May 5 1765 Octbr. 28 **BLEECKER, Anthony,** of Albany City, merchant. Jacob Bleecker (son?), sister Annatje Bleecker. House and lot in Schenectady, lands of Kanajoharie, share in Westenhook Patent, personal property. Executors mother Antie Bleecker and sister Annatje. Witnesses Jerh. van Rensselaer, William ver Planck and Abrm. Yates jun. Albany Co. Records, Wills, I., p. 304.

241 1772 Aug. 12 1779 Septbr. 3 **BRONCK, John I.,** of Albany Co. Wife Charlotta Amelia, children Peter, Coeymans, Jonas and Charlotta Amelia. Real and personal estate. Executors the wife and David McCarty. Witnesses Anthony ten Eyck, Henry Knoll, Doctor, and Daniel Schermerhorn, farmer. Albany Co. Records, Wills, I., part 2, p. 59.

242 1680–1 Febry. 9 March 1 Dutch **BECKER, Jochim Wesselsen,** of Rensselaerswyck Colony, and wife Geertruy Hieronimus. Catharine Hoffmayer, wife of Pr. Lassingh. Real and personal estate. The survivor executor. Witnesses Jan Verbeeck, Pr. Adriaensen and Robert Livingston, secretary. Albany Co. Records, Court Minutes, 1680–5, p. 87.

243 1682–3 Febry. 17 1683 June 5 Dutch **BACKER, Jan Harmensen,** and wife Barentje Gerrits Paws of Albany. Children of wife's sister, vizt: Roeloff Pietersen Letwoor and Aeltje Pieters Letwoor, living at Amsterdam. Real and personal estate. The survivor executor. Witnesses Dirck Wessells (ten Broeck), Lawrence van Ale and Robert Livingston, Secretary. Albany Co. Records, Court Minutes, 1680–5, p. 415.

244
1694
Aug. 31
Dutch

BECKER, Jan, senior, of Albany City. Children Johannes and Martina. Real and personal estate. Witnesses Lawrence van Ale, Evert Banker, alderman, and Warner Carstensen. Letters testamentary granted to da. Martina, wife of William Hogan of Albany City, Decbr. 16, 1697. The inventory mentions a silver spoon, 3 pairs of gold shirt buttons, 5 dozen and 10 silver buttons for shirt and 2 silver Scnuffies (?). Albany Co. Records, Wills, I., p. 58.

245
3d Ann. Reg.
Novbr. 22
1704-5
Febry. 9

BRIES, Anthony, of Albany City, yeoman. Wife Catharine, children Marritie, Nellitie, Hendrick, Catharina, Margrett and Eva. Real and personal estate. The wife sole executrix with her father Albert Ryckman and Anthony Rutgers as Tutors. Witnesses Johannes Lydius, David Schuyler, Justice, and Rt. Livingston jun. Albany Co. Records, Wills, I., p. 109.

246
1713
Aug. 22.
1722-3
Febry. 23
Dutch

BARHEYT, Jeroon, of Albany Co. Wife Rebecca, son Wouter and a da. not named. "Whole estate." Witnesses Jacob Schermerhoorn, Myndert Marseles and Hendrick van Wie. Albany Co. Records, Wills, I., p. 182.

247
1728
Decbr. 16
1732
Decbr. 2

BEEKMAN, Johannis, of Albany City, yeoman. Wife Eva, children Johannis, Susanna, Jacob, Marten, Johannis Jansen, Henery, Jannatie, Hillena, Maritie, Johanna, Alida and Neeltie. Land in Kayaderosseras Patent (Queensborough), personal property. Executor the wife. Witnesses Thomas Williams, Hendrik Minderse Roseboom and Daniel Hogan. Albany Co. Records, Wills, I., p. 194.

248
1738
Septbr. 9
1743
Octbr. 6

BRONK, Jan, of Cattskil, Albany Co., yeoman. Sons Peter, Leonard, Jonas, Philipp and Casparis. Land at Koxsakje. Executor son Casparis. Witnesses Sylvester Salisbury, William Salisbury and Jacob Freese. Albany Co. Records, Wills, I., p. 209.

249
1761
March 28
1770
Jany. 5

BLOOMENDAL, Cornelis Maase, of Albany City, brazier. Nephews Maas and Albertus, sons of bro. Jacob Bloomendal, Maas and Cornelius, sons of bro. Jan, nieces Leah, wife of Cornelius van Deusen, Jacomyntie, wife of Jacob Ostrander, daughters of sister Gertruy, who has also sons Cornelius and Jacobus Ostrander. Real and personal estate. Executors nephews Maas, son of bro. Jan, and Maas, son of bro. Jacob, with Cornelius van Deusen. Witnesses Staats van Santvoord, gunsmith, John van Valkenburgh, joiner, and John Roorback, alderman, all of Albany City. Albany Co. Records, Wills, I., p. 334.

249a
1763
Febry. 10

BEBEE, Samuel, of Plumb Island, Suffolk Co. Children Samuel, Elizabeth, Elnathan, Theophilus, Lucretia, Hannah, Anne, Jemima, Jerusha and Silas. Real and personal estate. Executors the four sons. Witnesses Experience Griffing, Thomas Prince and Ezra L'Hommedieu. Copy. N. Y. Col. MSS., XCI., p. 140.

250
1765
March 11
1770
Novbr. 19

BRAT, Arent, surviving patentee in trust for the Township of Schonectady, Albany Co., leaves to his son Harmanis Brat, Jacobus van Slyck, John Sandersen, Isaac Swits, Isaac Vrooman, Nicolas van Petten, Jacob Swits, Jacob Vrooman, Frederik van Petten, Nicolas Groot, Tobyas ten Eyck, Reyer Wimple, Samuel Art. Brat, Nicolas van der Volge, Abraham Wimple, Abraham Mabie, Jacobus Mynderse, John B. van Eps, Gerrit A. Lansing, Peter Mabie, Harme van Slyck, Isaac S. Swits and Abraham Fonda the Township of Schonectady in trust for the freeholders and inhabitants thereof. Executors Jacobus van Slyck, Nicolas van Petten, John Sanderse and Abraham Wimp. Witnesses Hendrick Brower, cordwainer, Elias Post, gunsmith and Cornelius Vroman, cooper, all of Schonectady. Albany Co. Records, Wills, I., part 2, p. 64.

251 1788 Jany. 15 1818 March 10 **BARRET, Thomas,** of Albany City. Wife Elisabeth, bro. Peter, sisters Mary, wife of Daniel Hewson, Jude, wife of Peter I. Hilton and Nancy, wife of Richard Dun. Real and personal estate. The wife sole executrix. Witnesses Edw. S. Willett, Mat. Visscher and Lydia Visscher. In the proceedings to prove this will Nehemiah B. Bassett of Albany City, goldsmith, says, that Richard Dunn and his wife Nancy, sister of Thomas Barret, had children James, Mary, wife of Jacob Salsman, and Sally, wife of Bartholomew Schram; Peter I. Hilton and wife Jude, also sister of testator, had Elizabeth, wife of William Brown and Margaret, wife of George Brown junior; Daniel Hewson and wife Mary Barret, sister of testator, had Daniel, Thomas, John, Mary, wife of David Melick Burger dec'd, who left widow Nancy (Mary?) and children William, John and Maria, and that Mary van Kleeck, wife of Richard van Kleeck, Ann, the wife of Casparus F. Pruyn, Elisabeth, the wife of Jacob Lansing, who are the daughters of Robert, the son of said Mary Hewson and Robert Dunn, Thomas Dunn and Peter Dunn, the sons of said Nancy, wife of Richard Dunn, are the heirs of said Thomas Barret. Albany Co. Records, Wills, I., part 2, p. 75.

252 (C 1) 1694 Decbr. 11 1709 June 7 **CROON, Catrina Jansen,** of Albany, widow of Anthony Cornelissen van der Poel. Children Elisabeth, wife of Benoni van Corlaer, Mary, wife of Anthony van Schaick, Johanna Anthonis, wife of Jan van Stryden. Whole estate. Executors the three daughters and Johannes Abeell. Witnesses Dirck Wessells (ten Broeck), Evert Bancker, Robert Livingston jun.

252a (C 2) 1699 Novbr. 7 1706 June 29 **CROM, Floris Willemsen,** of Oringe Co. Wife Leyntie Aryaensen, children William, Argen, Tuentie, Geysbert, Mary and Dirck. Real and personal property, (land at Haverstraw). The wife executrix. Witnesses Hendryck ten Broeck, Jaques Fontyn, Samuel Bayard.

253 (C 3) 1702 Jany. 12 1713-14 March 3 Dutch

CREGIER, Martin, of Kanestagione (Niskayuna), Albany Co. Wife Jannetie, sons Martin and Samuel, daughters Lysbet, Marytje, Katrina, Johanna and Geertruy. Real and personal estate. The wife executrix. Witnesses Mattys Boffie and Johannes Quackenbos.

254 (C 4) 1704 May 10 June 10

CORBIN, William, of Boston, New England, clerk. Rev. George Hatton, late Minister of the Church of England at New Providence, now of Boston, Mrs. Katharine Ball of Boston, widow, Mrs. Mary Greggory of Boston, spinster, daughter-in-law of Thomas Newton of said place, Mrs. Jane Allen of Newbury, New England, spinster, daughter of Honorable Samuel Allen. Real estate in England, personal property includes one silver mugg, three silver spoons, and a diamond ring. Executors Thomas Newton, esquire, James Oborne and Thomas Newton, merchant. Witnesses George Thorold, Habijah Savage, Anna Thorold. Copy, will proved at Boston.

255 (C 5) 1708 Novbr. 17 1728 March 28

CASPERSON, Isaac, of Albany City. Wife Dorithy, sons Jacob, Hendrick, Gerrit, daughters Marritie, wife of Wouter Vrooman, Elizabeth, Rachel and Hannah. Island in Hudson R. above Albany and other land, personal property. The wife executrix. Witnesses Hendrick Hansen, Jan Rosie, Thos. Williamsen.

256 (C 6) 1714 Febry. 4 1717 May 4

CORBETT, John, of Orange Co., Captain. Cousin John Jordaine, niece Anna Morris, sister Elizabeth Jordaine, kinswomen Elizabeth and Mary Anna Jordaine, nephew Isaac Corbett, wife Mary residuary legatee and sole executrix, daughter Mary. Plantation called Rockland, Orange Co., house and lot in N. Y. City, personal property. Witnesses Davis de Klerck, Cornelius Herring, Bartholomew Vouck. Two copies, one on parchment.

257 (C 7) 1721 July 5 Aug. 9 **COTTIN, Jean,** of Ulster Co., merchant. Brother Daniel Cottin of Bohein, near St. Quentin, France, sisters Susanna, widow of Louis Libot of the same place, Mary, wife of Philipp Gilliat senior, cousins (nephews) Daniel Libot, Jacques Libot and their sister, being children of sister Susanna, nephew Philipp Gilliot of N. Y. City, servant Maria Folbreght, Susanna and Elizabeth Peviet, Marie Droilhet, Ann Droilhet, Susanna Droilhet, Eliza-Droilhet, French Reformed Church, Dutch Refd Churches in N. Y. and Kingston. Only personal property. Executors Thomas Bayeulx and Augustus Jay of N. Y. City merchants and Johannes Wynkoop of Ulster Co. Witnesses Elias Pelletreau jun., Ebenezer Grant, Abraham Gouverneur.

258 (C 8) 1725 May 6 1735 April 23 **CASPERSEN, Jan,** of Albany Co., yeoman. Wife Rachel, son Casper Janssen Haalenbeeck, daughters Elisabeth, wife of Jacob Evertsen, Rachel, wife of Jan Jacobsen van Hoesen, Marritie, wife of Jurriaen (George) Clauws, Rebecca, wife of Jan van Loon. Real and personal estate. Executors the wife and son. Witnesses Abraham Cuyler, Nicolaes Bleecker, Rutger Bleecker.

259 (C 9) 1731 May 1 1738 Febry. 24 **CASWALL, John,** of London, merchant. Wife Keziah, son John and a daughter, wife of Jno. Warnar. Real and personal estate. The wife, the son, the son-in-law and brother Henry Caswall executors. Witnesses William Snell, Benjamin Parkidge, Edmund Baugh jun. Copy.

260 (C 10) 1733 June 21 **CARLE, John,** of Hemstead, Queens Co. Sons of dec'd son Jacob and wife Miriam, viz. John and Jacob Carle; daughters Sarah, wife of Daniel Pine, and Hannah, wife of John Leminton, all of Hemstead; grandson J. Jacob Carle, son of John dec'd. Real and personal estate. Executors George, son of Joseph Balding and daughters Sarah and Hannah. Witnesses Sarah Clowes, Willemtie Langdon. Much Worn.

261 (C 11) 1735 June 17 June 27 **COE, John,** of New Town, Queens Co. Brothers Jonathan and Samuel, nephews Robert and Samuel, sons of dec'd brother Robert; Rebecca Furman; Benjamin Hinckman, Abigail Coe, Mary Denton and Hannah Wood, "my nephews," sisters Mary and Hannah. Land at Hemstead and in Jamaica, personal property. Executors Benjamin Fish of New Town and Benjamin Hinckman. Witnesses Timothy Wood, Judith Wood, Edward Howard.

262 (C 12) 1735 Febry. 19 **COSBY, William,** Governor of New York and New Jersey. Wife Grace, sons William and Henry. Land in Cosby Manor on the Mohawk, at Rochester, Ulster Co., houses and lots in Soho Square, London, and at St. Leonard's Hall and personal estate. Executor the wife. Witnesses James de Lancey, John Felton, Jos. Murray, Charles Williams. Copy.

263 (C 13) 1735 Septbr. 6 1736 Septbr. 15 **CURE, John,** of New York City, vintner. Children Anne, John, Robert, William, Sarah and Belicha. Real and personal estate. Executors son John Cure and brother-in-law Cornelius Cousen. Witnesses Rachel Saunders, Samoon Pells, H. Demeyer.

264 (C 14) 1737 June 8 1743-4 Jany. 13 **CROOKE, John,** of Kingston, Ulster Co., shopkeeper. Wife Catharine, sons John, William, Robert, Charles, daughters Gertruyd, wife of Evert Bogardus, and Mary. Real estate (some in Dutchess Co.), personal property includes a silver tankard, of 3 pints, given to son John to descend to next eldest son. Executors sons John, William and Robert and son-in-law Evert Bogardus. Witnesses Petrus Bogardus, Heyltie Deckers, Abr. Gaasbeeck.

265 (C 15) 1738-9 Jany. 29 1740 Decbr. 1 **CARPENTER, John,** of Goshen, Orange Co., house carpenter. Wife Elizabeth, children John, Wait (?) and Rebecca, also an unborn child; brothers Joseph, Samuel, Benjamin and Timothy. Real and personal

property. Executors Joseph Carpenter, Wait Smith junior, and Benjamin Carpenter. Witnesses Wm. Smith, Salomon Smith, Wm. ffinn.

266 (C 16) 1739 Aug. 30 1741 Octbr. 21 **CLAESSEN, Lowrens,** son of Clas. Lowretse (van der Volge), alias Lowrens Clasen van der Volge, of Schenectady. First wife Geertruy van Petten had children Neeltie, wife of Sander van Eps, Eva and Marytie, second wife Susanna Wolleven, also dead, had Catherine, Elizabeth, Ariaantie and Geertruy. Sons Claus Lowernsen, Petrus. Real estate in Schenectady, personal property includes a gold seal ring, a silver cup, marked L.V.V. and other silver. Executors Cornelis Cuyler and Simon Vroman. Witnesses Hendrick Roseboom, Cornelis Cuyler and Jams. Stenhouse.

267 (C 17) 1741 May 11 1742 Octbr. 30 **COE, Samuel,** of Havestraw Prect., Orange Co., yeoman. Wife Margaret, sons Samuel, John, Benjamin, William, Isaac, Mathew and Daniel; daughters Margaret, wife of Benjamin Skillmon of Newtown, Queens Co.; Sarah, wife of More Woodward of the same place, and Abigail. Real and personal estate. Executors the wife and sons Samuel and John. Witnesses Cornelius Cuyper, Jeremiah Seamon, Jonas Holsted.

268 (C 18) 1742 May 11 1747 Octbr. 10 **CUYLER, Abraham,** of Albany City. Sons Hendrick, Johannis, Abraham jun., Nicolaes, daughters Margrita, wife of Dirk ten Broeck, Sarah, wife of Johannis Beeckman, and Catharina wife of Jacob Coenraets ten Eyck. House and lot in Pearl Str., 2d Ward, Albany, do. on Jonkers (State) Str. on the hill, 1st Ward, lot in Schonhechtade, land near Tieonondaroka Flats, Mohawks Country, do. at Skohary alias Huntersfield, do. in Westenhook Patent; personal property. Executors the four sons. Witnesses Ephraim Wendel, David van der Heyden, Jacobus Bleecker.

269 (C 19) 1742 April 5 **CORNEL, Giliam,** of Flatbush, Kings Co., farmer. Children Adriaen, Cornelius, Jacobus, Wilhelmus, Giliam, Johonas Simon and Maregretie, wife of Rem vander Bilt. Real and personal property. Executors sons Adriaen and Cornelius, brother-in-law Dominicus van der Veer and Christianus Lupardus. Witnesses Johannes Waldron, Rem van der Bilt, Peter Strycker. Copy.

270 (C 20) 1743 Septbr. 29 1743-4 Febry. 24 **CROM, Tuenes,** of Tappan, Orange Co., farmer. Wife Jannetje, nephew William, son of Brother Floris Crom. Real and personal estate. Executors the wife and brother Floris. Witnesses Cornelis Eckerson, John Perrie, Johannes Ferdon.

271 (C 21) 1743 Aug. 22 **CURE, John,** of Tappan, Orange Co. Wife Helena sole heiress and executrix of all real and personal estate. Witnesses Catalyna Crage, Abraham Kip, Rem Remsen.

272 (C 22) 1744 Octbr. 23 1745 June 29 **CONNER, Daniel,** of Ulster Co., labourer, now on board the man-of-war privateer *Hester*, Capt. Samuel Byard. Doctor William Allison, surgeon of the *Hester* and her consort *Polly*, Capt. Wm. Morgane, sole heir and executor of personal property. Witnesses John de Kay, Elij. Decay, Rebeker Morris.

273 (C 23) 1744-5 Febry. 1 1750 Septbr. 12 **CAMPBELL, Lauchlen,** of Campbell Hall, Ulster Co. Wife Martha, sons Daniel, George and James, daughters Rose and Margrett. Real and personal property. Executors the wife, Alexander Montgomery and Edward Graham. Witnesses Wm. Brownejohn, Daniel Masters, Jno. Alsop.

274 (C 24) 17th George 2d May 10 1745 June 21 **CRUM, Yeantea,** of Orange Co. Son Honnas Howencomp, son of Mindert Howencomp, sisters and brothers. Real and personal property. Executors father John Buckhoute, Mortines Howencomp and John Perry

senior? Witnesses Matthis Cauden, Jacob Bockheut, F. Bloodgood.

275 (C 25) 1745-6 Febry. 12 1755 June 17 **CURTICE, Benajah,** of Wallkill, Ulster Co., yeoman. Wife Mary, children, aged father. Real and personal estate. Executors the wife and the father. Witnesses S. Leonard, John Holly, Caleb Curtis of Ulster Co., farmer.

276 (C 26) 1752 Septbr. 22 1757 Febry. 2 **COLE, Hendrick,** of Crom Elbow Precinct, Dutchess County, yeoman. Wife Mary, her cousin Jacob Bresy, his own cousin Ury Cole. Real and personal estate. The wife sole executrix. Witnesses John Germond of Crom Elbow, carpenter, Eleanor Mullin, Patrick Mullin.

277 (C 27) 1752 June 21 Novbr. 1 **CARPENTER, Samuel,** of Goshen, Orange Co. Wife Patience, sons Samuel, William, Abraham, John, Joshua and Richard, daughters Abagail and Martha, one unborn child. Real and personal estate. Executors Wait Smith jun. and Benjamin Carpenter. Witnesses James Smith, Samuel Webb, Jonathan Webb.

278 (C 28) 1753 Decbr. 26 1754 Aug. 24 **CORY, John,** of Southold, Suffolk Co. Wife Dorothy, sons Abijah and John, daughters Elesebeth Lawes, Dorothea Dickinson, grandson Bradick Cory, granddaughter Mary Wigins. Real and personal property (a silver cup and *cam*). Executors the wife and son Abijah. Witnesses Samuel Case, Alse Corey, John Drake. Copy.

279 (C 29) 1753 Octbr. 6 **COSBY, Henry,** Captain of the *Centaur* man-of-war R. N. Mother, the Honble. Grace Cosby sole heiress and with brother-in-law the Honble. Joseph Murray executrix. Real and personal property. Witnesses Peter Renaudet, Samuel Breese, Fran. Costigan. Codicil of same date gives to sister Mary Murray a gold watch, a

diamond ring and a diamond heart, to cousin Philipp Cosby wearing apparel and to James Stuart, mate of the *Centaur* man-of-war a gun. Same witnesses.

280 (C 30) 1753 June 27 1765 Aug. 27 **CUYPER, Claes Jansen,** of Tappan Township, Orange Co. Wife Wellemintie, sons John, Nicklas and Jonathan, daughters Contriner, Rachal and Leaner. Real and personal property. Executors Cornelius Cuyper, Abraham Cole and John Mier. Witnesses Abraham Meier, blacksmith, Thomas Willson, shopkeeper, Yacob Kool, blacksmith.

281 (C 31) 1754 June 25 **COEYMANS, Samuel,** of Rensselaerswyck Manor. Wife Catrina, nephew Andries ten Eyck, children and grandchild of nephew Coenradt ten Eyck dec'd, viz. Jacob C., Anthony, Barent, Tobias, Margarittie, Gerritie, wife of Peter Gansevoort and Elizabeth Bradt, daughter of Gerret Bradt dec'd; Gerritie, widow of Coenradt ten Eyck; children of brother Andries Coeymans dec'd, of Peter Coeymans, of Johannes Bleecker, of Barent ten Eyck dec'd, and Nicholas van Patten, son of Maickie van Patten widow. Land near Achquetoch on N. side of Hanebraays Creek, personal property. Executors the wife and nephews Jacob C. and Anthony ten Eyck. Witnesses Isaac Bogert, Guysbert van Sante, David ver Planck. Copy.

282 (C 32) 1755 Aug. 4 Oct. 25 **COUSZENS, Jno.,** Ensign 51st Regt. R.A., commanded by Major General Sir Wm. Pepperell. Parents Samuel and Isabel Couszens of Dublin, Ireland, friend Mrs. Ann Hopper of South Sheels. Lots in the South Suburbs of Halifax, Nova Scotia, personal property. Executrix Mrs. Ann Hopper. Witnesses James Campbell, Lieut. 51st Regt., John Mills, Lieut., Capt. Hubert Marshall's Independent Company. Proved in N. Y. City. Copy.

283 (C 33) 1755 Septbr. 4 1759 April 23

COLON, John, of Schnectady, felt maker. Wife Elizabeth, son William, daughter Catherine. House and lot in Schnectady, personal property (a silver hilted sword). Executors Nicholas Folkertsen Veeder and William Schermerhorn. Witnesses Pieter Bosie, Harmans Peck, Thomas Nichson.

284 (C 34) 1757 March 2 March 30

CARTER, James, mariner belonging to the Snow *Hull Merchant*, Peter Dobins master, friend William Dowers of N. Y. City blocks with sole heir and executor of personal estate. Witnesses Emanuel Abrahams, Souering Sybrandt, George Clapham. Copy.

285 (C 35) 1757 April 17 May 5

CLARK, Eaphraim, of Floredy, Orange Co. Wife Mary, daughters Rebecca, Mary, Hannah, Martha, Deborah and Abigail, son James. Real and personal property. Executors the wife and Daniel Shepard of Floredy. Witnesses James Miller, Ananias Whitman, Wm. Denn.

286 (C 36) is a letter from John Crooke, dated Kingston March 10, 1757, to Deputy Secretary Goldsboro Banyar, complaining of Levi Pawling as executor of James Scott's estate.

287 (C 37) 1757 April 13 May 13

CHURCHILL, Edward, of Rumbouts Precinct, Dutchess Co. Wife Wentje, sons Abel, John, Robert, daughters Anna, widow of Isaac Coffin, and Levina, wife of John Totten, grandsons John, Joseph and Edward, sons of son John. Real and personal estate. Executors son-in-law John Totten and William Roe. Witnesses Chauncey Graham, Dirck Brinckerhoff, Joseph Wright.

288 (C 38) 1757 Aug. 4 1762 June 3

CAMPBELL, John, of Rumbout Prect., Dutchess Co. Wife Margret sole heiress and executrix of real and personal property. Witnesses Samuel Mills, Petrus Kip.

289 (C 39) 1757 Febry. 19 1758 July 5

CLINTON, Alexander, of Ulster Co., Surgeon-Apothecary. Brother George, Jane McClaughry, the poor of Highland Precinct, James and Catharine McLaughry. Personal property. Executors James and Catharine McLaughry. Witnesses John McLaughry of Ulster Co., carpenter, John Davis.

290 (C 40) 1757 Octbr. 2 1767 Septbr. 23

CUYPER, Tunis, of Naringshaw, Orange Co. Wife ——, sons Cornelius, Abraham, Tunis, daughters Altje and Maritie, wife of Hend. Teneur, granddaughter Gritie, child of da. Gritie. Real and personal estate. Executors the three sons. Witnesses Cornelius Eckerson, Cornelius Eckerson jun., Theodor Valleau.

291 (C 41) 1758 May 28 Aug. 14

CORNELL, Richard, son of Richard of Scarsdale Manor, Westchester Co. Wife Mary, son Peter, granddaughter Mary Cornell. Real and personal estate. Executors son Peter and brother Benjamin Cornell. Witnesses Ebenezer Haviland, Abigail, wife of Benjamin Cornell, Hannah Cornell. Copy.

292 (C 42) 1759 July 30 1760 April 7

CARR, George, of Floredy, Orange Co. Wife Jean, son George, daughters Hannah, Elizabeth, Mary Bull, Margaret Howell, Ann, Phebe, Sarah and Jean. Real and personal estate. Executors the wife and sons-in-law Matthew Howell and Thomas Bull. Witnesses George Bloem, Wm. Denn and John Martin.

293 (C 43) 1759 May 24 Octbr. 30

CUYPER, Cornelius, of Orange Co. Wife Derike, son Lambert, daughters Altie, Sarah and Lena, grandchildren Stephen and Mary Stephenson. Homefarm and land in Cakeyat Patent; personal property. Executors Lambert Smith, Cornelius Eckerson and Lambert Cuyper. Witnesses Abram Kool, Andries Onderdonck, Andries Onderdonck jun.

294 (C 44) 1759 March 17 1767 Jany. 31

CRAWFORD, Samuel, of Wallkil, Ulster Co. Wife Ann, children Alexander, Margaret, Rachel and an unborn child. Real and personal estate. Executors the wife and brother James Crawford. Witnesses John Crawford, Joseph Crawford, James Fulton.

295 (C 45) 1759 Jany. 19 June 11

CHILDS, Thomas, of New Windsor, Ulster Co., bricklayer. Wife Cateren, an expected child and Thomas Lines. Real and personal estate. The wife executrix. Witnesses Isaac Hodge, Saml. Bartlet, Francis Purdy.

296 (C 46) 1759 May 23 1768 Feby. 15

CHRIST, Henry, of Ulster Co., yeoman. Son Jacob, daughters Elizabeth, wife of Jacob Sinsinbough, Catherine, wife of Christian Rockeefellow, and Margaret, wife of John McClean. Farm on West side of Wallkil River, land on East side of said river. Witnesses Peter de Lancey jun, Richard Bull, David Colden. Letters testamentary granted to Julian, the widow, and Jacob, the son of Henry Christ Decbr. 18, 1768.

297 (C 47) 1760 April 28 June 11

COLLINS, Margaret, widow of Edward, of Albany City. Bro. John Rutsen Bleecker and Jacobus Bleecker, Marten Gerritsen van Bergen, widow Anganita Scott and her sister Elisabeth Williams. Real and personal property. Executor brother John R. Bleecker. Witnesses Barent H. ten Eyck, Staats van Santvoord, Cathalina van Ness.

298 (C 48) 1760 April 29 1761 April 18

COOPER, William (son of Obadiah), of Rumbout Precinct, Dutchess Co., carpenter. Wife Sarah, and six children, not named. Real and personal estate. Executors brother John Cooper, Jonathan Dubois and Eliza Dubois. Witnesses Lucas Wynkoop, Evert Brown, Thomas Schoonmaker.

299 (C 49) 1760 Septbr. 3 1761 May 10

CASE, Daniel, of Goshen, Orange Co. Wife Abigail, sons Daniel, Phineas, and Zacheus, da. Martha, grandsons David and Daniel Case, granddaughters Mary and Sarah Case. Real and personal estate. Executors brother-in-law George Thompson and cousin Joshua Brown. Witnesses Martha Case, David Moore jun, Wm. Denn.

300 (C 50) 1760 April 19 Decbr. 20 **CREGO, Stephen,** of Crom Elbow Precinct, Dutchess Co. Wife Margaret, sons Richard and John, daughters Jane and Anna, mother Ann Crego. Land at Crom Elbow and in Beekmans Precinct; personal property. Executors the wife and the two sons. Witnesses Joseph Haff, John Barto, Benjamin Barto.

301 (C 51) 1760 Octbr. 3 Novbr. 8 **CARPENTER, John,** of Goshen. Wife Elener, son Anthony, daughters Hannah and Eunice. Homefarm, share in Wawayanda Patent, land near Sugarloaf, do. in Connecticut Purchase on the Susquehannah River; personal property. Executrix the wife. Witnesses Solomon Carpenter jun, Thomas Wickham, Nehemiah Carpenter.

302 (C 52) 1760 May 15 Novbr. 11 **CARRICK, Thomas,** late of Newry, Ireland, now of N. Y. City. Wife Martha, children Charles and Martha. Personal estate. William Gilliland of N. Y. City, merchant, executor. Witnesses Andrew Hook and Richd. Stephens.

303 (C 53) 1760 March 31 1761 June 6 **CORNELL, John,** of Rumbout Precinct, Dutchess Co. Wife Mary, son Mertin (to be educated in the knowledge of physics), daughters Jane and Mary. Storehouse at Fishkil Landing, called Frankford's Store, personal property. Executors the wife, Mertin Wiltse and John Smith. Witnesses Henry Cornell, Michael Stilwill, John Couch.

304 (C 54) 1760 Jany. 30 1764 Jany. 10 **CYPHER, William,** of Poughkeepsie Prect., Dutchess Co. Wife Nelle, sons David, William, Lodwyck, daughters Elizabeth, wife of Carel Hoffman, Mar-

griet, Altie, Annatie and Sarah. Real and personal estate. Executors son-in-law Carel Hoffman, John Concklin, Tunis Tappen and son David. Witnesses Henry Livingston, Roelof Westervelt, Jacob Concklin.

305 (C 55) 1761 Octbr. 7 Novbr. 10 **CAMPBELL, Hugh,** of New York, mariner. Friend William Scott of N. Y. City, victualler, sole heir and executor of personal property. Witnesses James Ferguson, David Philipse, Philipp Fogerty. Copy.

306 (C 56) 1761 Septbr. 11 1762 July 7 **CARPENTER, Solomon,** of Goshen, Orange Co. Children of sons John and Anthony dec'd.; sons Solomon and Nehemiah; daughter Mary ffinn. Personal property. Executors sons Solomon and Nehemiah. Witnesses Benjamin Corey, James Little, M. Duning.

307 (C 57) 1761 March 11 1767 March 17 **CUYLER, Hendrick,** of Albany City, merchant. Wife Margreta, son Abraham, daughters Catreentie, wife of Jacob van Schaik, Elizabeth, Catelina, wife of Hendrick Bleecker jun. Real and personal estate (a silver tankard, a silver teapot). Executors son Abraham and brother Nicolaas Cuyler. Witnesses Johs. Roseboom, Jno. Glen, Abm. Yates jun.

308 (C 58) 1762 June 7 1763 Decbr. 16 **CHRYSTIE, George,** of New York, Sergeant Capt. Barneby Byrn's Company. William Mooney, butcher, sole heir and executor. Witnesses James Mackenzie, Daniel Durland, Elizabeth Flanigan. Copy.

309 (C 59) 1762 Aug. 10 1764 Jany. 5 **CROOKE, Charles** jun., of Crooke's Delight, Charlotte Precinct, Dutchess Co., merchant. Wife Cornelia, children of brother-in-law Petrus Edmundus Elmendorph, viz.: John, Catharina, Blandina Elizabeth and Sarah. Real estate, partly inherited from brother-in-law Evert Bogardus; personal estate. Executors brother-in-law P. E. Elmendorph and Everardus Bogardus. Witnesses John Dowzenberry, Cornelis Ostrander, John Wynkoop.

310 (C 60) 1762 Septbr. 25 Novbr. 3

COOLEY, Daniel, of Goshen, Orange Co., yeoman. Sons Daniel, Isaac, Samuel, Jonathan and David, daughter Sarah, granddaughter Mary Jayn. Land at Goshen and in Wawayanda Patent, personal estate. Executors son Jonathan, Matthew Howell and Daniel Everett. Witnesses William Knap, John Chandler, James Knap.

311 (C 61) 1764 March 20 1786 April 5

CURTICE, Mary, of Otterkill, Ulster Co. Four sons, of whom the two youngest, Jeremiah and Noah, are only mentioned by name. Personal estate. Executors Benjamin Booth and Wm. Denn. Witnesses Phebe Booth, John Booth, Elizabeth Hopper.

312 (C 62) 1764 Septbr. 6 1765 Octbr. 2

CUYPER, Johannis, of Orange Town, Orange Co., yeoman. Wife Sarah, grandson Cornelius Cuyper, daughters Catherine, Altie, Nellie and Sarah, son Johannes. Real and personal property. Executors the wife and son and Aaron Smith of Haverstraw. Witnesses James Spock, John Cuyper, boatman, and Andries Onderdonck jun., farmer.

313 (C 63) 1764 Aug. 20 Novbr. 16

CHAMBERS, John. Wife ——, sons Silas and Daniel. Real and personal property. Executors John Young and William Young. Witnesses John Flack of Orange Co., labourer, John Gilchrist and Sarah Flack.

313a (C 63) 1764 Jany. 20 May 1

CHAMBERS, John, of New York City, esquire. Wife Ann, da. of Col. Jacobus van Cortlandt, Corporation of Trinity Church, Augustus van Cortlandt ("whom I brought up"), John, son of brother-in-law Peter Jay, Mrs. Eve (van Cortlandt) White, sister of aforesaid Augustus, and her daughter Ann White, James van Cortlandt and Frederick van Cortlandt, brothers of Augustus, Colonel Vincent Mathews, John Bartow of Westchester, Lambert Moore. Land in Cheescock Patent, Orange Co., houses and lots in N. Y. City, personal estate (lawbooks, manuscripts). The wife sole executrix and after her death brother-in-law Peter Jay, nephews John Livingston of N. Y. City merchant, James van Courtlandt and Augustus v. Cortlandt. Witnesses Richd. Nicholls, John Kelly and Benjamin Helme all of N. Y. City, gentlemen. Copy.

314 (C 64) 1764 Febry. 23 1767 Octbr. 10 **CARPENTER, Benjamin,** of Orange Co. Wife Mary, sons Gilbert, John and Samuel, "three youngest daughters," Sarah, Mary and Rhoda. Real and personal property. Executors the wife and cousin Samuel Carpenter. Witnesses Henry Wisner, John Carpenter Smith, Isaiah Hallsted.

315 (C 65) 1765 Jany. 26 June 17 **CAMPBELL, Archibald,** of New York City. Wife Cathrin, son James, daughter Mary. Real and personal estate. Executors Alexander MacDugal and Christopher Schuyler. Witnesses Jacob Stoutenburgh, Harmanis Schuyler of N. Y. City, painter, John van Pelt. Copy.

316 (C 66) 1765 March 12 May 18 **CUYLER, Cornelius,** of Albany City, merchant. Sons Henry, Cornelius and Abraham, daughters Elizabeth, wife of Colonel James van Cortlandt, and Margaret, wife of Isaac Low. House and lot 2d Ward Albany and other real estate; personal property. Executors the three sons. Witnesses David Groesbeeck, Pieter de Garramao, cordwainers, Pieter Silvester, attorney-at-law, all of Albany.

317 (C 67) 1766 Jany. 13 1767 Octbr. 10 **CARPENTER, John I.,** of Blooming Green, Orange Co., merchant. Wife Jane, son Matthew, daughters Julia, Rachel and Amira, brothers Elijah and William Carpenter, brothers-in-law Hezekiah Howell jun., Stephen Howell and Charles Howell, sisters-in-law Phebe Howell, Susanna Howell and Abigail Howell. Real and personal property. Executors the wife, Michael Jackson and Hezekiah Howell jun. Witnesses Thomes Greag, Samuel Smith jun., Wm. Carpenter.

318 (C 68) 1767 March 9 1771 Aug. 16 **CRISPELL, Anthony,** of Hurley, Ulster Co. Sons Johannes and Cornelius, daughter Neeltie, wife of Dirck Roosa. Real and personal estate. Executors the two sons, son-in-law Dirck Roosa and Adrian Wynkoop. Witnesses Heyman Roosa, Lucas Elmendorph, Petrus Wynkoop, all of Hurley, farmers.

319 (C 69) 1768 April 14 April 7 **COLEMAN, Curtis,** of Blooming Grove, Cornwall Precinct, Orange Co., tailor. Wife ——, son Abner, daughters Amey and Eunice and an expected child. Apparently only personal estate. Executors Joseph Coleman and Thomas Coleman jun. Witnesses William Hudson, Caleb Coleman, Lewis Donnovan, schoolmaster. N. B. This will is dated April 14, the certificate by Surrogate John Gale of Orange of swearing the witnesses is dated April 7. The same Surrogate has sworn in the executors April 14, and the will is marked probated May 25, 1768.

320 (C 70) 1768 Decbr. 10 1770 Febry. 11 **CORY, Jonathan,** of Orange Co. Wife Patience, sons Elnathan, Jonathan, daughters Mary Smith, Lowis More, Temperance Sheppard, grandsons John, son of Elnathan Cory, and Jonathan, son of Abraham Sheppard. Real and personal property ("my grate bible"). Executors Doctor Nathaniel Elmer of Floreday and Samuel Carpenter of Goshen. Witnesses Charles Carroll, David Sheppard, yeoman, and William Seely.

321 (C 71) 1768 Octbr. 25 1769 March 22 **CARSKADAN, Robert,** of New Windsor Precinct, Ulster Co. Sons Andrew, John, Robert and Thomas, grandsons Caleb Wily, William Carskadan Case, daughters Margery Case and Lydia Jain; Joseph Paterson. Real and personal property (a chest brought from Havanna). Executors Patrick and James McClaghry. Witnesses David Parshall, William Gage, Robert Carskadon.

322 (C 72) 1769 April 4 1771 March 25 **CARMAN, John,** of Beeksmans Precinct, Dutchess Co. Sons Thomas, Joshua, son-in-law Joseph Doughty, daughters Mary Sleght and Martha. Real and personal estate. Executors son Joshua, sons-in-law William van Wyck and John Henry Sleght. Witnesses Dobson Wheeler, Garshom Martin, John Dorlon.

323 (C 73) 1769 April 28 1771 May 31 **CINNEY** (probably Kinney), **Andrew,** of Hurley, Ulster Co., farmer. "The Old English Church in the City of New York, who being kept according to the Constitution of the Church of England." Executors Andries DeWitt jun. and Levi Pawling. Witnesses John P. Dumond and Tjerck C. DWitt, of Kingston, farmers.

324 (C 74) 1770 May 1 Aug. 15 **COLLINS, Adam,** of Blooming Grove, New Cornwall Precinct, Orange Co. Mother, brother-in-law Nathaniel Seely, nephews Jeremiah Colman and Samuel Seely, brother Jacob Gale. Real and personal estate. Executors Nathaniel Satterly and brother-in-law Nathaniel Seely. Witnesses Nathan Marvin and Colman Curtice.

325 (C 75) 1770 April 27 **CAMPBELL, John.** Sisters Margaret Campbell, Catharine McArthur and Ann Campbell, brothers Archibald, Alexander and James Campbell, mother Ann Campbell, cousins Duncan and Alexander Campbell of Kingston, Jamaica, Rev. Mr. Mason, widow Mary Mackie. Lots 36, 37 and 38, lately purchased from Goldsborrow Banyan, personal property. Executors Peter Middleton, Johnston Fairholme and Walter Buchanan. Extract of a will dated as above, May 12, 1770 and June 25.

326 (C 76) 1770 April 25 1772 Decbr. 1 **CROOKE, Charles,** of Charlotte Precinct, Dutchess Co., yeoman. Wife Jannitje, wife's sister Banshe van Valkenburgh, son Charles, daughter Annaka, the Church of England at Poughkeepsie. Real and personal property. Executors the wife, brother John Crooke, brother-in-law Gabriel William Ludlow, wife's brothers-in-law Lawrence Funda and John Oosterhout. Witnesses Ananias Cooper, Hannah Walker, Bartholomew Crannell.

327 (C 77) 1771 Jany. 13 June 13 **CONKLING, Joshua,** of Newburgh Precinct, Ulster Co. Wife Mary, sons William, Joshua and Edmond, daughters Mary, Keziah Jean, Ester, Hannah, Ruth, Rachel and Sarah. Real and personal estate. Executors the wife, Arthur Smith and Stephen Wiggens. Witnesses Elijah Carman, David Purdy, Leonard Smith.

328 (C 78) 1773 Jany. 30 1780 Octbr. 5 **CAMPBELL, Samuel,** of Ulster Co., farmer. Wife Mary, sons Samuel, Daniel, Nathenal, Jonathan, Joel, Levi, Nathan, Ruben. Real and personal estate. The wife executrix. Witnesses Neal Anderson, of Wallkil, weaver, Mary Norris, wife of Wm. McDowel of Hannover Precinct, Ulster Co., and Samuel McCollam.

329 (C 79) 1773 March 19 1774 Septbr. 5 **CONYN, Peter,** of the Mohawks River, Tryon Co., esquire. Wife Rabaca, sons Petrus, John and Abraham, daughters Ally, wife of Adam Zielen, and Deborah (a widow), granddaughter Ariaentie Zielen. Land in Wilson, Abeel and Hansens Patent, do. on S. side Mohawk R., personal property (a silver cup marked P. W., silver spoons). Executors Christopher Yates, brothers Myndert and Andrew Wemple. Witnesses Hendrick Hansen, Simon Veeder, and John Wemple.

330 (C 80) 1774 Septbr. 24 Decbr. 16 **COLDEN, Alexander,** of Brookland, Kings Co., esquire. Wife Elizabeth, children Richard Nicholls Colden and wife Harriot, sons-in-law Archibald Hamilton and wife Alice, John Antill and wife Margaret, Anthony Farrington and wife Elizabeth, daughter Jane, son John, brothers Cadwallader and wife Elizabeth and David with wife Ann, brother-in-law Doctor William Farquhar, Rev. Samuel Auchmity, Doctor Peter Middleton, grandsons Alexander Colden, son of Richard, Alexander Mark Ker Hamilton, John Collins Antill and Charles Farrington; granddaughters Mary Elizabeth Jane Douglas Hamilton, Alice Margaret Campbell Hamilton, Elizabeth Farrington. House and lot in Brookland, do. at Newburgh, Ulster Co., lot called Beaver Dam in Alexander Baird's

Patent, lots in Geo. Harrison's Patent in Ulster Co., land on Mohawk R., adjoining Huntersfield, do. at Schohary, part of Johannes Lawyers et al. Patent, land in Cambridge Township and in Pittstown Township, in Magin's Purchase on Canada Creek, in Schuyler's Purchase, personal property ("two Ear'd Silver Cups, known by the name of the Cawdle Cup," a silver tobacco box and plate). Executors the wife, son Richard Nicholls Colden, son-in-law John Antill, trustees sons-in-law Archibald Hamilton and Antony Farrington. Witnesses Joseph Keys of Bedford, Kings Co., tailor, John McDonald, Bartholomew Besly, Copy.

331 (C 81) 1774 March 18 1775 April 4 **COSINE, Cornelius,** of the Out Ward, N. Y. City, farmer. Mother Deborah Cosine, sister Sarah, wife of William Swanser, brother Balm Johnson Cosine and his children, viz. Sarah, John, Hannah, Deborah, Nicholas, Cornelius and Catharine. Real and personal estate. Executors John Hopper jun. and Wessel Hopper. Witnesses Gerardus Hardenbrook, John Krouss, G. Furman. Copy.

332 (C 82) 1775 May 20 1776 March 7 **CHRIST, Stephanus,** of Hanover Precinct, Ulster Co., tavernkeeper. Wife Eva, sons Daniel, Frederick, Christian, Simeon and Jonathan, daughter Hannah. Real and personal estate. Executors the wife, Philipp Christ and Martinas Christ. Witnesses Jacob Crist, Samuel Smith and William Stewart.

333 (C 83) 1775 Aug. 18 1778 July 29 **CRISPEL, Cornelius,** of Hurley, Ulster Co. Wife Geertje. Real and personal estate. Executors Petrus Roosa, Egbert Roosa, both of Hurley, and Seth Curtiss of Kingston. Witnesses Petrus Crespel, Hendrick Konstapel, farmers, and Benyamen Roosa.

334 (C 84) 1775 March 4 July 31 **CLARKSON, Elizabeth,** of N. Y. City, widow. Sons David jun. and Mathew Clarkson, brother James de Peyster, sisters Catharine, wife of John Livingston, Mar-

garet, wife of Honble William Axtell, Mary, wife of John Charlton, and Eve de Peyster, brother-in-law David Clarkson, Mrs. James van Cortlandt. Lots in Great George Str, commonly called the Pasture, personal property. Executors son David Clarkson jun, William Axtell and Doctor John Charlton. Witnesses Robert Towt of N. Y. City cordwainer, William Harriss, Hester Harriss. Copy.

335 (C 85) 1775 May 10 1781 April 19 **CONKLIN, Kasparus,** of Orange Town, Orange Co. Wife Huyly, son Matthew, daughters Ritie, Castina, and Saffiaw; Rachel Wandler, Elizabeth Blauvelt and Altie van Dorson. Real and personal property (silver spoons). Executors Abraham Ricker and Daniel Lawrence. Witnesses Edward Briggs, Aury Campbell, Daniel Lawrence.

336 (C 86) 1775 June 8 July 11 **CARPENTER, Joseph,** the 3d, of Goshen Precinct, Orange Co. Wife Ruth, son Daniel, daughters Hannah and Ruth, an expected child. Real and personal property. Executors Daniel Vail and John Smith, cooper. Witnesses Michael Jackson, William Oldfield, Hannah Smith.

337 (C 87) 1775 March 18 1776 Jany. 25 **CONCKLIN, Mathias,** of Orange Town, Orange Co. Wife Sophica, sons Liverance, Abraham, Casparus, daughters Elizabeth Reyker, Anna Briggs, grandson John Stagg jun, son of dec'd daughter Rachell, granddaughter Sophia Sitchett, da. of son Abraham and her two natural daughters Syela Halsey and Polly Ackerman, daughter-in-law Margrett, wife of son Abraham. Real and personal estate. Executors the wife, sons-in-law John Stagg of New York and Abraham Reyker. Witnesses John Campbell of Orange Co. schoolmaster, Aury Campbell, David Archibald.

338 (C 88) 1777 May 20 1778 Novbr. 4 **COLEMAN, George,** of Little Britain, Ulster Co. Wife Keziah, sons George, Gideon, John, David and James, daughters Keziah, Sarah, Catharine, Hannah,

Mary and Lydia. Real and personal estate. Executors the wife and Nehemiah Carpenter of Newburgh. Witnesses David Belknap, Moses Hunt, of Ulster Co. yeoman, and Benjamin Robinson.

339 (C 89) 1777 Octbr. 31 1781 Decbr. 21 **CARPENTER, John,** of Fredericksburgh, Dutchess Co., yeoman. Wife Hannah, son of son Gabriel viz Caleb Carpenter, grandson Benjamin, son of Ame, wife of Caleb Carpenter, grandson Joseph Crane, son of daughter Thamar, wife of John Crane, grandson Joseph Lewis, son of da. Sarah, wife of Henry Lewis. Real and personal property. Executors Caleb Carpenter and John Crane. Witnesses Caleb Carpenter, John Crane, Henry Lewis.

340 (C 90) 1774 Novbr. 5 1775 April 4 **COSINE, Deborah,** widow of Cornelius, of Bloomingdale. Daughter Sarah, children of son Balm Johnson Cosine, viz: Sarah, John Hannah, Deborah, Nicholas, Cornelius and Catherine. Real and personal estate. Executors John Hopper jun. and Wessel Hopper. Witnesses Henry Gulick, Phebe Gulick, G. Furman. Copy.

341 (C 91) 1777 Jany. 8 1783 Febry. 10 **CRAWFORD, James,** of Wallkil Precinct, Ulster Co. cooper. Wife Elizabeth, brother Thompson, nephew James, son of brother Samuel, children of brothers David and Joseph. Real and personal estate. Executors brothers David and Joseph Crawford. Witnesses John McGowen, Samuel Moffat of Orange Co. weaver, Samuel Bodel.

342 (C 92) 1777 Octbr. 11 1782 Novbr. 7 **COE, Daniel,** of Orange Co. Wife Rachel, sons John, Matthew, Daniel, Samuel, Allaxsand (?), daughters Sarah Elizabeth, Mary and Rachel. Real and personal property. Executors son John and nephew Benjamin Coe. Witnesses John Coe, Jacob Cole, William Crom.

343 (C 93) 1777 Febry. 18 1779 March 26 **COX, Ebenezer,** of Tryon Co. Wife Elizabeth, sons and daughters. Real and personal estate. Executors Robert Cox, Jacob G. Klock and John Frey. No

witnesses. Will proved by testimony of William Petrie of Kingsland District, Tryon Co., physician, and Jacob G. Klock of Palatine Distr, same County, esquire, as to handwriting.

344 (C 94) 1778 June 19 1786 Octbr. 23 **COOL, Cornelius,** of Hurley, Ulster Co., yeoman. Wife Maria, son Cornelius, daughter Catherine. Land on Dove Kil, do. in Hurley, in Patentees Woods; personal property. Executors the wife, the son, brother Jacobus Cool, brother-in-law Johannis Schoonmaker and Levi Pawling. Witnesses Jan van Duesen, John I. Dubois, Ch. DWitt.

345 (C 95) 1778 July — 1786 Jany. 27 **CONDERMAN, Frederick,** of Canajohary District, Tryon Co., yeoman. Wife ——, sons Johannes and Fredrick. Real and personal property. Executors Conrat M. Conterman and Nicholas J. Pickerd. Witnesses Marcus Conderman, Friedrich Wallratha, John Pickerd.

346 (C 96) 1778 May 6 Octbr. 7 **CLARK, Lewis,** of Newburgh, Ulster Co. Wife Cornelia, daughter Derendia, nieces Juliana, daughter of sister Lydia, Lydia Smith, da. of sister Eleanor, and nephew William Smith, son of sister Martha. Real and personal estate. Executors the wife, Anning Smith and Stephen Case. Witnesses Samuel Stratton, John Stratton, Joanna Stratton.

347 (C 97) 1779 Octbr. 12 1784 June 12 **CRAGE, John,** of Mamacatting Precinct, Ulster Co., esquire. Wife Jane, children James, David, John, Martha, Margaret and Isabel. Real and personal estate. Executors the wife, Daniel Graham and Capt. William Cross. Witnesses James Fulton, David Crage, Adam Crage.

348 (C 98) 1779 March 10 May 13 **COLEMAN, Jonathan,** of Goshen Precinct, Orange Co., yeoman. Wife Charity, son Jonathan, an expected child, brothers Joseph and Nathan Coleman and

five sisters not named. Real and personal property. Executors Silas Horton, yeoman, and Doctor Jonathan Swazey, both of Goshen Prect. Witnesses Benjamin Tusten, Peter Clowes and Isaac Denton.

349 (C 99) 1780 May 15 1781 Decbr. 3 **CLEMENTS, Johannes,** of Beekmans Precinct, Dutchess Co. Sons Tobias, Thomas, Peter, daughters Cate, wife of Deliverance Mabey, Rachel, wife of Giddeon Hall, children of dec'd son John, viz: Thomas, Mariche and Cornelius, children of dec'd daughter Hannah, viz: William and Gabriel Strang. Real and personal property. Executor son Tobias Clements. Witnesses Jesse Oakley, trader, William Hall, Daniel Whitehead.

350 (C 100) 1781 Febry. 24 **CORNELL, Samuel,** of Newbern, North Carolina, merchant, now at New York. Daughters Mary Edwards, Susannah, Sarah, Hannah and Elizabeth, granddaughters Susannah and Rebecca Edwards, sister Hannah Browne, church at Flushing, L. I. Real and personal estate. Executors Thomas Hasslen (?), Jacob Blount, Wm. Low, all of North Carolina and Honble. Henry White of N. Y. City. Witnesses Arch. Hamilton, James Barclay, Saml. Camfield. Copy.

351 (C 101) 1781 Septbr. 10 Decbr. 1 **CLINCH, Robert,** of Schenectady. Wife Hannah, sons Ralph, Benjamin, Thomas, daughters Rebecca, Elizabeth and Euretta, brother-in-law John Vernon and his little daughter Polly. Real and personal estate. Executors the wife, John Brown and James Ellice, both of Schenectady. Witnesses Hermanus Bradt, Henry Glen, Wm. van Ingen.

352 (C 102) 1781 Novbr. 5 1782 Jany. 22 **COOLEY, Nathan,** of Cornwall Precinct, Orange Co., yeoman. Wife Keziah, sons Nathan, Justus, Daniel, daughters Hannah, wife's daughter Peniner. Real and personal estate. Executors the wife, brother-in-law John Carpenter and Thomas Moffat. Witnesses George Durya, blacksmith, Garret Duryea, Enos Ayres.

353 (C 103) 1787 March 25 May 24 **CINCEBOE, Philipp,** of Beekmans Precinct, Dutchess Co., yeoman. Wife Margaret, son Andrus, daughter Gade (Jade, ? Hade ?) and wife's children by first husband. Real and personal estate. Executors the wife, Andrus Buck and William McDowel. Witnesses James van der Burgh, Tillinghast Bentley and Nicholas Emig.

354 (C 104) 1782 March 4 Octbr. 23 **COE, John,** of Haverstraw, Orange Co., gentleman. Wife ——, daughters Abigail Gornee, Margaret van de Woort, Hannah Smith, Sarah Coe, sons Benjamin, Samuel, John, Jonas, Halsted and Matthew. Real and personal estate. Executors sons Benjamin, John and Jonas. Witnesses Gilbert Cooper, Peter Read, John D. Coe.

355 (C 105) 1782 July 11 1783 Jany. 3 **CLYNE, Jacob,** of Charlotte Precinct, Dutchess Co. Leaves all his "worldly" estate to Frederick Clyne, Hendrick Sleght and John Freeligh, his executors, in trust for the payment of his debts. If anything remains it is to go to sister Orshal, wife of Wm. Ward, Benjamin Akely and Frederick Cline, if they, after notice given, come to claim it within 12 months. Witnesses Wm. Terry and Walter Simpson.

356 (C 106) 1782 Octbr. 18 Novbr. 12 **COOK, John,** of New Windsor. Wife Sarah, daughter Mary. "My estate." Executor Patrick Burnet. Witnesses George Huggan, Mary Coleman, Patrick Burnet. Proved in Dutchess Co.

357 (C 107) 1783 Febry. 26 April 2 **CLOSE, David,** clerk. Wife Hannah, nephew David, son of sister Sarah Delivan, John Tomkins, son of brother John Close. Real and personal estate. Executors the wife, brother John Close and brothers-in-law Thomas Comstock and Timothy Delivan. Witnesses Alexander Kidd, of Fredericksburgh, Dutchess Co., Saml. Mills and Nathaniel Fisher, of Fredericksburgh, millwright.

358 (C 108) 1783 July 26 Septbr. 17 **CRIST, Henry,** of Montgomery Precinct, Ulster Co., yeoman. Wife Ann, sons David, Adam, Henry, wife's son Johannis Crist, daughters Hannah, Elisabeth,

Mary, Eve, Ann, Sally. Real and personal estate. Executors Stevonis Crist, Abraham Crist, Johannes Millar. Witnesses Johannes Neukerk, Jost German and John McKinstry.

359 (C 109) 1783 May 3 Aug. 18 **COOKE, Samuel,** of Pokeepsie Precinct, physician. Wife Temperance, sons William Hedges, George, Samuel, daughters Temperance and Anna. Real and personal estate. Executors the wife and John Bailey. Witnesses Wm. Terry, hatter, Sebre Fish, tailor, James Livingston.

360 (C 110) 1783 June 16 July 25 **CARPENTER, Nehemiah,** late of Jamaica, L. I., now of Goshen, *Ulster* Co., blacksmith. Wife Pracilla, sons Nehemiah, Nicholas, daughters Phebe and Sally. Land at Jamaica, L. I., personal property. Executors the wife and sons. Witnesses Joseph Carpenter, Amasa Mathews and John Kortright.

361 (C 111) 1784 Septbr. 18 1785 Janry. 1 **CARPINTAR, Weight,** of Wallkil Prect., Ulster Co., blacksmith. Wife Mercey, daughters Mary, Elizabeth White, Rebecca, son Weight. Real and personal estate. Executors Doctor Jonathan Sweezey and son-in-law James White. Witnesses Ino. McCamly, cordwainer, Nicholas Carpenter, blacksmith, Elizabeth Smith.

362 (C 112) 1784 Septbr. 15 1785 March 15 **CLARK, Abigail,** of Fredericksburgh, Dutchess Co. Son William, daughters Abigail, Mary, Elizabeth and Sarah. Real and personal estate. Executors Elias Cornelius and Isaac Seacor. Witnesses Peter Beadeau sen, of Dutchess Co., farmer, Isaac Badeau.

363 (C 113) 1784 June 17 1785 Febry. 4 **COCK, Catharine Margaret,** of German Camp, Albany Co., spinster. Friend (brother-in-law?) Wessel ten Brook of Livingston Manor and niece Nancy, da. of Wessel ten Brook. Personal property (six silver spoons). Executor Wessel ten Brook. Witnesses Abraham Bogardus, Mary Bogardus, John Fletcher.

364 (C 114) 1784 March 13 1786 Octbr. 12 **CRAWFORD, John,** of Pinpack Precinct, Ulster Co., yeoman. Nephew John, son of brother Samuel Crawford. Real and personal estate. Executors John Barkley and Samuel Crawford, both of Montgomery Precinct yeomen. Witnesses Henry Palmer jun, laborer. John Linderman, Wm. Steuart, John Crawford of Mamacatting Prect. made administrators.

365 (C 115) 1785 June 28 July 16 **CHAPMAN, Samuel,** of Stephentown District, Albany Co. Wife ——, brothers Daniel and Robert Chapman, sisters Mary, Susannah, Temperance, Chloe and Nance. Homefarm and land at East Haddam, personal property. Executor Jonathan Niles. Witnesses Joel Curtis, Ichabod Cone, cordwainer, Caleb Chapman, blacksmith.

366 (C 116) 1785 Aug. 5 Decbr. 31 **CONCKLIN, John,** of Poghkeepsie Precinct, captain. Wife ——, sons John, Lawrence, David, Abraham, Isaac, Jacob and Matthew, daughters Susanna, Anna and her daughters Johanna and Mary, Hester, wife of Teunis Tappen. Real and personal estate (a Dutch bible). Executors the seven sons. Witnesses Mathew L. Concklin, farmer, John L. Concklin, Jacob Westervelt.

367 (C 117) 1786 Septbr. 30 1787 March 24 **COLE, Myndert,** of Beekmans Prect., Dutchess Co., farmer. Wife Teatte, sons Aurea, Peter, Tunis, John, Jacobus, Myndert, Abraham, daughters Elizabeth, Cornelia and Margaret. Real and personal estate. Executors son Aurea Cole, Moses van Valey and Richard Knights. Witnesses Martin Overocker, Samuel Nights, farmers, Bartholomew Noxon.

368 (C 118) 1786 May 30 1787 March 24 **COMINS, John,** of Pawlings Precinct, Dutchess Co. Wife Elizabeth, sons John, Simion, Samuel, Gaylord, Abel, daughters Elizabeth, Abiah, Johanna, Silance, Anna and Irena. Real and personal estate. Executors sons Gaylord and Abel. Witnesses Joseph Weaver, Peter Talman, Isaac I. Talman, trader.

369 (C 119) 1793 Septbr. 9 Septbr. 17 French

CANHÉPÉ, Jean Bertram, jun. of New York City. Christian Matthias Heil of New York and slave girl Marguerite Françoise Catrone, now in France. Personal estate. Executor C. M. Heil. Witnesses R. J. van den Broek, St. Mainié, Fredrich Shanewolff.

370 (C 120) 1791 Febry. 22 1800 Septbr. 24

CRUGER, Nicholas, of New York City, merchant. Wife Ann, born Markoe. Sons and daughters by present wife and former wife Ann, daughter of Major and Madame de Nully, who died on the Island of St. Croix. Real estate (partly on said Island), personal property. Executors, the wife, Robert Watts, John Watts and Cornelius Stevenson, all of N. Y. City. Witnesses Chas. Haight, James Codwise, Mich. D. Henry. Codicil, dated at St. Croix January 16, 1800, supplies maiden names of the two wives and unimportant changes. It is witnessed by John Gordon and Henry N. Cruger. Copy.

371 1782 June 22 1787 Jany. 18

COOPER, Samuel, of Southampton, Suffolk Co. Wife Abigail, sons Zophar, Samuel, daughters Abigail Hathway, Mary Ayres and Phebe Juggar, grandson ——, son of son Stephen Cooper. Real and personal estate. Executors sons Zophar and Samuel Cooper. Witnesses Timothy Peirson, Matthew Rogers, Stephen Rogers. Recorded Vol. I. Wills and Probates, p. 26.

372 1783 May 21 1787 Febry. 12

CARMAN, Silas, of Oysterbay, Queens Co. Wife Hannah, sons Silas, Samuel and Joshua. Homefarm, land on Lattins Neck, Oysterbay Township, do. on Seas Neck, Huntington Township, do. on Hempstead Plains, personal estate. Executors the wife, Benjamin Tredwell of Hempstead, surgeon, and son-in-law Zophar Smith. Witnesses Enoch Plummer, Lieut. 3d Battaillon, 60th Regt., David Batty of South Hempstead yeoman and John Batty. Recorded ibidem, p. 44.

373 1786 20th day, 4th month 1787 Febry. 26

CARPENTER, Joseph, of Jericho, Oysterbay Township, Queens Co. Wife Elizabeth, daughters Elizabeth and Abigail Cook, sons Thomas, Joseph, Benjamin and Henry, grandchildren Freelove, daughter of son

Isaac, Joseph, son of son-in-law William Cook. Land in Limington Township, Vermont and other real estate; personal property. Executors son Thomas Carpenter, Thomas Willets and Jacob Willets, both of Jericho. Witnesses Samuel Willis of Jericho, carpenter, Daniel Dodge and Elias Hicks. Recorded ibidem, p. 56.

374
1779
Septbr. 25
1787
March 22

CANTINE, Jane, of New Rochel, Westchester Co., *youman*. Sister Susannah Cantine and niece Francies Jones sole heiresses and executrices. Witnesses John Shute, John Bonnet, yeoman, Jane Bonnet. Recorded ibidem, p. 84.

375
1776
Novbr. 30
1786
June 23

CLARKE, George, of Hyde, County Palatine of Chester, England, esquire. Great nephews George Clarke, Edward Clarke, George Hyde Clarke, great niece Jane, daughter of Letitia Penelope Crispis, nephew-in-law William Sanford and wife, niece Mary of Manchester, "my dear unhappy and much injured niece Mrs. Catharine Clarke, wife of my abandoned, profligate nephew Charles Hyde Clarke," nephew Mathew Cock, clerk of the Exchequer, servants John Ridley, stewart, Mary Burgess, housekeeper, William Cockerton, body servant. Lands in Province of New York, on the Island of Jamaica, and in England. Thomas Birch of Ardwick and Thomas Butterworth Bayley of Hope, Lancaster Co., England, trustees, Robert Crispin of Lincoln's Inn and William Sanford of Manchester, executors. Witnesses Mary Drenton, Thomas Sidebotham, John Whitehead. Probated at New York, April 20, 1787. Recorded ut supra, p. 110.

376
1777
Jany. 7
1781
March 13

CADWALADER, Thomas, of Philadelphia, practitioner in physic and surgery. Wife Hannah, daughters Rebecca, Elizabeth, son Lambert (of New Jersey), cousin Margaret Stevenson. Real and personal estate. No executors. Will executed at Shrewsbury, County of Kent, Maryland. Witnesses Margaret Stevenson, Wm. Gough, Henry Bruce. Codicil, dated Hunterdown Co., and executed at Trenton, Novbr. 2, 1779, makes a change in legacy to cousin Margaret Stevenson. Witnesses Mary Dagworthy, Abrm. Heint, Philimon Dickinson. Letters testamentary granted to Lambert Cadwalader March 13, 1781, at Philadelphia. Probated at New York, Novbr. 28, 1786. Recorded ut supra, p. 159.

377 1784 April 14 1790 Aug. 11 **COOLEY, Jonathan,** of Goshen Precinct, Orange Co., yeoman. Wife Ruth, wife's daughter Hurldey, sons Jonathan and David, daughters Mary, wife of Benjamin Smith, Eunice, wife of Andrew Wilson, Beulah, wife of Increase Mathers; apparently only personal estate. Executors son-in-law Benjamin Smith, Joseph Halsted and John Bradnor. Witnesses Alexander Campbell, farmer, Henry White, John White. Recorded ut supra, p. 241.

378 1776 Octbr. 17 1781 Aug. 14 **CAMPBELL, Archibald,** of Fredericksburgh, Dutchess Co., bachelor and Captain of the New York Company of Volunteers at Long Island, "my two boys left at my farm at Fredericksburgh" are given the farm, stock and mill with £100. "Mr. Monson, Daniel Chase and Mathew Patterson are to settle for Archd. and Duncan, brother Tom, Arch is to have Sara for Duncan." No executors or witnesses. Will proved at London, England, by testimony of Duncan Campbell, of Well Str., Parish of Saint Mary le Bone, carpenter, and Archibald McDuff, of Silver Street, Parish of St. James, Westminster, Cabinet maker. Letters testamentary granted to Duncan Campbell, of Aldergate Str., London, victualler, and John Campbell, of High Holborn, upholsters, brothers of testator. Will is dated "Brookland Fort" and probated in New York February, 1791. Recorded ut supra, p. 258.

379 1780 Novbr. 6 1782 Febry. 13 **COEJMANS, Samuel Staats,** son of Andries, of Somerset Co., N. J. Son Andries, daughter Gertruyd. Homefarm in Somerset Co., claims to land in State

of New York, personal property. Executors nephew Colonel John Neilson and neighbour William Patterson. Witnesses Charles Cox, John Y. Noel, Rob. Troup. Will proved at Barnards Town, N. J. Probated in New York April 1, 1791. Recorded ut supra, p. 300.

380 1793 Aug. 5 Aug. 16 **CLARKE, Jonathan,** of Savannah, Georgia. Wife Herodias, brother William Clarke. Land in District 96, New Purchase in South Carolina, (Winton County), personal estate (plate). Executors the wife and Ebenezer Hill, of Savannah, merchant. Witnesses Jas. Belcher, Abraham Leggett, of N. Y., blacksmith, Wm. Erving, of Savannah, Ga., auctioneer. Proved at New York. Recorded ut supra, p. 398.

381 1788 March 16 1795 March 25 **CAMPBELL, Pryse,** of Essex Co., N. J. Wife Magdalena Maria. Real and personal estate. No executors named. Witnesses James McIntosh and John McQueen. Letters testamentary granted to widow at New York March 25, 1795. Recorded ut supra, p. 465.

382 1775 Septbr. 3 1796 Febry. 6 **CRANE, Joseph,** of Essex Co., N. J., surveyor. Wife Sarah sole heiress and with John Range, of New Ark, N. J., and Richard Kep sen., of New York, executors. Real and personal estate. Witnesses Richard Kip jun., Daniel Ebbets jun. In the probate, dated as above, Sarah Crane has become Sarah Scudder. Recorded ut supra, p. 530.

383 1796 March 3 March 10 **CALLAGHAN, Nabby,** now of New York City, widow. John Leonard, of New York City, boarding house keeper, sole heir and executor of real and personal property. Witnesses Charles Dougherty, Bryan Conner, Laurence Courtney. Recorded ut supra, p. 537.

384 1796 April 12 Aug. 19 **COLDEN, Alexander,** now of New York City. Mother Henrietta M. Colden, brother Cadwalader R. Colden, cousin Captain Thomas Colden, friend Wm.

Alves, a native of Scotland, now of Island of St. Vincent, James Dole, of Lansingburgh, merchant. Lands at Pittstown, Rensselaer Co., and Cambridge, Washington Co., personal estate. Executors the mother and James Dole. Witnesses James Inglis jun., J. Blair Linn, John William Patterson. Recorded ut supra, p. 601.

385 1798 March 11 March 20 French **CORTET (Coatet, Gortel), Jeanne,** resident of L'Artibonte, Island of Sto. Domingo. Sons Valentin, 14 years, Cabaril, 12 years, daughters Perpignette, 4½ years, Tite, 2 years, and a daughter, born 8 days ago at New York. Personal property (six silver table spoons, five do forks, one do soup ladle, 12 do teaspoons, a do silver tongs and other silver). Executor Mr. Labouisse. Witnesses Messrs. Laffiteau, merchant, and de Neufville, habitant. Recorded ut supra, Vol. II., p. 69.

386 1795 April 2 1798 Decbr. 17 French **CUYALAU, Pierre,** a native of Pau, Bearn, 30 years old, now of St Marc Vignier Plantation, Parish of St. Pierre de L'Archaye, Quarter of Boucassin, Seneschalery of Port au Prince, Island of Sto. Domingo. Miss Fanny Remoussin of St. Marc, Mr. Parage of Boucassin and lawful heirs in France. Real estate in France, personal property on the Island. Executor Mr. Parage. Witnesses Elie Martin, millwright, John Jolly, carpenter, both of the same Parish. Recorded ut supra p. 180.

387 1795 May 20 Novbr. 14 **COCKROFT, William,** of Halifax, County York, gentleman. Henry Cockroft of Nest in Errington, son of late nephew William, nephews John Cockroft of Southerhouse, Thomas Cockroft of Holcome, near Bury, Lancashire, Grace, wife of John Ramsden of Highfield in Ovenden, nephew Thomas Mason of Eshton in Craven, nieces Sarah, wife of Thomas Foster of Hollings, near Heptonstall, Elizabeth, wife of Robert Holstead or Hallstead of Burntacres near Todmorden, children of William Grimshaw dec'd, son of late sister Mary, children of dec'd nephew John Gibson, viz: Thomas, Abraham and Eliza-

beth, niece Susan Gibson widow, nephew James Cockroft of N. Y. City, cousins Grace, wife of Thomas Holt of Wheatly, Nancy, wife of Mr. Jones, late Clergyman of Warley, now in Wales. Real estate in North America, personal property. Executors James King of Myth holme, Parish of Halifax, merchant, Thomas Murgatroyd of Willow Edge, same Parish, gentleman, James Oldfield of Harwood Well, same Parish, gentleman. Witnesses Rt. Parker, Ino. Lockhead jun., Noah Mellin. Recorded ut supra, p. 176.

388 1800 March 24 May 17 **CUYLER, Richard,** of Albany City. Mother Lydia Cuyler, sister Catharine Staats, sisters-in-law Ann, wife of brother Jacob Cuyler, Maria, wife of brother Glen, brothers Cornelius of Cayuga Co., John, of Albany, attorney-at-law, Jacob of Otsego Co., Tobias V., late of Schoharie Co. Personal property. Trustees and executors Nicholas Bleecker and Dudley Walsh, both of Albany, merchants. Witnesses Richard Lush, John Maley, Teunis Ts. van Vechten. Recorded ut supra, p. 242.

389 1799 Novbr. 11 1804 Septbr. 27 **CHANCELLOR, James H.,** formerly of St. James, Island of Jamaica, now of Stillwater, N. Y. Wife Cecilia sole heiress and executrix of "the estate." Witnesses John V. Henry, of Albany, counsellor-at-law, H. Bleecker, R. R. Henry. Recorded ut supra, p. 286.

390 1807 Aug. 21 1809 May 23 **CADMUS, Deborah,** formerly of Somerset Co., N. J., now of Watervliet, Albany Co. Andrew Cadmus, grandson of late husband Andrew Cadmus, son Richard Cadmus of Somerset Co., N. J., niece Catharine Bratt, daughter of brother John F. Bratt, sister Vroutye Bratt, w. of Peter Bratt. Personal estate. Executors brother John F. Bratt and nephew Dirck, son of Peter Bratt. Witnesses Ino. Fonday jun. John L. Winne, Paul Spencer. Recorded ut supra, p. 298.

391 1813 Jany. 26 June 10 **CROCKER, Sarah,** widow of Ebenezer, of Kinderhook, Columbia Co. Daughters Ann, Sarah, wife of John Barlow, Amelia, wife of David Blunt. Real and personal estate. Trustees and executors James van der Poel and Ebenezer Crocker. Witnesses David Carshore, Robert McDonnell, Matty Ames. Recorded ut supra, p. 316.

392 1815 April 13 June 22 **CRABTREE, John,** leaves to Mathew Crabtree 14 months pay due from U. S. and 160 acres of land. Witnesses A. Hansen, Henry Wright, sergeant, Thos. Williams. Recorded ut supra, p. 324.

393 1817 Jany. 23 June 10 **COPELAND, Jacob.** Wife Sally, sons Abraham, Isaac, Jacob, Benjamin, William and Lloyd, daughters Matilda, Phebe, Maria, Frances and Sally. Real and personal estate. Executors Enoch Sayre and son Abraham. Witnesses Platt Adams, William Chapman, Amoz Cornwall. Recorded ut supra, p. 338.

394 1818 Decbr. 31 1820 Septbr. 2 **CULLEN, John,** native of Dutchess Co., N. Y., of Aux Cayes, Haity, commission-merchant. Miss Maria Jeanne Chaillon of Port-au-Prince and his natural children by her, viz: Maria Magdalene Elmine and Jean, Mrs. James van Rensselaer jun, whose maiden name was Cullen, of Utica, N. Y. and her children. Personal estate. Joseph Kernochan of New York trustee for sister Mrs. James van Rensselaer jun. Executor Guillaume Chegaray of Aux Cayes. Witnesses John Cullen Dupon, A. Avignon and G. Malereil (?). Recorded ut supra, p. 352.

395 1775 May 20 1779 March 15 **COLDEN, Cadwallader,** Lieut. Governour of the Province of New York. Grandson Richard Nicolls Colden, sons David, Alexander, dec'd, Cadwallader, daughters Elizabeth de Lancey, and Alice Willett dec'd. Lands in the Lewis Morris Patent on Mohawks R., do. on Westside of Katskil Mts., do at Coldingham, Ulster Co., do at Flushing, L. I., farm at Springhill, personal property. Executors sons David and Cadwallader and

da. Elizabeth de Lancey. Witnesses Robert Doughty of Queens Co. yeoman, Benjamin Underhill, Edmund Underhill. Recorded vol. III., p. 16.

396 1784 Octbr. 13 **CAMPBELL, Duncan,** of Washington Co., farmer, letters of administration granted by Thomas Tredwell, Judge of the Probate Court at New York to, on the estate of his dec'd daughter Margaret of the same place spinster. Recorded ibidem, p. 130.

397 1770 April 27 July 25 **CAMPBELL, John,** late of the Island of Jamaica, planter, now of New York City. Sisters Margaret Campbell, Catharine McArthur, Ann Campbell, brothers Archibald, Alexander and James, cousins Duncan Campbell and Alexander Campbell, both of Kingston, Jamaica, merchants. Lands in New York Province, personal property. Executors Peter Middleton of N. Y. City physician, Johnstone Fairholme of Jamaica and Walter Buchanan of N. Y. City, merchant. Witnesses Samuel Jones, Isaac Noble, Uzal Johnson. Codicil of May 12, 1770, gives legacies to Rev. Mr. Mason of the Scotch Presbyterian Congregation in N. Y. City, to widow Mary Mackay of N. Y. City and to nurse Margaret Gilles. Same witnesses. Codicil of June 25, 1770, revokes legacy to Margaret Gilles. Witnesses Jean Guerinay and Isaac Noble. Recorded ibidem, p. 146.

398 1793 Febry. 19 1805 Aug. 15 **CAMPBELL, Archibald,** of Albany City, surveyor. Wife Christena, son John, Jacob, and four others; daughters Margaret, wife of Thomas Brissbrown, Hannah, Sarah, Caty and Elizabeth. Lands in New Jersey and near Sacondaga, house and lot in Albany; personal property. Executors the wife and sons John and Jacob. Witnesses Robert Hewson, William Fryer, P. Sternbergh. Recorded vol. IV., p. 24.

399 1782 June 12 Septbr. 3 **CROGHAN, George,** late of Pittsburgh, now of Passayunk, Philadelphia Co., Penna. Nephew John Ward, kinsmen Wm. Powell and Thomas Smallman, friend John

Campbell of Pittsburgh, "formerly my clerk," James Forrest, Barnard Gratz and his da. Rachel, daughter Susannah, wife of Augustin Prevoost. Lands on Robinson Run and on Chartier Creek. Executors Barnard Gratz and Michael Gratz of Philadelphia, merchants, Thomas Smallman of Pittsburgh, William Powell of same place coppersmith and James Innis of Washington Co., Pa. Witnesses Ann Gallagher, Jacob Seler, Lewis Weiss. Recorded ibidem, p. 29.

400
1801
July 16
1825
Febry. 21

CAMPBELL, Daniel, of Schenectady. Wife Angelica, brother John Campbell and his children Edward, Alexander and Sally. Had son David, who is now dead. Real and personal estate. Executors the wife and Joseph C. Yates of Schenectady. Witnesses Joseph Mynderse, Lowrans van Boskerck, Henry Yates jun. Recorded ibidem, p. 153.

401
1811
May 27
1825
Febry. 21

CAMPBELL, Angelica, of Schenectady. Margaret, wife of Simon Vrooman, Eve, wife of Simon Vedder, Angelica, wife of Jacob Schermerhorn, nephews Arent and Cornelius, sons of brother Samuel Bradt, brother Abraham Bradt, children of Abraham's son Arent, niece Helena, da. of bro. Frederick Bradt, nephew Arent, son of bro. John Bradt, and his two sons, Ann ten Eyck and Angelica Campbell, both daughters of Cornelius Vrooman dec'd, John, son and Susanna da. of Margaret Vrooman, Arent Vrooman and wife Elizabeth, Eve Vedder, her son Daniel Campbell and da. Angelica, Catharine, w. of Myndert Vedder, Catharine, wife of John Schermerhorn and da. of brother Jacobus, Daniel David Campbell, son of Jacob and Angelica Schermerhorn, Eve, da. of bro. Jacobus and w. of Takareus Vedder, Catharine Burt, Susanna, w. of Wyngart Veeder, niece Eve, da. of sister Susanna and w. of Daniel Peak, the Episcopal Church at Schenectady, Daniel Campbell Lambert, David Campbell Burgess, Mary Duncan, Michael commonly called John Bouderick, Daniel Martin, William

Boorland, Gennet Killey, Daniel Banter. Personal property (plate), saw and grist mill at Milton, Saratoga Co. Executor Jacob Schermerhorn. Witnesses Maus van Vranken, James Bailey, Cornelius S. Groot. Recorded ibidem p. 157.

402 1828 March 29 Octbr. 22 **CAMERON, Dugald,** of Bath, Steuben Co., now at Albany. Wife Frances, son Charles, daughters Lydia, wife of Ira Davenport and Elizabeth Whitney, brother Charles Cameron, of Greene, Chenango Co., father, sister Elizabeth, nephew Archibald McLauchlin, grandson Emanuel Coryell. Farm on Conhocton R. in Bath, personal property. Executors son-in-law Ira Davenport, brother Charles and son Charles. Witnesses James McNaughton, Azel Fitch, C. D. Townsend. Recorded ibidem, p. 256.

403 1825 Novbr. 5 1826 Aug. 7 **CLARK, Erastus,** of Utica, Oneida Co. Wife Sophia, sister Jerusha Clark. Real and personal estate. Executors the wife, Jesse W. Doolittle and Walter King. Witnesses James Dean, James Platt and I. H. Ostrom. Recorded Vol. V., p. 39.

404 1645 April 17 Dutch **CELES, Jan,** of Manhatans Island. Wife Maritie Robbers, brother-in-law Tonis Mysen. Real and personal estate. Witnesses Thomas Hall, Abraham Watson, Cosyn Gerritsen, Hendrick Pietersen, Jeurian Pratel and Cornelis van Tienhoven, Secretary. N. Y. Col. MSS., II., 146.

405 1663 July 3 Dutch **CRUYFF, Eldert Gerbertsen,** of Rensselaerswyck Colony, born at Hilversen in Gooylant, Holland, and wife Tryntie Jans, born at Noortstrant, Oostland. Son by first husband Jan Jansen Ryckman, vizt: Albert Jansen Ryckman. Real and personal estate. No executor named. Witnesses Adriaen van Ilpendam, Harmen Jansen Ryckman and Notary v. Schelluyne. Albany Co. Records, Notarial Papers, I., p. 337.

406 1676–7 Dutch **CORNELISSEN, Maerten,** of Claverack, born in the City of Ysselsteyn, and wife Maeyeke Cornelis, born at Barrevelt. Children mentioned, but not by name. Real and personal property. The survivor executor. Witnesses Jan Verbeeck, Pieter Loockermans, at whose house the will is executed, and Adriaen van Ilpendam, Notary Public. Albany Co. Records, Notarial Papers, I., p. 606.

407 1683 July 23 Dutch **CLAESSEN, Frederick,** of New Albany, born at Westenes, District of Drent. Mother Roelofie Willems, sister Hilletie Claes, living at Staphorst, Jannetie Gerrit of Rensselaerswyck Colony. "Estate." Executor Gerrit Gysbertsen. Witnesses Commissary Jan Jansen Bleecker, Barent Meyndersen and Adrian van Ilpendam, Notary Public. Albany Co. Records, Notarial Papers, II., p. 456.

408 1683 July 23 1684 Decbr. 11 Dutch **CLUTE, (Cloet), Captain Johannes,** of Albany. Present wife Bata van Slichtenhorst, cousin (nephew) Johannes Cloet jun., brothers Jacob, Barent, Evert, Clement, sisters Annetje and Engel Cloet, living at Nieuen Roy, District of the Mark. Farm at Canastagioene (Niskayuna), personal property. No executor named. Witnesses Mr. Cornelis van Dyck, Magistrate Dirck Wessells (ten Broeck) and Robert Livingstone, secretary. Albany Co. Records, Court Minutes, 1680–5, p. 618.

409 1689 Novbr. 16 —— Dutch **CALIER, Michiel,** of Kinderhook, Albany Co. First wife Engeltie, da. of Dirck the Swede, who had da. Magdalena, 2½ yrs. old, second wife Tretie, da. of Jeurian van Hoesem. "Estate." Guardians of the daughter and other prospective children Jeurian van Hoesem and Frenck Herdick. Witnesses Jochem Lammertsen, Willem Hoffmeyer and J. Becker. Albany Co. Records, Notarial Papers, II., p. 572.

409a 1691 Octbr. 8 **CARSTENSEN, Theunis,** of Shinnechtady, Albany Co, letters of administration on the estate of, granted to his widow Maritje. Albany Co. Records, Wills, I., p. 1.

410 1709 Aug. 5 Septbr. 20 **COLE, Henry,** of Middletown, Monmouth Co., N. J., cordwainer. Friend Benjamin Kellum of Huntington, Suffolk Co., L. I., farmer, sole heir and executor of real and personal estate. Witnesses Isaac Verplanken, Elisabeth van Corlaer and Jonathan Rumney. Albany Co., Records, Wills, I., p. 127.

410a 1720-1 March 3 1727 June 7 **CONYN, Casper Leendertsen,** of Claverack, Albany Co., yeoman. Wife Alecteka, children Leendert, Casper, Anganitie, wife of Gerret van Wie, Janaka, wife of Harma van Salsberge, Maritie, Commertie, Elizabeth, Ragell, Eava, children of dec'd son Peter. Real and personal estate. Executors Samuel ten Broeck, Peter Bronck and Thomas Williams. Witnesses Flip Conyn, Flip Conyn jun., Casparis Bronck and Tho. Williams. Albany Co. Records, Wills, I., p. 183.

410b 1734 Aug. 20 1741 June 10 Dutch **CREGIER, Jannetie,** widow of Martin, of Albany. Sons Martynus, Samuel, daughters Elizabeth, wife of Daniel van Olinda, Annatie, wife of Victoor Becker, Geertruy, wife of Ulderick van Francke, children of dec'd da. Marya, vizt. Enogh and Marya Vreelandt. Real estate at Kanistagone (Niskayuna) Albany Co., personal property. Executors all the children. Witnesses Stephanus van Rensselaer, Gerardus Banker and Ino. de Peyster. Albany Co. Records, Wills, I., p. 276.

411 1746 May 15 1747 June 1 **CLOET, Gerardus,** of Albany Co., yeoman. Wife Maghtell, children Johannes, Dirck, Jacob, Gerardus, Bata, Elizabeth and Claertie. Farm in the Boght of the Cahoos, personal property. The wife sole executrix. Witnesses Cornelius Onderdonk, Johannis J. Lansing, both of said Co. farmers, and James Stenhouse. Albany Co. Records, Wills, I., p. 317.

411b 1763 Septbr. 14 1771 June 15 **COEYMANS, Catriena,** da. of Anthony van Schaick and widow of Samuel Coeman. Margritia ten Eyck, Gerritie, wife of Peter Gansevoort, Elizabeth, wife of Thomas Peebles, nephew Jacob ten Eyck, sister Garritie, widow of Coenraet ten Eyck, Maritie, da. of Anthony van Shaick jun. dec'd., Chnotiantie, wife of Anthony van Schaick, Annatie, wife of Henry ten Broeck, Anthony Goose van Schaick, nephew Goose, son of bro. Goose van Schaick, Anthony ten Eyck, Barent ten Eyck, Andries ten Eyck, Barent ten Eyck, Tobias ten Eyck. Real and personal estate. Executors nephews Jacob, Anthony and Barent ten Eyck. Witnesses John Macob, Daniel Stall and Peter Silvester. Albany Co. Records, Wills, I., p. 353.

412 1765 Octbr. 30 1771 Octbr. 2 — Dutch **CONYN, Casparus,** of Claverack, Albany Co., farmer. Wife Eva, children Casparus, Lawrans, Maria, Jannietje, da. of dec'd. da. Alida, vizt. Maria. Real and personal estate. Executors the two sons and Henry van Rensselaer. Witnesses Nicklas Brissie, Peter Muller, both of Claverack, farmers and Stephen van Dyck. Albany Co. Records, Wills, I., p. 358.

412a (D 1) 1671 Septbr. 14 — Dutch **DU FOUR, David,** from Bergen, Henegau, and wife Jannetje Frans from Guevrerin near Valencyn, living at Deudelbay, N. Y. The survivor, the sons David, Pieter and Glaude and a son Jan by the first wife Maria Boulyn. Real and personal property. The survivor to be executor, Witnesses Cosyn Gerrits, Jan Bastiaens, Johannes Kip, Elias Provoost, Pieter Houss. Copy, no evidence of proof, except an endorsement, "Johannes Kipp, p^mo^ May 1699."

413 (D 2) 1672 June 4 — Dutch **DE FOREEST, Isaack,** of New York City, brewer, and wife Sarah de Truix. The survivor, daughters Susanna, wife of Pieter Riemer, Maria, sons Johannes, Philipp, Isaacq, Hendricus and David. Real and personal

property. Executors and guardians cousin Jacob Kip and Symon Janssen Romeyn. Witnesses Isaack Kip and Arent Isacksen. Original copy signed by testators, witnesses and notary. No proof.

413a (D 3) 1688 April 13 — **D'KEY, Jacob Teunis,** of New York. Wife Hellegonda, sons Teunis, Jacob, daughters Janneke, Angenitie and Maria, grandson Jacob, son of Teunis. Houses and lots in New York, land in the Highlands, personal property. The wife sole executrix. Witnesses Peter Jacobs Marius, P. D. Lancey. Copy. No proof.

414 (D 4) 1694 March 27 1696 Recorded June 23 Dutch — **DU BOIS, Louys,** of Kings Towne, Ulster Co. Wife Catrina, sons Abraham, Jacob, David, Solomon, Louys and Matthew, children of son Isaacq (dec'd?), daughter Sarah, wife of Joost Jansen. Real and personal property. The wife sole executrix. Witnesses John Ward, S. Valleau, Wm. D'Meyer. No proof.

415 (D 5) 1695-6 Febry. 22 1696 Recorded June 23 Dutch — **DU BOIS, Louys,** of Kingstowne, Ulster Co., same as preçeding, revokes the former testament and makes different disposition of his estate. Farm at Hurley, house and lot in Kings, land at New Paltz. Witnesses W. D'Meyer (Major) Jacob Rutsen, Jan Burhans, Mattys Slecht. Proved March 26, 1696. The widow Catrina sworn as executrix July 16, 1697.

416 (D 6) 1698 Octbr. 21 — **DUMARESQ, Nicholas,** of New York City, mariner, son of Elias Dumaresq and wife Mary of St. Saviours Parish, Garnesey (Guernsey) Island. Children Sarah, Nicolas, Jacob and John. Real estate in Europe and America; personal property (one silver cup old fashioned guilded). Executors Thomas Noell, Jacob van Cortlandt and Jacob Mayle. No witnesses. Incomplete copy. No proof.

417 (D 7) 1702 Aug. 20 1708 Septbr. 1 — **DE KEY, Theunis,** of New York City. Wife Helena, son Jacobus, and other children not named. Real and personal estate. Executors the wife, Major

Brandt Schuyler, brother Captain Jacob de Key and brother-in-law Peter van Brough. Witnesses A. Bonnin, Philipp Jouneau, William Huddleston.

418 (D 8) 1702 Octbr. 14 1709 June 20 **DE BRUYN, John Hendrick,** of New York City, merchant. Wife Johanna, children of dec'd sister Catherina Margerita, late wife of Halbertus Browers of Amsterdam, viz: John Hendrick, Dorothea and Maria, children of niece Maria Elizabeth, da. of sister C. M. Browers, John Hendrick, son of Lancaster Symms, Lutheran Church of N. Y., Gratia Anna Busch and her son John Hendrick, Hannah, da. of Hendrick ten Eyck by Peternela de Witt, Abraham Staats of Albany. Real and personal property. The wife sole executrix. Witnesses Gysbert van Imborgh, Benjamin Wynkoop, Johannes van der Huse (?). Copy.

419 (D 9) 1707 March 11 **DE KEY, Hellegonda,** of New York City, widow. Daughters Jane Tuthill, widow, Angnetta, wife of William Jannaway, brewer and Mary, wife of Sampson Broughton, son Jacobus, daughter-in-law Helena, widow of son Teunis. "Worldly estate" (an Indian slave). Executors daughter Jane Tothill and Rip van Dam of N. Y. merchant. Witnesses Robert Parkins, Par: Parmiter, Cornelius Lodge. Copy.

420 (D 10) 1711 Novbr. 1 — **DICKMAN, Cornelius,** of N. Y. City. Wife Jannetie, sons George, and Cornelius. Land and plantation; personal property. Executors Edward Blagge, Johannes Jansen and David Menosa (?). Witnesses Nicolas Somerdick, Teunis Cornelius, Johannis Pietersen Bass. Copy indorsed: "The Executors not sworn & noe administration granted."

421 (D 11) 1704 Jany. 10 1710–11 Jany. 8 Dutch **DE MEYER, Wilhelmus,** of Kingstown Corporation, Ulster Co. Wife Catrina, daughters Anneke, Catrina, Lidia, wife of Andries Dow, and Deborah, son Nicholas. Real estate in America and Europe; personal

property. The wife sole executrix. Witnesses (Colonel) Jacob Rutsen, Captain Thomas Garton, Thomas Noxon and William Nottingham.

422 (D 12 & 13) 1721 March 9 March 15

DU MORRISSEY, John, of New York City, but now in Barbados. Jacobus van Cortland, John van Horne, George Gass, George Hunter, Dutch Church in N. Y., nephew Nicolas Elsworth of N. Y. Real estate in New York, Barbados, England and elsewhere, personal property (bonds of Capt. Lancaster Symes, Col. Robert Lurting, Abram Bass, John Hunt, John Clemons, Odle Turneux, Jackman More, John Merritt, Richard Miles & Co. of Madeira, merchants). Witnesses Edward Oxnard, J. Phripp, Robert Hancock, George Maddey. Proved in Barbados.

423 (D 14) 1724 Novb. 6 Decbr. 3

DIGHTON, John, of New York City, tanner. Wife Bridget, sons John, Henry Foot, William, nephew Henry, son of dec'd brother William, kinsman Henry Foot Dighton. Real estate in St. James Parish, Bristol, England, house, lot, and tanyard in N. Y. City; personal property (plate). The wife sole executrix. Witnesses Thomas Hodgins, Anthony Webb, Abrah. Gouverneur. Copy.

424 (D 15) 1728 Novbr. 15 Novbr. 27

DEBONME, Etienne (Stephan), of Kingston, Ulster Co., perewigmaker. Father Stephen Debenne, mother Janne Lowis, friends John Tebenne of New Paltz and Aryantje Oosterhout. Personal property. Executors Major Johannis Hardenbergh, Anthony Sleght and Samuel Borhanse. Witnesses Harman Pick, Hendrickus van Steen Burgh, Arejantje Oosterhouts.

425 (D 16) 1731 Septbr. 14 1732 Novbr. 21

DAVIS, John, of New York. Wife Abigail (she has son John Hannes), sons Matthew, Joseph, Edward, daughter Elizabeth. Real and personal estate. Executors son Matthew and Charles Clinton. Witnesses James Thomson, Samuel Luckie, John Young.

426 (D 17) 1731 Octbr. 1 Octbr. 22 Dutch

DU BOIS, Abraham, of New Paltz, Ulster Co. Wife Margaret, sons Abraham, Joel, daughters Sara, wife of Roelof Eltinge, Lea, wife of Philipp Fires, Rachel and Catharine. Land on Raritans R., N. J., on the S. side of the Paltz (Wallkil) R., house and lot in New Paltz, land at Canestoga; personal property. Executors son Abraham, son-in-law Roelof Eltinge and Major Johannis Hardenbergh. Witnesses Daniel du Bois, Thomas Beekman, Ino. Crooke jun.

427 (D 18) 1734 Octbr. 20 1734-5 March 10 Dutch

DE LAMETER, Abraham, of Kingston, Ulster Co. Wife Elsie, da. of Jurian Tappen, sons Cornelius, Johannis, David, Jacobus and Abraham, daughters Ariantie, wife of Albert Kierstede, and Jannetje, wife of Willem Eltinge. Land on N. side of Ronduytkil, do. in Kingston Corporation, h. and l. in Kingston Village; personal property. Executors the wife, the five sons and the two sons-in-law. Witnesses Hans Kierstede, Christoffel Wamborne, Jacob Marius jun., Jacobus van Dyck.

428 (D 19) 1735-6 Jany. 31

DE KEY, Helena, widow of Teunis, late of N. Y., merchant. Daughters Helena Sheffield widow, Hillegond Bayard, children of dec'd daughter Catharine Wendell, son Johannis. Real estate in N. Y. City and Province; personal property (wrought plate). Executors daughter Helena, William Hamersly and Abraham van Vleck. Witnesses Paul Richard, Benj. Thomas, E. Blagge. Copy. No proof.

429 (D 20) 1736 April 13 July 19

DUNBAR, John, of Schenectady Township, vintner. Sons Robert, John, Alexander, daughters Mary, Catharine and Willempje. Houses and lots at Schenectady, land in the Mohocks Country, held in company with Stephanus Groesbeck and now occupied by Benj. Lenyne; personal property (a large silver tumbler, 10 silver spoons, two eared silver cup, a silver snuff box, a small silver tumbler, portraits of testator and wife). Executors Peter Wenne, mariner and John Waters vintner, both of Albany. Witnesses Gerret van Brakel, Arent Arat, Ed. Collins.

430 (D 21) 1736 Aug. 26 1741 June 3 **DE LAMETER, Jacobus,** of Marbletown, Ulster Co., yeoman. Wife Geertje, sons Glowdie, Isaak, Marte, daughters Bata, Ester, Jannetje and Susannah. Farms at Marbletown and at Claverrack; personal property. Executors sons Isaak and Marte, Thomas Jansen and Cornelis de Lameter. Witnesses Gil. Livingston, Hendrecus van Kuren, R. G. Livingston.

431 (D 22) 1736 Aug. 5 — **DE BONREPOS, Martha,** of Staten Island, widow. Daughters Frances Britain, Ann Biller (Billow) and her daughter Rachel, Rachel Britain, great granddaughter Martha, daughter of granddaughter Ann, granddaughter Martha, Jacob Biller, sons children. Personal property (two silver cups, each of £5 price). Executors John Lay Count and Captain Richard Stillwell. Witnesses Margaret Johes, Ebenezer Salter, and Safty Borden. Copy. No proof.

432 (D 23) 1736-7 March 9 1746 Novbr. 13 **DECKER, Lawrance,** of Warwick, Orange Co., yeoman. Wife Nielche, sons Benjamin, Lawrence, Daniel, Cornelius, David, daughters Beleche, Lisanna, Elener and Sarah. Real and personal estate. Executors Joseph Perry and Richard Edsall. Witnesses Thomas Wright, Thomas de Kay, Daniel Brown.

433 (D 24) 1737 Septbr. 20 1748 Decbr. 2 **DUMON, Igenas,** of Kingston, Ulster Co., farmer. Wife Catherine, sons Jan Baptist junior, David, Petrus, Hermanus, Cornelius, Minder, Anthony, daughter Elsie and an expected child. Real and personal property. Executors the wife and father Jan Baptist Dumon. Witnesses Tyerck de Witt, Johannis Dumon, Jarman Pick. See No. 436.

434 (D 25) 1740 Novbr. 5 1741-2 March 18 **DU MONT, John,** of Kingston, Ulster Co., merchant. Wife Rachael, children Johannes, Egbert, Petrus and Catherine. Real and personal estate. Executors

the wife, brothers Wallerand and Peter Du Mont and Cornelis Schoonmaker. Witnesses Tyerck van Keuren, Jan Slecht, Hendrecus van Kuren, Cornelis van Keuren jun. See No. 468.

435 (D 26) 1741 April 3 — **D'HARRIETTE, Benjamin,** of New York (?). Son Benjamin. This is only an abstract of part of the will, mentioning "the aforesaid John D'Harriette Smith, the aforesaid Elizabeth Groesbeeck, Magdalen Groesbeeck, another da. of the said John Groesbeeck, Ann, Catherine, Mary and Susannah, also daughters of said John Groesbeeck. This abstract mentions a house and lot on the N. side of Queen Str., purchased from George Duneau, Michall Duneau and William Ludlow.

436 (D 27) 1741 Novbr. 8 1749 Octbr. 2 Dutch — **DUMON, Janbatist,** of Kingston, Ulster Co. Grandsons Jan Batist, David, Petrus, Harmanus, Cornelius, Myndert, Anthony, granddaughter Elsie and Neeltie, all children of dec'd son Igenas (supra, No. 433), daughter Sarah, wife of Roelof Kip. Real and personal property. Executors son-in-law Roelof Kip, Albert Paling and Myndert Schuyler jun. Witnesses Cornelis de Lameter, Abra de Lamater, Cornelius de Lamater jun. Vide No. 433.

437 (D 28) 1742 May 29 1748 Novbr. 17 — **DAVIS, Mathew,** of Hunting Grove, Ulster Co., farmer. Wife Ruth, sons John, Jeams and Joseph. Real and personal estate. Executors Robert Burnet and Patrick McClaghry. Witnesses Arthur Beatty, Walter McMichal, Margaret McCool. Testator incidentally refers to his sister Elizabeth and brother Joseph. Confer supra, No. 425.

438 (D 29) 1743 June 7 1759 Febry. 15 — **DU BOIS, Salomon** (son of Lewis, dec'd), of Ulster Co., yeoman. Children Jacomyntje, wife of Barent Du Bois, Benjamin, Cornelius, Sarah, Hendricus and Helena, children of dec'd eldest son Isaac, vizt: Catherine, Margaret and Rebecca, children of dec'd daughter

Catherine, wife of Peter Low. Land at Perkieama, Penna., at Katskil, N.Y., at New Paltz, in Kingston Corporation, personal property. Executors the sons Benjamin, Cornelius and Hendricus. Witnesses Benjamin Hasbrouck jun., Jonathan Hasbrouck, J. Bruyn jun. A second will of the same testator, dated June 26, 1756, calls daughters Jacomyntje a widow, Sarah, wife of Simon van Wagenen and Helena, wife of Josiah Eltinge, makes sons Benjamin and Hendricus with John Eltinge of Kingston executors and is witnessed by Noach Eltinge, Lowis J. Dubois and Andris Dubois.

439 (D 30) 1743 April 16 1744-5 March 2 Dutch

DECKERS, Heyltie, of Kingston, Ulster Co. Children of brother Johannis Decker dec'd, vizt: Cornelius and sisters; sister's child Maria de Lametter (da. of Johannis de Lametter); sister Mary, brothers children viz: Gerret (?), Geerte, Elsie, Ragel, Maria and Catharina. Personal property (silver spoons). Executors brother-in-law Johannis de Lametter and uncle Johannis ten Broek. Witnesses Thomas Beekman, M. Edward Thompson, Cornelius Lambertsen Brinck.

440 (D 31) 1746 July 14 1749 Octbr. 4

DU BOIS, Jonathan, of New Paltz Precinct, Ulster Co., yeoman. Wife Elizabeth, sons Lewis, Andries, Nathaniel, Jonas, daughters Rachel, Cornelia and Maria. Land in New Paltz Patent; personal property. Executors brother Nathaniel Du Bois, brothers-in-law Johannis Hardenbergh and Wessel Brodhead. Witnesses Cornelius Dubois, Evert Terwelger jun., J. Bruyn.

441 (D 32) 1746 Octbr. 10 1760 March 18

DAVENPORT, Thomas, of Philipps Precinct, Dutchess Co. Wife Elizabeth, sons Thomas, William, Oliver, Robert and Stephen, children of daughter Mary, "which she had by Jacobus Hamōn," children of da. Elizabeth Nellson, daughters Charity, Phebe, Hanah and Abigail. Real and personal property. Executors the wife, son Thomas and John Nellson. Witnesses Joseph Goecocks, Hannah Sobee, who at the date of proof of this will is the wife of Oliver Davenport of Orange Co., yeoman, John Cuer.

442 (D 33) 1746 June 6 1764 Febry. 1 Dutch

DEDERICK, Frederick, of Albany Co., farmer. Wife Eiesie (?) sons Johannis, Wilhellemus, Henderieckis, Peturus and da. Eliesabeth. Real and personal property. Executor son Johannis. Witnesses Martin Gerson van Bergen, Pieter Sachs, Davd. van Dyck.

443 (D 34) 1747 April 4 April 27

DISBROWE, Henry, of Mareneck, Westchester Co., yeoman. Wife Hannah, daughters Mary, Deborah, Elizabeth and Margret, sons Henry, Benjamin, Joseph, Josiah. Real and personal property. Executors brother-in-law William Barker and cousin Henry Griffin. Witnesses Obadiah Palmer, Mary Griffin, James Scholefield. Copy.

444 (D 35) 1749 June 6 1751 Aug. 12

DOUW, Hendrick, of Rensselaers Wyck Manor. Wife Neeltie, sons Volkert jun., Johannis, daughters Doortie, wife of Jan Newkerk, Pietertie, wife of William Hogan, and Neeltie. Land on Papsknees Island (Renssaelaer Co.) and in Albany Co.; personal property (a silver tankard, a silver cup and silver spoons). Executors sons-in-law Gerrit, Marten and Petrus van Bergen. Witnesses Gerrit Gersen van den Bergh, Martin Gerritsen van Bergen, Hitchen Holland.

445 (D 36) 1749-50 March 23 1750 June 27

DICKESSON, Samuel, of Dutchess Co. Wife ———, children Christofer, Charles, Eacobud, Gideon, George, Willem and Mary. Real and personal property. The wife sole executrix. Witnesses John Paddock, James Rodes, Samll. Monrow. Proved in Westchester Co.

446 (D 37) 1749-50 Jany. 13 1753 Jany. 31

DU BOIS, Gualtherus, Minister of the Refd. Church in N. Y. City. Son Gualtherus, daughter Elizabeth, children of son John, vizt: Peter and Gaultherus, children of dec'd son Isaac, vizt: Gualtherus, Helena, and Margaret. Real and personal property (plate). Executors son Gualtherus and da. Elizabeth. Witnesses John Everson, Nicholas Bogert, George Duncan jun. Copy.

447 (D 38) 1750 July 30 Novbr. 7 **DENTON, Daniel,** of Goshen, Orange Co. Wife Sarah, daughter Sarah, sons Samuel, Gilbert, Joseph, James, Jonas, John, Daniel, Thomas. Real estate in Goshen, at Newborough, Ulster Co.; personal property. Executors sons Samuel and John and brother-in-law Daniel Everett. Witnesses John Samuel Denton, John Bradner.

448 (D 39) 1751 Aug. 28 Novbr. 13 **DISBROW, John** jun., of Rye, Westchester Co. Sisters Sarah, wife of Roger Perk jun. and Anne Disbrow; Anne, da. of Hannah Ferris. Real and personal property. Executors sister Anne Disbrow and Ebenezer Kniffin. Witnesses J. Wetmore, Hannah Carman, Susannah Leveridge. Copy.

449 (D 40) 1751 May 9 1755 May 29 **DE LANG, Francis,** of Beakmans Prect., Dutchess Co. Wife Mary, children (son) Arre, Rachel, Nicolas, Lawrence, Jean, Mary, Liddiah, Elizabeth, Catherine, Elias, Geshee and Egie. Real and personal property. Executors the wife, Benjamin Hosebrook (Hasbruck) and Peter van de Waters. Witnesses John Winslow and Wm. Huff.

450 (D 41) 1752 July 1 — **DITMARS, Dowe,** of Jamaica, L. I., yeoman. Son Dowe jun., children of dec'd sons Johannis and Abraham, do. of dec'd da. Ariaentie, wife of William van Duine, grandson Johannis Ditmas, children of dec'd son Peter's daughter, vizt: Peter Monfort, Antie Monfort, Sarah Monfort and Catherine Monfort. "Worldly estate." Executors son Dowe and grandson Johannis Ditmars. Witnesses Nathan Furman, Johannes Eldert, Hendrick Eldert. Copy.

451 (D 42) 1752 Octbr. 20 1753 Octbr. 31 **DE WITT, Henry,** of Kingston, Ulster Co., merchant. Wife Maria, sons Tjerck, Jacob, John and Henry, daughters Elizabeth and Ann, brothers Petrus and Andries.

Land on the Kingston-Hurley road; personal property. Executors the wife and the brothers abovenamed. Witnesses William Burhans, Tyerck de Witt, Dirck Janson. Mother's name Anne.

452 (D 43) 1753 Decbr. 29 1762 Decbr. 2 **DE WIT, Tjerck,** of Kingston Corporation, Ulster Co. Wife Deborah, children of dec'd son Henry, vizt: Tjerck Claesen, Jacob, John, Henry, Elizabeth and Hannah, sons Petrus, Andries, children of da. Neeltie, by Wessels Jacobsen ten Brock, vizt: Jacob, Tjerck and Elizabeth, granddaughter Ann, wife of Richard Stout and daughter of da. Neeltie, wife of Samuel Stout, son John dead. Land at Staatsburgh, Dutchess Co., home farm in Kingston Corporation, farm on Esopus Creek; personal property. Executors the two sons Petrus and Andries. Witnesses Joseph Gasherie, H. van Keuren, J. Hasbrouck.

453 (D 44) 1756 July 28 1758 Septbr. 12 **DOUGHTY, William,** of Kingston, Ulster Co., blacksmith. Wife Nanney sole heiress of "temporal estate" and with Johannis de Lametre and Abraham de Lametre executrix. Witnesses Thomas Beekman, Adam Swart, Matthew Edward Thompson.

454 (D 45) 1756 May 29 Aug. 4 **DUBOIS, Elias,** of Poughkeepsie Precinct, Dutchess Co., esqre, Commander of a company of N. Y. provincial forces for the expedition against Crownpoint. Wife Susannah, children Lewis, Helena, Gerret, Jannetje and Henry. Real estate includes a share in a mine at Newtown, New England; personal property. Executors the wife, father Lewis Dubois and James G. Livingston. Witnesses Isaac Bull, John Sackett, John van der Burgh, Barent Bond.

455 (D 46) 1756 April 26 1758 April 20 Dutch **DE LAMETTER, Johannis,** of Kingston, Ulster Co. Wife Marytje, son Abraham, daughters Marytje, Elisabeth, Anna, Cornelia, wife of Cornelius Low, Elsje, wife of Dirck Schepmoes, Catherina, wife of Wilhelmus van

Gaesbeek. Real and personal property. Executors son Abraham, sons-in-law Cornelius A. Low and Wilhelmus van Gaesbeek, brother David de Lametter and John Eltinge. Witnesses Teunis Swart, Thomas Beekman, M. Edw. Thompson.

456 (D 47) 1756 July 22 1762 Aug. 21 **DEPUE, Jacobus,** of Rochester, Ulster Co. Wife Sarah, son Jacobus, Ephraim, Cornelius, Benjamin, Daniel, Joseph and Jacob, grandson Jacobus, son of Jacobus, daughters Antie, widow of Benjamin Schoonmaker jun., Elizabeth, wife of Peter Eltinge, Cathrina, Susannah, Sarah, granddaughter Sarah, da. of da. Maria, dec'd, late wife of Jacobus Elmendorph Koole and another child of her. Real and personal property. Executors sons Jacobus, Ephraim, Cornelius, Benjamin and brothers Cornelius and Moses Depuy. Witnesses Hendrick Krom, Benjamin Depuy, Elias Depuy.

457 (D 48) 1757 Decbr. 15 1758 May 22 **DEKAY, Thomas,** of Orange Co. Wife Christiana, sons Jacobus, Thomas, William Willet, Michael and Charles, heirs of son George dec'd, daughters Sarah Aurnold, Jenney Morris, Christiana Gale, Elizabeth, Mary, Hilio and Frances, granddaughter Frances Sackett. Real and personal property. Executors the wife and sons Jacobus, William Willet and Thomas. Witnesses David McCamly, miller, John Decker, Jacobus Decker, Elisabeth Hauser, spinster (German).

458 (D 49) 1757 Febry. 20 1767 May 26 **DUBOIS, Hezekiah** senior, of Saugerties, Ulster Co. Sons Hezekiah jun., Mathew, David. Real and personal estate (a large bible). Executors son David and Jacobus Post. Witnesses Abraham Post, Egbert Schoonmaker, John Post jun.

459 (D 50) 1757 Septbr. 4 1784 Jany. 17 **DU BOIS, Josaphat,** of Rochester, Ulster Co., yeoman. Wife Tiatje, daughters Maria, wife of Hendrikus Hornbeck, Corneleja, wife of Johannis Grad. Hardenbergh, and Catharenna. Real and personal property. The wife

and daughters executrices. Witnesses Lawrens Cortright, Jacobus van Keuren, of Shawangunk, yeoman, A. van Keuren.

460 (D 51) 1758 July 13 1761 May 7 **DE WITT, Egbert,** of Nepenack, Rochester Township, Ulster Co. Wife Mary, sons Andries E., Jacob, William, John, Steven, Egbert, Thomas, Benjamin, Ruben, daughter Mary. Real and personal estate. Executors sons Anderies E., Jacob, William, John and Steven. Witnesses Jan van Duesen, Jacob Roosa, Charles D. Witt.

461 (D 52) 1758 Septbr. 20 Decbr. 16 **DUFFIE, Duncan,** of N. Y. City, carpenter. Wife Barbara, daughter Anne, stepchild Margaret Workman, da. of dec'd wife. Real and personal property. Executors Alexander Montgomery of Orange Co., schoolmaster, Eanis Graham of N. Y. City, tailor, Jasper Cropsie of Kings Co., yeoman. Witnesses Thomas Chadwick, John McArthur, John Bowie. Copy.

462 (D 53) 1759 July 4 1769 Febry. 20 **DEMYER, Nicolas,** of Kingston Corporation, Ulster Co. Wife Elsie, sons Wilhelmus, Jeremiah and Benjamin, da. Catherina, wife of Christopher Kiersted. Land on Papaweys Kil, Ulster Co., on the Saw Kil, house and lot in Kingston, land at Schohary, personal property (a silver mug marked W. M. C.) Executors sons Jeremiah and Benjamin and son-in-law Christopher Keirsteden. Witnesses Jacob Burhans, Hendricus Post, both of Kingston Corporation, farmers, David Burhans jun. and A. Hasbrouck. Codicil dated "Near the Esopus Creek" February 10, 1766, adds grandson Nicholas Kersteder to the heirs and is witnessed by Lawrence Salisbury, John Walker, William Keffer.

463 (D 54) 1759 Octbr. 17 Decbr. 24 **DEVEL, Christopher,** of Crumelbow Precinct, Dutchess Co. Wife Mehitabel, sons Israel and Jonathan, daughter Sarah Mosher, granddaughter Patience, da. of dec'd son Joseph. Real and personal estate. Executors the wife and son Israel. Witnesses Stephen Hicks and Samuel Mabbett, both quakers. Copy.

464 (D 55) 1760 Septbr. 3 1764 Octbr. 20 **DEWITT, Andries,** of Rochester, Ulster Co., carman. Wife ———, children Andries A., Jannetje, Garton, Catherine, Thomas, Henry, Mary and Levi. Real and personal estate. Executors nephew Andries de Witt jun. and sons Andries and Garton, nephews Andries de Witt jun., Stephen de Witt and Richard Broadhead to be trustees for the minor children. Witnesses John Brodhead, R. Brodhead, William Brodhead.

465 (D 56) 1760 Novbr. 7 —— **DEVORE, David,** of N. Y. City, yeoman. Wife Jane, son David, daughters Elizabeth, wife of John Burger, Jane, wife of Nicholas Burger. Houses and lots in the East Ward and in Montgomery Ward; personal property. Executors brother John Devore and Thomas Smith, attorney-at-law. Witnesses Abrm. Montagne, William Bockee, Jacob Gerrebrants. Copy.

466 (D 57) 1760 June 14 Decbr. 25 **DURYE, Joost,** of Goshen Precinct, Orange Co. Wife Sarah, children Joost and four others, not named, daughter-in-law Peternelle Wood. Real and personal estate. Executors the wife and Abimal Yongh. Witnesses Silas Benjamin, Christian Benjamin and Nathaniel Jayne.

467 (D 58) 1760 Novbr. 28 1785 Jany. 7 **DE LAMETTER, Cornelius,** of Kingston, Ulster Co., esqre. Sons Abraham, Benjamin, Cornelius, daughters Selitje, wife of Matheus van Keuren, and Anna Catrina, wife of Ephraim Dubois. Real and personal property. Executors sons Abraham and Benjamin. Witnesses Wilhelmus Hoogtyling, Rebeca du Bois (wife of Jan Dubois) of Kingston, Jan Eltinge.

468 (D 59) 1760 Novbr. 18 1765 Febry. 15 **DUMONT, Rachel,** of Kingston, Ulster Co. (daughter of Egbert Schoonmaker). (Vide No. 434.) Sons John, Egbert, daughter Cathrina. Real estate in Ulster Co.; personal property includes "Law and History Books," a silver tea pot and a silver milk pot. Ex-

ecutors son Egbert, da. Cathrina and Andries T. de Witt. Witnesses A. Hasbrouck, A. van Keuren, Joseph Gasherie.

469 (D 60) 1760 Decbr. 25 1763 Aug. 9 **DEWEY, Martin,** of Crum Elbo Precinct, Dutchess Co. Son Martin, daughters Elisabeth, Rhoda, Mary, Lucretia and Grace, brother Jedediah Dewey. Real and personal estate. Executor the son and the brother. Witnesses Elnathan Smith, Elkanah Holmes, Timothy Shepherd.

470 (D 61) 1760 Novbr. 5 —— **DUMONT, Henry,** of N. Y. City, merchant. Wife Catherine, sons Peter and John, da. Mary, an expected child. Land in Somerset Co., N. J., the "Lottery House" at Piscataway Landing and another house and lot there at the waterside, house and lot in Duke Str., Montgomery Ward, N. Y. City; personal property. Executors brother Peter Dumont, John Alstine, Eronimus Alstine and John Oothout. Witnesses Joris Brinckerhoff, John Oothout, Joseph Finman. Copy. No proof.

471 (D 62) 1760 March 10 Oct. 7 **DE NORMANDIE, Daniel,** Ensign 44th Regt., Sarah de Normandie and Ann, da. of Edward Williams, dec'd, Pennsylvania Hospital. Real and personal property. Executors Anthony de Normandie and John van Vacty (this name obliterated by pencil). Witnesses Gerard de Peyster of Albany, merchant, and James Daly. Proved at Albany. Seal.

472 (D 63) 1765 Decbr. 18 1767 Aug. 21 **DEWITT, Deborah,** widow of Tyerck. Granddaughters Catherine Vroom and Deborah. Personal property (a gold ring with a stone and a silver snuff box). Executors John du Mond and Johannis Sleght. Witnesses Egbert Dumond, Jacobus de Lametter of Kingston, yeoman, Catharine, wife of William Wells of Kingston.

473 (D 64) 1762 May 20 1767 Febry. 2 **DUBOIS, Benjamin,** of Catts Kil, Albany Co., yeoman. Wife Catherinetie, sons Isaac, Curnalius, Huibartus, daughters Sarah, widow of Christian Overbagh, and Trintie, wife of John van Orden, grandchildren Benjamin, son, and Catelintie, Sarah and Rachel, daughters of eldest son Solomon dec'd and daughter-in-law Margriet Dubois. Farm on S. side of the Cats Kil in a bent above Hopsnose Point, adjoining land of Catherine, widow of Johan Jury Overbagh, and other lands in the present Greene Co., personal property. Executors the three sons. Witnesses Samuel van Vechten, Sylvester Salisbury, Abraham Salisbury.

474 (D 65) 1762 Septbr. 5 1785 Jany. 10 **DENTON, Daniel,** son of Daniel dec'd (supra No. 447), of Goshen, Orange Co. Brothers Jonas, Samuel, Gilbert, James and Thomas, sister Sarah Denton, nephews John Denton, Joseph Denton. Real and personal property. Executors brothers Jonas and Thomas. Witnesses Daniel Everett, William Drake of Goshen, carpenter, John Everett.

475 (D 66) 1763 May 7 June 13 **DUBOIS, Nathaniel,** of Orange Co., yeoman. Wife Gertruy, sons Lewis, Zachariah, Jonas, daughters Rennaltje, Hester, wife of Jesse Woodhull, Rachel, wife of Andries La Fevour. Real and personal estate. Executors the three sons. Witnesses Edward Wilkins, Gamaliel Conkling, George Clinton. Seal.

476 (D 67) 1763 March 30 1764 June 29 **DUBOIS, Philipp,** of Rochester, Ulster Co. Dec'd wife's name was Esther. Daughter Esther, children of dec'd daughter Mary, viz: Philipp, Cornelius, Isaac, Jacob and Lodewick. Real and personal property (plate). Executors daughter Esther, son-in-law Louis Bevier, nephew Simon Dubois, cousins Jacob Hasbrouck jun., Abraham Hasbrouck and Abraham Dujow. Witnesses Johannis Bevier jun., Johannes G. Hardenbergh, both of Rochester, yeomen, Marygriet Klyne. Seal.

477 (D 68) 1763 May 23 1764 July 9 Dutch **DEWITT, Tjerck,** of Ulster Co. Wife Ariantie, children Annatie, Elizabeth, Catherine and Grietie, Jacob and Teunis Oosterhout, sons of da. Annatie. Real and personal estate. Executors da. Elizabeth de Witt, Petrus Koole, Jacob G. Louw, Johannis Rosekrans and Teunis Oosterhout. Witnesses John Tack of Marbletown, Petrus Burger of Rochester and John Schoonmaker.

478 (D 69) 1764 Aug. 22 1769 Octbr. 2 **DENNISTON, Daniel,** of Ulster Co., merchant. Wife Sophia, brothers Joseph and Hugh Denniston. "Worldly estate." The wife sole executrix. Witnesses John Monck and John Fendell.

479 (D 70) 1764 Septbr. 25 1785 May 20 **DEPUY, Jacobus,** of Rochester, Ulster Co. Wife Sara, sons Jacobus, Simon, Moses and Jacob, da. Sara. Real and personal estate. Executors the wife, brother Cornelius Depuy, brother-in-law Salomon van Wagenen, cousin Jacob Hoornbeeck. Witnesses Moses Miller, Jacobus Bos jun., of Rochester, blacksmith, Annatje van Wagenen (at the date of proof wife of John Depuy of Rochester).

480 (D 71) 1764 April 11 June 29 **DURYEE, Abraam,** of Rumbout Precinct, Dutchess Co. Wife Sarah, nephew George, son of brother Charles Duryee of Oysterbay, L. I., Charles, son of Tunis Duryee of N. Y. dec'd, Abraham, son of brother Jacob Duryee of Bushwick, L. I., brother Dirck Duryee of New York, brother-in-law Cornelius van Wyck. Real and personal estate (silver headed sword). Executors brother Jacob Duryee and uncles-in-law Richard and Cornelius van Wyck. Witnesses Abraham Adriance, Gerret Storm and Johannes Wiltse.

481 (D 72) 1767 Octbr. 29 1784 June 3 **DEMAREST, Peter,** of *Bargain* (Bergen) Co., N. J. Wife Elenor, daughter Mary, wife of Abraham Ely. Real and personal estate. Executors the wife and son-in-law Abr. Ely. Witnesses William Ely, Elizabeth Ely, Mary Demarest.

8

482 (D 73) 1765 March 3 **DECKER, Cornelius,** of Orange Co., yeoman, letters of administration on the estate of, granted by Cadwallader Colden, Lieut.-Govr. of the Province of N. Y., to Catherine his widow.

483 (D 74) 1765 Septbr. 29 Octbr. 17 **DONHAM, Ephraim,** of Beekmans Prect., Dutchess Co., merchant. Wife Abigail and children. Real estate "within this or any of the neighboring Provinces;" personal property. Executors the wife, Jeams Morgen of South Perth Amboy, N. J. and Barnet Stilwill of Beekmans Prect. Witnesses Assa Johnson, Jonas Allen, William Marsh. Copy.

484 (D 75) 1766 Novbr. 20 Novbr. 22 **DEAN, John,** of Wayayanda, Goshen Prect., Orange Co. Father William and mother Catrine Dean, brothers William, Joseph and Nicholas, sister Mary Dean. Real and personal estate. Executors Richard Edsall and Samuel Edsall. Witnesses David McCamly, John McCamly, John Edsall.

485 (D 76) **DUDLEY, Stephen,** of Albany. Missing.

486 (D 77) 1768 June 2 Septbr. 19 **DOUW, Volkert,** of Albany City, merchant. Wife Ragel, (niece of Isaac Bogert), son Andries, daughter Lidia. Real and personal property. Executors the wife and children. Witnesses Johannes Vol. Douw, Cornelius Douw, Abraham Oothout.

487 (D 78) belongs under letter V.

488 (D 79) 1768 Octbr. 18 Decbr. 26 **DE LAMETTER, Martin,** of Marbletown, Ulster Co. Wife ——, son Jacob, daughters Elizabeth, Margret, Maria, Batan and Hester, grandson Moses Cantine jun., child of dec'd daughter Geertje. Real and personal estate. Executors son Jacob, sons-in-law Abraham Cantine and Coenrad Du Bois. Witnesses Petrus Dumond of Marbletown, cooper, Cornelius Bogart of the same place, farmer, Ch. D. Witt.

489 (D 80) 1769 June 17 1770 Octbr. 27 **DE LAENGE (de Long), Arrie,** of Charlotte Prect., Dutchess Co. Wife Anne, sons Francis, Elias, Martin, Jeams, Lawrence, daughters Mary Cronkright and Jene Ismul. Real and personal estate. Executors the wife, sons Francis and Elias and David Sotherland. Witnesses Comer Bullock of Charlotte Prect., cordwainer, Deliverance Bullock, Ellis Bullock.

490 (D 81) 1770 Octbr. 15 Novbr. 1 **DUNNING, Jacob,** of Goshen Prect., Orange Co., yeoman. Sons John, Jacob and Benjamin, daughters Bathsheba, Mehitabel and Mary. Real estate, some in Wawayanda Patent; personal property. Executors the three sons. Witnesses James Carpenter of Orange Co., schoolmaster, John Conkling and Elisabeth Dunning.

491 (D 82) 1770 July 19 1771 Decbr. 17 **DE LAMETTER, Jacobus,** of Kingston, Ulster Co. Wife Catherine, Jacobus, son of Egbert Bogardes, Abraham I. Delametter, Abraham A. Delametter, David D. Delametter, Egbert Bogardes, Egbert Dumond, Anneke, wife of Abraham Post. Real and personal property (a silver hilted sword). Executors Abraham I. Delametter, Egbert Dumond and Dirck Wynkoop. Witnesses Cornelis Viele of Kingston, cordwainer, Elias Hasbrouck, D. Wynkoop jun.

492 (D 83) 1771 May 14 July 15 **DOUGHTY, William,** of Charlotte Precinct, Dutchess Co. Wife Margaret, sons William, James, Barnerd, Oliver and Samuel, daughters Phebe, Mary. Real and personal estate. Executors sons William and James. Witnesses Israel Green, Jacob Tobias and Alexander Chaucer.

493 (D 84) 1771 June 13 1772 Febry. 20 **DIEL, Henry,** of Rhinebeck Prect., Dutchess Co., yeoman. Children Johannes, Carl, Jacob, Elizabeth, Anna, Catherine, Anna, Mary, Henry, Zacharias, William, Lawrence and Cornelius. Real and personal estate. Executors Helmus Teller, Frederick Neher and Cornelius

Miller. Witnesses Jury Adam Zufeldt, John Schultz, Christian Schultz.

494 (D 85) 1771 Jany. 12 1780 July 10 **DENTON, Benjamin,** of Amenia Precinct, Dutchess Co. Wife Ruth, sons Benjamin and John, daughters Sarah, Ann and Rachel. Homefarm, land in Sharon Township, Connt. Executor son Benjamin. Witnesses Roswell Hopkins, Ruth Peck and Hannah Purdy.

495 (D 86) 1772 March 14 1781 Septbr. 15 **DU BOIS, Peter,** of the Wallkill, Ulster Co. "My very dear most excellent and amiable wife Catharine" sole heiress of real and personal property. Executors the Honble. Henry White, James Duane, Jacob Walton and Samuel Ver Planck. Witnesses John Bowles, Wm. Banyar and Cream Brush.

496 (D 87) 1772 June 12 1774 May 17 **DE VREESE, Jacobis,** of Orangetown, Orange Co., yeoman. Annetje, youngest da. of Jacob A. Blauvelt, Jacobis, son of Giles Hooper of Burlington, Jacobis Durie, Johan Martinhague; John, son of the late Colonel Haring residuary legatee of all real and personal property and sole executor. Witnesses Gerret Eckerson of Orangetown, yeoman, Johannes Quackenbos and John Eckerson.

497 (D 88) 1772 Septbr. 2 1776 Jany. 26 **DEWITT, John,** of Rochester, Ulster Co. Wife Ann, sons Jacob and Henriekus. Real and personal estate. Executors the wife, son Jacob, cousins Andries and Charles Dewitt. Has brother Jacob Dewitt. Witnesses Hendrikus Hoornbeek, Michael Enderle and Jacob Hoornbeek.

498 (D 89) 1772 March 24 1783 Aug. 20 **DIEFENDORF, Henry,** of Canajohary, Tryon Co., yeoman. Wife Anna Rosina, son Jacob and other children. Real and personal estate. Executors the wife and John Pickerd. Witnesses Peter Miller, Henrich Sander and Johan Henrich Meyer.

499 (D 90) 1773 Septbr. 8 Septbr. 21 **DUBOIS, Isaac,** of Green Kil, Kingston Township, Ulster Co., miller. Wife Jannetje, sons Jacob and Johannes, daughters Rachel, wife of Andries de Witt jun., Sarah, wife of Tobias van Beuren, Jannetje, wife of William Eltinge jun. Real and personal property. Executors son Jacob, sons-in-law Andries de Witt jun. and Tobias van Beuren. Witnesses Gerret Freer, Nicholas Kierstead. Christopher Tappen, all of Ulster Co., yeomen.

500 (D 91) 1773 July 8 Aug. 6 **DRAKE, Gerardus,** of Beekmans Prect., Dutchess Co. Wife Sarah sole heiress and with Benjamin Griffin executrix of "all my estate." Witnesses Jonathan Thorn, Ann Brown, Gabriel Smith.

501 (D 92) 1773 Aug. 2 Decbr. 1 **DUTCHER, David,** of Rumbouth Prect., Dutchess Co, yeoman. Wife Elisabeth, son Barneth, grandson David, son of son David Dutcher. Real and personal property. Executors son Barneth and Johannes Dubois. Witnesses Nathaniel Dubois, Jacob Coapman and Simon Leroy jun.

502 (D 93) 1774 Febry. 24 1784 Decbr. 21 **DECKER, Mathew,** of Shawangunk Prect., Ulster Co., yeoman. Wife Magdalena, children Johannis, Abraham and Maria, sister-in-law Catherine Bevier, Catherine, da. of Benjamin Smedes, nephew Jacob Hasbrouck, son of brother Johannis Decker. Real and personal property. Executors the wife, brother Johannis Decker, Captain Thomas Jansen of Shawangunk and Mathew Jansen. Witnesses James Fulton, Robert Hunter, Matthew Hunter jun.

503 (D 94) 1774 Octbr. 23 1775 March 15 **DE NOYELLES, John,** of Orange Co, esqre. Wife Rachel, sons John, Peter and Edward William, daughter Charlotte. Land in Durham and Deerfield Townships, Charlotte Co., do in Tryon Co. and on Lake Champlain, i. e. 1000 acres granted to Trevor Newland, a reduced officer, personal property. Executors the wife,

Goldsborow Banyar, Thomas Duncan, Isaac Low and Edward William Kiers (?). Witnesses Peter van Schaack, Waldron Blaau of N. Y. City innkeeper, John Kelly.

504 (D 95) 1774 Febry. 2 1782 May 24 **DEFOREST, Philip,** of Rensselaerswyck Manor Albany Co., yeoman. Wife Maria, sons David and John, daughter Rebecca. Real and personal property. Executors the wife, brother Martin Deforest and brother-in-law Maas Bloemedal. Witnesses Henry Beasley of Albany City, cordwainer, Jno. Ostrander of the same place, schoolmaster and Abraham Roseboom.

505 (D 96) 1775 Septbr. 26 1780 Septbr. 2 **DIETZ, Adam,** of the Beverdam, Albany Co., husbandman. Wife Geertruy, brothers Johannis and William Dietz (sister?) Elisabeth, wife of Juri Sible, Adam Dietz jun. and his son Adam, Geertruy Sybel and Anna Eker. "Whole estate." Executors brother William Dietz and John R. Bleecker. Witnesses Nalley Schuyler, Jno R. Bleecker and Barent Bleecker.

506 (D 97) 1775 April 26 May 15 **DU BOIS, Jonas,** of Cornwall Prect., Orange Co., yeoman. Wife Hannah, daughters Easther, Hannah and Gertruy, son Nathaniel. Real and personal property. Executors the wife, brother Zacharias Du Bois and brother-in-law Jesse Woodhull. Witnesses Rennelche Parkhurst, Elsy Wilkins and Thomas Moffat of Orange Co., merchant. Vide No. 475.

507 (D 98) 1775 March 8 1779 April 18 **DEPUY, Elias,** of Rochester Township, Ulster Co., esqre. Wife Rachel, sons Moses, John, Elias, Jesaia and Josia, daughters Sarah, Mary, wife of Joseph Depuy, and Grietie. Land in Ulster Co., personal property. Executors the wife, sons Moses and John, brother Benjamin Depuy, brother-in-law Jacob Hoornbeek. Witnesses Johannis G. Hardenbergh, Petrus Schoonmaker and Joseph Hasbrouck jun. of Marbletown, farmer.

508 (D 99) 1776 Aug. 20 1782 June 6 **DECKER, Joseph,** of Shawangunk Prect., Ulster Co., yeoman. Wife Rachel, children Benjamin, Jacob, Joseph, David, Rachel, Catherine and Elizabeth. Farm at Shawangunk, personal property. Executors the wife, Jacob Smedes, Matthew Smedes and Cornelius C. Schoonmaker. Witnesses George Smith of Shawangunk Prect. innkeeper, Teunis Terwilligen and Elizabeth Smedes, who at date of proof is wife of John Taylor.

509 (D 100) 1776 May 25 1779 April 23 **DUNNING, Samuel,** of Goshen, Orange Co. Wife Elizabeth, sons Samuel, Ephraim, Isaac, Matthew, Abijah and David, daughters Mary and Margaret. Real and personal property. Executors sons Samuel and Ephraim, and cousin Jacob Dunning. Witnesses William Denn of Ulster Co, schoolmaster, Loes Dunning and Ketum Dunning.

510 (D 101) 1776 Aug. 21 1786 Decbr. 22 **DECKER, Gerrit,** of Shawangonk Prect. Ulster Co., yeoman. Sons Manasa, Elias, Ruben and Petrus jun., daughters Geertie, wife of Lewis Gasherie, Elisabeth, wife of Cornelius Decker, Janneke, wife of William Goodjyon. Real and personal estate. Executors sons Manasa, Elias and Ruben. Witnesses Abraham Decker, Joshua Decker, Cornelius C. Schoonmaker.

511 (D 102) 1777 Decbr. 13 1782 Jany. 28 **DOUW, Johannes Vol.,** of Albany Co. Son Cornelius, da. Margaretje. House and lot in Albany City, land at Sachendage, Albany Co., personal property. Executors son Cornelius and nephew Volkert Oothout. Witnesses Hendrick Bogert, Henry Oothout jun., Ino. Jost Zabriskie.

512 (D 103) 1777 July 16 1782 April 6 **DEYGERT, Werner,** of Canajoharie Distr., Tryon Co., yeoman. Wife Lana, sons Han Jost (has wife Marilla), Zepherenus, daughters Mary, Catherine, Anna, Elizabeth, Lana and Mary Catherine. Real and personal property. Executors Nicholas Herckheimer,

Peter Deygert and George Henry Bell. Witnesses George Henrich Bell, Nicholas Bell and Isaac Johnson.

513 (D 104) 1778 May 1 Septbr. 1 **DAVIS, Frederick,** of Marbletown, Ulster Co. Sons Jacobus, Isaac, Andries, and Samuel, daughters Jane, Mary, Elizabeth, Rachel and Sarah. Real and personal property. Executors son Jacobus and David Bevier. Witnesses Levi Pawling, Robt. Harper late of N. Y. City, now of Dutchess Co., esqre., John Davis of Marbletown, blacksmith. Letters testamentary granted to Johannis Oostrander of Hurley Town, farmer, Moses Pattison of Marbletown carpenter and William Hume of the same place schoolmaster, all sons-in-law of testator March 24, 1783, the above named executors declining to act.

514 (D 105) 1778 Febry. 8 1779 Febry. 1 **DOLSEN, James,** of Goshen Prect., Orange Co. Wife Phebe, sons James, Asa and Samuel, daughters Mary and Abigail. Real and personal estate. Executors brothers-in-law Isaiah Veal and Abraham Harding. Witnesses Henry White, Benjamin Whitaker and James Little.

515 (D 106) 1778 July 28 1782 March 30 **DUSINBERE, Silvanus,** of New Windsor, Ulster Co. Wife Mary, son Samuel. Farm and personal property. Executors the wife or Samuel Sands or Benjamin Westlake. Witnesses William Cumming of New Windsor, yeoman, Agnes Cumming, his wife and Elizabeth Westlake.

516 (D 107) 1778 April 18 Octbr. 10 **DE WITT, Jacob,** of Rochester Township, Ulster Co., yeoman. Nephew Jacob, son of brother Cornelius DeWitt, and Hendrikus De Witt. Real estate in Rochester Township. Executors Moses Depuy, Benjamin Cortreght and Hendricus De Witt. Witnesses Philip Hoornbeek, Ino. Sleght, Christ? Tappen.

517 (D 108) 1779 Febry. 6 1780 Jany. 28 **DRAKE, John,** of Goshen Prect., Orange Co., yeoman. Wife Martha, sons Benjamin, Joseph, Samuel, William and Zephaniah, heirs of son John, daughters

Martha Jackson, Mary Holly and Esther Knap, granddaughters Martha and Mary, das. of Joseph Holly. Home farm, land in Queens and Kings counties, inherited from grandfather Adam Brewer; personal estate. Executors Captain Colvil Bradner and son Joseph. Witnesses Daniel Vail of Goshen, weaver, Isaac Smith and W. Thompson.

518 (D 109) 1779 Octbr. 12 1780 April 17 **DENTON, Samuel,** of Newburgh Prect., Ulster Co., farmer. Wife Phebe, daughters Abigail and Sarah, wife of John H. Scheutz, nephew Samuel, son of brother Thomas Denton, brothers Thomas, Daniel, James and Jonas, sister Sarah Wickham. Real and personal estate. Executors the wife, son-in-law John H. Scheutz and brother Daniel Denton. Witnesses Hope Mills, Monson Ward and Lewis Donnovan of Newburgh Prect., schoolmaster.

519 (D 110) 1780 Novbr. 3 1784 Febry. 19 **de PEYSTER, William,** late of N. Y. City, now a refugee at Albany. Children John, William, Gerard, Nicholas, Abraham, James, Ann and Margaret. Real and personal estate (two silver teapots, nine silver tablespoons, gold sleeve buttons, silver salt cellars, a silver tankard, six silver teaspoons). Executors sons William and Abraham with Egbert Benson. Witnesses Evert Bancker, Henry Rutgers and Gerard Bancker.

520 (D 111) 1780 June 6 1782 April 8 **DE LAVERGNE, Nicolas,** of Charlotte Precinct, Dutchess Co. Wife Mary, sons Giles, Joseph, Nicolas, James, Ebenezer and Walter, daughters Mary, Sarah, Elisabeth, Hannah, and Susanna. "Wordly estate." Executors the wife with Richard Snedicker as overseer. Witnesses Silas Devel, Joseph Woolley and Aaron Haight jun., farmer.

521 (D 112) 1780 Novbr. 26 1781 April 23 **DUBOIS, Cornelius,** of New Paltz, Ulster Co., Esqire. Wife Margaret, son Cornelius, daughters Tryntje, Jannetje, Jacominetie, Saretie, children of da. Rachel

dec'd, viz: Nathaniel Dubois, Wilhelmus Dubois and Polly Dubois, children of da. Leah dec'd, Dirck and Lea Wynkoop. Real and personal estate. Son-in-law Cornelius D. Wynkoop guardian of the grandchildren. Executors son Cornelius, son-in-law Jacob Hasbrouck jun., grandsons Josiah Hasbrouck, Nathaniel Dubois and Cornelius Hasbrouck. Witnesses Denie Ralyea, yeoman, David Louw, blacksmith and Joshua Dubois.

522 (D 113) 1780 Jany. 22 1787 March 14 **DE LAMETER, Abraham,** of Kingston, Ulster Co., miller. Wife ——, sons Cornelius and John, daughter Sarah. Real and personal estate. Executors the two sons. Witnesses Antye Hasbrook, Abraham W. van Gaasbeek, John Dumont.

523 (D 114) 1781 July 14 Aug. 9 **DE WITT, John,** late of New York Island, now of Poghkeepsie Prect. farmer. Wife Ann, son William, daughters Ann, wife of John Quackenbush, Nancy, wife of Peter Ogilvie and Gertruyd, wife of Samuel Harris. Real and personal property. Executors the wife, and sons-in-law Quackenbush and Ogilvie. Witnesses William Barns, Peter Tappen and Gilbert Livingston.

524 (D 115) —— 1782 Decbr. 2 **DUNNING, Jacob.** Memorandum given by, relative to his property. Had wife Jeeturah (?) two sons, brother John Dunning and William Hollis, who are named as executors. He disposes of a homefarm and land on the W. side of the Wallkil, Ulster Co. His intentions are proved by the testimony of Caleb Smith, yeoman and wife Abigail and of Lois, wife of Jabez Noble.

525 (D 116) 1787 22d Day 5th Month 1782 Febry. 27 **DAVIS, Joseph,** of Beekman's Prect., Dutchess Co. Wife Jemima, sons Joseph, Abner, David, daughter Mary. Personal property (4 silver tablespoons). Executors the wife, Joseph Davis and Robert Moone. Witnesses Joseph Clapp, John Lee and William Moore.

526 (D 117) 1781 July 20 Novbr. 17 **DEAN, Jedediah,** of New Paltz Prect. Wife Ariontyea, sons Gideon, Jedediah, Isaac, Jonathan, Daniel and Abraham, daughters Jenny Ellsworth, Elizabeth Wolsey and Mary Laroe. Real and personal property. Executors sons Gideon, Jedediah and Isaac. Witnesses Benjamin Ely of New Marlborough, Ulster Co., physician, Andries Dubois jun., of New Paltz, farmer and Simon Doiau.

527 (D 118) 1782 March 25 June 6 **DIETZ, William,** of Schohary, Albany Co., yeoman. Children William, Johannes, Adam, Johan Jost, Eva and Marilis, wife of Hendrick Ball. Real and personal property. Executors sons William, Johannes and Johan Jost. Witnesses David Sternbergh, Peter Vroman, Abraham Sternbergh.

528 (D 119) 1782 Febry. 4 1785 Aug. 17 **DAVIS, Ann,** of Fishkil Landing, Dutchess Co. widow. Daughters Elizabeth and Ann, sons John and Andreas. Real and personal property. Executors Richard Snediker of Poughkeepsie Precinct, gentleman, Peter Bogardus jun., of Fishkil Landing, skipper and John McCabe of Stony Kil, Rumbout Precinct, yeoman. Witnesses John Young of N. Y. City, schoolmaster, Petrus Bogardus and Shibboleth Bogardus.

529 (D 120) 1783 Novbr. 30 1784 June 4 **DEMOTT, James,** of Newborough Precinct, Ulster Co., yeoman. Wife Catherine, sons James, Michael, daughters Hannah, wife of Eliezer Lusee, Elisabeth. Real and personal estate. Executors the wife, Eliezer Lusee and Gilbert Jones. Witnesses Isaac Demott, David Keech and William Buckingham.

530 (D 121) 1783 June 21 1786 May 17 **DEAL, Laurentz,** of Rhinebeck Prect., Dutchess Co., yeoman. Stepdaughters Catherine, wife of Peter Freer, Eva, wife of Thomas Omfrey, Margaret, wife of Matthew van Steenbergh, son-in-law Jacob Tremper, grandchildren Laurentz, Jury, Helmus, Jacob, Manus

and Mary Tremper. Real and personal property (four silver teaspoons). Executors son-in-law Jacob Tremper, cousin Carol Deal, and John Ryckert Shell. Witnesses Joseph Reichert, John Francis Ellistone and Christian Schultzs.

531 (D 122) 1783 Octbr. 20 1786 Octbr. 16 **DUBOIS, Elisha,** of Rumbout Prect., Dutchess Co., farmer. Wife Sarah, grandson Elisha, son of dec'd son John, children of da. Sarah, wife of Duncan Graham and of da. Barbara, wife of Adriaen Couenhoven. Real and personal property. Executors Mathew van Benschoten, Obediah W. Cooper and Adriaen Couenhoven. Witnesses Isaac van Hook, John Hauk and William Cooper.

532 (D 123) 1785 June 1 1786 Septbr. 15 **DECKER, Joshua,** of Shawangunk Prect., Ulster Co. Wife Geertie, and children. Real and personal property. Executors Severyn T. Bruyn and Johannis A. Hardenbergh. Witnesses Daniel Wackman of New Paltz, farmer, Adna Heaton and Cornelius Schoonmaker.

533 (D 124) 1785 Febry. 27 March 4 **DODGE, Jeremiah,** of Pauldings Precinct, Dutchess Co. Sons Stephen, Daniel, Robert, Jonathan and David, daughters Rebecca, Lidia and Elisabeth (?). Apparently only personal property. Executors sons Daniel and Robert. Witnesses Caleb Lamb, Joseph Lamb and Elisha Champlin. Nuncupative will, written March 2 after the death of testator from recollection of witnesses.

534 (D 125) 1785 Novbr. 19 1786 July 15 **DENNISTON, Hugh,** of Albany City, innkeeper. Sons Daniel, James, Isaac, John and Hugh, daughters Isabella, Lydia, Margaret and Annie. Real and personal property. Executor John Taylor of Albany City, esquire. Witnesses Stephen Lush of Albany, attorney-at-law, Herman ten Broek and Neal Shaw.

535 (D 126) 1785 Octbr. 1 **DWIGHT, Stephen,** of Newark, N. J. Wife Hannah, daughter Martha, son Stephen, children of brothers and sisters, vizt: Thomas Dwight, Catherine and Mary Dwight, Joseph Monnel, Gennet Monnel, sister Catherine Monnel. Real estate in Newark and in State of New York (grandfather Eagles estate), personal property. Executors Richard Davis of New York and Isaac Alling of Newark. Witnesses Israel Reach, James Green and William Lee. Copy from N. J. records.

536 (D 127) 1786 Septbr. 14 Decbr. 30 **DEMLER, Henry,** of Ulster Co. Mother Susanna. Real and personal estate. Executors David Brooks and Richard Platt of New York. Witnesses Adolph de Grove sen., Isaac Belknap sen., John Du Bois sen.

537 (D 128) 1786 Novbr. 11 1787 Jany. 31 **DIEDERICK, Jury William,** of the West Camp, Ulster Co. Sons William, Matthise, Zacharias, Jacobus, daughters Hannah, wife of Jacob Conies, Maria, wife of George Carl, Eve, wife of Johannes Falkenburgh, Margerit, wife of Frederich Marda, Elisabeth, wife of Johannes Moore, Catherine, wife of Jeremiah Wolf, grandchild Altge, da. of dec'd da. Sarah. Real and personal estate. Executors sons Matthise and Jacobus. Witnesses Peter P. Eygner of the West Camp, weaver, Peter Myndertse and Philipp Rockefeller.

538 (D 129) 1794 July 4 1801 May 4 **DOUW, Volkert P.,** of Greenbush, Rensselaer Co. Son John de Peyster Douw, daughters Rachel, wife of Henry I. van Rensselaer, Magdalena, wife of John Stevenson, Mary, wife of John de Peyster ten Eycke, grandchildren Martin Hoffman and Catherine, wife of Barent T. ten Eycke, both children of dec'd da. Catherine Hoffman. Real and personal estate. Executors son John de P. Douw, and sons-in-law Henry I. van Rensselaer and John Stevenson. Witnesses H. Woodruff, Jacob van Loon, Ab. van Vechten.

539 (D 130) 1794 June 15 July 17 **de SEGUR—Pitray,** Vicomte Louis Antoine, Chevalier de l'ordre de St. Louis, late of the Province of Perigord, France, now of the State of New York. Wife Marie Nicole Ralin, two eldest sons Claude Nicolas Louis and Joseph Cyprien, and other children. Real estate in U. S., Island of St. Domingo and in France. The wife guardian of minor children and sole executrix. Witnesses Antide Menyin, late priest of St. Emilion (?), Charles Adams and Noel John Barbarin.

540 1785 June 18 1786 Decbr. 21 **DELAVAN, Samuel,** of Salem, Westchester Co., going on a long journey. Wife Agnes, daughters Annes, Cornelia and Levisee, brothers Cornelius, Timothy 3d, children of brothers Abraham and Nathan. Real and personal estate. Executors the wife and brother Daniel Delavan. Sister-in-law Hannah, wife of brother Abraham Delavan, to be guardian of the children, should their mother die before they are of age. Witnesses Barthw. Ryan, Nathan Delivan. Recorded in Wills and Probates, Vol. I., p. 36.

541 1784 Septbr. 2 1787 Febry. 28 **DENNISON, Frances,** of N. Y. City, widow. Daughter Deborah and husband, Richard Norwood, Isaac Hubbel, Catharine and husband James Kairns. Houses and lots in Goold and Fair Str. N. Y. City, personal property. Executors son-in-law Richard Norwood and Marinus Willett. Witnesses Hercules Mulligan, merchant, D. Niven and Elias Nexsen. Recorded ut supra, p. 51.

542 1787 March 10 March 26 **DURYEE, Sarah,** of N. Y. City, spinster. Mother Sarah Duryee of N. Y. City widow, brother Jacob heirs and executors of "worldly estate" (one silver sugar pot, one silver milk pot, six table spoons, five tea spoons). Witnesses Neal McIntire, Jas. N. Roosevelt, Wm. Carman jun. Recorded ut supra, p. 76.

543 1784 July 2 1787 March 26 **DURYEE, Magdalen,** of N. Y. City, spinster. Mother Sarah Duryee of N. Y. City, widow, and sisters. Real estate in State of New York and Great Britain, personal property. Executors the mother and Harry Peters of N. Y. City, merchant. Witnesses Jno. D. Crimsheir, Wm. de Peyster and Peter Demilt of N. Y. City tailor, a quaker. Recorded ut supra, p. 78.

544 1786 April 25 1787 Febry. 21 **DRAKE, Garrardus,** of Southampton Township, Suffolk Co. Wife Martha, son Aaron, daughters Loraney Thompson, Martha Brown and Elizabeth Becket. Real and personal property. Executors the wife and son Aaron. Witnesses Daniel Gibbs, Joseph Russell and Edmund Perry. Recorded ut supra, p. 85.

545 1786 Jany. 30 1787 May 11 **DALTON, Richard,** late of the City of Kilkenny, mariner. Friend John Dalton of N. Y. City, surgeon, sole heir and executor. Money due from owners of ship *Empress of China*, Capt. Green master. Witnesses Charles Norris and James Gilchrist of N. Y. City surgeon. Recorded ut supra, p. 145.

546 1793 Decbr. 7 1794 Jany. 3 **DAINTY, Joseph,** late of Dunington Wood, Parish of Lillyshore, County of Salop, Great Britain, now of New York, miner. Mary Felton, spinster, late of Chesele Hill, Parish of Longford, County of Salop, now of N. Y. City, da. of William Felton of Chesele Hill, husbandman, brothers and sisters James, John, Ann, Elizabeth and Mary Dainty. Real estate in Shifner and Lillyshore Parishes, Salop Co., now occupied by Edward Emery and Richard Johnson resp. George Hewlett, personal property (money in hands of Renwick and Hudswell of William Str., N. Y., merchants, Major William Shaddock of Niagara, Canada, Michael Cowan of Schenectady merchant, Willard Farmer of York, Canada). Executors Mary Felton and Robert Glover of Burlington, Stafford Co. Witnesses Joseph Smith, James Darrow and Edwd. Wilson. Recorded ut supra, p. 407.

547
1796
July 23
Octbr. 14
DROUGHT, Sherigley, of N. Y. City, leaves to wife Margaret "all my Right and Interest in the suit now pending in Commens Town, County Kildare. Likewise all my own Property in Plunkits Town and whatever Else property belongs to me." Witness Samuel Collins of N. Y. City. Letters testamentary granted to the widow. Recorded ut supra, p. 605.

548
1796
Jany. 26
Septbr. 7
DAVIS, Isaac, of Stamford, Fairfield Co., Connecticut. Wife Naomi, daughter Emma. Real and personal property. Executors the wife and father-in-law Daniel Tuttle. Witnesses Sarah Clock, Jacob Walesbury and Frederick Weed. Recorded Vol. II., p. 8.

549
1787
Febry. 1
1797
June 5
Dutch
de RAADT, William, of Zoetermeer, farmer. Wife Fryntje Bos and possible children, mother Adriana Huyser, formerly widow of Peter de Raadt, now wife of Cornelis Velthooven. Guardians of possible children Cornelis Huyser of Zoetermeer and Cornelis de Raadt of Rhoon. Real and personal property. No executor named and letters testamentary for lands in N. Y. State granted to testator's brother Adrian de Raadt of N. Y. City, farmer. Recorded ut supra, p. 30.

550
1793
April 18
1798
June 31 (?)
DREW, James, Captain Royal Navy, at present living in the Out Ward, N. Y. City. Wife Lydia sole heiress of real and personal estate and with her brothers Charles and Samuel Watkins executrix. Witnesses John Maunsell, Major General in his Britanic Majesty's service, Elizabeth Maunsell (at the time of proof widow). Recorded ut supra, p. 74.

551
1797
Novbr. 2
Decbr. 29
DICKINSON, Jonathan, of Philadelphia, Penna. Brother Isaac Dickinson. Real and personal property. Executors Jeremiah Bone and Joshua Dorsey, both of Philadelphia. Witnesses James Hussey and J. Waterman of N. Y. City. Recorded ut supra, p. 60.

552 1798 July 6 1799 Febry. 13 **DUFFIELD, Caesar,** of N. Y. City, son of Thomas Duffield, late of Burkstown, Parish of Tintern, Barony of Shilburn, County of Wexford, Ireland, dec'd and Bridget, his wife. Wife Margaret sole heiress and executrix. Farm at Ballatarsna, Parish of Tintern aforesaid; personal property. Witnesses Henry Forrest and Richard Clarke of N. Y. City, house carpenter. Recorded ut supra, p. 165.

553 1798 April 14 1799 April 3 French **DUBELLOIS, Pierre Robert Gabriel Despres,** inhabitant of the Island of Guadeloupe, now in N. Y. City, about 60 years old. The Chevalier de Bragelougne, cousin Desprèt, officer of the regiment of Guadeloupe, Toinette Dumoulin, my niece according to the custom of Bretagne, Mr. Laujol Desfonds, daughter Escudier of Madame Khouel, godson, *i. e.*, the son of Mr. Brageloughe Berlange. Madame Laroche of N. Y. City is given a legacy for her services to testator's son and daughter-in-law. Real estate on the Island of Guadeloupe; personal property. Executor for New York, Thomas Pasturin of Guadeloupe merchant. Witnesses Jh. Mercadier) Jn. Bte. Duclos and Desabraye. Recorded ut supra, p. 182.

554 1796 Aug. 24 1799 June 29 **DIES, Jane,** of Catskil Landing, Albany Co., widow. Children Mathew, Rebecca, Jacob, John, Catherine, grandchildren Mathew and John, sons, Jane, Margaret daughters, of son Mathew, Isaac, John Dies, James and and Jennet Dubois, children of dec'd da. Jane, children of son Jacob. Farms at Schoharie Kil, lot at Cats kil Landing, land in Femmenhook Patent; personal property. Executors John I. Dubois of Catskil Landing, who is also made guardian of his above named children by Jane, da. of testatrix, the three sons Mathew, Jacob and John and daughter Catherine. Witnesses John Lay, Lawrence Merkel and James Parker. Recorded ut supra, p. 200.

555 1811 Septbr. 24 1812 May 16 **DOUGLASS, Asa,** of Canaan, Columbia Co. Wife Sarah, sons Asa, Zebulon, Horatio G., daughters Sarah Wright, Olive Warner, Eliza Fordam, Nancy Pierson, Polly Pierson, heirs of son John. Real and personal property. Executors the wife with sons-in-law Daniel Warner and Nathan Pierson jun. Witnesses Harmanus ten Eyck, Peter van Loon and Joseph Russell. Recorded ut supra, p. 302.

556 1821 May 1 May 15 **DENNY, James,** of Albany, on board the schooner *Factor* of Portland, Isaac Knight commander. Daniel McNiell, brass founder, sole heir of real and personal estate. James Lindsay, carpenter, executor. Witnesses Philipp I. Quereau, Isaac Knight, Ezra Waring. Recorded ut supra, p. 354.

557 1806 Febry. 14 1808 Novbr. 11 **DAMPIER, John,** of Kingsdon, Somerset Co. Edmund Batten of Yeovil, John Reeves of Glastonbury, both in Somerset Co., Thomas Blake of Sherborne, Dorset Co., and William Raynolds of Charlton Adain, Somerset Co. Executors and trustees for testators sister Mary, wife of Joseph Mitchell, servant Jane Dawe, daughter Susannah and her husband Samuel Sparks. Witnesses Ino. Batten, Jas. Cruikshank and Fras. Robins. Recorded ut supra, p, 356.

558 1778 Aug. 12 1784 Septbr. 30 **DUNKLEY, Robert,** at present of N. Y. City, formerly of the City of Dublin, Ireland, hatter. Wife Celia, daughter Elizabeth, wife of Philipp Brooks of Norwich, Connt., bookbinder, heiresses and executrices of real estate in America and in Ireland and of personal property. Witnesses Charles White, Robert Johnston of N. Y. City shopkeeper, and Paul Hick. Recorded vol. III., p. 31.

559 1784 Decbr. 13 **de VISME, Peter,** of N. Y. City merchant. Letters of administration on the estate of, granted to his mother Anne de Visme of N. Y. widow. Recorded ut supra, p. 37.

560
1776
Octbr. 19
1785
July 13

DORAN, Paul, of Elizabeth Town, N. J. (late private American Army). Pierre de Peyster of Newark, N. J., sole heir and executor of real and personal estate. Witnesses Peter v.B. Livingston jun. of N. Y. City merchant, Josiah Banks and Daniel Ball. Letters testamentary granted to Cornelia de Peyster of N. Y. City widow, the mother and attorney of Pierre de Peyster, now in Great Britain. Recorded ut supra, p. 44.

561
1824
March 16
1825
Octbr. 29

DAVIDSON, Alexander, of Albany City, merchant. Wife Anna, da. of Gilbert Cumming, children Gilbert C(umming), Alexander jun. Susan and an expected child, brother James Davidson. Real and personal property. Executors Erastus Corning of Albany, merchant and brother-in-law Farquher McBain of Saratoga Co. Witnesses Robert O. K. Bennett (dead at date of proof), Alexander McKenzie, Ebenezer Baldwin. Recorded vol. IV., p. 169.

562
1825
March 7
1827
March 3

DOLE, Rebeccah, of Albany City, spinster. Sister Mrs. Sarah Nicholson, nieces Ann Eliza Nicholson, Sally Ann Clark, Catherine Clark, nephew James Nicholson; Euphemia, wife of James Daniel of Albany, George Dole, infant son of Rev. Staats van Santvoort of Bellevue, N. J., Rev. Wm B. Lacey, rector of St. Peters, Albany. House and lot corner Green and Beaver Str. Albany; personal property. Executors James Lamoureux of Albany and sister Sarah Nicholson. Witnesses John L. Tillinghast, Catherine Tillinghast, Catharine Leake. Recorded ut supra, p. 221.

563
1826
May 27
Aug. 7

DELVIN, Frances Marion, widow of James, of Utica, N. Y. Brother George Kinsella of N. Y. City, sisters Catherine Murphy and Jane Lyons, both of Schenectady, niece Mrs. Ann Haight, da. of sister Jane, brother-in-law John Delvin, Sarah Ann Martin, William Martin. House and lot corner John and Catherine St., Utica; personal property. Executor brother George

Kinsella. Witnesses Richard R. Lansing, Catherine de Graff and Otis Whipple. Recorded vol. V., p. 44.

564
1649
Decbr. 12
Dutch

DAMEN, Jan Jansen, of Manhatans Island. Wife ——, son of dec'd sister Hendrickie Jans, now living with testator and called Jan Cornelissen Buys, alias Jan Damen, brothers Cornelis Jansen Cuyper, Cornelis Jansen Damen, Willem Jansen Damen, sister Neltie Jans Damen, the Poor at Bunick, Diocese of Utrecht. Real and personal property. Witnesses Thomas Hall, Cornelis Cornelissen van Houten and Jacob Kip, clerk. N. Y. Col. MSS. III., 72 & 73.

565
1683
Novbr. 19
Dutch

DINGEMANS, Adam, of New Albany, born at Harlem, Holland, and wife Aeltie Jacobs Gardenier, born at New Albany. Children mentioned, but not by name. Real and personal estate. Executors Maas Cornelissen and Johannes Roos. Witnesses Jacob Theysen van der Heyden, Jan van Loon and Adriaen van Ilpendam, Notary Public. Albany Co. Records, Notarial Papers, II., p. 468.

566
1678
9 a.m.
July 24
Aug. 6
Dutch

de WINTER, Bastiaen, of Steenenhoek, Rensselaerswyck Colony, born at Middelburgh. Deacons of Reformed Church, Albany, sole heirs and executors. Witnesses Jan Jansen Bleecker, Jacob Staets and Adriaen van Ilpendam, Notary Public. Albany Co. Records, Notarial Papers, II., p. 41, Proceedings of Magistrates, 1676–80, p. 357, and N. Y. Col. MSS., XXVII., p. 171.

567
1705
June 20

de WANDELAER, Johannes senior, of Albany, merchant. Children Anderis, Johannis, Sara, Catharina, Anna, Alida, Adriaen and Pieter. House and lot in Queens Str., N. Y., land on the Plain, Albany, personal property. Son Johannis and Thomas Williams guardians of minor children and executors. Witnesses Hend. Hansen, Justice, Johannis Mingael, Justice, and Evert Jansen. Albany Co. Records, Wills I., p. 142.

568 1720-1 Jany. 21 March 14 Dutch

DINGMANS, Adam, born at Harlem, Holland, makes will at the house of Peter Cool in the Manor of Rensselaerswyck and leaves real and personal estate to daughters and sons, not named. Executor son-in-law Peter Cool. Witnesses Willem Halenbeek, Gysbert Osterhout and Dirk Halenbeek. Albany Co. Records, Wills I., p. 169. Vide No. 565.

569 1769 March 5 1771 Octbr. 2

DELAMETTER, Cloude, of Claverack, Albany Co. Wife Christina, sons Jeremiah, Dirck, Jacobus, daughters Geertruy, wife of Johs. Mingael van Valkenburgh, Cattelina, Ragel, widow of In. Legget jun., heirs of dec'd da. Christina, late wife of Johs. van Deusen, children of dec'd son John; Cloude Delamater. Real and personal estate. Executors sons Dirck and Jacobus, Gerrit Corneliusen van den Bergh and John Hansen. Witnesses Jeremias Hogeboom, merchant, Joghim Muller, farmer, both of Claverack, and Stephen Hogeboom. Albany Co. Records, Wills I., p. 361.

570 1779 March 30 1796 Octbr. 10

de GARMO, Jellis, of Albany City. Wife Rachel, son Jacob. Real and personal estate (a large Dutch bible). The wife sole executrix. Witnesses Abraham Minderse, Thomas Lansingh and Arie Legrange. Albany Co. Records, Wills I., part 2, page 70.

571 (E 1) 1709 May 16

EARLE, Edward senior, of Bergen Co., N. J. Wife Hannah, son Edward, grandsons Edward and Enoch Earle. Real and personal estate. Executors not named. Witnesses Martha Mompesson, Elizabeth Pinhorn, I. Pinhorn. Copy.

572 (E 2) 1714 Aug. 7

EMANS, John, of Gravesend, Kings Co. Children Johannes, Andrew, Abraham, Jacobus, Sarah Morgan and Cornelia Amerman. Real and personal property. Executors sons Andrew and Jacobus Emans, trustees Seger Gerritsen, John Lucassen, and Samuel Gerison. Witnesses Wm. Williamsen, Gerrit I. Lammertson, Benj. Holsaert. Copy.

573 (E 3) 1738 Jany. 31 — **EMONS, Abraham,** of Yonkers, Westchester Co. Wife Abigal, sons Stillwell, Isaac and Thomas. Real and personal property. The wife sole executrix. Witnesses Rogr. Barton, John Palmer, Benj'n Barnett. Copy.

574 (E 4) 1738-9 Jany. 30 1753 June 18 — **EGBERTSE, Elsie,** of Rensselaerswick, Albany Co., widow and executrix of Omy Lagransie junior. Brothers Albert, Klaas, Matyes and Jan van Loon, farmhand Pieter Franciscus, Antje, da. of Isaac Lagransie, Raghel, da. of brother Jan van Loon and wife of Egbert Egbertsen, Barent Sanders of Albany City, merchant. Personal property. Executor Barent Sanders. Witnesses John Sanders, Myndert Veeder, Symon Johs. Veeder.

574a (E 5) — **EMONS, Abraham,** 1738. E. 5 is missing. According to index it is the same as No. 573.

575 (E 6) 1743 Decbr. 7 1743-4 Febry. 13 Dutch — **ELTINGE, Willem,** of Kingston, Ulster Co. Children Jan, Jacobus, Hendericus, Elsie, wife of Isaak van Campen, Jacomyntie, wife of Noe Eltinge, Jannetie and Annatie. Real and personal estate. Executors the three sons. Witnesses Gil. Livingston, Johannes Masten jun., Cornelis Persen.

576 (E 7) 1745 Octbr. 29 1747-8 Jany. 13 — **ELTINGE, Roeloff,** of New Paltz, Ulster Co. Wife Sarah, sons Noah, John, Josiah, daughters Margaret, wife of Abraham Bevier, and Jacomyntie, grandson Roeloff, son of dec'd son Abraham. Real and personal estate. Executors the three sons. Witnesses Petrus Louw, Jean le Fevre, J. Bruyn.

577 (E 8) 1747-8 Jany. 15 1748-9 Jany. 17 Dutch — **ESSELSTYN, David,** of Albany Co. Brothers Johannes, Jacob and Willem, sister Batha van Duesen, heirs of dec'd brother Isack. Real and personal property (a bible). Executor Willem van Ness. Witnesses Gloude de Lametter, Cathalina Lametter, Barent Cammel.

578 (E 9) 1740 June 25 1748-9 Jany. 18 Dutch

ESSLESTEEN, Cornelis Martensen, of Claverack, Albany Co., farmer. Wife Cornelia, sons Willem, Jacob, David, Johannis, Isaac, daughter Bata, wife of Isaac van Deusen. Real and personal property (a large bible). Executors sons Willem, Jacob, Johannis and David. Witnesses Arent van Dyck, Justice of the Peace, Jeremyas Hogeboom, Ephraim van Alen (dead at date of proof).

579 (E 10) 1750 Septbr. 4 1755 June 5 Dutch

ELTINGE, Johannis, of Mormeltown (Marbletown), Ulster Co., farmer. Wife Jannetje, sons Petrus, Roelof, daughters Majeke and Sarah. Real and personal property (a large bible). Executors brothers Josias and Noah Eltinge and Hederikus Jansen. Witnesses Jan Eltinge, Rachel Eltinge and Willem Eltinge.

580 (E 11) 1759 July 17 1760 June 25

ETHERINGTON, Robert, mariner. Nephew Robert, son of brother Thomas Etherington sole heir and executor of real and personal estate. Witnesses Judson Coolidge, John Slater, Richard Lane, Phil. Young and David Arnold. Proved in Calvert Co., Maryland. Seal of Maryland.

581 (E 12) 1763 Jany. 12 —

ELTINGE, Jan, of Kingston, Ulster Co. Second wife Rachel, da. of Joseph Hasbrouck, first wife was Rachel, da. of James Whitaker. Children by first wife, viz: Willem, James, Petrus, Jannetie and Elizabeth, by second wife: Elsie. Real and personal property. Executors the six children. Witnesses Abraham Low, Robert Dunlap, and Cornelius J. Masten. Copy.

582 (E 13) 1760 Aug. 2 1771 Octbr. 21

EGBERTSEN, Egbert, of Albany City, mariner. Wife Maria, sons Benjamin, Anthony, Jacob Vischer, daughters Anna and Maria. Real and personal property. Executors the wife and Isaac Switts. Witnesses Hendrick M. Roseboom of Albany City, merchant, John Knickerbocker and Abrm. Yates junior.

583 (E 14) 1761 March 5 1768 Jany. 18 **ERWIN, Samuel,** of Ulster Co., yeoman. Wife Prudence, sons Samuel, Edward, George, John, William, daughters Phebe and Margaret, granddaughter Phebe. Real and personal property. Executors the wife and sons Samuel and Edward. Witnesses George Burne, Francis Burne of Wallkil Prect., yeoman, and Jane Morran.

584 (E 15) 1761 Jany. 29 May 25 **EDWARDS, Timothy,** of Northeast Precinct, Dutchess Co. Wife Ruth, sons Timothy, John, Henry, David and Jonathan, daughter Ruth. Real and personal property. Executors the wife, brother Henry Edwards of New York and Stephen Caswel. Witnesses Hector Gambold of North East Prect., clerk, Jacob Decker and Hester Decker.

585 (E 16) is the Dutch original of No. 581.

586 (E 17) 1762 Febry. 23 April 17 **EGGMONT, Nicholas,** of Coxsakie, Albany Co., yeoman. Stepgrandson Anthony Winne, niece Maritie van Valkenburgh, da. of sister Annatie Schermerhoorn, nephew Luke Schermerhoorn, son of said sister Annatie, Marytie, wife of Mathys Boom, the poor of the Protestant Church at Coxsakie. Real and personal property. Executors Anthony Winne, Anthony van Bergen and John L. Bronk. Witnesses Anthony van Bergen, Henry van Bergen and Jacob Freese.

587 (E 18) 1763 Febry. 15 1784 Septbr. 24 **EGBERTS, Mary,** widow of Egbert of Albany City. Children Benjamin, Annatie, Maria, Antony and Jacob Visher Egbertsen. Share in house and lot on Crown Str., N. Y., personal property. Executor Jacob Ja. Lansing. Witnesses Hendr. Roseboom, Jelles Clute and Abrm. Yates jun.

588 (E 19) 1764 Jany. 28 Febry. 21 **ELLEMS, George,** of Wallkil Prect., Ulster Co. Grandchildren John Shay, Elizth. Shay, George Shay, children of da. Hannah, sons George and John, children

of dec'd son William, viz: Robert and Hannah, children of da. Charity, vizt. George, James and Mary Davis, granddaughter Charity Hood. "Whole estate." Executors son John Ellems and William Thomson. Witnesses Cad. Colden jun., Wm. Thompson and Nathan Sanders.

589 (E 20) 1767 April 4 1784 May 19 **ELTINGE, Josiah** (son of Roelof), of New Paltz, Ulster Co. Wife Magdalena, children Abraham, Roelof J., Solomon, Cornelius and Catherintje. Real estate in Maryland, in New Paltz Patent in Somerset Co., N. J., in New Paltz Village, personal property. Executors the five children. Witnesses Jacob Hasbrouck jun., David Hasbrouck, Joseph Coddington.

590 (E 21) 1769 May 19 1785 May 19 **ECKERSEN, Cornelius,** of Haverstraw Prect., Orange Co. Wife Lena, children John, Dirckje, Cornelia, Jacob. "Worldly estate." Executors Petrus Blauvelt and Abraham Stevesen. Witnesses Abram Kool, Johannes Isaac Blauvelt of Haverstraw, yeoman, Johannis Hogenkamp.

591 (E 22) —— 1774 April 20 **ELWELL, Samuel,** of *Sout* Precinct, Dutchess Co. Wife Mercy, son Samuel and other children, not named. Real and personal estate. No executor named. Witnesses Robert Kean, Joshua Barnum jun., of South Prect., yeoman, and John Birdsell.

592 (E 23) 1775 April 5 1781 Aug. 16 **ELTINGE, Noah,** of New Paltz Prect., Ulster Co. Wife Jacomyntie, niece Annatje, da. of brother-in-law Jacobus Eltinge, son-in-law Dirk D. Wynkoop, granddaughters Cornelia Wynkoop and Geertje Wynkoop, grand-nephew Noah Eltinge jun., son of nephew Abraham Eltinge nephew Thomas, son of brother-in-law Jacobus Eltinge. Lands in New Paltz Patent, personal property. Executors the wife, son-in-law Dirk D. Wynkoop, and nephews Abraham Eltinge and William Eltinge jun. Witnesses Matthew Lefever, Jonathan Lefever, both of New Paltz Prect., farmers, and Joseph Coddington.

593 (E 24) 1776 Jany. 4 1784 Aug. 10 **ECKER, Adam,** of Mohawks District, Tryon Co., yeoman. Wife Margret, children by first marriage vizt: John, George and Mary, other children Adam, Henry, Peter, Abraham, Margaret, Catherine and Marilis. Real and personal estate. Executors John Eker, Richard Snell and Suphrines Tygart, all of Tryon Co., yeomen. Witnesses John McKinney, Elizabeth McKinney and John Phelleps. Proved in Montgomery Co.

594 (E 25) 1778 March 31 1783 Febry. 14 **ELLWELL, Samuel,** of South East Prect., Dutchess Co. Wife ——, heirs of son Samuel dec'd, sons Jabez and Isaac, heirs of dec'd daughters Mary, Esther and Sarah, daughters Elizabeth, Grissel and Deborah. Real and personal estate. Executor son Isaac. Witnesses Thomas Ragon of S. E. Prect., tailor, Mary Chapman and Moss Kent.

595 (E 26) 1780 Septbr. 20 1786 Decbr. 21 **EDMONSTON, James,** of New Windsor, Ulster Co., yeoman. Daughter Sarah McDonil, grandchildren James, William, Margaret Edmonston, son William and his wife Jane. Real and personal property. Executor son William. Witnesses John McConnell, of Ulster Co., blacksmith, Barzillai Tuthill and John Nicoll.

596 (E 27) 1780 Decbr. 6 1783 Septbr. 2 **ELIGH, Johan Yury,** of the Beverkil, Ulster Co., farmer. Wife Catherina, sons Andries, Jacob and Johannes, daughters Catherine and Margaret, six heirs of eldest da. Elizabeth, William, son of son Johannes. Real and personal property. Executors son Andries, Adam Beer and Jacob Moure. Witnesses Gysbert Diederick, Peter West, both of Sagerties, farmers, and Wilhelmus Rouw.

597 (E 28) 1781 May 5 1783 March 27 **ECKERSEN, Cornelius,** of Orange Township, Orange Co., yeoman. Wife Rachel, sons Jacob, Garrit and David, heirs of dec'd son Mathew vizt: Rachel and Sarah, daughters Willimpje, Catherine, Mary and Rachel. Real and personal estate. Executors John Perry and Isaac Debaen. Witnesses William Parsel, Thonis Cuyper and James Perry.

598 (E 29) 1781 Jany. 2 1783 Jany. 29

EVERSON, Thomas, of Cornwal Prect., Orange Co., yeoman. Wife Rhoda, son Thomas, four daughters, not named. Real and personal property. Executors brother-in-law David Corwin and Thomas Moffat. Witnesses John W. Tuthill, Joshua Davis and Thomas Moffat.

599 (E 30) 1781 Septbr. 28 1785 June 28

EVERITT, Robert, of New Marlborough Precinct, Ulster Co., farmer. Wife Esther, sons Daniel and John, daughters Nancy, Sarah, Frances, Patty, Esther and Jane, grandson John Manna. Real and personal property. Executors the wife, sons John and Daniel and son-in-law Elezer Freer. Witnesses William Car, Jehiel Semour and Benjamin Ely.

600 (E 31) 1781 May 25 1786 Aug. 31

EARLL, John, of Smiths Clove, Cornwall Precinct, Orange Co. Wife ——, daughter Elizabeth, sons Samuel, Richard, Benjamin, Peter, Ezra, Jonathan, grandchildren Joseph and Mary Holloway. Real and personal estate. Executors sons Benjamin, Peter and Ezra Earll and Jesse Woodhull. Witnesses John Weygant, John White and Wm. Thorn.

601 (E 32) 1782 Octbr. 20 1783 Decbr. 8

EMPIE, Adam, of Stoneraby, Tryon Co. Wife Anna Maria, sons John, Adam, stepson William Saltsman. Real and personal property. Executors Peter S. Deygert, Christopher W. Fox and Richard Young. Witnesses Nicholas Streder, Frederic Empie and George Saltzman.

602 (E 33) 1782 Aug. 14 1783 Octbr. 15

ELIGH, William, of the West Camp, Ulster Co., farmer. Wife Margriet, nephew Johannes Fearo, son of sister Margriet, Jeremiah, son of Andries Eligh, Rachel, wife of Hezekiah Dubois, William, son of Johannes Eligh, nephews Andries and Jacob Eligh; William and Saphiah, children of Ludwigh Rushel. Real and personal estate. Executors Andries Eligh, Jacob Eligh and Peter West. Witnesses Petrus Maurer, Adam Baur and Jacob Musier.

603 (E 34) 1784 Octbr. 20 1786 May 5 **EGBERTS, Jacob Visscher,** of Albany City, Doctor of Physics. Brothers and sisters, Benjamin Egberts, Ann Egberts, Mary ten Eyck and Anthony Egberts, niece Caty ten Eyck, nephews Egbert and Jacob ten Eyck. Real and personal property (seven silver table spoons, a silver mug, a pair of silver shoe buckles, a pair of silver knee buckles and stock buckle). Executors brother Benjamin Egberts, Anthony Egberts and Anthony ten Eyck. Witnesses Peter J. van Valkenburgh, Walter Baurhity, Thomas Barhydt. Vide supra No. 582.

604 (E 35) 1785 June 28 1786 Octbr. 18 **EVERTSEN, Jacob,** of Normanskil, Albany Co., cooper. Lutheran Church of Albany, sister Mary, wife of Christoyan Lagrange, children of brothers and sisters. Real and personal estate. Executors cousin Jacob Lagrange and cousin Jacob, son of John van Loon. Witnesses John Nightingale, schoolmaster, John Jackson and John Wands.

605 (E 36) 1785 Novbr. 29 1786 Febry. 16 **ENDERS, William,** of Schohary, Albany Co., yeoman. Wife Elisamargrate, sons John, Jacob, Peter, William, daughters Maria, Elisabeth, Margrita, Christina, Anna, grandsons Adam and Wilhelmus, sons of William. Real and personal property. Executors sons John and Peter Enders. Witnesses Peter Snyder jun., Petrus Man jun., both of Schohary, farmers, and Peter Vroman.

606 (E 37) 1786 Novbr. 2 Novbr. 16 **EDSALL, Samuel,** of Goshen Precinct, Orange Co. Wife Abigail, sons Jesse and Samuel. Real and personal estate. Executors the wife, brothers Richard Edsall and Jacobus Edsall. Witnesses George Rankin, Julia Armstrong and Robert Armstrong.

607 (E 38) 1786 Octbr. 25 Novbr. 13 **ELIAS, Jacob,** of the City of Hudson, Columbia Co. Wife Rachel, son Henry, daughters Abigail, Elizabeth, Rachel and Mary, an expected child, Thomas Whitlock. Real and personal estate. Executors Peter

Silvester, Caleb Lobdell and Thomas Whitlock. Witnesses William Coventry of Hudson District, yeoman, Timothy Allen and William Martin.

608 (E 39) 1787 July — Octbr. 21 **ELLIS, James,** of the Parish of St. James, Island of Jamaica. Brothers William and George Ellis of Great Britain, halfsisters Mary and —— Ellis. "My estate." Executors James Leslie, John Little and Charles Hanson, all of St. James Parish aforesaid. Witnesses Jas. Wauchope and Alexander Gordon.

609 (E 40) 1764 March 9 **EVERITT, Richard,** of Dutchess Co., house carpenter. Letters of administration granted to his son Clear Everitt of Dutchess Co., esquire.

610 1783 March 13 Octbr. 2 **EVERSON, Nicholas,** of South Amboy, Middlesex Co., N. J. Wife Susannah, sons George and Jacob, children of son John, children of dec'd da. Susannah, wife of Joseph Ellason, daughters Margaret Morgan and Mary Case, children of da. Elizabeth, wife of William Buckalew, granddaughter Margaret Ellason, grandsons Nicholas, son of son Jacob Everson, and James Morgan. Land in 9 Partners Patent, Dutchess Co., in Minisink Patent, in South Amboy, personal property. Executors son-in-law James Morgan senior and son Jacob Everson. Witnesses John Herbert, Jacob Johnson and Peter Burling. Recorded in Vol. I., Wills and Probates, p. 201.

611 1794 July 4 1795 April 20 **ELLIS, Samuel,** of Bergen Co., N. J., farmer. Wife Mercy, children of son Samuel dec'd, vizt: Mary, Avis and Dolly, Catharine, da. of da. Mary dec'd, late wife of Peter van Why, Nantie and Mary, children of da. Elizabeth, wife of George Ryerson, Samuel Ellis Ryley, son of kinsman William Ryley, godchild Jane, da. of Elias Burger, Catherine, wife of Daniel Daniel Westervelt of N. Y. City, weaver, and her daughters Catherine and Jane, daughter Rachel Ellis, wife of

John Cooder and her children John Edmond and Rachel. Lots leased from Trinity Church, N. Y., Oyster or Ellis Island, farm in Bergen Co., N. J., purchased from Jacob Etsel, personal property. Executors Elias Burger of N. Y. City, dockbuilder, Simon van Antwerp of N. Y. City, ironmonger, and Wm. Ryley, living on the Island in Hudson R. Witnesses Margaret Ryley, Abraham Lines jun., and John Mollineux. Recorded ut supra p. 473.

612
1796
Septbr. 17
Octbr. 17

EGAN, Robert, of Edenton, North Carolina, merchant, now in New York. Housekeeper Sarah Cotton, asst. housekeeper Frances Price, clerk John Wheate, John Haycock Coates and wife Elizabeth. Real and personal property. Executors John Haycock Coates of New York City, gentleman, Allen Ramsay and Alexander Miller, both of Edenton, N. C., merchants. Witnesses John Byrne, Granville Smith and Isaac Sharples. Recorded ut supra Vol. II., p. 1.

613
1819
July 23
1825
March 7

EDEN, Medcef, of Westchester Co. Wife ——, daughters Sally Ann, Elizabeth and Rebecca, who are not to marry without the consent of Aaron Burr; John Pelletreau. Real and personal property. Executors the wife and John Pelletreau. Witnesses John Dix, Samuel White late of N. Y. City, now (date of proof) of Poughkeepsie, grocer, and Benjamin P. Kissam. Recorded ut supra Vol. IV., p. 166.

614
1815
Aug. 31
1826
March 3

ELY, Justin, of West Springfield, Hambden Co., Mass. Wife Mary Ann, sons Theodore, Justin and Heman. Real and personal estate. Executors the three sons. Witnesses Pelatiah Bliss, John Ely, Edmund West. It is stated in the will, that testator gives to his wife "the annuity mentioned in the jointure with Matthew Griswold before our marriage." In the proof testator's age at date of will is given as about 70 years. Recorded ut supra p. 177.

615 1823 Decbr. 31 1826 Octbr. 18

ELLICOTT, Joseph, of Batavia, Genesee Co. Sarah, widow of brother Andrew Ellicott, sisters Ann, Letitia and Rachel Evans, Charles Augustus Henry, grandson of sister Mary Brown, Joseph, son of nephew Andrew A. Ellicott, John B. Ellicott, Lewis E. Evans, Trustees of Meth. Ep. Society in Batavia, Wardens of St. James Church, Batavia, Trustees of First Congregational Society, Batavia, nephew David E. Evans, Jonathan Brown, brother to sister-in-law Sarah Ellicott, brother Benjamin Ellicott, son Joseph and other children of brother Andrew Ellicott dec'd, of sisters Ann, Letitia and Rachel Evans. Mill tract in Town of Shelby, Holland Purchase, and other lands there, farms in Towns of Batavia and Pembroke, Williamsville Farm on East side of Ellicotts Creek, lots in Batavia village, land in Town of Royalton, Niagara Co., personal property. Executors Benjamin Ellicott, David E. Evans, William Peacock, Nathaniel C. Griffith and Andrew A. Ellicott. Witnesses Ebenezer Mix, James Milner jun., and Oliver G. Adams. Recorded ut supra p. 193.

615a 16?3 May 30

ELLET, Richard, of N. Y. City, cooper. Wife Susannah, children Robert, Joseph, Henry, John, sister-in-law Sarah Hart, godsons John Tuder and Joseph Hudleston, goddaughter Mary Fromantle. Real and personal estate (gold rings, silver westcoat buttons, do. buckles, two do. spoons). The wife sole executrix. Witnesses Edward Graham, Alice Allison and Thomas Clark. An inquisition, made Decbr. 18, 1721, before Gilbert Livingston, Escheator General of the Province of N. Y., says, that testator had then been dead 28 years, his widow 7 to 8 years, three sons had died without issue, the fourth Henry had gone to sea twenty years ago and had not been heard from since. N. Y. Col. MSS. LXIV., p. 10.

616 (F 1) 1711 Jany. 24

FOWLER, William, of Flushing, Queens Co., yeoman. Wife Mary, sons William, John, Joseph, Benjamin, Jeremiah, Thomas and Henry, daughters Mary

Dusenbury, Rebecca, Sarah, Hannah. Land in Harrisons Patent, Rye, Westchester Co., a tract on Blind Brook adjoining Thomas Merit, farm at Flushing, land in Pennsylvania, bought from Major William Lawrence, personal property ("money due by Father Thorne's Will"). Executors the wife, Jeremiah Fowler of Eastchester and William Thorne of Flushing. Witnesses Joseph Hunt, Thos. Cooke and Daniel Clarke. Copy.

617 (F 2) 1711-12 Febry. 16 1725 April 19 **FFISKER** (probably Vischer), **Tierck Harmensen,** of Albany City, sawyer. Wife Ffemitie, son Jacob, daughters Hester, wife of Cornelis Switts, Anke, Gertruide and Lena. Real and personal estate. The wife sole executrix. Witnesses John Collins, Evert Jansen and Gysbert van den Bergh.

618 (F 3) 1725 Aug. 21 1726 May 5 **FLENSBURGH, Daniel,** of Albany City, shoemaker. Wife Johanna, son Johannis, daughter Anna. Real and personal estate. Executors the wife, brother Mathew Flensburgh, Christophel Staats and Baarent Bratt. Witnesses Tobias Ryckman, Frederick Myndersen and Rutger Bleecker. Proved before Phil. Livingston, one of his Majesty's Council, who happened to be in Albany.

619 (F 4) 1726-7 March 18 March 29 **FREEMAN, Marmaduke,** late of the Morant, Parish of St. Thomas, Island of Jamaica, now of New York City, gent. Mother Mary Freeman, wife Eleanor, daughter Mary. Real and personal property in Jamaica. Executors the wife, father-in-law Jacob Swan of New York, and Colonel John Coveleir of Jamaica. Witnesses John Bend, Samuel Dunscombe, Matthew van Durzen and Johannes Degrave. Inventory enumerates gold rings with diamonds, gold shoe buckles, a gold chain 7 or 8 chains thick, with a gold locket flowered and marked M + F., one silver tankard holding a gallon, two do. holding a quart each, three silver salt cellars, six silver spoons and forks all new, 3 or 4 old silver poringers. Copy.

620 (F 5) 1727 Novbr. 30 1729 Aug. 9

FONSECA, Jacob, of N. Y. City, merchant, intending to go to the Island of Jamaica. Wife Rebecca, sons Isaac, Abraham, Joseph, daughters Rachel, Esther, Judith and Sarah. Real and personal estate. Executors the wife and Daniel Nunez da Costa. Witnesses Wm. Walling, Gabriel le Boyteulx and David le Tellier. Codicil of July 28, 1728, disposes of a house and lot at Spanish Town, Jamaica. Witnesses Abraham Rd. Dermera, Moses Lopez d Fonseca, David le Tellier. Copy.

621 (F 6) 1748 June 15 1749 April 18

FFINCH, Isaac (son of Abraham and grandson of Isaac), of Goshen, Orange Co. Wife ——, sons Samuel, Abraham, Daniel, John, Nathaniel and Salomon, daughters Hannah, Ruth and Elizabeth. Real and Personal estate. Executor son Isaac. Witnesses James Butler, Timothy Wood and Ant. Carpenter.

622 (F 7) 1753 Decbr. 15 1755 Octbr. 30

FRYER, Isaac, of Albany City, weaver. Wife Elizabeth, sons John, Isaac and William, daughter Catherine. Real and personal estate. Executors the wife and Jacobus Hilton. Witnesses Jakobis Hilton, Luykas Wit Buck (Witbeek), carpenter, and Richard Cartwright.

623 (F 8) 1755 Feby. 25 April 30

FELTEN, William, of Oringe Co. Wife Susanna, grandsons Peter and William Felten, daughter Maritie Trumper, granddaughters Elizabeth Trumper and Carstena Hopper. Real and personal estate. Executors Cornelis Cuyper and Lambert Smith. Witnesses Johannes Much, Johannes Snyder and Abraham Onderdonk.

624 (F 9) 1757 Novbr. 17 1758 June 14

FOWLER, William, of Crom Elbow Precinct, Dutchess Co. Sons William, Henry, Jacob, Benjamin. Real and Personal estate. Executors son William and William Doughty senior. Witnesses Jacob Haight, of Crom Elbow yeoman (a Quaker), Joseph Denton, yeoman, and Hannah Thorne.

625 (F 10) 1757 Novbr. 8 1758 June 9 Dutch

FRILINGHUYSEN, Henricus, minister of the three united congregations of Marbletown, Rochester and Nawarsink, Ulster Co. Sisters Margrita, wife of Rev. Thomas Romyn, Anna, wife of Rev. William Jekson, children of dec'd brother Rev. Johannes Frielinghuysen vizt: Frederik and Heva. Executors cousin Jacobus Vaniste and Isaac Hasbrouck jun. Witnesses Samuel Bevier jun., Elias Depuy and Jacob Hoornbeek.

626 (F 11) 1759 June 7 July 7

FFINN, William, of Goshen Precinct, Orange Co. Wife Mary, sons Solomon, Robert, James, Anthony and Nehemia, daughters Hannah, Mary Broderick. Real and personal property (*fisacal*-books). Executors the wife and Benjamin Carpenter. Witnesses William Thompson, blacksmith, William Knap, planter, and Michael Jakson.

627 (F 12)

FOLKERTSON, Nicholas, extract made April 1, 1762, from will of, disposes of real estate in Boswick Township, Kings Co., for the benefit of *four* children, viz: son Folkert and daughters Dina, Broca, Anatie, wife of Dirck Woortman and Marigritie, wife of John van Dyck.

628 (F 13) 1762 July 30 —

FONDA, Abraham, of Claverack, Albany Co., merchant. Present wife Jannetie, da. of Jermia Muller, sons Stephanis, Pieter, Lourens and Abraham, children by first wife Elbertie, da. of Stephanis van Alen: Johannes, Jeremia, Dowe and Cornelis, children by second wife. Real and personal property. Executors the wife, sons Pieter and Lourens, Abraham Yates jun. and Stephanis van Dyck. Witnesses Francis her Dyk jun., Petrus van Hoezen, Hendrik van Hoeze. Codicil of Aug. 3, 1762, disposes of land at Keesje Hook and is witnessed by John van Loon, Hendrick van Hoesen and Johannes van Hoesen. Translation from the original Dutch made June 1, 1763.

629 (F 14) 1764 July 14 1770 Febry. 10

FIERER, Vallentyn, of the Catsbaen, Albany Co. Wife Catherine, sons Johannes, Christian and Henrich, daughters Christina, wife of Johannes Trumpbour and Margretha, wife of Zachary Snyder. Real and personal estate. Executors the wife and sons Christian and Henrich. Witnesses Pat Clemens of Albany Co., weaver, and George Rhynhard, schoolmaster.

630 (F 15) 1767 Octbr. 28 Novbr. 9

FLANSBURGH, David, of the Mohawk River, Albany Co., carpenter. Wife Bautche, children David and Mary: John Clements of the Mohawk River, carpenter. Real and personal estate. Executors John Johnston and John Clements. Not signed nor witnessed, but proved by the testimony of William Johnston, whitesmith, Peter Davis, cordwinder, and Stephen Umbrat, cordwinder, all of Albany Co.

631 (F 16) 1767 March 11 Aug. 18

FOWLER, John, of Newburgh Precinct, Ulster Co., farmer. Sons Nehemiah (has wife Abigail), Samuel and Isaac, grandchildren James, John, Daniel and Sarah, children of son Daniel, children of son John, vizt. Thomas and Catherine, granddaughters Mary Merritt and Elizabeth Clark, grandson Isaac, son of son Isaac, daughter Elizabeth Wiggins, granddaughters Sarah Conklin, Elizabeth and Abigail Kniffin; Phebe and Abigail Bloomer, Daniel Kniffin and Stephen Wiggins. Real and personal property. Executors sons Samuel and Isaac and Thomas Woolsey. Witnesses Leonard Smith, Reuben Tooker of Ulster Co., farmer, and Cornelious Gail.

632 (F 17) 1767 Octbr. 15 —

FRESNEAU, Peter, of Middletown, Monmouth Co., N. J. Agnes Fresneau and John Morin Scott of N. Y. City executors and trustees for the children. Land in Albany, Orange and Westchester Co. N. Y., Sunbury and Stamford, Connt., Monmouth and Middlesex Co., N. J., personal estate. Witnesses Nonas van Pelt, David Watson and Jo. Burrowes. Copy.

633 (F 18) 1770 June 13 Novbr. 9 **FULTON, David,** of New Windsor Prect., Ulster Co., yeoman. Wife Ann, daughters Jane Harris, Ann Patten, sons Alexander, David, John, Hugh, grandchildren Thomas, son of David, David, son of Hugh, Ann, da. of Hugh, brother James Fulton, sister Hannah Fulton (apparently living at Cold Revier, Ireland). Real and personal property. Executors Mathew McDowel of New Windsor and Jonathan Brooks of Orange Co. Witnesses John Dean, farmer, Beriah Palmer and Jacob Devo, farmer.

634 (F 19) 1771 Septbr. 2 1775 Septbr. 25 **FONDA, Peter,** of Schonectady, Albany Co. Wife Alida, son Jellis, daughter Angenitje, stepdaughter Janeca Truex. Real and personal estate. Executors brothers Abraham and Jacob Fonda of Schonectady and nephew Christr Yates. Witnesses John Peeck, wheelwright, John Myndersen, blacksmith, and Isaac Rosa.

635 (F 20) 1771 Aug. 28 1772 April 10 **FORGUSON, Ephraim,** of Rumbout Precinct, Dutchess Co. Wife Hannah, sons Ephraim, Peter and Robert, daughters Susannah Farrington, Elizabeth Soper, Abigail Bogardus and Sarah. Real and personal estate. Executors the wife, son Robert and Michael Vinsent. Witnesses Nathl Sacket of Rumbout Prect., merchant, Robert Mills and John Bogardus.

636 (F 21) 1771 Aug. 14 1774 Septbr. 12 **FRANK, Johan Conrad,** of Burnetsfield, Albany Co. Wife Elizabeth, sons Frederick, Timothy, Conrad and Johannes, daughters Margaritta, Elizabetha, Anna Maria, Anna and Eva. Real and personal estate. Executors Augustinus Hess and Frederic Arendorph. Witnesses Augustinus Hess, Johannes Peter Bellinger and Frederic Arendorph.

637 (F 22) 1773 10th Day 6th Month 1779 Jany. 21 **FERRISS, Zebulon,** of Dutchess Co. Wife Ruth, daughters Phebe, Urania, Susannah, Ruth, sons David, Reed, and Zebulon. Real and personal property. Executors the wife and the two brothers Reed Ferriss

and Jonathan Akin. No witnesses. Proved by the testimony of Jonathan G. Tompkins of Westchester Co., esquire, Jonathan Akin and Reed Ferriss of Dutchess Co., yeomen (Quakers).

638 (F 23) 1773 July 27 Oct. 16 **FALLS, Alexander,** junior, of Little Britain, Ulster Co., yeoman. Wife Easter, nephew Alexander, son of brother Edward Falls, brothers Samuel and Edward Falls, nephews William, son of brother George Falls, Alexander, James, Arthur, George, Jane, Isabella and Elizabeth Buchanan, children of sister Elizabeth, niece Isabella, da. of bro. George. Real and personal property. Executors bro. Edward Falls, bro.-in-law James Denniston and Jesse Woodhull. Witnesses Charles Clinton jun., of New Windsor, surgeon, Elizabeth Denniston of the same place, spinster, and George Clinton.

639 (F 24) 1772 April 27 1775 April 1 **FREER, Jonas,** of New Paltz Prect., Ulster Co. Wife Catherine, sons Johannes, Eliza, Jonas, Simon, Petrus, da. Maria, wife of Gerrit Freer. Real and personal estate. Executors the five sons. Witnesses Col. Abrm. Hasbrouck of Kingston, merchant, Gerrit van Keuren of same place, blacksmith, and Jos. Hasbrouck.

640 (F 25) 1774 Novbr. 29 1775 Jany. 3 **FLAGLER, Simon,** of Charlotte Precinct, Dutchess Co. Wife Hester, sons Zachariah, Peter, Simon and John, daughters Joanna, wife of Henry van Voorhis, Elizabeth, wife of Jacob Lester, Sarah, Jane and Halanah. Real and personal estate. Executors John Carpenter, Reuben Hopkins and Jacob Smith. Witnesses Adrian van Ander, David Carpenter and Peter Coonly.

641 (F 26) 1775 June 23 1784 Aug. 8 **FOLK, Johannis,** of Churchland, Ulster Co., yeoman. Wife Mary, sons Wilhelmus, Johannis, Aaron, Jacob, daughters Mary, wife of Thomas Bexter, Christy, wife of James Jones, Leah, children of daughter Raenah, Jonas, son of son Wilhelmus, Laurance Folk. Real and

personal estate. Executors Wilhelmus Folk, Johannis Folk and Aaron Folk. Witnesses Jacob Maurer, Petrus Maurer and Lenerd Maurer, all of Sagerties, farmers.

642 (F 27) 1776 Jany. 16 Febry. 19 **FALLS, Edward** (bro. of No. 638), of Little Britain, Ulster Co., innholder. Wife Catherine, sons Alexander and George, daughters Esther and Frances, brother Samuel, nephew William, son of dec'd bro. George. Real and personal estate. Executors the wife, Archibald Little of Oxford and David Holliday of New Windsor. Witnesses Thomas Belknap, Jane Wilson and Daniel Goldsmith jun.

643 (F 28) 1778 Octbr. 20 —— **FELTON, Lewis,** of Captain Motts Co., Col. Lambs Artillery, leaves his clothing and four months pay due to his comrade Joseph van Amburgh. Witness Chs Laino?

644 (F 29) 1779 Aug. 12 1782 Jany. 13 **FINGER, Johannis,** of Livingston Manor, Albany Co. Sons Michael, David, Coenrat, Jacob and Petrus, daughters Elisabeth, wife of Hendrick B. Smith, Anna, wife of Jacob Blass, grandson Johannis, son of dec'd da. Catherine, late wife of Peter M. Blass, children of son Michael. Real and personal estate. Executors sons David, Coenrat and Jacob and Dirck Jansen. Witnesses Albertus Simon, Jesaias Lup, farmers, and Neal McFall.

645 (F 30) 1779 Aug. 13 Novbr. 1 **FERDON, John,** of Poghkeepsie Prect., Dutchess Co. Son Johannis, daughters Mary, Catherine, Phebe, Elizabeth and Gertruy, son-in-law Henry Scott. Real and personal estate. Executors brothers Zachariah and Jacob Ferdon. Witnesses Zachariah fferdon, yeoman, Johannis fferdon and Richard Snedeker.

646 (F 31) 1780 April 25 1781 March 10 **FINN, Robert,** of Orange Co., esquire. Wife Patience, son William, daughter Dinah. Real and personal property (a large bible). Executors brother Anthony Finn. Witnesses Constant Rowley, yeoman, and Robert Armstrong.

647 (F 32) 1781 May 9 Octbr. 10 **FLINN, David,** of Charlotte Prect., Dutchess Co. Cousins Zebulon and Jacob, sons of Hezekiah Mills. "Worldly estate." Executors uncle Hezekiah Mills and Thomas Stilwell of Charlotte Precinct, yeoman. Witnesses Richard Amberman, James Weeks and Thomas Stilwell.

648 (F 33) 1781 Aug. 6 1783 Decbr. 22 **FILKINS, Isaac,** of Charlotte Prect., Dutchess Co. Sons Peter, Isaac, Henry, Abraham, Jacobus, da. Lanah, Joseph Slicks and Enuch Lefler. Real and personal estate. Executors son Peter and John W. Allen. Witnesses John W. Allen, Reuben Sarles and Catren Allen.

649 (F 34) 1783 Novbr. 11 1784 Novbr. 6 **FRYER, John,** of Albany City, mariner. Daughters Sarah, wife of Edward Willett and her son Samuel, and Lydia, wife of Matthew Visscher and her son Bastian. Real and personal estate. Executors sons-in-law Edward Willett and Matthew Visscher and Robert Yates. Witnesses Bastejan Visscher, Peter W. Hilton, cooper, and John N. Visscher, gentleman.

650 (F 35) 1783 Septbr. 11 1784 Decbr. 23 **FAULKENDER, William,** of Wallkil Precinct, Ulster Co. Wife Mary, sons James, Joseph, William, Samuel. Real and personal estate. No executors named. Witnesses James Caldwall, John Dill and Eben'r Clark.

651 (F 36) 1784 March 16 1785 Octbr. 10 **FOULGER, Thomas,** of Currys Brook, Schenectady Distr., Albany Co. Daughter Reb'h, wife of William Fuller of Albany, sons Thomas and Benjamin. Real and personal estate. Executor Charles Martin of Schenectady, merchant. Witnesses Thomas Thornton, yeoman, James Wasson and John Wasson.

652 (F 37) 1785 Febry. 12 May 6 **FOWLER, Nehemiah,** of Newburgh Precinct, Ulster Co. Wife Abigail, nephew Samuel, son of bro. Samuel Fowler. "Worldly estate." Executors the wife

and Nehemiah Smith. Witnesses Henry ter Bush and Thurston Wood, yeoman.

653 (F 38) 1786 Novbr. 16 1787 Febry. 26 **FIERO, Johann Christian,** of Kingston Corporation, Ulster Co., yeoman. Sons Valentine, David, Christian, Peter, daughters Margaret, wife of Yurry Hommel, Anna, wife of Hieronimus Gernreyk, Lydia, wife of Coenrad Lesher, Esther, wife of Lourence Falk, Rosina, wife of Johannes Fitzel and Catherine, grandson Jeremiah Fitzel. Real and personal estate. Executors Peter Backer, Ludwigh Roessell and Wilhelmus Falk. Witnesses Hermanus Rechtmeyer of Sagerties, blacksmith, William Davenport of the same place, farmer, and John Davenport.

654 (F 39) 1786 Septbr. 8 Octbr. 16 **FORT, Johannis,** of Poughkeepsie Precinct, Dutchess Co. Wife Rebeccah, sons Abraham and John I., daughters Elizabeth, wife of James Bussing, Hannah, wife of Aaron Low, Deborah, wife of Casparus Westervelt, Francintje, wife of Andrew Low, and Aleda. Real and personal property. Executors son Abraham, Casparus Westervelt and Samuel Mathers. Witnesses Benjamin Westervelt, James Elderkin, farmers, and Gileath Hunt.

655 (F 40) 1786 Decbr. 30 1787 Febry. 8 **FISH, Thomas,** of Armenia Precinct, nuncupative will of, leaves personal estate to wife Maryann. Witnessed by Jonathan Deuel, Jacob Bockee, John MacDonald, Gabriel Douzenbery and Joseph Tar Bush.

656 (F 41) 1800 May 26 July 9 **FITSGERALD, Thomas,** of Albany City. Stepson John Lowry, Thomas Main and Richard Allanson. Real and personal estate. Executor Richard Allanson. Witnesses George McElcheran, William Hannagan and John van Ness Yates.

657 1787 Aug. 30 **FITCH, Abel,** of Yarmouth, Barnstable Co., Mass. Letters of administration on the estate of, granted to Naomi Fitch of the same place. Recorded Wills and Probates, Vol. I., p. 173.

658 1795 Octbr. 15 Octbr. 21 **FLETCHER, Thomas,** of N. Y. City, stone-cutter. Susannah Bowers, "my dearly beloved friend." "Worldly estate." Executors Robert Baird and Jonathan Wilder. Witnesses Michael Fullam and Robert Elliott. Recorded ut supra p. 508.

659 1795 Septbr. 19 Octbr. 16 **FARRELL, James,** of N. Y. City. James Ryan sole heir of real and personal estate. No executor named. Witnesses Alex. Anderson, of N. Y. City, physician. Caleb Fowler of N. Y. City, butcher, appointed administrator. Recorded ut supra p. 526.

660 1795 Decbr. 22 1797 Jany. 13 French **FAURE, Ppe.** Codicil to a will, made at Leoganne in January or February 1794, which it annuls. Wife and three children in France. Plantations known by the names of Baville, Parish of Fond des Negres La Croix des Palmistes, in the Parish of Baynet and in that of Tapion, near Petit Goave. The wife executrix and guardian of children. No witnesses. Recorded Vol. II., p. 14.

661 1798 Octbr. 4 1799 Jany. 3 **FARREL, John,** of N. Y. City, leaves outstanding debts, amounting to $56. 2 sh. to Patrick Lynch executor and Thomas Hollahan. Witnesses John Hobin and Thomas Hallahan. Recorded ut supra, p. 155.

662 1816 Octbr. 28 Decbr. 10 **FOWLER, Stephen,** of Brunswick, Rensselaer Co. Parents Isaac Fowler and wife Mary, wife Elizabeth, children Ammon, Abraham G. and Delilah. Real and personal property. Executors brother Gilbert Fowler of N. Y. City merchant and William McManus of Troy, counsellor-at-law. Witnesses Jacob Schermerhorn, James Roberts, Charlotte Fowler. Recorded ibidem, p. 335.

663 1807 Febry. 17 1827 Octbr. 18 **FRANKLIN, Samuel,** of N. Y. City merchant, "being of advanced age." Sons Abraham and John, son-in-law William I. Robinson. House and lot in Pearl Str. N. Y., running to Cliff Str., land on Greenwich Road, lot between Water and Front Str., N. Y. Executors the two sons. Witnesses Henry Franklin of Middleburgh, Schohary Co. (Quaker), Peter Hawes, Benjamin Clark, both of N. Y. City counsellors at law, the last a Quaker. Son Abraham had been dead at date of proof for two years, leaving widow Ann and ten children viz: Eliza T., Esther, widow of Thomas Walden of N. Y. City merchant, William Henry, Benjamin T., James T., Catherine, Abraham, John C., Anna T., wife of Philip W. Engs of N. Y. City merchant, and Maria Matilda Franklin. The daughter Sarah, wife of William T. Robinson, has been dead 20 years, leaving eight children vizt. Hester, wife of Jonas Minturn of N. Y. City merchant, Emma, wife of John Grimshaw of N. Y. City merchant, Mary, wife of Wm. Hunter of Rhode Island lawyer, Ann, wife of John B. Toulmin of Alabama, Abigail, wife of Joseph Pierce of Massachusetts, Franklin Robinson of Alabama, Roland R. Robinson of Indiana and William R. Robinson of Indiana. Recorded Vol. IV., p. 226.

664 1703-4 March 21 1706 May 11 **FREDRICKSEN, Myndert,** of Albany City, blacksmith. Wife Pietertie, sons Burger, living in New York, Fredrick, Johannis, Reynier, da. Neeltie, wife of Hendrick Dow, who has da. Pietertie. House and lot hard by the Church in Cow Street, Albany, garden behind the Fort, personal property (a great silver tankard, church book with silver clasps and chain, a silver tumbler, marked M. F). The wife sole executrix. Witnesses Albert Ryckman, Evert Bancker, I. Abeel and Robert Livingston jun. Albany Co. Records, Wills I., p. 122.

665 1824 April 10 1825 March 7 **FRYER, John,** of Guilderland, Albany Co. Wife Maria, sons John, Jacob, Abraham, Alexander, Derick, and William, daughters Hannah, wife of Peter Mesick, Maritie, wife of John van Wagenen, Elisabeth, wife of

Hendrick Crounse jun., and Barbara. Real and personal estate. Executors sons John and Jacob with Wm. McKown, Abel French and James McKown. Witnesses Peter van Auken, N. v. Valkenburgh and Peter Wormer. Albany Co. Records, Wills I., part 2, p. 130.

666 (G 1) 1685 Aug. 14 — **GLEN, Jacob Sandersen,** of Albany City. Present wife Catharina and her children Joannis, 10 years old, Annetje, about 8 years, Jacob about 6 years, Helena, about 2 years and an expected child. Land in the jurisdiction of Shanegtade and elsewhere, personal property. No land to be sold or alienated to persons not nearest in blood. Brothers Sander and Johannis to be tutors of children and executors. Witnesses Dirck Wesselsen ten Broek and Johannes Wendel. Copy of translation from original Dutch.

667 (G 2) 1770 July 4 1771 May 28 **GOETCHIUS, Johannis Mauritius,** of Shawengunk Precinct, Ulster Co., minister of the gospel. Wife Catharina, nephews Henricus and Mauritius, sons of bro. Henricus Goetchius, George, son of sister Ann and Rev. Coenraad Wirtz dec'd. Land in Shawengunk Precinct and in New Paltz Patent. Executors the wife, Johannis Jansen jun., and Benjamin Smedes jun. Witnesses Henricus Schoonmaker, Elias van Bunschoten and Joseph Coddington of New Paltz, schoolmaster.

668 (G 3) 1705 Febry. 14 1710 Aug. 21 Dutch **GOES, Jan Tysen,** of Kinderhook, Albany Co. Wife Steyntje Jans, sons Tys, Jan, Dirk, daughters Teuntie, Anna Jans, Judith, Meutje and Maycke. Real and personal property. Executors not named. Witnesses Pieter van Buuren, Dirck van der Kar, Paulus van vieg, Notary Public. John Goes appointed administrator.

669 (G 4) 1706 Septbr. 26 1707 Octbr. 4 **GLEN, Johannis,** of Schonectady, Albany Co., yeoman. Wife Janneke, sons Jacob Sandersen and Johannis, bro. Sanders Glen. Real and personal estate.

Executors bro.-in-law Abraham Cuyler and Johannis Beakman, both of Albany City. Witnesses Reyer Schermerhoorn, Johannis Glen and John Collins. Proved at Albany before the Gouvernour, Lord Cornbury.

670 (G 5) 1709-10 Jany. 28 1740 Novbr. 6 Dutch

GARDINER, Samuel Jacobs, of Albany Co. Wife Helena, son Dirck and seven other children, not named. Real and personal estate. No executor named. Witnesses Luycas Gerrit Wyngaert, Pieter van Slyck and Pieter van Alen (the first two dead at date of proof).

671 (G 6) 1711 May 10 ——

GARDNER, Benjamin, of West Farms, Westchester Co. Wife Elizabeth, sisters Elizabeth Hunt, Margret Hadden, Mery Oakley and Hannah, wife of John Hedger, cousins Elizabeth Dickerman and Sarah Hedly. Real and personal property. Executors sisters Elizabeth, Margret, Mercy and Hannah. Witnesses John Bartow and Cirely Legate. Copy.

672 (G 7) 1721 Febry. 21 1727 March 4

GENOUNG, Margaret, of Flushing, Queens Co., widow. Sons John, Jeremiah, daughters Hannah Hedger, Susannah Louerser, granddaughters Hannah Debreas and Charity Fiero. Real and personal property. Executors Stephen Ryder and James Clement. Witnesses Gabriel Luff, Joel Burroughs and J. Smith. Signatures missing.

673 (G 8) 1724 April 10 1729-30 Febry. 24

GIRARD, Abraham, of N. Y. City, sailmaker. Wife Anne and friend Michael Vaughton of N. Y. City sailmaker, heirs and executors of real and personal property. Witnesses Jacobus Kip, Abra. Boelen and Abrah. Gouverneur.

674 (G 9) 1726 Septbr. 24 1732 Octbr. 4

GUIMARD, Paiere, of Wagachkemeck, Ulster Co. Son Paiere (Pierre), daughters Hester, wife of Philipp du Bois, Anna, wife of Jacobus Swartwout, Elisabeth and Mary. Real and personal estate. Executors the son with sons-in-law Philipp du Bois and Jacobus Swartwout. Witnesses Louis Bevier, Stephen Nottingham and W. Nottingham.

675 (G 10) 1740 April 29 1760 March 17 **GROENENDYCK, Peter,** of Schonectady, Albany Co., trader. Wife Margrita, sisters Mary and Anna Groenendyck and Sara Stevenson, nephew John Stevenson, niece Sara Stevenson. Personal estate (six silver spoons). Executors Philipp Livingston and James Stevenson, both of Albany, merchants. Witnesses Ino. de Peyster, John Beeckman jun. and William Livingston.

676 (G 11) 1745 Octbr. 30 1748 June 16 **GESSENER, Hendrick,** of Tappan, Orange Co. Wife Elizabeth, daughter Grietje, wife of Jacob Vallentine, son John. Real and personal estate. Executors the wife, Isaac Blaewvelt and Johannes Ferdon. Witnesses Johannis Waldron, Gerrit Eckercen and Jacobus Vlierboom.

677 (G 12) 1745 Septbr. 19 1748 June 2 Dutch **GERRETSEN, Maria,** widow of Jan, of Albany City. Sons Adam and Cornelius van den Bergh, daughters Anna, wife of Adam Staats, Maria, wife of Wissel van Schaick. Real and personal property (a large silver cup, three silver spoons, one do from Margrieta ten Broek, a silver cup). Mother's name Anna van Woort. Executors son Cornelius and da. Maria. Witnesses Thomas Sharpe, James Sharpe and John Schuyler.

678 (G 13) 1746 May 3 1750 Octbr. 24 **GALE, John,** of Goshen Prect., Orange Co., gent. Wife Mary, sons John, Daniel Thomas, Abraham, Hezekiah, Samuel and Benjamin, da. Catherine Ludlum. Real and personal property. Executors the wife and sons John and Samuel. Witnesses Silas Leonard, Noah Holly and William ffinn.

679 (G 14) 1749 Decbr. 20 1751 Novbr. 21 **GIVEEN, John,** junior. Sisters Sarah and Mary, two nieces, daughters of sister Martha and Andrew McDougall; father still living. Real and personal estate.

Executors Michael Jackson of Goshen, Orange Co. and John Whorry of Ulster Co., both refusing to act, Sarah McMasters, sister of dec'd, is appointed administratrix. Witnesses Samuel Crawford, Janet McNeal of New York City and John McNeal. See No. 681.

680 (G 15) 1750 Octbr. 17 1752 Septbr. 15 **GONSALUS, Manuel,** jun., of Mammecatting, Ulster Co., yeoman. Wife Rymerigh, children Manuel, Daniel, Johanna, Elizabeth, Maria, Jacobus and Samuel heirs and executors of real and personal property. Witnesses Philippus Meller, cordwainer, Counrat Grs. Elmendorph, yeoman and P. Edmundus Elmendorph.

681 (G 16) 1751 Aug. 23 1755 Novbr. 24 **GIVEN, John,** of Hunting Grove, Ulster Co., cordwainer. Wife Margaret, son John and Robert, daughters Mary, Margaret and Sarah, grandsons John Wool and John McDoual. Real and personal estate. Executors the wife, Charles Clinton and John Young. Witnesses James Green, Arthur Beatty and Henery McNelley. Vide No. 679.

682 (G 17) 1752 May 20 1763 Novbr. 24 **GARTON, Anna,** of Marbletown, Ulster Co., spinster. Nephew Daniel Broadhead of Dansbery, Bucks Co., Penna. sole heir and executor of real and personal goods. Witnesses Evert Bogardus, Gerrit van Buren and John Crooke.

683 (G 18) 1755 May 11 May — **GREEN, JOHN,** of Crumelbow Prect., Dutchess Co. Wife Elizabeth, sons John and Tobias, daughters Mary Elizabeth and Ann. Real and personal estate. Executors father-in-law Christian Tobias and cousin Israel Green, both of Crumelbow Prect. Witnesses Joshua Haight, Daniel Tobias and Adomiah Newcomb. Copy made March 15, 1768.

684 (G 19) 1755 April 9 1758 Decbr. 1 **GREAG, Hugh,** of Blagg's Clove, Goshen Prect., Orange Co. Wife Jane, "eldest" son Robert, no other children mentioned. Real and personal estate. Execu-

tors the wife, James Bartley of Wallkil, Alexander Falls of Little Britain and Henry Smith of Newbourgh. Witnesses Samuel Moffat of Orange Co., farmer, John Carpenter and Samuel Smith.

685 (G 20) Original of No. 683.

686 (G 21) 1755 April 19 1760 April 18 **GILBEART, Caleb,** of Orange Co., yeoman. Sons Ebenezer, Stephen, John and Joshua, daughters Phebe Goldsmith and Hannah Gilbert. Real and personal property. Executors Silas Person and Samuel Birds Eye. Witnesses Luke Clarke, Mary Mosure and Fletcher Mathews of Ulster Co., attorney-at-law.

687 (G 22) 1756 Febry. 14 1757 Febry. 28 **GALE, Samuel,** of Goshen, Orange Co. Wife Elizabeth, sons Samuel, Asay and Richard, daughters Julianna, wife of George Dekay, Dorothy and an expected child. Real and personal property. Executors the wife, William Worthrinton of Saybrook and John Gale of Goshen. Overseers Benjamin Carpenter of Goshen and Henery Wsonow (??). Witnesses Joseph Wood, Israel Parshall and Jonathan Cory junior.

688 (G 23) 1757 July 3 Septbr. 27 **GALE, Daniel,** of Goshen, Orange Co. Wife Dinah, sons Daniel and Moses, brothers John, Benjamin, Samuel and Coe Gale, nephew and niece William and Temperance Gale. Real and personal estate. Executors brother John Gale and William Denn, both of Goshen. Witnesses Nathaniel Bayles, wheelwright, Isaac Smith, planter, both of Goshen, and James Thomson.

689 (G 24) 1759 Jany. 19 1761 Septbr. 4 **GREEN, John,** of Goshen Prect., Orange Co., yeoman. Wife Sarah, children John, Sarah Belden, Abagal Coray and Mary Hait, grandchildren James and Rode, children of da. Elizabeth and Jeams Moser dec'd. Real and personal property. Executors the wife and Jacob Dunning. Witnesses Thomas Pain and Elijah Reeve of Orange Co., blacksmith.

690 (G 25) 1760 Octbr. 10 Novbr. 4 **GALE, John,** of Goshen, Orange Co., yeoman. Sons Doctor John, Benjamin, Koe, and Samuel, daughters Sarah and Cuzziah. Real and personal estate. Executors sons Doctor John and Benjamin. Witnesses John Everett, John Ludlum and Sam Gale of Orange Co., shopkeeper. See No. 721.

691 (G 26) 1760 Decbr. 18 1761 March 5 **GREEN, William,** of Crum Elbo Prect., Dutchess Co. Wife Marther, sons Stephen, William and Joseph. Real and personal estate. Executors son Stephen, William Doughty and Israel Green. Witnesses John Roberts, Susannah Pudney and Zephaniah Platt.

692 (G 27) 1760 June 13 1763 May 20 **GERMOND, Isaac,** of Crom Elbow Prect., Dutchess Co., yeoman. Sons Isaac, Peter, John, James, daughters Mary Filkin and Sarah Hewstead and her children Susannah Smith and Germond Hewstead, grandson Isaac, son of Isaac Germond. Real and personal estate. Executor son James. Witnesses Hobart Hanbrough, Richard Post and Clear Everitt.

693 (G 28) 1762 Septbr. — 1763 Aug. 6 **GANSEVORT, Leonard,** of Albany City, brewer. Wife Catherine, sons Harmen, Johannis, Peter. Real and personal estate (a silver tankard). Executors sons Harmen and Johannis. Witnesses Abraham Douw, Pieter de Wandelaer and Volkert Am. Douw.

694 (G 29) 1763 11th Day 4th Month 1764 Febry. 20 **GOULD, John,** of Charlotte Precinct, Dutchess Co. Wife Mary, sons William, Adam and James. Real and personal estate. Executors son William Gould and Ruben Palmer. Witnesses Joshua Haight, Aaron Vail, William Palmer jun.

695 (G 30) 1763 May 3 May 19 **GILLETT, Joel,** of Amelia Precinct, Dutchess Co. Wife Mary, sons Abner, Moses and Eli, daughters Lucy Dunham, Mary and Sarah. "Worldly estate," all personal. Executors the wife and Nicholas Delavergne. Witnesses Daniel Barn, William Barker and Daniel Roberts.

696 (G 31) 1763 May 1 1775 Aug. 22 **GRIGG, Thomas,** of N. Y. City, joiner. Wife Hannah, "eldest" son Thomas, no other children mentioned. "Whole estate." Executor the wife. Witnesses Edward Man, Abraham Quick and Joseph Hildreth of N. Y. City, schoolmaster. Copy.

697 (G 32) 1765 Septbr. 11 1767 April 9 **GARDENIER, Dirk,** of Kinderhook, Albany Co., yeoman. Barrentie, widow of bro. Samuel Gardenier and her children Derick, Cornelia and Johanna; Johanna, widow of bro. Jacob G., sister Josina Gardenier, nephews Samuel S. Gardenier and his sisters, Samuel H. Gardenier, Derick Gardenier jun. and sisters; sister Angeltie, widow of Johannis Schermerhoorn. Real and personal estate. Executors Peterus van Slyck and Johannis van Slyck. Witnesses Jacob D. Vosburgh, Johannes Vosburgh, and Jacob Freese.

698 (G 33) 1765 Jany. 13 1770 Novbr. 1 **GELSTON, Samuel,** of Goshen Precinct, Orange Co. Wife Elizabeth, children of son William, vizt: Samuel, Elizabeth and Lucy, grandson Samuel Curry. Real and personal estate. Executors Michael Jackson and Thomas Welling, both of Orange Co., yeoman. Witnesses Timothy Back (Buck?), Rachel Cleark and Joseph Clarke.

699 (G 34) 1768 Septbr. 27 Novbr. 1 **GALE, Jacob,** of Orange Co. Wife Rebecca and an expected child; brothers Peter, David and Abraham Gale. Real and personal property. Executors brothers Peter and David Gale. Witnesses John Gale, Margaret Woodworth and Wm. Denn.

700 (G 35) 1768 Septbr. 16 1771 Septbr. 27 **GARDINIER, Andries,** of the Mohawk River, Albany Co., yeoman. Sons Nicholas, Matthew, daughters Rachel, Rebecca, Esther and Catherine. Real and personal property. Executors Samuel Gardinier and Dow Fonda, both of the Mohawk River, yeomen. Witnesses John McKinney, Adam Gardenyr, Saml. Gardener.

701 (G 36) 1769 Septbr. 20 1770 March 31

GLEN, Johannis, of Albany City, merchant. Children of brother Jacob Glen dec'd, vizt: John, Hendrick, Cornelius and Jannetje, wife of Abraham C. Cuyler, children of sister Catherine, wife of Johannis Cuyler, vizt: Elsje, wife of Barent ten Eyck, John Cuyler jun., Cornelius Cuyler jun. and Jacob Cuyler. Real and personal estate. Executors John Glen jun., Hendrick Glen, Cornelius Glen, John Cuyler jun., Cornelius Cuyler and Jacob Cuyler. Witnesses John Cuyler, Isaac Verplanck and Abraham Yates jun.

702 (G 37) 1769 March 4 March 31

GILLASPY, Neal, of Wallkil Precinct, Ulster Co., yeoman. Wife ——, sons Neal, Daniel; Alexander Campbell; da. Catty, wife of William Goodjon. Land in Scotch or Argyle Patent, personal property. Executors Alexander Kidd and David Jager. Overseer Cadwallader Colden jun. Witnesses Thomas Beatty, Samuel Haines of Ulster Co., yeoman, and Archibald McNeal.

703 (G 38) 1771 Septbr. 17 1781 June 25

GOVERNEUR, Jacoba, of N. Y. City. Sister Maria Farmer, niece Hester Governeur, Nicholas Governeur and sister Magdalen Hall, Isaac Low of N. Y. City merchant, nephew Abraham Governeur, Frances, wife of Jacob Sharpe, Rineir Skates, Peter Farmer, Jasper Farmer. "My estate," part of which came from sister Elizabeth, plate including a silver tankard, on which is engraved the Governeur coat of arms, china, an Arabian gold piece, a small picture, burnt on glass. Executors Nicholas Governeur and Isaac Low. Witnesses Gerard Walton of N. Y. City, gentleman, Richard Ray, Samuel Ray. Copy.

704 (G 39) 1772 April 23 June 3

GRIFFIN, Jonathan, of Charlotte Precinct, Dutchess Co., farmer. Wife Mary, daughters Sarah and Dorothy, an expected child. Real and personal estate. Executors brother Bartholomew Griffin and bro.-in-law Jacob Thorn, both of Charlotte Precinct. Witnesses Thos. Barker, James Jackson, yeoman, and Daniel Smith.

705 (G 40) 1772 Septbr. 26 1784 Aug. 6 **GARDINIER, Jacob,** of Klynekil, Kinderhook Township, Albany Co., farmer. Sons Johannis Jacobsen and Hendrick Jacobsen Gardinier heirs and executors of real and personal estate. Witnesses Samuel H. Gardinier, Elisabeth Cantine and Peter Cantine jun. Printed form of will.

706 (G 41) 1772 Octbr. 9 Decbr. 17 **GOURLAY, James,** of Albany City, merchant. Father James Gourlay, brothers Robert, Samuel and John, sister Margret. Excludes "my putative wife Ann Schuyler and the male child she has (the same being none of my begetting)." Real and personal estate. Executors the father, brothers, sister and Hugh Gray. Witnesses Alex. Cruikshank, Mathew Watson and Joseph Anderson, all of Albany. On parchment.

707 (G 42) 1773 Decbr. 25 1774 Febry. 10 **GRAY, William,** of Cambridge Township, Albany Co., husbandman. The father, brothers Hugh, Matthew, Jacob and David, sisters Dorothy Gilmore, Esther and Phebe. "Worldly estate." Executor James Cowdin of Cambridge. Witnesses Robert Gillmore, Hugh Gray and John McClung.

708 (G 43) 1774 Octbr. 1 1786 Octbr. 25 **GARDENIER, Josina,** of Kline Kil, Kinderhook, Albany Co., spinster. Nephew Dirk Gardenier sole heir and executor of personal estate. Witnesses Samuel Gardenier, farmer, Arthur B. Nugent and John C. Holland.

709 (G 44) 1776 Septbr. 20 1784 July 5 **GILCHRIST, Alexander,** of Argyle Township, Charlotte Co. Wife and sons mentioned, but not by names, daughters Jane, Catherine, Agnes, Flora and Margret. Real and personal estate. Executors Duncan Gilchrist and John McNeil. Witnesses John McDougall and Alexander McDougall, farmers. Proved in Washington Co.

710 (G 45) 1776 May 2 1787 Novbr. 20 **GOES, Christina,** of Kinderhook District, Albany Co., widow, da. of Peter van Alen. Daughters Jane, wife of Cornelis J. Sebring and Josina, wife of Thomas Wittbeek, sons Lowrens D. and Dirck Goes. Personal estate. Executors bro.-in-law Luykas I. Goes and friend Henry van Schaack. Witnesses John D. Goes, farmer, Johannis Goes and Elizabeth Huyck.

711 (G 46) 1777 Octbr. 19 1778 June 15 **GOLDSMITH, Benjamin,** of Goshen, Orange Co. Wife Jamima, da. Mary, sons James, Benjamin, Daniel and John. "My estate." Executors father Richard Goldsmith, brother Richard Goldsmith and Bimuel Youngs, all of Orange Co. Witnesses Brinton Paine of Dutchess Co., Major Viner van Zandt and Joseph Winter. Proved in Dutchess Co. See No. 720.

712 (G 47) 1777 Septbr. 15 Septbr. 24 **GRAHAM, Ennis,** late of N. Y. City, merchant, now of Middlesex Co., N. J., born in North Britain. Wife Elizabeth, sons Ennis, Alexander, John, James, Edward, Charles and William, daughters Sarah, Elizabeth and Jane. "Worldly estate" (plate). Executors the wife, Walter Buchanan of N. Y. City, merchant, and John Thomson of N. Y. City, sadler and merchant. Witnesses Israel Read, Michael Field and Peter Cockran. Proved in Middlesex Co., N. J. Copy.

713 (G 48) 1779 Octbr. 15 **GETTY, James,** of New Perth, Charlotte Co. Testimony of John Rowan, Patrick Wilson and Wm. McFarland, that James Getty signed on Feby. 10 or 11, 1772 a will leaving real and personal property to wife Jean and children Robert, Ebenezer, Isaac and Sarah, appointing John Rowan and Wm. McFarland executors. It was signed by Doctor Thomas Clark, Patrick Willson and John Livingston.

714 (G 49) 1779 July 20 Septbr. 4 **GRIDLEY, Noah,** of Albany Co., yeoman. Wife ——, children Mary, Noah, Rebecca and Nathaniel. Real

and personal property. Executors the wife and Matthew Adgate. Witnesses Mat. Adgate of Kings District, Albany Co., esquire, Allen Beach, and Timothy Buck. Proved in Ulster Co.

715 (G 50) 1779 Novbr. 3 1782 Decbr. 5 **GRIGGS, John,** of Newburgh, Ulster Co., yeoman. Wife Martha, sons Samuel, John, Ferdinand, daughters Elizabeth, Sarah and Mary. Real and personal estate. Executors the wife, son Samuel, and Colonel Thomas Palmer. Witnesses Cattrin, wife of Moses Ward late of N. Y., now of Newburgh, carpenter, John Foster and Samuel Edmonds.

716 (G 51) 1779 March 4 1785 Decbr. 19 **GAULT, William,** late of Chery Valy, yeoman, "being of a grate age." Natural son William sole heir and executor of real and personal estate. Witnesses William Harper, John Harper, Hanry Bogart and Archibald Harper. Proved in Montgomery Co.

717 (G 52) 1780 April 10 1785 April 15 **GINSALIS, John.** Present wife and son by her John, other children Peter and Hannah, grandsons John Miles, son of a daughter, Imanuel, son of son Joseph; Tiney Bulson. Real and personal property. Executors son Peter Ginsalis and Cornelius Bulson. Witnesses Peter Blane and Tunis. Proved in Albany Co.

718 (G53) 1781 Septbr. — Octbr. 10 **GILBORT, Josiah,** of Gray Court, Orange Co. Wife Hannah, children Elizabeth (and children), Mary (and two children), Calip (and three children), Hannah Brasted, Sara Person, Bethia Seely; Elizabeth and Hannah Person, Martha Gilbert, grandsons Gilbert Seely, James Davisson Seely and Josiah Breasted. Real and personal property. Executors the wife, Siles Person of Hamtinborough and Birdeyes Youngs. Witnesses Phil. Doyle of Orange Co., schoolmaster, John Carpenter and Jonas Seely.

719 (G 54) 1781 Novbr. 28 1784 May 8

GILLDERSLEEVE, Benjamin. Wife Hannah, sons James, Joseph, Elkanah, Benjamin and Thomas; Nathaniel Gildersleeve (doubtful, whether a son, brother, nephew or cousin). "Temporal estate." Executors the wife and Nathaniel Gildersleeve. Witnesses Francis Hasbrouck of Rombout Precinct, yeoman, and Mathew Valentine. Proved in Dutchess Co.

720 (G 55) 1781 March 3 1780 June 16 (*sic.*)

GOLDSMITH, Richard, senior, of New Cornwall Precinct, Orange Co. Son Richard, grandchildren James, Benjamin, Daniel, Richard, John and Mary Goldsmith, daughters Susannah, Abigail and Anne. Real and personal property. Executors son Richard Goldsmith jun., Edward Neely, Henry Winsner and John Seers. Witnesses William Hudson, James Mathews and James Martin. Copy. Vide No. 711.

721 (G 56) 1782 Febry. 28 1786 March 22

GALE, Benjamin, of Goshen Co. Wife Eleanor, mother Hannah Gale, nephews John, Moses and Benjamin, sons of brother Coe Gale, daughter Keziah Gale, nephew Benjamin, son of bro. Samuel Gale, niece Sarah, da. of Roger Townsend. Real and personal property. Executors brothers Doctor John Gale and Coe Gale and Anthy. Carpenter. Witnesses Jared Eliot, William McMillian, Jane Barker and Reuben Hopkins of Orange Co., attorney at law. See No. 690.

722 (G 57) 1782 Octbr. 12 Novbr. 18

GREEN, Joseph, of the Fishkils, Dutchess Co. Daughter Sarah Cooper, granddaughters Mary and Sarah Green, sons Joseph and Jeremiah, grandsons of James Green, vizt: Joseph, Daniel and James, daughters of John ter Boosh, vizt: Elisabeth and Sarah. Real and personal property. Executors the two sons Joseph and Jeremiah Green. Witnesses Silvanus Pine, yeoman, Philipp Pine and Teunis du Bois, cooper.

723 (G 58) 1782 6th Day 6th Month 1785 Novbr. 21 **GRIFFIN, Obadiah,** of the Nine Partners, Dutchess Co. Wife ——, sons Edward, Bartholomew and Mical, daughter Dorrity, grandson Obediah Hallock. Real and personal estate. Executors Jonathan Holms and Nathaniel Brown. Witnesses Jonathan Griffin, Samuel Doughty, farmer, and Ann Lockward.

724 (G 59) 1781 Septbr. 1 1782 June 5 **GODWIN, Henry,** of Rumbouts Prect., Dutchess Co. (has been prisoner of war). Wife Catelina, children Abraham Gates Godwin, daughters Phebea, Helena and Henrietta Godwin. Real and personal property. Executors the wife and "trusty friend and brother Samuel Demarest." Witnesses James Cooper, merchant, Adolphe Degrove jun. and Stephen Seaman. Codicil of March 9, 1782, names "trusty friend and brother Obadiah Cooper" as additional executor. Witnesses James Wills, farmer, William Brewer and Daniel le Dew.

725 (G 60) 1782 May 25 Novbr. 7 **GORSLINE, Samuel,** of Rumbouts Precinct, Dutchess Co., farmer. Sons Samuel, William, James, Richard and Jose, daughters Martha, Elizabeth, Sarah and Ruth. Real and personal estate. Executors sons Samuel, William and Richard Gorsline and son-in-law George Adriance. Witnesses Obadiah Cooper, merchant, Stephen Smith, hatter, both of Rumbouts Precinct, and Michael Tremper.

726 (G 61) 1783 March 19 1785 March 10 **GARNSEY, John,** of Amenia Precinct, Dutchess Co. Wife Anna, sons John, Nathan, Daniel, Peter, Noah, daughters Anna, Dorcas, wife of Job Thurston, Eunis. "Worldly estate." Executors the wife and son Daniel. Witnesses Roswell Hopkins, Grover Buel, farmer, and John Garnsey jun., son of testator.

727 (G 62) 1783 May 5 1785 Septbr. 2 **GREEN, Joshua,** of New La Bunun, Kings District, Albany Co., about 60 years old. Sons Daniel, Tones, Joshaway, daughters Mary Fox, Catharine Tabor,

Abigill (?) Hogkins, Elisabeth Sciner, Susannah Fox. Real and personal estate. Executor son-in-law Josiah Skiner. Witnesses Robert Havens, yeoman, Richard Thurber and John Bivins.

728 (G 63) 1784 Decbr. 12 1785 June 17 **GREEN, John,** of Wallkil, Ulster Co. Wife Patience, sons Israel, Ebenezer, John and Daniel, daughters Patience and Elizabeth. Real and personal estate. Executors sons Israel and John Green and Henry Wisner jun. Witnesses Timothy Smith, tailor, Samuel Wickham, yeoman, and Daniel Green, carpenter.

729 (G 64) 1784 Aug. 20 Novbr. 12 **GALE, Hezekiah,** of Wallkil, Ulster Co. Wife Martha, sons Abel, Moses and Samuel, daughters Hanna Smith, Mary Gale and Martha Lewes. Real and personal estate. Executors the three sons. Witnesses Jesse Brockway of Wallkil Precinct, innholder, Ino. McCamly and Jas. Crawford.

730 (G 65) 1786 May 10 1792 July 28 **GOELET, Catharine,** of N. Y. City, spinster. Goddaughter Elizabeth, da. of bro. Peter Goelet, sister Jane, wife of John Zebriska of Hackensack, N. J., children of bro. Francis Goelet, vizt: James and Peter, children of bro. Peter Goelet, vizt: Elizabeth, Alice Lott, Jennet, John, Peter, Robert Ratsey, Thomas Billopp and Christopher Billopp Goelet, son of sister Jane Zebriska, vizt: John Zebriska jun. Real and personal estate (plate). Executors nephews John and Peter Goelet of N. Y. City, merchants. Witnesses Theophilus de Bow, Thomas Hicks, both of N. Y. City, gentlemen, and Vincent Mathews.

731 (G 66) 1786 Octbr. 11 1787 Jany. 2 **GENSHIMMER, Christian,** of Rombout Prect., Dutchess Co., farmer. Sons Frederick, Peter and George, daughters Maria, Elizabeth and Betty. Real and personal estate. Executors John Robinson, Rudolph Philipp senior and Doctor Casparus Mancius, who all renounce their rights as executors, whereupon Daniel ter Boss and

John Luyster, principal creditors of dec'd, are appointed administrators. Witnesses Robert Sweet, farmer, George Barnes and Jasper M. Gidley.

732 (G 67) 1765 Febry. 13 **GELSTON, William,** of Orange Co., farmer. Letters of administration on his estate granted to his father, Samuel Gelston of same Co., farmer.

733 (G 68) 1786 April 17 **GIGO, Francis,** late private in Colonel Moses Hazen's Regt. Bond of Moses Hazen as administrator on Gigo's estate, given in N. Y. Co.

734 1786 Novbr. 13 1787 Aug. 23 **GOSS, Christopher,** seaman on board ship *Hope Wampo.* Brother Tobias Goss of Charleston, S. Carolina, to have all the wages due from the ship *Hope*, James Magee, commander, and other personal property including a pair of silver knee buckles. David F. Barber executor. Witnesses Abel Fitch, 2d mate, and Joseph Hunt, surgeon. Recorded Wills and Probates, Vol. I., p. 153.

735 1786 Octbr. 20 1787 April 18 **GOUVERNEUR, Nicholas,** of Newark, N. J. Wife Mary, son Isaac, da. Gertruyda Burnet, bro. Isaac Gouverneur, grandsons Anthony Rutgers, Nicholas Gouverneur Rutgers, Herman Gouverneur Rutgers, Isaac Burnet and Staats G. Burnet, granddaughters Alida Gouverneur, Mary Rhea and Cornelia Gale. House and lot in Newark, lands on W. side of and on an island in Lake Champlain, in Lyman Township, New Hampshire, personal estate (plate, gold knee buckles, family pictures and landscapes formerly belonging to Col. Peter Schuyler, a picture of Mrs. Winkler of Batavia, drawn on silver, a silver tankard, a silver bread basket). Executors the wife, brother Isaac Gouverneur, nephew Nicholas Low, Nicholas Gouverneur jun., Isaac Gouverneur jun. and Lewis Ogden. Witnesses Sarah Wallace, Uzal Ogden and Robert T. Kemble. Proved in N. J. Recorded ut supra, p. 162.

736 1790 Octbr. 9 Octbr. 23 **GOULD, Daniel,** of Kentucky, gentleman. Daniel Geno sole heir and executor of real estate in Kentucky and personal property. Witnesses Ino Dalton of N. Y. City, physician, William C. Thompson and Robert King. Recorded ut supra, p. 253.

737 1792 Octbr. 10 Octbr. 30 **GREEN, David,** of East Greenwich, R. I., mariner. Wife Eunice, children Martha, Mary, Edwin and Phebe. Real and personal estate. Executors the wife and father-in-law Jonathan Hopkins. Witnesses John G. Bogert, Joshua Sayer and Salley Durfee. Proved in N. Y. City. Recorded ut supra, p. 370.

738 1791 Aug. 4 1794 Septbr. 24 **GOUVERNEUR, Isaac,** of Mount Pleasant, Essex Co., N. J., gentleman. Nephews Isaac Gouverneur of N. Y. City, merchant, Samuel, Anthony, Joseph, Nicholas, sons of bro. Samuel, Gouverneur, son of Peter Kemble, Mary, widow of bro. Nicholas, children of Dr. Burnet, vizt: Isaac, Staats and David, Margaret, wife of Lewis Ogden, Mary, wife of Rev. Uzal Ogden, Hannah, wife of Charles Ogden, Rebecca, wife of Thomas Bibby, Sarah, wife of Samuel Reading, Isabella, wife of Isaac Wilkins, Effie, wife of Samuel Ogden, Gitty, wife of Alexander Wallace, Sarah, widow of Hugh Wallace, Allida Gouverneur, Mary, wife of William Ludlow of Claverack, N. Y., Gouverneur Morris, Isaac Low, Nicholas Low, Isaac Ogden, Samuel Ogden, Abraham Ogden, Nicholas Ogden, Peter Ogden, Sarah, wife of Nicholas Hoffman, children of sister Magdalena Hall, Anthony Rutgers, Nicholas Rutgers, Herman Rutgers, Gitty, wife of Peter Kemble, godchildren Gouverneur, son of Abraham Ogden, Lewis M., son of Samuel Ogden, Isaac G., son of Isaac Ogden, George, son of Thomas Bibby. Houses and lots in Front Str., in Water Str., in Gouverneurs Alley, in Smith Str., real estate in N. J., and in the West Indies, personal property. Executors nephews Nicholas and Isaac, sons of bro. Samuel Gouverneur, Gouverneur Morris, Lewis

Ogden and Peter Kemble. Witnesses Charles Smith, Peter Hill, both of N. Y. City, merchts, Viner van Zandt and Philipp Kearsey. Proved in N. Y. City. Recorded ut supra, p. 431.

739 1795 Septbr. 23 Octbr. 22 **GLOVER, Hester,** of N. Y. City, widow. Son William, godchild Margaret, da. of John Wood and his wife Margaret of Staten Island. "All my estate." Executor Jacob Heart of N. Y. City, grocer. Witnesses Hugh McDowle of N. Y. City, baker, James Russell and William Reid. Recorded ut supra, p. 510.

740 1796 March 4 July 22 **GENERY, George,** native of Old England, at present mariner on board the ship *Sampson*, John Esmond commander, in China. Sister Mary Sterling of Colchester, Essex Co., sole heiress. Executors Thomas Smith, mariner and William Sterling, mariner, both natives of Old England. Witnesses John Leonard and Ebenezer Williams. Proved in N. Y. City. Recorded ut supra, p. 552.

741 1797 April 6 April 20 French **GEOFFROY, Marianne,** widow Collien, born at Tournon in Vivarais, 60 years old, now living at New York. François Barbier, youngest son by her first husband, Henry Barbier, the elder son. No children by second and third husband. Mrs. Henry (wife of eldest son?) House at Roseau Quarter of Jeremie and personal property (seven silver table spoons, 11 do. coffee spoons, a pair of silver shoe buckles, a pair of gold earrings). Executors Henry Purcardy. Witnesses Hubert de la Massue, Antoine Marchand, B. Vieusse. Recorded Vol. II., p. 21.

742 1804 July 3 1805 Febry. 13 **GOETSCHIUS, John M.,** owner of the Brig *Venus* about to sail from New York for Lisbon, Cadiz, Geneva and Marseilles. Youngest brother Rynier, nephew Levi, oldest son of bro. John, nephew John

Maurice, oldest son of bro.-in-law. "Property." Executors Henry Post, Sylvanus Miller both of N. Y. City and John Elmer of Ulster Co. No witnesses, but will proved by the testimony of Daniel D. Tompkins of N. Y. City, esquire, as to handwriting. Recorded ut supra, p. 287.

743 1817 Novbr. 3 Decbr. 10 **GREGORY, Daniel,** of Carmel, Putnam Co. Wife Elizabeth, sons Ezra, James, Samuel, Lewis, Horace, Elnathan and Alva, daughters Hannah, wife of John Crain jun. and Mary, wife of Michael Sloot. Real and personal estate. Executors sons James and Alva Gregory and Joel Frost of Carmel. Witnesses Joel Frost, Jacob Gonong and Joseph Ganung. Recorded ut supra, p. 342.

744 1742 Septbr. 9 Decbr. 31 **GRIFFITH, Thomas,** of New York City, formerly of St. James, London. Wife Elizabeth, child or children, not named, Joseph Simson of N. Y. City, merchant. Real estate at Helver Green near Hungur, Essex, England and at Winyou, Carolinah, personal property. Executors the wife and Joseph Simson. Witnesses Jos. Simson, Thos. Eatton and Jacob Parsell. Recorded ut supra, Vol. III., p. 38.

745 1781 June 6 **GILBERT, John,** of N. Y. City, leather breeches maker. Letters of administration on his estate granted to his widow Sarah Gilbert of Port Rosaway, Nova Scotia. Recorded ut supra, p. 40.

746 1765 April 22 **GELSTON, James,** of N. Y. City, cooper. Letters of administration on his estate granted to his brother John Gelston of N. Y. City, house carpenter and next of kin. Recorded ut supra, p. 75.

746a 1689 Septbr. 24 **GARDENIER, Jan Jacobsen,** of Albany Co. Wife Sarah, children Jacob, Jannetje and four others, not named. Land at Shotack. Witnesses Andries Huyck and Hendrick Ridderhaes. Letters testamentary granted to widow June 21, 1695. Albany Co. Records, Wills, I., p, 32.

747 1690 July 19 — Dutch

GLENN, Sander, Captain, of Shinnechtady. Wife Antje, nephew Sander, son of bro. Johannes and children of dec'd bro. Jacob. Real and personal estate. Witnesses Willem Ketelheyn, Johannes Becker jun. and J. Becker. Letters testamentary granted to widow Febry. 20, 1696. Albany Co. Records, Wills, I., p. 40.

748 1695 April 7 —

GARDENIER, Hendrick, of Albany Co., letters of administration on the estate of, valued at 6390 florins ($2556 00/00), granted to Andries Gardenier and Cornelis Claessen. Widow's name Neeltie Claessen. Albany Co. Records, Wills, I., p. 30.

749 1696-7 Febry. 9 Recorded 1705-6 Febry. —

GOES, Jan Tysen, of Kinderhook, Albany Co., yeoman. Wife Styntje, children Tys Jansen, Jan, Dirck, Mayke, and 3 other daughters, not named. Real and personal estate. The wife sole executrix with Captain Johannis Schuyler and bro.-in-law Volkert van Hoese as overseers and trustees. Witnesses Johannes Beekman, Robert Livingston and Isaac Verplank. Albany Co. Records, Wills, I., p. 118.

750 1706-7 Jany. 3 Recorded 1712-3 March 20

GROESBEECK, Claes Jacobsen, of Albany City. Wife Elizabeth, children Jacob, William, Barber, wife of Gysbert Marcelis, Rebecca, wife of Dominicus van Schaak, Johannis and Stephanus, children of dec'd da. Catrine, late wife of Jacob Teunissen. Real and personal estate. The wife sole executrix. Witnesses Willem Jacobsen, Claes Vonda and Robert Livingston. Albany Co. Records, Wills, I., p. 135.

751 1709 Octbr. 30 — Dutch

GERRITSEN, Luycas, and wife Anna. Sons Gerrit, Luycas, and seven other children, not named. The survivor executor. Witnesses Pieter Vosburgh, Justice, Jacobus Turck and Yohannes van Alen. Albany Co. Records, Wills, I., p. 138.

752 1704 July 1 1717 Aug. 13 Dutch **GARDINIER, Andries,** of Kinderhook Village, Albany Co. Wife Eytje, sons Andries, 11 yrs. old, Jacob, 9 yrs. old, Arie, 7 yrs. and stepson Jan van Wye. Real and personal estate. Executors the wife, bro. Samuel Gardinier and Andries Coeymans. Witnesses Johannes Rooseboom, Justice, Johannis Cuyler, Justice, and Abraham Cuyler. Albany Co. Records, Wills, I., p. 150.

753 1732 June 1 Aug. 5 Dutch **GOES, Dirck,** of Kinderhook, Albany Co. Wife Elizabeth, sons Johannis, Luyckas, da. Anna, wife of Tobias van Beuren. Real and personal estate. The wife sole executrix. Witnesses A. v. Dyck, Cornelis van Schaack and Jan Tysen Goes. Albany Co. Records, Wills, I., p. 191.

754 1747 Aug. 10 1752 Novbr. 4 **GERRETSEN, Ryer,** of Albany City. Wife Geertruy, cousins Hendrick, son of Elbert Gerretsen, Gerardus, son of Stefanus Groesbeck, John Lansingh, Gerret Lansing, Peter Lansing and Philipp Lansing. Real and personal estate. Executor bro. John Lansing. Witnesses John Beasley, Henry van Dyck and John de Peyster. Albany Co. Records, Wills, I., p. 229.

755 1746 April 17 1755 Jany. 15 **GROESBECK, William,** of Rensselaerswyck Manor, shipwright. Wife Catherine, sons Gerrit, Nicholas, da. Maritie and an expected child. Real and personal estate. The wife sole executrix. Witnesses Gerrit van Ness, Jesse de Foreest and James Stenhouse. Albany Co. Records, Wills, I., p. 231.

756 1747 June 1 1750 Decbr. 31 **GERRITSEN, Elbert,** of Albany City, tailor. Children Hendrick, Annatie, Alida Greveraat, grandsons Gerrit Ryersen Gerritsen and Elbert Grevenraat. Real and personal estate. Executors son Hendrick, Johannis Jacobsen Lansing and Wessel van Schaick. Witnesses Hendrick Bleecker, Nicolas Cuyler and Rutger Bleecker. Albany Co. Records, Wills, I., p. 268.

757
1756
June 1
1759
April 11
GARDENIR, Niclaes, of the Mohox River, Albany Co., farmer. Wife Ragel, sons Hendrick, Adam, Andries, Jacob, Samuel, daughters Neelty van Falkburgh, Anneke van Alstyn, Sara de Garmo, and Ragel Quackenboss. Land near Fort Hunter on S. side of Mohawk R., adjoining John Schot Quackenbous, do. on Schotack Island near Albany; personal property. No executor named. Witnesses Joseph Yates, Christopher Yates, both of Schenectady, and Peter Krurs (?). Albany Records, Wills, I., p. 274.

758
1758
Jany. 31
1776
Febry. 15
GOES, Matthew, of Kinderhook, Albany Co., yeoman. Wife Jannatie, sons Matthew, Johannis, daughters Angenitie, Konelia, Eitie, Helena and Katharina. Real and personal estate. The wife sole executrix. Witnesses Katharina van Dyck, David van Schaack and Corns. van Schaack. Albany Co. Records, Wills, I., part 2, p. 19.

759
1783
Aug. 8
1784
Octbr. 15
GROOSBECK, Johannis, of Rensselaerswyck Colony, blacksmith. Wife Elizabeth, sons Gysbert, Johannis, Gerrit, daughters Gertie and Neltie. Real and personal estate. Executors Wouter Knickerbacker and Johs. van der Heyden jun. Witnesses Philipp de Forest, cooper, Levinus Dunbar, Christopher Bogart and Ino. R. Bleecker, gentleman. Albany Co. Records, Wills, I., part 2, p. 46.

760 (H 1)
1679–80
Febry. 16
——
HUTCHINSON, Ralph. Wife of Captain Nicolls, Peter Alrichs, sons of John Ogle, James Walliam, Thomas Woollaston, and wife, Mary Woollaston, John Darby, da. of Mr. Darby, Ann Woollaston, brother Robbart Hutchinson, Amond Bedford, uncle John Bedford, brother and sister in "ould England." Land at Poplar Neck, plantation on Cristeen (Christina) Creek, land in Major Fenwick's Colony (all on Delaware River), personal property in hands of Daniel Silleuant of Fair-

field, John Cockse, Lockart and Jonas Arskin, John Garritsen, John Smith, John Anderson of Cristina, Swart Jacob, Benjamin Nettelship. Executors Peter Alrichs, James Walliam and Thomas Woollaston of New Castle. Witnesses Tymen Stidden, Edm. Cantwell, Will Shill and Ph. Pocock. Copy certified by Ephr. Hermans, Clerk of the Court at Delaware.

761 (H 2) 1691 Novbr. 17 1692 May 26 Dutch

HANSEN, Pieter, about to sail for Barbadoes. Nephew Pieter Gerretsen, son of brother Gerret Hansen, sole heir, and after him the Poor at New Amersfort. Apparently only personal property. No executor named. Witness Pieter Jacobsen Marius, at whose house in N. Y. City the will is signed.

762 (H 3) 1704 Decbr. 15 1707 (*Torn*)

HARDING, Henry, of the Parish of St. Georges, Barbadoes, now in New York City. Wife Elizabeth, daughter Isabella, goddaughter Isabella, da. of aunt Jean Maverick of Barbadoes, cousin George, the son of John Barry of Barbadoes, cousins William, Thoms and Mary, children of Capt. Thomas Speight of Barbadoes, Jacob Drayton "my present writer (? blotted) on the Island of Barbadoes," Charles Egerton sen. of Barbadoes and his son Charles Egerton, cousin Grace, wife of Barne Cusens of N. Y. City. Real estate on the Island of Barbadoes, in New York and New Jersey, personal property. Executors the wife, Colonel William Battin and Capt. Thomas Speight. Witnesses Dan. Honan, Michael Hauden (?), Thomas Davenport and Edmond Kingsland. Codicil of Febry. 1, 1704-5 makes Elias Boudinot additional executor and is witnessed by Dan. Honan, Wm. Teller and David Jamison. Copy.

763 (H 4) 1710 Novbr. 14 Novbr. 24

HEATHCOTE, George, of Bucks Co., Penna., merchant. Children of dec'd daughter and John Barker of London, sisters Hannah Browne and Anne Lupton in England, Thomas Carlton and three brothers, cousin Caleb Heathcote of New York. Real estate (500 acres near Shrewsbery and elsewhere); personal property. Executor cousin Caleb Heathcote. Witnesses Willoughby Warder, Mary Blackshaw and William Biles. Copy indorsed "The Original Will proved in Pensilvania."

764 (H 5) 1711 Septbr. 19 Septbr. 25 **HAY, William,** of Port Royal, Island of Jamaica, surgeon. Thomas Robinson and Doctor John Dupuy heirs and executors of all real and personal property (plate). Witnesses Thos. Tanner, Stephen Gabaudan and William Perse. Copy, David Lyell of N. Y. City, merchant, attorney for executors.

765 (H 6) 1741-2 Jany. 13 March 3 **HARRIS, Mary,** of Goshen Precinct, Orange Co. Bro. John Harris; sisters Catherine, Elisabeth Leonard, children of dec'd sister Jane Lynsen, nieces Mary Leonard, Jane Leonard. Real estate, houses and lots in N. Y. City, i. e., in the fields, large house at the corner, in Stone Str., near the Old Slip, personal property (a silver tankard, a do. cup, a do. large spoon, six do. teaspoons, three gold rings, a do. necklace, a pair of do. buttons and two do. of earrings). Executors brothers-in-law Rev. Eabenezar Pemberton and Rev. Silas Leonard. Witnesses William ffinn, Daniel Everett and John Stephenson. See infra, No. 769.

766 (H 7) 1718 Decbr. 14 1719 Octbr. 12 **HONYWELL, Israel,** of the Town of Westchester. Wife Mary, da. Sarah, and Mary Baxter, sons Israel and Samuel. Real and personal estate. Executors the wife and son Israel. Witnesses John Mash, James Allisson and Daniel Clarke. Copy.

767 (H 8) 1723 Septbr. 2 1727 May 1 **HANSEN, Hendrik,** of Albany City, yeoman, Wife Deborah, sons Hans, Nicolas, Peter and Richard, daughters Deborah, wife of Jacob Beekman and Maria Hansen. Lots in Albany City, farmland on the Maquase River over against Tionondoroga, lots in Schenectady, land on E. side of Hudson R. between Nuttenhoek Kil

and Marmahits Kil, land on Canada Creek near Anthony's Nose, personal property. Executors the wife and sons Hans, Peter and Nicolas. Witnesses Johannes Pruyn, Jacob Staats, Jacob Lansing, Robert Livingston junior. Seal.

768 (H 9) 1723 Octbr. 20 1724-5 March 11. Dutch

HEERMANS, Jan senior, of Kingston, Ulster Co. Daughter Margarieta, children of dec'd son Jan, vizt: Jacob, Jan and Engeltie, wife of Cornelis Elmendorf, sons Hendricus and Andries. Real and personal estate. Executors the two sons. Witnesses Tobias van Bueren, Barent Nukrik (Newkerk), Willem Swart and Wm. Nottingham.

769 (H 10) 1730 Aug. 29

HARRIS, John, of N. Y. City, baker. Wife Jane, daughters Elizabeth, Mary, Catherine, wife of Rev. Ebenezer Pemberton, Jane, wife of Gideon Lynsen, son John. Real and personal property. Executors the wife, son John and son-in-law Rev. Ebenezer Pemberton. Witnesses Johannes Hyer, Edward Gatehouse and Richd. Nicholls. Copy, Vide No. 765.

770 (H 11) 1732 Septbr. 18 1739 April 7

HOGAN, William and wife Martiena, of Albany City. Sons Jurrian, William and Daniel, daughters Mary, wife of Edward Williams, Margaret, wife of Derrick Hunn, Hannah, wife of Folckert Douw jun., and Jude, wife of Abraham Pelts, six grandchildren. Real and personal property. Executors sons Daniel and William and son-in-law Edward Williams. Witnesses Thomas Williams, Tobyas Ryckman and John Beasley.

771 (H 12) 1733 Septbr. 13 1743 June 16

HAERRING, Cozyn, of Tapan, Orange Co., yeoman. Wife Marytie, son John, daughters Maretie, wife of Johannes Boogert, Grietie, wife of Jacobus Demarest, children of dec'd da. Mariah, vizt: Gerret, Cornelius and Willempie Eckessen. Real and personal estate. Executors the wife and son John. Witnesses David Demarest, Jacob Flierboom and John Fleerboom.

772 (H 13) 1734 Aug. 3 **HARRIS, Jane,** of N. Y. City, widow. Son John, daughters Jane, wife of Gideon Lynsen, Catherine, wife of Ebenezer Pemberton, Elizabeth and Mary, William Smith, son of da. Catherine Pemberton. Lot in the Commons of N. Y. City near the Freshwater, personal property. Executors David Abeel and Richard Ray. Witnesses Peter Zenger, Jesse Defforeest and Henry Deforreest. Copy made Decbr. 12, 1759. See No. 769.

773 (H 14) 1736 April 16 1750 June 27 **HERINGH, Peter,** of Tappan, Orange Co., yeoman. Wife Margaret, children Abraham, Elbert, Margeret, Pietertie, Breckje, Jeannetie, Catherine and Claesje, grandchildren Peter and Richard Truman. Real and personal estate (a "great nether Dutch bible"). Executors the wife and brother Abraham Heringh. Witnesses Johannes Fardon of Dutchess Co., farmer, Jacop Fardon and Johannes Ferdon.

774 (H 15) 1738 Jany. 30 1743-4 March 6 **HOGENCOMP, John,** of Orange Town, Orange Co., yeoman. Wife Gerritje, sons Minard, Honnes and Martynes, daughters Catharina, Jannetje, wife's children vizt: Flowrus, Tunes and Wilhelmus Krom. Real and personal estate. Executors the wife and the three sons. Witnesses Fridericus Muzelius, Myndert Hogencamp and Gabriel Ludlow jun.

775 (H 16) 1742-3 Febry. 13 1743 May 4 **HEUY (Hughy) Robert,** of Wallkil Precinct, Ulster Co., merchant. Wife Annevosall, sons James and John, three daughters, the youngest child Margaret. Real and personal estate. Executors Jeacobas Bruyn jun. and Charles Clinton. Witnesses Johannes Miller, Johannis Neukerk and Adam Graham.

776 (H 17) 1743-4 Febry. 25 1744 May 8 **HOFFMAN, Zacharias,** of Shawangunk, Ulster Co., yeoman. Children Zacharias, Jacob, Geertruyd, wife of Nathaniel du Bois, Ida, wife of Cornelius Bruyn, Janneke, wife of William Roosenkrans, Margaret, wife of

Thomas Jansen and Ida, granddaughter Ester Roosenkrans. Homefarm, land on Shawangunk Kil, on Mary Kil, in Graham and Griggs' Patent on Hudson R., mill on the Wallkil, land at Newburgh and in Kingston Corporation. Executors son Zacharias and sons-in-law Cornelius Bruyn and Nathaniel du Bois. Witnesses Yosua Smedes, Cornelius Schoonmaker jun. and J. Bruyn jun.

777 (H 18) 1745-6 March 1 1748 Jany. 4 **HAGERMAN, Francis** jun. of Nine Partners, Dutchess Co., blacksmith. Father Francis and mother heirs and executors. Witnesses William Gay and John Gay.

778 (H 19) 1747 Septbr. 25 1760 Septbr. 15 French **HASBROUCK, Jacob,** of New Paltz, Ulster Co. Wife Esterre, sons Benjamin, Isaac and Jacob. Real and personal estate. Executors the wife and the three sons. Witnesses Samuel Bevier, Daniel Hasbroucq and Yohannis Matyse Lou of New Paltz, blacksmith.

778a (H 20) 1748-9 March 4 1765 March 19 **HALLOCK, William,** of Brookhaven, Suffolk Co., yeoman. Wife Dinah, sons Jesse, William, Richard and David, daughters, Mary wife of Wm. Long, Dinah, Sarah and Elizabeth. Real and personal estate. Executors the wife and son Jesse. Witnesses Samuel Davis, George Davis and Jesse Willits. Copy.

778b (H 21) 1750 March 23 Octbr. 17 Dutch **HEERMANSE, Hendrikus,** of Rynbeek Precinct, Dutchess Co. Wife Antje, son Hendrikus, Philippus, Wilhelmus, Anderies, daughters Margriet, wife of Jacobus Ostrander ("given to drink") and Jannetje, wife of Cornelius Oosterander. Real and personal estate. Executors the four sons. Witnesses Hendrikes Sleght jun., Petrus van Aken, Andries Heermans (bro. of testator), and Jan Eltinge.

778c (H 22) 1752 Febry. 15 1754 Last Tuesday in April. **HOFMAN, Haramanus,** of Orange Co. Wife Gertruye, sons Haramanus and Jury, daughters Crestena, Rachel, Catrena Snider and Laya Geslar. Real and personal property. Executors Lambert Smith, Abraham

Onderdonck and Johannes Snedeker. Witnesses Johannis Mudge, Peter Geslar and Willem Fenton.

778d (H 23) 1752 March 10 1772 May 5 **HARINGH, Abraham,** of Orange Co., yeoman. Wife Derica, sons Abraham, Daniel, Cornelius, daughters Margaret Demories, Braca Ferdon, Rachel. Homefarm and other lands in Orange Co., land on Hackensack Creek, personal property. Executors three sons. Witnesses Casparis Mebie, Cornelis Meyer of Orange Co., farmer and John Dewint.

779 (H 24) 1753 Febry. 3 —— **HOGG, Rebecca,** of N. Y. City, widow. Daughter Margaret, wife of William Flanagan, from whom she lives separated, sister Rachel Boswell, whose husband lives in the West Indies, John Beekman, the son of widow Boulla, John Bard. Real and personal estate. Executors John Beekman, John Bard and Benjamin Nicoll. Witnesses John Tuder, Peter Middleton and Abr'm van Deursen jun. Copy.

780 (H 25) 1753 Septbr. 12 1754 Febry. 13 **HINCHMAN, Obeidiah,** of Jamaica, Queens Co., Children Thomas, Ann, Elizabeth, Obeidiah, John and Sarah. Real and personal estate. Executors son Thomas and cousin John Willet jun. of Flushing. Witnesses B. Hinchman, John Waters and Robart Hinchman. Copy.

781 (H 26) 1753 Jany. 15 Febry. 12 **HAFF, Lawrence,** of Crum Elbow, Dutchess Co., farmer. Wife Hannah, children Ellis, Susannah, Isaac, Elizabeth and William. Real and personal property. Executors the wife, father Jacob Haff, brothers Joseph and Jacob Haff and William Humfry. Witnesses Jacob Haight, Martines Wiltse and Hendrick Cole.

782 (H 27) 1754 Novbr. 20 1756 Decbr. 22 **HERTELL, Christian,** of New Windsor, Ulster Co. Son John, John, son of Amos Helms of N. Y. City. Glasshouse at New Windsor and other real estate, personal property. Executors bro.-in-law Cornelius Tiebout

of the Out Ward, N. Y. City, Hewark van Vlack of N. Y. City, merchant and Charles Clinton of Ulster Co. Witnesses John Thompson of Ulster Co. storekeeper, John Kennon and Frederic Melcher.

783 (H 28) 1754 Novbr. 24 1755 Jany. 9 **HARRIS, William,** of Orange Co. Wife Abegiel, daughters Mary (Mercy ?), Sarah, da.-in-law Jean and other children. Wife has been married before. Real and personal estate. Executor Richard Edsall jun. Witnesses Joseph Hercull of Goshen Prect., yeoman, Israel Wood and Daniel Simkeins.

784 (H 29) 1754 July 26 1756 Aug. 17 **HALENBEEK, Casper Jansen,** of Loonenburgh, Albany Co., yeoman. Wife Maddalena, sons Jan Caspersen, Merten, William, daughters Mary, wife of Johannis Klaw and Rachel, wife of Jacob Halenbeek, granddaughter Catrine Klaw, grandson Casper, son of Jan Caspersen, grandson Casper, son of Merten, grandda. Catrine, da. of Jacob Halenbeek, grandson Casper, son of William. Farm at Coxsakje, homefarm on the Flats, share in Loonenburgh or Coniskeek Patent and land at Freehold, Albany Co., personal property (house bible). Executors the wife and son Merten. Witnesses Nicholas Pare, Daniel Pare, both of Albany Co., yeomen and Jacob Freese.

785 (H 30) 1756 Novbr. 8 1759 Febry. 12 **HOLLAND, Edward,** of N. Y. City, merchant. Wife Frances, son Henry, daughters Magdalen Mary Nicoll, Jane and Elizabeth, grandson Edward Nicoll. Land near Schoharie, Albany Co., and other real estate, personal property (plate). Executors brother Henry Holland and son-in-law Benjamin Nicoll. Witnesses Theod. van Wyck, Cornelius Duane and Anthony Abramsen. Seal.

786 (H 31) 1756 March 10 1757 April 25 **HANSEN, Hans,** of Albany City, merchant. Wife Sarah, sons Peter, Johannis, grandda. Sarah, only child of dec'd eldest son Hendrick. Real and personal property. Executors the wife and the two sons. Witnesses Jacob

Lansing jun., Anthony G. van Schaick and Johannis Knickerbacker.

787 (H 32) 1756 May 13 Novbr. 5 **HARKER, Joseph,** of Orange Co., yeoman. Wife Jeann, Garrardus Townson. Real and personal property. Executor Richard Edsall jun. Witnesses Richard Edsall, Richard Johnson and John Minthorn.

788 (H 33) 1757 June 23 — **HOLT, William,** of N. Y. City, *merranr*. Brothers Ralph and John Holt, sisters Susannah and Mary Holt. Real and personal property. Executors bro. Ralph and Joseph Danlafs of N. Y. City, carpenter. Incomplete copy.

789 (H 34) 1757 Novbr. 8 — **HORTON, Joseph,** of White Plains, Westchester Co., yeoman. Daughters Bethia, Ann, Pashance, children of dec'd da. Mary, sons William, Joseph, Azariah and Ambros. Homefarm, farm in Cortlandt Manor, personal property. Incomplete copy.

790 (H 35) 1757 April 20 1767 Febry. 21 **HAINS, Benjamin** senior, of Wallkil Prect., Ulster Co., yeoman. Children Susannah Goaldsmith, who has son Benjamin and da. Susannah, Nathan, Benjamin, David and Samuel, grandchildren vizt: Susannah, da. of son Benjamin, Abagail, da. of David, David and Benjamin, sons of Samuel, daughter-in-law Susannah, wife of Samuel Hains. Homefarm and personal property. Executor son Samuel. Witnesses William Stitt, John Perry, both of Wallkil Prect., yeomen, and John Thompson.

791 (H 36) 1757 Octbr. 26 Decbr. 22 French **HARBORD, Alexander,** Captain 4th Bat. Royal Americans, a native of Switzerland, now at Albany in camp. The poor of Albany, Lieut. Gallot, Samuel Coigny, innkeeper at the Hague, Holland, children of David Fouetter of New York. Personal property. No executor named, administration granted to Daniel Christian Fueter of N. Y. City, goldsmith. Witnesses A.

Delliend, Samuel Engell, Quarter Master, and George Turnbull, Lieut. Royal Americans, by whose testimony this nuncupative will was proved at N. Y. City.

792 (H 37) 1757 May 29 1758 Jany. 15 **HAFF, Jacob** junior, of Crum Elbow Prect., Dutchess Co. Wife Mergit, sons Jacob, William and Lawrence, daughters Anna, Elisabeth. Land in lot No. 10 Great 9 Partners, personal property. Executors brothers-in-law Goris Storm and Thomas Noxon, brother Joseph Haff and Peter Storm. Witnesses Isaac Germond, James Germond and James Doughty. Vide No. 781.

793 (H 38) 1758 March 9 1767 Febry. 19 **HOPKINS, Stephen,** of Crum Elbow Prect., Dutchess Co. Wife Jemima, sons Noah, Roswell, Michel, Stephen, Benjamin and Ruban. Real and personal estate. Executor son Roswell. Witnesses Ephraim Paine, Enoch Slosson, and Elisbeth Lyman (at date of proof wife of Nathaniel Pinney of Amenia Prect., yeoman).

794 (H 39) 1758 Aug. 19 Septbr. 5 **HAFF, Lawrence,** of Rumbouts Prect., Dutchess Co., yeoman. Wife Sarah, children Winche, Anthony, Peter, Lawrence, Susannah, John and Mary. Real and personal property. Executors Peter Monfort, William Roe and Joseph Thirsten. Witnesses Johannes de Wit, Justice of the Peace, Cornelius Luyster and Gerrett Noortstrant.

795 (H 40) 1758 May 22 Octbr. 19 **HELM, Willam** junior, of Gorshen, Orange Co., yeoman. Wife Elesebeth, sons William and Vinsent. Real and personal estate. Executors the wife and bro. Finnias Helm. Witnesses James Tuthill of Orange Co., farmer, Benjamin Strong and Selah Strong.

796 (H 41) 1759 July 12 1769 May 11 **HARDENBERGH, Charles,** of Kingston, Ulster Co. Wife Catherine, children Johannes and Catherine. Real and personal estate. Executors father Johannis Hardenbergh and father-in-law Petrus Smedus.

Witnesses Adam Persen, tailor, Dirk Wynkoop jun., merchant, both of Kingston, and Wilh. Mancius.

797 (H 42) 1759 May 19 1762 April 28 **HALLSTED, Jonah,** of Orange Co., yeoman. Wife Martha, sons Caleb, Jonah, John, Benjamin, daughters Martha, Sarah Gurney, Hannah Coe, Abigail van der Voort. Real and personal property. Executors sons Caleb, Jonah and John and son-in-law John Coe. Witnesses Thomas Hallsted, Henry Hallsted and Gershom Rose.

798 (H 43) 1760 Octbr. 28 1771 April 30 **HESS, Johannes,** of Canajohary, Albany Co., farmer. Wife Margaret, sons Johan, Friderick, Dewald (?) and Daniel, three daughters. Real and personal property. No executor named, eldest son Johannes appointed administrator. Witnesses Andries Reber of Canagorie, farmer, Philipp Helmer and Johs. Bellinger.

799 (H 44) 1761 Octbr. 10 1764 Febry. 11 **HUTCHINGS, Richard,** of North Castle, Westchester Co. Wife Dinah, children Pheby, Sarah, Isaac, Jacob and John. Real and personal estate. Executors the wife, James Hunter and Zepheniah Birdsill. Witnesses Peter Huggeford, Hezekiah Kinnicutt and Caleb Huestis, schoolmaster. Copy.

800 (H 45) 1761 June 17 1762 Jany. 4 **HOLLING, Elisabeth,** of Albany City. Brother Barnardus Bratt, niece Jannitie, da. of bro. Gerrit Bratt. Personal estate. Executors John Lansing, Jacob van Schaick and John van Aelen, all of Albany City. Witnesses Isaac Swits, skipper, Gisbert Marselis and Abrm. Yates, attorney-at-law.

801 (H 46) 1761 Febry. 6 1762 July 31 **HOLLAND, Hitchen,** of Rensselaerswyck Colony, gentleman. Sons John Còllins and Philipp, daughters Margarett and Jane, wife of Henry van Schaack. Real and personal estate. Executor son-in-law Henry van Schaack and his wife and Volkert P. Douw. Witnesses Barnardus Brat junior of Albany City, yeoman, John Rostine and Johs. van der Heyden.

802 (H 47) 1762 Novbr. 23 1763 Septbr. 3 **HAASBROOK, Benjamin,** of Rumbout Prect., Dutchess Co. Wife Jonetje, sons Daniel, Francis, Benjamin and Jacob, daughters Mary, wife of John Halsted and Hettje. Real and personal estate. Executors William van Wyck, Doctor Theodorus van Wyck and Cornelius van Wyck, all of Rumbout Prect. Witnesses Rev. Chauncey Graham, John Carman and John van Vlackeren jun.

803 (H 48) 1762 May 12 — **HOPSON, Samuel,** of the Ferry, Brookland Township, Kings Co., victualler. Wife Alice, daughters Ruth, Rebecca, Jane, Sarah and Mary, son Samuel. Real and personal estate (5 silver spoons). Executors Jacob de Beavois and Robert Gilmore, both of Brookland. Witnesses Benjamin Everit, John Cox and Noah Rhodes. Copy made Aug. 10, 1764.

804 (H 49) 1763 April 23 Aug. 15 **HOORNBEEK, Cornelius,** of Rochester Township, Ulster Co. Wife Annatje, sons Lodewick, Jacob, Hendricus, da. Mary, wife of Jacob Hasbrouck, children of dec'd da. Ariaentie, late wife of Cornelius Schoonmaker, vizt: Cornelius, Abraham, Isaac and Mary. Real and personal estate. Executors the wife, the three sons, son-in-law Jacob Hasbrouck and cousin Johannis Oosterhoudt jun. Witnesses Mattheus Kortright, Johannis Hoornbeek, both of Ulster Co., yeomen, and Joseph Gasherie.

805 (H 50) 1764 May 4 1767 May 26 **HOGAN, Jurian,** and wife Maria, of Albany City. Children William, Anna, wife of John Trotter, Eva, wife of Dirck Becker, Margaret, wife of Johannis van Valkenburgh, Alida, widow of Andris van Schack, Maria and Susannah, wife of John de Gardimo, da. of dec'd son Marten, vizt: Maria, son John dead. House and lot on W. side of Pearl Str., 2d Ward, land on Foxes Creek, personal property. Wife's father has been Johannis Beekman. Executors son William, and John Trotter. Wit-

nesses Ino. R. Bleeker, Henry I. Bogert and Henry Merselis. Also in Albany Co. Records, Wills, I., p. 307.

806 (H 51) 1764 June 8 1776 April 3

HUN, Johannes, of Albany City. Daughter Else, wife of Philipp Lansing, son Thomas, grandchildren Annatie Hun and Annatie Lansing. House and lot in Albany, land at Sakondaga, personal property (a large bible). Executors son Thomas and son-in-law Phil. Lansing. Witnesses Abraham Douw, Dirk Hun and Abrm. Yates jun.

807 (H 52) 1765 March 14 1783 Decbr. 1

HELMER, Gottfried, of Canajoharie, Albany Co. (Second) wife Ann Margaretha, son Leonhart, sons by second wife Johannes, Godfried, Joost and Henry, daughters (apparently also by second wife) Elizabeth, Margaretha, Christina and Catherina. Real and personal property. Executors Daniel Miller and Jacob Kraus, who refusing to act, John Helmer of Canajoharie Distr. Montgomery Co., yeoman, son of testator, is appointed administrator. Witnesses Andreas Reber, I. Daniel Miller and Jacob Krausz.

808 (H 53) 1765 April 9 1770 March 30

HOORNBEEK, Lodewyck, of Rochester, Ulster Co. Mother Annatje Hoornbeek, wife Naomi, sons Philippus, Cornelius, Isaac, Jacob, Lodewyck, Hendricus and da. Maria. Real and personal property. Executor sons Philippus and Cornelius, brothers Jacob and Hendrick Hoornbeek and bro.-in-law Jacob Hasbrouck. Witnesses Jacob Tornaer of Rochester, labourer, Cornelius Chambers and Jacobus Turnaar. Vide No. 804.

809 (H 54) 1766 March 4 1769 March 6 Dutch

HEERMANS, Andreas, of Rhinebeck Prect., Dutchess Co., farmer, "being aged." Children of dec'd eldest son Jan, vizt: Jan, Abraham, Goze, Jacob and Jacomyntie, sons Jacob, Gerrit, Petrus, Hendricus, Wilhelmus, Nicolaas and Philipp, daughters Clara and

Catharina, son of dec'd da. Jannetje, vizt: Philipp Heermans. Farm on S. side of Wappaensche Creek (Wappingers Kil?) and other land, personal property. Executors sons Jacob, Gerrit, Petrus and Hendricus. Witnesses Cornelius Fynhout, Aarent Fynhout, both of Rhinebeck, yeomen, and Christian Schultz.

810 (H 55) 1766 Decbr. 29 1775 Octbr. 18 **HOGHTEYLING, Wilhelmus jun.,** of Kingston, Ulster Co., esquire. Wife Blandina, sons Philipp and Abraham, daughter Ariaentie. House and land in Kingston Corporation, house and lot in Kingston Village, personal property. Executors the two sons and Abraham Low of Kingston. Witnesses Christophel Kierstede jun., Johannis van Bunschoten and George Clinton. Sealed with Clinton coat-of-arms.

811 (H 56) 1767 June 5 1771 April 10 Dutch **HOORNBEEK, Tobias,** of Rochester, Ulster Co. Wife Elisabeth, sons Elisa, Warnaer, Gideon, Joel, da. Maria, wife of Lawrence Hoornbeek. Real and personal property. Executors the four sons. Witnesses Hendr. Sleght, Cornelius Swart jun. and Willem Eltinge.

812 (H 57) 1767 July 10 1768 Novbr. 25 **HUNTLY, John,** of Charlotte Prect., Dutchess Co., yeoman. Wife Lowes, daughter Elisabeth, sons Williams, Raner and John. Real and personal property. Executors the wife and Joshua Champion of said Prect., yeoman. Witnesses Joseph Green, Zophar Green, blacksmith and William Doughty.

813 (H 58) 1768 May 7 1770 March 1 Dutch **HASBROUCK, Jan,** of New Paltz, Ulster Co. Wife Rachel van Wagenen, eldest son and two other children, not named. Real and personal estate. Executors father-in-law Johannis van Wagenen, brothers Abraham, Jacobus and Petrus Hasbrouck. Witnesses Abraham Ein, Johannes Lefever, both of New Paltz, farmers, and Abraham Krom, of Hurley, cooper.

814 (H 59) 1768 May 9 1770 May 15 **HAGEMAN, John,** of Flatbush, Kings Co., farmer. Greatnephew John, son of Adrian Hageman jun., niece Heatrich, spinster, da. of Adrian Hageman senior. Real and personal estate. Executor Andrew Gautier of N. Y. City, house carpenter. Witnesses John Elliot, John Gelston, of N. Y. City, house carpenter, Jonathan Skinner and John C. Knapp. Copy.

815 (H 60) 1769 April 25 Decbr. 9 **HUGHSON, George,** of Dutchess Co. Wife Susannah, sons James and Joshua. Real and personal estate. Executors the wife and sons. Witnesses Thomas Huson, Eborn Haight, both of Dutchess Co., yeomen, and Robert Weeks.

816 (H 61) 1770 Febry. 6 April 23 **HUYCK, Andries B.,** of Kinderhook, Albany Co. Brother Johannes Huyck, sons of dec'd bro. Jacobus, vizt: Arent and Burger Huyck, Burger, son of Dirk Huyck, Burger, son of Burger Huyck, Andries, son of William Clawson, Moyaca, da. of Jacobus Huyck dec'd, Moyaca, Bata and Rachel, da. of Dirk Huyck. Real and personal property (4 silver spoons). Executors Dirk Huyck, Peter B. Vosburgh and Elizabeth Huyck. Witnesses Johs. Schrom, of Kinderhook, tavern keeper, Elizabeth Huyck and Andries L. Huyck, farmer. Executors dead at time of proof Aaron Huyck, of Kinderhook, yeoman, nephew of testator is appointed administrator.

817 (H 62) 1770 June 13 Novbr. 21 **HULSE, Simon,** of Orange Co. Wife Charity, sons Silas, James and Jonas, daughters Anner, Charity, and Martha. Real and personal estate. Executors the wife and son Silas. Witnesses William Knap jun., George Little and James Little, yeoman.

818 (H 63) 1771 April 5 1783 Octbr 4. **HERCHHEIMER, Johan Jost,** of Burnetsfield, Albany Co. Wife Catherine, sons Nicholas, John, George, Henry, Jost. Real and personal property. Executors sons Nicholas, Henry, and Jost junior. Witnesses Thos. Porter, Han Jost Herchheimer jun. and

Wm. Petry of the German Flats, Tryon Co., surgeon. Proved in Tryon Co.

819 (H 64) 1771 Septbr. 22 1761 (*sic.*) Octbr. 1

HOWELL, James, of Goshen Prect., Orange Co. Wife Juliana, sons Joshua, William, Thomas, daughters Mary and Christion. Real and personal estate. Executors Samuel Gale and John Evirett. Witnesses Daniel Denton, John Kinner and Thomas Denton. Probate dated July 2, 1772.

820 (H 65) 1771 Jany. 14 July 15

HARCOURT, Richard, of Newburgh Prect., Ulster Co. Mother Esther Harcourt, five daughters not named, sons Nathaniel and John. Real and personal estate. Executors son Nathaniel, John Mory and John Yong. Witnesses Elijah Lewis, mariner, Zadick Lewis and Peninnah Springer.

821 (H 66) 1771 Septbr. 22 1772 March 14

HARDENBERGH, Abraham, of Guilford, Ulster Co., esquire. Wife Mary, sons Johannis, Nicholas and Elias, daughters Sarah, wife of Charles W. Brodhead, Marritie and Rachel. Wife was da. of Nicholas Roosa and wife Sarah. Real and personal estate. Executors sons Johannis, Nicholas and Elias, son-in-law Charles W. Brodhead and stepson Joseph Gasherie. Witnesses John Terwilger, Peter Deyoo jun., both of New Paltz Prect., yeomen, and Daniel Freer jun.

822 (H 67) 1772 Febry. 19 1786 June 14

HOOGLAND, William, of Rombout Precinct, Dutchess Co., farmer. Wife Altje, sons Dirck, William and Abraham, daughters Neeltje, Altje, Maria, Dinah, Antje, Susannah. Real and personal property. Executors Mathys Lyster, Jacobus Swartwout and Stephen D. Derye. Witnesses Isaac Adriance, Jacob Griffin, both of Dutchess Co., farmers, and Dirck Brinkerhoff junior.

823 (H 68) 1772 Decbr. 3 1773 July 1

HUYCK, Dirk, of Kinderhook, Albany Co. Wife Sarah, son Burger, daughters Rachel, Bata and Majeke. Real and personal estate. Executors the wife, brothers-in-law William Klauw, Cornelis van Deusen, and Matthew

Goes jun. Witnesses H. v. Schaaik, Johannes Huyck, and Elizabeth Huyck. Vide No. 816.

824 (H 69) 1773 Jany. 5 1774 Novbr. 18 **HOGAN, Isaac,** of Albany City, blacksmith. Wife Mary sole heiress and executrix of real and personal estate. Witnesses Jelles de Garmo, shoemaker, Harmen Hun and Jacob de Garmo.

825 (H 70) 1773 Febry. 25 June 11 **HOLBROOK, Nathaniel,** of Hartford, Cumberland Co., N. Y. Wife Eunice, six sons, not named, and three daughters of whom only the name of the eldest, Sarah, is given. Real and personal estate. Executors the wife and Eleazer Robinson of Hartford. Witnesses Charles Hill, John Slapp jun. and Ino. Wheatley.

826 (H 71) 1773 Septbr. 4 1774 March 9 **HOFF, Daniel,** of Tryon Co., farmer. Mother Cornelia Hoff, brothers Nicholas and Burgun, sister Jane. Real and personal property. Executor the mother. Witnesses William Schuyler, Willem Mambrut and Maria Mambrut.

827 (H 72) 1774 Decbr. 2 —— **HARSING, Johannis,** of Bloomingdale, Out Ward, N. Y. City, farmer. Children Jacob, Cornelius, Cornelia Maria and Ann. The Dutch Church at Haerlem is to have a large Dutch bible. Mother-in-law Ann Cowenover is mentioned as still living. Real and personal estate. Executors son Cornelius and Martinus Schoonmaker. Witnesses Richard Somarindyke, Tunis Somandyke and Hendrick van Bramer. Copy made July 8, 1775.

828 (H 73) 1774 May 18 July 4 **HOLT, John,** of Westminster, Cumberland Co., N. Y., gentleman. Wife Sarah, daughters Hannah Spencer and Sarah, son John. Real and personal estate. Executor the son. Witnesses Ephraim Wilcocks, William Crook, both of Westminster, yeomen, and Noah Sabin.

829 (H 74) 1774 March 17 1775 March 17 **HULSE, Benjamin,** of Hempstead, Queens Co. Wife Rebecca, daughters Rebecca, Hannah and Phebe, sons John and Richard. Real and personal estate. Executors Valentine Hewlitt Peters and Jehu Mott. Witnesses Israel Smith, James Searing and David Batty, yeoman. Copy.

830 (H 75) 1774 May 5 1785 Decbr. 1 **HOLSTED, Richard,** of Goshen, Orange Co. Wife Esther, sons Richard, Joseph, Isaiah, Benjamin and Michael, daughter Sarah Seely, grandson Samuel Holsted. Land in Wawayanda Patent; personal property. Executors the wife and sons Joseph and Michael. Witnesses Henry David, Daniel Everett and Susannah Hue (?).

831 (H 76) See **MOYR, Philipp Hendrick.**

832 (H 77) 1774 Oct. 8 Octbr. 26 **HALLSTED, John,** of Haverstraw Precinct, Orange Co., farmer. Wife Mary, daughters Elisabeth and Sarah, son Jonah. Real and personal property. Executors John Coe and William Coe. Witnesses Wm. Smith, of Kakiat, merchant, Jonah Hallsted of same place, miller, and John Seaman.

833 (H 78) 1774 Febry. 26 Octbr. 26 **HALLSTED, Caleb,** of Haverstraw Precinct, Orange Co., farmer. Brother Benjamin Hallsted, daughters Martha, Margret, Abigal, Serah, Hannah, Phebey, Elizabeth, Mary, Rachel and Cathrine. Real and personal estate. Executors William Coe and Thunis Cooper. Witnesses John Hallsted, Peter van der Voort and Cornelius Smith, the last two of Kakiat, yeomen.

834 (H 79) 1774 Septbr. 3 Septbr. 27 **HAMBLY, Joseph,** of Cornwall Precinct, Orange Co. Nuncupative will leaving all property to Thomas Swafford, to the exclusion of a brother in England. Proved by the testimony of Ebenezer Seely of Cornwall Prect., yeoman, Salomon Teed and Jemimah Tidd.

835 (H 80) 1774 Septbr. 21 1776 April 29 **HOLMES, Soloman,** of Bedford, Westchester Co., farmer. Wife Rachel, daughter Rachel Mills, other heirs of equal shares are Rebeccah Mills and Dorothy Holmes. Real and personal property. Executors the wife, Ebenezar Miller and Peter Fleming. Witnesses Increse Miller, farmer, John Elliott and Daniel Holmes. Copy.

836 (H 81) 1774 July 5 1776 Jany. 16 **HAWKINGS, Benjamin,** of Brookhaven, Suffolk Co., yeoman. Wife Desire, sons William H(avens), Benjamin, Eleazar, daughters Sarah, Desire and Martha. Real and personal estate. Executors the wife and son William Havens Hawkings. Witnesses Joseph Denton, Nathaniel Denton, both of Suffolk Co., yeomen, and Elizabeth Longbotham. Copy.

837 (H 82) 1774 April 9 June 7 **HILL, William,** of Hanover Prect., Ulster Co., hatter. Wife Sarah, da. Mary, son William. Brother Samuel to have his passage to Ireland paid, if he wants to go. Real and personal estate. Executors the wife and Robert Monnel. Witnesses David Monnell, Francis Lush of Ulster Co., labourer, and William Steuart.

838 (H 83) 1764 April 23 1776 May 4 **HONEYWELL, Gilead,** of Westchester Borough, Westchester Co. Wife Mercy, son Gilbert, daughters Elizabeth and Mary, Mary, wife of Joseph Pell, Thaddeus and Alpheus, sons of Joseph Avery. Real and personal estate. Executors the wife, James Ferres and Ebenezar Haviland. Witnesses Philipp Palmer, farmer, Josiah Quinby, storekeeper, and Solomon Hunt. Codicil of April 7, 1775, makes provision for son James, born since, and adds John Ferris as executor. Witnesses Benjamin Ferris, Samuel de la Plaine and Elijah Pell. Copy.

839 (H 84) 1775 Novbr. 22 1783 June 17 **HUNTER, Robert,** of Shawangunk Precinct, Ulster Co., yeoman. Wife Anne, da. of James Neelly, sons James, John, David, William, Mattheus, Samuel and Robert, daughters Lilly and others not named. Real

and personal property. Executors son James and Matthew Rea. Witnesses Edward Neely, of New Windsor, farmer, George Knox, of Shawangunk, weaver, and James Fulton.

840 (H 85) 1775 April 6 1779 Novbr. 12 **HAIGHT, Caleb,** senior, of Charlotte Prect., Dutchess Co. Wife Elizabeth, sons Caleb, Benjamin, Josiah and Nathanel, daughters Elizabeth, Abigail and Elanor. Real and personal estate. Executors son Josiah and Caleb Mosher. Witnesses John Nelson and Aaron Haight jun.

841 (H 86) 1775 June 27 1786 May 20 **HOUGHTAILING, John,** senior, of the Little 9 Partners, Dutchess Co., farmer. Wife Yanakee, sons John, Jacob, Isaac, Abraham, Adam and Peter, daughters Yanakee, wife of Ruluff Shearer, and Rachel, wife of William Snider. Real and personal estate. Executors the wife and sons John and Jacob. Witnesses David Bostwick, John Bortell and Hugh Orr, of North East Prect., Dutchess Co., blacksmith.

842 (H 87) 1776 April 1 May 4 **HARRISON, Elizabeth,** of Ulster Co. Daughters Phebe Peterson, Mary Sampson, son Isaac. Real and personal estate. Executors David Corwin sen. and David Moore jun. Witnesses William Denn of Wallkil Prect., yeoman, Mary Moore and Mehitabel Dunning.

843 (H 88) 1776 Decbr. 28 1782 Febry. 9 **HEERMANSE, Evert,** of Rhinebeck Prect., Dutchess Co. Wife Ackamanchee and sister Elizabeth Heermanse heiresses and executrices of all real and personal property. Witnesses Andries P. Heermanse, yeoman, Goze Heermanse and John Coates.

844 (H 89) 1772 Novbr. 24 — **HASBROUCK, Jonathan,** of Newburgh, Ulster Co., merchant. Wife Tryntje, sons Cornelius, Isaac and Jonathan, daughters Rachel and Mary. Real and personal estate. Executors the wife, son Cornelius, bro. Abraham Hasbrouck and Joseph Gasherie. Witnesses

Geo. Clinton, James Gregg and Geo. Denniston. Codicil of Jnly 20, 1776, disposes of newly bought land and is witnessed by Robert Hunter, William Hunter and S. Robinson. Copy.

845 (H 90) 1776 Febry. 29 1782 Decbr. 27 **HUNT, Lewis,** of Dover, Pauldings Prect., Dutchess Co., yeoman. Wife Alice, daughters Susanah Briggs, Mary Stevens and Sarah Hunt. Real and personal estate. Executors Elkana Briggs and Saml. Stevens. Witnesses Ephraim Pray, Ebenezer Preston, both of Paulings Prect., yeomen and Agrippa Martin.

846 (H 91) 1777 Jany. 6 1783 July 23 **HAUCK, Peter,** of Knieskern Dorph, Albany Co. Wife Christina, sons Henrich, Peter, Jacob, daughters Anna, Elisabeth and Catrine. Homefarm and lands on Schoharry River, personal property. Executors brothers-in-law Doctor Jacob Werth and Peter Endors. Witnesses Henrich Simor, Casper Krisler and George T. Reinhard of Albany Co., schoolmaster.

847 (H 92) 1777 Novbr. 9 1783 Septbr. 16 **HOLSAPPEL, Philipp,** of Claverack, Albany Co., yeoman. Wife Gertruy, daughters Maragret and Mary. Real and personal estate. Executors father Johannis Holsapple and Hendrick Klapper. Witnesses Rich'd Esselstyn, esquire, Michael Horton, captain, both of Claverack and Henrich Zeubel.

848 (H 93) 1777 Decbr. 15 1799 Septbr. 4 **HEWSON, John,** of Albany City, cordwainer. Wife Annatie, sons Daniel and Casparus. Real and personal estate. Executors bro. Daniel Hewson and Rutger Bleecker, both of Albany. Witnesses Harms. A. Wendell, Jacob A. Wendell and Rutger Bleecker.

849 (H 94) 1777 Febry. 7 1783 Octbr. 4 **HERCHHEIMER, Nicholas,** of Canajoharie, Tryon Co. Wife Maria, da. of Peter S. Tygert, brothers Henry and John Herchheimer, sisters Elisabeth Barbary, Gertraut, Magdalene, Curtelia, Anna Maria, Elisabeth, Anna and Catharine, nephews Nicholas, Hanjoost, George

and Henry, niece Elisabeth, all children of bro. Henry, nephew Nicholas, son of bro. Hanjoost, godsons Nicholas, son of Peter D. Schuyler, Nicholas, son of Rev. Abraham Rosecrants, Nicholas, son of Peter ten Broeck; Rudolph, son of Rudolph Shoemaker, children of Jurry Henry Bell, vizt: Nicholas, Hanjoost, Anna and Maria, daughters of Rudolph Shoemaker, vizt: Catherine, Elizabeth and Gertraut, godchild Mary Catherine, da. of Werner Tygert, and her sister Magdalene, Nicholas, son of Peter Tygert, Maria, da. of John Tygert, Peter S. Tygert, wife's brother, Johannes Bierhausen, miller. Brother George residuary legatee. Real and personal property (3 silver spoons, four do. teaspoons). Executors Hanyoost Shoemaker, John Eisenlord and John Tygert. Witnesses Johann Jost Koch, George House and Wm. Stine of Canajohary, labourer.

850 (H 95) 1778 Jany. 5 1779 April 13

HOORNBECK, John, of Rochester Township, Ulster Co., esquire. Wife Elizabeth, da. Hannah, nephew Jacob jun., son of bro. Lodewick Hoornbeck. Real and personal estate. Executors bro. Hendricus Hoornbeck, bro.-in-law Jacob Hasbrouck, nephew Jacob Hoornbeck jun. and da. Hannah Hoornbeck. Witnesses Benjamin Merkell of Rochester, farmer, Lauerens Hoornbeck and Christopher Tappen.

851 (H 96) 1778 Aug. 17 1783 Septbr. 9

HERCHHEIMER, Henrich, son of Hon Yost of Burnettsfield, German Flats Distr., Tryon Co. Wife Catharine, sons Han Yost, Nicholas, Abraham, Henry and George, daughters Catherine, Elizabeth, Magdalene, Anna and Gertrude. Land on Lake Coneadrago in Croghans Patent, homefarm, personal property. Executors Ritcut Bligart of Albany City, attorney-at-law, sons Hon Yost and Nicholas. Witnesses Peter Bellinger, of Little Falls, yeoman, Johannes Hess and Isaac Johnson. Supra, No. 818.

852 (H 97) 1778 Febry. 25 1781 April 14 **HOORNBECK, Hendricus,** of Rochester Township, Ulster Co., yeoman. Wife Maria, nephew Cornelius C. Schoonmaker, Cornelius P., son of nephew Phipp, son of bro. Lodewick Hornbeck heirs and executors of real and personal estate. Witnesses Patrick Connolly, Jacob Hoornbeck jun., farmer, and Cornelius Oosterhout jun., carpenter.

853 (H 98) 1778 July 25 1782 Novbr. 18 **HOUCK, Hendrick,** of Schoharie, Albany Co., yeoman. Children of eldest son Peter dec'd, vizt: Hendrick, Peter, Jacob, Elizabeth, Catherine and Anna, daughters Catherine Elizabeth, w. of Harme Sidnigh, Maria Elizabeth, Maria Hester, Catherine and Margaret, children of son Hendrick dec'd, vizt: Jurie, Anna and Hendrick, whose mother's name is Catherine. Homefarm, land at Knieskern Town, Schoharie, personal property. Executors son-in-law Harme Sidnigh of Schoharie and Rutger Bleecker of Albany. Witnesses Ino. R. Bleecker, Barent Bleecker and Abrm. Verplanck.

854 (H 99) 1779 March 30 1784 July 26 **HOWEL, Stephen,** of Cornwall Prect., Orange Co., carpenter. Brother Charles Howel sole heir and executor of real and personal property. Witnesses Mathew Carpenter, Susannah Moffat and Thos. Moffat.

855 (H 100) 1779 May 1 1786 April 26 **HOWEL, Matthew,** of Goshen Prect., Orange Co. Sons Matthew, Theophilus, Philetus, William, daughters Mary, Margaret, Elizabeth and Jane. Real and personal estate. Executors Isaac Ludlow and Coe Gale, who refusing to act, Theophilus, son of testator, is made administrator. Witnesses Enos Smith, blacksmith, Jonathan Smith and John Conner.

856 (H 101) 1779 Aug. 8 1782 May 2 **HAIGHT, Jonathan,** of Fish Kils, Dutchess Co. Wife Elizabeth, children Martha, Samuel, Cornelius, Susan, Jacob and Elizabeth. Real and personal estate. Executors the wife, brother Benjamin Haight of Connecticut, Petrus Bogardus, William van Wyck and Jacob

van Voorheess jun. of Dutchess Co. Witnesses Zacrias van Voorhes, Thomas Skinner and Henry Schenk.

857 (H 102) 1781 May 24 1782 Decbr. 5 **HUTCHINS, John Nathan,** late of N. Y. City, now of Newburgh, Ulster Co., schoolmaster. Wife Mary sole heiress and executrix of "worldly estate." Witnesses Henry Smith, yeoman, Robert Morison, physician, both of Newburgh Precinct, and Wm. Albertson.

858 (H 103) 1781 May — 1782 Octbr. 10 **HAMMOND, Aaron,** of Philipps Town, Albany Co. Wife Meacey, daughters Sarah Creamer and Rebeccah. Real and personal estate. Executors John Dusenberry and Robert Bullis. Witnesses Abraham Holmes of the East Distr., Rensselaerswyck Manor, farmer, Sarah Holmes and Elizabeth O'Neal.

859 (H 104) 1782 Decbr. 21 1784 Jany. 16 **HOGEBOOM, Jeremiah,** of Claverack Distr., Albany Co. Wife Annatie, daughter Christina, wife of Gideon R. Hubbart, son Peter. Real and personal property includes "parts or parcels of the estates of Jurrian van Hoesen and David van Hoesen, both deceased, as I am entitled to in right of my wife." Executor son Peter. Witnesses Thomas Hop, James Hogeboom and Thomas Williams jun. of Claverack, gentleman.

860 (H 105) 1782 Decbr. 15 1783 March 28 **HUBNER (Hevener), Daniel,** of Rhinebeck Precinct, Dutchess Co. Wife Eve, children Susana, Rodia and Elizabeth. Real and personal estate. Executors the wife, her father Hendrick Shup and Lodewick Elsefer. Witnesses Peter Shop, trader, Valentine Trumport and Ananias Cooper.

861 (H 106) 1782 Jany. 22 May 6 **HALL, John,** of Beeckmans Prect., Dutchess Co. Wife ——, John, son of Benjamin Hall, Gideon Hall, Benjamin Hall, William Hall, daughter Mary, wife of

Daniel Ketcham; Abigail, wife of John Mott, Wait, wife of Austin Titus. Real and personal estate. Executors Benjamin, Gideon and William Hall. Witnesses Ebenezer Cary, Physician, Thomas Clements, yeoman, Benjamin Rogers and Abner Scidmore.

862 (H 107) 1782 27th Day 12th Month 1783 Octbr. 30 **HALLOCK, Samuel,** of N. Marlborough Prect., Ulster Co. Wife Sarah, Elijah Hallock, John Hallock, Anna Sands, Phebe Hallock, Deborah Hallock, Foster Hallock, Clement Hallock and James Hallock (probably the children, although not called sons and daughters). Real and personal estate. Gives 3 acres to 9 Partners Monthly Meeting in case they will build a Meeting House. Executors the wife, John Young, Nehemiah Smith, Caleb Merritt and Benjamin Anthony. Witnesses John Moore, John Moore jun. of Marlborough Prect., farmers, and Thomas Hallock.

863 (H 108) 1782 Febry. 19 1786 Septbr. 20 **HARDENBERGH, Johannes,** of Rosendall, Hurly Township, Ulster Co. Sons Johannes and Jacob Rutsen, son of dec'd son Charles, vizt: Johannes C., grandson Johannes H. Meier, da. Rachel, wife of Domine Meier, children of da.-in-law Nensie Riese dec'd, vizt: John, Catie, Pallie, Ellenger, Racel, Benjamin, Pagie, Nensie, Thomas, Harmanus and Elesabet. Real and personal property. Executors sons Johannes and Jacob R. Hardenbergh. Witnesses Abraham Krom of Hurly, cooper, Elesabeth Ca——, Jacob Heermanse of same place, innholder. Very dilapidated document.

864 (H 109) 1782 Octbr. 9 Decbr. 9 **HORTON, Barnabas,** of Goshen, Orange Co., yeoman. Wife Mary, sons Silas, Barnabas, Mathias, da. Mary. Real and personal property. Executors sons Barnabas and Silas. Witnesses Jonathan Swezy, John Taylor and Eusebeus Austin, of Goshen, physician.

865 (H 110) 1783 12th Day 4th Month 1786 March 8

HOAG, David, of the Oblong, Paulings Prect. Dutchess Co. Wife Keziah, sons William, David, Samuel, daughters Hannah and Keziah. Real and personal property. Executors sons William and Samuel. Witnesses Tristram Russell, John Hoag 3d, farmer, and Abel Hoag.

866 (H 111) 1783 April 19 1784 March 11

HOGEBOOM, Peter, of Beekmans Prect., Dutchess Co., farmer. Wife Elizabeth, children John, Jacob, Elizabeth, Sarah, Peter, Margaret, Hannah, James, Polly, and Catrin; Bartho'w Hogeboom, who (they call my son, crossed out) goes by that name. Real and personal estate. Executors the wife and Barth'w Noxon. Witnesses Smiten Tripp, yeoman, Jones D. Long and Samuel Irish.

867 (H 112) 1783 Jany. 6 Septbr. 19 Dutch

HARDICK, Francis, jun., of Claverack, Albany Co. Wife Margarieta, sons William, Pieter and David, daughters Anna Catharina, Maria, Elizabeth, Annatje, Margarieta and Gerritje. Real and personal estate. Executors the wife and sons William and Peter. Witnesses Justus H. van Hoesen of Claverack, Gerrit Hardick and Stephen van Dyck of Coxhacky, esquire.

868 (H 113) 1783 Octbr. 6 1786 Febry. 23

HILTON, Peter, of Sarotogo, Albany Co. Wife ——, son Richard and other children, not named. Real and personal estate. Executors Abraham Eights and Jacobus Vansanti. Witnesses Peter W. Douw, Jacob van Shaick and John Sheperd.

869 (H 114) 1784 June 22 Octbr. 5

HAGEDORN, Jacob, of Rhinebeck Prect. Wife Maritie, sons Peter, Francis, Jacob, Jury, David and Johannis, da. Annatie. Real and personal estate. Executors son Francis, Everardus Bogardus and Isaac Davis. Witnesses John Wels jun., farmer, Ruliff Ostrom and Isaac van Fradenburgh.

870 (H 115) 1784 May 25 1785 Decbr. 19

HARPER, John, of Harpersfield, Tryon Co., gentleman. Wife Rebeccah, da. Abigail, who has a da. Eunice, wife of John Tudle (?), Mary, Margaret and Meriam, sons William, John, Alexander and Joseph. Real and personal estate. Executors son Alexander and son-in-law William McFarland. Witnesses David Earll, Elihu Curtis and Josiah Throop of Johnstown, surveyor.

871 (H 116) 1784 July 13 Septbr. 30

HOWELL, Hezekiah, of Cornwall Prect, Orange Co., esquire. Wife Susanna, sons Hezekiah, Charles, daughters Phebe, Jane, Susanna and Abigail. Homefarm in Blaggs Clove, land in New Windsor Township, Ulster Co., personal property. Executors the wife and son Hezekiah. Witnesses Sylvanus White, Francis Brewster, yeoman, and Anselm Helme.

872 (H 117) 1784 Febry. 6 1785 Jany. 13

HOFFMAN, Anthony, of Kingston, Ulster Co., blacksmith. Wife Catherine, sons Nicholas, Abraham and Anthony, daughters Catherine, Saretie, Jannetie and Maritie, child of da. Annatie dec'd, vizt. Saretie. Houses and lots in Kingston, land in Dutchess Co., personal property. Executors son Anthony and sons-in-law John Addison and Hans Kierstede. Witnesses Cornelius Elmendorph jun., James Roe, both of Kingston, yeomen, and Joseph Gasherie.

873 (H 118) 1784 March 9 1785 July 8

HERMANS, Jacob, of Red Hook, Dutchess Co. Wife Catherina, sons Andrew, John, Jacob, Martin, daughters Neiltie, wife of Peter Cantine, Annatie, wife of Isaac Stoutenburgh and Dorothea. Real and personal property. Executors sons Andrew, John and Jacob. Witnesses Martin Vosburgh, Johannes Klum and Wm. Wheeler, physician.

874 (H 119) 1784 March 19 1786 Septbr. 11

HOGEBOOM, Thomas, of Claverack, Albany Co., yeoman. Wife Albertge, sons Johannes, Lawrance, Cornelias, Bartholomew, Abram, James, da. Janitje and Albertge, children of dec'd da. Sarah Muller, vizt. John and Sarah Muller. Real and personal property. Executors sons Lawrance, Abram and Bartholomew. Witnesses George Weismer, Caty Wiesmer and Peter Wiesmer. Copy.

875 (H 120) 1785 Aug. 11 Aug. 27 **HUEY, James,** of Montgomery Prect., Ulster Co. Wife Mary, da. Mary, an expected child, children of sister Ann, vizt: Leah and Rachel Dubois. Land at Jermantown and in New Windsor Prect., personal property (money in Continental Treasury). Executors Nicholas Hardenbergh of Shawangunk Prect., Abraham Caldwell and William Cross, both of Montgomery Precinct. Witnesses Henry Rump, yeoman, William Ross, labourer, and John Colter, yeoman.

876 (H 121) 1785 Septbr. 7 1786 Novbr. 11 **HALSTED, Jacob,** (of Ulster Co.). Wife Riahel, sons Jacob, John, Iaec (Isac), Aberham and Stphson (? ?). Land in Orange Co. personal property. Executors the wife, son Jacob and Elly Pheleps. Witnesses Robert Ross and Jacob Tremper.

877 (H 122) 1786 12th 7th Month Octbr. 3 **HUESTIS, Jonathan,** of Pawlings Precinct, Dutchess Co. Wife Rachel, son Solomon, Jonathan, Moses, Jacob, Joseph, and Isaac, daughters Mary Butts, Rachel Frost and Phebe Sutton. Real and personal estate. Executors sons Jonathan and Moses Heustis. Witnesses Brittan Tallman, farmer, Gilbert Browne and Alvin Browne.

878 (H 123) 1787 Jany. 13 March 20 **HATHAWAY, Jacob,** of Kinderhook, Columbia Co. Wife Thankful, sons Guilford, Abner, Elisha, Daniel, grandson Cornish, son of Guilford, da. Hulda, wife of Elijah Kent, Ruth, wife of Eleb Phaxon and Lydia. Only money devised. Executors son-in-law Elijah Kent and son Daniel. Witnesses Samuel Clark, yeoman, Ralph Austin and John Nichols Berry.

879 (H 124) **HOFFMAN, Anna C.,** of New York, missing.

880 (H 125) 1799 June 3 Aug. — **HANSEN, Dirck,** of Greenbush, Rensselaer Co. Wife Helena, and children not named. Real and personal property. Executors the wife, Wm. Beeckman of Schoharie Co., esquire, Jacob Staats of Rensselaer Co. and James van Rensselaer of Albany Co., esquire. Witnesses Neeltie Bleecker, Nichs. Bleecker and Jas. van Ingen.

881 (H 126) 1757 Febry. 28 **HOPE, Alexander,** of N. Y. City, mariner. Letters of administration on the estate of, granted to Joseph Haynes of N. Y. City, merchant.

882 (H 127) 1782 Novbr. 11 **HAMANOND, Aaron,** bond of administrator of estate of, to-wit Hezekiah Coon.

883 (H 128) 1736 Novbr. 26 **HOLLAND, Henry,** late Captain Independent Comp. of Fusileers at Albany. Certificate, that his eldest son Edward Holland, Mayor of Albany City, has been made administrator of the estate of.

883a (H 129) 1758 April 22 Decbr. 11 **HEPWORTH, Thomas,** now of N. Y. City, mariner. Wife Martha sole heiress and executrix of real and personal estate. Witnesses Lawr. Wessels, James McCartney, innholder, and Bartel Miller, cordwainer.

884 1774 March 4 1786 Febry. 23 **HEMPSTED, Robert,** of Southold, Suffolk Co. Wife Meheteble, sons Thomas, Joshua, daughters Abigail, Elisabeth, Mary and Experience. Land in Southold, inherited from father Benjamin Youngs, father of first wife Mary Younge, and bought from Benjamin Youngs Prime, land in Colchester, Connt., personal property. The wife sole executrix. Codicil of Febry 30 (*sic*), 1779 mentions bro. John Hempsted. Witnesses Joseph Prince, William Horton junior, both yeomen and Benjamin Prince, silversmith all of Southold. Recorded Wills and Probates, Vol. I., p. 16.

885 1786 Decbr. 9 1787 Jany. 9 **HAVENS, Amy,** widow, (of Suffolk Co.). Nuncupative will of, gives personal property to John Havens, Phebe Havens, Clarissa Havens and grandchildren, William and Jany Nicoll (one silver snuff box, a gold ring, two large and seven small silver spoons). Proved by evidence of Phebe Havens widow, Phebe Havens jun. spinster and Henry Halsey, yeoman, all of Suffolk Co. Recorded ut supra, p. 18.

886 1783 Novb. 1 1788 Febry. 11 **HAYNES, John,** of Philadelphia, late of the Continental ship of war *Alliance*, gives to Thomas Halfpenny, breeches maker, all real and personal estate, including prize money due and makes him executor. Witnesses Isaac Howell and James Jordan of N. Y. City, where the will was proved, proof calling the deceased "of Baltomore." Recorded ut supra, p. 178.

887 1788 Febry. 8 March 11 **HOLT, Elizabeth,** of N. Y. City, widow. Grandniece Elizabeth, da. of Colonel Eleazar Oswald and his wife Elizabeth, Mary Hall, David Mandeville Westcot, Elizabeth Hoogland, Hanna January; Colonel Oswald and da. residuary legatees of real and personal property. Executors Col. Oswald and wife. Witnesses J. McCree, Leonard Yundl and Assheton Humphreys. Proved in Philadelphia, Penn. Recorded ut supra, p. 182.

888 1791 Decbr. 5 1792 Febry. 11 **HARDY, Susannah Margaret,** wife of John Oakes Hardy, Captain Royal Navy, and daughter of Doctor Peter Middleton of N. Y. City dec'd. The husband sole heir and executor. Witnesses Robert Hurdy (Sturdy?) of Kirby Str., Parish of St. Andrew, Holborn, Middlesex Co., gentleman, Richard Blackford of Walworth, Parish of St. Mary, Barrington, County of Surry, gentleman, and Thomas Atkinson. Proved in London. Recorded ut supra, p. 349.

889
1792
Septbr. 25
Octbr. 30

HICKS, Jacob Johnson, of Pennsylvania, esquire. Sister Catharine Ceronio and her sons William, James and Edward, cousin Violetta, da. of Isaac Hicks, John and Mary, children of Mrs. Catherine Carey, brother William, children of John Barcley of Philadelphia, esquire, by his present wife, vizt: John Mortimer, Mary, Harriet and Sophia. Real and personal property. Executor John Barcley. Witnesses A. I. Dallas (secretary of the Governour), John Woods and Mich. Reynolds. Proved in Penna. Recorded ut supra, p. 376.

890
1793
Decbr. —
1795
Jany. 5

HAWEY, Thomas, of St. Elizabeth Parish, Cornwall Co., Island of Jamaica, esquire, now at New York. Brother-in-law George Young of N. Y. City, esquire, Patrick White and James Davy, both of St. Elizabeth Parish, Jamaica, trustees and executors of all real and personal estate for sister Ann, wife of George Young, her infant da. Ann Elizabeth and sons George and Brook Young. Witnesses Wm. Neilson, Wm. Neilson jun. and E. Watson. Proved in N. Y. Recorded ut supra, p. 455.

891
1794
May 23
1796
Decbr. 7

HUNTER, William, of Bristol, warehouseman. Wife Susanna, sole heiress and executrix of real and personal estate, lives at date of proof at Philadelphia, Penna. Witnesses Thomas Morgan, attorney at Bristol, Wm. Gurnsey, John Turnpenny jun. Proved in England. Recorded Vol. II., Wills and Probates, p. 29.

892
1792
28th Day
12th Month
1793
Septbr. 5

HAINES, Reuben, of Philadelphia, brewer. Wife Margaret, sons Casper W(ister), Josiah and Reuben, daughter Catherine. Real and personal property. Executors the three sons, nephew Bartholomew Wister and step brother Josiah Matlack. Witnesses Lawrence Seckel, Peter Thomson and Peter Thomson jun. Codicil of 12th. day 4th month 1793 leaves legacy to contributors to Pennsylvania Hospital. Witnesses Lawrence Seckel, Geo. Pennock and Nathan Matlack jun. Proved in Philadelphia. Recorded ut supra, p. 41.

893
1795
March 27
1798
Jany. 20

HANSON, John, of the Island of Antigua, at present in N. Y., grandson of John and Mary Wilkinson of Antigua dec'd, and son of Thomas Hanson and wife Elizabeth, who married as second husband John Braham of said Island. Wife Mary, son Robert and da. Martha, nephews James, Hughes sons, of br. James Hanson jun. dec'd, John Brooke Halloran and Thomas Hanson Halloran. Mentions property derived from kinsman James Hanson senior and wife Elizabeth. Real and personal property. Executors the wife, Lawrence Kortright, Abraham Brasher, and Anthony Van Dam of N. Y. City, merchants, Cornelius Henderickson, John Heylegar and Thomas Lille. Witnesses John Roome, Ino. van Dam and Moses I. Hays. Recorded ut supra, p. 63.

894
1793
April 11
1800
May 12

HUN, Harme, of Albany City. Wife Elsie, grandson Harme Bogert, daughters Cathelina, wife of Isaac Bogart, Maycka, wife of Cornelius van Buren, and Jannetie, wife of Thomas Lansing. Lot on S. side of Fox Creek, house and lot in Court Str., Albany, personal property. Executors the wife and the three daughters. Witnesses Henry R. Lansing, John Bogart and Gerrit Bogart. Recorded ut supra, p. 279.

895
1807
Octbr. 24
1809
Febry. 13

HILLS, John, of Charlotte, Chittenden Co., Vermont. Sons Zimri, and Lewis, daughters Ester Clarren —and Olive. Real and personal estate (gunsmiths shop and tools). Executors Zimri Hills and James Beers. Witnesses Joseph Allen, Jeremiah Barton and Jobe Smith. Recorded ut supra, p. 295.

896
1813
Febry. 11
April 14

HUYCK, Burger J., of Kinderhook, Columbia Co. Wife Margaret, son James and other children, not named. Real and personal estate. Executors and trustees Henry L. van Dyck and James van der Poel. Witnesses Ino. Doll, John van der Poel and Peter T. van Slyck. Recorded ut supra, p. 310.

897
1780
Octbr. 1
Novbr. 18
HICKS, Whitehead, of Flushing, Queens Co. Wife Charlotte, sons John, Thomas and Elias, da. Margaret. Real and personal estate. Executors the wife, Henry Brevoort, Honble William Smith, chief justice of the Province of N. Y. and David Colden of Flushing. Witnesses Joseph Lawrence, Scott Hicks, both yeomen and Tho. Willet. Recorded, Vol. III., p. 9.

898
1727
Novbr. 12
1730
April 28
HICKS, John, of Flushing, Queens Co., yeoman. Wife Elinor, sons Robert, Ellis, William and Thomas. Real and personal estate. Executors the wife, brother Isaac Hicks, brothers-in-law Thomas Ellison, John Tallman and Benjamin Thorn. Witnesses Samuel Stringham, William van Wyck and D. Cumphrey. Recorded ut supra, p. 65.

899
1788
Jany. 1
HEATH, William, mariner, who died out of the State and was not an inhabitant thereof; Letters of administration on his estate granted to Sarah, his widow. Recorded ut supra, p. 83.

900
1782
May 18
Aug. 20
HYLTON, John, of New York City. Deceased wife's name had been Ann and had daughters Sarah and Mariam Combs, sister Mary Hylton, sons Ralph and Thomas. Real estate partly derived from John Combs dec'd of Jamaica, L. I., personal property. Executors son Ralph, Thomas Braine and Stephen Skinner. Witnesses Sally Byvanck, Edward Laight and Mary Hylton. Codicil of July 29, 1782 adds sister Mary Hylton to the executors and disposes of an obligation from Robert Randolph and Daniel L. Hylton of Virginia. Witnesses Edward Laight, of N. Y. City, merchant, Catharine Skinner and Margt. Gautier. Recorded ut supra, p. 90.

901 1790 Septbr. 2 **HENDORFF, Frederick Christopher**, late Ensign 3d Batt. New Levies, Col. Abraham van Buskirk. Letters of administration on the estate of, granted to Frederick Westfall of N. Y. City, sugar baker, as creditor. Recorded ut supra, p. 121.

902 1746 July 5 1799 Octbr. 25 **HALLENBEEK, Jacob**, of Clinkenberg, Albany Co., yeoman. Wife Maria, children Jacob, Naning, Johannis, Hendrick, Alida, wife of Johannis Staats, Maria, Johanna and Gertruy. Real and personal estate. Executors sons Jacob, Naning, Johannes and Hendrick. Witnesses David van der Heyden, Johs. Rutsen Bleecker, who testifies, that testator was at time of signing will 50 or 60 yrs old, and Rutgar Bleecker. Recorded Vol. IV., p. 5.

903 1813 Jany. 2 1814 Jany. 6 **HATCH, Asa**, of Brutus Township, Cayuga Co. Wife Lucy, sons Charles, Warner, Jonathan, Asa, daughters Lucy Carpenter, Polly Whipple, Fanny Todd, Betsey Bascom, and Lydia. Real and personal estate. Executor son Jonathan. Witnesses Saml. Porter, John Dorrance and James Porter. Recorded ut supra, p. 67.

904 1800 Decbr. 13 1814 Aug. 15 **HUN, Thomas**, of Albany City, esquire. Wife Elizabeth, daughter Ann, wife of Rev. John Bossett, son Abraham. Houses and lots on Market Str., Albany, land in Greenbush, Rensselaer Co. and in Montgomery Co., personal property. Executors the wife and two children. Witnesses Barent Bleecker, Ino. R. Bleecker jun., Abraham R. ten Eyck and Rensselaer Westerlo. Recorded ut supra, p. 71.

905 1811 Septbr. 30 1814 Aug. 15 **HUN, Abraham**, of Albany City, counsellor-at-law. Wife Maria, da. of Leonard Gansevoort junior, son Thomas, da. Elizabeth. Houses and lots on Market and Dock Str. and on Union and Hannibal Str., Albany, personal property. Exectors the wife, father-in-law Leonard Gansevoort junior, brother-in-law Rev. Dr. John Basset

and wife (see No. 904), and Rensselaer Westerlo. Witnesses Ino F. Evertsen, Abrm. A. Lansingh and Isaac Hutton. Recorded ut supra, p. 77.

906
1804
Jany. 24
1815
Aug. 18

HAGADORN, Samuel, of the Town of Galloway, Saratoga Co. Wife Sophia, sons Jonathan, John, Cornelius, Henry, Samuel, daughters Elizabeth, wife of Henry R. Hagedorn, Leah, Maria, wife of John Ross, and Margaret. Real and personal estate. Executors son Jonathan and Henry A. Oothout. Witnesses Abrm. Oothout, Abrm. Santvoord and John M. Marselus. Recorded ut supra, p. 91.

907
1823
Aug. 23

HARRIS, Joseph, proceedings of the Supreme Court at Utica in proving the will of, by Ann Harris, executrix, Lemuel I. Page and wife Sarah, William James and wife Elizabeth, Margaret Harris and Joseph Harris, who are cited as heirs at law. Recorded Vol. V., p. 7.

908
1823
March 3
1825
Aug. 11

HIGBY, Joseph, of Whitestown, Oneida Co., farmer. Sons Joseph, Asahel, Enoch and Elisha, daughters Abigail, wife of Salmon Stanley, Olive, wife of Ebenezer R. Hawley, Asenath, wife of Matthew N. Tillotson, Mary, da. of da. Mary, greatgrandson Lewis Richardson, son of preceding grandda. Mary. Real and personal estate. Executors the four sons. Witnesses Jonathan Richardson, Saml. Dakin and Polly Dakin. Recorded ut supra, p. 31.

909
1821
Septbr. 12
1828
Aug. 21

HALL, John, of the Town of Benton, Ontario Co. Wife Sarah, children Moses, Rachel, wife of Jacob Hall, John, Joseph, Jacob B., Mary, wife of Stephen Whitaker, Catherine, wife of Amzi Bruen. Real and personal property. Executors sons Moses and Jacob B. Hall with advisory committee of Henry Dwight, Gavin L. Nicholas and Daniel Hudson, all of the Town of Seneca, Ontario Co. Witnesses W. W. Watson, Perez Hasting junior, and Joshua Gray. Recorded ut supra, p. 58.

910
1644
Jany. 18
Dutch

HENDRICS, Hans, from Traecx (?). Jochim Pietersen and wife. Real and personal estate. Witnesses Cornelis van der Hoykens, fiscal, Adam Roelantsen, Jan Dircksen and Jan Evertsen Bout. N. Y. Col. MSS., II., p. 93.

911
1678
Decbr. 24
4 P.M.
Dutch

HARDENBERGH, Gerrit, of New Albany, born at Maerssen, and wife Jaepie Schepmoes, born at New York. Children mentioned, but not by name. Incomplete. Albany Co. Records, Notarial Papers, II., p. 69.

912
1680-1
Jany. 5
1693-4
Recorded
Jany 18
Dutch

HEYNDRICSEN, Andries, of Kinderhook, born at Ootmars in Twent. Jan Gilbertsen of Albany and wife Cornelia. "Temporal estate." No executor named. Witnesses Jacob Maertensen, Evert Wendell and Adriaen van Ilpendam, Notary Public. Albany Co. Records, Notarial Papers, II., p. 324.

913
1693-4
Febry. 13

HENDRICKSEN, Hans, of Albany City, yeoman. Wife Eva, children Hendrick Hansen, Margriete, wife of Frederick Harmensen, Johannes and Elsie Hansen. Real and personal estate. The wife sole executrix. Witnesses Frans Pruyn, Barent Albertsen Bratt and Abram Kip. Albany Co. Records, Wills, I., p. 19.

914
1705
Aug. 23

HUYGH, Andries Hansen, of Kinderhook, Albany Co. Wife Catharine, children Johannis, Lambert, Burger, Cate, Jochem, Cornelis, Anna, Andries, Maria and Margaret. Real and personal estate. The wife sole executrix. Witnesses David Schuyler, Justice, Abraham Schuyler and Robert Livingston jun. Albany Co. Records, Wills, I., p. 146.

915
1737
Decbr. 19
1742
Novbr. 3
Dutch

HARDIK, Francis, of Claverack, Albany Co. Children Jan, Willem, Sarah, wife of Jonathan Rees, children (3) of dec'd da. Gerritie, late wife of Do. Justus Valkenaer. Real and personal estate. Executor son

Willem. Witnesses Samuel ten Broeck, D. W. ten Broeck and Evert Bout. Albany Co. Records, Wills, I., p. 206.

916 1747 June 20 1758 Febry. 23 Dutch

HOGENBOOM, Peter, of Claverack, Albany Co. Children Peter, Rachel, Cornelis, Bartholomeus, Catrynte, wife of Ph. Conyn, Hilletie, wife of Jochem Radcliff, Arriatie, widow of Lours. van Alee, Geertruy, wife of Willem van Ness, Johannis, Jeremyas, Marytie, wife of Jochem van Valckenburgh, and Annatie. Real and personal estate. Executors sons Bartholomeus, Johannis and Jeremyas. Witnesses Johannes ten Eyck of Livingston Manor, Abrm. Vosburghen and Pieter Lounhard. Albany Co. Record, Wills, I., p. 240.

917 1764 Novbr. 19 1766 Aug. 18

HALENBEEK, Hendrick, of Albany City, yeoman. Wife Susannah, children, Isaac, Dorothy, Elizabeth, wife of William Helling, Daniel, Garret, Jacob, Anthony and Barnardus, children of son Isaac, vizt: Hendrick, Nicolas and Daniel. Real and personal estate. Executors the eight children. Witnesses Jacob Cooper, William Fryer and Johs. Roorback, all of Albany City. Albany Co. Records, Wills, I., p. 309.

918 1816 Novbr. 27 1821 Octbr. 29

HOGTELING, Gerrit, of Bethlehem, Albany Co., farmer. Wife ——, children Hilmas, David, Peter, Hannah, wife of Garret van Alen, Maria. Real and personal estate. Executors sons David and Helmas. Witnesses Henry Creble, John Leedings and Gerrit Hogan. Albany Co. Records, Wills, I., part 2, p. 81.

919 1817 Septbr. 18

HOGAN, Neeltie, of Albany City. Nieces Dorothy and Eleanor Brown, Matilda, da. of John Brown dec'd, nephew William Brown. Real and personal estate. Executors nephew William and nieces Dorothy and Eleanor Brown. Witnesses Ebenezer Platt, Harman Jenkins and I. V. N. Yates. Codicil of Aug. 19, 1820, appoints the executors, named in will Trustees for Matilda Brown, now wife of James Gibbons jun. Witnesses Ira Jenkins, I. W. H. Smoll (?) and I. V. N. Yates. Albany Co. Records, Wills, I., part 2, p. 104.

920 (I 1) 1727 Aug. 21 Octobr. 5 1st George 2d **JANSEN, Mattys,** son of Jan Mattyson dec'd, of Kingston, Ulster Co., cordwainer. Children Johannis, Thomas, Cornelius, Jacobus, Grietie, wife of Lewis de Bois, Marritie, wife of Johannis Decker, Magdalena and Ragel. Real and personal estate (three silver cups and twelve do. spoons). Executors son Johannis, brother Thomas Jansen and brother John Crooke jun. Witnesses Petrus Vos, Hendrick Jansen and Gilbert Livingston.

921 (I 2) 1734-5 Jany. 3 **JOHNSON, Albert,** of Richmond Co., yeoman. Wife Catharine, sister Rachel, wife of Matthew van Brakell, niece Mary, da. of bro. Robert Johnson dec'd, daughter Martha, children of sister Rachel van Brakell, vizt: Martha, Rachel and Mary, Mary Gould. Real and personal estate. Executors John Lecount and Paul Mushow. Witnesses Nicolas Lozzlere, Stephen Wood and Adam Mott. Copy made April 14, 1763.

922 (I 3) **JACKSON, James,** of Orange Co., missing.

923 (I 4) 1746 Septbr. 15 Octbr. 17 **JACKSON, Hanoch,** of Goshen, Orange Co. William Gelston, his sisters Jane Currey and Elizabeth and bro. Hugh Gelston, Thomas Jackson, Thomas Gate, Thomas Smith and Samuel Gelston. Land in Wawayanda Patent; personal property. Executors Thomas Smith and David McCamly, both of Orange Co. Witnesses Henry Weesner jun., John Martin and William Thomson.

924 (I 5) **JACKSON, William,** of Orange Co., missing, 1746.

925 (I 6) 1749 Decbr. 31 1754 June 21 **JEWELL, Anne,** of East Chester, Westchester Co., widow. Sons William, Hezekiah and Amos. Real and personal estate. Executor Walter Briggs of West Chester. Witnesses Ino. Barlow, Thomas Sherwood and Mary Sherwood. Copy.

926 (I 7) 1753 May 22 1755 May 24 **JONES, Evan,** of Hermitage, Ulster Co., practitioner of physics. Wife Bridget, sons John, Thomas, Evan, James and Edward, da. Mary. Homefarm of 2000 acres, land at New Windsor; personal property. Executors the wife and sons John and Thomas. Witnesses Enos Ayres of Orange Co., minister of the gospel, Martha Ayres and Charles Clinton.

927 (I 8) 1759 Aug. 16 1760 Octobr. 3 **JANSEN, Thomas,** of Marbletown, Ulster Co., farmer. Wife Majeke, son, Hendrekus, Johannis, da. Annatje, children of dec'd da. Sarah, late wife of John Chrispell, da. Janitje, wife of Johannis Eltinge, Rebecca, Catherine, and other children, not named. Real and personal estate. Executors sons Johannis and Hendrekus. Witnesses Martin de Lametter of Marbletown, farmer, Dirck Wynkoop jun. of Kingston, merchant, and Nicholas Rosa.

928 (I 9) 1760 Jany. 26 April 10 **JENNINS, Richard,** of Goshen, Orange Co. Wife Phebe, sons Isaac, Benjamin, Richard, daughters Ann, Jerusha, Elizabeth, Ruth and Phebe. Real and personal property. Executors the wife and sons-in-law John Wood and John Carpenter. Witnesses Rebecca Allison, William Denn and Busul Seely of Goshen Prect., planter.

929 (I 10) 1762 Octbr. 29 1765 March 10 **JAYN, Samuel,** of Floroday, Orange Co. Wife Dinah, son Samuel, da. Mary. Real and personal estate. Executors the wife and son. Witnesses Isaac Ludlum, Ebenezer Holly jun. and Saml. Gale, merchant.

930 (I 11) 1764 Decbr. 17 1765 Jany. 29 **JONES, Thomas,** near Fort Edward, N. Y. Wife Sarah, sole heiress and executrix. Witnesses Richard Lockwood, Joseph Gillett, both of Fort Edward, yeomen, and James Dunsee. Proved in Albany Co.

931 (I 12) **JACKSON, William,** of Orange Co., 1765, missing.

932 (I 13) 1766 Decbr. 25 1767 April 8 **JINENS, Joseph,** of Beekmans Prect., Dutchess Co. Wife Hannah, grandsons Joseph Whitely, Pardon Whitely, granddaughter Judah Lake, da. Martha, wife of Robert Whitely. Real and personal property. Executors Benjamin Deuile and Elijah Doty, both of Beekmans Prect. Witnesses Matthew Ferriss, Philipp Allen, both Quakers, and Susannah Doty.

933 (I 14) 1766 July 1 1769 April 11 **JANSEN, Johannis,** jun., of Marbletown, Ulster Co. Wife Geertje sole heiress of real and personal estate. Executors the wife and bro.-in-law Benjamin Rosa. Witnesses Sara Sleght, Willem Eltinge, yeoman, and Hend. Sleght of Kingston, merchant.

934 (I 15) 1768 Decbr 20 1769 Novbr. 25 **IRISH, Smiton,** of Dutchess Co. Wife Elizabeth, children Samuel, Mary, Jonathan, Amos, and George, cousin Sarah Reynolds and an expected child. Real and personal estate. Executors Joseph Irish and Zebulon Hoxsie. Witnesses Lot Tripp, Smiton Tripp, both of Dutchess Co., yeomen, and Smiton Brownell.

935 (I 16) 1768 Aug. 18 1782 Aug. 16 **JANSEN, Roelof,** and wife Elizabeth, of Schoodack, Albany Co. Grandchildren Roelof and Elizabeth Jansen, Mary I. and Roeloff I. Huick. Real and personal property. Executors not named. Witnesses Andries ten Eyck of Albany Co., farmer, Kasper Springsteen and Ino. Fitzgerald.

936 (I 17) 1774 July 15 1782 Novbr. 13 **JONES, Jonathan,** of Beekmans Prect., Dutchess Co., yeoman. Wife Hannah, children Lewis, Mary, Hannah, Elisabeth, Nathaniel, Rhoda, Sarah, Levinah, Dorcas. "Worldly estate." Executors the wife and bro. Daniel Jones. Witnesses Mary Smith, John Platt of Charlotte Prect., yeoman, and Benjamin Paddock.

937 (I 18) 1774 May 25 1785 Septbr. 15 **JANSEN, Cornelis,** of Rochester, Ulster Co., yeoman. Wife Cattriena, children Matthewis, Teunis, Cornelis, Benjamin and Aentje. Real and personal estate. Executors the wife, the four sons and Johannis Snyder. Witnesses Adam Swart, Wilhelms Swart, both of Kingston, carpenters, and Petrus Swart.

938 (I 19) 1776 March 21 1782 Decbr. 21 **JOHNSTON, James,** of Shawangonk Prect., Ulster Co., yeoman. Wife Mary, sons James, George, William and Michael, daughters Elisabeth and Christian, an expected child. Real and personal estate. Executors bro. Michael Johnston and bro.-in-law James Graham. Witnesses David Winfield, Abraham Terwilliger of said Prect., farmers, and George Graham.

939 (I 20) 1777 April 6 1784 July 5 **JONES, Samuel,** jun., of Goshen Prect., Orange Co., farmer. Wife Hannah, sons Andrew and Samuel, da. Mary; Martha Vachte. Real and personal property. Executors William Allison and Capt. John Jackson, both of Goshen Prect. Witnesses Michael Jackson of Goshen Prect., esquire, James Sawyer and Michael Allison.

940 (I 21) 1777 April 12 1780 Jany. 31 **JUDSON, Samuel,** of Amenia Prect., Dutchess Co. Wife Abigail, children Azariah, Samuel, Noah, Elizabeth, Hannah, Sarah, Susannah and Mary. Land "at home and abroad," personal property. Executors Deacon Moses Barlow and bro.-in-law Noah Pratt. Witnesses Azariah Pratt, Ebenezer Knibloe, of Litchfield Co., Connt., clerk, and David Judson.

941 (I 22) 1778 Aug. 2 1785 Novbr. 28

JANSEN, Joachim, of Lonenburgh, Albany Co. Sons Johannes, who has wife Mary, Peter, Ruloff and Coenraed, daughters Fytje, Mary, Geesje, Eytje and Lena. Real and personal estate. Executors sons Johannis and Peter. Witnesses Henry Knoll of Coxhacky Distr., surgeon, John Burghert 3d and Rulif Ryan.

942 (I 23) 1781 Octbr. 4 1784 June 3

JOHNSON, Robert, of Amenia Precinct (Dutchess Co.). Wife Jane, sons Samuel, George and Robert, Sarah Kelsey, Ruth Cleaveland. Real and personal estate. Executors son Samuel and Isaac Darrow. Witnesses James Reynolds, Silas Marsh jun. of Poghkeepsie, gentleman, and Silas Marsh.

943 (I 24) 1781 April 20 Novbr. 3

JONES, Josias, of Dutchess Co., yeoman. Wife, ——, nephew Ananias Jones, niece Mary Jones, son of brother Nathaniel Jones, Gilbert Caregain. Only personal property mentioned. Executors bro. Samuel Jones and John Rhoad. Witnesses James Rhoads, Mary Shaw, spinster and Hannah Post.

944 (I 25) 1781 May 15 1784 Febry. 28

JONES, Samuel, senior, in the Drowned Lands, Goshen Prect., Orange Co. Grandson Nathan Jones, son Cornelius, grandson Michael Allison Jones, granddaughter Elenor Sheridan, grandsons Samuel, Andrew, George and Cornelius Jones, granddaughters Rebeckah Chandler and Hannah Jones, da. Hannah Sheridan. Real and personal property. Executors Hannah Jones, grandson Nathan Jones and Peter Gale. Witnesses John Conner, schoolmaster, Anthony Dobbin, labourer, both of Goshen Prect. and Michael Jackson.

945 (I 26) 1782 April 23 Novbr. 19

JOHNSON, James, soldier in Col. Philipp van Cortland's Regt. Jacobus Freer of Poughkeepsie Prect. farmer, sole heir and executor of real and personal estate. Witnesses William Hyer, William Wilsey of Dutchess Co. yeoman, and Barent Frear. Proved in Dutchess Co.

946 (I 27) 1785 Febry. 19 1786 March 3 **JAYNE, Daniel,** of Cornwall Prect., Orange Co., yeoman. Wife Hannah, da. Sarah, wife of John Carpenter, granddaughters Rachel and Hannah Tucker. Real and personal estate. Executors son-in-law Jonah Carpenter and Captain Ebenezer Woodhull, both of said Prect. Witnesses Jonah Tooker, William Shepard and Nathan Cooly.

947 1779 Septbr. 22 1780 March 21 **JANDINE, Charles,** of Staten Island, Richmond Co. Daughters Susanna Jandine, Cathrine Lamb, Mary Lamb, Hannah Lawrence and Martha Allicocke, granddaughters Cathrine and Sally Davis. Real and personal estate. Executors Joseph Allicocke and Wm. Smith of H. M. Council. Witnesses Daniel Crocheron, Moses Clendenney of Richmond Co., blacksmith and Benjamin Cole. Recorded Wills and Probates, Vol. I., p. 61.

948 1773 Septbr. 28 1787 March 10 **JOHNSTON, Lewis,** of Perth Amboy, N. J., Doctor of physick. Children John, Heathcoat, Ann and Margaret. Shares in eastern division of N. J., personal property. Executors son Heathcoat Johnston, James Parker and John Smith. Witnesses Ino. Johnston, John Thomson, both of Perth Amboy, gentlemen, and Peter Barberie. Proved in N. Y. Recorded ut supra, p. 66.

949 1790 Octbr. 16 Decbr. 18 **JUDSON, David,** late of Kinderhook, now on the way to New Haven, Connt. Sons Philander and David. Real and personal estate. Executors bro.-in-law Ebenezer R. White, Oliver Burr, both of Danbury, Conn. and bro.-in-law Sturgis Burr of New Haven. Witnesses Nathl., merchant, James Cebra, gentleman, A. Moor jun. gentleman, all of N. Y. City. Recorded ut supra, p. 254.

950 1790 Novbr. 18 Decbr. 30 **JACKSON, Joseph,** on board ship *Francisca*, in or nigh Boston Bay. John van Doren and Thomas Smith heirs of "my goods of all kindes." Witnesses Thos. Hadaway and Powel Nebor, mariners. Recorded ut supra, p. 255.

951 1780 Septbr. 5 1785 Febry. 24 **JOHNSON, Warren,** of the City of Dublin, esquire. Daughters of late uncle Sir Peter Warren, children not named. "Worldly substance." Wife insane. Executors bro. John Johnson, Robert Caddell and Daniel McGusty. No witnesses, proved by testimony of testators bro. John Johnson at Dublin. Recorded ut supra, p. 394.

952 1803 April 29 1820 March 27 **JOHNSTON, James,** of Salisbury, Litchfield Co., Connt. Present wife —— Daughter Sally Mix, son Walter (by second wife). Land on Cayahoga R., Connecticut Reservation on S. side of Lake Erie, personal property. Executor son Walter Johnston. Witnesses Adonijah Strong, Thankful Collins and Meriam Gleason. Recorded Vol. II., p. 350.

953 1791 April 5 **JUDAH, Samuel,** formerly of N. Y. City, late of Philadelphia, merchant, letters of administration on the estate of, granted his widow Jessy and son Benjamin S. Judah. Recorded Vol. III., p. 127.

954 1774 Jany. 27 July 25 **JOHNSON, Sir William,** of Johnson Hall, Tryon Co., Baronet. Son Sir John Johnson Kt., daughters Ann, wife of Col. Daniel C. Claus and Mary, wife of Col. Guy Johnson, natural children by housekeeper Mary Brant, vizt. Peter, Elisabeth, Magdalene, Margaret, George, Mary, Susanna, Ann Johnson; Young Brant alias Kaghnechtago and William alias Tagawirunte, two Mohawk lads, both of Canajohare; brothers John and Warren Johnson, sisters Dease, Sterling, Plunket and Fitzsimons; Mary, da. of Christopher McGrah of Mohawk Country; nephew Doctor John Dease; Robert Adams of Johnstown, William Byrne of Kingsborough, Patrick Daly "now living with me," Joseph Chew of Kingsborough and sons Joseph and William Chew, grandson William Claus. Land near Fort Johnson, do. in Kingsland or Royal Grant, Kingsborough Patent, in Klock and Nellus Patent, on Onondaga Lake,

in Sacondaga Patent, house and lot in Albany, at the German Flats, lot in Schenectady, in Nine Partner's Patent (Dutchess Co.), in Harrison's Patent, farm near Anthony's Nose on Mohawk R., land in Stoneraby Patent, do. near Canajohare Castle, do. In Adageghtcinge Patent, called Charlotte River, do. in Byrne's Patent at Schohare, do. on Lake Champlain, purchased from Lieut. Augustine Prevost, formerly the location of Lieut. Gorrel, personal property. Executors son Sir John Johnson, sons-in-law Daniel Claus and Guy Johnson, brothers John and Warren Johnson, Daniel Campbell of Schenectady, John Butler, Jeles Fonda, Capt James Stevenson of Albany, Robert Adems, Samuel Stringer of Albany, Doctor John Dease, Henry Fry and Joseph Chew. Guardians of children by Mary Brant, John Butler, Jelles Fonda, John Dease, James Stevenson, Henry Frey and Joseph Chew. Witnesses Wm. Adems, Gilbert Tice, Moses Ibbitt and Samuel Sutton. Recorded Vol. IV., p. 35.

955
1811
Aug. 7
1818
May 13

JOHNSTONE, Sir John Lowther, of Wester Hall, Dumfries County, Baronet. Appoints His Royal Highness Ernest Augustus, Duke of Cumberland, Charles Herbert Pierpoint, commonly called Viscount Newark, David Cathcart, advocate in Edinburgh, and Masterton Ure, writer to his Majestys signet in Edinburgh heirs and executors [really trustees] of real estate in America and elsewhere on behalf of legal heirs. Witnesses John Burch Dawson, testators Secretary, Sam: Jeyes, surgeon, Baker Str., London, and W. R. Reeder, testators servant. Proved before Richard Rush, Envoy Extraordinary of the U. S. at London. Recorded ut supra, p. 103.

956
1642
——
Dutch

JACOBSEN, Pieter, of Fort Orange, born in Rendsburgh, and wife Gysje Pieters. Daughter Tunitje Alberts. Real and personal estate. Witness Bastiaen Krol. N. Y. Col. MSS., II., p. 22.

957 1690 June 11 1722 May 22 Dutch **JANSEN, Marcelis,** of Albany City. Wife Annetie, children Gysbercht, Huybertje, Sytie, Judith and Aasverus. Real and personal estate. No executors named. Witnesses Cornelis Swart of Kingston, at date of proof 70 years old, Johannis Becker senior and junior. Albany Co. Records, Wills, I., p. 179.

958 1725 April 8 1733 Decbr. 28 **JANSEN, Evert,** of Albany City, cooper. Wife Maria, sons John, Hanns, Jacob. Real and personal estate, a large bible. Executors the three sons. Witnesses Cornelius van Schelluyne, Leendert Gansevoort and John Collins. Albany Co. Records, Wills, I., p. 198.

959 (K 1) 1703-4 Jany. 21 1704 Septbr. 7 **KEETELL, Jermy,** of Marbletown, Ulster Co. Wife Elizabeth, sons Jermy, and Richard, daughters Susan and Elizabeth; William Ennis. Real and personal estate. Executors John Cock and Captain Charles Brodhead. Witnesses John Cock, Charles Brodhead, John Noble, Captain Richard Brodhead and Wm Nottingham.

960 (K 2) 1726 Novbr. 3 —— **KIP, Jacobus,** of N. Y. City, esquire. Wife Catalina, sons John, Jacobus, William, Henry, Belthazier and Benjamin, daughters Catherine and Cornelia. Real and personal estate. Executors the wife and son John Kip, overseers bro. John Kip, Abraham van Vleecq and Balthazier D'Hart. Witnesses Samuel Kipp, Jacobus Kiersted and H. Demeyer. Copy made Aug. 18, 1762.

961 (K 3) 1734 Aug. 9 1746 Septbr. 25 **KETELHUYN, William,** of Saraghtogue, Albany Co. Wife Marie, Killiaen D. Ridder, children of Wouter van der Zee, of Albert van der Zee and of Antje Beckers dec'd, brothers and sisters of wife Marie, children of Walraven Clute, vizt. Antje, Mary and William. Real and personal estate. The wife sole executrix. Witnesses Ph. Livingston, Ja. Stevenson and Johannis de Foreest.

962 (K 4) 1737 Octbr. 21 1738 June 27 **KEYSERREYCK, Reynyer,** of Orange Co., yeoman. Wife Maria sole heiress and executrix of real and personal estate. Witnesses Yan Hagel, Jacobus Blavelt and Gabriel Ludlow jun.

963 (K 5) 1743 April 20 Novbr. 12 **KROM, Gisbert,** of Haverstraw, Orange Co. Wife Cornelia, children Lena, ffloris, Peter and Johannis. Real and personal estate. The wife sole executrix. Witnesses Philipp Verplanck, James Verplanck and John Verplanck.

964 (K 6) 1744 May 25 1762 Jany. 21 **KONINCK, Ary,** of N. Y. City, bricklayer. Wife Rachel, sons Johannis, Ary, Geysbert, daughters Mariah, Elizabeth, Rachel and Anna. "Worldly estate." Executors the three sons. Witnesses Lewis Bourdett, Alburtus van de Water, Tobias Stoutenburgh of N. Y. City, bolter. Copy.

965 (K 7) 1744 Octbr. 19 1748 Octbr. 31 **KERR, Charles,** Doctor at Oswego. Thomas and Walter, sons of Lieut. Walter Butler, Daniel Obryan. Personal property. Lieut. Walter Butler executor. Witnesses John Philipps, Edward Trivett and John Duffy, Proved in Albany, when Lieut. Butler being dead his son Thomas became admr.

966 (K 8) 1747 Jany. 12 March 17 Dutch **KIP, Jacob,** of Dutchess Co. Children Jacobus, Marretie, Sarah, Rachel and Jenneke. Real and personal property (a large bible). Executors Gerrit van Wagenen, Henderickes Heermansen and Abraham Kip. Witnesses Ruelof Kip, Abraham Kip and Isaac Kip.

967 (K 9) 1748 Decbr. 1 1758 June 9 Dutch **KIERSTEDEN, Aldert,** of Mormel (Marbletown), Ulster Co., farmer. Wife Arjaentje, daughters Catharina, wife of Nathan Smedus, and Blandina, wife of Wilhelmus Hoogteling junior. Real and personal estate. Executors the wife, bro.-in-law Davidt de Lametter and Jan Eltinge. Witnesses Hendrick Krom, Cornelius Cole and Benjamin Krom.

968 (K 10) 1750 Decbr. 20 1750-1 Febry. 27 **KILLBURN, Abner,** of New Windsor, Ulster Co., cooper. Wife Hannah and a daughter not named. Real and personal estate. Executors Ebenezer Seely and Barnard Lynch. Witnesses Thomas Ellison, James Kilburn and Judah Harlow.

969 (K 11) 1751 Decbr. 12 1754 Decbr. 14 Dutch **KIP, Hendrick,** of Fishkil, Dutchess Co., farmer. Wife Jacomintie, nephew Hendrick, son of eldest bro., nephew Matteus Slecht son of eldest sister, bro.-in-law Gerret Newkerk and his son Cornelius, cousin Cornelius, son of Jan Newkerk. Real and personal estate. Executors Jacob du Bois and Theodorus Cornelius van Wyck. Witnesses Evert Brown, Alexander Schofield and Joh: Cooper. The widow Jacomintie Kip has become wife of Peter Dubois Octbr. 9, 1755, when she is made administratrix, one of the executors being dead, the other refusing to act.

970 (K 12) 1755 Novbr. 13 1756 March 12 **KIP, Abraham,** of Rhinebeek Prect., Dutchess Co., yeoman. Son Jacob, da. Amelia, both minors, placed in the charge of mother-in-law and bro.-in-law Johannes Pruyn. Real and personal property (a great bible). Executors brothers-in-law Johannes Pruyn and Gerrit van Wagenen and cousin Jacob Johan Kip. Witnesses Jurry Kaas (Haas?), William Scott and Christian Schutzs. Endorsed among others "Stephen Winants wife Amelia herein named."

971 (K 13) 1755 April 30 1757 Octbr. 18 Dutch **KAST, Jurreje,** of Albany Co. Children Hans Jurreje, Grietie, wife of Willem Fox, Mary, wife of Jurreje Rechtmayer, Elisabeth, wife of Niklas Mattys, Sarah, wife of Teedy Magien, Jurreje, grandchildren vizt. Marie, da. of da. Doortie and Hendrick Heegar, children of Frederick Kelmer and da. Marie Barber. Apparently only personal estate. Executors Thomas Schoenmaker and Johannis Volkertsen Douw. Witnesses Barent Bratt, Marten Beekman and Volkert Douw.

972 (K 14) 1758 April 27 Novbr. 21 **KIP, Petrus,** of Dutchess Co., currier. Wife Maria, sons John, Benjamin and Abraham, da. Maria Margaret. Real and personal property. Executors the wife, Elieas Duboys and Jacob J. Kip (a brother). Witnesses James Duncan, John Bailey jun. and James Bayley.

973 (K 15) 1758 Jany. 26 1759 May 12 Dutch **KIERSTED, Hans,** of Kingston, Ulster Co., Doctor. Children Christoffel, Sara, wife of Henderikus Slegt, Catharina, wife of Henderik Bos, Lena, wife of Petrus A. Low, Cornelia, wife of Domine Mancius, Arjaentje, children of dec'd son Roelof, vizt. Christoffel, John, Luykis, Anna and Arjaentje, children of dec'd da. Anna, wife of Isaac Keuning, vizt. Hans, Abraham and Marytje. Real and personal estate. Executors son Christoffel, son-in-law Hend. Slegt and Domine Georgius W. Mancius. Witnesses James Eltinge, Johannes Masten and Jan Eltinge. Seal.

974 (K 16) 1759 May 6 1775 Octbr. 21 **KIP, Balthazar,** of New York, mariner. Wife Jeane sole heiress and executrix. Witnesses Hugh Ryder, Daniel Old and Benjamin Moore, of N. Y. City, sailmaker. Copy.

975 (K 17) 1760 April 15 May 3 **KETCHAM, Thomas,** of Batemans (Beekmans?) Prect., Dutchess Co. Wife Rabeker, sons Thomas and Isaac, daughters Leuinor, Pamela, Mary and Deborah. Real and personal property. Executors Joseph Haff and Samuel Adget. Witnesses Hobart Stanbrough, Peter Doty and William Doughty.

976 (K 18) 1760 June 7 June 11 **KYER, Coenradt,** of Albany City, carpenter, makes friend Adam Ramser heir of all his pay "due in the Kings work" and other outstanding money. Witnesses Samuel Larue, Henry Cole, both of Rensselaer Manor, and William Otto.

977 (K 19) 1763 Octbr. 5 Octbr. 17 **KIP, Jacob,** late of Saddle River, Bergen Co., N. J., now of New York. Wife Geesje, da. of Cornelius Brinckerhoff, Elizabeth Kip, wife of Claes Danielsen Romyn, Rynier Bordan and the children of his sisters and brothers, brothers Hendrick, Peter and Isaac Kip, children of dec'd sister, vizt. Annatje van Voorhees, Catherine ter Hune and Elizabeth Brinckerhoff. Real and personal property. Executors Hendrick Kip, Peter's son, and Claes Danielson Romyn, both of Hackensack, Bergen Co., N. J. Witnesses Peter Lot, bolter, William Brede, yeoman, and Evert Byvanck, merchant, all of N. Y. City. Copy.

978 (K 20) 1764 April 5 June 18 **KEATER, Arei,** of Marbletown, Ulster Co., weaver. Wife Cornelia, nephew Johannis, son of bro. Johannis Keater. Real and personal estate. Executors bro. Johannis Keater and and bro.-in-law Petrus Smith. Witnesses Ephraim Chambers, Andries de Witt, both of Marbletown, yeomen, and Andries van Luven.

979 (K 21) 1764 March 23 1769 Decbr. 2 **KROM, Henderikus,** of Marbletown, Ulster Co., yeoman. Sons Gysbert, John, William, Henderick, Benjamin, who has son Henderick, daughter Elisabeth, wife of Isaac Davis, Dina, da. of son Gysbert, Dina, da. of Elizabeth Davis, Henderick, son of William. Real and personal property. Executors the five sons and son-in-law Isaac Davis. Witnesses Lewis Bevier, Tuenis Kool and Nathan Smedes, farmer.

980 (K 22) 1765 May 25 1785 March 7 **KIP, Roeloff,** of Rhinebeck Prect., Dutchess Co., yeoman. Wife Sarah, children Jacob, John Baptist, Isaac, Ignas, Abraham, children of dec'd da. Grietje, wife of Philipp van Ess, vizt. Gerrit and Catalyntje, children of dec'd da. Sarah, wife of Baltus van Cleek, vizt. Peter, Franz, Sarah, Chatarina, Grietje and Elisabeth. Real and personal estate. Executors the five sons. Witnesses Jan Pir, George Trimper and Christian Schultz, schoolmaster.

981 (K 23) 1765 Febry. 14 1771 Octbr. 9 **KIP, Isaac,** of Albany City, merchant. Nephew Abraham, niece Gesie Staats, both children of Simon Veder, and four sisters, not named, resp. their children. Real and personal property. Executors Simon Veder and Joaigim, son of Isaac Staats. Witnesses George Feilding, silversmith, Hendrik M. Roosbom, merchant, and Abraham Roosbom, shopkeeper, all of Albany.

982 (K 24) 1767 June 3 1785 Jany. 22 **KLAWE, Johanis,** of the Flats of Loonenburgh, Albany Co., husbandman. Wife Mary, sons Jury, William, Francis, John, and Casper, daughters Rachel, Cornelia and Leah, granddaughter Elizabeth. Real and personal estate. Executors the wife and son Casper, overseers William Hallenbeek and Captain Jacob Hallenbeek. Witnesses Jury van Loon, Casper Hallenbeek, both of Coxhaky District, yeomen, and Hans Koning.

983 (K 25) 1768 Septbr. 12 Novbr. 1 **KNICKERBOCKER, Harmen,** of Schotta Coak, Albany Co., yeoman. Nephew John, son of bro. John Knickerbocker, sister Elizabeth Quockenbos, nephew Darieh Vanfactor and his sister Hannah Kipp, brother Woughtor Knickerbocker, sister Nealcha Knickerbocker, cousin Hannah, wife of Cornelius Vanfaiter, cousin Hannah, wife of Lewis T. Vieley, cousin Hannah, wife of Egmon (?) Kipp. Real and personal property (a silver teapot, 6 do. spoons, 6 do. tablespoons). Executors brothers Woughter and John Knickerbocker. Witnesses Johannes D. Wandelaer, Jacob Viele, both of Schachhok farmers, and Johannis Quackenbos. Also in Albany Co. Records, Wills I., p. 332.

984 (K 26) 1769 Febry. 16) June 21 **KOONS, Philipp,** of Livingston Manor, Albany Co. Wife Barbara, sons Nicholas, Philipp, Johan Jurry, Matthys, Adam and Johannis, daughters Catherine, Margriet, heirs of da. Claritje Treever, da. of dec'd son Firdenand vizt: Elizabeth. Real and personal estate. Executors the wife and sons Johan Jurry and Philipp Koons. Witnesses Johannis Peter Russ, Ruliff Kidnie jun., farmer, and James Elliott.

985 (K 27) 1771 Septbr. 28 1774 May 9 **KNAPP, Daniel,** son of Benjamin, of Haverstraw Precinct, Orange Co., yeoman. Wife Susanna, sons Daniel, Benjamin. Real and personal property. Executors bro.-in-law Abraham Thew, and Jeremiah Williamson. Witnesses Gilead Hunt of Poughkeepsie, boatman, David Pye, third name illegible.

986 (K 28) 1771 Jany. 19 May 2 **KNIGHTS, Thomas,** of New Cornwall Prect., Orange Co. Wife Mary, da. Alleda, wife of Zopher Teed, and 7 other children not named. Real and personal estate. Executors the wife and Zopher Teed. Witnesses Joseph Willcox, yeoman, Sarah Willcox and Nathaniel Jayne.

987 (K 29) 1772 Febry. 11 1773 Jany. 29 **KLAPPER, Hendrik,** of Claverack, Albany Co., blacksmith. Wife Anna Margaritha, eldest son William, "a degenerate and prodigal son," sons George, Frederick, Hendrick, Coenrad, Adam and Peter, daughters Anna, wife of Jost Kellder, Elisabeth, wife of Richard Blameless, Barbara, wife of William Snyder, Catharina and Gertruyd, Reformed Churches at Claverack and Rhinebeck. Real and personal estate (a great German bible). Executors Esqre John van Alen and Capt. Richard Esselstyne. Witnesses Francis Hardyck jun., Benedictus Valkenar and Peter Wiessmer.

988 (K 30) 1772 Aug. 22 1778 Aug. 5 **KIDD, Alexander,** of Wallkil Prect., Ulster Co. Wife Jane, sons Robert, Alexander, James, daughters Ann, widow of Samuel Crawford, and Hannah, wife of Alexander Wilson. Real and personal property. Executor son Robert. Witnesses Patrick Barber, esquire, William Wood, hatter, both of Ulster Co., and William Hill. Proved in Dutchess Co.

989 (K 31) 1772 Decbr. 11 1785 April 20 **KOWENHOVER, Johannes,** of New Marlborough Precinct, Ulster Co., yeoman. Daughter Anna and her husband David Ostrander. Real and personal estate. Executors son-in-law David Ostrander, Peter Os-

trander and Christopher Ostrander. Witnesses Daniel Freer junior, Wilhelmus Ostrander and Jacob Conklin of Newburgh, yeoman.

990 (K 32) 1772 Aug. 5 Octbr. 23 **KNAP, Benjamin,** of Haverstraw Prect., Orange Co., "being aged." Wife Susanna, sons Benjamin, Samuel, two children of dec'd son Daniel, daughters Elizabeth, Susanna, Rachel, Mary, Hannah, Debrah, and Rebeckha. Real and personal estate. Executors the wife and Jeremiah Williamson. Witnesses Henry Palmer, Susannah Knap, and David Pye, of Orange Co., clothier.

991 (K 33) 1773 June 27 Aug. 7 **KNAP, John,** of Goshen Prect., Orange Co. Wife Abigale and children, not named. Real and personal estate. Executors the wife, Jeames Knap and Benjamin Tusten jun. Witnesses Joshua Brown jun., Carman Carpenter and Benj. Tusten.

992 (K 34) 1773 Decbr. 8 1774 June 29 **KING, Thomas,** of New Windsor Prect., Ulster Co. Wife ——, sons Samuel and Steven, daughters Lydia, Roda Hardon, Prudance, grandchildren Benoni Right, Luke Haris, Jane King, Nathan Cook, Thomas Given. Real and personal estate. Executors the wife and the two sons. Witnesses William Young, Robert Cross and Andrew Dickson.

993 (K 35) 1773 Jany. 27 1774 Septbr. 28 **KETLETAS, Jane,** of N. Y. City. Son Abraham, daughter Jane Beekman. Real and personal estate. Executors Peter van Brugh Livingston, Peter Ketletass and William Nicoll. Witnesses Daniel Sickles, Thomas Colgan, silversmith, and Garret Ketletas, merchant, all of N. Y. Copy.

994 (K 36) 1774 May 30 1784 June 11 **KESELAR, Paulus,** of Haverstraw Prect., Orange Co., yeoman. Wife Maria, sons Peter and Philipp, daughters Maria and Christian. Real and personal estate. Executors Daniel Gero and Cornelius Hannium. Witnesses Joannis Snedeker, Jacob Polhemus and Gertie Polhemus.

995 (K 37) 1774 Decbr. 2 1775 June 22 **KAIN, Robert,** of Shawangonk Prect., Ulster Co., yeoman. Wife Mary, sons Francis, James, Robert, John, daughters Margaret, wife of Andrew Graham, Catharine, wife of John Lawrance, Elisabeth, wife of Michael Johnson, Mary, wife of Robert Dunlap. Real and personal estate. Executors the wife, and sons Robert, James and John. Witnesses John Graham, Samuel Irwin and James I. Graham of Ulster Co. merchant.

996 (K 38) 1775 March 26 Octbr. 9 **KNICKERBACKER, Neeltje,** of Schaghtakakock, Albany Co. Dirk T. van Veghten and son Teunis, Cornelia, da. of Igenas Kip and her brother Teunis, Annatje, wife of Igenas Kip, Annitje, wife of Lewis T. Viele and her da. Maria, Elezibeth, wife of John Tort, Neeltje, da. of Harme Quackenbush, Annaite Viele, da. of Johannis Knickerbacker, Margrita, da. of Dirk T. van Veghten. Personal property (six silver teaspoons, gold earrings). Executors Johannis S. Quackenbass and Dirck T. van Veghten. Witnesses John Davenport, Peter Benwa (Beneway) both of Schatekok, yeomen, and Dirck Swart.

997 (K 39) 1777 Octbr. 12 1784 July 17 **KING, Samuel,** of Amenia, Dutchess Co. Wife Rebackah, sons Samuel and Nathaniel, daughters Deborah and Rebeckah. Real and personal estate. Executors the wife and Ephman Pain, who refusing to act, John King of Berkshire Co., Mass., principal creditor, is appointed administrator. Witnesses Robert Hebard of Dutchess Co., farmer, and Jesse Pike.

998 (K 40) 1778 July 16 1785 June 7 **KLAUW, Frans,** of Kinderhook, Albany Co., yeoman. Wife Maritie, daughters Judith, wife of Johannis Legrange and Rachel, wife of Casper M. Hallenbeck, son Jurjii Frans. Real and personal estate. Executors the son and Gerrit van Hoesen. Witnesses Peter Vosburgh, Joggum Johs. van Valkenburgh, yeoman, and Peter van Schaack. Executors refusing to act, William Klauw, farmer, is made administrator.

999 (K 41) 1770 June 13 1780 March 20 **KUECHERER (Kickler), Friderich,** of Rumbouts Precinct, Dutchess Co. Wife ——, son-in-law William Burnet, grandson Fredrick Burnet, daughters Ann Maria, Elizabeth and Dority; Elizabeth is expected to become the wife of Matthew Burnet. Real and personal estate. Executors Cornelius Luyster, Tise Luyster, Peter I. Monfort and Johannes Duboys. Witnesses Joseph Gonsaules, Gerret Noortstrant and Dominicus Monfoort, yeoman.

1000 (K 42) 1778 Jany. 5 1782 Decbr. 21 **KAIN, John,** of Shawangonk Prect., Ulster Co. Wife Idah, and an expected child, brothers and sisters, not named. Real and personal estate. Executors the wife, bro. James Kain and James G. Graham. Witnesses Jane Graham, Francis Kain and James G. Graham, both yeomen.

1001 (K 43) 1780 May 8 1784 Aug. 4 **KNIESKERN, Henrich,** of Shoharry, Albany Co., farmer. Wife Elizabeth, sons Peter, John, Jacob, Henrich, Willem, Martinus, daughters Elisabeth, wife of Philipp Kayser, Catrina, wife of Joost Bekker. Land at Knieskern Dorph and in Duanesburgh; personal property. Executors sons John and Jacob Knieskern and son-in-law Joost Bekker. Witnesses Jost Kniskern, Hannes Merckel and George F. Reinhard, schoolmaster.

1002 (K 44) 1782 Decbr. 19 1783 April 18 **KROM, Jacob,** of Hurley Town (Ulster Co.). Wife Catharina, son Abraham and other children not named. Real and personal property. Executor the wife. Witnesses Benjamin Krom, Matthew Blanshan jun. and Jacob Blanshan jun., all of Hurley, weavers.

1003 (K 45) 1783 July 8 Aug. 21 **KNIFFIN, Israel.** Wife Esther, daughter Elizabeth, grandchildren Israel and Abraham Kniffin, children of son Jonathan Kniffin and Catherine Kniffin, sons Jozarel, Samuel, Daniel and Lewis. Real and personal estate. Executors bro. Lewis Kniffin and Jeremiah Cooper. Witnesses Jeremiah Cooper, physician, Petrus Bogardus, yeoman, both of Rumbouts Prect., and Henry van Voorhis.

1004 (K 46) 1783 June 20 1785 June 7

KORTZ, John, of the German Camp, Albany Co. Wife Elizabeth, sons Christopher and John, daughter Margaret and Christina. Homefarm, land in N. Y. City; personal estate. Executors the two sons. Witnesses Johannes Salbach, Pitter Blass of German Camp, yeoman, and Johannes Salbach.

1005 (K 47) 1783 Decbr. 17 1784 April 8

KIERS, Edward William, of Haverstraw Prect., Orange Co., dealer and chapman. Common Law wife Greetie and her children Rachel, William, Ufame and Elizabeth. Real and personal property. Executors John Robert, David Pye and John Suffern. Witnesses George Briggs of Haverstraw, yeoman, Dirck Ackerson and Abraham Cooper.

1006 (K 48) 1785 July 6 Septbr. 6

KETCHAM, Joseph, of Beekmans Prect., Dutchess Co., yeoman. Children Joshua, Samuel, Joseph, Daniel, Micah, Abija, Youngs, Isabel, Ruth, Rebeccah, Sarah, Abigail. "Worldly estate." Executors Jonathan Dennis, esqre, and Major William Clark, both of Beekmans Prect. Witnesses Britton Tallman, farmer, Nathaniel Soule and Mary Soule.

1007 (K 49) 1776 April 19

KNIFFEN, Nathan, of Memarneck, Westchester Co., mariner. Letters of administration granted his father Nehemiah Kniffen of Rye, same Co., yeoman.

1008 1787 Jany. 16 March 10

KETCHAM, Joshua, of Huntington Township, Suffolk Co. Wife Jerusha, sons Israel, Zebulon, Ruben, Joshua, Philipp and David, grandson Ketcham Terry, daughters Rebeck Buffet, Margaret Brush and Phebe Purdy. Real and personal property. Executors Wilmot Oakley, John Oakley and Nathaniel Whitman. Witnesses Thomas Powell, Jonah Powell, yeoman, and Philipp Ketcham. Recorded in Wills and Probates, Vol. I., p. 77.

1009
1804
July 24
1817
Novbr. 21

KANE, Archibald, of Canajoharie, Montgomery Co., merchant. Brother and partner in trade James Kane of Albany City sole heir and executor of real and personal estate. Witnesses Gerrit la Grangie, John Arden jun. and Joseph Leavens. Recorded ut supra, Vol. II., p. 340.

1010
1816
Decbr. 12
1821
Septbr. 15

KIDD, Christina, wife of John Kidd, late Commander of H. M. Packet *Elizabeth*, of Budock Parish, Cornwall Co., England, and late widow of Edward Hall. Son Capt. Edward Hall, R. N., mother Anna Maria Maudeline Wiler, infirm brother Mathias Wiler, widowed sister Mary Maudeline Burk, who has youngest child Michael, sister Catherine Gross, daughter Christina Anna Elizabeth Kidd. Bankstock. Trustees and executors William Rhinelander, Philipp Rhinelander, both of New York, Charles King of Paris and Edward Hall. Codicil of January 9, 1817, adds husband's mother Mrs. Mary Grainger, sister Ann and half brother John Grainger and children of late sister-in-law Hannah to beneficiaries under will. "The relations of my late beloved husband resided at Robinhoods Bay near Whitley, Yorkshire." No witnesses to will, witnesses of codicil J. Perry, John Richards, Wm. Carne and John Carne. Recorded ut supra, p. 362.

1011
1787
May 11

KEELING, Charles, of N. Y. City, merchant, who died at the Bay of Honduras. Letters of administration on the estate of, granted his widow Catharine Keeling. Recorded ut supra, Vol. III., p. 76 and 78.

1012
1707-8
Jany. 17
Dutch

KNICKERBACKER, Harmen Jansen, of Dutchess Co. Wife Elizabeth, children Johannis, Lowrens, Cornelis, Evert, Pieter, Jannetie, widow of Hendrick Lansing jun. and Cornelia. Real and personal estate. Executors the wife and sons Johannis and Lourens. Witnesses Jan Ploeg, Peter Pile and D'Meyer, clark. Albany Co. Records, Wills, I., p. 175.

1013 1722 June 8 — **KIDNEY, John,** of Albany City, letters of administration on his estate granted to Maritie, his widow. Albany Co. Records, Wills, I., p. 178.

1014 1753 Aug. 11 1760 March 29 — **KASS, Lodewick,** of Albany Co. Niece Hannah, oldest da. of sister Sarah and Teady Maginnes. Land at Burnetsfield, in the patent, granted to testator, his mother and sisters. Executor Teady Maginnes. Witnesses Abraham van Arnem, Yan van Buren, Richard Cartwright. Albany Co. Records, Wills, I., p. 253.

1015 (L 1) 1682 Octbr. 25 Dutch — **LAMBERTS, Thomas,** and wife Sarretie Jans, of Bedford, L. I. The survivor, daughters Elisabeth, Engeltie, wife of Jacobus van de Water, children of dec'd da. Elisabeth Juriaens, wife of Isaacq Grevenraet, children of dec'd son Andries Juriaens and wife Annetie ——. Real and personal property. The survivor to be executor. Witnesses Jan Vincent and Pieter Stevens. Notarial copy.

1016 (L 2) 1691-2 Febry. 10 1692 March 30 — **L'HOMMEDIEU, Peter,** of Kingston, Ulster Co., mercht. Mother Martha l'Hommedieu, living in London. "Worldly estate." Executors Steven Valloo and Steven de Lance of N. Y. Witnesses Jean David, St. Valleau and Humphry Davenport.

1017 (L 3) 1706 Novbr. 3 1707 Octbr. 3 — **LAFORD, alias LIBERTEE, John,** of Nistagajone, Albany Co., yeoman. Wife Maragrieta, sons John, Daniel, Abraham, Nicolaes, Jacob and Isaac, daughters, Mary, wife of John Vedder, and Anna. Real and personal estate. Guardians Gysbert Marselies and Johannis Beekman of Albany. The wife sole executrix. Witnesses John Sandersen Glen, Philipp Schuyler and Dirck Arentsen Brat.

1018 (L 4) 1709 Septbr. 17 1710 May 12 — **LYDIUS, Johannis,** son of Hendricus Lydius, late Minister at Maesdam, S. Holland, Minister of the Dutch Reformed Church at Albany. Wife Isabella, son John Hendrick, 5 yrs. old, daughters Geertruy Isabell, 14 years old, Marya Ennatte, 12 yrs., Margarieta Johanna, 7 yrs., and Susanna Catharina, 2 yrs. Real estate in the City of Onderwater, County of Leerdam, Jurisdiction of Tarley, personal property. Executors "my well beloved Spouse," Col. Killian van Rensselaer and Evert Bancker esqre. Witnesses Hend. Hansen, Johannis Mingael and Robt. Livingston jun. Seal. At date of probate April 17, 1716, widow Isabella Lydius has become wife of Jacob Staats of Albany.

1019 (L 5) 1724-5 Jany. 22 March 15 **LE GRANGE, Omy** jun., of Renselaerswyck Colony. Wife Else, Johannis Le Grange jun., brothers Isaac and Jabob Le Grange, nephew Barnardus, son of bro. Jacob, and Omy, son of bro. Isaac. Real and personal estate. The wife sole executrix. Witnesses Phil. Verplanck, Luycas Winegaert and Peter Bratt.

1020 (L 6) 1725 April 14 1750 April 30 **LIVINGSTON, Robert** junior, of Albany City, esquire. Wife Margaret, sons James, Peter and John, daughter Angletie, grandchildren Henry and Margaret Beekman. Real estate in Albany City, at Schoherah, Schenectady, Saratogah, Kinderhook and elsewhere, personal property. The wife sole executrix. Witnesses Jacob Staats, Jacob Roseboom and John Collins.

1021 (L 7) 1730 May 19 Octbr. 24 **LEGG, William,** of Kingston, Ulster Co. Children William, Henry, Catherin, Joanna, Leah, sister-in-law Giertie Ploegh. Real and personal estate. Executors son William, bro. John Legg and brothers-in-law John Davenport and William Ploegh. Witnesses Jakobus du Bois, James Whittaker, Kryn Oosterhoudt and Abraham Burhans.

1022 (L 8) 1734 March 25 —— **LAKEMAN, Abraham,** of Richmond Co., gentleman. Wife Anje, children Hester, wife of Nicholas Lazelier, Catharine, wife of John Morgan, Elizabeth, wife of John van Deventer, Jacob, Mary, wife or widow of

Nicholas Matison. Houses and lots in Wall Str. and in Dock Str., N. Y. City, land at Great Kil, Staten Island, personal property. Executors Gosen Adriaens, Rem van der Beck, Hendrick van Lawa, all of Richmond Co., gentlemen, Jacques Cortelyou sen. of New Utrecht, Kings Co., and the three sons-in-law N. Lazelier, John Morgan and John van Deventer. Witnesses Jacob Bergen, Nicholas Stilwell and Samuel Thirston. Copy made April 2, 1760.

1023 (L 9) 1739 June 15 Aug. 11 **LOW, William,** of Poughkeepsie, Dutchess Co., merchant. Wife Elezabeth sole heiress and with bro. Petrus Low executrix. Witnesses Jacob Louw, Abraham Freer jun. and Henry van der Burgh.

1024 (L 10) 1742 Septbr. 7 Octbr. 24 **LANE, Henry,** of N. Y. City, merchant. Wants to be buried in the Churchyard very privately two hours after dark. Sons Henry, lately married to da. of Henry Cuyler, Thomas, brother Joseph Lane. Lot in King Str., N. Y. City, personal property. Son Henry sole executor. Witnesses Jos. Murray, Wm. Searle and James Emott. Copy.

1025 (L 11) 1746 July 24 1746-7 Jany. 7 **LANSINGH, Gerrit Jan,** of Rensselaerswyck Manor, cordwainer. Wife Elizabeth, son to be baptized Gerrit, daughters Helena and Catharine. Real and personal estate. Executors bro. Hendrik Lansingh of the Boght in said Manor and bro.-in-law Abraham van Arnem of the same place. Witnesses Hendrick Lansingh, Abraham van Arnem and Jas. Stenhouse.

1026 (L 12) 1747 Decbr. 28 1756 May 25 **LE CONTE, John,** of Richmond Co. Wife Mary, son John, da. Frances. Real and personal property (a silver tankard, rings and jewels). Executors Nicholas Larzelere, John Morgine, Abraham Cole and son John le Conte. Witnesses Isaac Cole of Richmond Co., farmer, Nicholas Larzelere jun. and Ester la Tourette. Copy.

1027 (L 13) 1749 Jany. 8 1770 April 21 **LOW, Peter,** of N. Y. City, merchant. Wife Rachell, sons Peter, Cornelius, Nicholas and John, daughters Hellena, Margaret, Jane, Rachel and Elizabeth. Real and personal estate. Executors the wife and sons Peter and Cornelius. Witnesses John van Cortlandt, Cornelius Wynkoop and Benjamin Wynkoop. Copy.

1028 (L 14) 1752 May 13 1753 Febry. 21 **LITTLE, John,** of Stonefield, Ulster Co., gentleman. Wife Frances, daughters Frances Nicoll, Elisabeth, Elinor McGarrah, Hannah Galatian, who has sons John and David Galatian, Margaret Moffat, grandson John McGarrah. Real and personal property. Executors Jacobus Bruyn of Shangham, Michael Jaction of Goshan and son-in-law John Moffat, minister of the gospel at Wallkil. Witnesses Alexander Kidd, James Hunter and John Wharrey.

1029 (L 15) 1757 June 14 1759 Aug. 9 **LEWIS, Leonard,** of Poghkeepsie Prect., Dutchess Co., yeoman. Wife Rachell, son Thomas, two other children not named, brothers and sisters, except brothers Richard, Thomas and Barent Lewis. Land in Orange and Ulster Co., personal estate. Executors the wife and her father Abraham Swartwout. Witnesses Heinerig Busch, John Hickey and Bartholomew Crannell, att'y-at-law.

1030 (L 16) 1757 Decbr. 18 1762 Aug. 11 **LEATHEM, William,** Probate of will of, naming Robert Alexander of N. Y. City, merchant, sole executor.

1031 (L 17) 1757 Septbr. 5 Decbr. 10 **LITTLE, Frances,** widow of John, of Wallkil Prect., Ulster Co. Granddaughter Frances Galatian, daughters Hannah Galatian, Elioner McGarrah and Margaret Moffat. Personal property. Da. Hannah Galatian sole executrix. Witnesses Mary Hedon and Agness Deuenny. Vide No. 1028.

1032 (L 18) 1758 June 1 **LODGE, Abraham,** of N. Y. City, esqre., att'y-at-law. Sisters-in-law Catharine Morris and Rachel Fisher, a daughter, infirm of body. Personal property (plate, rings and jewels). This is a memorandum for a will, which upon testimony of John Kelly, att'y-at-law, John Chetwood, clerk of Abr. Lodge and Richard Morris, attorney-at-law, all of New York City, was admitted as a will. Abraham Lodge had married Margaret, da. of John Kelly, and died March 27, 1758.

1033 (L 19) 1758 Febry. 17 1786 Aug. 30 **LYON, Joseph,** of Whiteplains, Westchester Co., yeoman. Wife Mary, sons Joseph, Daniel, James, Reuben, Jeremiah and Thomas, daughters Mary, wife of Elnathan Ha——(?), Hannah, Susannah and Ann; an expected child. Real and personal property. Executors the wife, son Daniel and Charles Theall. Signatures cut off. Much faded. Proved by Elisha Horton of Harrisons, John Carhartt and Jane Carhartt.

1034 (L 20) 1759 May 3 **LAWRENCE, Mary,** widow of Daniel, of Flushing, L. I. Daughter Mehitabel Hilton and grandda. Mary Hilton, da. Mary, wife of James Thorn. Personal property. Executors da. Mehitabel Hilton and grandson John Hilton. Witnesses Jacob Goelet, John Talman and Jane Dies. Copy made January 18, 1763.

1035 (L 21) 1760 March 10 1765 Jany. 29 **LAWYER, Johannes,** of Schoharry, Albany Co., merchant. Wife Elizabeth, sons Johannes, Jacob Frederick, Lowrence, daughter Elizabeth, widow of Marcus Reckert and now wife of Hendrick Hayns, children of dec'd da. Sophia, late wife of Jeost Belinger and Christian Zehe. Real and personal estate. Executors the three sons. Witnesses Peter Nicolas Sommer, Lutheran minister at Schoharry, Johannes Scheffer and Franz Otto. Affidavit of Joseph Bevin shows, that testator was deprived of his senses and left out of his will his wife's da. Hannah Mitchell, when he signed the will in March, 1762.

1036 (L 22) 1761 June 27 Septbr. 18 **LEWIS, William,** of Albany. William Chase of Albany, victualler, sole heir and executor of "worldly effects," including money due for wages from Mr. John Farrel of Albany, merchant. Witnesses Jos. Deniston, Jo. FitzPatrick, Jno. Moore and Cornelis Creeden. Printed form.

1037 (L 23) 1761 Aug. 4 Novbr. 26 **LITTLE, John,** of Poughkeepsie Prect., Dutchess Co., carpenter. Thomas Dearing sole heir and executor of real and personal estate. Witnesses William Parks, Robert Luckey and Robert S. Butcher, schoolmaster.

1038 (L 24) 1762 March 9 1763 Jany. 18 **LOTT, Henry,** of Dutchess Co., esquire. Wife Hester, children Abraham, Mary and Sarah. "Worldly estate." Executors bro. Peter Lott of New York and his son, nephew Abraham. Witnesses Jacob R. Everson, Benj. Knight and Paulus Mauerer.

1039 (L 25) 1763 March 21 April 11 **LEGG, Samuel,** of N. Y. City, house carpenter. Wife Elisabeth, sons Henry, Samuel, daughters Sarah, Else and Phebe. Real and personal property. Executors son Henry and son-in-law Jacob Loveberry. Witnesses Philipp Pelton, carpenter, William Oglvie, cordwainer, and John Woods esqre. Copy.

1040 (L 26) 1764 March 20 May 21 **LEONARD, Silas,** of Newburgh Prect., Ulster Co., gentleman. Wife Elezebath, sons Silas, James, John, William and George, daughters Jane Carpenter, Elezebath Smith, Cateran Smith, Temper and Abigail. Real and personal property. Executors the wife, son Silas and Benjamin Carpenter. Witnesses Gilbert Denton, farmer, James Denton and Leonard Smith.

1041 (L 27) 1766 Octbr. 30 1767 Aug. 1 **LUDLUM, Isaac,** of Goshen, Orange Co., yeoman. Wife Catherine, sons Isaac, John, Benjamin, daughters Mary, Sarah and Elizabeth, son-in-law Samuel Denton. Homefarm, land in Wawayanda Patent, personal property. Executors son Isaac and son-in-law Samuel Denton. Witnesses Danl. Everett, John Gale jun., and John Garner, farmer.

1042 (L 28) 1766 Novbr. 8 Decbr. 2 **LYLE, Abraham,** of Albany City, merchant. Wife and two children. Real and personal estate. Executor bro.-in-law John van Alen, David Edgar and Peter Silvester. Witnesses Joseph Young, doctor, David Bary, tobacconist, both of Albany, and Richard Rea.

1043 (L 29) 1768 Decbr. 20 1770 March 14 **LOSEE, John,** of Beekmans Prect., Dutchess Co. Sons Lawrence, John and Abraham. "Worldly estate." Executors sons Lawrence and Abraham and Bartholomew Noxon jun. Witness Barthw. Noxon jun., yeoman, Tishe Losee and Losee.

1044 (L 30) 1768 March 17 May 16 **LOUNHART, Philipp,** of Rinebeck Prect., Dutchess Co., yeoman. Wife Anna Catrina, son Petar, daughters Eva, wife of Johannes Pest and Catrine, wife of Nicolas Traver, who has deserted her, grandson Philipp Traver and four more grandchildren Traver. Real and personal estate. Executors son Petar, son-in-law Johannes Pest and William Beam. Witnesses Peter Scott, John Morres and Benjamin Vredenburgh, all of Dutchess Co., yeomen.

1045 (L 31) 1768 May 14 Aug. 15 German **LAUNERT, Johan George,** of Witenkley's Kil, North end of Dutchess Co., farmer. Wife Anna Catherine, nephews Pitter, son of eldest bro., Johannes Mohr, son of a sister, godsons George Schneider, and George Seegendorff, Anna, wife of Heinrich Hoff, David Winkeler, Philipp Henrich Mohr, bro. Pitter Louks. Real and personal estate. Executors bro. Pitter Laux, Caspar Schult and Willem Betzer. Witnesses Jacup Mor, Carel Neher and Jacob Bitzer, all of said Prect., yeomen.

1046 (L 32) 1769 Novbr. 2 1770 Jany. 12 **LESSLEY, Mary,** of N. Y. City, widow. Son John, daughters Eleanor, wife of Thomas Yarrow, ship carpenter, Elizabeth and Mary. Real and personal estate. Executors Isaac Marschalk, baker, and Charles Philipps, cooper, both of N. Y. City. Witnesses John DLmontonje, painter, Evert Wessels and Charles Morse.

1047 (L 33) 1769 Octbr. 16 1770 Decbr. 3 **LANSINGH, Alexander,** of Schonectaday Township, Albany Co., yeoman. Wife Neeltie, sons Cornelius, Johannis and Harmanus, daughter Jannetje, wife of John van Eps. Real and personal estate (a Dutch bible). Executors John Visger esqre, Cornelius Lansing and Dirk van Ingen. Witnesses Abraham Grod, yeoman, Francis Osburn and Abraham Truax.

1048 (L 34) 1769 Novbr. 4 1770 Septbr. 26 **LYNOTT, Thomas,** of Potomocassock, Albany Co. Wife Elizabeth, daughters Elizabeth and Margaret, nephew Hubert, son of bro. Luke Lynott, cousin Sibby Lynott, of Dublin, Ireland, children of sister Mary Hutchinson. Real and personal estate. Executors Joseph Griswold of N. Y. City, distiller, and James Barker of Woodstock, Albany Co., gentleman. Witnesses Hugh Deniston, of Albany Co., innholder, Marten G. v. Bergen and Rachel Deniston.

1049 (L 35) 1770 Decbr. 12 1771 April 9 **LECOUNTE, Bowdewine,** of Poughkeepsie Prect., Dutchess Co. Wife Elesabeth, grandson Bowdewine Lecounte Yelverton, daughters Sisco and Sary, John Keep, Bowdewine Keep, Rachel Keep, Mary Keep. Real and personal estate. Executor John Stinboughrough (van Steenbergh). Witnesses John Carman of Poughkeepsie carpenter, and Thomas Newcomb.

1050 (L 36) 1771 April 20 Novbr. 27 **LAVINUS, Philipp,** of Rochester, Ulster Co. Andries D. Witt of Neponagh, Ulster Co., sole heir and with Dirck Hoornbeek and Mattheus Cortright executor of real and personal estate. Witnesses Charles de Witt of Marbletown, esquire, Arie Oosterhout and Hendericks Oosterhout.

1051 (L 37) 1771 March 19 1785 June 13 **LITTLE, Thomas,** of Corrysbrook, Albany Co., yeoman. Wife Jane, daughters Jane, wife of John Glasford, Unice, wife of Duncan Quinten, Dorothy, wife of John Wason, Elizabeth, wife of James More, sons Thomas and James, grandsons Thomas, son of son William, and Thomas Wason, four youngest children of William Thorington viz. Thomas, John, Mary and Samuel, Sarah, da. of son William. Real and personal estate. Executors Daniel Campbell and Reynier Myndersen. Witnesses Caleb Beck, Benjamin Young and Seth Young. Codicil of April 10, 1772, adds grandson John Little to heirs and is witnessed by William Johnston, William Butler and Thomas Thornton.

1052 (L 38) 1772 Jany. 2 1786 April 12 **LEVY, Joseph Israel,** of Calcutta, Kingdom of Bengal. Daughter Abigael Israel Levy, mother Rosey Israel, living in Houndsditch near Algate, London, Jews *Callige* at Jerusalem, "mother of my child named Jabeca," brothers and sisters in London. Real and personal property. Executors Abraham Levy of London, merchant, Charles Wiston, Joseph Pollard and Robert Brown. Witnesses Anth. O'Brien and James Miller. Hebrew Seal. Copy.

1053 (L 39) 1773 Novbr. 22 1775 April 15 **LYON, George,** of Ulster Co., farmer. Children Robert, Mary, Jean, Elizabeth and Sarah. "Worldly estate." Executors John Davis and James McMunn. Witnesses Henry McNeeley, Joseph Davis, yeoman, and Sarrah McNeeley.

1054 (L 40) 1743-4 March 8 1745 May 30 **LEGG, William,** junior, of Kingston, Ulster Co. Wife Marytie, children William, Samuel, Barent and Margret. Homefarm called Jacobs Hook and an island, personal property. Executors brothers-in-law Wilhelmus Burhans, Richard Davenport and Philip Vele jun., and neighbour Edward James Whitaker. Witnesses Hendr. Schoonaker, John Whitaker and Tobias Wynkoop. Codicil of Octbr. 11, 1744, empowers executors to sell estate derived through mother Gessie and aunt Giertie from grandfather Hendrick Ploegh and is witnessed by Jan Pyetersen Osterhoudt, John Whitker and Jacob Burhans.

1055 (L 41) 1774 March 15 Septbr. 24

LOW, John, late of Newark, N. J., now of Albany Co. Wife Sarah, grandsons Peter and John, sons of dec'd son Cornelius, John, son of Nicholas Low, and Jacob Farrand, John, son of da. Sarah Low, son-in-law Kilian van Rensselaer, husband of da. Mary, daughters Johanna Frankin, Margred Hedden, Elizabeth, wife of James Gray, grandda. Elizabeth, da. of dec'd son Cornelius, Margaret, widow of said son. Real and personal property (Dutch bibles). Executors the wife, sons-in-law Kilian van Rensselaer, Nicholas Low and Hendrick Andriessen Frankin. Witnesses Abrm. A. Lansing, Christan Abrims and John Roorbach.

1056 (L 42) 1774 Febry. 28 March 31

LINKLON, Samuel. Wife ——, an expected child, father Jeremiah Lincklon. "Worldly estate." Executors Samuel Bages or Bangs and David Crosby jun. Witnesses David Crosby jun. of Frederick Borough, Dutchess Co., cordwainer, John Waring and Thomas Benedict. Proved in Dutchess Co.

1057 (L 43) 1775 Aug. 4 1782 Novbr. 16

LIPE, Caspar, of Conajohary Distr., Tryon Co. Wife Catharina, sons Adam, John, Jost, da. Anna Maria, wife of Jacob van der Werken, Maria Elisabetha and Anna, children of dec'd da. Margaretha, late wife of Adam Conderman. Real and personal property. Overseer John Daniel Gross, the wife executrix. Witnesses William Seeber, Jacob Seeber and Johannes Wohlgemuth jun., farmer.

1058 (L 44) 1775 June 11 1776 Febry. 1

LESHER, Bastiaen, of Livingston Manor. Wife Elizabeth, sons Bastiaen, Samuel and Marks, daughters Hannah, wife of Peter Bain, and Helena, wife of Jurry Rosman. Real and personal estate. Executors bro. Coenrat Lesher and Dirck Jansen. Witnesses Martinus Shoech, Marks Coen and Henry Polwer.

1059 (L 45) 1775 Octbr. 5 1784 May 24 **LANGENDYK, Petrus,** of the Platte Kil, Town of Kingston, Ulster Co., yeoman. Wife Catherina, sons Cornelius and Petrus, da. Maria, niece Annatje, da. of sister-in-law. Real and personal estate. Executors the wife and bro.-in-law Christian Valkenburgh. Witnesses Petrus A. Winne, Arent Winne of Sagerties, farmer, and Christopher Tappen of Kingston, esquire.

1060 (L 46) 1775 Aug. 18 1776 Jany. 2 **LOSEE, John,** of Beekmans Prect., Dutchess Co. Wife Elenor, sons John and William. Real and personal estate. Executors the wife, Stephen van Vorhase and Mical Vincent. Witnesses Jacob Hesnor and Barthow. Noxon junior.

1061 (L 47) 1776 April 10 1784 March 6 **LYONS, Robert.** Sisters Elisabeth, Marthew, Searey and Jean, nephew ——, eldest son of sister Searey. Only personal property. Executors Richard Colman and George Denniston. Witnesses James Greer, Alexander Denniston of Wallkil, Ulster Co., and George Denniston. Proved in Orange Co.

1062 (L 48) 1776 Octbr. 22 —— **LEVY, Isaac,** of N. Y. City. Son Asher, da. Esther, otherwise called Henrietta, "both borne of Elizabeth Pue," bro. Samson Levy, sister Rachel, wife of Isaac Seixas. Real and personal property. Executors son Asher, when of age, bro. Samson Levy and his son Moses. Witnesses Walter Shee, Benj. Condy and Edmund Nihell. Copy made in Philadelphia Novbr. 8, 1785.

1063 (L 49) 1776 April 13 1786 April 11 **LAMON, Elisabeth,** of Ulster Co. Son William Lamon, grandchildren: two daughters of the son and John Wast, son of da. Mertha Wast. "Worldly estate." Executors Samuel Miller and John Black. Witnesses Arthur Barbor, James Downs and Samuel Miller of Montgomery Prect., farmer.

1064 (L 50) 1777 Febry. 7 1784 Septbr. 23

LANGDON, Thomas, of Beekmans Prect., Dutchess Co. Wife Femmetje, children Thomas, Abraham and Eleoner. Real and personal estate. Executors bro. Johannis Langdon, bro.-in-law Rem Adriance and neighbour John Wilkeson. Witnesses Isaac Adriance, Rem Adriance jun. and Jacob Horton of N. Y. City, grocer. Proved in N. Y. City.

1065 (L 51) 1777 Jany. 25 —

LOWAREAR, Michael, of N. Y. City, cooper. Son Edward, da. Mary Banks, bro. Henry Lowarear, nephew Benjamin Goff. Personal effects. Executor Dr. Middleton. Witnesses Thomas Davis, Martin Cregier and John Clarke Cooke. Printed form.

1066 (L 52) 1777 Febry. 12 1779 Jany. 1

LITTLE, Archibald, of Oxford, Cornwall Prect., Orange Co. Wife Sarah, sons James, Timothy, Archibald, Joseph and John, da. Sarah. Real and personal estate. Executors son-in-law Seth Marvin, Henry Wisner and Jesse Woodhull. Witnesses William Harper, Zebadiah Mills, Robert Benson and John McKesson.

1067 (L 53) 1778 May 10 July 4

LEWIS, James, of Smith Clove, Orange Co. Wife ——, Samuel Lewis, Isaac, Joseph and William Lewis, John Lewis, Mary Pilgrim, James and Jacob, Elizabeth Lewis, apparently all children of testator. "Worldly estate." Executors the wife and bro.-in-law Wm. Miller. Witnesses Adam Gilchrist, tailor, William Miller and James Gilchrist.

1068 (L 54) 1778 May 18 1779 March 20

LIVINGSTON, Philipp, of New York, now of York, Penna. Wife Christina, children Philipp, Catherine, Richard, Margaret, Sarah, Abraham and Henry. Real estate in Township of Brookland, Kings Co., houses and lots in N. Y. City, personal property. Executors the wife, Abraham ten Broeck and Walter Livingston. Witnesses Nathaniel Scudder, Wm. Duer and Gouvr. Morris. Proved in N. J. Copy.

1069 (L 55) 1779 Septbr. 22 1784 Aug. 20 **LEAYCRAFT, Viner,** late of N. Y. City, now of Tappan, Orange Co., mariner. Wife Elizabeth, sons William, Christopher, John and George, da. Mary. Son William disinherited, if he marries Elizabeth Devou. "Temporal estate." Executors da. Mary and sons John, George and William. Witnesses Garrat Paulding, Thomas Kelly and Thomas Goldstrap of Haverstraw, yeoman.

1070 (L 56) 1780 May 10 1783 Aug. 29 **LITTLE, Archibald,** of Oxford, Orange Co. Wife Susanna, brothers Joseph Little, John Little, James Little, Timothy Little, sisters Hannah, Mary and Sarah. Real and personal estate. Executor bro.-in-law Seth Marvin and bro. James. Witnesses Elihu Marvin, Samuel Racket and Sarah Marvin. See No. 1066.

1071 (L 57) 1780 Decbr. 6 1781 Jany. 8 **LEWIS, Gertrude,** widow of Jonathan, late of North East Prect., Dutchess Co. Daughters Anna, Johanna and Mary, son Jonathan. Real and personal property. Executors Daniel Lewis, Isaac Smith and bro.-in-law John Reyley. Not signed nor witnessed. Proved by testimony of Isaac Smith of Amenia Prect., esquire.

1072 (L 58) 1780 Septbr. 6 1783 April 15 **LANSING, Elizabeth,** late of Albany City, widow. Son Garret, daughters Annautie and Helenah. Real and personal estate. Daughter Annautie Lansing sole executrix. Witnesses Evert W. Swart, Cornelius Cooper, both of Rumbouts Prect., yeomen, and Nathaniel Sackett. Proved in Dutchess Co.

1073 (L 59) 1780 Jany. 8 1784 Jany. 19 **LUDLOW, Henry,** late of N. Y. City, now of Claverack Distr., Albany Co. Children William Henry, Gabriel Henry, Thomas, Sarah, wife of Richard Morris, Martha, son of dec'd da. Elizabeth, vizt. Gabriel Gillan Shaw, children of dec'd son John Corbet Ludlow, vizt. Henry Bayley, Peter Robert and Mary Corbet Ludlow. Real and personal estate. Executors sons Gabriel Henry and William Henry, sons-in-law Richard Morris and Charles Shaw. Witnesses George Monell, Jeremiah D. Lamater and W. T. Wemple of Claverack Dist., Doctor.

1074 (L 60) 1781 May 22 1784 Aug. 25

LEROY, Petrus, of Poughkeepsie Prect., Dutchess Co. Wife Deborah, children Francis, Simeon, Peter, Saletje, wife of Leonard Lewis, Maria, wife of François van de Bogert, Rachel, wife of Johannis Pels and Annatje; sons Francis and Peter are in N. Y. and have probably adhered to the King of Great Britain. Real and personal property. Executors brothers-in-law Johannis Teerpenning and Peter van Kleeck. Witnesses Thomas Pinkney, Richard Snedeker, both of Dutchess Co., gentlemen, and William Low.

1075 (L 61) 1783 Decbr. 19 1784 Febry. 14

LEAKE, Thomas, of Little 9 Partners, Dutchess Co., yeoman. Wife Lidia, daughters Sarah, Mary and Lydia (?), sons Stephen, David, Peleg, Daniel and Abraham, grandson Benjamin, son of son Isaac. Real and personal estate. Executors the wife and son Daniel. Witnesses George Huddleston, Samuel Dean jun., yeoman, and Lydia Leake, spinster.

1076 (L 62) 1784 April — 1788 March 28

LIVINGSTON, Philipp Philipp, of Kingston, Surrey Co., Isld of Jamaica. Wife Sarah, children Philipp Henry, George, Catherine, Christina, Sarah, Edward and Jasper Hall. Real estate on the Island, personal property (plate). Executors for Jamaica Richard Grant, Thomas Cargill, Richard Batty, William Dillworth and William Ross of Richmond, all of the Island; executors for New York Philipp Peter Livingston, Robert C. Livingston and brothers-in-law Thomas Jones and John H. Livingston. Witnesses William Young, James Braithwaite and Chas. Stewart of St. Mary Parish, planter. Proved in Jamaica. Copy.

1077 (L 63) 1784 Jany. 22 June 19

LOSEE, Simeon, of Charlotte Prect. Dutchess Co. Wife ——, sons James and Nathaniel, daughters Sarah, Phebe, Anna, and an expected child. Real and personal estate. Executors bro. James Losee and Jesse Oakley. Witnesses John Platt, farmer, James Pettet and Elizabeth Golden.

1078 (L 64) 1785 Decbr. 22 1786 Jany. 20 **LATTIMORE, Benoni,** of New Burgh Prect., Ulster Co. Sons Benoni, William Freeman and Job, daughters Bridget Marcy and Hannah, oldest child of da. Abigail. "Worldly estate." Executors Wolvert Ecker and Thurston Wood. Witnesses Henry ter Boss, yeoman, Thomas Jacockes, Thurston Wood and Wolvert Ecker.

1079 (L 65) 1785 July 7 1786 May 1 **LEYDT, Jennecke,** of Orange Co. Helletje, widow of Jonathan Debois, Sarah, widow of Albert Leydecker, Elizabeth, wife of John Hutton, Sarah, wife of Richard Blauvelt, William Sickles and wife Marretje, William and Henry van Dalsem. Lot in Courtlandt Str. N. Y. City, personal property (a silver teapot). Executors William Sickels of Orange Co. and Henry van Dalsem of N. Y. City. Witnesses John Hodson, weaver, Thunis Cuyper, yeoman, both of Orange Town, and M. Hogenkamp.

1080 (L 66) 1786 Jany. 14 Febry. 14 **LOOP, Marte,** of Livingston Manor. Wife Mary, son Johannis, daughters Maregreta and Mary. Real and personal estate. Executors the wife, Wm. Harder jun. and son-in-law Jurry T. Snyder. Witnesses George Dippel, yeoman, Coenrat Myer and Ino. W. Fonda.

1081 (L 67) 1790 April 26 May 22 **LUDLOW, Elizabeth,** wife of James, of N. Y. State and da. of Elizabeth Harrison, late of Rhode Island. Da. Frances Mary. Real estate in New London, Connt., derived from sister Hermione, wife of Captain Robert Cargey, late of London, lands in R. I., personal property. Executors kinsmen Gabriel William Ludlow, Thomas Ludlow, Cary Ludlow, George Ludlow, William Ludlow and Charles Ludlow of N. Y. City, gentlemen. Witnesses Richard Bayley, physician, Abraham Ludlow, gentleman, both of N. Y. City and John Davis.

1082 (L 68) 1796 Jany. 3 — **LOCKMAN, Frederick,** of New York. Hanniken Lilienthal, bro. Mathew and sister Alheid Lockman, not far from Bremen. "What I leave behind me." No executor named. Witnesses Conrad Croeder, Fredk. Trackman, Hy. Eichel and Hy. Gear. No evidence of proof.

1083 (L 69) 1744 Aug. 27 1749 March 25 — **LEWIS, John,** of Albany City, yeoman. Wife Hillegond, da. Mary. Personal estate. Executor Peter Winne. Witnesses Thomas Williams and Abraham Douw.

1084 1783 April 2 1787 Jany. 24 — **LYON, Jonathan,** of North Castel, Westchester Co. Wife Elizabeth, sons Jonathan, Elnathan, Israel, David, Peter, grandsons Jonathan, son of Elnathan, Jonathan, son of Peter, Jonathan, son of da. Phebe. Land at North Castel, personal property. Executors sons Israel and Peter. Witnesses Silas Sutherland, yeoman, Enoch Miller and Samuel Miller. Recorded in Wills and Probates, Vol. I., p. 7.

1085 1780 May 21 1781 June 29 — **LABOYTEAUX, John,** of Philadelphia. Wife Hannah, children John, Samuel Smith, Peter, Gabriel, William, Hannah and Nancy. "Worldly estate." Executors the wife, Thomas Pearsall of N. Y. City, merchant, and Benjamin Helme of N. Y. City, attorney-at-law. Witnesses Timothy Brundige, William Kennan and John Vandegrist. Proved in Pennsylvania. Recorded ut supra, p. 107.

1086 1785 Aug. 11 1785 Septbr. 9 — **LEVY, Joseph Israel,** of Leman Str., Goodmansfield, Parish of St. Mary's, White Chapel, London. Wife Polly, da. Sarah, brothers Samuel, Israel and Benjamin Jacobs, sisters Abigail Jacobs and Rachel Israel. Portuguese Synagogue, Jews College at Jerusalem. Rachel Cohen Medeco and Sarah Cohen Medeco, widow Fanny Myers of Elizabeth Square, St. Botolphs. Nine houses in Colbrook Square, personal property. Executors the wife and Isaac Moran of George Str., Minories. Witnesses Samuel Baker, Jos. Legros and S. Lazarus. Recorded ut supra, p. 215.

1087 1790 June 30 Septbr. 16 **LIVINGSTON, William,** of Essex Co., N. J. Children Brockholst, Susannah Catherine, widow of Matthew Ridley, Mary, wife of James Linn, Sarah van Brugh, wife of Honble. John Jay, and Judith, wife of John Watkins; son William disinherited. Real and personal estate (map of N. J. by John Hills, "Chronology and History of the World," by Rev. John Blair, LL.D.). Executors Honble. John Sloat Hobbart, Judge of the N. Y. Supreme Court, Robert Watts and Matthew Clarkson, both of N. Y. and da. Susannah. Witnesses Isabella Bell, Patrick Dennis and Wm. P. Smith. Proved in N. J. Recorded et supra, p. 262.

1088 1789 Jany. 3 1792 April 10 **LOYD, Henry,** at present of N. Y. City, mariner, bound on a voyage to the East Indies. Friend Joseph Keens of N. Y. City, innholder, sole executor of personal estate. Witnesses John Balton, John Anderson, auctioneer, and John Wood. Recorded et supra, p. 337.

1089 1792 Febry. 9 Aug. 21 **LIVINGSTON, Catharine,** late of Rhinebeck, Dutchess Co., now of N. Y. City, widow of Robert Gilbert Livingston. Sons Henry G., Gilbert R., daughter Catharine, wife of John Reade, da.-in-law Margaret, widow of son Robert G., grandchildren Samuel and Helena Hake. Real and personal estate. Executors Gilbert Livingston, attorney-at-law, and son Gilbert R. Witnesses Martin S. Wilkins, Valentine Nutter and James Lashman. Recorded ut supra, p. 356.

1090 1792 June 6 July 2 **LEVY, Moses,** of New Port, R. I., merchant, "advanced in age." Moses, son of nephew Hiam Levy, Margaret McMahone, and her da. Anna, Moses Seixas and Simeon Levy, Bilhah, da. of Moses Seixas. Real and personal estate. Executors Hiam Levy, Moses Seixas and Simeon Levy. Witnesses Jona. Willson, John Anthony and Edmund I. Ellery. Proved in R. I. Recorded ut supra, p. 360.

1091 1792 Septbr. 18 1793 Jany. 9

LIVINGSTON, Peter van Brugh, late of N. Y. City, now of Elizabeth Town, N. J. Wife Elizabeth, son Philipp, children of da. Catharine Bayard, daughters Sarah Ricketts, Susannah Kean, son of da. Mary vizt. George van Brugh Brown, Mary, da. of son Peter dec'd and his wife Susan, Eliza, da. of dec'd da. Eliza Otto. Real and personal property. Executors Gerrard Bancker, Treasurer of N. Y. State, and son Philipp. Witnesses Walter Rutherford, Margareta Marshall and Aaron Ogden. Codicil of Octbr. 2, 1792, leaves legacies to grandda. Maria Pen Ricketts, grandsons Philipp Ricketts, James Otto Ricketts, Peter Kean; also to Rachel Hansen and her sister Elizabeth McCleaf, sister Sarah, Catherine, widow of bro. John. Witness Aaron Ogden. Recorded ut supra, p. 382.

1092 1792 May 13 1793 March 18

LEE, John, of Essex Co., born in the Town of Buxton, England, now of Faulkland Islands and the brig *Hope*, George Farmer, master, of N. Y., bound on a sailing voyage. Shipmate Robert Robinson sole heir and executor of personal property. Witnesses John Baxter, David Utt, butcher, and Jacob Hyer. Recorded ut supra, p. 386.

1093 1792 Decbr. 4 1794 18

LEWIS, John, of N. Y. City, mariner, going on a voyage to the East Indies. Friend George Potter of N. Y. City, innholder, sole heir and executor of personal estate. Witnesses John Galloway and Wm. Collins. Recorded ut supra, p. 429.

1094 1795 Aug. 23 Aug. 29 French

LEMAY, William Theodorus, of Plaisance Parish, St. Domingo, now of N. Y. City, son of Guilleaume Lemay and Marie Catherine Renullard of St. Germain en Laye near Paris. Sister Catherine Lemay, Benedictine nun at the Convent of Villarseau, near Magny, in the French Voxin, godda. Marguerite Ballou, M. Couet de Montarand, member of the Council. Real estate in the

Isld. of Sto. Domingo and in France, personal property. Executor Couet de Montarand. Witnesses Claude de Barras, Jean Pierre Cossié and Jean Leonard de la Boisserie. Recorded ut supra, p. 496.

1095 1795 May 31 Aug. 15 **LAWSON, John,** of Workington, Cumberland Co. (England), merchant. Wife Sarah, daughters not named. Real and personal estate. Trustees and executors bro.-in-law Robert Jackson of Rawtonhead, said Co., William Eckford, bookseller, and John Tye, tailor, both of Workington. Witnesses Joseph Tye, William Salkeld and John Askew, who certify that dec'd had goods, chattels and credits in the Province of N. Y. Recorded ut supra, Vol. II., p. 4.

1096 1797 April 22 April 27 French **LAMARQUE, Jean,** of Areahaye, Island of St. Domingo, now in N. Y. City. Codicil to a last will, made in St. Domingo, names Pierre Laffiteau as executor and gives a legacy to Madame Rosalie Gabrielle Pault, widow of Simon Voisin and to Marie Rose le Blanc. Witnesses R. J. van den Brock, notary public, Jouve and Michel. Recorded ut supra, II., p. 24.

1097 1792 Octbr. 11 1798 Novbr. 30 French **LOTBINIÈRE, Michel Chartier de,** Marquis de Chartier de Lotbinière, Marquis de Lotbinière in Vaudreuil, Lord of the Seigneuries de Vaudreuil, Deux Rigauds and Villechauve in Lower Canada, Knight of the Royal and Military Order of St. Louis. Son Eustace Gaspard Michel Chartier de Lotbinière, whom testator calls ungrateful and whose wife he designates as monster, cousin and pupil Michel Alain Chartier, Knight and Lord of Allainville, daughter in the U. S. Real and personal property in Canada. Executors (honoraires et onéraires) Rt. Rev. Jean François Hubert, Bishop of Quebec, Honble Wm. Smith, Chief Justice of Canada, Jean Baptist Deguin, priest at Vaudreuil, and Louis de Salaberry. Proved by the testimony of Simon Nathan, auctioneer, and Chartier Allainville, clerk, both of New York, as to handwriting. A long letter to Chief Justice Smith is added. Recorded ut supra, p. 99.

1098 1790 Jany. 4 1791 June 8 French **LARRESET, George,** native of Bayonne, France, about going to Isle de France. Sister Gracieuse Larraset, of Bayonne, the three children of M. Dingisart and wife, nephew and nieces of testator. Real and personal estate. Executor Dominic Lynch of N. Y. City, merchant. Witnesses V. A. Le Prince, Secretary to Count Moustier, and N. A. de Champgrillet. Testator died at Cape of Good Hope in January 1791. Recorded ut supra, p. 216.

1099 1785 July 9 **LIVINGSTON, Henry,** late Ensign N. Y. Levies. Letters of administration on the estate of, granted to his father John Livingston of N. Y. City, gentleman. Recorded ut supra, Vol. III., p. 47.

1100 1810 Febry. 21 1820 Aug. 19 **LAWRENCE, Jonathan,** of New York City, merchant. Wife Ruth, daughters Margaret, Judith Ireland, sons Jonathan, Samuel, Richard M., Abraham Riker, Joseph, John L., William Thomas. 14 Houses and lots between Arundel, Delancey and Suffolk Streets, personal property. Executors the seven sons. Witnesses Abraham Brinkerhoff jun., Danl. Rapelye and Charles Rogers. Recorded ut supra, Vol. IV., p. 113.

1101 1825 April 11 1826 Octbr. 16 **LUSH, Stephen,** of Albany City, esquire. Wife Lydia, daughters Rachel, Gertrude, widow of Robert James, Mary, wife of John M. Bradford, sons Samuel Stringer, William and Richard. House and lot on N. Market Str. (Broadway) Albany, land on Sakendaga R., in Township No. 3 & 11 Old Military Patent, No. 27 Totten and Crossfield Purchase, in Montgomery County, in lot No. 77 Jersey field, in lot No. 73 on Scaroon Lake, personal property. Trustees for da. Mary Bradford sons

Samuel S. and William. The wife sole executrix. Witnesses Richard S. Treat, Henry van den Bergh and C. Y. Lansing. Recorded ut supra, p. 180.

1102 1814 Jany. 27 1827 Octbr. 26 **La GRANGE, Christian,** of Bethlehem, Albany Co. Wife Elizabeth, daughters Ann, wife of John Hallenbake and Angelica, wife of Andrew Hallenbake, Janet, wife of James McClasky. Real and personal estate. Executors Jacob ten Eyck, James D. la Grange and James McClasky. Witnesses James Rodgers, Thomas Spencer and I. A. Quackenboss. Recorded ut supra, p. 234.

1103 1683-4 Jany. 6 1684 June 3 **LOVERIDGE, William,** of Albany. Wife Temperance, sons William, Samuel, daughters Hannah, wife of Henry Slaide, of Carolina, Temperance, wife of Isaac Molyn, of New York and Sarah, wife of John Ward of Esopus. Land at Catskil and personal property. No executor named. Witnesses Jacob Sanders Glen, Mr. Richard Pretty, at whose house the will is executed, and Robert Livingston, secretary. Albany Co. Records, Court Minutes, 1680-5, p. 549.

1104 1685 April 2 Dutch **LESPINARD, Anthony,** of Albany, burgher. Wife Abeltie, children Johannis, 10 yrs. old, Cornelia, Margarita and Abeltie, 6 months old. Real and personal estate. The wife sole executrix and guardian. Witnesses William Teller, Cornelius van Dyck and J. Becker, Notary Public. Albany Co. Records, Notarial Papers, II., p. 540.

1105-1107 1761 April 16 1767 Septbr. 26 **LAGRANGE, Isaac,** of the Normanskil, Albany Co., yeoman. Wife Maria, sons Omey, Isaac, Koonradt, daughters Geezee, wife of Johannis Look, Antje, wife of Anthony Quackenboss. Real and personal estate. Executors sons Omey and Isaac. Witnesses John M. Veeder, Volkert Veeder, both of the Normanskil farmers, and Jacob Jacobson. Albany Co. Records, Wills, I., p. 326.

1108 1761 June 12 1766 July 24 **LAGRANSE, Jacobus,** son of Omey, of the Normanskil, Albany Co. Wife Engeltie, children Omey, John, Arie, Myndert, Barnardus, Susanna, Annatie, Debora, grandson John Blomendal, son of dec'd. da. Christean. Real and personal estate. Executors sons Barnardus, Omey and John. Witnesses Volkert Veeder, Simon M. Veeder and Jacob Jacobson. Albany Co. Records, Wills, I., p. 364.

1109 1747 June 18 1750 May 9 **LAGRANGE, Johannis,** late of Rensselaerswyck Manor, yeoman. Children Johannis, Christiaen, Annatie, Margaret and Christientie, granddaughters, "which are Christened after my wife deceased towit Eytje," daughters of son Christiaen and daughters Annatie and Christientie. Real and personal estate (a silver cup, a do. tankard, engraved I L G, a do. do. engraved O. L G, plate). Executors the two sons. Witnesses Robert Sanders, Jacob Evertsen and Myndert van Jeveren. Albany Co. Record, Wills, I., part 2, p. 1.

1110 (M 1 & 2) 1692-3 March 16 — **MEYER, Martin Jansen,** and wife Hendrikje of New York City. The survivor, children Johannes, Harman, Martin, Elsje, wife of Burger Meyndertz, Beeltje, wife of Claas Gysbertz, Helenah, wife of Edward Cock, Catherine and Hannah. Real and personal estate. The survivor executor. Witnesses W. Bogardus, Peter de Mill and Dirk Bensen. Translated Aug. 15, 1713.

1111 (M 3) 1717 May 1 1719 June 27 **MATHEWS, Colonel Peter,** of Albany City. Wife Bridgett sole heiress and executrix of real and personal estate. Witnesses Robert Lurting, Wm. Sharpas and Gerard Clows. Seal.

1112 (M 4) 1723 Septbr. 6 — **MULL, Abraham,** of N. Y. City, yeoman. Wife Jackamintye, children Adriana, wife of Francis Harrison, Susanna, Ryartye, grandchildren, vizt. Walter, Abraham and William Hyer, sons of dec'd da. Katerlyntye, Abraham Stephens, son of da. Ryartye, Hendrick van Bonwell, son of da. Susannah. Real and personal estate. Executors Uynant Vinsant, blockmaker, and Nicholas Matthieson, blacksmith, both of N. Y. City. Witnesses Johanness Banc, William Hier and John Breested. Copy.

1113 (M 5) 1719 Octbr. 10 1724 Novbr. 24 Dutch **MATTYSEN, Jan,** of Kingston Corporation, Ulster Co. Wife Maddeleen, sons Mattys Jansen, Thomas, Jan, Hendrick, David, Margrieta, wife of Barent Burhans, Catrina, wife of John Crooke jun., grandson Daniell, son of dec'd. da. Magdalena, wife of Richard Broadhead, children of dec'd. da. Sara, wife of Elias Bunschoten, vizt. Teunis Johannis and Gerritie. Real and personal estate. Executors sons Mattys, Thomas, Hendrick and David Jansen, Jan having gone to England and believed, to be dead. Witnesses W. ten Broeck, A. Gaasbeek Chambers, Johannis ten Broeck and William Nottingham.

1114 (M 6) 1725 April 3 Septbr. 13 **MABEE, John,** of Schenectady Township, Albany Co., yeoman. Children Peter, Jacob, Abraham, Margret. Land on both sides of Mohawk R., "lands, " where da. Margret now lives, called Kadoritha," h. and l. in Schenectady; personal estate. Executors Jacobus van Dyke and Caleb Beck. Witnesses Jan Danielsen, Johannis Peck and Harme van Antwerp.

1115 (M 7) 1727-8 Febry. 25 1728 Novbr. 20 **MACK GREGORY, Patrick,** of Orange Co., yeoman. Daughter Mary, wife of David Southerland of Ulster Co. and her sons Patrick and David, grandson Gregor MacGregory. Real and personal estate. Executors son-in-law David Southerland and John Alsop of Ulster Co. Witnesses Frances Jaycocks, Ino. Alsop and W. Gale.

1116 (M 8) 1729 Aug. 1 1731 May 19 Dutch **MINGAEL, Johannes,** of Albany City. Wife Maria sole heiress and executrix. Witnesses Johannis Hansen, Gerrit van den Bergh and Arendt Pruyn.

1117 (M 9) 1732 Aug. 18 1751 March 10

MINTHORNE, Philipp, in the Bowree, Out Ward, N. Y. City, yeoman. Wife Johanna, children Philipp, Johanna, Hillegonda and Margaret, sisters Geertje, Sarah and Hannah. Land on Manhattan Island, called the Negroes Cagee, tanyards on the Freshwater; personal property. Executors the wife, bro. John Minthorne and bro.-in-law John Roll. Witnesses Andryes ten Eyck, Samuel Beekman, cordwainer, and H. Demeyer. Copy.

1118 (M 10) 1740 Jany. 22 — Dutch

MICHAL, Moses, widower of Catharina Hasher, of the Jewish Nation, of Curaçao. Children Johevit, wife of Judah Means, Rachel, wife of Samuel Meyer Cohen, who has children Elkaley and Hayah, Rebecca, wife of Judah Ehays and Bloeme, wife of Aron Louzada y Zulex. Real and personal property. Executors the four sons-in-law in New York, Isaac Levy Maduro and Cohen Henriquez jun. of the Island of Curaçao. Witnesses Nicolaus Henricus and Laurents Laan. Copy, endorsed "Admn. granted here the 10th June 1740."

1119 (M 11) 1744 May 28 Octbr. 4

MULDER, Cornelius, son of Cornelis Stevensen Mulder of Claverack, Albany Co., yeoman. Wife Janetie, nephew Johannes Tobise van Dusen, brothers Christopher and Jacob Mulder, sons of dec'd bro. Johannis Mulder, vizt. Cornelis, Isaac, Jacob and Jeremiah. Real and personal estate. Executors the wife, William van Ness and Jacob Freese. Witnesses Samuel ten Broeck, Wyllem Esselstyn and Jacob Freese.

1120 (M 12) 1746 Septbr. 6 1748 April 25

MOORE, Benjamin, of Goshen, Orange Co., tailor. Sons Benjamin and Nathan, daughters Anna, Margat and Martha. Real and personal estate. Executors Joseph Allison and Richard. Witnesses Alexr. Smith, Hendry Wesener and Anthony Carpenter.

1121 (M 13) 1746 Aug. 9 — **MORRIS, Isabella,** widow of his late Excellency Lewis Morris. Daughters Euphemia, widow of Matthew Norris, Mary Pearse, Anne Antill, Arabella Graham, Margaret Morris, Elizabeth White, children of dec'd da. Kearney vizt. Isabella Kearney, Mary van Horn, Euphemia, Arabella Kearney and Graham Kearney, children of dec'd da. Isabella, late wife of Richard Ashfield, vizt. Lewis, Mary, Isabella, Patience, Richard and Pearse. Real and personal property. Executors sons Lewis and Robert Hunter Morris. Witnesses Ino. Cox, Ino. Frehock, D. Martin and Sarah Robinson. Letters of administration granted to Lewis Morris, April 20, 1752. Copy.

1122 (M 14) 1748 June 28 1749-50 March 2 **McNEAL, James,** of Wallkil Prect., Ulster Co., yeoman. Wife Margarett, daughters Hannah, Aner and Mary, son James. Real and personal estate. Executors Alexander Milleken and Jacobus Bruyn. Witnesses Samuel Haines, Alexander Milliken jun. and John Milliken.

1123 (M 15) 1751 May 21 1768 Jany. 14 **McNEALL, John,** jun., of Wallkil Prect., Ulster Co. Wife Martha, children Thomas, John, Edward, Susanna, Jane Butterfield, Martha, Ann, Rebecca, Mary and Lydia. Real and personal estate. Executors bro.-in-law William Bowland and son-in-law Daniel Butterfield. Witnesses Thomas Neley, James Crawford jun., both of said Prect., yeomen, and Samuel Crawford, jun.

1124 (M 16) 1753 Septbr. 9 — **MORE, Robert,** of Southampton, Suffolk Co., yeoman. Wife ——, son Henry and other children not named. Real and personal estate. Executors the wife and Capt. Theophilus Howell. Copy.

1125 (M 17) 1754 May 4 1757 May 17 **MYNDERSE, Johannes,** of Schenectady Township, Albany Co., blacksmith. Sons Myndert, Jacobus and Reynier. H. and lots in Schenectady, land in Stone Rabie, personal property. Executors the three sons. Witnesses Yacobus Peeck, Hendricus F. Veeder and Maes van Vranken.

1126 (M 18) 1755 June 14 Novbr. 5 **MCGINNIS, William,** Captain of a Company of Militia in the Cruyn (Crown) Point Expedition of Schonectady. Mother-in-law Annitje Veeder, son Alexander, bro. Robert Maginnes of N. Y. City, joiner, and his son William. Real and personal estate. Executors John Sanders of Schonectady, merchant, and Levi Pawling of Ulster Co., gentleman. Witnesses Gerrit A. Lansing of Schenectady, merchant, Isaac Is. Truax and John Sanders.

1127 (M 19) 1756 Octbr. 9 1763 July 18 **MYNDERSE, Myndert,** of Schonectady Town, Albany Co., blacksmith. Wife Maria, sons Johannes, Barendt and Harme, daughters Geertruyd, Margarieta and Sarah. Houses and lots in Schonectady, personal property. Executors the wife and brothers Jacobus and Reynier. Witnesses Arent Stevens, Ino. Brown, merchant, and Johannis Veeder. See No. 1125.

1128 (M 20) 1757 March 9 April 29 **MUTS, Johannes,** of Haverstraw Prect., Orange Co. Wife Cathereen, Dutch Church at Haverstraw for a free school. Real and personal estate. Executors Powlas Hopper, Lucas Stephanson, Ondris Onderdonck and Wm. Campbell jun. Witnesses Paulus Hopper, Luykas Stephanson, William Campbell jun. and Andries Onderdonck.

1129 (M 21) 1758 Novbr. 30 1775 April 21 **MULLER, Cornelis,** of Rensselaerswick Colony, yeoman. Children, all under age, not named, Real and personal estate. Executors bro. Isaac Muller and bro.-in-law Johannis Jacobs van Valkenburgh. Witnesses Andries Kittel of Kinderhook, blacksmith, Johannis van Valkenburgh and Arent van Dyck.

1130 (M 22) 1758 Aug. 7 1759 March 2 **MOTT, Gershom,** of New Hempsted, Orange Co., yeoman. Wife Ruth, sons Solomon, Gershom, Charles, Benjamin, daughters Moley, wife of Peter Lott, and Elizabeth Clark, grandson Gershom Lott. Real and personal estate (a bible). Executors son Benjamin and Jacob Hallsed. Witnesses Joseph Seaman, Caleb Seaman and Gershom Rose, farmers.

1131 (M 23) 1758 May 10 1759 April 18 **MILL, Aurelius,** of Flushing, L. I., joiner. Daughter Elizabeth. Real and personal property. Executor Thomas Thorn of Flushing. Witnesses Huybert van Wagenen of N. Y. City, shopkeeper, Jesper Drake and John Ketchum. Copy.

1132 (M 24) 1758 July 13 Decbr. 18 **McEUEN, Danel,** of Ulster Co. Daughter Mary, Mikem, son of John Euen of N. Y., carman, and Richard, son of Richard Lues of Ulster Co. "Worley estate." Executors Francis Purdy and John McEuen sen. of N. Y., carman. Witnesses Henery Smith of Ulster Co., farmer, John Young and Richard Lewis.

1133 (M 25) 1758 Jany. 4 July 13 **MATTHEWS, Robert,** of Poughkeepsie Distr., Dutchess Co., yeoman. Wife ——, son Samuel and an expected child. "Worldly estate." Executors bro. James Lucke and Matthew van Kuran. Witnesses David Fulton and Wm. Irwin.

1134 (M 26) 1759 Febry. 12 Febry. 26 **MILLS, Samuel,** of Smithtown, Suffolk Co. Wife Ruth, sons Timothy and Samuel, daughters Mary, Sary. Homefarm, land in Brookhaven bounds, personal estate. Executors brothers Jonathan Mills and Eleazer Hockings. Witnesses Isaac Mills, David Biggs and Jonathan Mills.

1135 (M 27) 1757 Decbr. 24 1760 Novbr. 15 **MERTEN (Martine), John,** of Haverstraw Precinct, Orange Co., yeoman. Wife Affie, daughters Elesabeth, Affie and Hannah, sons Daniel and Jerimah. Real and personal property (a silver *baker*). Executors James Declark and Thomas Wilson. Witnesses William Campbell jun., Peter Maberry and Johannes Vanderbelt of Orange Co., farmer.

1136 (M 28) 1759 Jany. 25 March 23 **MERITT, George,** of Hilands Prect., Ulster Co., youman. Wife Glorande, sons Caleb, Umphere, Samuel, George, David, Gabrill, Josiah, daughters Elizabeth, Glorande and Jen. Homefarm, land near Robins Point, do. in the Whiteplains inherited through mother from grandfather Umfree Underhill, personal property. Executors the wife, Samuel Fowler and son Umpheree. Witnesses Thomas Merrit of Ulster Co., miller, John Bloomer and Joseph Bloomer sen., miller.

1137 (M 29) 1759 Decbr. 2 1765 Octbr. 18 **MERITT, Glorin,** of Hilands Prect., Ulster Co. Daughters Elizabeth, Glorin and Jan., sons Josiah and Caleb. "Worldly estate." Executors son Umpherey Meritt and bro. Samuel Purdy. Witnesses Martha Latting, Stephen Purdy of Dutchess Co. farmer and Joseph Bloomer. See preceding No.

1138 (M 30) 1760 May 21 Octbr. 1 **MEAD, Nehemiah,** of Crom Elbow Precinct, Dutchess Co., yeoman. Wife Sarah, sons Nehemiah, Joseph, Philipp and Noah, da. Sarah. Real and personal estate. Executors brothers Enos and Jonathan Mead, both of Crom Elbow Prect. Witnesses Samuel Barker, Samuel Barker jun., both of Dutchess Co., yeomen, and Freelove Barker.

1139 (M 31) 1760 Novbr. 19 1762 Aug. 5 **MORRIS, Lewis,** of Morrisania. Wife Sarah, sons Lewis, Staats Long, Richard, Gouverneur, daughters Mary, wife of Thomas Lawrence, Isabella, Sarah, Euphemia and Catherine, wife's niece Johanna Hall, bro.-in-law James Graham, bro. Robert Hunter Morris. "My desire is, that nothing be mentioned about me, not so much as a single Line in a News Paper, to tell the World I am dead." . . . "It is my Desire that my son Gouverneur Morris may have the best Education that is to be had in England or America, but my Express Will and Directions are, that he be never sent for that purpose to the Colony of Connecticut, Least he should imbibe in his

Youth that Low Craft and Cunning, so Incident to the People of that Country, which is so interwoven in their constitutions, that all their art cannot Disguise it from the World, Tho' many of them under the Sanctified Garb of Religion have Endeavour'd to Impose themselves on the World for Honest Men." Farm at Morrisania, lots on Broadway, N. Y. City, land on Pisaick River, personal property (plate, family pictures). Executors bro. Robert Hunter Morris, son Richard and William Smith junior. Witnesses Francis Lewis of N. Y. City, merchant, Samuel Gilford and Stephen Sayre. Copy.

1140 (M 32) 1761 Octbr. 14 1762 Novbr. 13

MILSPAH, Peter, of the Wallkil. Wife ——, son Benjamin and other children not named. "Worldly estate." Executors and trustees William Comfort and Jacob Milspah. Witnesses Lorentz Christ, Necolas Melsbagh and John McClean.

1141 (M 33) 1761 Novbr. 6 1762 Aug. 14

MUCH (Mutts), Catherine, widow of Jehais, of Haverstraw Prect., Orange Co. Children of kinswoman Onnor Christion of Scorhary, Alboney Co., Nicholas Cooper sen. of Haverstraw. Personal property. Executors Philipp Servent and Thunis Declark both of Haverstraw. Witnesses William Taylor of Orange Co., carpenter, Nathl. Barmore & Gershom Rose. Codicil of January 19, 1762 gives legacies to Philipp Servent, Mary Servent, Tunis Clark and William Taylor. Witnesses Susannah Knapp, William Kemp and Johannes Snyder.

1142 (M 34) 1761 March 28 1770 Jany. 5

MAESEN, Cornelis, of Albany City, brazier. Nephews Maas and Albartus Bloemendal, sons of bro. Jacob Maas, and Cornelius Bloemendal, son of bro. Jan, nieces Leah, wife of Cornelius van Deusen, Jacomyntie, wife of Jacob Ostrander, both daughters of sister Gertruy and nephews Cornelius and Jacobus Ostrander, sons of the same sister. Houses and lots in Albany. Executors nephew Maas, son of bro. Jan, nephew Maas, son of bro.

Jacob and Cornelius van Deusen. Witnesses Staats van Santvoord, gunsmith, John van Valkenburgh, joiner, and John Roorback, alderman.

1143 (M 35) 1762 Septbr. 28 1765 Febry. 16 **MOTT, Joseph,** of Sharlotte Prect., Dutchess Co. yeoman. Wife Chatharina, sons Joseph, who has son Joseph and other children, Samuel, Richard, Jacob, daughters Martha, wife of James Vollentine, Jane, wife of Timothy Smith, Elisebeth, wife of Samuel Smith, and Jemima, wife of John Connon. Land in Great Nine Partners, personal property. Executors bro. Jacob Mott of Queens Co. and Lawrence Maston of L. I. Witnesses Tobias Stoutenburgh of Charlotte Prect., merchant, Johann George Rimpp and Catharina Stoutenburgh.

1144 (M 36) 1762 Septbr. 11 Septbr. 15 **MELSON, Charles,** of N. Y. City, mariner, going on board the Snow *Boscawen,* Edward Spain, master. Alexander Mack Bain sole heir and executor of all property. Witnesses Alexander Bayne, Sergt. 77th Regt., John Rodey and Hectour Taylor of N. Y. City, mariner. Copy.

1145 (M 37) 1762 Jany. 8 Febry. 4 **McINVIN, John,** of N. Y. City. John Anderson sole heir and executor of real and personal estate. Witnesses James McKenzie of N. Y. City, innholder, and Hector McKenzie. Copy.

1146 (M 38) 1763 March 20 1765 Aug. 27 **MACEY, Mary,** widow, formerly of the Island of Jamaica now of N. Y. City. Widow Elizabeth Moore of N. Y. City and her da. Mary, nephew Isaac Wilkins, son of dec'd sister Johanna, late wife of Martin Wilkins, formerly of Jamaica, last of N. Y. City dec'd, Isabella, wife of nephew Isaac and da. of Lewis Morris, late Judge and Commissary of the Admiralty. Real and personal estate. Executor nephew Isaac Wilkins. Witnesses Catherin Ludlow, Anthony Hoffman and William Smith jun. Copy.

1147 (M 39) 1763 June 20 Aug. 23

MULLER, Jeremiah, of Claverack, Albany Co., yeoman. Wife Elizabeth, sons Cornelis, Jacob, Johannes, daughters Hendrickje, widow of Bartholomeus Hogeboom, Heyetje, wife of Jan de La Matre, Maria, wife of Jacobus de La Matre, Jannetje, widow of Abraham Fonda. Real and personal estate. Executors the three sons and Stephanus van Dyke. Witnesses J. v. Rensselaer, Laurance Hogeboom of Claverack and Philipp Schuyler of Albany.

1148 (M 40) 1763 May 14 ——

MURRAY, William, of N. Y. City, mariner. Wife Mary, son Charles. Marine property. Has brother John Murray. Executors Malcolm Campbell and Peter Pra van Zandt, both of N. Y. City, merchants. Witnesses Thos. Grigg jun. and Thos. Moore. Copy made June 16, 1763.

1149 (M 41) 1763 Jany. 10 1765 Febry. 25

MIER, Eda, of Orange Township, Orange Co., yeoman. Children Johannes, Anitie, Elisabeth, Altie, Wellemintje, Cornelius, Andries, Abraham, Garret, Jacob, Isaac, John and Daniel. "My estate." Executors son Johannes and Johannes Josephson Blawfelt of Orange Township. Witnessess Gerrit van Cleff, Andrs. Onderdonck jun., of Orange Co., farmer, and Lambert Cuiper. Printed form.

1150 (M 42) 1764 April 16 1768 Septbr. 28 German

MUELLER, Hans Joerg, living on Mr. van Benthuysen's land in Dutchess Co. Wife Anna Barbara *née* Trumbur, sons Christian, Heinrich, Johannes, and Jacob, da. Elizabeth. Real and personal estate. Executors Caspar Schult, Jacop Maul and Willem Betzer. Witnesses Philipp Henrich More of Rinebeck Prect., blacksmith, Jorg Klum and William Mohr.

1151 (M 43) 1765 Octbr. 2 1784 June 1

MESIER, Peter, of N. Y. City, bolter. Sons Abraham and Peter, da. Elezabeth, wife of Abraham Bussing, grandchildren Jacob and John, sons of dec'd da. Catherean, late wife of Jacob van Voorhis. Houses and lots on Cortlandt and Mesier Str., West Ward, N. Y. City, personal property. Executors sons Abraham and Peter. Witnesses John van Dalsem, mason, Marselus Gerbrandts and Henry Sickels.

1152 (M 44) 1764 June 29 1766 May 27 **MARSH, Witham,** His Majesty's Secretary for Indian Affairs, Clerk of the City and County of Albany, Clerk of the Common Pleas and Clerk of the Peace for said City and County. Bro. John Marsh of Richmond, Surrey Co., Mary, da. of William Whitaker of Leachlade, County of Gloucester, England, the Earl of Halifax, Lewis Lord Sondes, Sir Wm. Johnson, Bart., Edward Waldo, merchant in Abechurch (?) Lane. Personal estate. Executors Sir William Johnson, Robert Leake, H. M. Commissary General at N. Y. and Peter Silvester of Albany. Wishes to be buried under the belfry of Albany Church with the epitaph, "Withamus de Marisco, alias Marshe, natus die Maij 17 . . . ex matre sui Patris nobilissime oriundus. Denatus idem Withamus—die—176—." Proved by the testimony of John McKesson of N. Y. and Gilbert Burger, clerk of John Morin Scott, as to handwriting.

1153 (M 45) 1766 Novbr. 20 1769 Jany. 15 **MILLS, Ephraim,** of Charlotte Prect., Dutchess Co., yeoman. Sons Ephraim, Samuel, daughters Bathiah, Susannah, Mary, Hannah, and Phebe, grandchildren Susannah, Stephen and John, children of dec'd son William Mills, son-in-law John Earls. Real and personal estate. Executors Obe Griffin and Joshua Height. Witnesses James Germond of Dutchess Co., yeoman, John Haddan and Isaac Huff.

1154 (M 46) 1766 Febry. 5 May 28 **MERSELIS, Gerret Joh.,** of Albany City. Mother, brothers Gisbert and Henry, sisters Eva, Barbara and Maria. H. & l. in Albany, real estate in Schonectady, personal property. Executors the two brothers. Witnesses Marten Mynderse of Albany, blacksmith, Cornelius Beekman and Abr. Yates jun.

1155 (M 47) 1767 Aug. 10 Septbr. 10 **MILLER, Andrew,** of Goshen Prect., Orange Co., yeoman. Daughters Ann Armstrong, Elizabeth Miller, sons Andrew, James, John, William, David and Alexander, brothers-in-law James Jackson of New Windsor, and Alexander Jackson. Real and personal estate. Executors son Andrew, bro.-in-law James Jackson and da. Elizabeth. Witnesses Michael Jackson, William Armstrong, farmer, and William Jackson.

1156 (M 48) 1767 July 4 Novbr. 6 **McINTIRE, James,** of Littel Brittain "and so-forth." Children of sister vizt. Jean, Nancy and Mary Wallace. "Worldly goods." Executor Joseph Davis, Witnesses James Umphry, carpenter, Arthur Beatty and Samuel Boyd.

1157 (M 49) 1767 Decbr. 17 1775 June 15 **MARVIN, Robert,** of Herricks, Hempstead Township, Queens Co., yeoman. Children John, Sarah, Mary, Hannah and Pheby, grandchildren Jacob and John Marvin, sons of John, Marvin Rowland, son of da. Mary, children of dec'd. da. Ruth, wife of Samuel Rowland of Dutchess Co. Son John's wife is Mary. Real and personal estate. Executors sons John and sons-in-law Jonathan Rowland and Isaac Smith. Witnesses Daniel Lawrence, practicioner of physics, Richard Wiggins, yeoman, both of Queens Co., and Uriah Smith. Copy.

1158 (M 50) 1767 July 14 1771 Novbr. 19 **MILLERD, Robert,** jun., of Beekman's Prect., Dutchess Co., tanner. Wife Phebe, children Temperance, Abiathar, Abigal, and Robert. Real and personal estate. Executors George Panny of Philipps Patent and Joshua Millerd. Witnesses Bennajah Millerd, of Pawlings Prect., yeoman, Abiathar Millerd and Zephiniah Eddy.

1159 (M 51) 1767 Decbr. 4 1771 May 24 **MOVIEL, Thomas,** of Newton, Queens Co., yeoman. Wife Kezia, sons Jonathan, Jacob, Samuel, Robard and Thomas. Real and personal property. Executors sons Jonathan, Jacob, Samuel and Robard. Witnesses James Way of Queens Co., farmer, Philipp Edsall and Nathaniel ffish. Copy.

1160 (M 52) 1769 Decbr. 12 1770 Septbr. 3 **MONTROSS, John,** of Rumbout Prect., Dutchess Co., yeoman. Wife Margaret, daughters Mary Langdon, widow, Margaret, wife of George Bloom, Rachael, wife of Joseph Thirstan, Leah, wife of Matthias Horton, grandda. Molly, wife of Dirck Hogeland and da. of dec'd son Peter. Real and personal estate. Executors William van Wyck, Theodorus van Wyck jun., and Jacob Dubois jun. Witnesses Jacob du Boys, Philipp Verplanck jun., and Peter Duboys.

1161 (M 53) 1769 Decbr. 6 1770 April 30 **MILSBACH, Mathias,** of Wallkil Prect., Ulster Co., yeoman. Son Jacob, children of dec'd son Peter, da. Christina, wife of Johannis Krans. Real and personal estate. Executor son Jacob. Witnesses Andrew Graham, Coonrod More and Johannes Bruyn.

1162 (M 54) 1769 Aug. 9 1785 Jany. 26 **MARSELIS, Annatje,** widow of Johannis, of Albany City. Children Gysbert, Eva, wife of Johannis M. Roseboom, Barbara, wife of Henry I. Bogert, Maria, wife of Henry Lansingh, and Hendrick heirs and executors of real and personal estate. Witnesses Jacobus Vinhagen, Abraham Vinhagen, of Albany Co., farmers, and Abraham Yates jun.

1163 (M 55) 1769 Jany. 10 June 2 **MILLER, Henry,** of New Cornwal, Orange Co., farmer. Wife Margret, sons John, William, Henry, James, Benjamin, Jesse and Peter, daughters Rebeckah and Mary. Real and personal estate. Executors the wife and Archibald Little of New Cornwal. Witnesses Hopkins Smith, Aaron Cunningham, labourer, and James Smith.

1164 (M 56) 1769 June 6 1782 Novbr. 14 **MANDEVIL David,** of New Cornwell Prect., Orange Co., gentleman. Wife Anna, sons Joseph, Jacob, Henry, Francis, Michael and David, da. Mary Wescoat. Real and personal estate. Executors bro. Francis Mandevil, Henry Wisner jun., and son Jacob. Witnesses Amos Mills, Langford Thorne and David Sands.

1165 (M 57) 1769 July 8 1784 June 12 Dutch

MOWRIS, Samuel, of Marbletoun, Ulster Co. Wife Geesje, sons Samuel, Henry, Petrus, Daniel, step-daughter Arjaentje Oosterhout, "the child of my present wife by former husband." Real and personal estate. Executors sons Henry and Petrus and Willem Eltinge. Witnesses Hend. Sleght of Kington, esquire, Abraham Hasbrouck jun., and Hend. I. Sleght of Kingston, yeoman.

1166 (M 58) 1769 March 25 1772 July 8

MABEI, Peter, of Orange Town, Orange Co. Wife Cathalintie, sons Casparus, Jeremiah, Abraham, Peter, Jost, Cornelius, grandson Isaac, son of Peter, daughters Elizabeth, wife of Abraham Haring, Sofiah, wife of Johannis Delamator and Mary, wife of John Westervelt. Real and personal estate. Executors bro. Johannes Mabei and Thomas Outwater. Witnesses Ebenezer Wood, William Hammon of Orange Co., shoemaker, and Gilm. Outwater.

1167 (M 59) 1770 Febry. 21 1784 June 3

McPHEADRIS, Helena, of N. Y. City, widow. Daughter Catherine, wife of Robert G. Livingston of N. Y. City, merchant, granddaughters Helena McLeod and Susannah McDonald, grandsons Andrew Myer jun. and his children, Simon Johnson Myer, John Myer and Gilbert Myer, children of dec'd da. Susanna Myer. "Worldly goods and estate." Executors son-in-law Robert G. Livingston and wife. Witnesses Margaret Stuyvesant, Peter Stuyvesant of N. Y. City, esquire, and John Mekel.

1168 (M 60) 1770 July 9 1771 May 22

McMENNOMY, Robert, of N. Y. City. Wife Elizabeth, sons John and Robert, da. Margaret. Lots 66 and 151 in Turner's Patent, Albany Co., personal property. Executors the wife and John Curry. Witnesses Joseph Dunkly, James Wilkes, shopkeeper, and James Hill. Copy.

1169 (M 61) 1771 Febry. 20 1773 April 20 **MULLENDER, Peter,** of Little Brittain, New Winsor Precinct, Ulster Co., yeoman, "fair advanced in years." Wife ——, children William, Elizabeth Olepher, Mary Wellings, Sarah Ball, Reachel Falls and Agnes Porter; Rev. John Scears or his successor, grandda. Isabelah Falls. Homefarm, land in the Hermitage tract, personal property. Executors son William and daughters Elizabeth, Mary, Sarah and Agnes. Witnesses Hugh Umphrey, John Peacock and James McClaghry. Codicil of April 12, 1771, makes slight change and is witnessed by Isabella Welling, Mary Welling, of New Winsor, spinster, and Thomas Porter.

1170 (M 62) 1771 Aug. 19 1775 May 22 **MARTIN, Manasah,** of Paulings Prect., Dutchess Co., carpenter. Wife Sarah, daughters Anner, Susannah Robinson, Deborah Nicobacker, Meribah, sons Mashar, Agrippa, Amaziah, Manasah, Ephraim, James, John, Asa, George and Aaron. Real and personal estate. Executor son Agrippa, who is also made trustee for da. Anner. Witnesses John Wickham, David Wickham, yeoman, and Elisha Allin.

1171 (M 63) 1771 Septbr. 5 Septbr. 24 **McCEW, William,** of Albany City, tailor. Wife Mary, his journeyman Ralph Miller and apprentice John Walton, little girl Jenny. "Worldly estate." Executors David Edgar and Thomas Shipboy, who refusing to act the widow is made administratrix. Witnesses Thos. Barry, John Sturgeon, of Albany, merchants, and Alexr. Chestnut.

1172 (M 64) 1771 Jany. 24 March 29 **MILLS, Catharina,** of Dutchess Co., widow. Father Peter Monfoort, niece Catharina Bush, da. of sister Anne ter Bush, who has da. Sarah and a not yet baptized da. "Worldly estate." Executors father Peter Monfoort and bro.-in-law Isaac ter Bush. Witnesses Abraham Lent, Jacobus Swartwout of Rumbouts Prect., gent., and Daniel Brinckerhoff.

1173 (M 65) 1771 Aug. 5 1778 June 26 **MONELL, John,** of New Windsor Prect., Ulster Co., yeoman. Wife Hannah sole heiress and executrix of real and personal property. Witnesses John Nicoll, William Cumming, weaver, and John Hays, yeoman.

1174 (M 66) 1772 May 23 1784 June 3 **McPHEADRYS, Helena,** of N. Y. City, widow. Codicil to No. 1167 makes some changes in the legacies and adds a gift for educating poor children in a Free English School belonging to the Dutch Reformed Church of N. Y. Witnesses John Keily, Ann McPherson and Mary Peterson, widow.

1175 (M 67) 1772 Octbr. 19 1773 Febry. 9 German **MOCHIE, Johann Michel,** of Livingston Manor, Albany Co. Wife Anna Eva, 5 children, Johannes, Hermanus, Marcus, Eva, Anna Maria, 6 stepchildren, Adam Killmer, Niklas, William, Elisabeth, Catharina and Gert. "Wordly goods" (a bible). Executors George Best, Auiustinus Schmit and Petrus Meyer. Witnesses Conradt Schauerman, Johan Bartelmeus, labourers, and Emrig Schauerman.

1176 (M 68) 1773 Febry. 17 1782 Octbr. 2 **MOSSER, Jury,** of West Camp, Albany Co. Wife ——, sons Jacob, Thomas, daughters Elizabeth, wife of Peter Young, Christina, wife of Harme Fritts, Margret, wife of Michel Finger, Helena, wife of Johannis Petrie, Lea, wife of Christian Petrie, Susanna, wife of Christian Sax, granddaughters Elizabeth Kerker and Christina Chishem. Real and personal estate. Executors Harme Best, Johannes Michael and Dirck Jansen of Livingston Manor. Witnesses Petrus van Gaasbeek, Christian Valkenburgh, yeoman, of Livingston Manor and John Habs.

1177 (M 69) 1773 March 15 1783 May 8 Dutch **MYER, Christiaen,** of Kingston Corporation, Ulster Co., farmer. Sons Willem, Johannis, Stophanis, Benjamin, Petrus and Tobias, children of dec'd son Christiaen vizt. Annatje, Christiaen and Benjamin, heirs of dec'd da. Marytje, late wife of Hieronimus Valkenburgh, heirs of dec'd da. Christina and of dec'd da. Cattriena, da. Geertje, wife of Hendrick Fiero. Real and personal estate (a Dutch Bible). Executors sons Willem, Johannis, Stophanis and Johannis Snyder. Witnesses Arent Winne, Petrus Backer of Sagerties, farmer, and Johann Heinrich Meyer.

1178 (M 70) 1774 Octbr. 17 1775 March 17 **MITCHELL, Robert,** jun., of Madnans Neck, Hempstead Township, Queens Co., farmer. Wife Sarah, daughters Sasannah, Phebe and Martha, sons William and Allen, reputed son Henry. Real and personal estate. Executors bro. John Mitchell, bro.-in-law John Allen and Henry Stocker. Witnesses John Morrell, Thomas Smith and Danl. Kissam. Copy.

1179 (M 71) 1774 Octbr. 25 1775 Novbr. 1 **MONTAGNE, Rebecca,** widow of Thomas, of N. Y. City, shopkeeper, children Peter, Auriantche Lefay, Hannache, wife of Morris Earl, Jane, wife of John Wright, John, Pelonch, wife of Elbert Aumermann, Benjamin, Eleanor, wife of Isaac Vreedenburgh, grandson Thomas, son of da. Martha Allenor, five children of son Vincent. "Worldly estate." Executors sons Peter, John and Benjamin and son-in-law Morris Earl. Witnesses Robert Manley, of N. Y. City, coachmaker, Wm. W. Gilbert and David Shaddel. Copy.

1180 (M 72) 1774 July 21 1782 Septbr. 30 **MASTEN, John,** of Shawengunk Prect., Ulster Co. Wife Marytie, sons Matthew, Cornelis, Art, Ezekiel, Johannis, Abraham, daughters Elisabeth, wife of Johannes Roos, Jatie, wife of Johannis Weller, and Mary, wife of Philipp Rank. Real and personal property. Executors bro. Ezekiel Masten of Kingston and sons Ezekiel and Cornelis. Witnesses Johannes Bevier, Cornelis ter Willgen and Johs. Hardenbergh jun., farmers.

1181 (M 73) 1774 June 23 Septbr. 19

McCOBB, James, of Handover Prect., Ulster Co., merchant. Wife Jane, daughters Elizabeth, Mary, and Jane, James McClaghry jun., father William McCobb in Ireland, Samuel, son of John Finley, George, son of Alexr. Trimble, James Latta, trustees James Wilkin and Thomas Beatty of the new Wallkil meeting house, father-in-law Patrick McClaghry. Real and personal estate. Executors the wife, George Clinton and James Barkley. Witnesses Robt. McCuchan, Andrew Willson and James McClaghry, yeomen.

1182 (M 74) 1774 Feby [illegible] 17[illegible] June 7

MESICK, Jacob, of Claverack, Albany Co., yeoman. Wife Cathariena, sons Hendrick, John or Johannis, Peter, Jacob, da. Cathariena. Real and personal estate. Executors sons Hendrick, Johannis and Peter. Witnesses Michel Pulffer, Michel van de Water and David Browver, weaver.

1183 (M 75) 1775 6th Day, 5th Month May 25

MacFARLAND, Jane, late of N. Y. City, now of Elizabeth Town Raway, Essex Co., Eastern Division of N. J. Son John MacFarland, Susannah Loverage and Susannah Sutten, both of N. Y., widows. Real and personal estate. Executors John Drummon and Alexander Oglesbee, both of N. Y. Witnesses Joseph D. Camp of Elizabeth Town Raway, surveyor, Hope Moore of the same place, physician, both Quakers and Enoch Moore. Copy.

1184 (M 76) 1775 Aug. 29 1776 April 30

MILLER, Abram, of Bedford, Westchester Co., yeoman. Wife Comfort, sons Joseph, Abram and Isaac. Real and personal estate. Executors the three sons. Witnesses Ezra Wilson of said Co., surgeon, Josiah Miller, farmer, and Isaac Holmes. Copy.

1185 (M 77) 1775 April 12 1780 Aug. 23

MILLER, James, of Chearlotte Prect., Dutchess Co., yeoman. Wife Elezebath, son James, da. Mary Hunt, grandson Willem Baerd. Real and personal property. Executor the wife. Witnesses Lewis Barton, James Hall of said Co., wheelwright, and Kezia Hall.

1186 (M 78) 1775 Decbr. 30 1776 Jany. 17 **MERRITT, Gabriel,** of New Marlborough Prect., Ulster Co. Brothers Caleb, David and Josiah heirs and executors of real and personal estate. Witnesses Isaac Brown, surgeon, Mary Merritt, spinster, and Leonard Smith of Newburgh, yeoman.

1187 (M 79) 1776 July 6 1779 March 2 **MANDAVIL, Francis,** of New Windsor, Ulster Co., blacksmith. Wife Mary, children David, Martha, Corneliouse, John, Jacob and Frances. Real and personal property. Executors the wife and sons David, Corneliouse and John. Witnesses John Nicoll, Samuel Arthur of said Co., miller, and Leonard D. Nicoll. Proved in Dutchess Co.

1188 (M 80) 1776 April 26 1779 Octbr. 29 **MOORS, Johannes,** of Dutchess Co., yeoman. Wife Elisabeth, son Philipp and other children, not named. Real and personal estate. Executors the wife, son Philipp and William Bitcersen. Witnesses Zacharius Hoffman, Volkert Witbek and Adam Segendorpfs of Albany Co., yeoman.

1189 (M 81) 1777 Octbr. 5 1778 June 13 **MILLER, Garrett,** of Smiths Clove, Cornwall Precinct, Orange Co. Wife ——, children Joshua, Mary, Elizabeth, Garret, Nathan, Sarah, Samuel, Ann, Hampton and Jeremiah. Real and personal estate. Executors the wife and Nathaniel Seely. Witnesses John Fell, Benjamin Goldsmith and Abram Skinner.

1190 (M 82) 1777 Septbr. 14 1779 Jany. 30 **MILLER, Adam,** of Cornwall Prect., Orange Co., yeoman. Wife Abigail apparently second wife, sons Philipp, John, da. Elizabeth McGown, grandda. Lydia McGown. Real and personal estate. Executors James Peters of Orange Co., esquire, and John Harris of Ulster Co., yeoman. Witnesses Oliver Peterson, Thomas Moffat of Orange Co., esquire, and George Felmore.

1191 (M 83) 1778 May 12 1780 June 29 **MILLS, Timothy,** of New Windsor Prect., Ulster Co., yeoman. Wife Margaret, sons John, Daniel, Jonathan, daughters Anah, wife of Nathan Serjeant, and Johannah. Real and personal property. Executors the wife and Col. Thomas Palmer. Witnesses Thomas Neeley jun., Thomas Palmer, both of said Co., yeomen, and James Smiley.

1192 (M 84) 1778 Jany. 12 1785 March 10 **MULFORD, David,** of Rhynbeek Prect., Dutchess Co., yeoman. Wife Phebe, sons David, Job and other children, not named. Real and personal estate. Executors the wife, son Job and Ananias Cooper. Witnesses Jno. Younglove and John Brown.

1193 (M 85) 1779 Septbr. 1 1783 Decbr. 2 **MOUNTGOMERY, William,** late of New York City, now of Newindsor Prect., Ulster Co. Friend Margaret, da. of Samuel Mountgomery of Armagh, Ireland, merchant, *cousin* William, son of John Mountgomery, brothers Joseph, John, James and Robert Mountgomery, Mrs. Agnes Lightbody and da. Elizabeth. Personal estate. Executors brothers James and Robert. Witnesses William Edmonston of New Windsor and Gabriel Lightbody of Cornwall, yeoman. Copy.

1194 (M 86) 1779 June 22 1781 Octbr. 4 **MORRIS, John,** of Rhynbeck Prect., Dutchess Co., yeoman. Sons Jacobus, John, Abraham and Isaac, da. Annatje, wife of Johannis B. van Vredenburgh. Real and personal estate. Executors the four sons. Witnesses Peter Westfall, John Wels jun., both of Dutchess Co., yeomen, and Zacharius Weydman.

1195 (M 87) 1780 May 19 1781 April 11 **McCALLUM (McCalm), John,** of Amenia Prect. Peter Gilchrist of Woodbury, Connt., sole heir and executor of "all my estate." Witnesses Job Mead, captain, and King Mead, yeoman, both of Amenia Prect.

1196 (M 88) 1780 Decbr. 9 1786 Aug. 23 **MASTEN, Benjamin,** of Kingston, Ulster Co., weaver. Wife Mariea, sons Johannis, Benjamin, Cornelius, daughters Mariea, wife of Cornelius Tack jun., Cattriena, wife of Jeremiah Dubois, Margriet and Elizabeth, wife of Cornelius Persen. Real and personal estate. Executors the three sons. Witnesses Tobyas van Stenbrgh jun., Abraham Elmendorph and Johs. Snyder.

1197 (M 89) 1782 May 27 1786 Septbr. 15 **MULLER, Killian,** of Claverack, Albany Co. Children John, Hellitie, Cornelius, Joakim, grandchildren Jenny Hogeboom, Mary Hogeboom, son-in-law Stephen Hogeboom. Real and personal estate. Jacobus, son of Johannes Hogeboom, and Hendrick Muller guardians of son Cornelius. Executors son Joakim and son-in-law Stephen Hogeboom. Witnesses John Bay, counsellor at law, David Culley and Thomas Williams jun.

1198 (M 90) 1782 Novbr. 3 1783 April 10 **MOOR, James,** of Great White Creek, N. Y. Wife Margaret, who has son Thomas and da. Christian Harvy; sons David, James, Hugh Moor, daughters Jane and Isbell, grandda. Nancy, da. of son Hugh Moor. Real and personal estate. Executors the wife and son James Moor. Witnesses John McMullen of Charlotte Co., farmer, John Williams, John Connor and Hugh Martin. Codicil of same day appoints John McMullin guardian of da. Isabell. Same witnesses. Proved in Charlotte Co.

1199 (M 91) 1782 April 24 1782 Septbr. 13 **MEYER, Abraham,** of Newhemstead, Orange Co. Wife Margeret, children Jacobus, Charity, Annatje, Sarah, Elisabeth, Marya, Grytye, Altie and Hyllitie. Real and personal estate. Executors brothers Isaac and John Meyer. Witnesses Abraham Blauvelt of Haverstraw Prect., Abraham D. Haring and Harmanus Blauvelt.

1200 (M 92) 1782 July 26 1783 Novbr. 7 **MESICK, Thomas,** of Claverack, Albany Co., yeoman. Wife Mary, children Hendrick, Fite, Johannes, Catharina, Rosiena, a widow, Mary, Thomas and Elizabeth. Real and personal estate. Executors sons Fite and Johannis. Witnesses Dirck van der Kar, Abraham Brower, farmers, and David Brouwer.

1201 (M 93) 1782 Septbr. 23 1784 Febry. 10 **MABIE, Casparus,** of Orange Town or Tappan, Orange Co., yeoman. Wife Willempje, sons Cornelius, Peter, Abraham, daughters Mary, Cathaline, Catharine, Margaret and Elizabeth. Real and personal estate. Executors son Peter and son-in-law Johannis Bogert. Witnesses Jacobus Da. Blauvelt, John Johnston, and John Haring of Orange Co., esquire.

1202 (M 94) 1782 March 7 1784 June 25 **MUZELIUS, Fredericus,** of Orange Town, Orange Co. Doctor Gardner Jones and Joost Mabee, heirs and executors of real and personal estate in America, Europe and elsewhere. Witnesses Cornelius C. Roosevelt of N. Y. City, merchant, Joseph Withten and Anthony Polishie.

1203 (M 95) 1783 Septbr. 20 —— **MONCRIEFFE, Thomas,** Major of Brigade in H. M. Army in N. A., now at New York. Sons Edward Cornwallis and Thomas Barclay Moncrieffe, brother Richard Moncrieffe of Dublin. Land in Nova Scotia and elsewhere; personal property. Executors bro. Richard and bro.-in-law Augustus van Cortlandt. Witnesses Margaret Jay, Charlotte Amelia Bayley and Fred. Jay. Endorsed "Not proved."

1204 (M 96) 1783 March 12 1784 June 21 **MATHEWS, Vincent,** of Mathewsfield, Cornwall Prect., Orange Co., esquire. Children Fletcher, James, Bridget Jones, Elizabeth Beekman, children of son David. Wife's name was Elizabeth, first wife was Catalina Abeel. Land in Westenhook Patent, do. in Connecticut and "elsewhere"; personal property. Executors son James and son-in-law Theophilus Beekman. Witnesses William Hudson, Richard Goldsmith and Thomas Moffat.

1205 (M 97) 1783 Aug. 29 1785 Octbr. 11 **MASTEN, Aart,** of Charlotte Precinct, Dutchess Co., yeoman. Wife ——, sons Jacobus, Samuel, Jeremiah, Abraham, Peter, John, daughter Maria, wife of Johannis van Aken, Geertje, Elizabeth, wife of Gidion van Aken, Anateje, wife of John Cammel, grandchildren Mary, Marretje and Elizabeth, daughters of son Dirck. "Worldly estate." Executors Dirck van Vliet, Abraham Freligh and son Samuel. Witnesses Johannes Freligh, Moses Powell and Abrm. Freligh of Dutchess Co., farmer.

1206 (M 98) 1783 April 5 1784 Jany. 17 **McKINLEY, Nathaniel,** of Hurley, formerly of N. Y. City, tailor. Wife Rebecca, children Catharine, wife of Alexander Crooksank, Jane, Elizabeth, Sarah and Mary. House and lot in N. Y. City, land in Bamp Patent; personal property. Executors the wife, bro. William McKinley and son-in-law Alexander Crookshank. Witnesses Garrit Harsin, baker, John Newkerk, gentleman, both of N. Y. City and Huybert Ostrander.

1207 (M 99) 1784 April 4 Aug. 4 **MERCKEL, Nicolas,** of Shoharry, Albany Co. Nephews and nieces Nicholaus, son of brother Johannis Merckel, "my Lovely" Maria, da. of bro. Henry Merckel, Jabob, son of bro.-in-law Willem Sittnich, Nicholaus, son of bro.-in-law Christian Richtmeyer, children of bro. Peter, vizt. Cathrine and Jacob, sister Barbel, wife of Christian Sandt, sister Elizabeth, wife of Christian Richtmeyer, Lissaketh, wife of Willem Sittnich. Real and personal estate. Executors brothers-in-law Christian Richtmeyer and Willem Sittnich. Witnesses Ludwig Bremer, yeoman, Lawrence Schoolcraft and George T. Reinhardt, schoolmaster.

1208 (M 100) 1785 April 29 1786 March 17 **McCURDY, Archibald,** of Wallkil Prect., Ulster Co. Wife Margret, son Archibald, da. Agnes, wife of Wm. Wilson, grandchildren Margrit, Jane and Isabell Wilson. Real and personal estate. Executors sons Archibald, Capt. Samll. Watkins and Samll. Crawford. Witnesses Ino. McCamly, Daniel Butterfield and DavidCrawford, all yeomen.

1209 (M 101) 1785 March 24 Octbr. 21 **McLEAN, John,** of Montgomery Prect., Ulster Co., farmer. Wife Margrett, sons John, Cornelius, Jonas, daughters Charity, Sarah, Hannah Sutherland, Piggy Lewis, Cathrine Moor and Mary Moor. Real and personal estate. Executors the wife and James Barkley jun. Witnesses John Blake, George Smith and Christian Rockefeller of said Prect., blacksmith.

1210 (M 102) 1785 Septbr. 1 Novbr. 7 **MUNNEL, Hannah,** of New Windsor Prect., Ulster Co. John Munnel, Rosanna Dinnastan, William Weare jun., son of Rachel Sparks, and his bro. John, sister Mary McCay, George Munnel and his da. Jane, Martha Pennear and da. Betsey. Real and personal estate. Executors John Robbison, George Harris and William Jackson. Witnesses Benjamin Smith, Catherine Smith and Leonard D. Nicoll, yeoman.

1211 (M 103) 1786 Decbr. 22 1787 Jany. 6 **MILLER, Jacobus,** of Montgomery Prect., Ulster Co. Wife Mary, sons James and George, daughters Sarah, Susannah Watson, Jemima and Mary. Real and personal estate. Executor not named. Witnesses James Fitzgerald, Johannis Fetter and Philipp Crist.

1212 (M 104) 1789 Febry. 9 1790 Septbr. 7 **MATTISON, Aaron,** Sergeant 1st U. S. Regt., General Harmars. Brother Joseph Mattison. Personal property. Executor Wm. Price. Witnesses Henry Burbeck, John Peirce, Lieut. in Capt. Burbecks Artillery Comp., and W. Moore.

1213 (M 105) 1793 April 1 1795 Aug. 17 **MAUNSELL, John,** Major General in H. M. Army, now in N. Y. City. Codicil to last will of Aug. 2, 1790, giving to wife Elizabeth real estate at Harlem, Out Ward, N. Y. City. Witnesses Hugh Gaine, Philipp ten Eyck and Charles Watkins.

1214 (M 106) 1763 June 1 **McNEIL, Donald,** Lieut. 78th Regt., letters of administration on the estate of, granted to David Shaw of N. Y. City, merchant.

1214a 1774 May 2 Octbr. 2 **MOHR (Moyr), Philipp Hendricksen,** of Rynbeek Precinct, Dutchess Co., farmer. Wife Ariel, sons Philipp, Christian, Petrus, John, Jacob, Nicholas, Andries, da. Catherine. Real and personal property. Executors sons Philipp, Petrus and John. Witnesses Johannes Klum, farmer, Johannes Miller and Philipp I. Livingston. Seal. In Index of Court of Appeals misplaced under H. 76.

1215 1786 Septbr. 30 1787 April 30 **MORTIER, Martha,** widow of Abraham, of N. Y. City, esquire. Grandda. Elizabeth, wife of William Jephson, who has son William Henry, da. Elizabeth Banyer and children, vizt. Martha, Hariot and Goldsborough Banyar. Real and personal estate. Executors Gabriel William Ludlow, John Thurman, Captain Anthony Rutgers and Daniel McConnick, all of N. Y. City. Witnesses John Kelley, esqre., Hugh McClellan and J. van Benthuysen. Recorded in Wills and Probates, Vol. I., p. 135.

1216 1781 Octbr. 6 1782 May 27 **MOORE, Michael,** of New York. Wife Caty, children Michael, Samuel and Jacob, a daughter. Real and personal estate. Executors Michael Moore, Jacob Moore and Caty Moore. Witnesses Benjamin Huggett, grocer, John Devine, cordwainer, both of N. Y. City and John Hardenbergh. Recorded ut supra, p. 189.

1217 1781 March 6 1788 Novbr. 28 **McCLELLAR, William,** at present in N. Y. City. Mother Margaret Wallace, brother James Wallace, children of sister Mary, wife of Alexander Norris of Glasgow, Michael Wallace, John Wallace and William Maxwell. Personal property. Executors Michael Wallace, John Wallace and William Maxwell. Witnesses Alexr. Telfair, David Telfair and Wm. Maxwell jun. Recorded ut supra, p. 199.

1218 1792 Septbr. 20 1793 March 19 French **MASSON, François,** at present in N. Y. Declares, that he married Miss Marie Therese Legrettier, of the Parish of St. Rose de Laugane, Island of St. Domingo, in the Parish of Clery near Orleans, Jany 10, 1771, and has children Desiré, Florinand, Edward, Johannes, Charles and Therese; Miss Doizé, the children's nurse. Sugar Plantation at Laugane, coffee plantation at La Montagne de Rocheloin, Parish of St. Michael du Fond des Negres, personal estate. Executors Messrs. Commarque and Barichereau, merchants at the Cape, with Messrs. Sheridan, Fitzgerald and Co. merchants, Henry Goguet and Mr. Hamory, merchant at Miregoane as advisory committee. No witnesses. Will proved by the testimony of Jean Louis Jauvin as to handwriting. Recorded ut supra, p. 388.

1219 1762 Febry. 1 1795 Aug. 19 **MANN, John,** of N. Y. City cordwainer. Wife Ann, children John, James, Ann, wife of Abraham Wilson, Elizabeth and Sarah. Real and personal estate. Executrix da. Ann. Witnesses Josiah Bagley, Samuel Lester and Vincent Tilyou of N. Y. City, turner. Recorded ut supra, p. 487.

1220 1795 Octbr. 17 Decbr. 2 **MONEY, John,** of N. Y. City, ropemaker. Mother. Personal property. Executor Nicholas Devenport; proceeds to be sent to mother by John Fitzsimons. Witnesses Nicholas Devenport, painter, John Fitzsimons, blacksmith, both of N. Y. City and Rachel Devenport. Recorded ut supra, p. 524.

1221 1795 May 22 1796 March 7 **MELCHER, Jacob,** of Philadelphia, Penna. "Amiable little friend," Mrs. Theresa Waters, late of Greenwich Co., N. J., John Hide of N. Y. City, sister Maria Hasenclever. Real and personal estate. Executors the sister Maria Hasenclever and John Hide. Witnesses John Tice and Caty Tice. Recorded ut supra, p. 534.

1222 1796 March 17 **MOWATT, George,** of N. Y. City, letters of administration on the estate of, granted to Lawrence Yates and Alexander Thompson, executors named in his testamentary codicil, which leaves legacies to George, son of Professor John Stuart of Mareschal College, Aberdeen, to Margaret, wife of said Professor, to Marjory, wife of Rev. Alexander Peters of Logie and Pert, County of Angus, North Britain. Recorded ut supra, p. 539.

1223 1796 June 7 July 2 **McMAUNIS, Peter.** Mother Anna van Horne, brother John McMaunis, sister Mary Pryor. Personal effects. William Stephens executor. Witnesses William Stevens, John McCornell and Jesse Woodhull. Recorded ut supra, p. 542.

1224 1796 Jany. 15 July 29 **MAUGUEN, Matthieu le,** at present of N. Y. City. Mother and sister. Real and personal estate. Executor James Dupuy. Witnesses John H. Remsen of N. Y. City esquire, de Seulle, Hilaire Gaubert and John Jukes. Recorded ut supra, p. 557.

1225 1796 Septbr. 28 Octbr. 13 French **MANET, Jean Baptiste Nadaud,** native of Limoges, France, about 23 years old, son of Jacques Nadaud and Marie Rose Manet, resident of the Island of St. Domingo. Legal heirs Uncle Manet. "My property and goods of whatever kind." Executor Hilaire Gobert, M.D. Witnesses Joseph Marcadier, François Laurence and Baptiste Vieusse. Recorded ut supra, p. 603.

1226 1795 Decbr. 10 1796 Decbr. 13 **MARSH, Hannah,** widow of ——, sailor on board the *Falkand,* Sir Francis Drake commander. Richard B. Marsh, Mary Darrell, Samuel, Jane and William Riley, Margaret, widow of William Riley. Personal effects. Witnesses John Burt of N. Y. City and Simon Swartwout. Recorded ut supra, Vol. II., p. 6.

1227 1797 Octbr. 19 Octbr. 30 French **MARÉS, Jean,** of St. Marc, Island of St. Domingo, now in N. Y. City. Brother Jean Paul Marés of Philadelphia, Penna., Jean Paul Mary, natural son of Marguerite Mary, sister Catherine Marés. Real and personal estate. Executor Jean Baptiste Bacqué. Witnesses P. Maurin, Julien Veron and Reiner John van den Broch, Not. Public. Recorded ut supra, p. 47.

1228 1796 March 28 1797 Decbr. 29 **McLEOD, William,** of N. Y. City, mariner and mate of the schooner *Dispatch.* Wife Margaret sole heiress and with John R. Harrington executor of real and personal estate. Witnesses, John Anderson, mariner and Edward Dodsworth. Recorded ut supra, p. 62.

1229 1798 Novbr. 12 Novbr. 23 **MURFIN, Angle,** late mariner of the brig *Porcupine,* Captain Butler. Capt. William Lowndes of N. Y. City sole heir and executor of " my estate." Witnesses Philipp Parison, of N. Y. City, miniature painter and Ann Black. Recorded ut supra, p. 86.

1230 1799 Jany. 18 Febry. 18 **McKAY, Jane,** widow of James, of N. Y. City. Son-in-law Robert Patterson, son George McKay, grandson James McKay, grandda. Alexie, da. Jane Patterson. Personal property. Robert Patterson executor. Witnesses Peter Ogilvie and James Riker of N. Y. City, gentleman. Recorded ut supra, p. 169.

1231 1798 May 31 1799 April 12 **MILLS, Hannah,** of Elizabeth Town, N. J. Sister Mary Halstead, brothers John Reading Mills, Isaac Mills, William Mills and Thaddeus Mills. Real and personal estate. Executors bro. Thaddeus Mills and sister Mary Halstead. Witnesses Daniel Comstock, Jonas Mills jun., and Hannah Woodhull. Proved in N. Y. Recorded ut supra, p. 189.

1232 1784 Jany. 8 Septbr. 11 **MURGITTROYD, Samuel,** of N. Y. City, grocer. Wife Esther sole heiress and executrix of real and personal estate. Witnesses Andrew Bowne of said City, shopkeeper, and Ann Letson. Recorded ut supra, Vol. III., p. 19.

1233 1784 Novbr. 27 Decbr. 18 **McNACHTANE, John,** of the Port of N. Y., mariner. Wife Cornelia sole heiress and executrix of real and personal estate. Witnesses Dirck Lefferts, merchant, James J. Beekman, Sarah J. Beekman. Recorded ut supra, p. 41.

1234 1776 Febry. 8 1778 Septbr. 12 **MARSTON, Nathaniel,** of N. Y. City, merchant. Da.-in-law Ann, wife of Augustus van Horne, Stephen Kibble, daughter Margaret Ogilvie and her sons Nathaniel, Frederick and Adolf Philippse, sons Johns Marston, Thomas Marston, who has son Nathaniel, grandson Nathaniel, son of John, granddaughters Frances and Mary, daughters of dec'd son Nathaniel, sisters Mary Marston and Ann Grant. Prospect Farm on Horns Hook, lot in Kings Street, h. and l. in Hanover Square and other real estate in N. Y. City, personal property (plate). Executors sons Thomas and John. Witnesses Jas. Jauncey of N. Y. City, gentleman, Evert Bancker and Zacharias Sickels. Codicil of Septbr. 12, 1778, gives legacy to the Episcopal Church in N. Y. for the use of the Charity School and adds Thomas and John, sons of son John to legatees. Witnesses Beverley Robinson, Robert R. Waddell and Samuel Jones. Recorded ut supra, p. 52.

1235 1793 Febry. 5 **McLAREN, Duncan,** of Georgia, mariner, letters of administration on the estate of, granted John McLaren of N. Y. City, merchant, a relation of deceased. Recorded ut supra, p. 129.

1236 1796 June 4 1799 Jany. 17 **MILLER, Burnet,** of Stanford Town, Dutchess Co. Wife Lucretia, sons Jason, Guidon, John, Thomas, Eleazer, grandson John, son of da. Phebe, daughters Mary, Elizabeth, Phebe and Ruth, grandda. Harriet Lucretia Smith, children of dec'd son Burnet, vizt. Elizabeth, Moriah, Marget and Lucretia. Land near Plattsburgh, personal property (plate). Executors sons John, Thomas and Eleazer. Witnesses Lot Carman, William Carskadan and Jonathan Marriot. In certificate of proof testator is called as about 70 years old and late of the Town of Plattsburgh, Clinton Co. Recorded ut supra, Vol. IV., p. 1.

1237 1823 April 15 Aug. 6 **MUIR, John,** of Sherburne, Chenango Co. Wife Molly, son John, James, David and William, Phylinda Goodell, "the young lady, that has lived in my family," son Catlin Stockbridge alias Muir. Homefarm, land in Hamilton Township, Madison Co., personal property. Executor James M. Cassels of Sherburn. Witnesses David Muir, Amos Pettit and J. B. Eldridge. Recorded ut supra, Vol. V., p. 13.

1238 1816 Decbr. 11 1827 Aug. 6 **McVICKAR, Henry,** of N. Y. City, merchant. Godson William Henry Constable; brother Edward Corp McVickar principal heir and executor of real and personal estate. Witnesses Annah McVickar, Hannah Moore and Benjamin McVickar. Recorded ut supra, p. 52.

1239 1685 Aug. 7 Dutch **METSELAER, Teunis Teunissen de,** and wife Eghbertie Eghberts, of Rensselaerswyck. Children Maritje, wife of Harmen Lievesen, Eghbert, Gerritje, wife of Andries Hansen, Dirckje, wife of Bastiaen Harmansen, Willemtie, 23 years old, Anna, 21 yrs., Martin, 19 yrs. Real and personal estate. The survivor executor. Witnesses Cornelis van Dyck and Myndert Harmensen. Albany Co. Records, Wills, I., p. 6.

1240 1761 Septbr. 18 1764 Jany. 16 **MYNDERS, Johannis,** of Albany City, blacksmith. Wife Maria, children Elizabeth, Frederick and Rachel. Real and personal estate. Executors brothers Abraham and Marte Mynders. Witnesses Isaac Bogert, carpenter, Gerrit G. van den Bergh, and J. Roorbach, schoolmaster, all of Albany City. Albany Co. Records, Wills, I., part 2, p. 28.

1241 (N 1) 1702 Octbr. 4 — **NOELL, Thomas,** of N. Y. City. Wife Hannah, sons Noah Noell and Richard Hall. Real and personal estate. Executors the wife, Ripp van Dam and Capt. Lawrence Read. Witnesses Arent Schuyler, James Spencer, James Wright and Wm. Huddleston. Copy made Novbr. 14, 1770.

1242 (N 2) 1715 May 1 — **NORTON, George,** of N. Y. City, butcher. Wife Margaret, Edward Pennant, da. of Mrs. Skellen, Mrs. Stoaks. Personal property. Executor Captain Ebenezer Wilson. Witnesses Will. Bradford, Elie Pelletreau and Will Anderson. Copy.

1243 (N 3) 1724 July 25 Septbr. 30 Dutch **NEWKERK, Gerrit,** of Ulster Co. Wife Grietje ten Eyck, children Jannetje, Cornelius, Matheus, Benjamin and Coenraat. "My whole estate." Executors Cornelius Wynkoop and Timothy Louw. Witnesses Gerrit Nukerk jun., Jaco: Elmendorph, Samuel Burhans and Gert. van Wagenen.

1244 (N 4) 1730 Decbr. 7 1730-1 March 8 **NOTTINGHAM, William,** of Marbletown, Ulster Co. Wife Margaret, sons Stephen, Thomas and William, daughters Mary, wife of Egbert de Witt, Elizabeth, wife of Marten de Lametter, Bridget, Ann and Catherine, sister Ann Garton. Real and personal estate. Executors the wife, sons Stephen and Thomas, and the two sons-in-law. Witnesses Joris Middagh, Johannis de Witt, Abraham Post and Richard Pick.

1245 (N 5) 1746 Aug. 2 1747 July 1 **NORTHRUP, Moses,** of Beekmansberry, Dutchess Co., yeoman. Wife Abigail, daughters Sarah, Abigail Caulkings, sons Moses, Amos, Joseph, Benjamin and Cornwall. Real and personal estate. Executor son Moses. Witnesses James Brown, Richard Olmsted and Saml. Lobdell.

1246 (N 6) 1756 Septbr. 17 Decbr. 10 **NEELY, Robert,** of Neely Town, Ulster Co. Wife Isabell, children Addam, William, David, Matthew and Mary. Real and personal estate. Executors the wife and brothers William and John Neely. Witnesses Isaac Hodge of N. Y. City, shopkeeper, John Thompson and John Monell.

1247 (N 7) 1758 April 15 — **NICOLL, Benjamin,** of N. Y. City. Wife ——, son Edward and apparently other children not named. Real and personal estate. Executors the wife, Honble. John Chambers, William Nicoll of Shelter Island, John Watts and William Nicoll jun. Witnesses David Matthews, Cary Ludlow and D. Isaac Browne. Copy.

1248 (N 8) 1759 May 5 Novbr. 15 — **NEWMAN, Thomas,** of Ceacat (Kakiat), Orange Co., yeoman. Wife Philey, brothers Jeremiah Newman of North Castle, Westchester Co., Daniel of the same place, Steven of Kakiat, sisters Hannah Warring of Bedford, Westchester Co., Rebeccah Brown of Stamford, Fairfield Co., Connt. Real and personal estate. Executors John Rider of Ceacat and Charles Smith of Stamford. Witnesses Rem Remsen, Jacob Polhemus of Orange Co., farmer, and Johannis Tromper.

1249 (N 9) 1762 Aug. 23 Aug. 27 — **NELSON, John,** of N. Y. City, at present in Philadelphia, mariner. Mother Frances, sisters Sarah and Margaret. "Estate." Executors John Sears sen. and John Sears jun. Witnesses Paul Isaac Voto, Thomas Clarke and Esther Sayre. The executors named being out of the Province Francis Wade of Philadelphia, merchant, husband of testator's sister Sara is made administrator April 2, 1763. Copy.

1250 (N 10) 1763 Novbr. 30 1764 Febry. 1 — **NEWKERCK, Corneles,** of Fishkil, Dutchess Co. Wife Maria, sisters Annatie Cutler, Janitia van Etten, Engeltie Rickman and Cornelia van Kuren, nephew Abraham, son of John Heeremanse. Real and personal estate, including a legacy from Uncle Hendrick Kip, payable after the death of Aunt Jacomintie, wife of Captain Peter Duboyce. Executors the wife, William Humfrey, Nathaniel Sackett and John Cooper. Witnesses Abraham Heermans, Simon ter Bush and Isaac ter Bush.

1251 (N 11) 1769 Novbr. 5 1770 Novbr. 7 **NEELY, William,** of Wallkil Prect., Ulster Co., Captain. Wife ——, da. Sarah, Martha, wife of Benj. Hains, who has children John, William and Elizabeth Hains, Elizabeth Harlow, grandchildren William, Henry and Elizabeth Harrold, son William Neely. Real and personal estate. Executors son William and James McCobb of said Precinct, merchant. Witnesses William Young, William Stewart and Thomas Neely.

1252 (N 12) 1774 Septbr. 26 1775 Febry. 17 **NOBLE, James,** of Mamicoten Prect., Ulster Co. Wife Margaret, da. Mary, grandchildren vizt: James, son of John Crage, Stephen, son of Benjamin Homans and Jenat, da. of John McKinstry. Personal property. Executors John Crage and James Monell. Witnesses George Monell, David Monnell of Hanover Prect., schoolmaster, and Robert Henderson.

1253 (N 13) 1775 April 10 May 4 **NEATE, William,** of London, merchant. Wife Christiana, daughters Christiana, wife of Henry Chapman, Mary, Jemima and Phyllis, grandson William Neate Chapman, niece Mary Evans, bro.-in-law Henry Appleton and wife Susannah, who have children John and Susannah, bro.-in-law Thomas Shirley and wife Martha, John Prothero, clerks William Groile and Michael Touray, Samuel Stapleton of Wandsworth. Real and personal effects. Executors John Platt sen. of Cornhill, London, linendraper, bro.-in-law Henry Appleton, Sampson Wright of Northumberland Str. in the Strand esquire, son-in-law Henry Chapman and John Prothero. Witnesses Jas. Hutchinson, Edward Middlecott and Francis Knight. Proved in England.

1254 (N 14) 1776 Septbr. 6 1778 Aug. 25 **NOTTINGHAM, Stephen.** Wife Nealtie. Real and personal estate. Executors John Cantine and William Pick. Witnesses Jacob Keatter of Marbletown, farmer, Frederick Markle of the same place, weaver, and Frederick F. Markle.

1255 (N 15) 1776 April 30 1785 Octbr. 22 **NELSON, Reuben,** of Charlotte Prect., Dutchess Co., yeoman. Wife Elizabeth, sons Francis and Reuben R., daughters Zeba, wife of Smith Rowland, Susannah, wife of Henry Neely, Mary, Ann and Elizabeth. Real and personal property. Executors the wife and sons. Witnesses P. D. Witt, John Pauling of said Co., farmer, and Albartus Sickner.

1256 (N 16) 1781 Septbr. 11 1784 April 23 **NICOLL, John,** of New Windsor Prect., Ulster Co., esquire. Wife Hannah, sons John Dowden, Leonard William, Abimael Youngs, daughter Frances. Real and personal estate (a silver tankard). Executors the wife, his Excellency George Clinton and John McKesson, attorney at law. Witnesses John Cochran of N. Y. City, physician, John Barton and Isaac Mills.

1257 (N 17) 1781 March 26 Aug. 17 **NEELY, John,** of Hanover Prect., Ulster Co. Daughters Sarah, wife of James Wilkens, Mary, who is expected to become w. of Andrew Willson, nephew Samuel, son of bro. Matthew Neely. Real and personal estate. Executors da. Mary and Andrew Willson. Witnesses Alexander Trimble, John Trimble, farmer, and Patrick Barber, esquire. At date of swearing in the executors Mary is the wife of A. Willson.

1258 (N 18) 1781 Decbr. 12 1783 Febry. 14 **NEWKERK, Cornelius,** of Rochester, Ulster Co. Sons Gerret, Jacob, Matthew, Benjamin and Isaac, daughters Margrieth, Jannetje and Jacobmyntje, children of dec'd da. Cathrina, wife of John E. de Witt, vizt. Neeltje, Margrieth, Maria and Leah. Land in Rochester Township, personal estate. Executors sons Gerret, Matthew and Benjamin and Andries de Witt. Witnesses John Brodhead, Peter Contine of said Township, farmers, and Andries de Witt.

1259 (N 19) 1785 Aug. 2 1787 March 7

NEELY, Thomas, of Wallkil Prect., Ulster Co. Wife Margaret, daughters Rebecca, Jean and Alener, sons Thomas, John and Daniel, da. Margaret. Real and personal estate. Executors the wife, son John and John Monell. Witnesses Thomas Borland, yeoman, and Charles Borland.

1260 (N 20) 1785 Octbr. 31 1787 Febry. 3

NELSON, Theophilus, of Charlotte Precinct, Dutchess Co. Wife Mary, children Stephen, Joshua, Sarah, wife of Gilbert Williams jun., Mary, Charles, Theophilus, David, George and Catherine. Real and personal estate. Executors the wife, sons Charles and John D. Witt jun. Witnesses Rachel van Dyck, Francis Williams of Clinton Prect., Dutchess Co., yeoman, and Jno. DWitt jun.

1261 (N 21) 1785 Febry. 12 June 13

NICOLL, Hannah, widow of John, of New Windsor, Ulster Co. Sons Abimail, John Dowden, Leonard William, da. Frances. Personal property (a silver bowl, a do. teapot, six do. table and 12 do. teaspoons, a pair of silver tea tongs, a silver pepper box, a do. salt cellar, gold sleeve buttons). Executors Henry Wisner jun., Jeremiah Clark and Leonard D. Nicoll. Witnesses Abimail Youngs of said Co., yeoman, Mary Chandler and Sarah Case, widow, both of Orange Co. Supra, No. 1256.

1262 (N 22) 1786 March 17 May 31

NEELY, Samuel, of the Oblong, Dutchess Co. Aged mother Ginnet McMullen, sons Elexander and John, daughters Anna, Ginnet, Mary, and Rachel; bro. William Neely to be supported agreeable to contract made between Samuel Neely and Elexander McMullen in 1774, William being dumb and non compos mentis. "Worldly estate." Executors John Buttolph, David Lawrance and Silas Roe. Witnesses Hezekiah Buttolph of said Co., farmer, Ebenezer Knap and Josiah Knap.

1263 1792 Octbr. 5 Novbr. 30 **NICOLS, William,** of Hartford, Connt. Natural and adopted son William Nicols, sisters Mary Nicols, Caty Nicols, Sarah Jeffery. Real and personal estate. Executors John Dodd and John Porter. Witnesses Zebulon Seamour, Richard Skinner and Joseph W. Seamour. Recorded in Wills and Probates, Vol. I., p. 458.

1264 1798 July 6 1799 Febry. 2 **NELSON, Abraham,** now of N. Y. City. Daughter Martha, John Nelson of N. Y. City, physician. Land in a tract called Williamsburgh, on N. W. side of Allegheny River, in Westmoreland Co., Penna., personal property. Executors William Dunlap, merchant, and John Wells, attorney-at-law, both of N. Y. City. Witnesses Bezaliel Howe, Daniel D. Walters and John H. Field. Recorded ut supra, Vol. II., p. 171.

1265 1786 Novbr. 22 Decbr. 12 **NASH, Abner,** of North Carolina. Da. Margaret, wife of Thomas Haslin, son Abner, da. Justina, children of " my present wife." Land on Tar River, do. on West side of Apalacian Mts., personal property. Honble. William Blount, guardian of son Abner. Executors Jacob Blount senior, Alfred Moore, Thomas Pearson and William Blount. Witnesses John Cochran, Charles McKnight, Willie Blount, of N. Ca., student in the College of New York. Recorded ut supra, Vol. III., p. 69.

1266 1822 March 2 1828 Febry. 21 **NORTON, Samuel,** of Goshen, Litchfield Co., Connt., " advanced in age." Wife Phebe, das. Miranda, Diantha, wife of Eliphaz Bissel, an occasionally intemperate man, Eunice, widow of Stephen Goodwin, grandson Samuel Norton Bissel, grandda, Miranda Goodwin. Land in Litchfield Co., do. in Vernon, N. Y., personal property. Ashbel Norton, of Vernon, N. Y., trustee for da. Diantha. Executors da. Miranda, William Stanley and Lewis M. Norton. Witnesses George Stanley, of Goshen aforesaid, Clara Stanly and Henry Kimberly. By the certificate of proof it appears the heirs are Miranda Norton of Goshen,

Eunice Goodwin, Diantha Bissel, Phebe E. Bissel, Henry W. Bissel and Eunice C. Bissel, all of Vernon, Oneida Co., N. Y. Recorded ut supra, Vol. IV., p. 241.

1267 1829 May 9 June 30 **NORTHUP, Remington,** of Deerfield, Oneida Co. Sons William, Remington and John, daughters, not named. Real and personal estate. Executors bro. Stephen and son Remington. Witnesses John Northup, Stephen Northup and Isaac Bucklin. Recorded ut supra, Vol. V., p. 97.

1268 1673 April 21 — Dutch **NOORMAN, Jan Jansen,** of Albany, and wife Maritie Dirckx. Da. by first husband Dirck Dircksen Mayer, vizt: Susanna Dirckx, wife of Barent Albertsen, son Dirck Mayer. Real and personal estate. No executor named. Witnesses Pieter Ryverdingh, David Schuyler and Adriaen van Ilpendam, Notary Public. Albany Co. Records, Notarial Papers, I., p. 534.

1269 (O 1) 1738 Octbr. 11 1740 April 26 **OOTHOUT, Hendrick,** of Rensselaerswyck Manor, yeoman. Children Volkert, Jan, Jonaes, Dorothee, wife of Cornelis Boogard, Hendrickie, wife of Isaac Boogard, Margrita, wife of Domine Jan van Driesen, Annatie, wife of Pieter Wouters Quackenboss, grandson Hendrick, son of son Jan. Real and personal property. Executors son Jan and son-in-law Cornelis Boogard. Witnesses Peterus van den Bergh, Cornelys Ouderkerk and Rutger Bleecker.

1270 (O 2) 1739 June 14 1747-8 Febry. 2 **OOSTERHOUT, Teunis,** of Rochester, Ulster Co., yeoman. Children Jan, Petrus, Engeltie, wife of Nicolaes Keeter, Johannes, Henricus, Marytie, wife of Matheus Terwilliger, Annatie, wife of Cornelius Hoornbeeck, Ariaentie, wife of Harmen Rosenkrans, Arien and Kryn, children of dec'd son Aldert, vizt: Jacobus and Aldert Oosterhout. Real and personal estate. Executors sons Jan, Kryn and Hendricus. Witnesses Jacob de Witt, John Schoonmaker and Jacobus Bruyn jun.

1271 (O 3) 1741 May 14 1742 Novbr. 24 **OLDFIELD, Joseph,** of Goshen Township, Orange Co. Sons Joseph, Elias, Augustus, daughters Mary Smith, Martha Drake and Easter Holstead. Land in Goshen Township and at Jamaica, L. I., personal property. Executors son Elias and son-in-law Richard Holstead. Witnesses Danll. Denton, Henry Smith and Danll. Everett.

1272 (O 4) 1757 May 20 1766 March 7 **OCHTERLONY, David,** late of Montrose, now of Boston, mariner. Wife Thellrin (Catherine) sole heiress and executrix. Witnesses Saml. Minot, Miriam Tyler and Mary Tyler. Proved in Boston. Copy.

1273 (O 5) 1758 May 7 June 23 **ONDERDONCK, Abraham,** of Orange Co., merchant. Son Abraham, cousins Adriaen, son of Andries Onderdonck, Captain Gerrit, son of Gerrit Onderdonck, Rou Onderdonck. Real and personal estate. Executors brothers Captain Andries Onderdonck of Orange Co. and Gerrit Onderdonck of said Co., esquire. Witnesses Theodoros Snedeker, Rem Monfoort and Adriaen Onderdonck.

1274 (O 6) 1760 July 11 1762 March 9 **OOSTERHOUT, Theunis,** of Albany Co. Wife Eva, children John, Anna, wife of Eyston Munson, Alletua, wife of Lambert van Alstyn, Marytie and Trintje. Real and personal estate. Executors the wife, Casparus Coneyn and Henry van Rensselaer. Witnesses Jeremias ten Broeck, Andries Witbeck, both of Claverack, yeomen, and Lowrence Conyne.

1275 (O 7) 1761 Febry. 16 March 4 **OWEN, Timothy,** of Goshen Prect., Orange Co., cordwainer. Wife ——, children Timothy, John, Israel, Anning, Moubery, Sarah and Elizabeth (eldest son sometimes crazy). Real and personal estate. Executors Girshom Owen, Nathaniel Owen of Ulster Co. and Ebenezer Owen of Pochack. Witnesses Abner Brush, John Gale and James Little.

1276 (O 8) 1763 June 6 1765 March 28 **OBLENUS, Peter,** of New Hempstead and Kakiate Patent, Orange Co., yeoman. Wife Sarah, sons Hendrick, John, daughters Sarah, Jonitia and Maria. Real and personal estate. Executors Hendrick Oblenus, Abraham Stevens and Hendrick Nagel. Witnesses Myndert Hogenkamp, Jacob Meyer and David Pye of Orange Co., clothier.

1277 (O 9) 1767 Octbr. 6 1768 Febry. 23 **OVERTON, James,** of Corwell Prect., Orange Co. Wife Mary, son James and other children, not named. Real and personal estate. Executors the wife and Curtis Colman. Witnesses Thomas Clark, farmer, Daniel Curtis and Nathaniel Jayne.

1278 (O 10) 1769 May 16 1774 Septbr. 15 **OLIVER, David,** of Cornwall Prect., Orange Co. Wife Elizabeth, children Thomas, David, Elizabeth Shaw, Anne, Sarah and Margareth. Real and personal estate. Executors cousin James Oliver of Marvel Town, Ulster Co. and Thomas Porter of Orange Co. Witnesses Wm. Denn, of Ulster Co., yeoman, Phebe Denn and Daniel McCloud.

1279 (O 11) 1770 Aug. 15 Aug. 28 **OWENS, George,** of Goshen Prect., Orange Co. Wife Elizabeth, children, sons and daughters, not named. Real and personal estate. Executors the wife, Thomas Sayres and Thomas Wisner. Witnesses David McCamly jun., Isaac Sammis and Francis Baird of Orange Co., merchant.

1280 (O 12) 1770 Novbr. 30 Decbr. 17 **OSBORN, John,** of New Hempstead, Orange Co. Wife Ann, sons James, John, daughters Hannah, Mary, Elizabeth, Phebe, Sarah, Rachel, Martha and Nancy. Real and personal property. Executors son James and Gilbert Cuyper. Witnesses Caleb Halsted, farmer, Pieter Sisiyent, cordwainer, and Dirk Straet, farmer, all of Orange Co.

1281 (O 13) 1771 April 29 Septbr. 4 **OOSTERHOUT, Abraham,** of Kingston Corporation, Ulster Co. Catherine, widow of Teunas Oosterhout, Marritie, wife of Petrus T. Oosterhout, godchildren Cornelius Oosterhout, Abraham Borhans, Marrytie Oosterhout, wife of Johannis Meyer, Abraham, of son of Johannis Meyer, Abraham, son of Stiphanis Meyer, brothers Jan, William, Petrus and Hendricus, sisters Anneke, widow of Abraham Borhans, Arriantie, wife of Jonetan Dubois, Sarah, widow of Johannis Borhans. Real and personal estate (a bible). Executors Peterus t. Oosterhout, Tobias Meyer and Benjamin Snyder. Witnesses Nicolaes Miller, of Sagerties, Ulster Co., labourer. and Benjamin Snyder.

1282 (O 14) 1775 Septbr. 1 1784 April 2 **OUTWATER, Peter,** of Rumbouts Prect., Dutchess Co., farmer. Wife Balitje, grandson Daniel Outwater, grandda. Catherine Outwater, wife of Barendt van Kleeck. Real and personal estate. Executor grandson Daniel Outwater and grandson-in-law Barendt van Kleeck. Witnesses Johannis Schurry, Clement Cornell, yeoman, and Anthony Helst. Codicil of May 15, 1777, states, that wife Balitje is dead and makes a bequest to Peter, son of grandson Daniel. Same witnesses.

1283 (O 15) 1775 Aug. 30 1785 Febry. 26 **OTTO, Franz,** of Schohary, Albany Co., yeoman. Wife Maria Elizabeth, sons Gotlieb and Franz. Real and personal estate. Executors the two sons. Witnesses J. Gottlieb Boeckle, Anderes Feinaur, farmers, and Johanes N. Lawyer.

1284 (O 16) 1775 Decbr. 9 1776 March 1 **OSTERHOUDT, John Crinse,** of Sagerties, Ulster Co., carpenter. Sisters Anneke and Margaret, half sister Elizabeth, sister Anneke's oldest da. Mary, godsons John C. Persen and Samuel, son of Egbert Schoonmaker; Peter West, Edward Schoonmaker jun.; children of half brothers and sisters. Real and personal estate. Executors Edward Schoonmaker jun., William

Dederick jun. and John Brink jun., all of Ulster Co. Witnesses Cornelius Legg and Andrew van Leuve, both of Sagerties, farmers.

1285 (O 17) 1775 3d Day 11th Month 1781 Aug. 29 **OSBORN, Paul,** of Dutchess Co., yeoman, Wife Elizabeth, who is blind and has Mary R . nold as companion, cousins Isaac Osborn, Amos Osborn and Stephen Osborn. Real and personal property. Executors Salomon Height, John Hoag 2d jun. and Abner Hoag, all of Dutchess Co., yeomen. Witnesses Aaron Vail, Martha Vail, widow, and David Sands.

1286 (O 18) 1783 June 23 1784 April 30 **OAKLEY, Thomas,** junior, of Goshen Prect., Orange Co., late a soldier in Col. Lambs Regt. of Artillery. Brothers John, Jeremiah, Augustus, sisters Phebe, Marthar, Sarah and Julianah. Real and personal estate. Executors Uncle William Holly and bro. John Oakley, both of Orange Co. Witnesses William Holly jun., Samuel Holly and James Hennep.

1287 (O 19) 1785 Jany. 12 Febry. 23 **OWEN, Jonathan,** of Dutchess Co. Wife Jain, sons Jonathan, Samuel, Israel, Benjamin and Salomon, daughters Abbe and Mary. Real and personal estate. Executors the wife and Jesse Owen. Witnesses Joseph Bard, Joseph Chase of Dutchess Co., farmer, and Susannah Mangle.

1288 1786 Novbr. 16 1787 Jany. 25 **OSBORN, Joseph,** of Easthampton, Suffolk Co., yeoman. Son Joseph, grandsons Abraham and Stephimus, sons of dec'd son Lewis, da.-in-law Prusha Osborn and her sons Abraham and Septimus, da. Mary, granddaughters Hannah Dayton and Esther Osborn. Land at Easthampton, at Westplain Close, at Orchard Close, Norwest plain, personal property. Executors son Joseph and bro.-in-law Stephen Hedges. Witnesses Jeremiah Miller, Hunting Miller, yeomen, and John Chatfield. Recorded in Wills and Probates, Vol. I., p. 30.

1289 1792 Decbr. 6 1796 Jany. 1 **OCKERSON, Clayton,** of N. Y. City, mariner. George Copland of N. Y. City, grocer, sole heir and executor of real and personal estate. Witnesses James McKay and Richard Williamson, grocer. Recorded ut supra, p. 527.

1290 1800 Jany. 1 Febry. 19 **OSTRANDER, John,** jun., of Albany City. Wife Catherine, son John and other children, not named. Real and personal estate. Executors son John and Whiting Warner. Witnesses Joseph Caldwell, Charles Newman and Jared Skinner. Recorded ut supra, Vol. II., p. 234.

1291 1799 July 1 1800 Octbr. 28 **OGSBURY, David,** of the Town of Watervliet, Albany Co. Wife Elizabeth, children David, Anna, wife of Nicholas Conteman, John, Susannah, wife of Peter Wormer, Margreth, wife of Bartholomy van Alstine, Elizabeth, wife of Jacob Waggoner, "which said Jacob is now and has been for several years since a proper Tippler." Real and personal estate. Executors Barent Mynderse, John Schoolcraft jun. and Thomas Esmay. Witnesses Jacob Mans, Frederick Frydendall and Edward Ward. Recorded ut supra, p. 250.

1292 1797 Jany. 18 1801 Aug. 14 **OOTHOUDT, Henry,** of Catskil, Albany Co. Daughter Catherine, wife of David Bancroft, grandchildren Henry Oothoudt Demarest and Nelly Demarest. Homefarm on Corloskil, Catskil Township, land on the St. Lawrence R., in a patent granted to testator and Jeremiah van Rensselaer, personal property. Executor Gerrit Bogart of Albany City. Witnesses Elsie Lansing, Gerrit Lansing jun. and Jeremiah van Rensselaer. Recorded ut supra, p. 272.

1293
1796
May 27
OSBORNE, Samuel, late of St. John, Nova Scotia, mariner, letters of administration on the estate of, granted to his father Almer Osborne of Paulings (?), Dutchess Co., farmer. Recorded ut supra, Vol. III., p. 161.

1294
1687-8
March 13
1695-6
Jany. 3
OUTHOUT, Jan, of Greenbush, Rensselaerswyck Manor, brewer. Children Johannes, Hendrick, Mayekay, Ante, Jannetie and Arien 12 yrs. old. Real and personal estate. Executors son Hendrick and bro.-in-law Hendrick van Ness. Witnesses Cobus Janssen and E. D. Ridder. Albany Co. Records, Wills, I., p. 36.

1295 (P 1)
1691
Jany. 21
1695
March 25
PAWLING, Henry, of Marbletown, Ulster Co. Wife ——, children Jane, Wyntie, John, Albert, Ann and Henry. Wife's brother is Arien Rose, who with Gysbert Crum is to take an inventory of the real and personal property, of which the widow Pawling is sworn as executrix, on the 25th of March, 1695. Witnesses to will are Gysbert Crum and John Ward.

1296 (P 2)
1719
June 15
Aug. 3
PUIROE, Martha, of N. Y. City, widow of John. Children: Margaret Hall, Mary Leonard, who has son Jacob Leonard, Peter Puiroe, Joanna, who has son John Kearney, Catharine Kearney.* Apparently only personal property (plate, a silver tankard, a do. cup with cover, 5 pictures in black frames, and 5 do. in gilt frames). Executors sons-in-law John Hall and Thomas Kearney. Witnesses Hendrick Meyer, Harmanus Rutgers and H. Wileman.

1297 (P 3)
1734
Decbr. 26
1734-5
March 15
Dutch
PLOEGH, Wilhelmus, of Kingston Corporation, Ulster Co., cooper. Wife Barbara, sons Hendrick, Wilhelmus, daughters Geertruy and Catharina. Real and personal estate. Executors bro.-in-law Nicolas de Myer and cousin Powlis Ploegh. Witnesses Petrus Bogardus, Johannis Dumont, Walran Demon and Ino. Crooke jun.

* It may be Joanna Catherine Kearney.

1298 (P 4) 1736 July 5 **PERROW, Richard,** of the Boore near N. Y. City, miner, about going to the Island of Jamaica. Wife Katie, children John, Ann and Elizabeth. Real and personal estate. The wife executrix. Witnesses Gerardus Stuyvesant, Elizabeth Ustick and Edward Pennant. Copy made April 2, 1760.

1299 (P 5) 1739 Aug. 6 **PRAA, Peter,** of Buswick, Kings Co. Wife Mary, grandsons Peter Praa van Zandt and Johannes van Zandt, daughters Elizabeth Miserole, Annitie, wife of Daniel Boddie, Christiana Provoost. Two houses and lots in N. Y. City, North Ward, homefarm, land on Mespath Creek in Newtown, Queens Co., called Dominies Hook; personal property. Executors grandsons Jacobius Collier, Isaac Bergen and Johannes Albertse. Witnesses John Vanderspeigle, Abraham Lodge and Bartholomew Crannell. Copy made February 12, 1765.

1300 (P 6) 1740 Jany. 30 1766 Jany. 31 **PROVOOST, Abraham,** of Claverack, Albany Co. Sons Johannis, Hendrick, Samuel, Abraham, Isaac and Jacob heirs and executors of real and personal property. Witnesses Samuel Staats, farmer, the only witness living at date of proof, Neeltie Staats and Barent Staats.

1301 (P 7) 1741 Novbr. 24 **PALMER, Silvanus,** of Momaroneck, Westchester Co., yeoman. Wife Mary, children Silvanus, John, Marmaduke, Anne, Susannah, Mary, Charity, Edward, Robert, Edward. Land at New Rochelle and elsewhere, personal property. Executors the wife, Joseph Rodman of New Rochelle, Richard Cornwell sen. and John Griffin. Witnesses John Ray, Thomas Gilchrist and John Cuer. Copy.

1302 (P 8) 1745 April 8 1757 July 15 **PLASS, Johann Emmerich,** of Claverack, Albany Co., yeoman. Wife Agneta Flora, da. Elisabeth, wife of Hendrick Plass, grandsons Emmerich Plass and Hendrick Plass, Lutheran Church at Loonenberg (Athens).

Real and personal property. Executors Rev. William Christopher Berkenmeyer and Jacob Freese. Witnesses Piter van Buren, Piter Kool and Jacob van Hoise. Also in Albany Co. Records, Wills, I., p. 237.

1303 (P 9) 1747 July 29 1757 Novbr. 7 Dutch **POFFIE, Antie,** of Albany City, widow. Jannetie, da. of Jochem van Valkenburgh, Jannetie, da. of Jeremiah Hoogeboom, Jannetie, da. of Jochem Redliff, Jannetie, da. of Willem van Nes. Personal property (a gold chain, do. buttons). Executors Barent Brat and Willem van Nes. Witnesses David A. Schuyler, Will. Rogers jun., both of Albany and Elisabeth Brat.

1304 (P 10) 1748 July 5 1756 June 25 **PERSON, John,** of Kingston Corporation, Ulster Co. Wife Anna Catrina, sons Abraham, Jacobus, heirs of dec'd son Cornelis, viz: John and Marya Person, da. Jannitte, wife of Myndert Mynderse. Real and personal estate. Executor Jacobus Person and Myndert Mynderse. Witnesses Hiskia Dubois, Hiskia Dubois jun. and Martin Hoffman.

1305 (P 11) 1757 April 18 1760 Octbr. 20 Dutch **PEELEN, Petrus,** of Kingston, Ulster Co. Wife Elisabeth, children Gysbert, Ezechiel and Cathrine. Real and personal estate. Executors bro. Paulus Peelen and bro.-in-law Willem Legg. Witnesses Hendrick Ploegh jun., weaver, Abraham Burhans, farmer, and Jan Eltinge.

1306 (P 12) 1753 Octbr. 9 1764 March 22 **PAWLING, Catharina,** of Rhinebeek Prect., Dutchess Co., gentlewoman. Daughter Catherine, wife of Capt. Petrus ten Brook, grandda. Cornelia, da. of dec'd son Jacob Rutsen, grandson John Rutsen. Lands in Dutchess Co., in Ulster Co. and elsewhere, personal property. Executors da. Catherine, her husband Petrus ten Brook and bro. Henry Beekman. Witnesses Christian Schultz, Wilhelmus Heermans, yeomen, and Hannes Hendricksen. Seal.

1307 (P 13) 1754 March 11 July 8 **PLOGH, Henry,** son of Arent of Flatbush, Kingston Corporation, Ulster Co. Nephew Cornelius Swart, son of eldest sister Catherine, sisters Marretje, widow of Nehemia Duboys, Marya Plough, Elisabeth Plough and nephew Hendrick Palen, son of sister Catherine. Real and personal estate. Executors Evert Wynkoop, Abraham van Keuren and Poules Pelen. Witnesses Samuel Davis, James Whittaker and D. Wynkoop jun.

1308 (P 14) 1757 April 18 1760 Decbr. 22 **PARHAM, Thomas,** of Oswego Garrison, boat builder, signs will in the Castle of Denan, France, and leaves all his property to brothers and sisters (sic!) William and John Parham of Philadelphia. Witnesses John van Sise of N. Y. City, ship carpenter, John Young of Philadelphia, shipwright, and John Matthews. Proved in N. Y. City. A note at the foot of the will says: "Thomas Parham Died ye 21 of Aprill in the morning In Denan ospetal 1757."

1309 (P 15) 1757 Aug. 20 1765 Jany. 22 **PATTERSON, Joseph,** of N. Y. City, mariner. "Loveing friend" Cattren Manburt of N. Y. City, simster, sole heiress of real and personal estate. Executor James Wells of said City, cordwainer. Witnesses John I. de Meyer, William Young and Garret Abeel. Copy.

1310 (P 16) 1757 April 28 1763 July 6 **PAGE, John,** of Beekmans Prect., Dutchess Co. Wife Sarah, daughters Johanna, Patience, Elizabeth and Margot, grandsons Jeremiah Mott and Brier Carpenter. Homefarm and personal property. Executors sons-in-law Thomas Carpenter and Benjamin Lapham. Witnesses Isaac Germond, Susannah Haffe, at date of proof wife of James Doughty and Sarah Smith, at the said date, wife of Ebenezer Huested.

1311 (P 17) 1758 March 26 1759 June 4 **PHENIX, James,** of Shawangunk, Ulster Co., yeoman. Wife Geessie, daughters Sarah, wife of Barent Kool, who has son Philipp, Maritie, wife of William Harlow, who has da. Geessie, Rebecca, wife of Isaac Terwilligen, who has son James Phenis T., Grietie, wife of Arie Terwilligen, and Helena. Real and personal estate. Executors sons-in-law William Harlow and Isaac Terwilligen. Witnesses Johannis H. Jansen, Harmanis Ostrander jun. and J. Bruyn.

1312 (P 18) 1759 —— 27 1765 April 19

PETTER, Jost, of N. Y. City, cooper. Wife Elizabeth, son Petter and two daughters, not named. Real and personal estate. Executor the wife. Witnesses Daniel Fisher of said City, butcher, and George Gorgus. Copy.

1313 (P 19) 1760 May 10 1768 May 30

PITSIER, Adam, of Dutchess Co. Wife Catryn, sons Pieter, William, Harmon, Jacob; son Harmon is "hunting taverns and gitting drunk." Homefarm, land bought of the van Benthuysen, do. do. of Capt. Josiah Ross in North East Prect, Dutchess Co., land in the Camp or 6000 acres patent, personal property. Executors sons Pieter, Jacob and William. Witnesses Jacobus Persen, Lodewick Ensle of Rinebeek, miller, and Martin Hoffman.

1314 (P 20) 1760 March 8 1786 Decbr. 9

PIXLEY Joseph, of Claverack. Wife Ann, daughters Lidia and Mary, sons Aaron, Squire, Elijah, Nathaniel, Jonah, William and Ephraim. "Worldly estate." Executors Abraham Fonda and William White. Witnesses Peter A. Fonda, Lawrence Fonda and John Smith.

1315 (P 21) 1760 Febry. 27 1784 Febry. 5 Dutch

PHILIPP, Nickel, of Dutchess Co. Wife Christina, sons Zaghrias, Nickolas, Johann, daughters Catharina, wife of Johans Kool and Geertie. Real and personal estate. Executors the wife and sons Zaghrias and Nickolas. Witnesses Willem Betzer of Dutchess Co., yeoman, Aernout Veele and Joseph Niev (?).

1316 (P 22) 1762 Octbr. 3 Octbr. 27 **PAUL, Joseph,** of Haverstraw Prect., Orange Co., yeoman, Wife Hannah, sons and a daughter, not named. Real and personal property. Executors Garret Snedeker and Joannes Snedeker. Witnesses Willem Velter, Garret Myer of Tappen, farmer, and John Rider.

1317 (P 23) 1763 Novbr. 9 1764 Jany. 3 **PAINE, Joshua,** jun., of Dutchess Co. First Church of Christ in the Nine Partners, the parents, brothers Ephraim Paine, Ichabod Sparrow Paine, Barnabas Paine, sisters Rebacker Dyer and Pheba Hurd. "Worldly substance." Executor brother Ephraim Paine. Witnesses Isaiah Williams, Elisha Cleveland of Amenia Prect., farmer, and James Betts. Copy.

1318 (P 24) 1765 Febry. 13 1769 March 25 **PEET, William,** of Ulster Co. Wife Hannah, sons Gilbert and Stephen, daughters Sary Sherwood and Mary Gidney, grandda. Sary, da. of dec'd son William. Homefarm and land at Cacaot or New Hempstead, personal property. Executors the wife and sons. Witnesses John Nicoll, Leonard Nicoll, both of New Windsor Prect., Ulster Co., yeomen, and Nathaniel Sands.

1319 (P 25) 1765 Aug. 19 1781 Novbr. 27 **PINE, John,** of Fishkil, Dutchess Co., yeoman. Children Joshua, Silvanus, Philipp, Abigail Bailey. Homefarm, land on Long Island, personal property (a silver tankard and 6 do. spoons). Executors bro.-in-law John Carman and Cornelius van Wyck sen., both of Dutchess Co. Witnesses James Duncan, now of Dutchess, late of Queens Co., esquire, Henry Buys and James Bailey.

1320 (P 26) 1766 Octbr. 9 1770 Decbr. 3 **PURDY, Abigail,** of Newburgh Prect., Ulster Co., widow. Children Stephen, Abigail Fowler, Martha Merritt and Elizabeth Smith, grandda. Abigail Terbush. "Worldly estate." Executors son Stephen, Caleb Merritt and Arthur Smith. Witnesses James Pugsly, Mary Blamles and Leonard Smith, yeoman.

1321 (P 27) 1769 Aug. 8 Octbr. 16 **PERSEN, Cornelius,** of Kingston, Ulster Co. Wife Alleda, children Johannis, Matthevis, Cornelius and Jannetje, wife of Petrus Swart. Real and personal estate. Executors the three sons and the son-in-law. Witnesses Abraham Low, esquire, Christopher Tappen, both of Kingston, and William Eltinge jun.

1322 (P 28) 1770 19th Day 7th Month Septbr. 14 **PECKAM, Reuben,** of Charlotte Prect., Dutchess Co. Brother Samuel Peckam, friend Ruth, [wife of] Timothy Dakin of New Fairfield in the Colony of ——. Executor —— Haight. Witnesses ——. Part of this will is gone.

1323 (P 29) 1775 Decbr. 8 1786 Octbr. 29 **PALMER, William,** of Charlotte Prect., Dutchess Co., yeoman. Wife Reachel, sons William, Abraham, Reuben, Jacomiah, Gilburt, Edward, grandson Jeremiah, son of dec'd son Ezekiel, granddaughters Sarah and Ruth, da. of the same dec'd son, daughter-in-law Sarah, widow of son Ezekiel, daughters Mary, Esther, Ame, Reachel and Phebe, grandson James Palmer, son of da. Esther. Real and personal estate. Executors sons William and Reuben. Witnesses David Husted jun, Samuel Palmer jun of Washington Prect., Dutchess Co., a Quaker, and Amos Tubbs.

1324 (P 30) 1772 March 16 1773 March 5 **PLOEGH, Paulis,** of Kingston Corporation, Ulster Co., cooper. Wife Eliesabeth, da. Mariea, wife of Johannis B. Masten, son of dec'd son Petrus, vizt: Petrus. Real and personal estate. Executors son-in-law Johannis B. Masten and Johannis Snyder. Witnesses Johannes Masten, merchant, Anthony Frere, tailor, and James Richey.

1325 (P 31) 1774 Decbr. 10 1782 Jany. 19 **PALMER, Ephraim,** of Charlotte Prect., Dutchess Co. Wife Rachal, sons Silvanus, Uriah, Ephraim, daughters Abigail, Rachel, Gehannah, Darkis and Rebeckah. Real and personal estate. Executors brothers Nehemiah Reynolds and Edward Palmer. Witnesses David Hustead, Reuben Palmer and Silas Deuel jun., both of said Precinct, farmers.

1326 (P 32) 1774 Decbr. 12 1777 Febry. 3 **PARKER, John,** of Haverstraw Prect., Orange Co. Wife Jemime, sons John, Peter, Jacob, David, Isaac, da. Mary, grandda. Mary, da. of son John. Real and personal property. Executors the wife and son Isaac. Witnesses Thos. Osborn, Benjamin Furman and John Hitchcock.

1327 (P 33) 1774 June 16 1775 Octbr. 6 **PAINE, Joshua,** of Amenia, Dutchess Co. Wife, sons Ephraim and Barnabas, children of son Ichabod Sparrow Paine dec'd, vizt: Rebecca, Joshua and Ichabod Sparrow, das. Rebecca Dyer and Phebe Munro, bro.-in-law Elisha Paine of Long Island. Real and personal property. Executors the wife and son Barnabas. Witnesses Benjamin Doty of Amenia Prect., yeoman, Eunice Wheeler and Solomon Wheeler. Vide No. 1317.

1328 (P 34) 1775 Jany. 10 May 22 **PEARSALL, Henry,** of Hempstead, Queens Co. Wife Martha, grandsons Henry, son of son Hezekiah, Joseph, James, Henry and Daniel, sons of dec'd son James, William and John, sons of dec'd son Henry, grandson John Mugin. Homefarm, land adjoining Joseph Bedel, do. purchased from James Burtis adjoining Thomas Hendrickson, a patent right, personal property. Executors Richard Hewlett and Carman Dorlon. Witnesses Stephen Smith, Thomas Cornell, of said Co., yeomen, and Isaac Denton. Copy.

1329 (P 35) 1775 Aug. 15 1776 May 25 **PALMER, James,** of Haverstraw Precinct, Orange Co. Wife Deborah, mother Anna Palmer, da. Susanna, nephews Herry and William, sons of bro. Richard Palmer. House in N. Y. City, personal property. Executors Michael Cornelison of Nayak and Aury Smith of Haverstraw. Witnesses Jeremiah Williamson of Orange Co., yeoman, John Smith and Andries Onderdonk.

1330 (P 36) 1776 Aug. 20 1784 Septbr. 21 **PERKINS, Abijah,** of New Marlborough Precinct, surgeon. Wife Lucy, children Hannah and George Whitefield Perkins, brothers and sisters John, Isaac and Seth Perkins, Lucy Ely, Elisabeth Startin, Margaret Belden, Sarah Marvin, Hannah and Lydia Perkins; father lives at Lyme. Real and personal estate (books). Executors the wife, her bro. Willm Ely, son of George Whitefield and bro.-in-law Samuel Startin; overseers Stephen Case and Lewis Dubois. Witnesses Stephen Case of New Marlborough Prect., Ulster Co., Captain, Luff Smith and Deborah Smith. Lucy Cook, late Lucy Smith, sworn as executrix May 26, 1785.

1331 (P 37) 1776 Febry. 5 1778 Aug. 19 **PARIS, Isaac,** of Stonearabia, Palatine District, Tryon Co., merchant. Wife Catharine, sons Isaac, Peter, Francis and Daniel, da. Margaret, sister Margaret, wife of Doctor Bodo Otto of Reading, Penna. Land at Stonearabia, in Osquagoe Patent, Canajoharie District, houses and personal property. Executors the wife, Revd. Daniel Gross of Canajoharie Distr. and John Eisenlord of N. Germantown, Palatine Distr., merchant. Witnesses B. Higgins, Simon Baydeman of said Co., cooper, and John Smith of Palatine Distr., esquire.

1332 (P 38) 1777 Jany. 31 1783 May 3 **POYER, Thomas,** of Rombouts Prect., Dutchess Co., farmer. Wife Maregriet, children Thomas, Sarah, Marigret, Joseph, Hannah, Jacobmies. Real and personal estate. Executors the wife, Joseph Tuston and Jonis Halstead. Witnesses Otho Lawrence, Philipp Jacob Schaff and John Cooper of said Precinct, yeoman.

1333 (P 39) 1777 Septbr. 18 1782 Aug. 12 **PRESTON, David,** of Albany Co., farmer. Wife Sibbel, children David, Joseph, Abial, Anne and Sibbel. Real and personal estate. Executors the wife and Caleb Smith. Witnesses William Brown of said Co., farmer, and Betty Maleroy. Proved in Rutland Co., Vermont.

1334 (P 40) 1777 Septbr. 15 1783 June 4 **PATE, (Peet), Gilbert,** of Ulster Co. Wife Elisabeth, children Mary, Anny, Hana, William and Stephen. Home property, land in Orange, Ulster Co. or elsewhere, personal estate. .Executors the wife, bro. Stephen Pate and Samuel Arthur. Witnesses John Nicoll of New Windsor Prect., Ulster Co., esquire, Benjamin Thorne and Timothy White.

1335 (P 41) 1777 Febry. 4 1782 Decbr. 2 **PETERS, George,** of Charlotte Prect., Dutchess Co., yeoman. Wife Sarah, sons Abel, Richard, Charles, Morris, Hewlett, George, Samuel, daughters Jerushe, wife of Jesse Oakly, Ruth, Sarah, Jemima, Molly, wife of Joshua Halloc. Real and personal estate. Executors the wife, son Abel, son-in-law Jesse Oakley and Jacob Smith. Witnesses George Sands, James Scott of said Co., yeoman, and Jemima Sands.

1336 (P 42) 1777 Septbr. 18 1780 April 18 **POTTER, Job,** of Dutchess Co. Wife Desire, children Jenevery, Riscom, Sims, Lois, John, Eseck, Nathaniel, Elisebeth and Judah. Real and personal estate. Executors the wife and Benjamin Akins. Witnesses Israel Deuel, Samuel McHago and Daniel Jackson, yeomen. The wife is sworn as executrix as Desire Green, formerly wife of testator.

1337 (P 43) 1778 Septbr. 12 Novbr. 4 **PERSON, Silas,** of Goshen Prect., Orange Co. Wife Abigal, sons James, Silas. Real and personal estate. Executors the wife and George Thompson. Witnesses Thomas Horton, yeomen, Mehitabel Bayley and Anna Wickham.

1338 (P 44) 1780 Jany. 11 1784 June 1 **PEARCE, Nathan,** jun., of Pawlings Precinct, Dutchess Co. Wife Elizabeth, sons Daniel, Robert Gilbert and Charles, daughters Susanna and Hannah. "Worldly estate." Brother William Pearce to be guardian of children and with testators wife executor. Witnesses James Stark, yeoman, Sarah Pearce and Nathan Pearce.

1339 (P 45) 1781 June 29 1785 Febry. 3 **PERSEN, Abraham,** senior, of the Great Imbough, Albany Co., yeoman. Wife Catharine, sons John, Jacobus, Abraham, Henry, daughters Hannah, wife of Egbert Bogardus, Gethroy, wife of Evert de Witt, Deborah, wife of Lucas de Witt and Jenny, wife of Wessel ten Broecke. Real and personal estate. Executors sons Jacobus, Abraham and Henry and sons-in-law Egbert Bogardus, Wessel ten Broecke and Lucas de Witt. Witnesses James Tattersall, schoolmaster, John C. Persen, yeoman, both of Albany Co. and Sybrant van Schaick junior.

1340 (P 46) 1781 Decbr. 6 1782 June 28

PRATT, Jacob, of Beekman Prect., Dutchess Co., Wife ——, son John, daughter Nancy. Homefarm, personal property. Executors bro. Stephen Pratt and Jesse Oakly. Witnesses William Moore, Zebulon Green of Charlotte Prect., said Co., carpenter, and William Gray.

1341 (P 47) 1781 March 14 ——

PELL, Samuel T., late of Westchester Co. Father, mother, brothers and sisters, nephew Charles, son of bro. Philipp. Real and personal estate. Executor the father, brothers Philipp and David. Witnesses Thos. Thomas, Samuel Drake and Nathan Rockwell. Copy made Octbr. 29, 1790.

1342 (P 48) 1782 Jany. 26 June 2

PERKINS, Oliver, of Little Hoesock, Albany Co. Wife ——, sons Rufus, Moses, Silas, Oliver and Phineas, daughters Charity, Hannah, Susannah, Elisabeth, Prudence and Eunice. Real and personal estate. Executor Richard Brown. Witnesses Nathl. Niles, Nathan Tanner and Daniel Kinyon, farmers.

1343 (P 49) 1782 Decbr. 25 1784 July 21

PICKERD, Bartholomew, late of Palatine Distr., Tryon Co., now of Fort Plank, yeoman. Wife Philipbina, wife and sons of nephew Bartholomew Pickerd, vizt: Maria Catharina and Conrad and Christian. Land on N. side of Mohawks R. near Little Falls, personal property. Executor Abraham Copeman. Witnesses Abraham Copeman, Heinrick Eckler of Montgomery Co., farmers, and Jacob House. Proved in Montgomery Co.

1344 (P 50) 1782 Septbr. 22 1786 May 2

PADDACK, Seth, of Fredericksburgh Prect., Dutchess Co. Wife Ruth, sons Zachariah, Stephen, Seth, Judah, da. Deliverance. Real and personal estate. Executors son Seth and Doctor Joseph Crane senior. Witnesses Thomas Baldwin, Jonathan Smith, both of Dutchess Co., farmers, and David Baldwin.

1345 (P 51) 1782 Febry. 7 March 19

PAWLING, Levi, of Marbletown, Ulster Co., esquire. Wife Halana, children Albert, Henry, Levi and Margret. Real and personal estate. Executors sons Henry and Albert. Witnesses Nathan Smedes, Aldert Smedes and John Cantine of Marbletown, yeomen.

1346 (P 52) 1785 March 21 1786 Febry. 2

PATTON, William, of New Windsor Prect., Ulster Co. Wife Margaret, son James, grandda. Margaret and other grandchildren, not named. Real and personal estate. Executors James Kernaghan and Samuel Boyd. Witnesses George Huggan, schoolmaster, Miles Cavan, yeoman, and John Morrison, yeoman.

1347 (P 53) 1785 June 24 1786 June 21

PHILIPP, Christian, son of Peter, of East Camp, Albany Co. Catherine, da. of Diderich Dick, Peter Philipp, Reformed German Church at East Camp. Real and personal estate. Executors Peter Philipp, Peter Scherp and Philipp Rakkefeller. Witnesses Rev. Gerhard Daniel Cock of East Camp, John Cook and Johan Bernhart Faerber (?).

1348 (P 54) 1785 Aug. 8 1786 Novbr. 29

POLHEMUS, Cornelius, of Rumbouts Prect., Dutchess Co. Son Cornelius, grandson Daniel McGuin. Real and personal estate. Executors the son and John Hughson sen. Witnesses James Philipps, Walter Hughson and James Wells, schoolmaster.

1349 (P 55) 1785 Aug. 3 Decbr. 29

PATTERSON, John, of Wallkil Prect., Ulster Co., yeoman. Wife ——, da. Mary, bro. James. Real and personal estate. Executors William Faulkner and

William Bull. Witnesses Edward Campbell, shoemaker, Daniel G. Rogers, yeoman, and William Wilkin jun., yeoman.

1350 (P 56) 1785 Aug. 3 Octbr. 27 **PAINE, Ephraim,** of Amenia Precinct, Dutchess Co. Wife Mary, daughters Elizabeth, Mary, Sarah, Chloe and Lucy, sons Ephraim and Abijah. Homefarm, land in Whitesborough, Montgomery Co., personal property. Executors the wife, Ezra Thompson and Peter Garnsey. Witnesses Samll. Thompson, Rebecah King, widow and Barnabas Paine. See No. 1327.

1351 (P 57) 1786 June 20 Aug. 12 **PEYPHER, Peter,** of German Flatts Distr., Montgomery Co. Present wife Gertrude, sons Peter by "last wife," Andrew, heirs of son Jacob, daughters Catharine, Dorothy and Margaret, Elizabeth, wife of Ellis Henry, bro. Jacob Peypher, son-in-law Peter Orndorph. Real and personal estate. Executors Lodowick Campbell and Hanjost Shoemaker. Witnesses John Helmer, Thomas Cochel and Peter Marsh.

1352 (P 58) 1786 March 6 May 4 **POLHEMUS, George,** of the Pond Patent, Haverstraw Prect., Orange Co., farmer. Wife ——, sons Titus, Jacob, Daniel and George, daughters Matie, Jenny, Elizabeth, Ann, Hannah. Real and personal estate. Executors sons Titus and Jacob, Johannes Remsen and Closs R. von Hooten. Witnesses John Farrand, Geo. Douglas, schoolmaster, and Yury Pery.

1353 (P 59) 1787 Jany. 10 March 8 **PERRY, Roland,** of Saratoga Distr., Albany Co., farmer. Wife Bulah, sons Benjaman, Roland, Samuel, John, Absalom, Roseal, Artmus, Joseph, daughters Febey, Azubah, Mary. Real and personal estate. Executor son Benjamin. Witnesses Timothy Bloodworth, Nathaniel Stiels of Saratoga, yeomen, and Mary Bloodworth.

1354 (P 60) 1798 Febry. 20 1799 June 13 **PORTEOUS, John,** of Herkimer Co. Nephew John, second son of bro. Alexander Porteous of Perth, North Britain, Elizabeth, da. of James Cockburn of Dutchess Co., Henry Frey of Canajohary, Elinora Hawkins, "now bound to my da. Catherine Mary Alexander," grandda. Mary Porteous Alexander, da. Catherine Mary, wife of William Alexander, bro. David Porteous of Strageth, Parish of Muthel, County of Perth. Real and personal estate. Executors the da. and her husband, the two brothers, the nephew John and Henry Frey. Witnesses John Robison, William Robison and Cornelius W. Groesbeeck.

1355 (P 61) 1806 Octbr. 11 Novbr. 26 **PENNY, Timothy P.,** late of the Island of Jamaica, now of Lansingburgh, Rensselaer Co. Sister Arabella, wife of Dr. Moses Willard of Lansingburgh. Codicil, witnessed by David Allen, Lydia Bassel and Jonathan Meirnele Mott.

1356 (P 62) 1786 March 24 **PROVOST, Johannis,** late of Lonenburgh, Albany Co., yeoman, letters of administration on the estate of, granted to Stephen Haight of Coxhaky District, merchant, as creditor. Executors named in the will, to-wit Catrina Provost and John Jas. Roseboom are dead.

1357 (P 63) 1809 May 31 1811 May 9 **PULTENEY, Sir James,** Baronet, of Bath House, Picadilly, Middlesex Co., and Buckingham House near Thetford, Norfolk Co. Sisters Madeline Murray, spinster, Jane, wife of Sir Alexander Muir Mackenzie, Baronet, Susan, wife of Patrick Murray, bro. Rev. William Murray, children of dec'd cousin Wm. Hepburn, late Lieut. Col. 31st Regt. of Foot, vizt: William and Madeline Hepburn, sisters of Col. Hepburn, Ann, Christie and Grame Hepburn, spinsters, Dame Susan, widow of Sir Robert Murray, Colonel Robert Smith of Methoen, Porter Co., N. B., the Headmaster of the —— School at Clewar near St. Leonards Hill, County of Berks; brother

John Murray, Major General in H. Ms. service remainderman. Codicil of March 10, 1810, adds the names of Madame de Frouville, wife of President Frouville of Paris, Elizabeth Frances Markham, Henrietta Alicia Markham, Colicia Markham, Maria Markham, Ann Isabella Markham, George Markham, Frederick Markham, Sophia Markham, Edmund Markham and Sarah Markham, children of Mrs. Elizabeth Evelyn, wife of John Fawcett by the first husband Rev. George Markham, Dean of York. Mentions late wife Henrietta Laura Pulteney, Countess of Bath. Codicil of Febry. 14, 1811, adds name of Anna Rose of Duncan Place, Leicester Square. Codicil of March 9, 1811, adds children of Madame de Froudeville, formerly Countess of Beckers, of Paris. Witnesses Richd. Williams, and Francis Broderip.

1358 1786 Decbr. 23 1787 Febry. 3 **PENDLETON, Solomon,** of Chatham Co., Georgia, now in N. Y. City. Willempee Niefus, "a young woman in the State of N. Y. . . for kindness when I was a prisoner on Long Island and in want of money," Robert Montfort, esquire, Richard Wylly, esquire, William and James Bryan, Miss Nancy Eaton, brothers David, Daniel and William Pendleton, Mathew McAllister, nephew Edmund Pendleton. Land in Effingham Co. and elsewhere, personal property. Executors bro. Daniel P. of N. Y. City, Robert Montfort, Richard Wylly and Mathew McAllister of Georgia. Witnesses Samuel Bradhurt, physician, William Newton, shopkeeper, and Thomas O'Hara, gentleman. Recorded in Wills and Probates, Vol. I., p. 10.

1359 1779 Octbr. 30 1787 Jany. 31 **PEIRSON, Abraham,** of Southampton, Suffolk Co., farmer. Sons William, Zebulon, Matthew, da. Elizabeth, wife of Samuel Peirson. Real and personal estate. Executors sons Zebulon and Matthew. Witnesses Nathan Peirson, yeoman, Silvanus Peirson and Silvanus Tapping. Recorded ut supra, p. 28.

1360 1782 Septbr. 17 1787 Febry. 12 **PALDING, Joseph,** of Philippsburgh Manor, Westchester Co. Wife ——, sons William, Joseph, Peter, John, grandda. Catherine, da. of son William. Real and personal estate (a Dutch bible). Executors sons Joseph, William and Peter. Witnesses Jacob Ruamman, yeoman, Jacob van Wert and William Davis. Recorded ut supra, p. 54.

1361 1779 Jany. 24 April 19 **PERRINE, John,** senior, of Upper Freehold, Monmouth Co., N. J. Children Henry, James, Daniel, Joseph, John, William, Rebecca, wife of Joseph Storey, Hannah, wife of William Deye, Anne, wife of James Abrahams, children of son John, vizt: John, Peter, Matthew, Joseph, Anne, Rebecca and Hannah, children of son William, vizt: William, Mathew, John, Daniel, Catherine and Rebecca, children of da. Margaret dec'd, vizt: John, Henry, Andrew, Joseph, Daniel and Catherine Wilson. Lands in Upper Freehold and at Cranbury, personal property. Executors sons James and Joseph. Witnesses Richard Compton Joseph Compton, and Hugh Mannahan. Proved in New Jersey. Recorded ut supra, p. 99.

1362 1784 Novbr. 2 1787 Aug. 2 **PIERREPONT, Evelyn,** citizen of the State of Delaware. Joshua Waddington of N. Y. City, merchant, sole heir and executor of real and personal estate in U. S. Confirms testament made in England in 1780 or 81 not disposing of this property. Witnesses Benj. Waddington, Henry Waddington and Robert Harwood of N. Y. City. Recorded ut supra, p. 150.

1363 1790 July 9 Aug. 25 **PRICE, William,** of West Point, N. Y. Daughter and son, not named. Executors Jedediah Waterman, John Sullivan, of N. Y. and Robert Dunlap of West Point. Real and personal estate. Witnesses Tobias van Zandt, Joseph Browne and Gerret Keteltas, all of N. Y. City. Recorded ut supra, p. 245.

1364 1788 Novbr. 14 1790 Febry. 12 **PIERCE, Thomas,** of the City of Bristol, esquire. Wife Hester, sons Thomas and Charles. Real and personal property. Executors the two sons. Witnesses John Wilcox and Peter Ashmead. Proved in England. Son Thomas is merchant at Bristol, Charles of Oxford University, gentleman. Recorded ut supra, p. 306.

1365 1781 March 12 1783 Jany. 3 **PATTON, Elizabeth,** of Bermuda Islands, widow, da. of Eli Richard, heiress of sister Sarah Place and uncles Paul Richard and Stephen Richard of N. Y. Children of sister Sarah Place, children Susanna Parker, Francis Landy Patton, Elizabeth Patton and Eli Patton. Real and personal estate. Executor the four children, Theophilus Beach and Mills Sherbrook. Witnesses Daniel Hubbard Outerbridge, Francis Zuile and Sarah Woolen. Proved in Bermuda. Recorded ut supra, p. 325.

1366 1793 Decbr. 30 1794 May 30 **PHILLIPS, Francis,** of N. Y. City. Son Francis Michel Phillips. Real and personal estate (2 violoncelli and 2 violins). Executors George Garland and Simeon Bailey. Witnesses Abrm. Beach, of N. Y. City D.D., and William Wright.

1367 1794 Febry. 5 1795 June 19 **PREISSAC, Pierre Joseph,** late of the Island of St. Domingo, now of Red Hook, Dutchess Co., son of Henry Preissac, heretofore Marquis de Cardillac, Chevalier de St. Louis, who died on his plantation in the Parish of St. Michael, Island of St. Domingo Jany. 6, 1793. Wife Catharine, *née* Livingston, her mother and sister Peggy Livingston. Real and personal estate. Executor Benadict Lebone, late of St. Domingo, now of N. Y., gentleman. Witnesses Pierre Masson-Neau, Stephen Nocus of N. Y. City, broker, and Dallebout de Perigny. Recorded ut supra, p. 479.

1368 1795 Septbr. 29 Octbr. 15 French **PACAUD, Jean,** of N. Y. City, tobacco merchant, native of Montlion, Department de Charente Inferieure, France, son of Gabriel Pacaud dec'd and Marie Jacoby,

33 years old, living at the corner of Front and Pine Str. N. Y. Dlle. Marie Fulton of N. Y. City. "Tout ce que je possède dans l'étendue des Etats Unis." Executor Citizen Navarre jun. of N. Y. City. Witnesses Joseph Marcadier, Jean Baptiste Lacoste, Louis Lestrade and Charles Bridgen, Not. Public. Recorded ut supra, p. 506.

1369 1795 Novbr. 1 Novbr. 10 French **PICHON, Julien Romain,** late of the Island of Guadeloupe, now of N. Y. City, born in the Parish of Petit Bourg, said Island, as son of Jacques Julien Pichon and his wife, Dame Mollard, about 40 years old. Wife and children, not named. Personal property. Executors wifes bro. Jean François d'Artignan of South Amboy and Thomas Pasturin of N. Y. City, merchant. Witnesses Baptiste Fouquet, Joseph Marcadier and Jean Antoine Berard Cap. Will made at the house of André Mathieu in Greenwich Str. Recorded ut supra, p. 519.

1370 1798 27th Day 9th Month Decbr. 5 **PROCTOR, James,** of Stockton upon Tuse, County of Durham, Old England. Bro. John Proctor of Stockton, aforesaid, grocer. "Worldly estate." Executors Nicholas Taylorson and Joseph Hopkins of New York, merchants. Witnesses Samuel Wood, John Underhill of Westchester Co. and Samuel Mott. Recorded ut supra, Vol. II., p. 150.

1371 1796 Octbr. 3 1797 June 5 **PARSON, Jasper,** late of Santa Cruz, now of Boston, Mass., planter. Wife Tabitha. Real and personal estate. Executor Dr. William Wheeler of Rhinebeek, Dutchess Co., physician. Witnesses Lucretia Parson, Philipp I. Schuyler and William F. Salter. Recorded ut supra, p. 291.

1372 1813 Septbr. 4 1815 Octbr. 11 **PASSAGE, George,** of Princetown, Schenectady Co. Wife Mary, children George, Mary and Margaret. Real and personal estate. Executors Benjamin Whitney, William Weller and James McDonald jun. Witnesses Michael van Wormer, Calvin Cheeseman and Benjamin Whitney. Recorded ut supra, p. 331.

1373 1817 Decbr. 31 1818 March 4 **PATTINSON, Richard,** of Montreal, Lower Canada. Children Mary Ann, Richard, Ellen Phyllis, halfbrother Hugh Pattinson, Mrs. Archange Askin and her da. Mrs. Therese McKee, Dr. William Caldwell of Montreal, Female Benevolent Society of Montreal, of which Mrs. Aird is treasurer, Jasper Tough. Real estate in Upper Canada, in Indiana and Michigan, personal property. Executors Robert Gillespie, George Moffat, both of Montreal, merchants, and William Gilkson of Glasgow, Scotland, merchant, with George Jacobs of Sandwich, John Askin and James Gordon of Amherstburg, Upper Canada, as agents. Witnesses H. Bleecker, J. W. Rockwell and Jas. van Ingen. Will made, executed and proved in Albany. Recorded ut supra, p. 346.

1374 1781 Octbr. 9 1782 Jany. 9 **PARKIN, Thomas,** Deputy Commissary General of Virginia. Mrs. Robert Muter, Mr. Mewburn of Yorkshire, William Robertson of N. Y., Adam Dolmage, nephew Thomas Parkin of Baltimore. Personal property. No executor named. Witnesses G. Robertson, Agent for Transports and Adam Dolmage, Deputy Commissary of Provisions. The preceding information is given in the letters of administration granted to Richard William Parkin of Jamaica, L. I., Asst. Commissary of Provisions as nearest of kin. Recorded ut supra, Vol. III., pp. 79 and 94.

1375 1823 June 2 Octbr. 29 **POWELL, Jacob,** of Newburgh, Orange Co. Bro. Thomas Powell, bro.-in-law Benjamin Townsend, his wife Patty, testators sister, nieces Betsy and Mary Townsend and Nancy Jenkins, children of B. Townsend and wife Patty, nephew Benjamin Townsend, nieces Margaret E. and Mary P. Seymour. Land in Marlborough Township, Ulster Co., personal property. Executors bro. Thomas Powell and Samuel R. Betts. Witnesses Daniel Tuthill jun., John W. Knevels and Aaron Belknap of Newburgh, Attorney-at-Law. Recorded ut supra, Vol. IV., p. 144.

1376 1640 April 10 — Dutch **PIETERSOON, Jan,** from Essendelft, now of Fort Amsterdam. Gerrit Bartelsen, bro. Adrian Pietersen, sister Anna Pieters. Personal property. Executor Mr. Hans Kierstede. Witnesses Ulrich Lupolt and David Provoost. N. Y. Col. MSS., I., p. 199.

1377 1670 10 o'clock a.m. — Dutch **PIETERSEN, Reyndert,** of New Albany. Mother Taet Joosten, wife Metie Jans, both living at Bolswaert, Friesland. "Estate." Executors in America Schout Gerard Swart and Adriaen van Ilpendam. Witnesses Gerrit van Slichtenhorst, Jan Evertsen and Adriaen van Ilpendam, Notary Public. Albany Co. Records, Notarial Papers, I., p. 510.

1378 1688 Octbr. 7 1688–9 Febry. 5 **PAPENDORP, Adriaen Gerritsen,** of Albany. Wife Jannetje Crom, niece Harmyntje Nagels, John Abeel and sisters Elizabeth, Magdalena and Mary Abeel, children of wife's niece, Elizabeth van der Poel, wife of Sybrant van Schaik, Adriaen, son of Gerardus Beeckman, Maria and Hannah van der Poel, Dirk van der Karre, Evert Banker. Real and personal estate (a gold ring, do. buttons, a silver tooth-pick, a do. tumbler, pictures). Executors the wife, Johannes Abeel and Anthony van Schaick. Witnesses Jan Jansen Bleecker, Justice of the Peace, Jan Lansink and J. Becker, Notary Public. Albany Co. Records, Minutes, 1686–1702, p. 116.

1379 1693 Novbr. 8 — **PIETERS, Volkie,** letters of administration on the estate of, granted to Hestertie Tiercks, widow of Harma Bastiaensen of Albany City. Albany Co. Records, Wills, I., p. 15.

1380 1751 Novbr. 5 1771 Jany. 14 **PROVOST, Johannis,** of Lonenburg, Albany Co. Wife Catarina, brothers Henderick, Samuel, Jacob and Isaac Provost. Real and personal estate. Executors the wife and John Jac. Roseboom. Witnesses Sybrant G. van Schaick jun. of Coxhachie, Ino. Beeckman and Jacob van Schaick. Albany Co. Records, Wills, I., p. 348.

1381 1752 March 27 1753 Jany. 26 **PRUYN, Samuel,** of Albany City, blacksmith. Wife Maritie, sons Frans S., Johannis S. and Jacob S. House and lot in 2d Ward, personal estate. Executor Abraham Bogart of Albany City. Witnesses John Ja. Lansingh, Phelip Muller and Richard Cartwright. Albany Co. Records, Wills, I., p. 219.

1381a 1771 April 2 —— **POST, Jacob,** senior, of the Younkers, Westchester Co. Sons Jacob, Anthony, Abraham, Isaac, Peter, Martin, daughters Johanna and Margret, grandson Mortimer (?) Cregier, grandda. Ann Cregier. Homefarm, land in Orange Co., personal property. Executors sons Isaac and Anthony. Not executed nor witnessed. N. Y. Coll. MSS., XCVII., p. 39.

1382 (Q 1) 1771 Septbr. 27 1775 Jany. 16 **QUACKENBOS, Johannes,** of N. Y. City, bolter. Wife Margaret, sons Walter, Nicholas, Petrus and John, da. Cornelia. Real estate in Rensselaerswyck Manor, personal property. Executors the wife and children. Witnesses Stephen Terhune, Chas. Morse of N. Y. City, scrivener, and Adam Dolmage. Codicil of Octbr. 14, 1774, disposes of land in Charlotte Co. Same Witnesses.

1383 (Q 2) 1777 April 24 1782 Jany. 16 **QUICK, Jacobus,** of Rochester, Ulster Co. Children Jacobus, Johanna, Magery, Elizabeth, Petrus. Real and personal estate (a bible). Executors sons Jacobus and Petrus with Richard Davis as overseer. Witnesses Cornelius Hoornbeck jun., Richd. Davis, both of Rochester Township, farmers, and Friederich Schoennig.

1384 (Q 3) 1784 Febry. 28 1786 July 6 **QUACKENBOS, Margritje,** widow of John, of New York City. Children Walter, Nicholas, Peter, John and Cornelia, wife of John P. Quackenbos, da. of son Walter, vizt: Margaret. Land on White Creek, Albany Co., East side of Hudson R., personal property. Executors sons Nicholas and John. Witnesses Henry I. Bogart of Albany, Matthew Trotter and Robert Yates. Supra No. 1382.

1385 (R 1) 1693-4 Febry. 15 1712 Octbr. 31

REYERSEN, Gerrit, of Albany City, yeoman. Wife Annetje Gerrits, children Elbert Gerritsen, John Gerritsen, a shoemaker by trade, Reyer Gerritsen, Annetje Gerrits and Marritje Gerrits. Real and personal estate (a large bible with annotations and copper clasps). The wife sole executrix, Egbert Teunisen and son Elbert guardians of minor children. Witnesses Teunis Slingerlandt, Anthony Brat and Robt. Livingston. Also in Albany Co. Records, Wills, I., p. 22.

1386 (R 2) 1696 May 30

REMSEN, John, of Flackbush, Nassau (Long) Island. Wife Martha, "my now lawful wife," children Sophia, John, Rem, Janneye, Martha and Cornelius. Real and personal estate. Brother Joris Remsen and Rem Remsen to be guardians, tutors, overseers or inspectors. Witnesses Denys Hegemans, Jacob Hendricks and Johannes van Ekelen. Copy.

1387 (R 3) 1700 April 1

RICHBELL, Ann, of Marronack, Westchester Co., gentlewoman. Children Elizabeth, Ann, grandchildren Anna Gidsey, Mary Williams, Mary Mott, James Mott, Adam Mott, son-in-law Capt. James Mott, Col. Stephen Cortlandt, granddaughters Anna, Mary, Grace, Elizabeth and Jane, Benjamin Collier. Personal property (a gold ring with an emerald stone). Executors Col. Caleb Heathcote, Richbell Mott and Lieut. John Horton. Witnesses John Stoakham, Jonathan Huestes and Obadiah Palmer. Copy.

1388 (R 4) 5th Anne June 28 1707 Octbr. 3

ROBERTS, Benjamin, of Schinnechtady, Albany Co. Wife Mary, stepchildren Peter, Joseph, Elisabeth and Fransyntje Clement. Farm at Maelwyck on the N. side of Schinnechtady River, personal property. The wife sole executrix. Witnesses John Sandersen Glen, Philipp Schuyler and Robert Livingston jun.

1389 (R 5) 1708 Aug. 23 Septbr. 9 Dutch

ROOSA, Heyman, of Horly, Ulster Co. Children Allert, Nicolaes, Gysbert, Jannetie, wife of Philipp Hooghtylingh, Wyntie, wife of Willem Crom, Ragel and Lea. Real and personal estate. Executors the three sons. Witnesses Jan Roosa, Mattys Low, Jacobus van Netten and Wm. Nottingham.

1390 (R 6) 1709 June 17 —

ROKEBY, Philipp, of N. Y. City, chyrurgeon. Present wife Elizabeth, son Joseph. House and lot in Queen Str., N. Y., now occupied by Samuel Bourdet, personal property. The wife sole executrix. Witnesses Peter Mathews, William Chambers and Will Sharpas. Copy made Decbr. 7, 1749.

1391 (R 7) 1712 May 8 March 24 1712-13

REYERS, Anatie, widow of Gerrit Reyersen of Albany (see No. 1385). Children Elbert, John Reyer, Maritie, wife of Harpert van Deusen. Real and personal property. Executors sons Elbert and Reyer. Witnesses Jan Lansingh, Anthony van Schaick and Thos. Williams.

1392 (R 8) 1724-5 March 5 1725 May 4

RUTSEN, John, of Knightsfield, Ulster Co. Wife Cathrine, son John and natural children, not named, wife's bro. and sister, vizt: Henry Beekman and Cornelia, wife of Gilbert Livingston, his own brother and sisters, not named. Real and personal property. The wife sole executrix. Witnesses Johannis Westbroeck, Joseph Wheeler and Johannis Schoonmaker.

1393 (R 9) 1726 June 17 Octbr. 27

ROSENKRANS, Sarah, of Ulster Co. Mother Magdalena Rosenkrans, brothers Alexander and his son Hermanus, Derrick and son Harama Rosenkrans, sisters Rachel van Garden and her son Harma, Johanna Devenport and her son John, Christenah Cortright and her son Hendrick, other children of bro. Alexander Rosenkrans vizt: Helenah and Johannes; Sarah Cole, Christenah van Garden. Real and personal estate. Executors brothers Hendrick and Derrick Rosenkrans. Witnesses Derick Krom, Derck de Witt and Willem Cortrecht.

1394 (R 10) 1732 Novbr. 1 — **ROUSLEY, Sarah,** of N. Y. City, widow of Christopher Rousby, late of New Jersey. Children Christopher, Henry, William, Sarah, widow of Joseph Lathem, late of N. Y., and Elizabeth, wife of John Troup. Real and personal estate. Executors son Christopher and son-in-law John Troup. Witnesses Benj. Hildreth, Ab. van Wyck and Christr. Robert. Copy made Aug. 13, 1765.

1395 (R 11) 1736 Decbr. 23 1739 May 1 **RYCKMAN, Albert,** of Albany City, brewer. Children Tryntje, Peter, Harmanus, Margaret, Tobias and Magdalena, 2 children of da. Mary, and "several" children of son Johannes. "My estate." Executors sons Harmanus and Tobias and Benj. Brat. Witnesses Gerrit van Ness, Cornelius van Dyck and Henry Holland.

1396 (R 12) 1737 June 14 Novbr. 8 **ROSIE, John,** of Albany City. Jacob Perse and wife Janetie, John Henry Lydius, Johannes van Vranken and wife Anatie, Gertruy Bareway, Jacob van Nosteram of Aequegenhoek, Jeremia van Rensselaer, Roelif Kidnie, Johannes, son of Jacob Perse, Barent Brat "my book keeper," Maritie Kidnie, Altie Milton, Reyer Gerritsen. Houses and lots in Albany, personal property. Executors Reyer Gerritsen and Barent Brat. Witnesses Willem van Allen, Jacob Rooseboom and Joseph Yates.

1397 (R 13) 1738 Jany. 26 — **REDDING, Jeremiah,** of N. Y. City, joiner. Father-in-law Thomas Beheunce (?) sole heir and executor of real and personal estate. Witnesses John Kilmaster, Walter Dobbs and Sarah Cure. Copy made May 14, 1761.

1398 (R 14) 1741 July 16 Septbr. 23 **REMSEN, George,** of Harvourstraw Prect., Orange Co., gentleman. Wife Elisabeth, children Tunis and Elisabeth, an expected child. Real and personal estate. Executors the wife, Thedorias Snedeker and Theodorios Remsen. Witnesses John Paterson, Paulus van der Voort and Jonathan Rose jun.

1399 (R 15) 1744 March 26 1748 May 12 **REMSEN, George,** of the Pond, Haverstraw Precinct, Orange Co. Wife Sarah, children Theodorus, Ram, Ann, Ariete and Lambatie, grandchildren George and Lambatie Perhelmus. Lands adjoining Johannis Muts, a lot at Kines Rige, do. on Demerees Kil, do. adjoining Jacob Perhelmus dec'd, on English Rige, personal property (a large bible). Executors the wife and son Theodorus. Witnesses William James, Poulus van der Vort and Johannis Cuyper.

1400 (R 16) 1745 July 18 1761 June 2 **RYPELE, John,** of N. Y. City, baker. Wife Catherine, Maria Catherine, da. of Martin Roehl dec'd, Sophia, da, of John Roerback, baker, Catharine, da. of John Francis Walter, dec'd, joiner, Johannes, son of William Speeder, of Somerset Co., yeoman. House and lot in Stone Str. N. Y., personal property (plate). Executors the wife, George Brenkerhof and Evert Byvanck. Witnesses Abraham Lodge, John van Cortlandt of N. Y. City esquire and William Williamson. Copy.

1401 (R 17) 1746 Aug. 2 — **RUTGERS, Anthony,** of N. Y. City, brewer. Wife Cornelia, children Anneke, wife of Charles Crooke, Catherine, wife of Abraham Lynson, who had first husband Thomas Thong, Elshe, wife of Leonard Lispanar, Mary Rutgers and Aletta, wife of Dirck Lefferts, children of son Petrus dec'd, son of da. Anneke Crooke, who is blind, Anthony, son of dec'd son Anthony and wife Margaret. Real (h. and lot on Maiden Lane) and personal estate. Executors the wife and daughters Elshe, Mary and Aletta. Witnesses John Roosevelt, Rapel. Goelet and John Chambers. Copy.

1402 (R 18) 1747 Septbr. 3 1749 Octbr. 21 **RYCKMAN, Peter,** of Albany City, tailor. Children Wilhelmus (cut off with three shillings), Petrus, grandda. Cornelia, da. of son Wilhelmus. Real and personal estate (silverplate). Executor son Petrus, but his widow Catharine is made executrix Septbr. 22, 1750, her husband being dead. Witnesses John Jas. Roseboom, Eghbert Brat and Ja. Stevenson.

1403 (R 19) 1749 Aug. 24 Octbr. 3 Dutch

RYCKMAN, Petrus, of Kingston, Ulster Co. Wife Catharina, son Harmanus, da. Cornelia. House and lot in Albany, personal property. Executors the wife and Isaac Bogart. Witnesses Doctor Christoffel Kierstede, Jan Eltinge and Willem Eltinge. See preceding No.

1404 (R 20) 1750 Aug. 28 1756 Octbr. 11

RYCKMAN, Harmanis, of Albany City, brewer (see No. 1395). Bro. Tobias Ryckman, nephew Harme, son of bro. Peter Ryckman, late of Esopus (Kingston) dec'd, children of bro. John Ryckman, of sister Margaret Kip, dec'd, of sister Maria Brat dec'd, sisters Cathrina Bries and Magdalena Brat. Real and personal property. Executors bro. Tobias Ryckman and kinsman John Ja. Rose. Witnesses Johannis van Sante, esqre., David van Sante, and Johannes Myndersen jun., blacksmith.

1405 (R 21) 1753 Jany. 11 April 9

RUMSEY, Simon, of Goshen Prect., Orange Co., yeoman. Wife Phebe, children Simon, Daniel, James, Finnis, Nathan, Abigal, Ruth, Sarah and Phebe. Real and personal estate. Executors Daniel Everett and John Yalvarton, both of Goshen. Witnesses Jonathan Cory, Ebn. Holly and John Carpenter.

1406 (R 22) 1757 May 16 ——

RUTTERY, Margt., of N. Y. City, widow. Cousin Henry Lane, sister Fommetje Hardenbrock, cousin Meliora Lewes, cousin Cornelia Norwood, cousin Elizebeth, da. of Richard Britton Deres, cousin van der Clif Norwood, cousin Catherin Lory. Real and personal estate. Cousin Cornelia Norwood sole executrix. Witnesses Richard Kip, David Honson and Lawr. Wessells.

1407 (R 23) 1758 Septbr. 18 1759 July 16

REYNOLDS, Elisabeth, of Florada, (Orange Co.), widow. Sons Austin Reynolds and Abraham Chanler; Sarah, da. of Timothy Clark; wife of Richard Clark, widow Phebe Baly, Abraham Chanler jun. "Worldly estate." Executor son Abraham Chanler (Chandler). Witnesses Anthony Bradrick, blacksmith, and Nathan Elmer, surgeon, both of Orange Co.

1408 (R 24) 1758 Decbr. 12 — **RODMAN, Joseph,** of New Rochel, Westchester Co. Wife Helena, son Samuel of Flushing, L. I., grandson Joseph, son of son William dec'd., daughters Mary Hicks, Anne Riche, Sarah Bowne, Deborah Hicks, Elizabeth Lispenard, grandson Joseph, son of son Samuel. Land at New Rochelle, bought of Anthony Lispenard, do. on Nehammany Creek, Bucks Co., Penna., do. in New Rochelle, bo't of Joseph Causten and Philipp Riche, do. bo't of Isaac Secord, do. in Flushing, L. I., do in Pelham Manor, Westchester Co. adjoining Benj. Bowne and Isaac Contine, personal property (a silver teapot, plate). Executors bro. Thomas Rodman, son Samuel and son-in-law David Lespinard. Witnesses Susanna Willett, James ffowler and Ino. Bartow. Copy made Septbr. 9, 1766.

1409 (R 25) 1760 Decbr. 25 1774 Novbr. 17 **RENNE, James,** of New Town, Queens Co., carpenter. Wife Mary, children Samuel, Hannah, Marget and Sarah Culver. Real and personal estate. Executors the wife, son Samuel and Samuel Culver, Joseph Lawrence and Robert Field jun. Witnesses John Gosline of said Co., yeoman, Jonathan Roberts and Robert Morrell. Copy.

1410 (R 26) 1760 May 22 1761 March 4 **ROE, William,** of Philipps Patent, Dutchess Co. Wife Eleanor, mother Margaret Roe, brothers James and Charles Roe, sisters not named. Real and personal estate. Executors the mother Margaret Roe and father-in-law George Corey. Witnesses Alexander Dowell of said Co., farmer, James Ackill and William Nelson.

1411 (R 27) 1760 Decbr. 9 — **RAVEAU, Daniel,** of N. Y. City. Daughters Jane, wife of John Pascot, Ann, wife of John King, son Daniel. Real and personal estate. Executors the three children. Draft of will, not executed nor witnessed.

1412 (R 28) 1762 June — Novbr. 20 **ROSS, James Isaiah,** of North East Precinct, Dutchess Co., merchant. Wife Margaret, brother Robert, of the Parish of St. John, Kilwarnon, Co. Down, Irld., son of testators father James Ross and wife Alice McGee, late of Ballyknock, Parish of (late Magheralin) now St. John, Co. of Down, dec'd, niece Margaret Parks, John McGarrah, goddaughter Geertruyd Crannell, sister Margaret Gilmore, sister Mary, children of dec'd sisters Catherine and Jane, half sisters Sarah, wife of John Shaw and Arabella, wife of McDole, near Carrick Fergus, both daughters of father James Ross by his second wife Arabella Brown, nephew John Dougherty. Real and personal estate (wrought plate). Executors Bartholomew Crannell and William Kennedy of N. Y., merchant. Witnesses Robert Hopkins, Petrus Knickerbacker and Adam Dings of Albany Co., yeoman.

1413 (R 29) 1766 Febry. 2 — **ROBISON, Jonathan,** of Upper Dublin, Philadelphia Co., Penna. Wife Elizabeth, children Robert, Jonathan, Rachel, wife of Doctor John Rockhill, Mary and John, merchant in Carolnioa, children of dec'd son Mauris Robison, grandda. Betsey, da. of Edward Robison. Real and personal property. Executors son Jonathan Robison of White Marsh, son-in-law Dr. John Rockhill of N. J. and da. Mary Robison. Witnesses Mary Yorke, David Morris and William Dewees. Copy made in Philadelphia Septbr 1, 1768.

1414 (R 30) 1767 Aug. 17 1785 Novbr. 15 **ROGERS, Israel,** senior, of Wallkill Prect., Ulster Co., yeoman. Wife Serrah, children Israel, Elizabeth, Marry, Daniel, Rachel, James, grandson Daniel Graham. Real and personal estate. Executors son James and son-in-law William Wilkin. Witnesses David Clark, William Reynolds, Peter Berry and William Wilkin.

1415 (R 31) 1768 April 2 1771 Aug. 30 **REID, John,** of New Winsor Prect., Ulster Co. Children Mary Reid alias McClahry, Anne Reid, alias Burnet, children of da. Jean Burns, vizt: William, Mary, Kathrine and Jean, James Burns, blacksmith, bro. Robert Reid and bro. Thomas Reid of Colerain, Co. of Derry, Ireland. Real and personal estate. Executors grandson James Burnett and da. Mary Reid alias Mc-

Clachry with her husband Patrick McClachry. Witnesses Mary McCahry, John McKnight and Thomas Clarke of Ulster Co., practicioner of physics.

1416 (R 32) 1768 July 12 1782 June 29 **REEDER, Josiah,** of Goshen, Orange Co., yeoman. Wife Sarah, sons Samuel, Jacob, Peter, Stepen and Philipp. Real and personal estate. Executors the wife and Thomas Wickham. Witnesses Daniel Denton, of Goshen Prect., esquire, Jonas Denton and Jonathan Swayze.

1417 (R 33) 1769 Septbr. 9 1770 April 26 German **ROCKENFELLER, Diell,** of the Camp, Albany Co. Wife Anna Gert, children Philipp, Simon, William, Diell, Christian, Piter, Elisabeth, Gert, Maria, Eva and Margret. Real and personal estate. Executors sons Simon, William, Peter, Diell and Philipp. Witnesses Pitter Heisler, Christian Philipp, both of East Camp, farmers, and Petrus Philipp of Claverack, farmer.

1418 (R 34) 1769 March 15 1771 April 29 **READE, Joseph,** of N. Y. City, esquire. Wife Ann, children Lawrence, Joseph, John, Ann, widow of Garret van Horne, Sarah, wife of James de Peyster, Mary, wife of Francis Stephens. Real and personal estate. Executors the wife and the three sons. Witnesses Gabriel Ludlow, David Clarkson, both of N. Y. City, merchants, and Henry Cuyler. Copy.

1419 (R 35) 1770 Decbr. 5 1774 March 28 **ROSEBOOM, Ahasverus,** of Albany City, merchant. Sons Dirck and Gerrit. Real and personal estate. Executors the two sons. Witnesses Dirk B. van Schoonhoven, Ragel Viser and Nanning Harmense Visscher.

1420 (R 36) 1770 Aug. 7 1785 Octbr. 20 **ROE, Nathaniel,** of Florada, Goshen Precinct, Orange Co., farmer. Wife Mary, children Jonas, Elizabeth Davis, Mary de Key, Abigail Allison, Deborah Knap and Nathaniel. Homefarm, land on the Long Ridge, said Precinct, personal property. Executors the two sons. Witnesses Michael Jackson esquire, John Thompson and Mary Jackson.

1421 (R 37) 1771 Septbr. 14 Novbr. 7 **ROW, John,** of Little Nine Partners, Dutchess Co., yeoman. Wife Christenia, children Lydia, Elizabeth Streight, Catharine, Mary, John, Bastian, Philipp and Mark. Real and personal estate. Executors Annias Cooper and William Stewart. Witnesses Ananias Cooper, George Zufelt, yeoman, and William Stewart.

1422 (R 38) 1773 May 19 Septbr. 27 **RICHARD, Stephen,** late of N. Y. City, now of Albany City, merchant. Wife Margaret, uncle John van Rensselaer, cousin Jeremiah van Rensselaer, mother Elizabeth Richard, cousins Stephen Randle and Stephen Brown, John H., son of Harmanis Schuyler. Houses and lots in N. Y. City and land, inherited from Uncle Paul Richard, personal property (a silver hilted sword, gold headed cane, gold sleeve buttons, do. stock buckle, silver shoe and knee buckles). Executors Philipp Livingston, John van Rensselaer and Abraham ten Broeck. Witnesses Peter W. Douw, Barent Rooseboom, mariners, and Robert Yates, attorney-at-law, all of Albany City.

1423 (R 39) 1773 Novbr. 15 1774 Janry. 7 **RENNE, Peter,** of Rumbouts Precinct, Dutchess Co. Wife Mary, son John, daughters Sarah, Mary and Elizabeth, son-in-law John Lossee. "My estate." Executors Samuel Dorland, John Lossee and John Renne. Witnesses Charity House, Hannah Allen and Gilbert Dorland.

1424 (R 40) 1774 Aug. 13 Septbr. 3 **RUNSHAW, Martha,** of N. Y. City, widow of John. Sons William and John, stepdaughter Margaret Runshaw, sister Mary Pell. Personal estate (gold sleeve buttons, marked M. S., large silver open work shoe buckles). Executors Peter Ricker and Aron Stockholm. Witnesses William Plowman, Adolph de Grove, hatter, and W. de Peyster. Copy.

1425 (R 41) 1774 Febry. 21 March 22 **RIDER, John,** of Dutchess Co. Wife Mary, children Ebenezer, Reuben, Zadoc, John, Christopher, Patience, Mary, Rebeccah, Mehitebel, Hannah and Zuwiah, grandchildren Elenor, Hulda and Thomas Regan. Real and personal estate. Executors the wife, bro. Simeon Rider and son Ebenezer. Witnesses Charles Cullen of South East Prect., Dutchess Co., merchant, Ebenezer Benedict and Stephen Rockwell.

1426 (R 42) 1776 Novbr. 5 1786 July 4 **ROGERS, John,** of Dutchess Co. Sons Richerd, John, Benjamin, daughters Charity Hustis, Easter Nelson, and Ann Worren. Real and personal estate. Executors son Benjamin and Capt. Calip Nelson. Witnesses Gilbert Budd, farmer, Richard Hopper and Nathaniel Sarles.

1427 (R 43) 1776 Septbr. 22 1783 May 15 **RAYNOR, William,** of Rumbout Prect., Dutchess Co., yeoman. Wife Margret, children Jacob, John and Martha, Real and personal estate. Executors Jacob Griffin, Ambros Lattin and Richard Southward. Witnesses Ambrose Latting, yeoman, George van Nostrand and Zephaniah Platt of Poughkeepsie Prect., esquire.

1428 (R 44) 1776 April 27 1781 April 14 **RUTSEN, Michael,** of Poghkeepsie Precinct, Dutchess Co. Wife Abigail, children, not named. House and lot, land in Charlotte Precinct, personal estate. Executors the wife, Henry van der Burgh, esq., and Richard Snediker, esq. Witnesses James Brooks, Ebenezer Badger, cordwainer, and Isaac Lothrop.

1429 (R 45) 1776 Decbr. 16 1779 April 23 **RICHARD, Elizabeth,** widow of John, late of N. Y. City (see No. 1422). Brothers Killian, John and Henry van Rensselaer, sons of Hendrick, nephew Stephen Ray, sister Lena Wendell, children of dec'd sisters Annatie Douw, Catharine ten Broeck, and Maria ten Broeck; nieces Mary Wendell and Mary, da. of bro. Killian van Rensselaer. Land on the Kinderhook Road, houses and lots on Broadway, near the Oswego Market, N. Y. City, and real property elsewhere, personal property. Executors the three brothers van Rensselaer. Witnesses Guysbert G. Marselis, Harmanus ten Eyck of Albany, skipper, and Jeremiah van Rensselaer, Paymaster 3d N. Y. Regt. Also in Albany Co. Records, Wills, I., part 2, p. 21.

1430 (R 46) 1777 March 31 1787 March 5 **RIKER, Abraham,** of Dutchess Co. Wife Margaret, da. Jane, brothers children, vizt: Samuel, Jonathan Lawrence, John and Cornelius Bradford; Caty Colings. Land on Long Island, personal property. Executors the wife and Jonathan Lawrence. Witnesses Catherine Bradford and Jonathan Lawrence of N. Y. City, esquire. Proved in N. Y. City.

1431 (R 47) 1678 May 8 — **RAYNOR, Joseph,** of Southampton, L. I. Wife Mary, children Thirston, Isaac, John, Josiah, Mary, Hannah and Elizabeth. Lands in the Great Plains, at Shinacock, at Great Neck, at Wicopague, personal property. The wife sole executrix. Witnesses Henry Peirson jun., and John Laughton. Copy.

1432 (R 48) 1778 May 5 1782 Febry. 6 **REITSER, Conrad,** of Livingston Manor, yeoman. Anna Stall (? Hall), nephew Hendrick Stall (Hall ?) senior. Real and personal estate. Executors Samuel ten Broeck and Antonius Sneider. Witnesses Richard McMullen, Casper Hamm, farmer, and William Lee.

1433 (R 49) 1779 April 10 1786 Octbr. 13 **ROCKEFELLER, William,** of the East Camp, Albany Co. Wife ——, sons William, Jacob, Harmen, John, daughters Hannah, Gertgen and Lana, an expected child. Real and personal property. Executors William Diederich of Ulster Co., Diell Rockefeller and Philipp Rockefeller. Witnesses Johannes Lasher, of the German Camp, said Co., yeoman, Margaret Holzapple and Christian Rockefeller.

1434 (R 50) 1780 Janry. 27 1784 May 1 **RODMAN, Thomas,** late of Flushing, L. I., now of Fishkil, Dutchess Co. Wife Martha, da. Elisabeth, the mother, sisters Ann Field, Hannah Hicks, Caroline Bown and Penelope Shoemaker, nieces Margaret Hicks and Elizabeth Tom; Clarissa, da. of widow Rachel North. Farm in Flushing, land in New York, personal property. Executors the wife, brothers-in-law Charles Hicks and James Bown, (bro. John mentioned). Witnesses Thomas Williams, jun. of Dutchess Co., trader, Aspinwall Cornwell and Robert Williams.

1435 (R 51) 1782 July 24 Octbr. 10 **ROOSA, Isaac,** of Schonectady, Albany Co. Wife Maria, children Johannes, Annatje, Reikert, Magtildie, Jacobus and Maas van Franken. Real and personal estate. Executors the wife, Christopher Yates and Dirk van Ingen. Witnesses Abraham Fonda, esquire, Seymen Schermerhoren and John Clute, blacksmith.

1436 (R 52) 1782 June 25 1783 June 1 **ROBBINS, Zebulon,** of Albany Co. Wife Louis, daughters Comfort Stillman, Sarah Douglas, Hannah Kellogg, Abigail Darrow and her husband Samuel Darrow "the last two having behaved in a very undutifull and Disrispectfull manner" are cut off, Mary Ketchum. Real and personal estate. Executors sons-in-law Josiah Stillman and Aaron Kellogg. Witnesses Mat. Adgate of Kings District, Albany Co. esquire, Ithamar Mallory and Lewis Graves. Endorsed "I Louis Robbins do hereby fully agree and consent to the last Will and Testament of my Dear and Beloved Husband Zebulon Robbins as it is Within Written in Witness whereof I have hereunto set my hand & Seal this —— day of June 1782.
in Presents of —— (not signed)

1437 (R 53) 1782 Octbr. 24 1784 Janry. 12 **REYFENBERGER, John,** jun, of Little Nine Partners, Dutchess Co. Wife Eva, children Johannis, Catherine, Anna, Eva, George and Daniel, father Johannes Reyfenberger, and bro. Daniel. Leasehold estate, personal property. Executors the father and the brother. Witnesses John I. Meyer, Lancaster Burting and Felix Lewis, yeoman.

1438 (R 54) 1783 May 7 May 12 **RANDALL, Marianne,** of N. Y. City, widow. Widow Lanah Brown, Mrs. Elizabeth Taylor, living in Barrack Street, N. Y. Houses and lots in N. Y. City. Nuncupative will, proved by the testimony of Catherine Eckart, Catherine Willis, widows, and Mrs. Abigail Cock, all of N. Y. City. John Cock, gardener, and Abraham Eckart, grocer, next friends to dec'd, appointed administrators. Copy.

1439 (R 55) 1782 April 19 Octbr. 5 **ROSECRANTS, Daniel,** of Goshen Precinct, Orange Co., farmer. Wife Catrein, six sons and one daughter, not named. Land on Lackewaney Line and other real estate, personal property. Executors son Mannes Couchendale and bro. Jacob Cole. Witnesses Alexander Campbell of said Prect., schoolmaster, and Benjamin Cole.

1440 (R 56) 1783 Decbr. 3 1785 July 5 **ROSEKRANS, Elijah,** of Rochester Township, Ulster Co. Wife Hannah, children Antje, Maria, Sarah and Peternella. Real and personal estate. Executors the wife, Derick Wesbrook, Cornelius Hardenbergh and bro. Zachariah Rosekrans. Witnesses John Depuy jun., Jacobus Davenport jun. of Marbletown and John Evans of Rochester, physician.

1441 (R 57) 1783 Decbr. 30 1784 July 22 **REICHERT (Rikard), David,** of Rhinebeck Prect., Dutchess Co., yeoman. Wife Mary, children Joseph, Johannes, Henry, Jacob, David, Philipp, Zacharia, Barent, Susannah, wife of Lodwick Elsefer, Mary, widow of Uury Siperly, and Catherine, wife of Wilhelmus Feller, stepdaughter Elizabeth Counes. Real and personal estate (" my Big Dutch Bible "). Executors son Joseph and sons-in-law Lodwick Elsefer and Wilhelmus Feller. Witnesses Will. Cockburn, James Cockburn, farmer, and Philipp Verplanck.

1442 (R 58) 1784 April 9 May 7 **RIDER, William,** of Cakeate, Haverstraw Prect., Orange Co., farmer. " I give and bequeath to Martha, daughter of my Lawful daughter Phebe, with Elizabeth, Suckey and Miller, my two twines the part of Lydias estate . . . , I give and bequeath this . . . on an Equal Division among my Lawful Daughters and Grand Daughter . . . to be Divided among the Boys, namely William, Joseph & Ino. and my Jemima to have her Liveing of the Boys place, till the Boys comes of Age and my Lawful Wife to have her Liveing of the whole Farm. . . ." Executors William Smith and John Palmer. Witnesses Mathew Coe, wheelwright, John Cox, yeoman and Isaac Smith.

1443 (R 59) 1789 Febry. 18 — French **ROTTENBOURG, Ernest Guillaume, Baron de,** late of Lausanne, Switzerland, now of N. Y. City. Kinsman Philipp August Hennequin de Rottenbourg, citizen of N. Y., but now at Lyons, France, sole heir and executor of real and personal estate. Witnesses R. J. van den Broek, Not. Public, Ph. Dubey and Sigismund Hugget. Seal. This instrument was sewn into a parchment pocket and was still sealed.

1444 (R 60) 1794 Decbr. 29 1795 April 14 **ROSSET, Ferdinand Antoine Henry,** late of Lausanne, Switzerland, now of N. Y. State. Wife Cecile Caroline Cazenove, children Antoinette Marie Sophie, Antoinette, Richard Frederic Theophile, Henry Nicholas Quirin; Antoine Auguste Theophile, Ernest Emile, and Cecile Henriette; Claudine Pointet, Jean Sutter. Real and personal estate. Executors the wife with the assistance of William Bayard and John Linklaen, both of N. Y. State, for the property in the U. S., of bro.-in-law Marc Antoine Cazenove d'Arlens of Lausanne aforesaid for property in Switzerland and France, of Charles Theophile Cazenove of London for property in England and bro.-in-law Theophile Cazenove of Amsterdam for the general direction of the children. Witnesses Noel John Barbarin, William W. Morris and Chles. Malenfant. Seal blurred, device: "Ardua Vincit Omnia Virtus (Virtue overcomes all difficulties).

1445 (R 61) 1802 June 7 1804 Febry. 7 **RALEIGH, Walter,** of Cambridge, Washington Co. Wife Abigail (second wife); children by first wife John, James, Edmund, Walter, Polly and Hannah, son by second wife not named. Real and personal estate. Executors Austin Wells, John H. Roll and son John N. Raleigh, of Westmoreland, Oneida Co., in 1804. Witnesses Ebenezer Allen, Austin Wells and James Wells.

1446 (R 62) **ROOSEVELT, Jacobus,** of N. Y. City, merchant. Children Isaac and Adolphus, children of dec'd da. Helena Barclay, grandchildren Nicholas Roosevelt, son of dec'd son Nicholas, James Cromeline, Peter Roosevelt and Jacobus Roosevelt jun., son of dec'd son Christopher, grandda. Catherine, wife of Abraham van Ranst of Bushwyck, L. I., who has son John Roosevelt van Ranst. Real property at Rariton Landing, East New Jersey, purchased from Evert Dayking, farm at Bushwyck, L. I., purchased from heirs of John Alberson, houses and lots in Roosevelt Str., Out Ward, N. Y. City, No. 69, 89, 169, 170 and 193 St. James Str., in John Str., North Ward, at Pecks Slip, Montgomery Ward. Draft of will, part missing.

1447 (R 63) **REGNIER, Jacob,** unsigned and undated part of the probate of the will of.

1448 1773 Febry. — 1787 Jany. 9 **REMSEN, Dority,** of N. Y. City. Nephews Henry and Joris, sons of bro. Henry Remsen, Jeronimus A., son of Aris Remsen, mother Catalina Remsen, brothers Joris and Henry Remsen, sister Phebe Remsen. "Worldly estate." Executors the two brothers and cousin Jeronimus A. Remsen. Witnesses John W. Vredenburgh, hatter, James Cobham and Dorithy Kip. Recorded in Wills and Probates, Vol. I., p. 13.

1449 1780 Jany. 22 1787 March 15 **RICH, Abraham,** of Mile Square. Wife ——, son Lewis and three others, not named, da. Sarah. Real and personal estate. Executors bro. Jacob Rich and Thomas Vollentine. Witnesses George Crawford of Westchester Co., Stephen Davis and Cornelius McCarthy. Proved in Westchester Co. Recorded ut supra, p. 71.

1450 1749 April 5 1787 April 7 **ROOMER, John,** of New Harlem, Out Ward, N. Y. City. Wife Margaret, da. Angenelia, eldest son of Beter Waldron of New Harlem. Real and personal estate. Executors Peter Waldron and Arent Bussing. Witnesses Daniel McGown, Cornelius Sickles of the Out Ward, tailor, and William Moore. Recorded ut supra, p. 117.

1451 1785 Decbr. 10 — **RENAUDET, Adrian,** of Philadelphia, Penna., gentleman. John James and James, sons of dec'd nephew James White, children of dec'd sister Ann, vizt: Sarah Furman, Townsend White jun., John White, Isabella Edgar and Ann Constable, bro. Peter Renaudet, sisters Jane Osborn, Elizabeth Beekman and Mary Chevalier. Real and personal estate. Executors nephew Moore Furman of Trenton, N. J., and John Duffield of Philadelphia. Copy of a copy, made at Philadelphia, July 3, 1787. Recorded ut supra, p. 173.

1452 1780 July 22 1788 Febry. 28 **RODGERS, Thomas,** of N. Y. City, mariner. Margaret Marsh sole heiress and executrix of personal estate. Witnesses John Evans of N. Y. City, lumber merchant, and Hester Marsh. Recorded ut supra, p. 179.

1453 1788 March 15 April 17 **RIPLEY, Eliphalet,** son of Joshua, of Windham, Connt., now in N. Y. City. Sister Polly Ripley and surviving brothers and sisters, S. & T. H. Delap of Bordeaux, France. Real and personal estate. Executors George Flagg, esquire, and Major Robert Alden. Witnesses John Ritsen, John de la Mater of N. Y. City, merchant, and M. Willett. Recorded ut supra, p. 191.

1454 1784 July 10 1788 March 22 **ROBERTSON, James,** of New Bigging, County of Fife, North Britain, and Wempole Street, Parish of St. Mary Le Bone, Co. of Middlesex, esquire, Lieut.-General of H. M. forces. Wife Anni, grandda. Anne Henderson. Real and personal estate. Executors and trustees the wife, John Melville of Cairne, Scotland, esquire, and William Lumsdane, of Edinburgh, writer to His Majesty's signet in Scotland. Witnesses Richard Carrigul, Samuel Willis and William Lancaster. Codicil of Septbr. 18, 1787, adds names of nephews John Cowe and John Melville. Witnesses Ja. Chalmer, Will Moncurr and William Dewer (?). Recorded ut supra, p. 193.

1455 1783 May 13 1790 June 11 **READ, Thomas,** of Philadelphia, Penna., mariner and merchant. Wife Mary sole heiress and executrix. Houses and lots at Christiana Bridge, Whitely Creek Hundred, New Castle Co., Delaware, do. in Bordentown, Chesterfield Township, Burlington Co., N. J. Witnesses James Nicholson of N. Y. City, gentleman, Clement Stocker and John Nicholson. Proved in N. Y. Recorded ut supra, p. 237.

1456 1789 Septbr. 13 1790 Aug. 5 **ROSS, Thomas,** seaman on board the ship *America*. Shipmate Malcolm Taylor, who is made administrator, heir of all effects. Witnesses Abraham Dawson, Robert Pearce, both mariners, and David Bridge. Recorded ut supra, p. 239.

1457 1794 April 18 Novbr. 17 **ROSE, William,** of Broms Grove, County of Worcester, Great Britain, tallow chandler. Wife Martha, children William, Thomas, Abigail and Sarah. Real estate " in Great Britain, America or wheresoever else in the known world," personal property. Executors the wife and Rev. William Wells, " late dissenting Minister of Broms Grove, but now of Medford, near Boston, America." Witnesses Isabella Hollowell, Elizabeth Hollowell and Jos. Brettell. Proved in N. Y. by testimony of the widow Martha Rose, the only son Thomas Rose and Martha Lea of N. Y. City, spinster. Recorded ut supra, p. 453.

1458 1792 July 17 1795 July 4 **RILLIET, Isaac Robert,** of Geneva, Switzerland, son of Isaac. Wife ——, nieces Madame d'Orvilliers, da. of bro. ——? Jane Marianne Diodati, wife of James Massi, grandnieces Annie Marie Holme Diodati, Anne Marie Hubbard Diodati, grandnephew Frederic, son of nephew Capt. de Stoutz, goddaughters Madame Turrettin, née Gremes, Anne Marie, da. of Mr. Masbon, Sarah, da. of the late Bartholomy Hermebez, niece Madame de Stoutz, Henrietta Brun, formerly waiting woman to the wife, sister widow Diodati, brother Jacques Rilliet, niece Madame Huber. Real and personal property. No executor named. Proved at London, and Captain Charles Frederic Laurent Stoutz, nephew of testator, made administrator with direction to render accounts to testator's sisters Marie Aimée Diodati, bro. James Rilliet, niece Marie Aimée, wife of Francis Huber and Jeanne Marianne Rilliet, testator's widow. Recorded ut supra, p. 544.

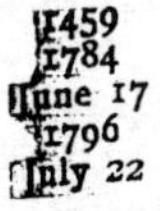

1459 1784 June 17 1796 July 22 **RAPALJE, Jeromus,** of Cow Neck, North Hempstead, Queens Co. The mother, sister Jane Thorne and her children, vizt. Stephen and Edward, half sister Sybel Thorne, reputed Uncle Jacobus Lefferts. "My estate." Executor uncle Jacobus Lefferts of N. Y. Witnesses David Brooks, Hannah Brooks and Thomas Thorn of N. Y. City, grocer. Recorded ut supra, p. 555.

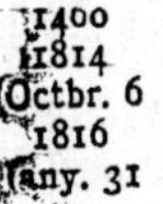

1400 1814 Octbr. 6 1816 Jany. 31 **ROLES, Myndert,** of Schenectady. Nicholas P. Veeder, sole heir and executor of real and personal property. Witnesses Myndert van Guysling, John McMichael and Harvey Church. Recorded ut supra, Vol. II., p. 334.

1461 1785 Novbr. 2 **RUSSELER, William,** late seaman in his Britannic Majesty's service, letters of administration on the estate of, granted to his mother Sophia Russeler of N. Y. City, widow. Recorded ut supra, Vol. III., p. 48.

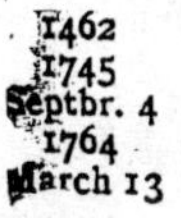

1462 1745 Septbr. 4 1764 March 13 **RAPALJE, Joris (George),** of the Ferry, Brookland Township, Kings Co. Wife Dina, sons John, Gerrit, daughters Cornelia, wife of Abraham Lott of N. Y. City and Antje. Real and personal estate. Executors bro. Jeronimus Rapalje and bro.-in-law John Middagh. Witnesses William Edmonds, Jacob Remsen, whose signature is proved by his son Rem Remsen, of Bruycklin merchant, and Adrian Hegeman, signature proved by his son Joseph Hegeman of Bruycklin Ferry, baker. Recorded ut supra, p. 66.

1463 1826 Novbr. 15 1829 March 23 **ROSEBOOM, John J.** Sister Elizabeth, wife of Conrad Gansevoort, of Albany City, esquire, bro. Abraham Roseboom. Land in Sacondaga Patent, h. & l. in Albany and other real estate, personal property. Executors the brother and his son John. Witnesses Gardner Blair, William Graham of Middlefield, Otsego Co., farmers, and James Brackett. Codicil of Feby. 2, 1826, is witnessed by James Brackett of Cherry Valley, Otsego Co., counsellor at law, Henry Lawrence of Cherry Valley, farmer, and James Ferris of the same place, labourer. Recorded ut supra, Vol. V., p. 67.

1464 1639 June 16 Dutch **ROELOFFSEN, Roeloff.** Laurens Pietersen van Tonsback sole heir of real and personal property. Witnesses Pieter Jansen and Hans Stam. N. Y. Col. MSS., I., p. 138.

1465 1643 May 19 Dutch **ROY, Jacob Jacobsen,** gunner, sick at the house of Hendric Westercamp. Jacob Reynsen and Teunis Jansen, sailmaker, sole heirs and executors of real and personal estate. Witnesses Pierre Pia, Ulderick Blauw (?) and Cornelis van Tienhoven, Secretary. N. Y. Col. MSS., II., p. 58.

1466 1646 Octbr. 18 Dutch **RINGO, Philipp Jansen,** from Flushing, Holland. Comrade Anthony Crol sole heir of common property. Witnesses Adriaen van Tienhoven, Jacob Hendricksen Kip and Cornelis van Tienhoven, Secry. N. Y. Col. MSS., II., p. 150.

1467 1662 Aug. 29 Dutch **RINCHOUT, Daniel,** of Beverwyck, bachelor, 36 years old. Brothers Jan Rinchout, of Beverwyck, and Aertman Rinchout, living in Pommerania. Real and personal estate. Witnesses Jan Verbeeck, Jan Koster van Acken, Dirck van Scheluyne, Notary. Albany Co. Records, Notarial Papers, I., p. 256.

1408
1702
Septbr. 14
Septbr. 24

REIMS, Edward, of Albany, victualler. Wife Elisabeth; Daniel Wilkeson, John Taylor, drummer in Capt. James Weemes' Company. Personal estate. Executor Lieut. Henry Holland. Witnesses John Collins, John Oliver and John Carr. Albany Co. Records, WIlls, I., p. 82.

1469
2d Ann
Febry. 2
1704
March 30

RINCKHOUT, Jurriaen, son of John, of Shinnechtady, Albany Co., yeoman. Wife Maria, children Teunis, 17 yrs. old, Effie, 12 yrs., Jan, 9 yrs., Daniel, 5 yrs., Jannetie, 3 yrs, Ida, 1 year. Real estate in Shinnechtady, N. Y., and elsewhere, personal property. The wife executrix with Capt. Johannis Bleecker and Jean Rosie as trustees. Witnesses David Schuyler, Justice, Robert Livingston jun. and Jean Rosie. Albany Co. Records, Wills, I., p. 104.

1470
1713–14
March 9

REYERSEN, Gerrit, and wife Annatie, children of, vizt. Jan Gerritsen, Reyer Gerritsen, Maritie and son-in-law Harpert Jacobsen, receipt to their eldest brother Elbert Gerritsen for their share of parents estate. Albany Co. Records, Deeds E, p. 223.

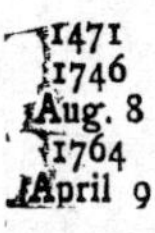
1471
1746
Aug. 8
1764
April 9

ROSEBOOM, Robert, of Albany City, merchant. Wife Ryckje, brothers Hendrick, Ahasverus, Geysbert and John, sister Elsje Roseboom. Real and personal property. The wife sole executrix. Witnesses Robt. Sanders, merchant, William Rogers and Abraham Wendell. Albany Co. Records, Wills, I., p. 295.

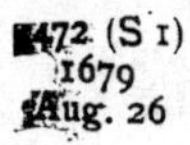
1472 (S 1)
1679
Aug. 26

SALISBURY, Silvester, of Albany Co., Captain. Wife Elizabeth, children Francis, 9 yrs. old, Silvester, 6 yrs. and Mary, 13 months. Real and personal estate. Executors the Right Honourable Sir Edmund Andros, Knight, Governour General, brother Peter Jacobsen Maurius and Jacob Tunissen Key. Witnesses Johannes Wendel andRobert Livingston. Copy.

1473 (S 2) 1683, O. S. May 1 1683-4 March 4 Dutch

SCHUYLER, Philipp, of Albany, late Magistrate, and wife Margarita van Slichtenhorst. The survivor, children Arent, 22 years old, Philipp, 17 yrs., Johannes, 15 yrs., Margriet, 11 yrs., Geertruy, wife of Stephanus van Cortlandt, Alida, wife of Robert Livingston, Peter, and Brant. Real and personal property. No executors named, letters testamentary granted to the widow. Witnesses Cornelis van Dyck and Dirck Wessells.

1474 (S 3) 1688 May 21 1694 April 11

SCHUYLER, David, of Albany City, merchant. Wife Catelyntie, children Peter, Geertruy, Abraham, Maritje, David, Myndert, Cobus and Catelyntje. Real and personal property. The wife sole executrix. Witnesses Dirck Wessells (ten Broeck) and Jan Peeck.

1475 (S 4) 1700 April 3

SYLVESTER, Nathaniel, of Easthampton, Suffolk Co. Wife Margret, children Nathniel, Grizell, Brinley, Margret. Land on Shelter Island, personal property. Witnesses James Brading, Matthias Burnat, John Merry and Abiel Carll. Codicil of April 24, 1705, appoints Benj. Newberry and Arnold Collins as executors and is witnessed by Francis Brinley, Caleb Arnold and Willm. Coddington. Proved at Newport, R. I., probated July 4, 1705, in New York. Copy.

1476 (S 5) 1701 May 24

SMITH, Joseph, of N. Y. City, merchant. Wife Mary, da. Ann. Real and personal estate. The wife sole executrix. Witnesses Jacobus Vanderspiegel, Wellem Seckerly and Will. Sharpas. Copy made Aug. 14, 1755.

1477 (S 6) 1701 April 1 1707 Octbr. 4 Dutch

SWITS, Isaac, of Schinnechtady. Wife Susanna Groot, children Cornelis, Symon, Abraham, Aryaentie, Rebecca, Isaac, Jacob, and Claes. Real and personal property. Executors son Cornelis Isaacsen, the wife and Captain Evert Banker. Witnesses Anthony van Schaick and Anthony Koster.

1478 (S 7) 1708 Aug. 17 1713 April 9 **STEPHENSON, Stephen,** of Port Royal, Island of Jamaica, mariner. George Hall of Port Royal, chirurgeon, sole heir and executor of real and personal property. Witnesses Edward Reeves, John Johnson and George Evans. Proved at St. Jago de la Vega, Jamaica. David Minvielle of N. Y. City, merchant, appointed attorney of executor.

1479 (S 8) 1712 —— —— **SELYNS, ——.** This is a paper, endorsed "Part of the will of ? Selyns 1712" and mentions Abraham Gouverneur, Isaac Gouverneur and Elizabeth Nessepat, children of sister Magtel Nessepat, to whom three-sixths of the residuary estate are bequeathed. Not dated nor signed.

1480 (S 9) 1717 April 5 1719 April 8 **SCHERMERHOORN, Reyer,** of Schonectady, Albany Co., esquire. Wife Aryantie, children John, Jacob, Aerent, Janneke, wife of Volkert Symonsen, children of dec'd da. Cataline, late wife of John Wemp, vizt. Mindert, Ryert and Ariantie, bro. Luycas Schermerhoorn, Willihelmus, son of Garrit Symonsen, Hannah, da. of the same, Aryantie Symonsen, wife of Daniel Danielsen. Real estate in Schonectady, in Albany Co., in the Raretons, East New Jersey, personal property. Executors the three sons. Witnesses Dowe Aukes, Capt. Philipp Schuyler and Philipp Verplanck. Seal.

1481 (S 10) 1717 Novbr. 10 1719 Octbr. 9 **STEVENSON, Thomas,** of Bucks Co., Penna. Wife ——, children Samuel, Edward, Ann, Sarah, Elie and Olif or Elie Ollif, children of brothers William and John. Real and personal estate, partly derived from father-in-law Jenings. Executors the wife and Joseph Kirkbride. Witnesses Anna Marriot, John Anford and Benj. Field. Proved in Pennsylvania. Copy.

1482 (S 11) 1720–1 Jany. 5 March 2 **SLOSS, John,** of Fairfield. Wife Esther, daughters Sarah, Ellen and Deborah, sister Anna, in Scotland. "My manour of Eatons Neck, L. I.," property in Scotland, personal estate. The wife sole executrix. Witnesses Nathaniel Whitehead, Elisabeth Whitehead and Major Peter Burr. Copy.

1483 (S 12) 1723-4 Febry. 15 1725 Septbr. 20 Dutch

SCHEPMOES, Dirck, of Kingston Corporation, Ulster Co. Wife Maragrietie Tappen, daughters Anna, Aryantie, Sara, Dirikye, Ragell, Leea and Rebecca, sons Willem, Johannes. Real and personal estate. Johannis Hardenbergh, Pieter Tappen and Hendrick Pruyn guardians, and with Willem Schepmoes, Thuenes Tappen, Barnardus Swartwout, Barent van Waagenen, Aldert Roosa, executors. Witnesses Gilbert Livingston, Ino. Rutsen, Salomon Davis and Jacobus van Dyck.

1484 (S 13) 1723 March 30 1729 Decbr. 1

SYMES, Lancaster, of New York City, gentleman. Wife Catherine, children Elizabeth, John, Hendrick, Lancaster, Richard, grandson Richard Gree*d*, son of dec'd da. Catherine Gree*n*. Real and personal property. Executors the wife, son John Hendrick and Adolph Philipps, esquire. Witnesses Samuel Bayard, Richard Stillwell and Fredk. Morris. Codicil of March 28, 1727, describes testator as late of N. Y. City, now of Albany, makes different disposition of land near Haverstraw, Orange Co., and appoints all his children and the grandson executors. Witnesses Edd. Holland, Jeremiah van Rensselaer and William Hopkins.

1485 (S 14) 1729 Decbr. 9 1730 Novbr. 7 Dutch

SCHOONMAKER, Joachim, of Kingston, Ulster Co. Wife Antje Hussey, sons Cornelius, Hendrick, Vredrick, Jacobus, Benjamin, Jan, Joachim, Daniel, daughters Tryntje, wife of Jacobus Bruyn, Elsje, widow of Joseph Haasbrock, Jacomyntje, wife of Johannis Miller, Grietje, wife of Moses Dupuis jun., Elizabeth, wife of Benjamin Dupuis, Antje, wife of Cornelis Wynkoop, Sarah, wife of Jacobus Dupuis. Real and personal property. Executors sons Cornelis, Vredrick and Jacobus. Witnesses Johannis Hardenburgh, Jurryan Tappen, Hendrick Sleght and Ger. van Wagenen.

1486 (S 15) 1732-3 Jany. 11 1733 June 2

SMITH, William, of Grey-Court, Goshen Precinct, Orange Co., yeoman. Wife Mary sole heiress and executrix of "worldly estate." Witnesses John Smith, Samuel Seely and Samuel Seely jun. At date of proof the widow Mary Smith has become the wife of William Jackson.

1487 (S 16) 1733 Aug. 7 1735 Decbr. 4 **SICARD, Ambroise,** senior, of New Rochelle, Westchester Co., yeoman. Wife Jeane, children Ambroise, Magdalen Williams, Judith Dubois, Daniel, Paul. Real and personal estate. Executors nephew Peter Sicard and John Badaux. Witnesses Danl. Giraut, Daniel Angevine and John Constant. Copy.

1488 (S 17) 1734 Septbr. 14 1735 April 28 **STAATS, Jacob,** of Albany City, chyrurgion. Wife Isabella, children Deborah, wife of Hendrick Roseboom, Catherine, widow of Gose van Schaik, grandson Jacobus van Schaik. Real and personal property. Executors son-in-law Hendrick Roseboom and grandson Jacob Roseboom. Witnesses Reyer Gerritse, Joseph Yates and Wm. Hopkins.

1489 (S 18) 1731 (?) Decbr. 27 1732 April 22 **SMITH, Caleb,** of Goshen, Orange Co., yeoman. Wife Phebe, sons Henry, John, Isaac, Elias, Jeremiah and Timothy, daughters Phebe and Sarah, an expected child. Real and personal property. Executors Wait Smith, Isaac Ludlow, both of Goshen, and Nehemiah Smith jun. of Jamaica, Queens Co. Witnesses John Thomson, James Tomson and Joshua Smith.

1490 (S 19) 1735 Septbr. 11 1753 Novbr. 1 **STILLWELL, Elizabeth,** of Jamaica, Queens Co., widow. Da. Meriam Marsh; Mary, wife of Samuel Southward of Hempstead, Easter, wife of John Sayre of N. Y. City, tailor; Elizabeth, da. of Samuel Southward, Elizabeth, da of John Saye, grandda. Elizabeth, da. of James Milward and dec'd da. Elizabeth. "Worldly estate (eighteen silver spoons of 2 ounces each). Executors John Sayre and Jarvis Mudge junior of Oyster bay, Queens Co. Witnesses W. Lawrence, Joost Lemsen and Hester Lawrence. At date of proof John Sayre is described as of Philadelphia, Penna., shopkeeper.

1491 (S 20) 1737-8 Febry. 21 1746 June 3 Dutch

SWYTS, Jannetie, widow of Cornelius, of Rochester, Ulster Co. Husband's sister Aploniea Aken, sister Rachel Bogardus, nieces Jenneke Wynkoop, Cathariena de Duytser, Margriet Oosterhout, friend Arieantie Hoornbeek. Personal estate. Executors cousin Egbert de Witt and niece Barber Tapper. Witnesses Maria Hoornbeek, Annetye Hoornbeek, and Cornelus Hoornbeek. Codicil of May 29, 1739, makes niece Jenneke Wynkoop residuary legatee and co-executrix. Witnesses Cornelus Hornbeek, Maria Hornbeek and Willem C. Kool.

1492 (S 21) 1737 Novbr. 10 ——

SHERMAN, Dorothy, of N. Y. City, widow. Elizabeth, wife of Alexander Hope of Philadelphia, mariner, who has son Francis Johnson, cousin Edward Cox and his da. Dorothy, Mary and Dorothy, daughters of John ten Brook, cartman, Hannah, wife of Peter Fleming, Thomas Ming, Elisabeth, da. of Thomas Corvin. Real and personal estate (a gold locket, do. sleevebuttons, 3 silver spoons, a gold ring). Executors Elizabeth Hope, Edward Man, of N. Y., cooper, and Abraham Lodge, attorney-at-law. Witnesses I. Brown, John Lyne and Law van der Spiegel. Copy made April 6, 1764.

1493 (S 22) 1737 Aug. 30 1747 Novbr. 2

SIMSON, Peter, of Batemans (Beekmans) Precinct, Dutchess Co., yeoman. Wife Mary, sons Joseph, Peter, Abel and Isaac. Real and personal estate. Executors John Carmon and Peter Simson. Witnesses Thomas Barker, William Humfrey and Joshua Champlin.

1494 (S 23) 1739 Aug. 13 Aug. 22

SCOT, James, of Kingston, Ulster Co. Wife Elizabeth, children William, Majory and Jannetie. Real and personal estate. Executors bro. William Scot, Major Johannis Hardenbergh and Abraham Hasbrouck. Witnesses J. Elmendorpf, Coernelus Elmendorph and Abraham Hardenbergh.

1495 (S 24) 1739 June 13 1747 Aug. 10 **SCHUYLER Philipp Johannissen,** of Saratoga, Albany Co., gentleman. Sister Margriet Schuyler, bro.-in-law Isaac Wendell, nephews John Johannissen and Philipp, sons of bro. John Schuyler, jun., Johannis Cornelissen and Philipp, sons of bro.-in-law Cornelis Cuyler. Real and personal estate. Executors bro. John Schuyler jun. and bro.-in-law Cornelis Cuyler. Witnesses Hans Hansen, Gulyen Verplaenck and Ja. Stevenson. Seal, but not the Schuyler arms.

1496 (S 25) 1739 March 27 1756 July 24 **SCHUYLER, Myndert,** of Albany City. Wife Rachel, da. Anna de Peyster, grandchildren Anna and Rachel de Peyster. Real and personal estate (plate). Executors the wife, the daughter, Rutger Bleecker, Henderick Cuyler jun., and Philipp Schuyler. Witnesses Abraham Cuyler, Nicolaes Bleecker and Johannis Rutger Bleecker, gentleman. Codicil of July 28, 1741, provides for grandson, lately born, Myndert Schuyler de Peyster. Witnesses Nicolaes Bleecker, John ten Eyck and Abraham Cuyler jun.

1497 (S 26) 1739 Novbr. 1 1758 April 13 **SANDERS, Barent,** of Albany City, merchant. Sons Robert and John. House and lot on Pearl Str., Albany, do. in Schonectady, land near Schonectady, do. at Pakeepsie, now occupied by bro. Thomas Sanders, land on Skohary River or Cadaridie Creek; personal property. Executors the two sons. Witnesses Johs. Roseboom jun., Ephraim Wendell and Gulyen Verplaenck.

1498 (S 27) 1741-2 Febry. 25 1757 July 25 **SCHUYLER, John,** of Albany City, Colonel. Children Philipp, Margrieta, wife of Col. Philipp Schuyler, Catalyntje, wife of Cornelius Cuyler, stepdaughter Sarah, wife of Jacob Glen, children of dec'd son John. Real estate at Saratogue, in Albany City and County, personal property (a portrait of testator and wife). Executors the son and two daughters. Witnesses Jeremiah Schuyler, Pieter Schuyler and Francisckys Lansyngh. Codicil of

Febry. 25, 1746-47, divides property, formerly left to son Philipp, since deceased. Witnesses Ino. de Peyster, Ja. Stevenson and Peter Lansingh. Schuyler seal. See No. 1495.

1499 (S 28) 1744 May 6 1764 May 3 **STRANG, Elisabeth,** widow of Henry, late of Rye, Westchester Co., saddler. Son Daniel, daughters Elisabeth, wife of Richard van Dyck, Hannah and Livina. "Estate." Executor bro.-in-law James Woods, of Rye. Witnesses Rog. Woods, Eliah Budd and Ino. Carhartt of said Co., schoolmaster. Copy.

1500 (S 29) 1744 Aug. 27 1744-5 Febry. 21 **SMITHREM, Esther,** widow. Cousins Anne, wife of Timothy Horsford, of Canaan, Connt., Elizibeth, wife of Abraham Halenbick. Personal estate. Executor Timothy Horsford. Witnesses Jochem van Valkenburgh, John McCay and Andrew Ellet. Proved in Albany.

1501 (S 30) 1744 Decbr. 14 1746 April 28 **SACKETT, Richard,** of Dover, Dutchess Co., yeoman. Wife Margery, children Josiah Crego, Richard, John, Catherine Margeson, children of dec'd da. Maria Dean. Real and personal estate. Executors the wife and sons Richard and John. Witnesses Henry Nase, William Hunt and Josias Crego.

1502 (S 31) 1744 Decbr. 1 1749 June 13 **SWARTWOUT, Jacobus,** of the Fish Kil, Dutchess Co., gentleman. Wife ——, children, Thomas, Cornelius, Adolphus Samuel, Jacobus, Elizabeth, Jannetie, Jacomyntje and Catherine. Real and personal estate. Executors sons Thomas and Cornelius Theodorus van Wyck and John Brinkerhoff. Witnesses Ino. Rowe, Stephen Ladou and Jacob Graver.

1503 (S 32) 1744 June 12 1749 Septbr. 15 **SMEDES, Benjamin,** of Shawangonk, Ulster Co., yeoman. Wife Magdalena, children Peter, Nathan, Benjamin, Rachel, wife of Nicholas Bogardus, children of dec'd da. Elizabeth, late wife of John Sleght. Land in

Shawangonk and Kingston, personal property (a Dutch bible). Executors the three sons. Witnesses Jacobus Bruyn jun., Jacobus van Keuren and John Bruyn.

1504 (S 33) 1744 Novbr. 12 1749-50 March 23 **SCHOOMAKER, Tyrick,** of Kingston Corporation, Ulster Co. Wife Doostie, sons Hendrick, Edward, John, Tyrick, daughters Margereth, Geertruy, Hiltie and Deborah. Real and personal estate. Executors Ezekiah du Bois and Myndert Myndersen. Witnesses Wm. Legg, John Legg jun. and John West.

1505 (S 34) 1745 May 15 1755 Decbr. 22 **SCHARS, Christoffel,** of Gouanus, Brookland Township, Kings Co., yeoman. Cousins Tuenis van Pelt, Alexander van Pelt, Pieter van Pelt, Johannis van Pelt, Jacomyntje van Pelt, wife of Samuel Berrie, and Grietje Bennett, wife of Jacob Bergen of Staten Island. Real estate in Brookland and at Nevesings, N. J., personal property. Executors cousins Pieter and Johannis van Pelt. Witnesses William Hoogland, Jacobus Lott of said County, farmer and Abraham Lott. Copy.

1506 (S 35) 1746 May 12 1748 Aug. 27 **SCHUYLER, Nicholas,** of Schenectady, Albany Co., gentleman. Wife Mary, sons Harmanus and Johannes, daughters Catrina, Lysbetie, wife of Jochem Staats, Arriantie, wife of Killian van Rensselaer. Real and personal estate. Executors the wife, son Harmanus and bro.-in-law James Stevenson. Witnesses Thomas Sharpe, Michael Bassett and Barent ten Eyck.

1507 (S 36) Misplaced, belongs under Veeder.

1508 (S 37) 1747 March 19 1755 Decbr. 5 **SIPKINS, Rebeccah,** of N. Y. City, widow. Christina, daughter of dec'd son Gerrit Breested, Cornelia, John, Rem and Rebecca Remsen, children of da. Elizabeth Griffith, Maria, da. of dec'd da. Johanna van der Heul, John Taylor, son of da. Rebeccah Griffith. Real and personal estate. Executors' names illegible. Witnesses Willem Bogert, Cornelius Boghart and Simon Johnson. Copy.

1509 (S 38) 1747 May 7 1764 Octbr. 4 Dutch **SMIT, Jurje Adam,** of Claverack, Albany Co., farmer. Wife Christiena, sons Coenraat, Johan Adam, Johannis, Jacob, Petrus, Jurje (George) and Teunis, daughters Maria, wife of Mathys Emmerigh, Elsje, wife of Hendrick Hoppelbeek, Christiena and Catharina. Real and personal estate. Executor sons Johan Adam, Jacob and Petrus. Witnesses Aarent van Dyck, Stephanis van Dyck and Elizabeth van Dyck of Kinderhook.

1510 (S 39) 1747 Febry. 25 1748 Octbr. 22 **SMITH, James,** of Newburgh, Highlands Precinct, Ulster Co. Wife Mary, sons Joseph, William, Benjamin, Ephraim and James. Homefarm, personal property. Executors the wife, Capt. Alexander Colden and Charles Clinton. Witnesses John Umphrey jun., William Ward and Thomas Ward.

1511 (S 40) 1748 Octobr. 3 1755 Octbr. 16 **SEAMAN, Jonathan,** of New Hampstedt, Orange Co. Jonathan, son of son Jonathan dec'd, of Fredericks Co., Virga., sons Jonas, John and Jacomiah, daughters Elizabeth Palmer, Hannah Coe, Martha van der Voort, Phebe Coe. Real and personal estate. Executors sons John and Jacomiah and son-in-law John Palmer. Witnesses Geysbert Cuypèr, John van der Voort and William Sarjant.

1512 (S 41) 1748 June 28 1758 June 6 **SCHUYLER, Philipp,** of Albany City. Wife Margrieta, brothers Jermey and Peter, sisters Margrita Livingston and Gertruy Lansingh, nephews Peter Lansingh, Peter Schuyler, Barent Staats jun., who has sister Anna van der Poel, Philipp, son of dec'd brother John. Share in Westenhook Patent, lots at Canajoharie on N. side of Mohawks River, land at the Flats, personal property (two large silver salt cellars). The wife sole executrix. Witnesses Ino. de Peyster, Nich. Schuyler and Ja: Stevenson.

1513 (S 42) 1749 May 26 — **SMITH, Daniel,** of N. Y. City, gardner. Wife Elizabeth, "undutifull and disobedient son John Conraat Smith" cut off with £5 N. Y., other children Barent, Elizabeth, Catharine, Maria. Real and personal estate. Executors the last named four children. Witnesses John Myer, William Bond and S. Johnson. Copy made May 10, 1762.

1514 (S 43) 1749 Septbr. 18 1756 June 21 **SALISBURY, Francis,** of Catskil, Albany Co. Wife Mary, sons Abraham, William, Lawrence, daughter Elizabeth, wife of Rensselaer Nicols. Real and personal estate. Executors the three sons and the son-in-law. Witnesses Benjamin Dubois, Theunys van Vechten, farmer, and Jacob Freese.

1515 (S 44) 1740 April 12 1750 Octbr. 8 Dutch **SCHEPMOES, William,** of Kingston Corporation, Ulster Co. Wife Catharina, sons Derick and Johannes, daughters Marytie, wife of Abraham van Stienbergh, Sarah, wife of Peter Dumon jun., Catharina, Maregrietie, Ariejantie. Real and personal estate. Executors the wife and the two sons. Witnesses G. Hardenbergh, Christoffel Kierstede and Jacobus van Dyck.

1516 (S 45) 1750 Septbr. 24 1753 Octbr. 12 **SMITH, Wait,** of Goshen, Orange Co., yeoman. Wife Charity, sons Wait, Samuel, Oliver, James, William, Joshua, Solomon, daughters Elizabeth Smith and Charity Thomson. Real and personal estate. Executors sons Wait and Samuel. Witnesses Daniel Everett, Daniel Gale and Gilbert Denton.

1517 (S 46) 1752 Octbr. 28 1767 July 27 **SCHERMERHORN, John,** of Schonectady, Albany Co., farmer. Wife Engelie, sons Reyer, Symon, Jacob, Johannis, Barnardus, daughters Catlyna, wife of John Dodds, Neeltie, wife of Claes Vielen, Magdalena and Janitie. Homefarm, land in East New Jersey, bought from brothers Jacob and Arent Schermerhorn, personal property. Executors sons Reyer, Symon and Jacob. Witnesses Hendereykes Feder, farmer, Hermanis ter Wellgen, cooper, both of Albany Co., and Jacob Vrooman.

1518 (S 47) 1752 Febry. 24 — **SMITH, William,** of Newburgh, Ulster Co. Wife Elizabeth, sons Henry, Thomas, Josiah, children of dec'd son James, son-in-law James Edmunston and wife Margriet. Real and personal estate. Executors the wife, Charles Clinton and Jonathan Hasbrouck. Witnesses Thomas Ward, Johannes Wandle and Nathan Furman. Filed March 3, 1805.

1519 (S 48) 1749 Jany. 11 1752 Septbr. 25 Dutch — **STAATS, Barent,** of Albany, Major. Wife Neltie, sons Joagim and Gerrit, daughters Annatie, wife of John Visser, Aryaentie, wife of Henderik van Deusen, Catarina, wife of Abraham Schuyler, Geertrui, wife of Jacobus Schuyler, Neltie, wife of Samuel Staats, Teuntie, wife of William Salsbury, Elizabet, wife of Johans. Bliker. Real and personal estate. Executors the wife and the two sons. Witnesses Sybrant G. van Schaick, Jacobus van Schaick and Killiaen v Rensselaer.

1520 (S 49) 1753 Septbr. 5 1754 June 3 Dutch — **SUYLANDT, Johannes,** of Horly, Ulster Co. Wife Eva, son Johannes, daughters Catharina, Maria, Lena and Elizabeth. Real and personal estate. Executors wife's bro. Derick van Vechten, Hendricus Sleght and Jacob Roosa. Witnesses Huybert Oostrander, Johannes Oostrander jun. and Johannis G. Hardenburgh.

1521 (S 50) 1754 Octbr. 21 1755 Aug. 19 — **SUYLANDT, Huybert,** of Hurley, Ulster Co., yeoman. Wife Sarah, grandson Johannes Suylandt and his three sisters; four daughters, not named. Real and personal estate. Executors sons-in-law Derick van Veghten and Benjamin Dubois, also grandson Johannis Suylandt. Witnesses Thobias van Steenbergh, John Ellison and John Crooke.

1522 (S 51) 1754 June 12 — **SEMPLE, James,** of New York City. Wife Rebecca, kinsman John Grigg. Real and personal estate. The wife executrix. Witnesses Thos. Candell, Samuel Bridge and James Emott. Copy made Octbr. 23, 1754.

1523 (S 52) 1754 Octbr. 4 1761 Novbr. 12 **SWARTWOUDT, Jacobus,** of Sandeohquen, Orange Co., gent. Wife Onake, grandson Jacobus, son of son Philipp, daughters Esther, wife of Abraham Cuddeback, Yonake, son Geradus. Real and personal estate. Executors the wife, son Philipp and Jonathan Westbrook. Witnesses Saml. Green, Jonathan Pettit and Joseph Willits of Minissink, N. J., farmer.

1524 (S 53) 1754 Decbr. 21 1755 March 29 **SCOTT, James,** of Hurley, Ulster Co., merchant. Leaves real and personal estate to Levi Palding as executor in trust for the support of an English schoolmaster at Hurley. Witnesses Isaac Roosa, Petrus Roosa and Egbert Roosa.

1525 (S 54) 1755 June 8 Octbr. 6 **STUART, Robert,** of Scoharre, Albany Co. Johannes Lawyer jun. sole heir and executor of "worldly estate," with a legacy to James Stevenson. Witnesses Peter Nicolas Sommer of Schohary, Minister of the Gospel, Johann Abraham Arbeiter and Johannes Lawyer.

1526 (S 55) 1755 April 13 1761 Novbr. 26 **SMITH, John,** of Ulster Co., yeoman. Wife Isabel, sons James, John, da. Mary, grandson Robert Smith. Real and personal estate. Executors the wife, da. Mary, John Neely and James Barkley. Witnesses Robert Neely, James Morison, farmer, and John Moffat. At date of proof Mary Smith is wife of Robert Calwall of Ulster Co., farmer.

1527 (S 56) 1755 Novbr. 4 1762 June 17 **SLEGHT, Hendrikus,** junior, of Rhinebeek, Dutchess Co., yeoman. Wife Rachel, children Matthewes, Cattaleyntie, Annatie and Majeke. Real and personal estate. Executors bro. Matthewes Sleght, brothers-in-law Henrickis Johnsen and Moses Conteyn and neighbour Gerrit van Wagenen. Witnesses Abraham Kip, Petris van Aake, yeoman, and Gerrit van Wagenen.

1528 (S 57) 1752 May 13 1756 Febry. 24 Dutch

SLEGHT, Mateys, of Rhinebeek Prect., Dutchess Co., farmer. Wife Catlyntje, children Mattewis, Hendricus, Antje, Marytje and Tryntje. Real and personal estate. Executors the two sons and son-in-law Moses Conteyn. Witnesses Isaac Kip, Isaac Kip jun. and Christian Schultzs. See preceding No.

1529 (S 58) 1756 Febry. 20 1760 July 16

SLECHT, Anthony, of Kingston, Ulster Co. Wife Neeltie, da. Cathrina, wife of Abraham Turk, grandda. Leïdia, da. of Johannis Schepmoes and dec'd da. Maria Magdalena, grandda. Catherina, da. of Johannis Stoffel Thomas and dec'd da. Jannetie, grandson Anthony Turk. Real and personal estate. Executors da. Cathrina, her husband Abr. Turk, son-in-law Johs. St. Thomas and cousin Abraham Hasbrouck. Witnesses Abraham van Keuren of Kingston, blacksmith, Cornelius Elmendorph jun. and Joseph Gasherie.

1530 (S 59) 1756 May 28 Septbr. 7

SALISBRY, Abraham, of Catskil, yeoman. Wife Rachel, sons Francis, Abraham, Wessel, da. Mary. Homefarm and land near it, land at Makwams Cassaick, at Tabagiget, at Batavia, at Kiskatamanati, personal property. Executors brothers Lawrence Saulisbury, Ransalar Nicols and David Lamater. Witnesses Casparis Bronck, John M. Connell and Henry Wabber.

1531 (S 60) 1756 Febry. 6 March 20

STILVIL (Stillwell), Nicholas, of Old Town, Richmond Co. Wife Mary, children Thomas, Nicholas, Mary, Catherine, Susannah, Ann, Francis and Sarah. Real and personal estate. Executors the wife and sons Thomas and Nicholas. Witnesses Tho. Walton, Jacob Berger, farmer, and Thomas Price. Copy.

1532 (S 61) 1756 May 25 1758 Octbr. 18

SMITH, Reuben, of Dutchess Co. Wife and children, not named. Real and personal estate. Executors the wife and brothers Nathan Smith and Jonathan Lockwood. Witnesses Daniel Wright, Isaac Burton and Joseph Powell.

1533 (S 62) 1756 March 17 1757 Novbr. 22 **SMITH, Arthur,** of Highlands Prect., Ulster Co. Wife Keziah, sons Joel, Arthur, David. Real and personal estate. Executors the wife, bro. Leonard Smith and David Holmes of Bedford, Westchester Co. Witnesses Jehiel Clark, Moses Fowler and Nathan Mills.

1534 (S 63) 1757 Septbr. 10 Octbr. 8 **SMITH, Henry,** of Goshen, Orange Co. Wife Joanna, daughters Abigail, Phebe, Joanna, Elizabeth and Hannah, sons Caleb, Henry, Stephen. Homefarm, land in Wawayanda Patent, do. in Menesink Patent, personal property. Executors the wife and bro. Jeremiah Smith. Witnesses Solomon Smith, Benjamin Drake and Danll. Everett.

1535 (S 64) 1757 July 15 1758 June 23 **SMITH, Richard R.,** of N. Y. City, schoolmaster and mariner. Wife Joanna, niece Mary Frogatt, da. of sister. Real and personal estate. The wife sole executrix. Witnesses Tobyas van Zandt, Richard Curson of N. Y. City, merchant, and Dond. Morison. Copy.

1536 (S 65) 1757 July 19 Aug. 5 **SEAL, Anthony,** of White Fryers Precinct, London, glassmaker. Cousin Elizabeth Batchelor, Edmund Shallett of Southwark, esqre., and Joseph Newdick of Cornhill, London, colourman, trustees for sister Maria, wife of Thomas Hanson, resp. children of John Perger of Lewisham, County of Kent, attorney-at-law; aunt Mrs. Deane, Anthony Blew. Executors the two trustees. Witnesses Cha. Searse of the Inner Temple, William Howard and John Hopton. Proved in London. Copy. N. Y. letters testamentary granted to Christian Jacobson, mariner, as attorney for trustees.

1537 (S 66) 1757 May 20 1761 Octbr. 12 Dutch **SCHOONMAKER, Antje,** widow of Benjamin S. junior, of Rochester, Ulster Co. Son Benjamin; sisters Elisabeth, Catharina, Susannah and Sarah. "Worldly estate." Executors bro. Jacobus Depuy jun. and bro.-in-law Joseph Schoonmaker. Witnesses Benjamin Depuy, Cornelius Depuy and Johannis van der Merker.

1538 (S 67) 1758 Novbr. 29 1762 Novbr. 24 **SCHUYLER, Cornelia,** of Albany, widow of John. Sons Philipp, Cortlandt, Stephen, da. Geertruyd, widow of Peter Schuyler. Land in Cortlandt Manor, houses and lots in Queen Str., N. Y. City, personal property. Codicil of Aug. 26, 1760, gives legacy to children of da. Geertruyd, vizt. Cornelia and Peter Schuyler. Witnesses to will Pr. Stuyvesant, John Stevenson and James Stevenson, both of Albany, merchants, who sign also as witnesses to codicil with William Ashton. Copy.

1539 (S 68) Misplaced, belongs to H. (Hepworth).

1540 (S 69) 1758 March 22 July 27 **SPARHAM, Thomas,** of N. Y. City, surgeon. Wife Margaret, sole heiress and executrix of real and personal estate. Witnesses John Bowie, Sarah Swanser and William Rhinelander, cordwainer. Copy.

1541 (S 70) 1758 Jany. 20 June 5 **SMITH, Joseph,** of Newburgh, Ulster Co. Wife Leuiny, da. Mary. "Worldly estate," part of which is derived from bro. William Smith. Executors the wife, Henry Smith of Newburgh and Daniel Thurston. Witnesses Daniel Denton, Sarah Conklin and Leonard Smith.

1542 (S 71) 1759 Decbr. 21 1760 Decbr. 22 **STEVENS, Timothy,** of the Oblong, Dutchess Co. Wife Lidiah, sons Matthew and Timothy, da. Lidiah. Land on Croton River, personal property. Executor bro. Nathan Stevens of Danbury. Witnesses Joshua Barnum of South Prect., said Co., farmer, Temperance Parkins and Joseph Crane.

1543 (S 72) 1759 July 17 1768 May 26 **SCHERMERHOORN, Reyer,** of Rynbeek Prect., Dutchess Co., blacksmith. Wife Marritje, sons Barent, Jacob, Johannis and Jan, daughters Gerritje, wife of Gerrit Heermans, Jannetje and Cathelina. Real and personal estate. Executors son Jacob and bro.-in-law Johannis B. ten Eyck of Livingston Manor. Witnesses Augustinus Turck, Barent John ten Eyck and James Stenhouse.

1544 (S 73) 1759 Novbr. 25 Decbr. 18 **SMITH, Zophar,** of Huntington, Suffolk Co. Wife Susannah, children vizt. two sons and also daughters not named. Real and personal estate. Executors bro. John Bailey and David Rusco. Witnesses Joseph Lewis of Huntington, merchant, and William Grlffes. Copy.

1545 (S 74) 1759 April 3 1764 Febry. 10 **SCHUYLER, David,** of Conajohary, Albany Co. Eldest son Peter D., second wife ——, and children by her, vizt. John, Adoniah, David, Philipp, Jacob, Anna Margreta, Alida and Cathalina. Homefarm, land in Rensselaerswyck Colony and in Surinam, personal estate. Executors Sir William Johnson, Bart., Sybrant van Schayk, "old Major" Petrus P. Schuyler, Dominie Johan Kasper Lappeus, Abraham Yeates, High Sheriff of Albany Co., Johannes Degarmoy and Conraet Matys. Witnesses Hendrick Eckler, Joseph Meyer, both of Albany Co., farmers, and Caspar Bauer.

1546 (S 75) 1759 March 25 1761 May 18 **SMITH, Nathan,** son of Nathan, of Crom Elbow Prect., Dutchess Co., yeoman. Wife Rachel, son Nathan and other children not named. Real and personal estate. Executors the wife and bro. James Smith. Bro. Isaac Smith mentioned. Witnesses John Adams, Samuel Bemon and Joseph Powell, yeoman.

1547 (S 76) 1759 Septbr. 1 Octbr. 8 **SUTTON, Benjamin,** of North Castle, Westchester Co. Wife Elenor, children Rachel, Abegell, John, Benjamin, Rukin, Charles, Josuah, Caleb, Mary. Real and personal estate. Executors the wife, son John and son-in-law Stephen ffaronton. Witnesses Benjamin Smith, Joshua Hutchings of said Co., farmers, and John Leverich. Copy.

1548 (S 77) 1760 July 6 1761 Novbr. 27 **STEPHANSON, Roulof,** of Haverstraw Prect., Orange Co. Wife Manche, sons Albert, Stepan, Roulof and William, daughters Mary, Elesabeth and Alche, an expected child. Real and personal property. Executors William Campbell and Abraham Stevenson. Witnesses Lucas Stevenson, Lammerdt Smith and Niklas Stevenson, farmer.

1549 (S 78) 1760 Septbr. 15 1768 Febry. 26 **SCHNEIDER (Snyder,) William,** of Rynebeek Prect., Dutchess Co. Wife Geertruy, sons Johannes Pieter, Harme, William, Adam, daughters Marya, Eva, Catryn, Geurtruy and Elsie. Real and personal estate. Executors sons William, and Adam and Pieter Sherp. Witnesses Jacob Bitzer, yeoman, Tryntie Hoffman and Martin Hoffman.

1550 (S 79) 1760 Octbr. 20 Decbr. 26 **STRONG, Benjamin,** of Gorshen, Orange Co., esquire. Children Catary, Elesabeth, Jerusha, Mary, Milesent and James. Real and personal estate. Executors bro. Selah Strong and John Bruster, both of Orange Co. Witnesses Daniel Tuthill, John Brewster jun., of Orange Co., planter, and Edward Brewster.

1551 (S 80) 1760 Septbr. 22 1761 June 18 **SCHOOLCRAFT, William,** of Schoharie, Albany Co., blacksmith. Wife Maria, heiress of all real and personal estate, including "what shall fall to me from my Grand Father William Cammer." Executor Sybrant G. van Schaick. Witnesses Jacob van Schaick, Evert John Wendell and Peter Lansingh.

1552 (S 81) 1760 Novbr. 19 1761 July 13 **SCHERMERHORN, Jacob,** of Livingston Manor, Albany Co., yeoman. Sons Cornelius, Jacob, Tunis, William and Martin, daughters Neeltie, wife of Johannes Radclift, of Livingston Manor, Polly, wife of Jerom Haulenbake. Real and personal estate. Executors sons Jacob, Tunis and William. Witnesses Dirck Jansen, Elias Hasbrouck and Peter Radclift.

1553 (S 82) 1761 March 21 1762 May 28 **SCHUYLER, Peter,** of N. Y. City, esquire. Wife Mary, sister Cornelia de Peyster, da. Catharine Schuyler. Real and personal estate. Executors the daughter and bro. John Schuyler. Witnesses William Smith jun., Samuel Jones and George Clinton. Copy.

1554 (S 83) 1761 May 20 1762 May 28 **SCHUYLER, Adoniah,** of N. Y. City. Wife Geertruy, children Ranslaer, Mary, Swan, John, Peter, Adoniah and Philipp. Land in the Provinces of N.Y. and N. J., personal estate. Executors the wife, brothers John and Peter and David Johnson of N. Y. City merchant. Witnesses James Melrose of Bergen Co., N. J., gardner, James Still and David Ogden. Copy.

1555 (S 84) 1761 Decbr. 22 1762 July 10 **SMITH, Oliver,** of Goshen Prect., Orange Co. Children Nehemiah, Benjamin, Martha, Mary, Pheby, Aimy, Oliver, Joseph. Real and personal estate. Executors brothers Joshua and Solomon Smith, both of Goshen Precinct, aforesd. Witnesses John Roe of Orange Co., planter, Thomas Denton and Isaac Roads.

1556 (S 85) 1761 June 25 1782 April 30 **SMITH, John,** of Orange Co. Wife ——, sons John, Edward, six daughters, not named. Real and personal estate. Executors the two sons and Thomas Halsted, all of Orange Co. Witnesses Delilah Smith, wife of Elihu Smith, Joseph Jones of Haverstraw, yeoman, and Adriaen Onderdonck. Testator had a *Frog* in his tongue and could speak only indistinctly.

1557 (S 86) 1761 Aug. 23 1762 July 12 **SLEGHT, Catlyntie,** of Kingston Corporation, Ulster Co., widow. Sons Mattheus and Hendricus, daughters Antje, Marytie and Tryntje, grandda. Johanna, da. of dec'd son Johannes. Real and personal estate. Executors the two sons and son-in-law Moses Cantyne. Witnesses Jacob S. Freer, Evert Bogardus and D. Wynkoop jun, all of Kingston, yeomen. See No. 1528.

1558 (S 87) 1761 Febry. 9 March 4 **SIMSON, John,** of Orange Co., yeoman. Wife Isabel, friends Benjamin Burt, Samuel Lobdon, Jonathan Knap, Daniel Brown, and William Blain, bro. Hennery Simson, nephew Robert Simson, John Blain, children, not named. Real and personal estate. Executors the wife and Richard Edsal. Witnesses Samuel Vance, planter, Hugh Killpatrick and Francis Armstrong (? paper torn out).

1559 (S 88) 1762 Octbr. 26 1763 Febry. 14 **SIMPSON, Isabella,** of Goshen, Orange Co., widow of John. Son Matthew Neely, da. Mary Neely, wife of Thomas Neely, and grandda. Isabella, da. of Thomas Neely. Personal estate. Executor Arthur Beatty of Ulster Co. Witnesses Donald Cameron, Thomas Neely and Archibald Beatty.

1560 (S 89) 1762 Novbr. 3 1763 June 6 **STEEL, Thomas,** of N. Y. City, merchant, "intending shortly for London in Great Britain." Wife Sarah sole heiress and executrix of real and personal estate. Witnesses Augt. v. Cortlandt, Benjamin Helme and John Crimpsheire of N. Y. City, gentleman. Copy.

1561 (S 90) 1763 Novbr. 4 1769 March 29 **STEVENSON, James,** of Albany City. Children Sarah, wife of Col. Gabriel Christie, John, James. Real and personal estate. Executor son John. Witnesses Abraham H. Wendell, Luycas Wit Beeck and P. Sylvester. Codicil of Decbr. 6, 1764, makes unimportant change in devices. Witnesses John McCrea, James van Rensselaer and Henry B. ten Eyck.

1562 (S 91) 1763 May 16 1767 March 7 **SEELY, Ebenezer,** of Goshen Prect., Orange Co., yeoman. Wife Unis, sons John, Bezael, Israel, Josiah, Nathaniel, daughters Mercy Bartlett and Susina Sayre, grandchildren Bezael Seely, Ebenezar, Mercy, Hannah, William, Jonas, Thaddeus, Elizabeth, Hannah, Susannah, Sarah and Mercy. Real and personal estate. Executors son Israel and son-in-law James Sayre. Witnesses Elias Ward, Eliet Ward, and Daniel Everett.

1563 (S 92) 1763 Jany. 9 March 10 **STAATS, Johanis,** of Rynbeck Prect., Dutchess Co. Wife Catrene, children Philipp, Johanis, Hendrick, Petrus, Elizabeth and Margaret. Real and personal estate. Executors Zachariah Smith, Hendrick Bender and Petrus Hermanse, all of Rynbeck. Witnesses Michael Scherp of said Co., yeoman, and Ananias Cooper.

1564 (S 93) 1763 June 28 1770 Jany. 15 **STORM, Thomas,** of Philippse Manor, Westchester Co., yeoman, Wife Annace, sons Garret, Gores, Abraham, John, Isaac, daughters Catherine, wife of Jacob Byse, and Engeltie, grandchildren Christina and Ann, daughters of dec'd son Thomas, Abraham, son of son Jacob dec'd. Real and personal estate. Executors sons Garret and Isaac and neighbour William Davis esqre. Witnesses Abraham Adriance, Dirck Hegeman and John Clements.

1565 (S 94) 1764 March 24 May 23 **SMITH, Lambert,** of Haverstraw Precinct, Orange Co. Wife Elisabeth, sons Aury and John. Real and personal estate (a Dutch bible). Executors Jacobus Vanderbelt, Andries Onderdonck and Derick Vanderbelt, all of said Precinct. Witnesses Benjamin Wise, farmer, Johannes Hase, labourer, and Andries Onderdonck jun., farmer, all of Orange Co.

1566 (S 95) 1765 Septbr. 4 1767 May 5 **SMITH, John,** of Ulster Co. Wife Mary, son William, bro. James Smith and nephew John Robert, son of bro. James. Land at Shangunk, personal estate. Executors John Neely jun., John Davidson and the wife. Witnesses Samuel King of New Windsor Prect., yeoman, Margaret Davidson of Wallkil Prect., widow, and Jenet Miller.

1567 (S 96) 1765 May 17 May 28 **SANDERS, Robert,** of Albany City, merchant. Children Peter, Maria, Catharina, Deborah and Elizabeth. Land in Ulster Co., in Albany City, on Brickers Island, Hudson R., in Dutchess Co., personal property (a large Dutch bible, silver tankards, one marked M. L., a do. teapot marked R. S., one with cypher of parents name, R E S, do. mugs, do. soup spoons, do. salt cellars, 24 do. spoons, do. wine server, do. tumbler, silver tankard marked R. G., a diamond ring). Executors bro. John Sanders and Stephen van Rensselaer. Witnesses Seymon Johs. Veeder, merchant, Peter Lansingh, alderman, and Gysbert Marselis jun., trader, all of Albany.

1568 (S 97) 1765 Jany. 12 June 11 **SOMERDICK, Exbarth,** of Rumbouts Prect., Dutchess Co. Wife Elizabeth, children Sarah, William and Jacob. Real and personal estate. Executor Tunis Somerdick of N. Y., Joseph Harris and Zacharias van Voorhis, both of said Co. Witnesses Nathl. Sackett, Isaac ter Bush and Thomas Ludlow.

1569 (S 98) 1766 May 2 Aug. 29 **SCOTT, Adam,** of Wallkil Prect., Ulster Co. Wife Sarah, sons Alexander and John, an expected child. Real and personal estate. Executors David Jaggers and John Millikin, both of said Prect. Witnesses Andrew Kidd, James Kid, both of Ulster Co., yeomen, and James Fulton.

1570 (S 99) 1767 Octbr. 3 1771 Octbr. 14 **STANTON, Jeremiah,** late Lieutenant, of Margaret Street, Cavendish Square, London, now of Richmond Co., N. Y., gentleman, "intending soon to embark for England." Wife Louisa Teresia, son George Augustus, daughters Diana Maria and Louisa. Real and personal estate. Executors the wife, bro. John Stanton, Captain R. N. and George Harrison of N. Y. City, gentleman. Witnesses Peter Marquis de Conty, James Leadbetter and Richard Harrison of N. Y. City, attorney-at-law. Codicil of June 19, 1769, provides for son William Edward, born since making will. Witnesses Morley Harrison, James Leadbetter and Richard Harrison. Copy.

1571 (S 100) 1767 April 11 April 17 **SAYRES, Joseph,** of Goshen Precinct, Orange Co. Wife Sarah, sons James, John, Benjamin, Daniel, Stephen, Jonathan, daughter Martha, Jost Daree, Garret Daree, Sarah Daree and Hannah Daree. Real and personal property. Executors sons James and John. Witnesses Derrick Smith, Daniel Reeve and Samuel Sayres.

1572 (S 101) 1767 Aug. 8 1768 Febry. 3 **SIMSON, Alexander,** of Orange Co. Wife Rachel, sons Robert, John, Samuel, Henry, stepson Garrit Smith. Real and personal estate. Executors son John and Richard Edsall, esquire. Witnesses Ino. McCamly, cordwinder, Charity Bowhanon and Bridgit Sullivan.

1573 (S 102) 1767 Octbr. 5 Novbr. 2 **SMITH, Henry,** senior, of Ulster Co. Children Mary, Margret, John and Elizabeth. Real and personal estate. Ann Wickham to be guardian of the children and with Leonard Smith executrix. Witnesses Jas. Kip, Richard Lewis of N. Y. City, innkeeper, and Ann Thompson. Proved in N. Y. City.

1574 (S 103) 1769 Febry. 27 1778 Novbr. 3 **SOUTHERLAND, David,** of New Cornwall Precinct, Orange Co., yeoman. Wife Mary, grandson Charles Southerland, sons Andrew, David, Alexander, granddaughters Mary and Jane, daughters of dec'd son Patrick, daughters Jane, wife of William Edminster, Lesbia (?), wife of Moses Clerk, Mary, wife of Robert Farrier; da.-in-law Margret, widow of son Patrick. Real and personal estate. Executors the wife, Andrew Southerland and Alexander Southerland. Witnesses Amos Mills, Patrick McDonell (Donald) and Thomas Palmer.

1575 (S 104) 1769 June 11 Decbr. 5 **SEELY, Eunis,** of Woodbury Clove, New Cornwall Prect., Orange Co., widow. Grandson Gideon, stepda. Hannah Devenport, grandson Peter, granddas. Mary and Deborah. Personal estate. Executor the stepson-in-law, grandson Oliver Devenport and Gideon Florance. Witnesses Johannes Snock, Hannah Snock and Lewis Donnovan of Orange Co., schoolmaster.

1576 (S 105) — **SMITH, Daniel,** of Smith Town, esquire. Draft of will, incomplete. Wife Mary, daughters Irene, Deborah, Sarah and Mary, sons Daniel, Salomon. Land on Smith Town—Brookhaven road, homefarm, personal property (a silver tankard, a do. cup).

1577 (S 106) 1769 Aug. 15 1770 Jany. 16 **SCHRYVER, Nicholas,** of Rhinebeck Prect., Dutchess Co., yeoman. Wife Anna Maria, sons Christian, Henry, Petrus and Jacob, daughters Eva, wife of Thomas Omfrey, Catherine, wife of Petrus Frere, Margriet; Dutch Refd. Church at the Flats, the Poor of Rhinebeck Prect. Real and personal estate. Executors son Henry, sons-in-law Thomas Omfrey and Petrus Freer. Witnesses Jost Weder, John Sickner and Nathaniel Conklin.

1578 (S 107) 1770 Jany. 24 1772 Decbr. 19 **STOUTENBURGH, Jacobus,** of Charlotte Prect., Dutchess Co. Wife Margaret, children William, Jacobus, John, Peter, Luke, Annatje and Margaret. Real and personal property (a silver tea pot to descend to the child or grandchild, etc., named Margaret). Executors sons William, John and Luke. Witnesses John Barrack, Christian Dob and James Livingston of Poughkeepsie, gentleman.

1579 (S 108) 1770 Aug. 16 Octbr. 16 **SMITH, Hannah,** of Ulster Co., widow. Children Daniel, Jesse, Phebe, Joshua, William, George, Tabith and Ann. "Worldly substance." Executors son George and William Denn. Witnesses Thomas Bull of Wallkil Prect., said Co., yeoman, Mary Bull and Agnis Umphrey.

1580 (S 109) 1770 Novbr. 10 1773 June 22 **SCHUYLER, Myndert,** of N. Y. City, merchant. Wife ——, children Ann Bogert and Myndert. Real and personal estate. Executors the wife, the daughter and her husband Nicholas Bogert, John Thurman jun. and Henry Remson jun. Witnesses Peter de Riemer, G. Duyckinck of N. Y. City, merchant, and Henry Holland esquire.

1581 (S 110) 1770 May 28 1775 Aug. 17 **SNUR, Barentie,** of Kinderhook, Albany Co. William, son of Peter van Slyck, Barentie, da. of Betson Krampton, Ledia, da. of Moses Engerson, Dorothy, wife of said William van Slyck, Cornelius, son of Michael Collons, Hannah van Slyck, wife of Francis van Buren, Eva van Slyck, wife of Harme van Buren, children of Joghem van Slyck, Peter, son of Peter van Slyck jun., Peter, son of Johs. van Slyck, Teunis, son of Isaac van Slyck, Johanna Engerson, wife of Samuel Hopkins. Money bequests, furniture, a gold chain, a large Dutch bible. Executor William van Slyck. Witnesses Dirck Gardenier and Johannis D. Vosburgh of Kinderhook, yeoman.

1582 (S 111) 1770 Jany. 28 1786 June 12 **STRAAT, Jacob,** of Tappan, Orange Co., yeoman. Wife Sarah, children Dirck, Sarah, Jacob, John. Land in Haverstraw Precinct, personal property. Executors the three sons. Witnesses Myndert Hogenkamp, Jan Myndert Hogenkamp, of Orange Town, yeoman, and Robert Pigot, of N. Y. City, schoolmaster.

1583 (S 112) 1770 Aug. 16 Octbr. 5 **STEWART, John,** of Goshen, Orange Co., blacksmith. Wife Elisabeth, sons John, Colvel, Asa, Nathan, Gilbert, daughters Mary, Elisabeth and Eunis. Homefarm, land bought from Benjamin Carpenter, from Elkana Fuller, dec'd, do. at Newborough, Ulster Co., do. in Newingland or Boston Government, do. in Ulster Co., bought of John Dill, personal property. Executors the wife, son John and bro.-in-law John Bradnor. Witnesses Danl. Everett, yeoman, James Steward and Silas Steward.

1584 (S 113) 1777 March 10 1783 Febry. 10 **SWARTWOUT, Rudolphus,** of Rombouts Precinct, Dutchess Co. Wife Sarah, sons Jacobus and Johannis, daughters Aeltie, wife of Cornelius Adriance, Elisabeth, wife of Francis Hasbrook, Killetie, wife of Theodorus (?) Adriance. Real and personal estate (4 silver table spoons, 6 do. tea spoons. Executors bro. Jacobus Swartwout, Abraham Schenck, George van Noordstrand and Thomas Burris. Witnesses Joseph Wood, Hendricus Wyckoff of said Precinct, esquire, and Hannah Pudney.

1585 (S 114) 1771 June 24 Novbr. 5 **SNEDEKER, Abraham,** of Haverstraw Prect., Orange Co. Abram Thew, Thunis, son of brother Johanias Snedeker, Abraham, son of bro.-in-law Harmanus Tolman, Peter and Naltye, children of sister Sarah and bro.-in-law Peter van de Woort (Naltye is the wife of Joseph Johnson), sister Elizabeth, wife of John Smith at the Hook, Naltye, wife of Jacobus de Klerck, bro. Garret Snedeker, children of dec'd bro. Theodorus Snedeker, sister Rebecca Tolman, children of sister Altye Cortie,

Thunis Thew and Harmanus Cortur (?). Real and personal estate. Executors Abraham Thew, David Pye and nephew Thunis Snedeker. Witnesses Rem Remsen, Paul Hesler and James Paul.

1586 (S 115) 1771 March 15 1773 Octbr. 6 **SHARPE, Thomas,** of Albany City. Son Jacobus, daughters Anne, Auriantie and Mary, wife of John Monier. Real and personal estate. Executors the three daughters. Witnesses Peter van Bergen, John Hilton and Thomas I. Williams.

1587 (S 116) 1772 Jany. 14 Octbr. 14 **SHAFER, Adam,** of Rhinebeck Prect., Dutchess Co., yeoman. Wife Geertruyd, sons Adam, Philipp and other children, not named. Real and personal estate. Executors son Jacob, bro.-in-law Wilhelmus Feller and son-in-law Johannes Sickner. Witnesses Petrus Krans of said Prect., farmer, Christian Schriver and Henry Schriver.

1588 (S 117) 1773 Novbr. 3 1774 Prob. March 30 **SNEDEKER, Thunis,** of Haverstraw Prect., Orange Co., yeoman. Bro. Theodorus Snedeker, Naeltie, wife of David Brown, Ariantie, wife of Solomon Waring, Sarah, wife of Luke Taller, Mary Snedecker, Rebecca Snedeker. Real and personal estate. Executors Abraham Thew and bro. Theodorus Snedeker. Witnesses William James, Altie Snedeker and David Pye of Orange Co., farmer.

1589 (S 118) 1773 May 6 1779 May 25 **SCHOONMAKER, Benjamin,** of Rochester Township, Ulster Co. Wife Jenneke, son Cornelius, grandson Benjamin Schoonmaker. Real and personal estate. Executors Jochem Schoonmaker jun. and son Cornelius. Witnesses Benjamin Depuy junior, Joseph Depuy, both of Rochester, farmers, and Jacobus Bos jun.

1590 (S 119) 1773 March 21 1774 July 8 German **SCHERTZ, Johannes D.,** of Livingston Manor. Wife Anna, da. Catrina, an expected child. Personal estate. Executors Henrich Schoeffer and Friederich Patz. Witnesses Johann Friederich Ries, Jonas Miller and Christoffel Hoener of Claverack.

1591 (S 120) 1773 Octbr. 3 1774 Febry. 15 Dutch

SCHOONMAKER, John, of Ulster Co. Sons Petrus, Jochem and Lodowyck. Personal estate (a Dutch bible). Executors sons Jochem jun. and Lodowyck. Witnesses Thomas Schoonmaker jun., Jochem D. Schoonmaker and John Schoonmaker.

1592 (S 121) 1774 July 8 1775 Jany. 9

SEBRING, Cornelius I., of N. Y. City, merchant. Father Jacob Sebring, brothers John, Jacob, Isaac and Joseph, sisters Femetie and Catharine, nephew John Suydam, son of dec'd sister Altie. Real and personal estate. Executors brothers John and Jacob junior and Nicholas de Peyster. Witnesses Wm. de Peyster, Henry Rutgers jun. and Abrm. W. de Peyster of N. Y. City, esquire.

1593 (S 122) 1775 Febry. 12 April 8

SIMERALL, Thomas, of Wallkil Prect., Ulster Co., farmer. Son-in-law Jeames Colwal, sons Robert Simerall and William Simerall, daughters Margaret, Christian and Elizabeth. Real and personal estate. Executors Jeames Colwall, James Kidd and Benjamin Booth. Witnesses Thomas Bull, John Booth and Absalom Bull.

1594 (S 123) 1775 March 14 1786 March 21

SMITH, John, of Rumbout Prect., Dutchess Co., yeoman. Wife Margaret, children Joseph, Mary, Martin, James, John, Jacob, William, Cornel. "My estate." Executors brothers-in-law Platt Rogers and Martin Wiltse, also friend Henry Cornell. Witnesses John A. Brinckerhoff, William Humfrey jun. of said Co., farmer, and Joseph Smith.

1595 (S 124) 1775 Octbr. 25 1778 Decbr. 15

SCHOONMAKER, Fredrick, of Marbletown, Ulster Co., yeoman. Sons Thomas and Fredrick, children of daughters Antje, wife of Harmanus Rosekrans, Elizabeth, wife of Abrm. Klaarwater, Rachel, wife of Samson Sammons, Lydia, wife of Benjamin Hasbrouck, Maria, wife of Andries Roosa, Sarah, wife of Johannis Rosekrans, Tesintje, wife of William Wood, grandson Jacob DWitt, son of dec'd son Jochem Schoonmaker,

Jacobus Elmendorph Kool, husband of da. Hester. Real and personal property. Executors the two sons. Witnesses Jacob Schneyder, Christopher Snyder, both of Marbletown, farmers, and Ch. D. Witt.

1596 (S 125) 1775 Febry. 21 March 27

SEGENDORPF, Jurie (George), of Dutchess Co., yeoman. Wife Anna, children Jurie and Harmanus. Personal estate. Executors Peter Segendorpf, Adam Segendorpf and David Shafer. Witnesses Frans Neher of Rhinebeck Prect., William Cramer and Frederick Cramer of Livingston Manor, all farmers.

1597 (S 126) 1776 29th Day 6th Month 1784 Febry. 28

SOULE, George, of Great Nine Partners, Dutchess Co., blacksmith. Wife Lydia, son Rouland, grandson Joseph, son of dec'd son George, daughter Margaret, who has five daughters, not named, children of dec'd da. Lydia, not named. Real and personal estate. Executor son Rouland. Witnesses John White and Elijah Hoag, yeoman.

1598 (S 127) 1776 Aug. 1 1783 April 19

SMITH, Jeremiah, of Orange Co. Wife Elizabeth, son Jeremiah, grandsons Jonas and Joel Smith, granddaughters Dorothy and Elizabeth Veal, da. Elizabeth Veal. Real and personal estate. Executors son Jeremiah and son-in-law Wait Carpenter. Witnesses Archibald McCurdy, Phebe Denn and William Denn of Ulster Co., schoolmaster.

1599 (S 128) 1776 June 12 1778 March 3

SMITH, Elizabeth, of Wethersfield, Hartford Co., Connt., widow of the Honble William Smith of N. Y. City. Elisha Williams, son of Rev. Dr. Solomon Williams, Samuel, son of Elisha Williams, Rev. Eliphalet Williams, his wife Mary, their son Solomon, and daughters Anne and Mary, Ezekiel Williams and wife Prudence, bro. John Scott of Norwich, merchant, Rev. Dr. Solomon Williams and his sons Colonel William Williams and Dr. Thomas Williams, his daughters Mary Salter and Christian Salter, Yale College, Rev. John Marsh, Mrs. Lockwood, Rev. Joshua Belding, Rev. Burragés Merriam, John Newson, John Treat, Mrs. Margaret Hancock, stepchildren of Honble. William Smith, Thomas Smith, John Smith, Joseph Smith, Mrs. Livingston, Mrs. Torrence (widow), Mrs. Margaret Smith; Rev. Abraham Ketteltas, Mrs. Katherine Gordon, Mrs. Hay, Andrew Bortwich, late husband's granddaughter Mary, da. of John Smith, merchant, Mr. Vandervoort and Miss Elizabeth Ledyard, his wife's sister, son of Rev. Bostwick, late Pastor of the Church at N. Y., Rev. John Brainard, missionary among the Indians, Col. Israel Williams of Hatfield, Mrs. Ashley of Deerfield, Mrs. Livingston, widow of Judge Livingston, Rev. Mr. Gordon, Sarah, widow of Colonel Chester, Mr. Edey, Colonel Wyllys of Hartford. Real and personal estate (6 silver spoons, a do. salver, a small do. waiter, a do. teapot, a set of do. knives and forks, two do. candlesticks, snuffers and snuffdish, a diamond ring). Executors Ezekiel Williams, brothers in England mentioned. Witnesses O. W., P. B. and T. N. Proved at Hartford, Connt. Copy.

1600 (S 129) 1776 June 20 1787 April 26 **SNEDEKER, Garret,** of Haverstraw, Orange Co., yeoman. Wife Altie, brother Johannis Snedeker, John Thew, son of sister Elcie Coerter, nephews Richard and Theodorus, sons of dec'd bro. Theodorus Snedeker, Theunis, John and Garret, sons of bro. Johannis. Real and personal estate. Executors the wife, John Thew and Richard Snedeker. Witnesses Theodorus Polhemus, Abraham Polhameus, of Haverstraw, weavers, and Theodorus Poulhameus jun.

1601 (S 130) 1777 April 30 1778 Octbr. 15 **STRONG, Nathaniel,** of Cornwal Prect. Orange Co. Wife Amy, sons Selah, Nathaniel, daughters Rachel, Hannah, Mary and Julianer. Real and personal estate. Executors Jesse Woodhull, esqre, and brothers Samuel and Nathan Strong, all of Orange Co. Witnesses James Mathews, James Tuthill and Thomas Moffat.

1602 (S 131) 1778 July 25 1784 March 8 **SEBRING, Cornelius,** of Dutchess Co. Wife ——, daughters Katherine, Margaret, son Isaac. House and lot in N. Y. City, personal property. Executors son Isaac and stepson Archibald Currie. Witnesses John Brinckerhoff, Theodorus van Wyck of Dutchess Co., esquire, and Chas. Young.

1603 (S 132) 1778 July 23 1779 May 13 **SWEZY, David,** of Goshen Prect., Orange Co. Wife Elizabeth, sons David and Jonathan, da. Elizabeth Satterly, grandda. Mary Dains. Real and personal estate. Executors the two sons. Witnesses Noah Carpenter, of said Co., blacksmith, Bethiah Aldrig and Mehetable Hallock.

1604 (S 133) 1778 Febry. 16 1779 Febry. 19 **SMITH, John Carpenter,** of Goshen Prect., Orange Co. Children Richard, Ama, John, Phebe, Jesse and Asa. Personal estate. Executors bro. Waid Carpenter and Samuel Gale. Witnesses Samuel Baly, yeoman, David Baly and John Conner.

1605 (S 134) 1778 July 3 1786 Septbr. 12 **SHOOK, Martinus,** of Livingston Manor. Wife Anna Elsje, sons Johannis and William, children of da. Geertruy, at present wife of Marte Miller, viz.: William Dennius, Johannis Dennius and Petrus Dennius, da. Eve Geertruy, wife of Peter Snyder. Real and personal estate. Executors the two sons and Dirck Jansen, who having renounced as executors John D. Robinson of Claverack, carpenter, is made administrator. Witnesses Christian Valkenburgh, Heinrich Polwer of said Manor, farmer, and Baltis Siemon.

1606 (S 135) 1779 Septbr. 6 1782 Septbr. 20 **SCHOONMAKER, Johannis,** son of Jacobus, of Rochester, Ulster Co. Wife Geertruy, daughters Maria and Helena, an expected child, nephew Johannis Low. Real and personal estate. Executors the wife, brothers-in-law John Cantine and Charles Brodhead and nephew Cornelius Cole. Witnesses John Evans, Louis Brodhead of Marbletown, farmer, and Christopher Tappen of Kingston, esquire.

1607 (S 136) 1779 Jany. 27 1783 Febry. 7 **SANDERS, John,** of Schonectady, Albany Co., merchant. Wife Debora, children Margerieta, Maria, wife of John Ja. Beekman, John, Sarah, wife of John Sanders Glen, who has son Jacob Sanders Glen, Elsje, wife of Myndert Schuyler ten Eyck, who has son John Sanders ten Eyck. Houses and lots in Schonectady, land near it, do. on Aries Creek in Tryon Co., do. on White Creek in the Patent granted to Lieut Henry Farrant, house and lot in 3d Ward, Albany, near the Church of England, personal property. Executors the wife and son John. Witnesses Alexander Vedder, Peter van Benthuysen, hatter, and Abraham Oothout, esquire.

1608 (S 137) 1780 Decbr. 13 1782 Febry. 20 German **SCHERP, Peter,** of the Camp, Albany Co. Children George, Petrus, Maria, wife of Peter Wissmer, Gertoje, wife of Frederick Maul, Margrita, children of dec'd da. Catharina, late wife of Philipp Rockefeller, vizt: Petrus, Eva and Catharina. Real and personal estate. Executors sons George and Petrus Scherp, Christian Philipp and Henrich Will. Witnesses Johannes Peter Russ, Abrm. J. Delameter of said Co., farmer, and Rev. Gerhard Daniel Cock.

1609 (S 138) 1781 June 3 1782 Febry. 9 **SCHOONMAKER, Godfrey,** of Claverack, Albany Co. Wife Annamaria, children Henry, Elisabeth, Margaret, Catherine, Johanes, John Mathias, Hannah and Godfrey. Real and personal estate. Executors George Lown and Johannes Stall. Witnesses Johann Goerg (George) Goebel, farmer, Wynant Mantil and Martin Delong.

1610 (S 139) 1781 Septbr. 17 Novbr. 1 **SIMSON, Joseph,** of Charlotte Prect., Dutchess Co., yeoman. Wife ——, a son and a daughter, not named. "My substance." Executors father Joseph Simson senior and brothers Peter and James Simson. Witnesses Ananias Cooper, Alexander B. Thompson and Frederick Haver of said Co., farmers.

1611 (S 140) 1781 Novbr. 22 1785 April 26 **STRAIGHT, Frederick,** of Rynbeck, Dutchess Co. Wife Catherine, children Frederick, Christina Ham, Margaret Ule, Catherine Lodawick, children of dec'd da. Maddalan Bander, of dec'd da. Mary Eckert, of dec'd son George, son-in-law Frederick Ham, grandsons Counradt Ham and Casper Ham, grandda. Maddleen Moor. Real and personal estate. Executors son Frederick and son-in-law (?) Counradt Ham. Witnesses Petter Eckert, Abraham Fredenburgh, both of said Co., yeomen, and Hugh Willson.

1612 (S 141) 1781 Febry. 22 1782 June 14 **SWART, Josaias,** of Schohary, Albany Co. Wife Geerdreuy, children Tenes, Bartholomaus, Sarah, Engel, Eva, Steynge, Maria, heir of dec'd da. Geertruy, viz: Josaias Clerk, heirs of dec'd da. Susannah. Homefarm, land in Smith Dorp on E. side of Schohary Kil and other land in Schohary Patent, personal property. Executors the wife, son Tenes and Johannes I. Lawyer. Witnesses Adam Seth Vrooman, farmer, Daniel McMichael, blacksmith, and William Schermerhorn.

1613 (S 142) 1782 Febry. 16 Novbr. 23 **SAYER (Sawyer), James,** of Orange Co., farmer. Wife Elizabeth, children Benjamin, Moses, Matthew, Sarah, March, Temperance. Real and personal estate. Executors the wife, John Steward and Benjamin Carpenter. Witnesses Anthony Dobbin, Michael Jackson and Thaddious Finch of Goshen Precinct.

1614 (S 143) 1782 Febry. 21 1783 Jany. 26 **SCHUYLER, Margaret,** widow of Colonel Philipp Schuyler of the Flats, Albany Co. Geertruy, wife of Dr. John Cochran, Philipp Schuyler, Stephen I. Schuyler, children of Cortlandt Schuyler dec'd, Henry Cuyler, Philipp Cuyler, Cornelius Cuyler, Abraham C. Cuyler, Elizabeth, widow of James van Cortlandt, Margaret, wife of Isaac Low. Real and personal estate. Executors Philipp Cuyler and Stephen I. Schuyler. Witnesses Myndert Roseboom, John A. Wendel and Mat. Visscher.

1615 (S 144) 1782 Aug. 11 1783 Jany. 10 **SERVICE, Peter,** of Tryon Co., farmer. Wife Madallaine, sons-in-law Jacob Kitts and Johannes Kitts. Real and personal estate. Executors the two sons-in-law. Witnesses James Platto of Cachnawage, Tryon Co., yeoman, Godfrey Shew and Stephen Shew.

1616 (S 145) 1782 June 11 1787 Febry. 1 **SMITH, James,** of Montgomery Prect., Ulster Co., surgeon. Son James, by first wife Anne Anderson, sons Thomas, Frederick, Abraham, and Charles Lynam by second wife Rebecca Neelly. Real and personal estate. Executors James Bartley, John Bartley, living on Gillaspy's former farm, and Robert McCurdy. No witnesses; proved by the testimony of Benjamin Sears, cooper, and James McClaughry, merchant, both of said Prect., as to handwriting.

1617 (S 145 bis) 1782 Decbr. 6 1783 Jany. 20 **SMITH, James,** of Goshen Prect., Orange Co. Wife Ruth, an expected child, niece Sarah Bradner, stepson Daniel Carpenter, nephews Asa, Richard, William and John, sons of John Smith, Jonathan, and Enus, sons of bro. William Smith, George and William, sons of bro. Joshua Smith. "My estate." Executors nephew John, son of William Smith, and Samuel Gale of Galesborough. Witnesses John Smith, cooper, Caleb Smith, weaver, and John Smith jun., all of sd. Prect.

1618 (S 146) 1783 Octbr. 28 1784 June 6 **STEVENS, Aaron,** of Albany Co. Sons Jonathan, Thomas and Hendericus, daughters Margaret and Mary. Real and personal estate. Executors the wife ——, William Stevens and Gerret Spitzer. Witnesses William Stevens, farmer, Gerrit Spitzer, weaver, both of Schenectady District, said Co., and Colen McLeland.

1619 (S 147) 1783 July 22 1785 April 21 **SPRINGSTEEN, Hermanus,** late Private 2d N. Y. Regt., now of Poughkeepsie Prect., Dutchess Co. Wife Altje, sons Coenrad and John, daughter Mary. Personal estate. The wife sole executrix. Witnesses Saml. Dodge, Comfort Johnson and Richard Dodge of N. Y. City, gentleman. Proved in N. Y. City.

1620 (S 148)
1783
March 22
Aug. 19

STEVENS, William, of Paulings Prect., Dutchess Co., yeoman. Wife Mary, sons Gideon, Samuel, Thomas, Ephraim, William, Joseph, Roger, daughters Keziah Reynolds, Hannah Shearman, Deborah Parks, Lydia, Susannah, Mary, grandsons Zebulon and Ebenezer Saule, sons of da. Keziah Reynolds. Homefarm, land on or near Otter Creek, N. H., personal property. Executor Elder Samuel Waldo of said Precinct. Witnesses John Robinson, Ebenezer Moor, yeomen, and Abner Chase.

1621 (S 149)
1783
Febry. —
Octbr. 13

SMEDES, Petrus, of the Green Kil, Kingston, Ulster Co., miller. Wife Catharina, son Petrus, daughters Gerritje, Sarah, Elizabeth, Jackamyntje, children of dec'd da. Magdelena, of dec'd da. Catherina, of son Benjamin, vizt. John, Petrus, Jacob and Elizabeth. Real estate includes a farm at Shawangonk, personal property. Executors the wife, son Petrus, grandson Coenradt I. Elmendorph and Albert Pawling. Witnesses Johannis van Wagenen jun., Petrus van Wagenen jun. and Jacob van Wagenen, all of Hurley Town, said Co., farmers.

1622 (S 150)
1783
Septbr. 6
Octbr. 7

STEPHENS, Alexander, of Haverstraw Prect., Orange Co., yeoman. Children Stephen, Peter, Abraham, Hendrick, Maria, Elizabeth, Jonitee and the wife of Dowe Vanderbelt. Real and personal estate. Executors sons Stephen and Peter, Jacobus van Orden and Resolvert R. van Houten. Witnesses Stephen Stephens, Hendrick Stephens, both of said Precinct and David Pye, esquire.

1623 (S 151)
1783
Novbr. 21
1784
Novbr. 17

SMITH, John, of Cornwall Prect., Orange Co. Children Keziah, John, Martha, Sarah, heirs of dec'd da. Ellethea. "My estate." Executor son Joseph. Witnesses Henry Mandeville, Jacob White and Jeremiah Clark of Cornwall Prect., esquire.

1624 (S 152) 1784 April 28 1785 May 10 **STURGIS, Nathan,** of Fredericksburgh Prect., Dutchess Co. Wife Mary, son Thadeus, daughters Rhodais and Sary. Real and personal estate. Executors the wife and Stephen Hurlbutt. Witnesses Humphrey Ogden jun. of said Co., farmer, David Sturgis and Humphrey Ogden.

1625 (S 153) 1784 Octbr. 23 1785 Jany. 8 **SCHRAM, William,** of Lonenburgh, Albany Co., yeoman. Wife Catharine, children Peter, Clement, Frederick, Veldte (Valentin), Johannis, Jeremiah, Maria, wife of William Halenbeck, Geertruy, wife of Jacob van Buskirk, Annatje, wife of Mathys Bronk. "Temporals." Executors sons Peter and Clement and son-in-law Mathys Bronk. Witnesses Henry Knoll, Frederick Lantman of Coxhacky Distr., farmer, and his wife Catharina.

1626 (S 154) 1784 May 28 Novbr. 4 **SHURRIE, Johannes,** of Rumbouts Prect., Dutchess Co., farmer. Children Elizabeth, wife of Jeremiah Jones, Catherine, wife of Laurence Haff, Maria, wife of John Conkland, Anitie, wife of Laurence Conkland, Lydia, wife of James Hicks, children of dec'd da. Rachel, do. of dec'd da. Sarah. Real and personal property. Executors sons-in-law Laurence Haff, John Conkland, Laurence Conkland and James Hicks. Witnesses Stephen Townsend, Thomas Rosekrans, yeoman, and Walter Scot.

1627 (S 155) 1784 April 17 May 6 **SMITH, Caleb,** of Goshen Prect., Orange Co. Wife Abigail, sons Henry Conkling, Stephen, John, Caleb, Joshua, da. Abigail. Real and personal estate. Executors sons Henry Conkling Smith and Stephen Smith, bro. Stephen Smith and Benjamin Conkling. Witnesess James Carpenter, John L. Moffat, Coe Gale and Reuben Hopkins.

1628 (S 156) 1784 July 13 1786 Jany. 23 **SLINGERLAND, Abraham,** of Rensselaerswyck Colony, yeoman. Wife Rebecca, sons Tunis, Peter, Albert, Abraham, Stephen, daughters Catriena and Marytje. Real and personal estate. Executors the wife and sons Peter and Abraham. Witnesses Christena Slingerland, Hester Slingerland and Jacob de Garmo of Albany Co., cordwainer.

1629 (S 157) 1784 Septbr. 17 Novbr. 11 **SMITH, Azariah,** of Amenia Prect., Dutchess Co. Wife ——, children Anna, Ezeriah, David, Elijah, children of da. Sarah. Homefarm, land in Saulsbury, personal property. Executor son Elijah. Witnesses Stephen Jones of said Co., farmer, George Sornberger and Ichabod Paine.

1630 (S 158) 1784 March 25 1787 Jany. 12 **SEARS, Benjamin,** of South East Prect., Dutchess Co. Wife Abigail, children Benjamin, Lydia, Abigail, Sunderlin, Stephen, Seth and Mercy. "Worldly estate." Executors son Seth, and son-in-law Shaw Young. Witnesses James Sackett, Joseph Sackett and Edmond Wright of said Co., farmer.

1631 (S 159) 1785 13th Day 3d Month June 25 **SPENCER, Benjamin,** of Beekmans Prect., Dutchess Co., yeoman. Wife ——, children, Henry, Elnathan, Amey, Lydia. "My estate." Executrix the wife. Witnesses Elnathan Sweet, Joseph Lancaster, both of said Co., farmers, and Samuel Whipple.

1632 (S 160) 1785 April 2 1786 Jany. 18 **SALISBURY, Sylvester,** of Kingston, Ulster Co., yeoman. Wife Elsie, children Rachel, Lawrence, John and Anna Marytje. Real and personal estate. Executors the wife, brothers-in-law Philip Hooghteling and James Roe, cousins Abraham Salisbury and Joseph Oosterhoudt. Witnesses Jacob Borhas, yeoman, Jacobus Hasbrouck jun., merchant, and John Eltinge, merchant, all of Kingston.

1633 (S 161) 1785 June 17 Novbr. 7 **SMITH, Samuel,** of Charlotte Prect., Dutchess Co., yeoman. Children Daniel, Robert, George, Samuel, Cattrain. "My estate." Executors sons Daniel and Robert and Samuel Mott. Witnesses James Valentine, William Gay, both of Dutchess Co., farmers, and John Laroy.

1634 (S 162) 1785 24th Day 3d Month 1786 April 10 **SOWLE, James,** of Saratoga, Albany Co., hatter. Wife Jemima, sons Jonathan, James, Robert, daughters Levina, Deborah, Lydia, Eunice and Hannah. Land at Nantucket, homefarm and personal property. Executor and guardian bro. Jonathan Sowle. Witnesses Gideon Mead, Asa Brown, yeoman, and Rebecca Leggett.

1635 (S 163) 1785 May 16 1786 May 17 **ST. JOHN, Abram,** of Fredericksburgh, Dutchess Co. Mother Experience St. John, wife Lucy, children Lucy, Sarah, Elizabeth, Eunice, Lydia, Abraham and John Reed. Real and personal estate. Executor the wife. Witnesses Nathaniel Hayes, Stephen Northrup, carpenter, and Ephraim Jones.

1636 (S 164) 1786 April 15 May 15 **SMITH, Samuel,** of Washington Prect., Dutchess Co. Wife Hannah, sons Samuel, Israel and Waters, daughters Hannah, Elizabeth and Mary. "My estate." Executors the wife, son Samuel and bro. Israel Smith. Witnesses James Jackson, William R. Sutherland and Henry S. Platt of said Co., farmer.

1637 (S 165) 1794 Decbr. 16 1795 Octbr. 12 **SMITH, William,** mariner. John Bill, of the Third Ward, N. Y. City, innholder, sole heir and executor of personal estate. Witnesses Benjamin Bates Smith and William Cummins of N. Y. City, marshall. Printed form.

1638 (S 166) 1794 April 17 —— **SHAW, Samuel,** U. S. Consul at Canton, now on board the ship *Washington* at anchor in the Bay of Sunda. Wife Hannah, bro. William Shaw of Boston, merchant. Real and personal estate. Executors the wife, the brother and Thomas Randall, commander of the ship *Washington*. Witnesses Samuel Hubbart, James Dodge and Benjamin Shaw. Not proved.

1639 (S 167) 1797 Octbr. 7 1798 May 13 **STEIN, Robert,** of Coxsakie Distr., Albany Co., mariner. James, son of bro.-in-law Ahasverus Turk, Ahasverus, grandson of said bro.-in-law, sister-in-law, widow Sarah Turk, Phoebe Burns, adopted da., da. Mary, wife of Henry Hoofteeling. Real and personal estate.

Executors bro.-in-law Ahasverus Turk, John P. Pearss of N. Y. City, merchant, and John Delamater of said city, merchant (son of Isaac D., dec'd). Witnesses John McMurray, John Smith and Francis Child.

1640 (S 168) 1795 March 24 **SHON, John.** The whole will under this No. reads: "I appoint my Father Mr. George Shon of South Patherton Bridgemills near Crookhom within the County of Somersetshire in the Kingdom of Great Britain my sole Executor and Mr. Richard Morris, Auctioneer of the City of New York executor in trust for my Father.

John Shon × his mark.

Done in the presence of
John Bamfield,
John Nichols (of New York City, cabinet maker),
Thomas Chapman.

1641 (S 169) 1711 June 27 **SCHUYLER, Margaret,** widow of Philipp, sometime of Albany, merchant. Children Peter, Geertruy, Alida, Arent, Philipp, Johannis, Margaret, children of son Brant vizt. Philipp, Oliver and Johannes. Real and personal estate. Executors sons Peter and Johannes, son-in-law Robert Livingston, husband of da. Alida. Witnesses Jonathan Rumney, Anthony Caster and John Dunbar.

1642 1786 March 9 1787 Febry. 6 **SANDS, Stephen,** of N. Y. City, clock- and watchmaker. Wife Mary, children Nathaniel, Philipp Bransen, Stephen, Elizabeth and Ann. Real and personal estate. Executors brothers Robert Sands of Rhinebeck, Dutchess Co., and Joshua Sands of N. Y. City, merchant. Witnesses Henry Rogers, merchant, William Lupton and Henry Mitchell, watchmaker. Recorded in Wills and Probates, Vol. I., p. 21.

1643 1787 March 27 April 11 **SICE, John,** of N. Y. City, baker. Father John Michael Sice, sisters Elizabeth Mathewman, Rebecca Dalgall, brother Michael Sice. Real and personal property. Executors Wendell Boos and Thomas Stagg, both of N. Y. City, bakers. Witnesses Cornelius I. Bogert, John Buxton and John Sticklen of N. Y. City, cordwainer. Recorded ut supra, p. 103.

1644 **STUYVESANT, Gerardus,** of the Bowery, Out
1774 Octbr. 26 Ward, N. Y. City. Sons Nicholas and Peter sole heirs
1786 Aug. 7 and executors with the Honble. John Watts, John van Cortlandt and James van Cortlandt as advisers. Witnesses Aug. v. Cortlandt, Thos. Wendover jun. and John Lasher jun. Recorded ut supra, p. 105.

1645 **SEARS, Isaac,** of N. Y. City, merchant. Wife
1775 April 27 Sarah, children Esther, Sarah, Mary, Rebecca, Isaac,
1787 April 24 Jasper and Abigail Drake Sears. Real and personal estate. Executors the wife and Paschal N. Smith. Witnesses Donald Campbell, esquire, Joseph Peirson and Eliakim Raymond, merchant. Recorded ut supra, p. 120.

1646 **SMYTH, John,** late of Perth-Amboy, N. J., now of
1784 Febry. 18 N. Y. City. Wife Susannah, son Andrew, niece Frances,
1787 Aug. 20 da. of Charles Moore, cousin James Johnston of the Fresh Ponds near Cranbury, Middlesex Co., N. J. Real estate or what the Americans have not confiscated of it, personal property. Father Lawrence Smyth and mother Margaret Smyth mentioned. Executors John de Hart and John Chetwood, both of Elizabeth Town, attorneys-at-law with James Parker and Walter Rutherford as advisers. Witnesses Thos. Skinner, Lambert Moore of N. Y. City, esquire, and I. Moore jun. Recorded ut supra, p. 151.

1647 **SHEARMAN, Uzail,** of N. Y. City, shipwright.
1773 Novbr. 24 Wife Aletty, children Uzail, Aletty, Edward, Hannah
1788 April 2 and John. Real and personal estate. Executors George Hopson, butcher, and William Elsworth, gunsmith, both of N. Y. City. Witnesses Huybert v. Wagenen, merchant, Simon Schermerhorn and I. H. van Wagenen. Recorded ut supra, p. 183.

1648 1772 Septbr. 21 1792 April 16 **STILLWELL, Richard,** of Middletown Township, Monmouth Co., N. J. Wife Lydia, children Gershom, Mercy, Mary and Catherine. House and lot in N. Y. City, homefarm, land at Neycake, do. in Shrewsbury Township, personal property. Executors the wife, Thomas Hartshorne and Robert Hartshorne. Witnesses Sarah Hartshorne, Elizabeth Hartshorne, at date of proof wife of Robert Bowne of N. Y. City, merchant, and Richard Hartshorne. Recorded ut supra, p. 339.

1649 1792 Febry. 28 June 5 **SHELDON, Aaron,** of Hudson, Columbia Co., trader. Mother Eunice Phelps of Great Barrington, Berkshire Co., Mass. "My estate." Executor Samuel Edmunds of Hudson. Witnesses John Farnam and W. King. Will signed at Great Barrington. Recorded ut supra, p. 343.

1650 1779 April 7 1792 Decbr 20 **STEVENS, John,** of Libanon Township, Hunterdon Co., N. J. Wife ——, son John, da. Mary, sister Sarah Stevens, bro. Richard Stevens. Homefarm, house and lot in N. Y. City, farms in the Society's Grant Tracts in Hunterdon Co., personal property (plate). Executors the wife, son and daughter. Witnesses Peter Garrabrants jun. of Bergen Co. N. J., saddler, Jacob Eick and William Eick. Recorded ut supra, p. 378.

1651 1793 July 25 Aug. 7 **SHERWOOD, William,** ropemaker, late of N. Y. City, now of the vicinity of Augusta, Georgia. Wife ——, children Moses and Mary. "Temporal estate." Executor Andrew Innes. Witnesses Jesse Newton, Yelvered Reardon and William H. Jack. Proved in Richmond Co., Georgia. Recorded ut supra, p. 405.

1652 1783 Novbr. 16 1794 April 10 **SMITH, William,** of N. Y. City. Wife and children, not named, except son William. John Blenderleath, husband of da. Janet. Land in Moore Town, personal property. The wife sole executrix. Witnesses Thos. Smith of N. Y. City, esquire, Robert Whyte and James S. Smith. Recorded ut supra, p. 410.

1653 1794 June 15 July 17 **SEGUR-PETRAY, Louis Antoine, Vicomte de,** Chevalier de l'ordre de St. Louis, late of the Province of Perigord, France, now of N. Y. Wife Marie Nicole Ralin, sons Claude Nicholas Louis and Joseph Byprien Segur. Real estate in France, U. S., and Island of St. Domingo, personal property. The wife guardian and executrix. Witnesses Antude Menyin, Charles Adams and Noel John Barbarin. Recorded ut supra, p. 426.

1654 1779 Decbr. 14 1791 Septbr. 5 **SPAVOLD, Mary,** of Bawtry, County of York, England, widow. Daughter Elizabeth, wife of James Barker, of Katskil, Albany Co., N. Y., niece Catharine Harrot; Mary, da. of Robert Spencer of Hodsark, George Gooddy of Bawtry, mercer and draper. Personal property. Executor George Gooddy. Witnesses Mary Howson and Thos. Thirkell, George Remsen of N. Y. City, merchant, attorney for Elizabeth Barker, made administrator. Recorded ut supra, p. 436.

1655 1794 Febry. 12 1795 Febry. 2 **STEUBEN, Frederick William, Baron de,** of N. Y. City. Former Aids-de-Camp Benjamin Walker and William North, adopted as children, John I. Mulligan. Real and personal property (gold hilted sword, given by U. S. Congress, gold box, given by N. Y. City). Executors Benjamin Walker and Wm. North. Witnesses Charles Williamson, Charles Adams and W. H. Robinson of N. Y. City, merchant. Recorded ut supra, p. 460.

1656 1784 April 26 1795 May 28 **SPRAGGS, Samuel,** of N. Y. City, schoolmaster. Wife Mary, sole heiress and with nephew Edward, son of Daniel Dunscomb, executrix of real and personal estate. Witnesses William Deane, Daniel Voorhis and Abraham Lynsen. Recorded ut supra, p. 471.

1657 1785 Aug. 29 Septbr. 27 **SCHUYLER, Philipp,** of New Barbadoes. Sister Swans Schuyler and her son John, nephews John Rensselaer and Peter, sons of bro. John Schuyler. Land on Passaic River, personal property (a silver bowl). Executors bro. John Schuyler, Arent Schuyler and nephew Adoniah Schuyler. Witnesses James Brown, John Marley and Pierre E. Fleming. Proved in Bergen Co., N. J. Recorded ut supra, p. 528.

1658
1815
July 20
Aug. 8

SHIELDS, Barnard, late U. S. soldier. Thomas Dexter and wife Lucy of Albany sole heirs and executors of real (?) and personal property. Witnesses Christr. Monk, Aaron Lyon and James Dexter. Recorded ut supra, Vol. II., p. 326.

1659
——
1795
Octbr. 2

SPRANGER, John, of N. Y. City, ship carpenter, letters of administration on the estate of, granted to his widow Sarah Spranger. Recorded ut supra, Vol. III., p. 158.

1660
1811
Decbr. 30
1818
Aug. 6

SMITH, James, of Broadalbin, Montgomery Co. Thomas Hewitt, of the same place, widow Anna Hewitt, also of Broadalbin. Land in lot No. 10 Milton, now Town of Genoa, Cayuga Co., personal property. Executors Thomas Hewitt and John Parsons. Witnesses James Ford, Daniel Stewart and Luther Wheeler. Recorded ut supra, Vol. IV., p. 99.

1661
1805
Decbr. 25
1823
Jany. 18

STRINGER, Samuel, of Albany City, physician. Daughters Lydia and Gertrude, wife of ? (not named). Houses and lots in Market Str., on West side of Middle Lane, lot No. 137 Pitts Town, Rensselaer Co., a silver coffeepot, marked on the bottom E. W., a do. oval bowled soup spoon, a do. teapot, a do. milkpot, 12 do. desert spoons, 2 do. salt spoons, 2 do. salt cellars, all marked I. T. E., a pair of do. pint mugs with the letters R. G. T., 6 do. large table spoons, all marked E. W., 3 do. large table spoons, marked S. W. E., one do. chased punch laddle, 2 do. salt spoons, 2 do. salt cellars, all unmarked, a fine library of medical works, about 160 titles, surgical instruments, bankstock, turnpike stock and other personal property. Trustees Honble. John Lansing jun., and Samuel Stringer Lush. Executors Stephen Lush and Barent Bleecker. Witnesses Isaac Truax, J. H. Wendell and John Brinckerhoff. Recorded ut supra, p. 123.

1662 1803 June 20 1827 March 2 **SCHUYLER, Philipp,** of Albany City. Children Philipp Jeremiah, Rensselaer, Angelica, wife of John Barker Church, Elizabeth, w. of Alexander Hamilton, Cornelia, wife of Washn. Morton, and Catherine, wife of Samuel B. Malcolm, grandsons Philipp Schuyler, son of dec'd son John Bradstreet Schuyler, and Stephen van Rensselaer, son of dec'd da. Margaret and Stephen van Rensselaer sen. Land at Saratoga, houses and lots on Market Str. and on Montgomery Str., Albany, personal estate. Son Philipp Jeremiah Schuyler, sons-in-law Alexander Hamilton and Stephen van Rensselaer guardians to grandsons Philipp Schuyler and Stephen van Rensselaer. Executors sons Philipp Jeremiah and Rensselaer, sons-in-law John Barker Church, Alexander Hamilton and Stephen van Rensselaer. Witnesses Abm. ten Broeck, G. W. Mancius, Catherine Mancius and Margaret ten Broeck. Recorded ut supra, p. 207.

1663 1821 May 30 1824 Aug. 9 **SWIFT, Elijah,** of Aurelius Town, Cayuga Co. Bro. Jarvis Swift sole heir of real and personal estate, George Casey of the Town of Aurelius executor. Witnesses Wm. I. Hopkins, Reuben Hawley and John Hawley. Recorded ut supra, Vol. V., p. 23.

1664 1824 April 20 1828 May 27 **STONE, William,** of Whitestown, Oneida Co. Wife Rachel, Nathan Richardson of the same place and wife Betsey. Real and personal estate. Executors the wife and Nathan Richardson. Witnesses John G. Weaver, I. H. Osborn and M. Talcott. Recorded ut supra, p. 78.

1665
1661
Decbr. 31
Dutch

SWART, Gerard, Schout (Sheriff), of Rensselaerswyck Colony and wife Anthonia van Ryswyck. The survivor, no children. Real and personal property. Witnesses Jan Labatie, Jan Dareth, Dirck van Schelluyne, Notary. Albany Co. Records, Notarial Papers, I., p. 188 (202).

1666
1673
April 19
Dutch

SANDERSEN, Robert, of Albany, and wife Elsie Barents. Children Elisabeth, Marytie, Saertie and Annetie. Real and personal estate. The survivor executor. Witnesses Claes Ripsen van Dam, William J. Nottingham and Adriaen van Ilpendam, Notary Public. Albany Co. Records, Notarial Papers, I., p. 530.

1667
1678
Septbr. 7
6 P.M.
Dutch

SCHERMERHOORN, Reyer Jacobsen, of New Albany, born there, and wife Ariaentie Arents, born in the Esopus. The survivor heir and executor. Children mentioned, but not named. Real and personal property. Witnesses Omy de la Gransie, Evert Jansen (Wendel) and Adrien van Ilpendam, Notary Public. Albany Co. Records, Notarial Papers, II., p. 49.

1668
1683
May 1
1683-4
March 4
Dutch

SCHUYLER, Philipp, old Magistrate of Albany, and wife Margareta van Slichtenhorst. Children Geertruy, wife of Stephen van Cortlandt, Alida, wife of Robert Livingston, Peter, Brant, Arent, Philipp, Johannes and Margriet. Real and personal property. Executor and guardian of minor children the survivor, in this case the wife. Witnesses Mr. Cornelis van Dyck and Magistrate Dirck Wessells (ten Broeck) and Robert Livingston, secretary. Albany Co. Records, Court Minutes 1680-5, p. 511. See No. 1473.

1669
1685
March 24
Dutch

SCHUYLER, Arent, of Albany, and wife Janneke Teller. Expected children. Real and personal estate. Executor the survivor. Witnesses Jan Verbeeck, Jacob Abrahamsen and Jan Becker, Notary Public. Albany Co. Records, Notarial Papers, II., p. 552.

1670 1688 May 21

SHERMERHOORN, Jacob Jansen, of Shinnechtady, Albany Co., yeoman. Wife Jannetje, children Ryer, Symon, Helena, wife of Myndert Harmensen, Jacob, Machtell, wife of Johannes Beeckman, Cornelis, Jannetie, Neeltie and Lucas. Real and personal estate (plate). The wife sole executrix. Witnesses Domine Gideon Schaets and Jacob Staets. Albany Co. Records, Wills, I., p. 26.

1671 1689 July 1

SMITH, Carsten Frederiksen, and wife Tryntje Warners, of Albany. Children Margaret, 20 yrs. old, Warner, 15 yrs, Anna Mary, 12 years, and Magdaleentje, 9 yrs. Real and personal estate. Executor the survivor. Witnesses Stoffel Jansen Abeel, Evert Jansen (Wendell) and Robert Livingston, secretary. Albany Co. Records, Minutes 1686–1702, p. 122.

1672 1692 Aug. 23

SCHOONHOVEN, Geurt Hendricksen, of the Half Moon, Albany Co., yeoman. Wife Maritje Cornelissen, children Jacobus, Hendrick, Hendrickie, Geertruy and Jacomyntie, heirs of da. Margriet. Real and personal property. The wife sole executrix. Witnesses Jacob Staets and Hendr. van Dyck. Albany Co. Records, Wills, I., p. 85.

1673 1708 Aug. 31 1730 July 27 Dutch

SYMONSEN, Pieter, of Rensselaerswyck Colony. Wife Neeltie, children Symon and Maritie. Real and personal property. Executors brothers Gerrit and Volkert Symonsen. van Rensselaer Manor Records, No. 1226.

1674 1709 Decbr. 15 Dutch

SCHUYLER, Abraham, of Albany City, freeman. Wife Geertruy, children David, 17 yrs. old, Christyna, 15 yrs., Dirck, 10 yrs., Abraham 5 yrs., and Jacobus, 3 yrs. Real and personal estate. Guardians and executors brothers David and Myndert Schuyler and brothers-in-law Wessel and Zamuel ten Broeck. Witnesses Andries Coeyemans, Johs. Cuyler and Pieter van Brugh. Albany Co. Records, Wills, I., p. 186.

1675 1712–13 Jany. 28 — Dutch **SLINGERLANT, Aarent,** of Rensselaerswyck Colony. Wife Geertruy, children Teunis, Gerrit, Engeltie and Sarah. Real and personal estate. Executors bro. Albert Slingerlant, Johannes Myngaal and Casper van Hoesen. Witnesses Johannis Myngal, Albert Slingerlant and Rutger Bleecker. Albany Co. Records, Wills, I., p. 160.

1676 1717 April 5 1719 April 8 **SCHERMERHOORN, Reyer,** of Schonectady Co., esquire. Wife Aryantie, sons John, Jacob, Aerent, daughter Janneke, wife of Volkert Symonsen, children of dec'd da. Cataline, late wife of John Wemp, vizt. Myndert, Ryert and Ariaentie, bro. Luycas Schermerhoorn, Hannah, da. and Wilhelmus, son of Garret Symonsen, Aryantie Symonsen, wife of Daniel Danielsen. Real estate in Schonectady, do. in the Raretans, East N. J., personal property. Executors the three sons. Witnesses Dou Aukes, Capt. Philipp Schuyler and Phil. Verplank. Albany Co. Records, Wills, II., p. 163. See No. 1480.

1677 1719 May 26 1720 June 3 **SPOOR, Gerrit,** of Albany. Wife Mary, children Johannes, Annmary, Cornelia, William and Abraham. Real and personal estate. Executors the wife and Claas van Woert. Witnesses Abraham Staats, Johannis Maesen and Rutger Bleecker. Albany Co. Records, Wills, I., p. 107.

1678 1725 June 7 1371 July 13 **SLINGERLAND, Albert,** of Niscothaa, Albany Co., yeoman. Wife Hester, children Johannis, Thomas, Engeltie, wife of Anderies Wittbeek jun., Teunis. Real and personal estate. The wife sole executrix. Witnesses Joh. Myngal, Jacob Roseboom and Rutger Bleecker, Albany Co. Records Wills, I., p. 188.

1679 1731 Septbr. 24 1739–40 Jany. 30 **STAATS, Abraham,** of Claverack, Albany Co., yeoman. Wife Elsje, da. of Johs. Wendell, sons Abraham, Samuel, Jochem, Johannis, Isaac and Jacob, daughters Maria, Catrina, Sarah, Elizabeth and Elsje. Real and personal estate. Executors sons Johannis and Isaac, Mr. Barent Staats, Robert Sanders and Johannis Provoost. Witnesses Jacob Staats, Abraham Provoost and Barent Sanders. Albany Co. Records, Wills, I., p. 224.

1680
1781
Octbr. 2
1782
June 19

STALEY, Hendrick, of Albany Co., yeoman. Sons Matthias, Haramanis, Hendrick, Jacob, George, Rulif, grandson John Staley. Real and personal property. Executors sons Hermanis and Hendrick. Witnesses John Manning, George Lin and Christyan Manning. Albany Co. Records, Wills, I., part 2, p. 35.

1681
1793
Decbr. 27
1794
Jany. 11

SCHUYLER, John Courtlandt, of Water Vliet, Albany Co. Wife Angelica, da. of Henry I. van Rensselaer, mother Barbara, widow of Courtlandt Schuyler. Real and personal estate. Executors father-in-law Henry I. van Rensselaer, uncle Stephen I. Schuyler for property in America and mother Barbara Schuyler for estate in Europe. Witnesses Francis Nicoll, Ozias M. Huntington and Ph. Schuyler. Albany Co. Records, Wills, I., part 2, p. 61.

1682 (T 1)
1672
May 14
1679
May 23

TITUS, Hannah. Sons Content, John, Samuel, Abiall, da. Susanna. Real and personal estate. No executors named. Witnesses Richard Williams and Thomas Skidmor. Proved at Huntington.

1683 (T 2)
1701
May 5
——

TAYLOR, Edward, of N. Y. City. Mrs. Elizabeth Plumley, children Mary, Edward and Charles. Real and personal estate (half a dozen silver forks, 6 do. spoons, 6 do. porringers). Executors William Nicoll, Ebenezer Wilson and John Hutchins. Witnesses Dan Bate, René Rezeau, Abraham Rezeau and Roger Jones. Codicil of Septbr. 16, 1701, makes William Nicoll, Ebenezer Wilson, Edward Antill and Elizabeth Plumley heirs, in case the children should die without issue, and the three first-named executors and guardians. Witnesses René Rezeau and Wm. Dalton.

1684 (T 3) 1708-9 Febry. 5 1717-8 March 6 Dutch

ten HOUT, Severyn, of Shawankonk, Ulster Co., farmer. Wife Geertruy, stepson Jacob Bruyn, who has son Severyn ten Hout, sole heirs and executors of real and personal property. Witnesses Col. Jacob Rutsen, Major Johannis Hardenbergh, Capt. Johannis Schepmoes and Johannis ten Broeck.

1685 (T 4) 1714-5 Febry. 4 1717-8 Febry. 6 Dutch

ten BROECK, Dirck Wesselsen, late of Albany, now of Livingston Manor. Wife Christyna, sons Wessel, Samuel, Johannes, Tobias, daughters Elsje, wife of Johannes Cuylaer, Catalyntje, wife of Johan Lissier, Cornelia, wife of Johannes Wynkoop, Geertruy, wife of Abraham Schuylaer, Christyna, wife of Johannes van Alen, Elizabeth, wife of Antny Costers, Lidia, wife of Volckert van Vechten. Houses and lots in Albany, land in Livingston Manor. Executors the wife and the four sons. Witnesses Jan Vosburgh, William Scott and Peter Vosburgh.

1686 (T 5) 1716 Septbr. 6 1736 July 10

ten EYCK, Geertie, widow of Jacob, of Albany. Children of dec'd son Barent ten Eyck, vizt. Jacob, Joannes, Geertie, Annetie, Maria and Barentje, sons Coenraat and Hendrick, daughters Mayke, wife of Andries van Petten of Schanegtade, and Jenneke; (Jacob ten Eyck of N. Y. City, bolter, above named as son of Barent, is called great grandson of Coenraat ten Eyck). Real and personal estate. Executors the two sons, Hendrick and Coenraat. Witnesses Jacob Staats, Geysebert Marcelis and Nicolaes Bleecker. Seal.

1687 (T 6) 1716 Decbr. 11 1722 Octbr. 29 Dutch

TITSOOR, Willem, of Dutchess Co. Wife Neeltje, da. of Teunes Swart, children Abraham, Stefanus, Jacob, Isaac, Elizabeth, wife of James Witte (?), Eghie, wife of Abraham Freer, Rebecca, wife of Jurean Quick, Helena, wife of Damon Palmetier, Areiantie, wife of Jacob van Kuykendal and her da. Maragrieta, and Marya Titsoor. Real and personal estate. Executors the wife, son Jacob and Capt. Barent van Kleeck. Witnesses Henry van der Burgh, Elias van Bunschooten and Leonard Lewis.

1688 (T 7) 1704 Decbr. 2 1716 June 26 **TEUNISSEN, Egbert,** of Albany City. Wife Marritie Brad, sons Teunis, Dirck, Benjamin, Barent, da. Susanna. Real and personal property (a bible, a silver cup). Brothers in-law Dirck and Daniel Brat mentioned. Executors not named. Witnesses Hendrick Hansen, Johannes Pruyn and Wouter Quackenbos.

1689 (T 8) 1718–9 Febry. 28 1719 June 5 **THOMPKINS (Tomkins), Edmond,** of Scarsdale Manor, Westchester Co., yeoman. Wife Hannah, sons Edmond, John, Eligia, Obadiah, Caleb, Roger, Joseph, daughters Susanna, Mary and Jane. Real and personal estate. Executors the wife, Noah Barton and Jonathan Odell. Witnesses Joseph Tomkins, Thomas Huddon and John Gifford. Copy.

1690 (T 9) 1724 June 12 1726–7 March 6 Dutch **TAPPEN, Teunis,** of Kingston, Ulster Co. Wife Sarah, children Jurriyaan, Marytie, Arriantie, Johannes, Catharina and Rebecca. Real and personal estate. Executors Jurriyaan and Johannes Tappen with Wilhelmus Hooghteylingh. Witnesses Pieter Tappen, Willem Schepmoes, Willem Eltinge and Steph. Gasherie.

1691 (T 10) 1730 Febry. 15 —— **TELLER, Andrew,** of N. Y. City, merchant. Second wife Mary, da. Catherine by first wife, children of uncle Oliver Teller dec'd. Real and personal estate (a Dutch bible, plate and jewelry). Executors the wife, bro.-in-law David Provoost of N. Y. City, merchant, son of William Provoost, Stephen Bayard, Jacob Goelet jun. and Abraham van Wyck, all of N. Y. City, merchants. Witnesses Simeon Soumain, Alex. Mills, Jacob Bergen and Direck van Allen.

1692 (T 11) 1732 June 16 Aug. 17 **TRAPHAGEN, Willem,** of Kingston, Ulster Co., yeoman. Stepmother Eva, sister Janitien, uncles Peter Winne of Kingston and William Traphagen of Dutchess Co. Real and personal estate. Executors cousins Abraham Burhans and Samuel Burhans. Witnesses Jan Pyetersen Oosterhoudt, Abraham Oosterhoudt and Peetervs Oosterhoudt.

1693 (T 12) 1734 Aug. 3 1742 May 1

ten EYCK, Mathys, of Hurley, Ulster Co., yeoman. Children Coenradt, Andries, Jacob, Abraham, Wyntie, wife of Jan Hendricksen, Maritie, wife of Tjerck van Keuren, Grietie, wife of Willem Burhans, Sarah, wife of Lawrence Cortreght, Ragell, wife of Cornelis Newkerk, grandda. Janneke, da. of eldest son Aldert dec'd. Real and personal property. Executors the four sons. Witnesses A. Gaasbeeck Chambers, Wessel ten Broeck and Gilbert Livingston.

1694 (T 13) 1738 April 28 1739 July 28

TALLAMAN, Tunis, of Nayack, Orange Co., carpenter. Wife Margret, sons Dowe, John, Tunis, Harmanus, daughters Greetje Blawvelt, Antye Hennion, Derrickye van Dolphsen, Maria Smith, Breahye Tallaman, Yannata Blawvelt. "My estate." Executors sons Dowe and Tunis. Witnesses Vint. Mathews, Peter Mathews, Klaes Yanson Cuyper. Seal.

1695 (T 14) 1739 Febry. 9 March 6

THOMSON, John, of Goshen, Orange Co. Wife Jean, daughters Sarah, Margret, Anna, Cathrin and Elisabeth, son William, father and mother. Real and personal estate. Executors brother Robert Thomson and bro.-in-law James Thomson, both of Goshen, overseers James Jackson, Daniel Everet and George Car. Witnesses David McCamly, William Car and David Car.

1696 (T 15) 1740 Febry. 4 Decbr. 1

THOMSON, James, of Goshen Prect., Orange Co. Wife Mary, sons George, John, James, da. Mary. Real and personal estate. Executors the wife, bro. Robert Thomson and bro.-in-law Michael Jackson. Witnesses Wait Smith, Henry Smith and Jeremiah Smith.

1697 (T 16) 1742-3 Jany. 29 1755 May 14

TAVEAU, Isaac, of N. Y. City, shipwright. Wife Sarah sole heiress and executrix of real and personal estate with legacy to sister Susannah Taveau. Witnesses John Dally, shipcarpenter, John Kip and Abel Hardenbrook. Copy.

1698 (T 17) 1743 April 27 1744-5 March 2 ten **BROECK, Wessel,** of Foxhall Manor, Ulster Co., yeoman. Children Sarah, Loweransie, wife of David Delamatre, Rachel, wife of Abraham Salsbury, Wessel, Coenraedt. Real and personal estate (a bible). Executors the two sons. Witnesses A. Gasbeek Chambers, Thomas van Gaasbeek and Gilbert Livingston.

1699 (T 18) 1745 Septbr. 17 1767 Novbr. 4 ten **EYCK, Richard,** of N. Y. City, cordwainer. Wife and children, not named. Real and personal estate. Executors the wife, father-in-law William Roome and uncle Abrm. ten Eyck. Witnesses John Riven, Cornelius Quick and John Kerfbyle. Proved by the testimony of Hester Elsworth and Sarah Bussing as to handwriting. Copy.

1700 (T 19) 1746 Octbr. 14 1751 Octbr. 26 **TENBRUCK, John,** of Poghkeepsie, Dutchess Co., shopkeeper. Wife Hannah, children Sarah and Hendricus, sister Mary. Personal estate. Executors the wife, brothers-in-law Henry Filkin and Tobias Stoutenburgh. Witnesses J. Elmendorph and Bartholomew Crannell.

1701 (T 20) 1746 March 31 May 18 Dutch ten **BROEK, Jacob,** of Kingston, Ulster Co. Wife Elisabeth, children Wessel, Cornelis, Judickje, wife of Teunis Van Vegten, Catharina, Jacob, Maria, wife of Henry de Wit, grandson Johannis, son of dec'd son Johannis. Real and personal estate. Executors the wife and sons Wessel, Cornelis and Jacob. Witnesses Counrat ten Broeck, Benjamin ten Broeck and Jan Eltinge.

1702 (T 21) 1746-7 March 14 1747 May 8 **TUTHILL, Mary,** widow of Jonathan, of Goshen Precinct, Orange Co. Son William Tuthill; Salomon Tuthill, Thomas Tuthill, John Tuthill. Personal estate. Executor James Tuthill. Witnesses Abigail Norton, Patrick Mullen and Alexander Smith.

1703 (T 22) 1746 May 6 1748 Novbr. 17 **TAREPENNING, Tunis,** of Kingston Corporation, Ulster Co. Wife Gritje, sons Gerrett, Jacobus, Abraham, Hendricus, daughters Esther, wife of Robert Hanna, Mary, wife of Petrus van Aken, Bridget, Hannah and Elisabeth. Real and personal estate. Executors the wife, son Jacobus and Abraham Hasbrouck. Witnesses Dirck Terepenning, Marynies van Aken and Jacob Tarpenning.

1704 (T 23) 1747 Aug. 1 1748 Octbr. 18 **TOLL, Daniel,** of Schonechtadie Township, Albany Co., yeoman. Grandson Carel Hanszen, son of son Johannes Toll dec'd, daughters Susannah, Hannah and Geertruyd, son-in-law Cornelius van Santvoord, da.-in-law Eva, widow of son Johannis, Sarah, da. of Peter Meby. Real and personal estate (a silver cup). Executors Peter Cornue and Rynier Mynderse. Witnesses John Visger jun, Claas van der Volgen and Joseph Drake.

1705 (T 24) 1748 July 1 1752 July 13 **ten BROECK, Dirck,** of Albany City, merchant. Wife Maragrita, children Abraham, Catharina, wife of Johs. Livingston, Christina, wife of Philipp Livingston, jun., Maria, wife of Gerardes Groesbeck, Sara, wife of Johannes H. ten Eyck, Maragrita and Dirck. Houses and lots in Albany, land in Serigtoge Patent, do. in Westenhook Patent, personal estate. Executors the wife and sons Abraham and Dirck. Witnesses John Jas. Rooseboom, Adam Yates and Johannis Spoor. The two sons qualify as executors March 18, 1768.

1706 (T 25) 1751 July 8 1758 July 18 **ten EYCK, John,** of Kinderhook, Albany Co., cordwainer. Wife Susanna sole heiress and with bro.-in-law Peter van Buren executrix of real and personal estate. Witnesses Jan Tyse Goes, Marthys Vasburgh and Arent van Dyck.

1707 (T 26) 1753 July 23 1759 May 16 **TELLER, William,** of South Precinct, Dutchess Co., yeoman. Wife Mary, children William, Jeremiah, Rachel, wife of John Lin, Anne, Mary, wife of Jacobus Buys, John, Jacobus, Isaac, Margrit, Gualterus and Sarah. Real and personal estate. Property derived from grandmother Sarah Roeloffse, otherwise called Sarah Stothoff, widow of Hans Kierstede and from father William Teller. Executors the wife, sons William, Jeremiah, John, Jacobus, Isaac and Gualterus and son-in-law Jacobus Buys. Witnesses Henry ter Bos, Cor. Osborn and James G. Livingston.

1708 (T 27) 1754 18th Day 5th Month Aug. 30 **TOWNSEND, Nathennel,** of Jericho, Oyster Bay Township, Queens Co., yeoman. Wife Martha, sons Stephen, John and Nathaniel, daughters Martha and Almey. Real and personal estate. Executors brothers-in-law Samuel Doughty and Benjamin Doughty and son-in-law Richard Willets. Witnesses William Seaman, Zebulon Seaman and Samuel Willis. Copy.

1709 (T 28) 1756 March 17 June 29 **TUTHILL, James,** of New Windsor, Ulster Co., yeoman. Wife Mary, children Joel, Thomas, James, Jamima and Mary. Real and personal estate. Executors father James Tuthill and Seely's Strong, both of Orange Co. Witnesses Ebener Seely jun, Moses Gale and John Thompson of New Windsor, schoolmaster.

1710 (T 29) 1758 Aug. 23 — **THURMAN, Susannah,** widow of Francis, of N. Y. City, mercht. Daughter Elisabeth, sisters-in-law Elisabeth, wife of Nicholas Roosevelt and Gertrude Thurman, aunts Agnes, wife of Joseph Lockwood, Grace, wife of William Williams, Sarah, wife of Isaac Brown, son Richardson Thurman, brothers-in-law Ralph and John Thurman. Real and personal estate. Executors bro.-in-law John Thurman, merchant, Nicholas Roosevelt, goldsmith, and Dirck Schuyler, merchant, all of N. Y. City. Witnesses Thomas Pettet, Abraham Bussing and John McKesson. Copy made Novbr., 1763.

1711 (T 30) 1759 March 10 1765 Octbr. 1 **TUTHILL, Freegift,** of New Windsor, Ulster Co. Wife Abigail, children Abigail, Nathaniel and Joshua. Real and personal estate. The wife sole executrix. Witnesses Col. Thomas Ellison of Ulster Co., John Ellison and William Ellison.

1712 (T 31) 1759 May 9 1762 Febry. 15

ter BOS, Henry, of Rombouts Prect., Dutchess Co. Wife Catharyna, sons Henry, Seymon, John, Isack, Benjamin, Lukas, Pieter, Jonas and Freer, daughters Elisabeth and Marya. Real and personal estate. Executors sons Henry, Seymon, John and Isack. Witnesses John Bailey, Samuel Mills of said Prect., cordwainer, and Jacobus Buys.

1713 (T 32) 1760 April 6 Octbr. 22

TELLER, John, of Dutchess Co. Wife Margret, son Jacobus, bro. Isaac Teller, sister Margret Teller. "Goods and chattels." Executors the wife and brother. Witnesses Samuel Anthoney, Charity Lumaree and Samuel Stakham.

1714 (T 33) 1761 Febry. 23 Septbr. 28

TUTHILL, Daniel, of Gorshen Prect., Orange Co., yeoman. Wife Susanna, sons Daniel, John, Phenias, Samuel, and apparently other children, not named. Real and personal estate. Executors the wife, son Daniel and Joshua Broun. Witnesses John Brewster of Orange Co., farmer, Samuel Smith and Selah Strong.

1715 (T 34) 1762 Octbr. 30 1771 Decbr. 24

TONGUE, John, of Haverstraw Prect., Orange Co., yeoman. Wife Tamason (Thomasine ?) son George, daughters Alice, Anna and Betse. Homefarm, land at Old Poundridge, Westchester Co., personal property. The wife sole executrix. Witnesses John June, Samuel Bird and David Stanley of Westchester Co., yeoman. James Clarke of Westchester Co., son-in-law of testator, made administrator.

1716 (T 35) 1765 Octbr. 30 1780 June 8

ten BROECK, Dirck, of Albany City, merchant. Wife Ann, bro. Abraham ten Broeck, sisters Catharina, wife of John Livingston, Christina, wife of Philipp Livingston, Marya, wife of Gerardus Groesbeck, Sarah, wife of John H. ten Eyck and Margaret, wife of Stephen Richard. Real and personal estate. Executors the wife, father-in-law Volckert P. Dow and bro. Abraham ten Broeck. Witnesses Peter Hansen, merchant, Stephen Groesbeck and S. v. Rensselaer. Supra, No. 1705.

1717 (T 36) 1767 Decbr. 13 1768 April 27

ter BUSH, John, of Orange Co. Wife Catherine, children John, Cornelis and Neeltie, mother Neeltie Bush. Real and personal estate. Executors the mother Neeltie Bush, Mrs. William Wickham, John de Noyelles. Witnesses John Anderson, Thomas Willson and Gabriel Winter.

1718 (T 37) 1769 Aug. 9 Novbr. 4

THORNE, Isaac, of Charlotte Prect., Dutchess Co. Wife Hannah, children Hannah, Jacob, William, Isaac, Phebe Griffin, grandson Isaac Deuel, cousin Phebe Smith, grandda. Patience Deuel. Real and personal estate. Executors sons Jacob and William with Mica Griffin. Witnesses Joseph Griffin, Edward Griffin and Joseph Thorn of Amenia Prect., yeoman.

1719 (T 38) 1769 Decbr. 8 1770 June 18

TREMPER, John George, of Rhinebeck Prect., Dutchess Co., yeoman. Wife Susanna, children Catherine, Jacob, Lena, wife of Abr. Roel. Kip, John. Real and personal estate. Executors the wife, son Jacob and son-in-law Abram Roel. Witnesses Adam Shever, Henry Diel and Christian Schultz of said Prect., schoolmaster.

1720 (T 39) 1769 Febry. 20 1784 Novbr. 4

TITSORT, Sarah, of Poghkeepsie Prect., Dutchess Co., widow. Children Leonard, Neiltie, Isaac, Thomas, Elizabeth, wife of Joseph Willson, grandda. Sarah Willson. Real and personal estate. Executors Leonard van Kleek and Leonard Lewis. Witnesses John Seabury of Dutchess Co., currier, Joseph Gale jun. and Jacob Conklin.

1721 (T 40) 1771 June 15 1775 May 24

TERNEUR, Michael, of Haverstraw Prect., Orange Co. Children Jacobus, Jannitje, wife of John Terneur, Efyee, wife of Dirck de Klerck, Sarah, wife of Edward Selyer, Mary, wife of William Dickman, Jemima, wife of William Chappel, Hendrick, children of son Jacobus, vizt: Michael, Lowrence, Jacobus, John, Hendrick, Jane, Mary, Marritye and Sarah. Real and personal estate. Executors son Hendrick and Johannis Jacobus Blauvelt. Witnesses Jacobus Turner of said Co., yeoman, Hendrick Jacobus Terneur and John Haring.

1722 (T 41) 1771 March 13 1773 April 17 **ten BROECK, Cornelius,** of Albany City, merchant. Wife Maria, son John, da. Catherine, wife of George Wray, grandson Cornelius ten Broeck jun., grandda. Jenney Wray. Real and personal estate (plate). Executors the wife and the two children. Witnesses Joseph Yates, blacksmith, Robert Yates, attorney-at-law, both of Albany and Thos. I. Williams.

1723 (T 42) 1771 Octbr. 10 1772 Jany. 2 **TERRY, William,** of Pokeepsie Prect., Dutchess Co., yeoman. Wife Ellenor, sons Edmond, William and James, step-children Peter and Frances Mullen. House and lot near the Court House and woodland, bought of James Livingston, personal estate. Executors son Edmond, James Livingston of Pokeepsie, esquire, and Myndert van Kleeck. Witnesses Jas. Livingston, Simeon Wright and Simon Newcomb of said Co., yeoman.

1724 (T 43) 1771 Jany. 16 Decbr. 11 **ter BUSH, Jonas,** of Rombout Prect., Dutchess Co., blacksmith. Brothers Henry, Simon, John, Isaac, Benjamin, Luke, Peter and Frayer ter Bush. "Worldly affairs." Executors Capt. Eleiza Dubois, Nathan Bailey, Zebulon Southard and Mathw. Brett. Witnesses Jacobus Cooper of said Prect., blacksmith, and Philipp Jacob Schaff. See No. 1712.

1725 (T 44) 1771 Jany. 31 Febry. 28 **TUTHILL, Solomon,** of Goshen Prect., Orange Co., yeoman. Children Jonathan, Mary and others, not named. Real and personal estate. Executors Abimil Yongs and Joseph Wodkins of Ulster Co. Witnesses Hugh Byrn, William Banker, Col. Benj. Tusten and Derrick Smith.

1726 (T 45) 1772 March 9 1781 Febry. 19 **ten BROECK, Petrus,** of Rhynbeek Prect., Dutchess Co. Wife Catherine Rutsen, sole heiress and executrix of "temporal estate." Witnesses James Smith, John Wm. Sutherland and Philipp Huc Manc.

1727 (T 46) 1773 Septbr. 18 1782 Septbr. 2 **ten BROECK, Johannis,** of Kingston, Ulster Co. Children Petrus, Margriet, wife of Coenraedt ten Broeck, Sarah, wife of Abraham van Gaasbeek, Catherine, wife of Jonathan Elmendorph, Geertruy, wife of John Dumond, Benjamin. Real and personal property. Executors the two sons and son-in-law Abraham van Gaasbeek. Witnesses Johans. Beekman, Jacob ten Broeck, yeomen, and Chs. D. Witt.

1728 (T 47) 1773 May 20 Septbr. 13 **TOMKINS (Tompkins), Samuel,** of Stillwater, Albany Co., yeoman. Wife Charity, sole heiress, and with John Black executrix of real and personal estate. Witnesses George Smeart and James Forbes of N. Y., tavern-keeper. Printed form.

1729 (T 48) 1773 June 29 Novbr. 22 **TOTTEN, John,** of Rumbout Precinct, Dutchess Co., farmer. Wife Lovinee, sister Rebeckah Brookes and children, sister's sons Thomas, Isaac and David Southard, sister's da. Phebe Weeks, bro. Jonas Totten and son Benjamin, da. of wife's sister Sarah van Wyck, sister's da. Lovinee Whiteman, Trinity Church at Fishkill for a bell. "Worldly goods and affairs." Executors wife, sister Rebeccah Brookes, Jonathan Brookes and Jeremiah Cooper, all of Dutchess and Albany Counties. Witnesses Samuel Mills, yeoman, John H. Sleght, merchant, both of Dutchess Co., and James Brumfield jun.

1730 (T 49) 1773 Jany. 30 April 13 **TERNEUR, Jacobus,** of Haverstraw Prect., Orange Co., yeoman. Wife Margaret, children Jacobus, Rachal, Jacamyntye, Margarit and David. Real and personal estate. Executors bro. Henry Terneur, son Jacobus and bro.-in-law Jacobus Blauvelt. Witnesses Johannes Poulhameus, Johannes van Dalfsen and John Haring of said Co., weaver. See No. 1721.

1731 (T 50) 1773 March 25 1784 Jany. 18 **TERWELLEGE (Terwillegen), Abraham,** of Shawangunk Prect., Ulster Co., yeoman. Children of nephew Teunis Terwillegen and wife Catharine, vizt. Sarah and Abraham. Real and personal estate. Executors Cornelius C. Schoonmaker, Matthew Jansen and Johannes Bruyn. Witnesses Cornelius Decker, Abraham Decker, of said Prect., farmers, and Johs. Bruyn.

1732 (T 51) 1774 Aug. 29 1785 April 16 **ten Eyck, Tobias,** of Schenectady Township, Albany Co., merchant. Wife Rachel, sons Myndert Schuyler, Henry, John Depyster, Jacob, Tobias and Barent. Real and personal estate. Executors the wife and sons. Witnesses Christr. Yates, Abraham Fonda, esquire, and John de Graef.

1733 (T 52) 1774 Octbr. 27 1784 April 17 **ter BOS, Jacobus,** of Rumbouts Prect., Dutchess Co. Wife Sary, children William, Jeames, Eleyas, Susana, Chaharyna, Sayry, Eleysabet. Real and personal property. Executors the wife, father Jacobus ter Bos, Elyas de Bouys and Isaac ter Bos. Witnesses Isaac ter Boss, of Dutchess Co., farmer, Thomas Surderd (Southard) and James Osborn.

1734 (T 53) 1774 Novbr. 10 1776 May 14 **TOBIAS, Christian,** of Charlotte Prect., Dutchess Co. Wife Ruth, sons Christian, Jacob, Frederick, Thomas, Isaac, Joseph, daughters Elizabeth, wife of Samuel Badgelly, Sarah, wife of Zacciues Newcomb, who has children James and Mary. Homefarm, land in Filkintown, personal property. Executors sons Christian and son-in-law Zaccheus Newcomb. Witnesses Abel Peters, Ezekiel Whitney and Daniel Hamill of said Prect., schoolmaster.

1735 (T 54) 1774 April 24 June 20 **ten EYCK, Anthony,** of Rensselaerswyck Manor. Wife ——, son Coenraed, daughters Cathereen, Gerritie, and Susan, children of da. Sarah dec'd. Real and personal estate, (land in Coeymans Patent, a large Dutch bible). Executors the son and daughters Cathereen and Susan. A statement appended to will calls da. Sarah Ernests, Gerritie, wife of William D. Faulkner. Witnesses James Waldron of Albany Co., blacksmith, Wilhelmus Rouw, and David McCarty, merchant.

1736 (T 55) 1726 Octbr. 24 1726-7 Febry. 23 **TRAPHAGEN, Johanis,** of Kingston, Ulster Co. Wife Eva, son William, daughter Janitie. Real and personal estate (a bible). Executors the son and cousin Abraham Burhans. Witnesses Kryn Oosterhoudt, Jan Pietersen Oosterhout, Edward Whitaker and Teunis Pietersen Oosterhoudt. See No. 1692.

1737 (T 56) 1776 March 7 1782 June 28 **TOLL, Simon,** of Schenectady Township, Albany Co. Wife Hester, children Charles H., John, Daniel, Jesse, Elizabeth, wife of John Farley, Alle, wife of John Mabie, Anneca, wife of William Kettelhun, Effie, wife of Lodewikes Fielen (Viele), Sarah, wife of Stephanus Vielen. Land at Maghquamehack on Scatecock Creek, personal estate (a large Dutch bible). Executors the wife and sons John and Daniel. Witnesses Claas de Graaf, Carel H. Toll jun., both of said Co., farmers, and Chris. Yates.

1738 (T 57) 1776 April 20 1781 April 5 **THOMPSON, James,** of Goshen Prect., Orange Co. Sons-in-law Joseph Luckey, Samuel Luckey, and John Luckey, daughters Agnes, who has children Robert and Nancy, Margaret Armstrong, Elizabeth Luckey, Catharine Luckey, Elener Newmans and Jane Luckey. Real and personal estate. Executors bro. George Thompson and cousin George Thompson, cooper. Witnesses William of said Prect., mason, Catharine McCalaughan and Wm. Thompson.

1739 (T 58) 1776 Septbr. 20 1784 May 20 **THORN, Jonathan,** of Beekmans Prect., Dutchess Co. Children Gilbert, Stephen, Samuel, Cornelia, Jeames, Cornelius, Robert and Catharine. Real and personal estate. Executors sons Stephen and Gilbert with John Cooke. Witnesses Robt. van Rensselaer, Samuel Smith of Charlotte Prect., merchant, and Killian van Rensselaer.

1740 (T 59) 1777 April 24 1778 July 30 **TOMSON, John,** of Goshen, Orange Co., yeoman. Jane and Mary, daughters of George Car, children of son-in-law Stephen Crane, Sarah Barker, grandchildren Lette and Mary Tomson. Real and personal estate. Executors sons-in-law Andrew McCord of Ulster Co. and Stephen Crane of Orange Co. Witnesses Samuel Newcomb Dod, Stephen Crane, cooper, and John Dod.

1741 (T 60) 1777 Decbr. 31 1783 Febry. 7 **ten BROECK, Catharina,** widow of Petrus of Rhynebeek Prect., Dutchess Co., esquire. Jacob Rutsen van Rensselaer, Petrus ten Broeck, son of Seymon Johnson Meyers by his wife Cornelia, da. of Jonathan Thorn, Catharina and Sarah, das. of John Rutsen dec'd, Cornelia, wife of Robert van Rensselaer, Refd. German Church at Rhynebeek, Henricus van Hoevenbergh, Catharine Hannion, John Dumont of Kingston, esquire, Petrus, son of Abraham Gaesbeek, Petrus, son of Benjamin ten Broeck, Catharina, da. of said Benj. ten Broeck, John Robert van Rensselaer. Land at Poghanaiwonk, Beekmans Prect., houses and lots in N. Y. City, personal estate (plate). Executors Robert van Rensselaar and wife Cornelia. Witnesses William Beam, William Beam jun. and Henry van Hoevenbergh, esquire.

1742 (T 61) 1778 Septbr. 18 1785 May 18 **TIETER, Hendrick,** of Rhinebeck Prect., Dutchess Co. Wife Catharine, children Catharine, Henry, William (imbecile), Philipp, John, Zacharias, Abraham, Margaret, Elisabeth. Real and personal estate. Executors sons Zacharias, Abraham and William. Witnesses Herman Hoffman, Philipp Teller and Egbert Benson.

1743 (T 62) 1780 Septbr. 19 1782 April 30 **THOMAS, Jacob,** of Rynebeck Prect., Dutchess Co. Wife Greitie, children Henry, Elizabeth, John, Mary, Sarah, Herman, Catharina and Ruliff; Jacob Yaugher and wife Elizabeth. Real and personal estate. Executors bro.-in-law Abraham Fetter, Matthew van Vradenburgh and Herman Hoffman. Witnesses Peter van Alen, yeoman, and Elizabeth Back.

1744 (T 63) 1782 Octbr. 28 1783 April 12 **TITUS, Timothy,** of New Perth, Charlotte Co., N. Y. Sons James, Timothy, Robert, Samuel and Ebenezar, daughters Lizzy and Sarah. Real and personal estate. Executors Wm. Read and Edward Savage. Witnesses Wm. Teller jun., Wm. Teller and Ahasverus Teller of Albany Co.

1745 (T 64) 1782 Aug. 9 Aug. 30 **THOMPSON, George,** of Goshen, Orange Co. Wife Elizabeth, children Elizabeth, George, James, other daughters mentioned, but not named. Real and personal estate. Executors William Allison, Doctor Daniel Wood and William W. Thompson. Witnesses Samuel Smith, Anthony Dobbin and Amaziah Bust.

1746 (T 65) 1782 Septbr. 13 1783 Septbr. 7 **ten BROECK, Catherine,** of Rhinebeck Prect., Dutchess Co. Codicil to No. 1741 calls Peter van Gaasbeeck, Petrus ten Broeck, Catherine ten Broeck, nephews and niece and leaves bequests to sister-in-law Geertruy, wife of John Dumont, father of John Dumont, mentioned in the will, nephew Jacobus J. Bruyn. Witnesses Henry van Hoevenbergh, esquire, John I. Feller and Johannis van Etten.

1747 (T 66) 1782 Jany. 29 June 4 **TOWNSAND, Robert,** of South East Prect., Dutchess Co. Wife Ama, children Rebekah Wood, Ama, Isaac, children of dec'd son Solomon, vizt: Deborah and Rebekah. Real and personal estate. Executors David Pamer (Palmer) and Thomas Veal (Vail), both of Salam. Witnesses Stephen Townsend of Salem, Westchester Co., yeoman, Joshua Lea and Thomas St. John.

1748 (T 67) 1783 Septbr. 4 Decbr. 23 **TABER, Thomas,** of the Oblong, Dutchess Co. Wife Annetherase, children Nathaniel, William, Jeremiah, Meribe Hazerd, Antheracy, Ruth, Saloma, Amey and Mary, children of dec'd da. Hannah, vizt: Thomas Taber and Hannah Farrest. Real and personal estate. Executors sons William and Jeremiah. Witnesses Abraham Thomas, Benjamin Deuel and Edward Shove of said Co., yeoman.

1749 (T 68) 1783 Decbr. 29 1784 June 4 **TRUMPOVER (Drumbauer), Andres,** of Montgomery Prect., Ulster Co., waggonmaker. Wife Elizabeth, children Elizabeth, wife of Matice Clearwater, Susannah, Mary, Cathren, Andrew, Peter, Nicolas, Margrit and Cristen. Real and personal estate. Executors Stufel Mool and Henry Cranss. Witnesses Jacob Newkirk, Adam Newkirk, of said Prect., farmers, and William Stewart.

1750 (T 69) 1783 Septbr. 5 Octbr. 14 **TELLER, Isaac,** of Rumbout Prect., Dutchess Co., farmer. Wife Sarah, children Jacobus, Oliver, Deborah, Mary and Isaac Depyster. Real and personal estate. Executors Oliver Teller, Martin Wiltsie, Peter M. de Bois and Jeremiah Cooper. Witnesses Mary de Peyster, Jeremiah Cooper of said Co., physician, and Martin Wiltse.

1751 (T 70) 1783 Decbr. 13 1785 Octbr. 18 **TAREPENNING, Hendrick,** of Shawangunk Prect., Ulster Co., husbandman. Wife Maria, sons Levi, Morenis, Eleazer, Moses and David, daughters Margaret, Jeseintie, Rachel and Elizabeth. Real and personal estate. Executors the wife, son Levi, Eliphaz van Auke and Bowdewine Tarepenning. Witnesses Boudewyn Terpenning, William Ralyea of New-Marlborough Prect., yeoman, and Jacob Conklin.

1752 (T 71) 1783 March 3 1785 June 28 **TRUMPBOUR, Johannes,** of Ulster Co., farmer. Wife Christine, sons Nicholaus and Jacob, other sons and daughters mentioned, but not by name. Real and personal estate. Executors the wife and sons Nicholaus and Jacob. Witnesses Stephanus Fiero, John Dods and Ludwigh Roessell of Sagerties, yeoman.

1753 (T 72) 1783 July 4 1785 Jany. 6 **TELLER, Jacobus,** of Schenectady, Albany Co. Wife Maria, son William, brother Gerrit T. Teller. Real and personal estate. Executors the wife, the brother and bro.-in-law Robert Yates. Witnesses Cornelius A. van Slyck, merchant, Dirck van Ingen and Jacobus van Ingen, gentleman.

1754 (T 73) 1784 Febry. 28 April 5 **THEW, John,** of Haverstraw Prect., Orange Co., yeoman. Second wife Elizabeth, son Jacobus and Thunis, three sons by first wife, not named. Real and personal estate. Executors bro. Abraham Thew and bro.-in-law Johanias Blauvelt. Witnesses Isaac Sherwood, Thomas Lawrence of said Prect., yeoman, and David Pye.

1755 (T 74) 1784 April 3 1785 June 23 **TRAVERS, Nathaniel,** of Pienpack Precinct, Ulster Co. Son Nathaniel and younger children, not named. "Substance and effects." Executor Joseph Ketchum of Wallkil Prect. Witnesses James Finch and William Denn.

1756 (T 75) 1784 April 12 July 8 **TOM, Nathaniel,** of Pawlings Prect., Dutchess Co., merchant. Wife Elizabeth, sons John and Nathaniel. Real and personal estate. Executors bro. Thomas Tom, Jonathan Lawrence and Isaac I. Talmon. Witnesses Potter Shelden, David Dunkin of said Co., farmer, and John Comins jun.

1757 (T 76) 1784 Jany. 10 April 5 **TRACY, Isaac,** of Goshen Prect., Orange Co. Wife ——, sons Zaavan and Solomon, daughters Keturah, Thankfull, Elizabeth, Mary, Ziporah, Bethsheba, Mehetable, Lois, Zirviah. Homefarm, land in Westmoreland, Suschohannah Purchase, do. in Delaware Purchase. Executors the wife and son Solomon. Witnesses James Steward, Joseph Hallsted and Henry White.

1758 (T 77) 1785 April 11 April 28 **TAYLOR, Isaac,** of Beekmans Prect., Dutchess Co., farmer. Wife Catherine, children Thomas, William, Richard, Daniel, Peter and Rachel. Real and personal estate. Executors Azariah Crandall and Jonathan Prosser. Witnesses Benjamin Prosser, of said Co., farmer, Azariah Crandall and Jonathan Prosser.

1759 (T 78) 1785 Aug. 3 Septbr. 2

TRIMBLE, Alexander, of Montgomery Prect., Ulster Co. Children William, John, George, Isabel Hill, Jane King, Elizabeth, Sarah, Alexander and Timothy. Homestead, land at Floraday, Orange Co., personal property. Executors sons-in-law Rev. Andrew King, Petter Hill and son William. Witnesses Patrick Barber of said Prect., esquire, and James Coldwell of Wallkil Prect., yeoman.

1760 (T 79) 1785 Novbr. 29 1786 April 11

TANNER, William, senior, of the Clove, Beekmans Prect., Dutchess Co., farmer. Sons William junior, Ruben, Samuel, James, grandson David Tanner, daughters Hannah Thompson, Martha Thomas, Margaret Radel, Maribe Thompson and Rachel McIntosh. Homefarm and personal property. Executors Jonathan Dennis, esquire, and Britain Talman, both of said Prect. Witnesses John Moores, Henrich Klein and Peter Cline, all of said Co., farmers.

1761 (T 80) 1787 Jany. 9 Febry. 19

TUTHILL, John, of Wallkil Prect., Ulster Co. Wife Nancy, sons Nathan, John, Daniel, daughters Fanny and Mary. Real and personal estate. Executors Samuel Wadkin and Jonathan Swezy. Witnesses Peter Stales of said Co., "laybourer," Daniel Marshall and Nancy Yates.

1762 (T 81) 1790 June 19 1801 Septbr. 2

TAYLOR, Samuel, of Albany Township and Co., farmer. Nephews Samuel, son of bro. James Taylor, Mathias, son of nephew Robert Taylor. Farm near New Scotland, personal property. Executor nephew Robert Taylor. Witnesses Elisha Hungerford, Guisbert Sharp and George Thompson.

1763 (T 82) 1799 Aug. 20 1800 March 29

TOLLY, John Frederick, of Coxsakie, Albany Co., physician. Wife Catharine, sons Henry, John, George, William. A farm, house and lot on North Str., Hudson, Columbia Co., land on Hoge Barrack or High Hill, do. in Loonenburgh Patent. Executors sons Henry and John with Henry Wells junior of Catskil, Ulster Co. Witnesses John W. Hollenbeck and Henry Wells junior.

1764 1786 Aug. 17 1787 Jany. 23 **TYLER, Margaret,** widow of Jonathan, of Bedford, Westchester Co. Abel Weeks, son-in law of dec'd husband, having married Abigail, Jonathans da., Zephaniah Miller, widower of testatrix dec'd, da. Jehannah, bro. John Williamson, who has son James, sister widow Leaner June, niece Jehanah June. "Worldly estate." Executors Lot Sarlls and Jehannah June. Witnesses Nehemiah Lounsbery of Bedford, yeoman, Stephen Lounsbery and Henry Ross. Recorded in Wills and Probates, Vol. I., p. 9.

1765 1787 Jany. 2 April 19 **TOPPING, Daniel,** of Southampton, Suffolk Co., yeoman. Wife Elisabeth, children Joseph, Seth, Abijah, Daniel, William, Elizabeth Howell, Prudence Tinnins, Martha Hildreth and Ziporah Cooper. House on "hum lot," land in Easthampton, personal property. Executor Daniel Howell. Witnesses John Norris jun., Stephen Howell and Simon Howell. Recorded ut supra, p. 116.

1766 1790 April 2 1792 June 27 **TUCKER, Robert,** late of Nova Scotia, now of Westchester Town, Westchester Co., physician. Wife Hannah, children Fanning Cobham, Cornelius Wortendyck, James, Susanna Maria and Caroline. Real and personal estate (a silver tankard). Executors the wife, Samuel Bayard of Westchester, sons Fanning Cobham Tucker, Cornelius Tucker and James Tucker, (the last two, when they have become 21 years old). Witnesses Peter de Mill, Jonathan A. Pell of N. Y. City, merchant, and Elijah Ferris. Recorded ut supra, p. 345 and Vol. III., p. 135.

1767 1789 Decbr. 2 1790 Octbr. 22 **THOMSON, John,** of Shelburne, mariner. Wife Elizabeth, children Robert and Elizabeth. "Movables and immovables." Executor not named and the widow made administratrix. Witnesses Timothy Hoody and Jonathan Baxter. Recorded ut supra, p. 514.

1768 1755 Aug. 13 1798 March 30

THOMPSON, James, of New Jersey, "resolved on a distant voyage." Wife Catherine sole heiress and executrix of real and personal estate. Witnesses Jacob Walton, Jonathan Fish and John Dunscomb, whose signatures are proved by Elenor Chambers, Henry Cruger, John Moore and Jacob Ricketts. Recorded ut supra, Vol. II., p. 73.

1769 1798 Jany. 6 Novbr. 15

THOMAS, William, of the Parish of Sangunnock, County of Carmarthen, South Wales, husbandman. Wife Hama, nephew John Robert, sisters son, (is not in the Old Country) niece Ann Robert, sisters da. Personal property in England, Wales and in America. Witnesses John Davis and David Williams of Westchester Co. farmer. Recorded ut supra, p. 83.

1770 1798 Aug. 1 Novbr. 28

TEMPLE, John, late of Great Britain, Baronet, now of N. Y. City. Wife Elizabeth sole heiress and executrix of real and personal estate; children mentioned, but not by name. Witnesses Sarah Sears, Paschal N. Smith and John L. Broom. Recorded ut supra, p. 95.

1771 1661 March 17 — Dutch

TEUNISSEN, Juriaen, of Beverwyck, and wife Wybrecht, da. of Jacobsen, brother of testatrix Jacob Cornelissen, sister of same Grietie Machielsen, son of testators sister Teunis Pietersen. Real and personal property. No executor named. Witnesses Rev. Gideon Schaets and Jacob de Hinsse, surgeon. Made before Notary Dirck van Schelluyne. Albany Co. Records Notarial Papers I., p. 57.

1772 1663 May 26 — Dutch

TOMASSEN, Harmen, from Amesfoort, shoemaker, and wife Catalina Bercx, of Beverwyck (Albany). Testatrix' children by first husband Dirck Bensing, to-wit: Dirck, 13 yrs old, Sampson, 11 yrs, Johannes, 8 yrs, Catarina, 6 yrs, Maria, 4 yrs. Real and personal estate. Guardians of children Mr. Adraien van Ilpendam and Jan van Aecken. No executor named. Witnesses Adriaen van Ilpendam, Jan Koster van Aaken, Jan Verbeeck and Dirck van Schelluyne Notary. Albany Co. Records, Notarial Papers I., p. 333.

1773 1677 Jany. 3 — **TOM, William,** of New Castle, Delaware, gentleman. Godson Richard Cantwell sole heir and executor of real and personal estate. Witnesses John Mall, Walter Wharton and Gysbert Dircx. N. Y. Col. MSS. XX., p. 151.

1774 1679 Octbr. 21 — Dutch **TOMASSEN, Jan,** of Paepsachanie, born at Witbeeck, Holstein, and wife Geertruy Andries, born at New York. The survivor sole heir and executor of real and personal estate. Children mentioned, but not named. Witnesses Captain Volckert Jansen Douw, Jan Andriesen and Adriaen van Ilpendam. Notary Public, Albany Co. Records, Notarial Papers, II., p. 103.

1775 1723 June 10 1752 Jany. 29 **ten BROECK, Wessel,** and wife Catharine, da. and heiress of Jacob Lokermans, of Albany City. Sons Dirck, Jacob, Cornelis, daughters Anna Catharyna, wife of Anthony van Schaick, Cristyna, wife of David van Dyck. Houses and lots on Brewers Street, Albany, farms in Lokere, West side of Hudson R., on Wanton Island Kil, on Catrix Kil, on Bever Kil (Greene Co.), personal estate. Executors the survivor with the three sons. Witnesses Johs. Myngall, Johs. Vinhaghen and Arent Pruyn. Albany Co. Records, Wills, I., p. 215.

1776 1756 Novbr. 19 1768 Octbr. 13 **ten EYCK, Gerritie,** widow of Koenradt, da. of Anthony van Schaick, of Albany City. Children Jacob C., Anthony, Barent, Tobias, Andries, Maragrieta, Gerritie, wife of Peter Gansevoort, grandda. Elisabeth, da. of Gerrit Bratt dec'd, heirs and executors of real and personal estate. Witnesses Wilhelmus van Antwerpe, Peter Yates and Ino. Rutse Bleecker. Albany Co. Records, Wills, I., p. 330.

1777 (U 1) 1709 Aug. 29 1710 Septbr. 11

URQUHART, William, Clerk, Rector of the Parish of Jamaica. Wife Mary, sole heiress and executrix of real and personal estate in America. Witnesses Gabriel Luffe, Thomas Hicks and Samuel Clowes. Copy.

1778 (U 2) 1746-7 Febry. 9 1762 May 1

USEELY, Peter, of Scoharre, Albany Co. Wife Anna, children Cornelia, Elizabeth, Engle, Maria, Anna, Janneke, Cathrina, an expected child. Real and personal estate (a large bible). Executors Johannis Lawyer jun. and Rayer Porter (?), who having refused to act, the widow is made administratrix. Witnesses Johannes Lawyer, Jost Bellinger and Roger Baxter of Schohary, farmer.

1779 (U 3) 1773 Aug. 28 Octbr. 6

UPHAM, John, of Claverack, Albany Co., yeoman. Children John, Gesey, wife of Yurry A. Smith, Mary, wife of Peter I. van Valkenburgh, and Elizabeth, children of son John, vizt. Emelia, Helene, Gesey, Mary, Elizabeth, Barta and Susanna, of da. Gesey, vizt. Yurry, John, Jeremiah, Richard and Charles, of da. Mary, vizt. Emelia, Jocham, Mary, and Susanna. Real and personal estate. Executors son John, sons-in-law Yurry A. Smith and Peter I. van Valkenburgh. Witnesses John Paterson, Wm. Legg and Richard Esselstyne.

1780 (U 4) 1777 April 10 1778 Octbr. 16

UPHAM, John, of Claverack, Albany Co. Wife Wintie, son John, daughters Eme, Magdalena, Gessie, Mary Elisabath, Bata and Susanna. Real and personal estate. Executors the wife, Richard Esselstyne, Jacobus Philipp, Michael Horton and John Price of Albany City. Witnesses Richard Norris, David Spoor and Lewis Morris, gentleman.

1781 1793 May 27 1794 June 9

UPTON, Francis, Lieutenant R. N., now in N. Y. City. Wife Joanna, bro. Clotworthy Upton of the British East India Company. Real and personal estate. No executor named. No witnesses. Will proved by the testimony of John Johnston of N. Y. City, counsellor-at-law, who had drawn the will, which testator copied. The widow made administratrix. Recorded in Wills and Probates, Vol. I., p. 422.

1782 (V 1) 1686-7 Febry. 22 1687 June 7

van RENSSELAER, Killian, of Watervliet, Patroon of the Lordship and Manor of Rensselaerswyck. Wife Anna, cousins Hendrick, son of uncle Jeremiah van Rensselaer, children of Jeremy, son of John Baptist van Rensselaer and of Domine Johannes Carlinnius, sister Nelle Maria, aunt Petronella van Twiller. The Manor, land in Gelderland, do. at Clein Overhoorst, District of Barnvelt in the Haspell van Voorthuysen, house and lot at Newkerk, personal property. No executor named. Witnesses Martin Gerritsen (van Bergen), Justice of the Peace, Hendrick van Nesse, Old Commissary, and Jacob Stadts, of Albany City, chyrurgeon. Copy.

1783 (V 2) 1714 May 20

VOLKERTSEN, Symon, of Schenectady, Albany Co., yeoman, letters testamentary on the estate of, granted Gerrit Symonsen, Johannes Symonsen and Volckert Symonsen, his sons.

1784 (V 3) 1696-7 Jany. 8 1713 April 13

VOLKERTSEN, Symon, of Shinnechtady, Albany Co., yeoman. Wife Engeltje, children Volkje, wife of Arent Wemp, Geesie, wife of Jan Hendricksen Vroman, Magdalena, wife of William Appel of N. Y., Peter Gerrit, Johannes, Volckert and Maria. Land on Normans Kil, called Tawassathaa, do. at Shinnechtady, personal property. Executor the wife. Witnesses Harmen Gansevoort, Volckert van Hoesen and Robt. Livingston.

1785 (V 4) 1698-9 Jany. 11 1707 Octbr. 28 Dutch

van BOCKHOVEN, Claes Jansen, of Schinnechtady Village, Albany Co. Wife Catalyntie Andries de Voss, formerly wife of Arent Bratt, stepgrandson Arent Andriessen, son of Andries Bratt dec'd, stepgranddaughters Catelyntie, wife of Teunis Dircksen, da. of Affie Bratt, wife of Claes van Petten, Catelyntie, da. of Ariaentie Bratt, wife of Ryer Schermerhoorn, daughters of Samuel and Dirk Bratt, Maritie, da. of Cornelia Bratt, late wife of Jan Pootman; Johannes, son of Cornelis Wyncoop of Kingston. Real and personal property. The wife sole executrix, Ryer Jacobsen Schermerhoorn and stepson

Dirk Arentsen Bratt trustees. Witnesses Hendrick Hansen, Isack ver Planck and Johannes Beeckman. Albany Co. Records, Wills I., p. 64. The above named wife of testator made her last will on the same day, mentioning the same heirs and legatees, except Johannes Wyncoop and appointing the husband executor. It is witnessed by Isack Swys, Jan Vroman and Cornelis Slingerlandt.

1786 (V 5) 1699 Novbr. 30 — **van ELMENDORP, Grietje,** of Kingstown, Ulster Co. Sons Conrad and Jacobus, daughters Geertje, wife of Evert Wynkoop, Antje, wife of Mattys Jansen, and Janneke. "Estate of goods and debts." Executor son Conrad. No witnesses. Copy and translation made Decbr. 9, 1714.

1787 (V 6) 1714-15 March 9 1715 June 10 — **van NES, Garrit,** of Albany City, wheelwright. Wife Marya dead. Stepson William van Alen, mariner, stepda. Jannetie, wife of Laurence van Schaick, niece Moyeke, wife of Thomas Harmensen of Albany City. Real and personal estate. Executors said Jannetie van Schaick and Moyeke Harmensen. Witnesses Reyer Schermerhoorn, John Collins, Tho: Martin. Seal.

1788 (V 7) 1714 March 25 1732 May 23 — **van den BERGH, William Gysbertsen,** of Albany City. Wife Catharina, William, son of eldest son Cornelius dec'd, sons Wynant, Wilhelmus, Gysbert, Gerrit, daughters Cathrintie, wife of Livinus Lievesen, and Geertie. Land on Vossen Kil, Albany City, lot in Rensselaerswyck Manor between Wouter Quackenboss and Jan Gerritsen, do. do. between Johannis Oothout and Cornelis van Ness, house and lot in Albany City between Jacobus Schoonhoven and Cornelis van den Bergh, personal property. The wife sole executrix. Witnesses Peter Bennewy, Samuel Prujen and Philipp Livingston.

1789 (V 8) 1699 Novbr. 30 1714 Octbr. 16 Dutch — **van ELMENDORP, Grietien.** Original of No. 1786, with the names of witnesses, to-wit: John Ward, Jan Heermanz senior, W. D. Meyer.

1790 (V 9) 1706 Novbr. 24 1713 April 22 **van den Bergh, Cornelis Williamsen,** of Albany City, carman. Wife Marike, son William and other children mentioned, but not by name. Land in the Manor, house and lot, personal property. Executors Winant Williamsen van den Bergh and Francis Winne. Witnesses Hend. Hansen, Abraham Staats and John Collins. See No. 1788. Seal same as No. 1787.

1791 (V 10) 1709 April 6 July 26 **van EXVEEN, Cornelis,** of Kingston, Ulster Co., son of Gerrit Cornelissen v. E. of N. Y. City. Wife Catrina, an expected child, wife's bro. Henricus Beekman, "father" Evert Byvanck, David, eldest son of Willem Provoost. Real and personal property. The wife sole executrix. Witnesses Major Jacob Aartsen, Teunis Ellisen and Willem Eltengh.

1792 (V 11) 1709 Novbr. 10 1709–10 March 23 **van NIEWENHUYSEN, Mourits,** of New Castle (Delaware?). Sisters Elisabeth van Niewenhuysen and Catrina Lamberts. Uncle Jacob Mourits of N. Y. and wife Elisabeth, Isak Grevenraet, Mary Syardin, Willem Ryniers, cousins Paul Maurits and Jacob Maurits jun. No executor. Witnesses Rd. Haes, Thomas Janvier and Edward Jennigs (?). Copy.

1793 (V 12) 1711 May 15 1713 Septbr. 1 **van HOESEN, Jurriaen,** of Claverack. Wife Katherin, sons Gasper, Jan, daughters Titje and Mary. Homefarm, personal property. Executor the wife. Witnesses Samuel Miller, *bieb schier* (in the certificate called Philipp Schifer) and Robert Livingston.

1794 (V 13) 1719–20 Febry. 6 1720 April 19 Dutch **van der POEL, Elisabeth,** of Albany City, widow. Daughters Margarietie, wife of Volckert Douw, Maria, wife of Jan Vinhagen, Maghdalena, wife of Abraham Lansing, Helena, wife of Jan Barentsen and Ariaentie. House and lot in Albany, personal property. Executors Olif Teller and Harmanis Wendell. Witnesses Stevanus Groesbeek, Jacob Beekman and Rutger Bleecker.

1795 (V 14) 1719 June 22 1727 July 1 Dutch

VERNOOY, Cornelis, senior, of Rochester, Ulster Co. Wife Anna, sons Cornelis, Johannis, daughters Cornelia, wife of David Dubois, Marytie, wife of Lodewyck Hoornbeek, Margariet, wife of Jacob de Witt, Geertruy, wife of Pieter Louw, Ragel, wife of Abraham Beviere, children of dec'd son Jacob, vizt: Anneke and Elizabeth, do. of dec'd da. Celitie, late wife of Abraham Delametter, viz: Cornelis, do. of dec'd da. Elizabeth, late wife of Jacob Dubois, vizt: Lena, wife of Peter van Nest. Real and personal estate. Executors sons Cornelis and Johannis. Witnesses Yaen van Vlyet jun., Cornelis van Aken and Capt. William Nottingham.

1796 (V 15) 1729 Septbr. 12 1730 June 13

VROOMAN, Adam, of Schonactendy Township, Albany Co., yeoman. Wife Margrieta, sons Barent, Henderick, Wouter, Bartholomewes, Tiemoty, Seth, Jacob Messen, Peter (disinherited) and Jan, daughters Maritie and Eva. Real and personal estate. Executor the wife. Witnesses James Banks, Arenout de Graef and Evert Wendell.

1797 (V 16) 1731-2 March 24 1736 Aug. 25

van der VOLGEN, Cornelis, of Schonaghtaday Village, Albany Co., farmer. Wife Elisabeth, nieces Jannetie, da. of bro. Tunus van der Volgen, Maritie Truax, da. of dec'd sister Neltie, nephews Gysbert van Brackel, son of sister Catryntie, Cornelis, son of bro. Lowerens van der Volgen, Cornelis Groot, son of sister Elesabeth Groot, Nicholas de Graaf, son of sister Arejaetie de Graaf. Real and personal property. Executors Cornelis van Dyck, Robert Jeatts and Symon Vrooman. Witnesses John Marselis junior, Joseph van Sice and Nich. Schuyler.

1798 (V 17) 1737-8 Jany. 13 1750 Octbr. 18

van der BURGH, Henry, of the Midle Ward near Poeghkeepsinck, Dutchess Co., gentleman. Wife Magdalen, sons Richard, Henry, John, Peter, William, Stephen, daughters Annamary, wife of Baltus van Kleeck, Hestor, wife of Johannis Lewis, Susannah and Magdalen.

"Worldly estate." Executors the wife with sons Richard and Henry. Witnesses Joseph Webb, Tuenis van Bunschoten and Elias van Bunschooten junior.

1799 (V 18) 1737 May 3 1738 May 5 **van SELLEA, France Abrahamsen,** of Orange Co., free negro. Wife Isabala, sons Abraham, Jan Prime, Casper Prime, France, daughter Anna Mary, stepda. Maryte Salomo (Salmon). Real and personal estate. Executor son France. Witnesses Johannes Remsen, Arie Koning, and Johannis de Grau (Graef).

1800 (V 19) 1727-8 Jany. 29 1738 Septbr. 20 **van DRIESEN, Petrus,** Domine, of Albany City. Wife Eva, sons Petrus, Hendrick, Johannis, da. Anna. House and lot in N. Y. City, land in the Maquase Country, personal property. Executors the wife and children. Witnesses Ph. Livingston, Dirick ten Broeck, Pieter Winne and Coen-Raet Reghtmyer.

1801 (V 20) 1739 April 16 1745 June 11 **van STIENBERGEN, Mattys,** of Kingston, Ulster Co., carpenter. Wife Marytie, da. Catherine, son Gerret and apparently other children. Real and personal estate. Executors sons Johannes, Abraham and Tobyas. Witnesses Ino. Crooke, Petrus Bogardus and John Crooke junior.

1802 (V 21) 1735 March 25 1740 Dutch **van SLYCK, Pieter,** of Kinderhook, Albany Co., farmer. Wife ——, children Thunes, Dirck, Pieter, Elizabeth, wife of Arie Gardenier, Catharyna, wife of Moses Ingersole, Anna, wife of Johann Jacob Eal, Barentje. Real and personal estate. Executors sons Thunes, Pieter and Dirck. Witnesses Aarent van Dyck, Lambert Huyck and Johannis Huick.

1803 (V 22) 1742 May 27 Septbr. 22 **van KEUREN, Tyerck,** of Kingston Corporation, Ulster Co. Wife Maritie, children Matheves, Benjamin, Sarah, wife of William van Vliet, Abraham, Jacobus, Jenecken, wife of Derick Westbrook, Tatie, wife of

Josaphat Dubois, Catherine, wife of Aronald Vielen, Maritie, wife of Pietrus Louw, Rachel, wife of Derick van Vliet, Elizabeth and Lydiae. Real and personal estate. Executors the four sons. Witnesses Tyerck de Witt; Adam Persen and Cornelis Persen.

1804 (V 23) 1743 Octbr. 14 Decbr. 6 — **van LOON, Jan,** of Loonenburgh, Albany Co., yeoman. Wife Rebecca, sons Johannis, Petrus, daughters Rachel, Elsie, Rebecca, Elisabeth, Lenoeir, Susanna, Marya and Catrina. Real and personal property. Executors Barant Staats and Johannis Provoost. Witnesses Willem Waelderon, Jacob Kydnye and Arent van Driesen.

1805 (V 24) 1744 Septbr. 18 1753 June 8 — **VISSCHER, Johannis,** of Albany City. Wife Annatje, children Neeltje, Nanning, Alida, Barent, John, Joachim and Gerrit. Real and personal estate. Executors the wife and bro.-in-law Joachim Staats. Witnesses Barent Staats, Jacobus Schuyler and Johs. Rutse Bleecker.

1806 (V 25) 1745 Novbr. 1 1746 Octbr. 22 Dutch — **van ALEN, Sarah,** widow of Johannis, of Kinderhook, Albany Co. Daughters Elbert, Alida, Elizabeth and Katarina, sons Adam, Evert, Abraham, Jacobus. "Worldly affairs." Executors son Jacobus and son-in-law Johannis Hoogboom. Witnesses James Panton, Mary Mathews and Gerrit Dingman.

1807 (V 26) 1742 Jany. 19 1746 Decbr. 4 Dutch — **van SCHELLUYNE, Johannes,** of Albany City. Sister Hester van Schelluyne, brothers Tieleman, Harmanus and Wellem sole heirs and executors. Witnesses Harme Bastiaensen, Jacob van Woert and Thuenes Visger.

1808 (V 27) 1746 Novbr. 4 1748 Novbr. 21 — **van SLYCK, Teunis,** of Coxsakie, Albany Co., yeoman. Wife Jannetje, children William, Hendrick. Andries, Gerrit Teunissen, Peter, Eybie, Alida and Chatrina. Real and personal estate. Executors the wife, son Peter and Jacob Freese. Witnesses Albert van Loon, Eghbert Ebberse and Jacob Freese.

1809 (V 28) 1746 March 17 1760 July 25 Dutch

van STEENBERGH, Benjamin, of Dutchess Co. Wife Rachel, sons Benjamin and Johannes, daughters Sarah, Maria, Catarina, Margrita, Johanna, Rachel and Elisabeth. Real and personal estate. Executors the nine children. Witnesses Maes Bloemendahl, yeoman, Johannes Nicoll and Isaac Kip. Copy.

1810 (V 29) 1746 July 15 ——

VEEDER, Johannes Seymonsen, of Rensselaerswyck Manor. Children Myndert, Seymon, Engeltje, Debora and Maria, stepson Johannis Wyngaard. Real and personal estate (Dutch bible). Executors sons Myndert and Seymon with Robert Sanders. Witnesses Barent Sanders, Johannis Lansing jun. and Nathl. Buell (?).

1811 (V 30) 1746 Septbr. 14 1747-8 Febry. 13

van LOON, Francis, "designed upon an Expedition against Canada." Father Nicholis van Loon, brothers and sisters. Personal estate (pay as soldier). The father executor. Witnesses Peter Heyden, Jacob Hilton and Jacob H. Decker.

1812 (V 31) 1747 March 26 1768 Aug. 22 Dutch

van DYKE, Cornelius, of Albany City. Wife Maria, son Hendrick. Real and personal estate. Executors the wife and cousin Johannis de Peyster. Witnesses John Beasley, Reyer Gerritsen and Barent H. ten Eyck, brewer. Seal.

1813 (V 32) 1746-7 Jany. 17 1756 May 18

van den BOGERT, Jacobus, of Dutchess Co., yeoman. Wife Maragrit, sons Myndert and Jacobis, daughters Catharine and Helena. Real and personal estate. Executors the wife and sons. Witnesses William Welling, Elcebeth Noxon and Barthow. Noxon.

1814 (V 33) 1746-7 Jany. 6 1754 Octbr. 7

van KLEEK, Johannes, of Dutchess Co., yeoman. Wife Catharine, children Tryntie, Baltus, Peter, Sarah, Jacobis, Johannis, Lawrence, and Myndert, children of dec'd. da. Elizabeth, vizt. Frans and Johannes. Real and personal estate. Executors sons Peter and Jacobis with

Myndert, son of Jacobes van den Boogert. Witnesses Elcebeth Noxon, Peter Windover of N. Y. City, cordwainer, and Bartholw Noxon.

1815 (V 34) 1746-7 Jany. 27 1750 April 5 **van VOORHEES, Johannes,** junior, of Rumbouts Prect., Dutchess Co. Wife Garritje, children Elias, Johannes, Barbaratje, Catrena, Sare and Jannetje. Real and personal estate. Executors the wife, bro. Coert van Voorhees and bro.-in-law Tunis van Bunscoten. Witnesses John Brinckerhoff, Catrina van Voorhees and Jannitje Brinckerhoff.

1816 (V 35) 1746-7 March 6 1752 June 2 **van SANTVOORD, Cornelius,** Minister of the Ref. Prot. Dutch Church at Schenechtady, Albany Co. "First wife" a da. of John Staats of Staten Island, second wife mentioned but not named, children Staats, Zeger, Cornelius, Jacoba, grandchildren Antje Veldtman and Ann Wendell; eldest da. of Geertje Metzelaar, wife of Ryk van der Bilt of Rariton, bro.-in-law (sister's husband) Zeger Hazebroeck of Leyden, Holland, Elisabeth, da. of Peter Cornu. Land on Staten Island, personal property (a silver seal, do. shoebuckles, 5 do. large spoons, 4 do. teaspoons, books and manuscripts). Executor Peter Groenendyk of Schenechtady, merchant. Witnesses John Sanders, Gerrit A. Lansingh and Gerrit van Antwerpen.

1817 (V 36) 1748 Septbr. 8 Novbr. 1 **van LOON, Nicholis,** of Loonenburgh, Albany Co., yeoman. Wife Rachel, sons Jurie (George), Isaac, William, Mathys, Abraham, daughters Mary, wife of Casper van Hoesen, and Elsie. Share in Loonenburgh Patent, personal estate. Executors the wife, bro.-in-law William Klaw and Jacob Freese. Witnesses Duloton, Jakobis Hilton and Jacob Freese.

1818 (V 37) 1748 April 15 1757 July 6 **van VECHTEN, Benjamin,** of Albany City, merchant. Mother Grietie van Vechten, brothers Thunis v. V., Harmen v. V. dec'd, mentioned. Wife Annatie, son Anthony, niece Alida, da. of sister Annatie, late wife of Hendrik Fonda. Real and personal estate. Executors the wife and Gerrit Gerritsen Lansingh of Albany, cooper. Witnesses Antony Brat, Ahas. Roseboom and Johs. van der Heyden.

1819 (V 38) 1748 July 25 1754 May 13 **van BRUNT, Cornelis,** of New Utrecht, Kings Co., gentleman. Children Rutger, Nicolas, Tryntie, Marrytie, Marragreet Neeltie, children of dec'd. da. Angenitie. Homestead, land adjoining Hendrick Smak, do. in Town of Gravesand, personal property. Executors the two sons. Witnesses Jan Jansen of said Co. farmer, Peter Lefferts do. farmer, and Cornelis Groenendeyck. Copy.

1820 (V 39) 1748 Octbr. 17 1748-9 Jany. 20 **van ALEN, Adam,** of Kinderhook, Albany Co., yeoman. Wife Tryntie, sons Johannis, Jacobus, Abraham, daughters Sarah, Maria and Lena. Farm at Claverack (van Rensselaer Lease), personal property. Executors the wife, bro. Jacobus van Alen and Edward Collins. Witnesses John Lansing, Zacharias Haas and Theunis van Slyck. Seal.

1821 (V 40) 1748 May 7 1757 April 18 **VROOMAN, Wouter,** of Schenectady Township, Albany Co., miller. Children, Adam, Jacob, Barent, Isaac, Nicholas, Engeltie, wife of Cornelius Veeder, Christina Vrooman, Rachel, wife of Abraham Wemp and Elizabeth Vrooman. Real and personal estate. Executors sons Adam and Isaac with Joseph Yates. Witnesses Ino. Chambers, Wm. Cosby jun., Lambt. Moore and Augs. van Cortlandt. Seal.

1822 (V 41) 1749 Octbr. 14 —— **van NORSTRANDT, John,** of Hemstid, Queens Co., turner. Wife Lamocke, sons Aron, Cornelias, Abraham, Morter, John, George, daughters Alche, Sarah, Jean and Onche. Real and personal estate. Executors the wife, son Aron and father-in-law Cornelias Rierson. Witnesses George Everit, George Rerson and James Turner. Copy.

1823 (V 42) 1750 April 18 1756 Septbr. 13

van DRIESEN, Eva, widow of Domine Petrus (No. 1800). Son Hendrick, da. Annatje, grandchild Marritie van Driesen. Personal estate (a silver teapot, 6 do. tea spoons). Executors the two children. Witnesses Ino. de Peyster, Ino. Beeckman of Albany, merchant, and Johannys deForeest.

1824 (V 43) 1750 Novbr. 7 1754 Febry. 11 Dutch

van CORLAER, Elisabeth, of Albany City, widow. Sons Gerret van Schajck, Jacob v. S., Abraham v. S., Anthony v. S., Arent v. S., grandson Sybrant Gosensen, son of dec'd eldest son Gose van Schajck, daughters Maria, widow of Johs. Glandorf, Debora, wife of Johannis Beekman, Johanna, wife of Nicholas Groesbeck of New Brunswyck, children of dec'd da. Catarina, to-wit Sybrant, Adriaen, Johannes, Anthony, Magtel and Catarina Quackenboss, do. of dec'd da. Alida, wife of Salomon Goewey, towit Benjamin, Johannis, Catalina, wife of Hendrick Bulsen, Elisabeth, wife of Andries Scherp; Sybrant, son of son Anthony. Real and personal estate (a large Dutch bible). Executors son Gerret van Schayck, grandson Sybrant Gosensen van Schajck and da. Maria Glandorph. Witnesses Richard Miller, James Willson and Johs. van der Heyden.

1825 (V 44) 1750 Octbr. 6 1754 July 11 Dutch

van den BOGERT, Myndert, of Poghkeepsie, Dutchess Co. Wife Neeltie, children Lena, Myndert, Neeltje, Jacobus, Peter, Ragel, Johannes and Cornelius. Real and personal estate. Executors the wife, Johannis Rynders, Johannis Swartwout and son Jacobus. Witnesses Roger Stevens, Josiah Gains and Teunis Tappen.

1826 (V 45) 1751 Decbr. 10 1752 Febry. 13

van SLYCK, Johannes, of Schonectady Township, Albany Co., farmer. Brothers Harme, Cornelis, nephews Cornelis, son of dec'd bro. Adreejan, Cornelis Petrus, son of bro. Petrus, Cornelis Antone, son of bro. Antone, nieces Clara, da. of dec'd bro. Hendrick, Margret and Elisabeth, da. of bro. Harme, Margaret, da. of bro.

Albert, Gertruy, da. of bro. Cornelis, Elizabeth, da. of Johannes Visger esqre., sisters Margaret Peeck and Lena van Antwerpe. Dec'd wife Lena was da. of Harme van Slyck. Land in said Township between Stene Kil and Plate Kil on S. side of Mohawk R., personal property. Executors brothers Harme and Cornelius van Slyck. Witnesses Joseph Yates, Arent van Antwerpen, and Jacob Peeck.

1827 (V 46) 1752 Jany. 26 1756 Novbr. 11 Dutch — **van ALSTYN, Sander,** of Kinderhook, Albany Co., Capt. of a Company. Wife Elbertje, sons Abraham, Pieter, Johannis, da. Maria, an expected child. Real and personal estate. Executors the wife and bro. Isaac van Alstyn. Witnesses Arent van Dyck, Adam van Alen and Andries Kittel of Schotack, Albany Co., yeoman.

1828 (V 47) 1751 March 12 1762 Febry. 22 — **van DRIESSEN, Petrus,** of Schonechtady Township, trader. Wife Engeltje, children John, Petrus, Mary and Anna. Real and personal estate. Executors the wife, Pieter Groendyck and Hendrick van Driessen. Witnesses Johannes S. Vroman, Maas van Vranken, both of Schonectady, shoemakers, and Johannes J. Vrooman.

1829 (V 48) 1751 July 19 1753 Novbr. 19 — **van DYCK, Francis,** of Crum Elbow Prect., Dutchess Co., yeoman. Sons Francis, Peter, Cornelius, grandson Jacobus, son of dec'd son Jacobus, bro. Richard van Dyck, daughters Magdalena, wife of Jost Garrison, Margaret, wife of Richard Williams and Catalintje. Homefarm, other land in said Prect., do. in Great Nine Partners, personal property. Executors the sons-in-law and the three daughters. Witnesses Edward Man of N. Y. City, cooper, B. Payne and Abrm. de Foreest.

1830 (V 49) 1752 Octbr. 23 1753 Octbr. 16 — **van WORMER, Johannes,** of Sagerties, Albany Co., mariner. Wife Engeltie (Anna), daughters Hannah, Aleda and Mary. Real and personal estate. Executors father John Conclin, Captain, and brother Henry G. Livingston. Witnesses Eghbert Brat, John Carrée and John West.

1831 (V 50) 1752 Octbr. 13 — **VIELE, Elizabeth,** of N. Y. City, widow. Da. Sarah Viele, cousins Andries Abrahams, Arientie Seymour, Sarah Leacraft, Elizabeth Beekman, Cornelia Bogart, Margaret Shourt, Cornelia Bowly, children of dec'd cousin Elizabeth Deforrest. Real and personal estate. (plate, jewelry). Executors cousins Andries Abrahams and Arientie Seymour. Witnesses Jasper Farmer, Luke Roome and Cornelius Sebring. Copy made Febry. 4, 1754.

1832 (V 51) 1753 July 24 Octbr. 25 **van ANTWERPEN, Gerret,** of Schonectady, Albany Co., tailor, son of Daniel D. Wife Catriena, children Daniel, Arejantie, Maria, Annaatje, an expected child. Real and personal estate. Executors father-in-law Cornelis Brower, bro. Wilhelmus van Antwerpen and bro.-in-law Ruben Horseford. Witnesses James Lythall, John Freeman and John Sanders.

1833 (V 52) 1751-2 Febry. 8 1753 Novbr. 5 Dutch **VEDDER, Albert,** of Schonechtade, Albany Co. Wife Marytie, sons Harmen, Sander, Aarent, children of dec'd son Johannes vizt. Albert, Catrina, Marya and Anna, do. of dec'd da. Anna. Bro. Corset Vedder dec'd mentioned. Real and personal estate. Executors the wife and the three sons. Witnesses Alsander van Eps, Tobyas ten Eyck and Ino. de Peyster.

1834 (V 53) 1753 June 19 1784 July 8 **VOSBURGH, Jacob Pietersen,** of Kinderhook, Albany Co., batchelor. Brothers Johannis and Isaac Vosburgh. Real and personal estate. Executors brothers Johannes and Pieter Vosburgh. Witnesses Jacob D. Vosburgh, Bartholomevous P. van Valkenburgh of Claverack, cordwainer, and Arent van Dyck.

1835 (V 54) 1754 Septbr. 26 — **van der BEEK, John,** of Richmond Co. Wife Hannah, son Rem and other children, not named. "Worldly estate." Executors Daniel Lake and Stephen Martino jun., both of said Co. Witnesses Wm. Walton, Thomas Stilwell and Gilbert White. Copy.

1836 (V 55) 1754 Septbr. 13 Octbr. 7 **van WYCK, Theodoros,** of Runbouts Prect., Dutchess Co. Wife Sarah, father Cornelius van Wyck, children Sarah, Cornelius, Abraham, Catalina and Antie. Real and personal estate. Executors brothers Francis Britt, George Adriance and Richard van Wyck. Witnesses Isaac Brinckerhoff, esquire, Robert Brett and James Willson.

1837 (V 56) 1754 Octbr. 14 1757 Jany. 4 **van ALEN, Jacobus,** of Kinderhook, Albany Co., yeoman. Wife Leena, sons Lowrens, Abraham, Johannis, daughters Mary, wife of Johannes van Alen and Catharina. Real and personal estate. Executors the wife with sons Lowrens and Abraham. Witnesses Anth. Quackenbos, Peter Vosburgh and Arent van Dyck. Copy.

1838 (V 57) 1755 Aug. 15 1758 Febry. 25 **van VOORHUIS, Johanne,** of Rombout Prect., Dutchess Co., yeoman. Wife Sarah, children Court, Zacharias, Jacob, Jannetie and Maria, children of dec'd. son Johannes. Real and personal estate. Executors sons Zacharias and Jacob with sons-in-law John Brinckerhoff and Elias du Boyse. Witnesses Petrus Bogardus, John Cambell and Egbert Bogardus.

1839 (V 58) 1755 July 15 1773 March 31 Dutch **van den BERGH, Gysbert,** of Kingston, Ulster Co. Son-in-law Benjamin van Wagenen, Cornelus, son of da. Divertje, daughters Cornelia Catharina, wife of Johannis Vielee, Elisabeth, wife of Benjamin van Wagenen, and Dievertje, wife of Johannis van Keuren. Real and personal estate. Executors the three sons-in-law. Witnesses Jan Eltinge, Catrinna Rycman and Rachel Eltinge.

1840 (V 59) 1755 Jany. 25 1762 June 26 **VERVEELEN, Gideon,** of Rumbout Prect., Dutchess Co., yeoman. Children Moses, Mary, wife of William Rodgers, Hester, wife of Johannes Roeger, Alida, wife of Isaac Cole, children of da. Mary Rogers, vizt. Jannetie and Susannah. Land in Rumbout Prect., bought from Stephen van Rensselaer, out of which farms have been sold to Simon Pells, Ezekiel Masten, Johannis Roeger, Arie van Vliet, Jan Ostrom jun., Jacob Westervelt, Jan La Roy, Thomas Vorse, Aert Middagh, Hans Joost Snyder, Elias van Bunschoten jun. and Migell Hoffman, homefarm on Wappingers Creek, personal estate. Executors Ezekiel Masten, Aert Middagh and Thomas Vorse. Witnesses Richard van der Burgh, Henry v. d. Burgh and Henry Livingston.

1841 (V 60) 1755 July 8 1758 Aug. 3 **van EPS, Alexander,** of Schonectady, Albany Co., innkeeper. Wife Neltye, children Jan Baptist Sander, Jacobes, Loweres, Leena, wife of Ebre (?) Thome (?) and Gertruy. Real and personal estate (a large Dutch bible). Executors the three sons. Witnesses Joseph Yates, Christopher Yates and Abraham Wempel.

1842 (V 61) 1756 Febry. 4 — **van VOORHIES, Johannes,** of Dutchess Co., draft of letters testamentary on the estate of, granted to his widow Gerritje, since intermarried with Lewis Dubois. His will, proved April 5, 1750, named Tunis van Buntschoten as executor with the wife.

1843 (V 62) 1756 Novbr. 26 1757 Jany. 18 **van RENSSELAER, Elizabeth,** widow of Stephen. Son Stephen, da. Elisabeth, nephews Stephen Schuyler and John Groesbeck. Real and personal estate (a silver tankard, a do. bowl and 12 do. spoons.) Executors son-in-law Abraham ten Broeck, da. Elizabeth, son Stephen and nephew Stephen Schuyler. Witnesses Catrena Schuyler, Philipp van Vechten, yeoman, and Hendrick Gardenyer.

1844 (V 63) 1757 Febry. 23 1763 March 17 **van ANTWERPEN, Johannis Sy.,** son of Seymon Danielsen, of Schonectady, Albany Co., waggoner. Wife Catriena, son Seymon, da. Engeltje. Real and personal estate. Executors the wife, bro. Lawies van Antwerpen, bro.-in-law Albert Johse. Vedder. Witnesses John Sanders, merchant, Elder Groot and Nicholas Groot, carpenter.

1845 (V 64) 1757 Novbr. 24 1763 May 21 **van WYCK, Cornelius,** of Rumbout Prect., Dutchess Co. Wife Hannah, children Richard, Cornelius, Phebe, wife of George Adriance, Margaret, wife of Francis Britt, Catherine, wife of Johannis ter Bos jun., children of dec'd son Theodorus vizt. Sarah, Cornelius, Abraham, Catalina and Antje. Real and personal estate. Executors sons Richard and Cornelius with son-in-law Francis Britt. Witnesses Johannes ter Bos, Theodorus van Wyck and John Brinckerhoff.

1846 (V 65) 1757 March 16 1758 May 15 **van WYCK, John,** of Newtown, Queens Co. Daughters Phebe and Sarah. Real and personal estate. Executors uncles John and Theodorus van Wyck, cousin Stephen van Wyck and bro.-in-law Edward Burling. Witnesses Benjamin Meyer, Lieut. Royal American Regt., William Betts and John Townsend. Copy.

1847 (V 66) 1758 July 25 1759 Feby. 5 **van BERGEN, Gerrit,** of Katskil, Albany Co., yeoman. Children Martin Garson, William, Deborah, wife of John Peers, Ann, wife of Wilhelmus van Bergen, Neeltie, wife of David Abeel, grandda. Annake, da. of Casparus Bronck dec'd, Refd. Church of Catskil. Land on the Single Kil, do. at Tabegeght, do. in Katskil Patent, do. in Rensselaerswyck Manor, derived from mother Neeltie Dow, do. on Plaat Island, do. called the Ryters Wey (Riders Pasture), do. now tenanted by Nicholas Brando, Wilhelmus Oosterhout and Peter Sax, do. at Batavia behind the Katskil Hills, do. in Corlars Kil Patent, personal property. Executors the two sons. Witnesses Wessel van Dyck, Joseph Nisbit and Henry Oothoudt.

1848 (V 67) 1758 Decbr. 6 1759 Febry. 15 **van DYCK, Cornelis,** of Schonectady, Albany Co., "dockter." Wife Margreta, children John Most, Henderick Most, Cornelis Lott, Jacamintye, wife of John Baptist Wendel, Jacobes, grandda. Marya, da. of da. Elisabeth, late wife of Haramanes Bratt. Real and personal property (a Dutch bible, a silver tankard). Executors Johannes A. Bratt and Joseph Yates jun. both of Schonectady. Witnesses Christopher Yates, John Vedder and Arent And. Bratt.

1849 (V 68) 1758 Aug. 28 1761 Septbr. 16 Dutch **van SCHAAK, Michiel,** of Loonenburg Flats, Albany Co., farmer. Wife Maria Magdalena, sons Niclaas and Arend, daughters Maria and Margaretha. Real and personal estate. Executors Johannes Brandow and Lourens van Boskerk. Witnesses Dirck van Vechten, Albert van Schaak, farmers, and Michael Christian Knoll.

1850 (V 69) 1750 Aug. 19 1768 Septbr. 22 Dutch **van GAASBEEK, Johannes,** of Foxhall, Ulster Co. Wife Antje, children Sarah, Catharina, Abraham and Thomas. Real and personal estate. Executors brothers Abraham and Lawrens van Gaasbeek, Lawrens Salsberry and Adriaan Wynkoop. Witnesses William van Gaasbeek of said Co., cooper, Henry Jansen and Thomas H. Jansen.

1851 (V 70) 1759 June 12 1783 Febry. 5 **van BENTHUYSEN, Gerrit,** of Rhinebeek Prect., Dutchess Co., gent. Children Jannetje, Barent and Peter. Real and personal estate (a silver teapot, six do. spoons, six do. teaspoons, a do. sugar tong, all marked F. L.). Executors the three children and bro. Peter van Benthuysen. Witnesses Jurry Haas, John Jurry Tremper and Christian Schultz, yeoman.

1852 (V 71) 1759 March 25 1761 March 5 **VIELE, Philipp,** of Kingston, Ulster Co. Wife Antje, children Helena, wife of Matheus van Keuren, Arenhoudt, Philipp, Cornelius, Gerret, Johannes, Marrea, wife of Cornelius van den Bergh, grandson Cornelius, son of dec'd son Petrus, Reformed Church at Kingston.

Real and personal estate. Executors the wife and sons Philipp and Johannes. Witnesses Johannis Jansen, Christophel Tappen and D. Wynkoop jun.

1853 (V 72) 1759 May 30 1760 March 5

VROOMAN, Adam, son of Wouter, son of Adam, of Schonactady Township, Albany Co. Wife Susanna, sons Wouter, Jacob, Isaac, daughters Maria, Lena, and Jannetje, niece Maria, da. of bro. Isaac. Real and personal estate. Executors Isaac Swits of Albany, John Sanders and bro. Isaac Vrooman. Mother's name was Maria Halenbeek. Witnesses Johannes S. Vroman, Johannes Fort and Isaac Jacobus Swits.

1854 (V 73) 1759 June 11 1769 Septbr. 12

van DYCK, Arent, and wife Heyltje, of Kinderhook, Albany Co., Doctor. Sons Stephanus, Hendrick and Laurens. Real estate, derived from "our father Stephanis van Alen," personal property. Executors sons Hendrick and Laurens. Witnesses Jacob van Schajck, Anth. Quakenbouss and Hend. van Dyck of Albany City, Doctor.

1855 (V 74) 1760 Aug. 15 1770 June 17

VELEN, John, of Schonectady Township, Albany Co., husbandman. Wife Debora, daughters Debora, Margrieta, Maria, Susanna. Real and personal estate. Executors Jacobus Peck, carpenter, and Albert Vedder, carpenter. Witnesses Hendricus F. Veeder, joiner, Barent Veeder and Caleb Beck, merchant, all of Schonectady.

1856 (V 75) 1760 Octbr. 9 1761 April 20

van HORNE, James, of Middlesex Co., N. J., gent. Late wife Margaret, sons John and James. Real and personal estate (plate, pearl necklace, diamond rings). Executors nephews James Mack Evers and William Cockerofft, both of N. Y. City, merchants, and John Berrian of Rockkey Hill, N. J., merchant. Witnesses Catharina van Horne, Catherine Cebra and James Cebra. Copy.

1857 (V 76) 1760 May 8 July 4 **van de WATER, Jacobus,** jun., of Beekmans Prect., Dutchess Co., farmer. Wife Maryah, nephew Jacobes, son of bro. Benjamin van de Water. Real and personal estate. Executors the wife, father-in-law Larrance Lose and Abraham Adriance. Witnesses Henry Wiltse, Johannis Wiltse, and Francis Lose, yeomen.

1858 (V 77) 1760 Septbr. 14 1773 April 5 **van JEVEREN, Mindert,** of Albany City, blacksmith. Wife Hariantie, children Ryneer, Garret, Hester, Hannah and Santie, grandda. Hittie Williams. House and lot in 2d Ward, Albany, between Frans Pruyn and Robert Sanders, personal estate. Executors sons-in-law Harme Visgher and Peter Williams. Witnesses Robt. Sanders, Frans Sa. Pruyn and Richard Cartwright of Albany City, vintner.

1859 (V 78) 1760 April 20 1775 May 16 **van EPS, Abraham,** of Schonectady, Albany Co., carpenter. Wife Susanna, daughters Marya and Effe. Real and personal estate. Executors the wife and da. Marya, who refusing to act John S. Glen, farmer, is appointed administrator. Witnesses Joseph Yates, Pieter Cornu and Cornelius Lansing of Schonectady, carpenter.

1860 (V 79) 1760 April 30 1769 Aug. 23 **van KLEEK, Lawrence,** of Poghkeepsie, Dutch-Co., esquire. Wife Jaepje, children Elizabeth, Baltus, Trintje, Leonard and Sarah, grandda. Jacoba, da. of Peter van Kleek. Real and personal estate (a great Dutch bible). Executors the wife with sons Baltus and Leonard. Witnesses Richard Snedeker of said Co., gent, Trintie Crannell and Barthw. Crannell. Copy.

1861 (V 80) 1761 Aug. 8 Octbr. 16 **VAUGHAN, David,** of Beekmans Prect., Dutchess Co. Wife Dinah, sons Benjamin, John, David, James, Henry, Daniel, Obediah and Anthony, daughters Sarah Willber, Elizabeth Wood, Mary Vaughan, Abigail Dunkin and Dinah Vaughan. Land in said Precinct and in New England, personal property. Executors the wife and bro.-in-law Benjamin Northrop of New-England, "formerly a Dweller in Exeter." Witnesses Emanuel Woolly, Thomas Dunkin, both of said Prect., yeomen, and Thomas O'Bryan.

1862 (V 81) 1762 Septbr. 20 1763 June 27

VEDDER, Harme Haramanes, of Schonectady, Albany Co., merchant. Da. Susanna, widow of Nicolas A. van Petten, bro. Johannes Haramanes Vedder. Real and personal estate. Executor the daughter. Witnesses Joseph Yates of Schonectady, blacksmith, Johans. Roseboom, silversmith, Symon Vroman and Mindert R. Wemple.

1863 (V 82) 1762 July 1 Septbr. 6

VEDDER, Jacobus, of Schonectady, Albany Co., yeoman. Wife Maria, brothers Harmen Vedder, Johannis Har. Vedder, sister Antje, wife of Harmanis Peeck, son of Johannis Peeck, Harmanis Franse, son of Nicolaes van den Bogert, children of dec'd sister Suffia Pieters, vizt: Harmanis Pieters and Margariet, wife of James Seuter, da. of dec'd sister Lydia, vizt. Margariet van Sleyck, children of bro. Arent Bradt vizt: Harmanis and Margrieta, widow of Cornelis van Dyck, do. of sister Batseba, vizt: Andries Burn, Catoleyn Burn and her grandchildren, *i. e.* children of dec'd son Samuel Burn and of Jacomeyn; Margrieta, wife of John Brown. Real and personal estate. Executors the wife and bro. Johannis Har. Vedder. Witnesses Thomas Brower Bancker, John van Sice and John Sanders.

1864 (V 83) 1762 Novbr. 10 1763 Octbr. 24

VISSCHER, Jacob, of Albany City. Gertruy, da. of Major Isaac Swits, Gerret van Vranke of Albany City, carpenter, children of sister Hester Swits, to wit Isaac, Sannake, wife of Cornelius van Ness, Anna, wife of Hendrik Beekman. Real and personal estate. Executors Isaac Swits, Jacob Ja. Lansing and John M. Beekman. Witnesses Isaac van Aernam, hatter, Peter W. Yates, yeoman, and Abrm. Yates jun., attorney-at-law,

1865 (V 84) 1762 May 1 1766 Novbr. 12 **van VECHTEN, Neeltie,** widow of Johannis, of Albany City. Sons Volckert, Johannis, Ephraim and Hendricus. Real and personal estate. Executors sons Volckert, Johannis and Ephraim. Witnesses John, son of Jellis de Garmo, Cornelus van den Bergh and Wm. Hogen jun., blacksmith.

1866 (V 85) 1762 May 13 1763 Octbr. 6 **van VEGHTEN, John,** of Albany City, Major in the N. Y. Forces. Wife Annatie sole heiress and executrix of real and personal estate. Witnesses Goose van Schaick, John Visscher, both of Albany, gentlemen, and Gerard de Peyster.

1867 (V 86) 1763 June 1 1764 June 20 **van FLEET, Cornelius,** of Shaloty Prect., Dutchess Co., gentleman. Cousin Cornelius van Fleet jun., sister Anna Ostrom, cousin Arey van Fleet, brothers Dirck, Johannes and Benjamin van Fleet. "Worldly goods." Executors Dirck van Fleet, John Ostrom and Thomes Garesen. Witnesses Jacob Clyne and Mary Hagaman.

1868 (V 87) 1763 Septbr. 16 1765 Jany. 25 **van RENSSELAER, Jeremiah.** Wife Judith sole heiress, and with brothers-in-law Philipp Schuyler and Nicholas Bayard executrix of real and personal estate. A son mentioned. Witnesses Hester, wife of —— van Cortlandt, of N. Y. City, James van Rensselaer and Wm. Smith jun. Proved at N. Y. City. Copy.

1869 (V 88) 1763 —— 1768 Febry. 1 **VELLER, Philipp,** of Rynebeek, Dutchess Co. Wife Catherine, children Wilhalmus, Johannes, Philipp and four more, not named. Real and personal estate. Executors the three sons named. Witnesses Everardus Bogardus of said Co., merchant, Jerge Jan Zufeldt and Petrus ten Broeck.

1870 (V 89) 1769 Aug. 17 —— **van RENSSELAER, John Baptist,** of Albany Co., gentleman, letters testamentary on the estate of, granted to John Schuyler jun., of the executors appointed in the will, made April 25, 1763, James Stevenson being dead, John Schuyler and Oliverde Lancey refusing to act.

1871 (V 90) 1764 May 10 1782 Febry. 8 Dutch **van VECHTEN, Dirck,** of the Flats, Loonenburg District, Albany Co. Wife Helena, sons Teunis, Hubartis, who has son Dirrik, daughters Jannetie, Sara, wife of Isack Kalier, Eva, wife of Abraham van Valkenburg, Maria, wife of Nicolaus Spoor, Catariena, wife of Lambert van Valkenburg. Real and personal estate. Executors son Hubartus and sons-in-law Lambert van Valkenburg and Nicolaus Spoor. Witnesses John ten Broeck, Martin Lydius, Jacob Roseboom and John H. Lydius.

1872 (V 91) 1764 May 5 1765 Febry. 20 **van NORDEN, Wessel,** of N. Y. City, *masenar.* Mother Ariantie van Orden sole heiress and executrix of "temporal estate." Witnesses Catherine McClean, widow, Attie Soomerendyck and Law. Wessells. Copy.

1873 (V 92) 1764 Jany. 4 1769 Novbr. 6 **van DURHEN, (Duehren), Sara.** Rev. John Albert Weygand and John Dealing of N. Y. heirs and executors of share in the patent granted to Christian Gerlog, Andreas Finck et al. Octbr. 19, 1723, at Stonarabie, Albany Co., derived from father. Witnesses Gerret van Gelden, of N. Y. City, chairmaker, Frs. Tetord and Anna Sophia Jaquery. Copy.

1874 (V 93) 1765 Octbr. 22 1767 May 11 **van ETTEN, Jacobus,** of Wachconck, Kingston Corporation, Ulster Co. Wife Catherine, sons Arie, Gysbert, Johannes, daughters Arreiantje, Catherine, Maria, Elizabeth and Leaja. Real and personal estate. Executors sons Johannis and Gysbert, Wilhelmus Hooghteeling jun., esquire and Johannis van Bunschoten. Witnesses Wilhelmus Hooghteelingh jun., Johannis van Bunscohten and Andries de Witt, all of Kingston, gentlemen.

1875 (V 94) 1766 Octbr. 14 1771 Febry. 9 **van der BURGH, William,** of Poghkeepsie Prect., Dutchess Co., yeoman. Wife Margit, children Henry, John, William, Magdelin, Elesabeth, Hester. Real and personal estate. Executors the wife, bro. Henry v. d. Burgh and Richard Davis. Witnesses Jacobes Frear, yeoman, Peter Frer, and Cornelus Westervelt.

1876 (V 95) 1767 March 16 1769 Octbr. 6 **van BENTHUYSEN, Jacob,** of Rynbeek Prect., Dutchess Co., yeoman. Children Abrehem, John, Catleyntie and Jenneke. Real and personal estate. Executors bro. Pieter van Benthuysen, Pieter van Benthuysen jun. and Barent van Benthuysen jun. Witnesses Augustinus Turcke, Gerrit van Benthuysen and Isaac Cole jun.

1877 (V 96) 1759 Jany. 27 1768 Septbr. 5 **VERNOOY, Cornelius,** of Rochester, Ulster Co., farmer. Sons Cornelius, Jacob and Wessel, Margerith, widow of dec'd. son Coenraet and his children vizt. Cornelius, Sarah, Andries, Simeon, Jonathan and Cornelia. Real and personal estate. Executors the three sons and grandson Cornelius, son of Coenraet. Witnesses Cornelius Joh. Vernooy, Johannis Vernooy jun. and Andries de Witt jun. Codicil of January 16, 1767 divides the share, given to grandson Simeon since deceased, and appoints Andries de Witt, Capt. Johannis Bevier and Cornelius I. Vernooy, to make the partition of the estate. Witnesses Johannis Vernooy, Nathan Vernooy and Jurry Mack of Rochester, labourer.

1878 (V 97) 1768 Octbr. 10 1771 Decbr. 30 **VROMAN, Peter,** of Schohary, Albany Co., yeoman. Sons Abraham, Barent, Cornelius and Isaac; Jonas, Peter and Simon, sons of dec'd eldest son Adam, Peter, son of son Barent, Dina, widow of son Adam, da. Engeltie, wife of David Uzile, Geertruy, Maria and Engeltie, daughters of dec'd. son Martynes, Lydia, da. of dec'd son Peter, Sara, Geertruy, Christina and Maria, daughters of dec'd, da Janetje, Elisabeth and Cathrina, daughters of dec'd. da. Cathrina. Real and personal estate. Executors son Barent, Cornelius and Isaac. Witnesses Laurentz Lawyer, of Schohary, farmer, Marteynys van Slyck and Conrad Brown.

1879 (V 98) 1768 Decbr. 24 1770 Aug. 28 **van LEUVEN, Andrias,** of Marbletown, Ulster Co., yeoman. Wife Margrit, sons Johannis, Christopher, Elias and Eliza. Real and personal estate. Executors the wife, bro. Gysbert van Leuven, and bro.-in-law Petrus van Leuven. Witnesses John van Luven of Marbletown, farmer, Ephraim Chambers and Thomas Schoonmaker jun.

1880 (V 98½) 1768 Novbr. 30 1769 Septbr. 25 **VOSBURGH, Jacob D.,** of Kline Kil, Kinderhook Township, Albany Co. Wife ——, sons John and Dirk and other children, not named. Land in Dorset, N. H., and in Kinderhook. Executors John Legget, Marte van Alstyne, Lowrence Hoogeboom and Tobyas Legget. Witnesses Johannis D. Vosburgh, Cathrine van Schaack and David van Schaack.

1881 (V 99) 1769 May 13 Aug. 24 **van der BURGH, Richard,** of Poughkeepsie Prect., Dutchess Co., blacksmith. Wife Mary, children Jacob, Leanah, wife of Thomas Pooley, Sarah, wife of Thomas Frear, and Mary. "My estate." Executors the wife, bro. John van der Burgh and son-in-law Thomas Pooley. Witnesses William van der Burgh, John Koapman, wheelwright, and Maurice Smith, cordwainer.

1882 (V 100) 1769 Novbr. 6 1772 Febry. 10 **van WAGENEN, Nicholas,** of Charlotte Prect., Dutchess Co., yeoman. Wife Hester, da. of Jan de Graff dec'd, sons Evert, John, Nicholas, Gerret, daughters Hellegontie, wife of Johannis Bush, Elizabeth, wife of Joseph Hagaman, Sarah, wife of Johannis van Enden, and Janneke. Brother Gerret van Wagenen mentioned. Real and personal estate. Executors the wife, the four sons and the three sons-in-law. Witnesses Enoch Lester, Samuel Cooke, of Dutchess Co., physician, and Hendrick Pele.

1883 (V 101) 1769 March 30 1770 March 7 **van ALEN, Jacobus,** of Claverack, Albany Co., yeoman. Johannis, son of dec'd bro. Adam, Johannis E. and Abraham E., Lourens E., Jacobus E., Dirck, Adam and Maria, children of dec'd bro. Evert and wife Margrieta, Mayeke Witbeck, da. of Peter Koeyeman. Land at Richmond, Berkshire Co., Mass., and at Clavarack, personal estate. Executors nephew Johannis E., Abraham E. and Lourens E. van Alen. Witnesses Lourens L. van Alen, Margrieta van Alen and Cornelius van Dyck.

1884 (V 102) 1769 Septbr. 27 1778 July 3 — **van VLIET, Aury,** of Poghkeepsie Prect., Dutchess Co., yeoman. Wife Janatje, sons Garret, Petrus, Tunis, Frederick, da. Nelly, wife of Isaac van Bunschoten, grandchildren, Janatje, Sarah and Aury Low, children of Petrus Low. Real and personal estate. Executors sons Garret, Petrus and Tunis. Witnesses Barnados Swartwout, Mindert Swartwout, yeomen, and Richard Snedeker.

1885 (V 103) 1769 April — 1785 Novbr. 22 — **VISSCHER, Barent,** of Albany City, Indian trader. Wife Sarah, daughters Anna and Sarah. Real and personal estate. Executors stepfather Johs. Roorbach and bro.-in-law Bastiaen H. Visscher. Witnesses Staats van Santvoord of Half Moon Distr, Albany Co., blacksmith, James Dole and Anna Schuyler.

1886 (V 104) 1769 Aug. 30 1770 July 16 — **van RENSSELAER, Stephen,** esquire, proprietor of the Manor of Rensselaerswyck, Albany Co. Wife Catherine, sons Stephen, Philipp, da. Elizabeth, sister Elizabeth, wife of Abraham ten Broeck, esquire, aunts Gertruyd Livingston and Ann Schuyler, kinsman John van Rensselaer. The Manor, land in Walomscock Patent, personal estate. Executors the wife, father-in-law Philipp Livingston, bro.-in-law Abraham ten Broeck, John ten Eyck of Albany esquire and Gerardus Groesbeck. Witnesses Philipp Schuyler, Lucas van Veghten and Peter Silvester, attorney-at-law. Codicil of Septbr. 7, 1769, makes unimportant changes and is witnessed by Thomas Hun, John ten Broeck and Rutger Bleecker.

1887 (V 105) 1770 Febry. 7 Aug. 13 — **van der HEYDEN, David,** of Albany City, merchant. Wife Geertruy, sons Dirck, David, Jacob, daughters Alida, wife of Rev. Barent Vrooman, Rachel, wife of Doctor Samuel Stringer. Real and personal estate.

Executors the wife and son-in-law Samuel Stringer. Witnesses Ino. N. Bleecker, Robert Yates of said City, attorney-at-law, and Jacob Lansing, gentleman.

1888 (V 106) 1770 March 9 May 16 Dutch

van STEENBERGEN, Abraham, of Kingston, Ulster Co. Wife Marytie, children Tobias, Wilhelmus, Mattheus, Abraham, Dirck, Catharine, Arjaente, Marytie, wife of James Eltinge, and Sarah. Real and personal estate. Executors sons Tobias, Wilhelmus and Mattheus. Witnesses Tobias van Steenbergh, barber, Jacob M. Groen, saddler, and Willem Eltinge, merchant, all of Kingston.

1889 (V 107) 1771 March 12 Aug. 5

van der HEYDEN, Johannis, of Albany City. Children John, Mary, Rachel and Jane. Real and personal estate (a large Dutch bible). Executors da. Jane, Harme Gansevoort, Volckert Douw and Garret van Sante. Witnesses Marten Mynderse, blacksmith, Peter Walderen, bricklayer, and John Bay, schoolmaster, all of Albany City.

1890 (V 108) 1771 April 2 1772 Septbr. 22

van GEYSELING, Myndert, of Schonectady, Albany Co., farmer. Wife Suster, sons Elias, Jacob, Cornelis, Pieter, daughters Catarien, wife of Samuel Ar. Bradt, Debora, wife of Issaac S. Swits, Jacomintje, wife of Arent Schermerhoorn. Real and personal estate. Executors sons Elias, Jacob and Pieter. Witnesses John Sanders, John Hall, cooper, and John J. Peeck, tailor, all of Schonectady.

1891 (V 109) 1771 Decbr. 3 1772 Jany. 9

VALENTINE, Jacob, senior, of Orange Town, Orange Co. Wife Margaret, children of dec'd son Hendrick, vizt. Jacob, John, Alexander, Peter and Margaret, sons Jacob and Johan Matthias, nephew John Briant. Real and personal estate. Executors Martin Poulus and Peter S. de Marest. Witnesses Jan Nagel (?), Barent Nagel and John Haring of said Co., yeoman.

1892 (V 110) 1772 Octbr. 8 1782 May 17 **van KLEECK, Elizabeth,** of Rumbout Prect., Dutchess Co., widow. Children Barent, Baltus, Maria, wife of John Freer, Neeltje, wife of Peter Fielen, Elizabeth, wife of John Laroy, and Antonetta, wife of Jacob Becker. Real and personal estate. Executor son-in-law John Freer. Witnesses John Robinson and Jacobes Frear, of Poghkeepsie Prect, yeoman.

1893 (V 111) 1772 Jany. 15 1782 Jany. 18 **van DEUSEN, Tobias,** son of Robert, of Claverack, Albany Co., yeoman. Children Robert, Johannis, Tobias, Heyltye, Ariantje and Mary. Real and personal property. Executors the three sons. Witnesses Robert van Deusen, Jacob Carrie (dead at date of proof) and David Brouwer of Claverack District, farmer.

1894 (V 112) 1773 Febry. 6 1785 April 30 **VERVELEY, Hester,** of Rumbout Prect., Dutchess Co., widow. Children Gideon, Moses, John, Daniel, Jeremiah, Elizabeth and Hannah. Real and personal estate. Executors Moses de Graff, Jacobus de Graff and Zephaniah Platt. Witnesses Matthias Cook, John Rugur and Zephaniah Platt of Poughkeepsie Prect., esquire.

1895 (V 113) 1773 Aug. 26 1776 April 3 **van WOERDT, Ariantje,** widow of Peter, of Rensselaerswyck Colony. Nephew Cornelius, son of bro. Nicholas?, Nicholas, son of bro. Johannis?, nieces Catharina, Rachel, Santie, Antie and Maria, daughters of sister Anna, grand niece Annatje, da. of Ariaentie, da. of sister Anna, nephew Peter, son of bro. Petrus, Santie, da. of bro. Johannis, Nicholas, son of bro. Cornelius, Santie, da. of bro. Cornelius, Antie, da. of sister Lanneke, Marytie and Alida, daughters of sister Sarah. Real and personal estate. Executors Cornelius C. van den Bergh and Nicholas Johs. van den Bergh. Witnesses Johannes Yates jun., tailor, and Abrm. Hooghkirk, brickmaker, both of Albany City.

1896 (V 114) 1774 Octbr. 2 1782 Septbr. 17 **van DUESEN, Martin,** of Pawlings Prect., Dutchess Co., yeoman. Sons Robert, Mellegert, who has sons Martin and Henderick, John. Real and personal property. Executors son John and son-in-law Abraham van Duesen. Witnesses Jacob van Duesen of said Prect., yeoman, Carolina Rose and David Rose.

1897 (V 115) 1774 Novbr. 30 1775 Aug. 28 **van HORNE, Cornelius,** son of Garret, late of N. Y. City, merchant, dec'd, of Richmond Town, Richmond Co. Bro. Garret van Horne, sisters Joanna, Ann, Alada and Mary van Horne. Real and personal estate. Executors uncles Augustus van Horne and Joseph Read with bro. Garret, when of age. Witnesses Joseph Lester, Matus Sweme (Sweem) of said Co., farmer, and Hannah Swaim. Copy.

1898 (V 116) 1774 June 6 July 14 **van AKEN, Gedion,** of Kingston, Ulster Co. Children Peter, Johannis, Abraham, Benjamin, Gideon, Catharina, wife of Abraham van Vliet, and Maria, wife of Conrad Wist. Real and personal estate. Executors sons Johannis, Abraham and Benjamin. Witnesses Francis Heyler, Jan van Aken of Kingston, farmer, and Petrus van Aken, of Dutchess Co., farmer.

1899 (V 117) 1775 June 17 1784 Septbr. 7 **van BENTHUYSEN, Peter,** junior, of Rynebeek, Dutchess Co., gentleman. Children of bro. Bornt van Benthuysen, vizt. Jacob, Mary, Bornt and Kethurah. Fast and moveable estate. Executor cousin Jacob van Benthuysen. Witnesses Patt Hogan of said Co., schoolmaster, Johannis Luyck and Petrus Cool.

1900 (V 118) 1775 Octbr. 1 1782 Aug. 14 **van WYCK, Theodorus,** of Rumbout Prect., Dutchess Co. Wife Janiche, sons William, Theodorus, son of dec'd da. Margaret, vizt: Albert Andriance, children of dec'd da. Latetia, vizt: Theodorus, Cataline, Ram, Isaac and John, children of dec'd da. Elizabeth, vizt: John Graham, Elizabeth, Chancey, Abigail, Theodorus van Wyck, Stephen Curtis, Zephaniah Platt and Sarah; da. Mary, wife of Zephaniah Platt. Real and personal estate. Executors sons William and Theodorus, sons-in-law Isaac Andriance, John Baylie and Zephaniah Platt. Witnesses John van Nostrand, of Brooklyn, Kings Co., grocer, Benjamin Hasbrook, Abraham Garrison. Codicil of April 23, 1776, makes an unimportant change and is witnessed by John Bedels of said Precinct, yeoman, John van Nostrand and Abraham Garrison.

1901 (V 119) 1775 July 31 1784 Febry. 8 **van SCHAACK, Cornelis,** of Kinderhook, Albany Co., esquire. Wife Lydia, sons Henry, Cornelis, David and Peter, daughters Margaret, wife of Lowrens L. van Alen, and Jane, wife of Peter Silvester, grandchildren Isaac van Vleck, Margaret van Vleck and Lydia van Schaack van Vleck, children of dec'd da. Lydia and husband Isaac van Vleck. Real and personal estate. Executors Laurens L. van Alen, Peter Silvester and Colonel Peter Vosburgh. Witnesses John Pruin of Kinderhook, blacksmith, Chrystina Pruin and Caty Prune.

1902 (V 120) 1776 July 19 1778 Febry. 17 **van WYCK, Theodorus,** of N. Y. City, merchant. Wife Helena, sons Abraham, David, daughters Helena Bogart, Catharine, wife of Rev. John Mason, Margaret and Anna-Mary. Land in Monckton Township, Albany Co., in Meklenburgh Township, same Co., house and two lots at Hackensack, Bergen Co., N. J., personal property (a large Dutch bible, a large silver salver or waiter, a present from Samuel Schuyler, William Lupon and Cornelius Switts, plate). Executors the wife, son Abraham, da. Helena Bogart and son-in-law John Mason. Witnesses Archibald Laidlie, Mathias Ernest and John Oothout. Proved at Bernards Town, N. J. Copy.

1903 (V 121) 1776 July 7 1785 March 5 **van BUNSCHOTEN, Teunis,** of Rhynbeek Prect., Dutchess Co., yeoman. Wife Elsje, sons Solomon, Egenas, Egbert, Harmanis, Jacobus and John, daughters Catharine, wife of Christian Bergh jun., Mary, wife of Stephanis Freligh, Neeltje, wife of Johannes P. Schryver, Elsje, Elizabeth and Annatje. Real and personal estate. Executors the wife with sons Solomon and Egenas. Witnesses Peter D. Witt, Johan Petter Froelich and Zacharias Weydman.

1904 (V 122) 1777 July 19 1781 May 1 **van den BOGERT, Margriet,** of Schonectady, widow. Grandson Frans, son of son Claas van den Bogert, da. Lena, wife of Richard Collins of Schonectady, children of son Harmanus van den Bogert, grandchildren Margriet and others not named, children of dec'd da. Agnitie Nixon, da. Suffia Voorhis, children of Cathrine Calvin, Marite Morrison. Real and personal estate. Executors Abraham Fonda and Takenas van den Bogert. Witnesses Alexander Vedder, Benjn. Young and Caleb Beck, merchant.

1905 (V 123) 1777 April 25 1778 Novbr. 25 **Van ETTEN, Anthony,** of Goshen Prect., Orange Co. Wife Annatje, children Levi, Henericus, Thomas, Jacob, Antje, Jannekie, Margaret, Alida, Blandina and Marie. Real and personal estate. Executors the wife, son Levi and bro.-in.law Jacob de Witt Gumaer. Witnesses Yohannes Decker jun., Samuel Davis and Thomas Kyte, of Ulster Co., schoolmaster.

1906 (V 124) 1777 May 19 1784 Septbr. 2 **ver PLANCK, Philipp,** of Rumbouts Prect., Dutchess Co., gentleman, only surviving son of Philipp ver Planck of van Cortlandt Manor, Westchester Co., dec'd. Daughters Catherine, Gertruyd, Margaret and Anna Maria, sons Philipp and William Beekman. Brother John dec'd mentioned. Front lot No. 2 in van Cortlandt Manor, land there over against Haverstraw, called

Managh, or Verplanck's Point, homefarm, personal estate. Executors Pierre van Cortlandt of the Manor, Philipp Schuyler of Albany City esqre., Samuel ver Planck of N. Y. City esqre., bro.-in-law Gerard G. Beekman of N. Y. City, merchant, bro.-in-law David Beekman of the Island of St. Croix, merchant, and John Cook of Rombouts Prect., esqre. Witnesses John Honson jun., Albert Monfoort and Jon. D. Crimsheir of N. Y. City, attorney-at-law.

1907 (V 125) 1779 May 4 1780 Decbr. 28 — **van BENTHUYSEN, Marya,** widow of Jan, of Rhinebeek, Dutchess Co. Nephews Johnbotist, son of bro. Roelof Kip, Doctor Isaac and Abraham, sons of bro. Isaac Kip, Johannis, sons of bro. Johannis Kip, and Thomas, son of sister Rachel Lewis. Real and personal estate. Executors Johnbotist Kip, Dr. Isaac Kip jun. and Abraham Kip jun. Witnesses Henry King, Everhard Rynders, of said Co., yeoman, and John Christopher Dorn.

1908 (V 125½) 1779 April 6 1781 Jany. 19 — **van BENTHUYSEN, Jacob,** of Rhynbeck Prect., Dutchess Co., farmer. John, son of Jacob van Benthuysen dec'd, "who now lives with me," sole heir. Homefarm, personal property (one silver tankard, a do. teapot, four do. salt cellars, six do. tablespoons, one do. sugar dish, one do milkpot, mahogany furniture). Executors mother Maria v. B., uncle Peter v. B. and Stephen Wynants. Witnesses Thoomes Luwis (Lewis) of said Prect., brewer, Johannes Kip jun., farmer, and Everhart Rynders.

1909 (V 126) 1780 May 6 1782 Aug. 17 — **van HOESEN, Cathariena,** of Claverack, Albany Co., spinster. Godchild Cathariena, da. of Stephen van Alen, Engeltije, da. of Casparus Huyck. Personal estate (six silver table spoons). Executor Casper Huyck. Witnesses Matthias Goes, John Jur. van Hoesen and David Brower.

1910 (V 127) 1780 Octbr. — 1783 Jany. 18

VOSBURGH, John D., of Kinderhook, Albany Co., yeoman. Wife Cornelia, sons Samuel and Dirck, da. Alida, an expected child. Real and personal estate (a large English bible). Executors the wife, bro. Evert Vosburgh and brothers-in-law Cornelius Hogeboom and Johannes Goes jun. Witnesses Peter A. Vosburgh, weaver, Mica Mudge, farmer, both of said Co. and Seth Rowlee.

1911 (V 128) 1781 March 13 Decbr. 29

van KEUREN, Mattheus, of Poughkeepsie Prect., Dutchess Co. Wife Saletija, sons Tjerck, Cornelius, Abraham, Benjamin and Mattheus, da. Mary Lawson, heirs of dec'd eldest da. Margaret Lawson. "Worldly estate." Executor son Mattheus. Witnesses Cornelious Brewer and Thomas Dearing of said Co., yeomen.

1912 (V 129) 1781 Octbr. 31 Decbr. 27

van TASSEL, William, of Philipps Prect. Dutchess Co., farmer. Wife ——, and adopted son Isaac van Tassel. Real and personal estate. Executors Joseph Bard, John Lickly and Ester van Tassel. Witnesses Philipp Steenback and Isaac Odle, both of said Prect., farmers.

1913 (V 130) 1781 Septbr. 14 1783 March 10

van LOON, Mathys, of Loonenburgh, Albany Co. Wife Annatje, son John, daughters Mary, Ida, Christina and Catherine. Real and personal estate. Executors the wife, son John and friend Jacob van Loon. Witnesses Henry Knoll, Coenradt Haake and William Adams of said Co., farmers.

1914 (V 131) 1781 Aug. 18 1782 April 3

van SCHAICK, Anthony, of the Island of Cahoes, Albany Co. Wife Christina, da. Anna, who has second son Anthony van Schaick. Cahoes or van Schaick, Haver and Platte Plate Islands, personal property. Executors the wife and son-in-law John G. van Schaick. Witnesses John van Vleck, of Charlotte Prect., Dutchess Co., blacksmith, Samuel van Vleck and Abraham van Vleck. Seal.

1915 (V 132) 1781 Novbr. 8 1783 Novbr. 6 **van ANTWERP, Wilhelmus,** of Canistagauna (Niskayuna), Albany Co. Wife Hility, Daniel G. van Antwerp, Marritje Groot, wife of Isaac van Vranka, Garret van Antwerp and sisters children. Real and personal estate. Executors the wife and friends Daniel G. van Antwerp and James van Vranka. Witnesses Cornelis Groot of said Co., farmer, Dirick C. Groodt and Cornelius Groot.

1916 (V 133) 1782 May 14 1787 Jany. 24 **van der VALGEN, Cornelis,** of Schonectady, Albany Co. Wife Rebecca, daughters Susanna and Elisabeth, son Lourance: bro.-in-law Johannes Fort to be supported. Real and personal estate. Executors brothers Claas and Petrus van der Volgen and Dirck van Ingen. Witnesses Henry Glen, esquire, Phineas Leach and Abraham A. Yates.

1917 (V 134) 1782 Novbr. 25 1784 Decbr. 21 **van ALEN, John,** of Claverack Landing, Albany Co. Wife Catherine, children Adam, Elbertie and Tryntje. Real and personal estate. The wife sole executrix. Witnesses Jacob F. van Hoesen of Claverack, yeoman, Justus H. v. Hoesen, merchant, and James Barker of Coxhacky, esquire.

1918 (V 135) 1782 March 7 1783 March 19 **VIELE, Cornelis,** of Kingston, Ulster Co. Wife Elizabeth, sons Petrus, Cornelius, Johannes, daughters Christina, wife of Tjerck van Vliet, Annatje, wife of Petrus van Wagenen, Elizabeth, wife of Abraham Vossburgh, and Marritje. Real and personal estate. Executors sons Johannis and Cornelius with son-in-law Abraham Vossburgh. Witnesses David de Lamettre jun., farmer, John van Steenbergh, silversmith, both of Kingston, and Christopher Tappen.

1919 (V 136) 1782 Decbr. 16 1783 Octbr. 2 **van SCHAICK, Wessel,** of Albany City, merchant. Wife Mary, sons John G. and Gerrit W., daughters Mary van Schaick, Catharine, wife of Peter

Gansevoort, esquire. Real and personal estate. Executors the wife, da. Mary, the two sons and the son-in-law. Witnesses Jacob van Schaick, Abraham Eights of said City, sailmaker, and Robert Yates.

1920 (V 137) 1782 July 13 1784 Novbr. 8 **VAIL, Benjamin,** of Goshen Precinct, Orange Co. Children William, John, Mary, Pain, Benjamin, Lidia, grandson Alsop, son of Benjamin, Lidia, da. of son John. Real and personal estate. Executors William and John Vail. Witnesses William Wickham of said Prect., yeoman, John Garey and William Jackson.

1921 (V 138) 1782 Aug. 7 1785 April 20 **van VECHTEN, Theunis,** of Catts Kil, Albany Co., yeoman. Wife Judith, sons Samuel, Jacob, Theunis, Abraham, da Elizabeth. Real and personal estate (a large Dutch bible and picture of uncle Samuel van Vechten). Executors the wife and sons. Witnesses Cornelius Dubois, Wilhelmus Dedrick and Henry Oothout of Catts Kil District, esquire.

1922 (V 139) 1782 June 12 —— **van VALKENBURGH, Lambert,** of Coxhacky Distr., Albany Co., yeoman. Wife Catherine, sons Jacobus, Dirck and Abraham, daughters Helena, Christina and Elizabeth. Real and personal property. Executors son Jacobus, Samuel van Vechten and Henry Oothoudt, all of said District. Witnesses John Demarest, John Shuneman jun., and Caty Demarest.

1923 (V 140) 1783 July 18 Octbr. 17 **van KLEECK, Leonard,** of Poghkeepsie Prect., Dutchess Co., esqre. Wife Janetje, da. of Hannah ten Bruck, children Lawrence, Leonard, Sarah and Gertrude, grandchildren John and Annatje van Kleeck. Real and personal estate. Executors the wife, John Davis, John Cooke, Myndert van Kleeck and John P. van Kleeck. Witnesses Teunis Tappen, Peter B. van Kleeck, Robert Noxon and Richard Snedeker. Copy.

1924 (V 141) 1783 Octbr. 2 1784 May 10 **van BUREN, Maas,** of the East District of Rensselaerswyck Manor, Albany Co., gentleman. Wife Cattalina, son Johannis, daughters Itie, Catherine and Aaryaentie. Real and personal estate (a silver cup). Executors son Johannis and Jochem Staats of Albany. Witnesses David McCarty, John H. Beekman and William Harrison, farmers. Codicil of Octbr. 4, 1783, enumerates furniture, left to the son, and is witnessed by Eyche van Buren and David McCarty.

1925 (V 142) 1783 April 29 1784 Jany. 12 **van BUNSCHOTEN, Elias,** of Poughkeepsie Prect., Dutchess Co. Wife Jacomyntje, sons Elias, John, Teunis, daughters Catherine and Rachel. Real and personal estate. Executors the three sons. Witnesses Peter Dubois jun., Jacobus Ostrom of said Co., yeoman, and James Elderkin.

1926 (V 143) 1783 Jany. 27 1784 Febry. 27 **van VOORHIS, Zacharias,** of Rombout Prect., Dutchess Co., yeoman. Nephews and nieces: Henry and Zacharia, sons of bro. Coart, John, son of bro. John dec'd, Jacob, John, sons, and Kathrine and Jane, daughters of Bro. Jacob dec'd, sisters Garachey Brinckerhoff. Real and personal property. Executors nephews Henry, Jacob and John (son of John) van Voorhis. Witnesses Daniel ter Bos, Peter Bogardus and Isaac I. Sebring, yeomen.

1927 (V 144) 1783 May 1 —— **ver PLANCK, Isaac,** of Hacketock, Albany Co., cordwinder. Leonard, John and Thomas, sons of John L. Witbeck, of Hacketock. Land near City Hall, N. Y., on the Schepe Wey, personal property. Executor cousin John Leonard Witbeck. Witnesses Isaac D. ver Planck, David Houghtaling and Jacobus Bleecker.

1928 (V 145) 1784 Octbr. 6 1785 Aug. 13 **VEDDER, John,** of Schonectady, Albany Co., gentleman. Andries van Petten, Geertruy Robinson, wife of John Robison, Annatie Cuyler, Harmanis Cuyler, John Ja. Peck, Jacobus Harmanus Peck, Margaritha, da.

of Harme van Slyck dec'd, Harms. Pietersen, Annatie Meldrum, Arientie, wife of Niclaus van Petten, Margaret, wife of James Shuter, Anthony van Slyck, Harmanis Bradt, Albert S. Vedder. Real and personal estate. Executors Andries van Petten and Albert S. Vedder. Witnesses Francina van Ingen, Betsey van Ingen and Dirck van Ingen.

1929 (V 146) 1784 March 8 March 23 ver **PLANCK, Abraham,** of Rensselaerswyck Colony, mariner. Wife Helena, daughter Ariantie, children of bro. William ver Planck. Real and personal estate. Executors the wife, bro. William v. P., Peter Dox and Jellis Winne. Witnesses John van Sante, Jac. Winney and R. Bleecker of Albany City, merchant.

1930 (V 147) 1785 June 1 1786 April 9 **VIELE, Myndert,** of Beekmans Prect., Dutchess Co., farmer. Sons Barent, Peter, Baltus, daughters Johanna, Rebecca, Helena, Neeltje and Jannetje. Real and personal estate. Executors sons Barent and Baltus with son-in-law Abraham A. Losee. Witnesses James Emott, Peter Tappen of said Co., esquire, and Gilbert Livingston.

1931 (V 148) 1785 June 30 1786 Jany. 28 van **PETTEN, Arent N.,** of Schenectady. Children Nicolas, John, Marya and Janetie. "My estate" (blacksmiths tools and utensils). Executors Abraham Oothout and Michel Tyme. Witnesses John Js. Wemple, Neicolaes van Petten, yeoman, and Adam Ecker.

1932 (V 149) 1786 Octbr. 11 Novbr. 16 van der **COOK, Michael,** of Cooksborough, Schaticoke District, Albany Co. Wife Sarah, sons Michael, Simon and Hendrick, da. Sarah and apparently other children. Farms, tenanted by Elisha Arnold, Morris Merrel and Jacob Stover, all at Cooksborough, personal estate. Executors the three "eldest" sons above named. Witnesses Peter van Aulen, Elisha Arnold and Manuel van Allen of Schachtecock District, yeomen.

1933 (V 150) 1795 March 17 **van VORST, Cornelius,** of New Barbadoes Prect., Bergen Co., N. J. Children Ary, Garrit, Anne. House on Chapple Str., N. Y. City, do. in Read Str., personal property. Executors the three children. Witnesses Caspauras van Iderstine, Henry P. Kip and Henry Berry.

1934 (V 151) 1798 June 13 1800 March 14 **van ALEN, Abraham,** of Kinderhook Landing, Columbia Co., yeoman. Wife Cathrine, children Ally, Catelina, Lanchey, Margaret, Sally and Catherine, grandson Adam Hogeboom. Real and personal estate. Executors the wife, Bartholemew I. van Valkenburgh and Abraham Vosburgh. Witnesses David van Ness jun. and John Lovett.

1935 (V 152) 1798 July 7 **van COURTLANDT, Philipp,** of Second River, Essex Co., N. J., gentleman. Sister Johanna, James, son of late nephew John van Courtlandt, nephew Stephen van Courtlandt, Philipp Jacob Prince, nieces Elizabeth and Gertruyd, surviving daughters of dec'd bro. John v. C. Real estate at Second River, on New Barbadoes Neck and in Cortlandt Manor, N. Y., personal property. Executors nephew Stephen v. Courtlandt, General Philipp van Courtlandt and Pierre van Courtlandt jun., both of the Manor. Witnesses Benj. Helme, Thomas Post and Abr. ? Copy.

1936 (V 153) 1800 Aug. 16 1801 Febry. 18 **VIELE, Lodewicus,** of Saratoga, Saratoga Co., yeoman. Wife Eavau, sons Jacob, Simon, Abraham, Jesse, Stephen, Charles John and Lodewicus, da. Hisse. Real and personal estate. Executors the wife with sons Jacob and Simon. Witnesses Abraham Viele, Jacob S. Viele and John A. Viele.

1937 (V 154) 1801 Jany. 11 May 18 **van HORNE, David.** Wife Sarah, da. Augusta. Real and personal estate. Executors the wife and father-in-law Christopher Miller. Witnesses Abm. A. Lansingh, Theodorus V. W. Graham, Enoch Leonard and Ab. van Vechten.

1938 (V 155) 1760 March 6 — **van CORTLANDT, Eva,** formerly the wife of Jacobus v. C. of N. Y. City, merchant, letters of administration on the estate of, granted to Abraham de Peyster, esqre., John Chambers, esqre., both of N. Y. City and Peter Jay of Westchester, esquire.

1939 (V 156) Fourteen Lines of the intended will of **Stephen van CORTLANDT** of N. Y. City, esquire.

1940 (V 157) 1833 June 29 — **van RENSSELAER, John,** receipt of Philipp Viele, Surrogate at Troy, for the will of.

1941 1784 Septbr. 7 1785 Febry. 23 — **VARICK, Ann,** of Second River, Essex Co., N. J. Mary Joralemon, wife of Teunis Joralemon, son Gilliam Varick of New York, da. Mary. Personal property. Witnesses David Demaree and Anna Davaul. Proved in N. J. and Teunis Joralemon with wife appointed administrators. Recorded in Wills and Probates, Vol. I., p. 25.

1942 1781 Febry. 17 1782 Febry. 18 — **van VARICK, Effee,** of N. Y. City, widow. Daughters Effee, wife of John B. Stout of N. Y. City, baker, Dinah, wife of Thomas Periam of said City, mariner, children of dec'd son James. Real and personal estate. Executors the two sons-in-law Stout and Periam and nephew John Walter, house carpenter. Witnesses Jacob Durye, Andrew Ricker and Peter Thompson of N. Y. City, bricklayer. Recorded ut supra, p. 147.

1943 1784 Decbr. 3 1785 Febry. 5 — **van VLECK, Henry,** late of N. Y. City, but now of Bethlehem, Northampton Co., Penna., merchant. Wife Elizabeth, sons Isaac, of Philadelphia, merchant, Jacob, of Bethlehem, clerk, Henry, of Lititz Village, Lancaster Co., Penna., hatter, who has wife Elizabeth, daughter Mary, wife of Emanuel Nitschman of Bethlehem, da.-in-law Elizabeth, widow of eldest son Abraham, who has children Lawrence, Henry, Judith and Maria Elizabeth. Real and personal estate. Executors the three sons with Thomas Bartow of Philadelphia, merchant, and James H. Kip of N. Y. City, merchant. Witnesses Andreas Wilhelm Boehler, silversmith, Christn. Rens. Heckeweller, merchant, and John Ohely, gent., all of Bethlehem. Proved in Pennsylvania. Recorded ut supra, p. 167.

1944 1793 Septbr. 19 1794 July 15

van VARICK, Richard, of N. Y. City, baker. Friends Abraham Varick, merchant, and Richard Varick, attorney-at-law, both of N. Y. City heirs and executors of real and personal estate in N. Y. and N. J. Witnesses Abraham Duryee, Gabriel Furman, Isaac van Hook and Abrm. Walton. Recorded ut supra, p. 424.

1945 1792 Decbr. 19 1796 Febry. 9 Dutch

van LENNEP, Aarnoud David, of Amsterdam, now of N. Y. City. Sons-in-law Jan Willink and Jan Pieter van Wickervoort Crommelin executors of personal estate in England, France and U. S. Witnesses Jan Frelich and Jan Angerman. Recorded ut supra, p. 534, from a copy made at Amsterdam by Notary Petrus Cornelis Nahuys, June 12, 1795.

1946 1799 Decbr. 4 1800 Febry. 5

van INGEN, William, of Albany City. Wife Elizabeth, son Henry Glen, nephews James and Dirck van Ingen Mercer, sons of sister Elizabeth, wife of Alexander Mercer. "Worldly estate." Executors brothers James and Abraham van Ingen. Witnesses Sebastian Visscher, John T. Spalding and Wm. Caldwell. Codicil of Jany. 9, 1800, adds bro.-in-law Cornelius Glen and youngest child of sister Betsey to legatees. Witnesses Elizabeth Glen, Aaron H. Bradt and Geltey Robeson. Recorded ut supra, Vol. II., 222.

1947 1803 June 22 1811 Novbr. 7

VUSBURGH, Isaac, of Watervliet, Albany Co. Children Abraham, Jacob, John, Hannah, wife of James Cornelia (?), Elisabeth, wife of Cornelius Letcher, Gertrude, wife of Philipp Wendell, Margaret, wife of Garret van Benthusen, William, heirs of dec'd da. Catherine. Real and personal property. No executor named. Witnesses John Liswell, Levinus L. Winne and Jacob L. Winne. Recorded ut supra, p. 299.

1948
1815
May 20
Septbr. 8

van SLYCK, Jesse, of Schenectady City. Children Peter, Elizabeth, Simon J., Hellen, Martin, grandchildren Jesse C. van Slyck, Jemima, da. of son Abraham, Jesse van Pettan, Jesse M., son and Jemima, da. of son Martin I. Real and personal estate. Executors son Martin van Slyck, Daniel J. Toll and John Yates. Witnesses Danl. J. Toll, Ahasverus Merselis and John J. Neff. Codicil of May 22, 1815, changes bequest to son Martin to that son's wife Margaret. Witnesses Aaron I. Stevens, Frederic P. Clute and Richard Clute. Recorded ut supra, p. 328.

1949
1784
May 6
—

van HUYSEN, John, late a Dragoon in Colonel Lee's Regiment of Light Horse, letters of administration on the estate of, granted to his bro. Hermanus van Huysen, of N. Y. City, grocer. Recorded ut supra, Vol. III., p. 131.

1950
1808
Septbr. 21
1809
Febry. 17

VISSCHER, Nanning H., of Waterford, Saratoga Co. Wife Alida, da. Rachel, wife of John Knickerbacker jun., who has son Nanning Visscher Knickerbacker, wife's nephew Alexander Fonda, friend Francis Drake of Waterford. Real estate in Albany City, at Watervliet, Albany Co. and at Waterford, personal property. Executors the wife, the son-in-law and Francis Drake. Witnesses John Haswell, Saml. D. Lockwood and Ino. Stewart. Recorded ut supra, Vol. IV., p. 49.

1951
1805
May 21
1814
Jany. 3

van ORDEN, John, of Great Imboght, Town of Catskil, Greene Co., yeoman. Children Benjamin, Peter, John, Trintje, wife of Benjamin Post, Sally, wife of Samuel van Vechten. Brothers Ignatius and William van Orden mentioned. Homefarm, land at Uky Hook, do. in Town of Windham and on the Mohawk River in Glen Patent, personal estate. Executors the three sons and two sons-in-law. Witnesses Abrm. Salisbury jun., Polly Person (at date of proof wife of Frederick Rockfeller) and James Tattersall. Recorded ut supra, p. 61.

1952
1798
Octbr. 6
1815
Aug. 18

van WOERT, Henry, of Albany City. Wife Catherine, children Elizabeth, Henry, William and Catherine. Real and personal estate. Executors bro.-in-law Abraham Eights and Gerrit W. van Schaick. Witnesses James la Grange, John I. Wendell and John W. Yates. Recorded ut supra, p. 85.

1953
1625
July 31
Dutch

van NES, Cornelis Hendricksen and wife Maygen, of the Havendyck, Vianen. The survivor heir of real and personal estate. Witnesses Gysbert Barentsen, Luycas Joriensen and Rudolph van Suylen van den Natewis of Vianen, Notary Public. Albany Co. Records, Notarial Papers, I., p. 425.

1954
1638
Septbr. —
Dutch

van den BOOGAERT, Harman Meyendersen, of New Amsterdam, surgeon, about to sail for the West Indies, leaves personal property to Jellisse Claes, daughter of Sirickse. Witnesses Ulrich Lupolt and Oloff Stevensen (van Cortlandt). N. Y. Col. MSS., I., p. 44.

1955
1642
March 8
Dutch

van NORDEN, Barent Dircksen, of Manhatans Island, and wife Lysbet. The survivor, niece Femmetje Alberts, wife of Hendrick Westercamp. Real and personal property. Witnesses Maurits Jansen, Oloff Stevensen (van Cortlandt) and Cornelis van Tienhoven, Secretary. N. Y. Col. MSS., II., p. 13.

1956
1663
Septbr. 7
Dutch

van der HEYDEN, Jan Cornelissen, of Beverwyck (Albany), free merchant, born at Sevenbergen, in Brabant, and wife Aeltie Jansen Wemp, born in Rensselaerswyck Colony, da. of Jan Barentsen Wemp. The survivor heir of real and personal property. No executor named. Witnesses Henderich Yansen Rooseboom, Aernout Cornelis Veilen, D. v : Schelluyne, Notary. Albany Co. Records, Notarial Papers, I., p. 372.

1957
1663
Novbr. 22
Dutch

van VOORHOUT, Cornelis Segersen, of Rensselaerswyck Colony, farmer, and wife Brechie (Brigitta) Jacobsen. Children Cornelis, Lysbet, wife of Sr.

François Boon, Jannetie, wife of Jacob Schermerhoorn, Neeltie, wife of Hans Carelsen, children of dec'd son Claes Cornelissen van Voorhout. Real and personal property. No executor named. Witnesses Wouter Albertsen, Harmen Thomassen from Amesfoort, D. v. Schelluyne, Notary. Albany Co. Records, Notarial Papers, I., p. 395.

1958 1664 March 21 — Dutch **van NESS, Cornelis,** member of the Council of Rensselaerswyck Colony, who is about to marry again, secures to the children by his first wife Mayeke Hendricx van den Burchgraeff, vizt. Gerritie Cornelis, wife of Roeloff Cornelissen, Hendrickie Cornelis, wife of Jan Jansen van Oothout, Hendrick, Gerrit, Jan and Grietie Cornelis, wife of Pieter Claessen of Amesfoort, L. I., their mother's property. Witnesses G. Swartt, Schout of the Colony, Cornelis van Schelluyne and Dirck van Schelluyne, Notary. Albany Co. Records, Notarial Records, I., p. 421.

1959 1668 Aug. 6 1675-6 Febry. 12 Dutch **van SCHAYCK, Goosen Gerritsen,** Commissary of Albany, and wife Annetje Lievens (married July 30, 1657). Children by first wife Geertje Brants, vizt. Geertje Goosens, wife of Hendrick Caster, 18 yrs. old, now in Holland, Sybrant, 15 yrs., Anthony, 13 yrs., children by second wife vizt. Gerritie, 11 yrs., Engeltie, 9 yrs., Livinus, 7 yrs., Cornelis, 5 yrs., Margarytie, 3 yrs., Barent 1½ yrs. Real and personal property. The survivor executor. Witnesses Commissaries (Magistrates) Philipp Pietersen Schuyler, Richard van Rensselaer and Notary Dirck van Schelluyne. Albany Co. Records, Proceedings of Commissioners or Magistrates, 1676-80, p. 13.

1960 1674 Octbr. 10 — **van RENSSELAER, Jeremiah,** and wife Maria van Cortlandt. Children Kiliaen, 11 yrs. old, Hendricus, 7 yrs., Johannes, 4 yrs., Maria, 1 year. Real and personal estate. Executor the survivor. Albany Co. Records, Court Minutes, 1675-84, p. 6.

1961
1676-7
Jany. 15

van CURLAER, Anthonia Slackboom, widow of Arent, letters testamentary on the estate of, granted to William Beeckman, senior, of N. Y. City. Albany Co. Records, Proceedings of Magistrates, 1676-80, p. 157.

1962
1678
Novbr. 30

van RENSSELAER, Nicolaes, letters of administration on the estate of, granted to his widow Alida. Albany Co. Records, Proceedings of Magistrates, 1676-80, p. 395.

1963
1678
June 4, 5 p.m.
Dutch

van den UYTHOF, Wouter, of Albany, baker, and wife Elisabeth Heyndricx. Children by first husband Aeltie Lansingh, Gysbertie Lansingh, Gerrit Lansingh, Heyndrick Lansingh, Johannes Lansingh and Hilletie Lansingh. Real and personal estate. The survivor executor. Witnesses G. Swartt, Albert Ryckman and Adriaen van Ilpendam, Notary Public. Albany Co. Records, Notarial Papers, II., p. 37.

1964
1678-9
Febry. 24
Dutch

van der ZEE, Storm, of New Albany, and wife Hilletie Lansinck. Children mentioned, but not by name. Real and personal estate. The survivor executor. Witnesses Jacob Jansen van Nortstrant, Steeven Jansen Coning and Adriaen van Ilpendam, Notary Public. Albany Co. Records, Notarial Papers, II., p. 73.

1965
1679
Novbr. 11
1681
May 10
Dutch

van SCHAYCK, Gerrit, of Albany, born at Albany and wife Alida van Slichtenhorst, also born at Albany, who at date of proof was daughter-in-law to David Schuyler. Children of brothers and sisters. The survivor executor of real and personal estate. Witnesses Johannes Provoost, Dirck Wessels ten Broeck, magistrate, and Adriaen van Ilpendam, Notary Public. Albany Co. Records, Court Minutes, 1680-5, p. 114.

1966
1682
Septbr. 4
Dutch

van WOGGELOM, Jan Pietersen, of New Albany, born at Amsterdam. Wife Styntie Jans, born at Ootmars near Pamars Mills, living on the Kil van Kol,

Staten Island, sole heiress and executrix of real and personal estate. Children mentioned, but not by name. Witnesses Commissary Cornelis van Dyck, Harman van Gansevoort and Adriaen van Ilpendam, Notary Public. Albany Co. Records, Notarial Papers, II., p. 404.

1967 1684 April 4 — Dutch **VROOMAN, Matthys Pietersen,** of New Albany, and wife Maria Aernouts Viele. Daughter Geertruyt. Real and personal estate. Guardians of child Jacob Meessen Vrooman and Willem Claessen Groesbeek. Executor the survivor. Witnesses G. Swartt, Jan Becker and Adriaen van Ilpendam, Notary Public. Albany Co. Records, Notarial Papers, II., p. 484.

1968 1684 July 9 — Dutch **van LAER, Jacob Gerritsen,** of New Albany, born in the Manor of Ruynen. Brothers Jan and Egbert, Gerritsen van Laer, sisters Grietie Gerrits, Albertie Gerrits, Juditie Gerrits, Roelofie Gerrits, children of dec'd sister Geertie Gerrits, son of dec'd sister Annetie Gerrits, to-wit Gerrit Jansen Ruytingh. "Temporal estate." Executor Jan van Vynaghen, Elder of the Reformed Church, Albany, and Marten Cregier junior. Witnesses Gerard Swartt, Gerrit Bancker and Adriaen van Ilpendam. Albany Co. Records, Notarial Papers, II., p. 494.

1969 1685 Septbr. 1 — Dutch **van der HOEVE, Cornelis,** of Albany City. Present wife Metie Beeckman, children mentioned, but not by name. Real and personal estate. The wife executrix. Witnesses Paulus Maartensen, Barent Meyndersen and J. Becker, Notary Public. N. B. Testator was buried January 10, 1688–9. Albany Co. Records, Notarial Papers, II., p. 568.

1970 1687 June 17 1688–9 Febry. 5 **van der POEL, Anthony Cornelissen,** of Watervliet, Rensselaer Manor. Wife Catrine Jans Crom, daughters Elisabeth, wife of Bennony van Corlaer, Mary, wife of Anthony van Schaick, Johanna Anthonis, wife of

Barent Lewis. Real and personal property. The wife sole executrix. Witnesses Hend. van Ness, Pr. Lokermans, Robert Livingston, secretary. Albany Co. Records, Minutes, 1686–1702, p. 119.

1971 1695 Febry. 29 1702 April 17

van der POEL, Wynant, late of Albany City, now of New York. Son Malegardt (Melchior) and son-in-law William van der Bergh. Real and personal estate. Executor Wm. van der Bergh. Witnesses Heyman Coninck of N. Y., bricklayer, Peter Bogart and William Huddleston of N. Y. City, gentleman. Albany Co. Records, Wills, I., p. 81.

1972 1687 April 4 1703 March 30 Dutch

van VECHTEN, Dirk Teunissen, of Katskil, Albany Co., farmer. Wife Jannetie Michiels, children Jannetie 27 yrs. old, Weyntie, 25 yrs, Michael 23 yrs, Neeltie, 22 yrs, Johannis, 20 yrs, Teunis, 18 yrs, Annetie, 16 yrs, Fytie, 15 yrs, Samuel, 14 yrs, Sara, 12 yrs, and Abraham 8 yrs. Guardians of minor children: Marten Gerritsen van Bergen, Gerrit Teunissen, Elias Michielsen and Enoch Michielsen. The wife sole executrix. Witnesses Gerrit Vislerse (?). Wouter Albertsen and J. Becker, Not. Public. Albany Co. Records, Wills, I., p. 89.

1973 1703 Aug. 2

van HOESE, Jan Fransen, of Albany Co., letters of administration on the estate of, granted to his eldest son Juriaen van Hoese and wife Volkie. Albany Co. Records, Wills, I., p. 94.

1974 1690 June 24 Dutch

VOSBURGH, Pieter, of Kinderhook, Albany Co. Wife Jannetie, children mentioned, but not by name, bro. Isaack, sister of wife Adriaantie. Real and personal estate. The wife executrix. Witnesses Aernout Cornelissen Viele, Johannis Becker jun. and J. Becker. Albany Co. Records, Notarial Papers, II., p. 564.

1975 1690-1 Jany. 6 — Dutch

van BERGEN, Martin Gerritsen, of Albany Co. Wife Neeltie Mynders, children Gerrit, 3 yrs. old, Myndert, 1½ yrs. Home farm, land at Katskil, personal property. Guardians of children Gerrit Teunissen (van Vechten) and Claes Siverzen. Witnesses Pieter Schuyler and L. van Schaik. Letters testamentary granted to widow Decbr. 3, 1696. Albany Co. Records, Wills, I., p. 50.

1976 — 1701 June 3 Dutch

van WIE, Hendrik. The wife sole heiress and executrix, children mentioned, but not by name. Whole estate. Witnesses Gerrit Gysbertsen and Helmer Jansen. Albany Co. Records, Wills, I., p. 80.

1977 1691 July 23 —

VROOMAN, Jacob Meesen, of Albany City, carpenter. Wife Elizabeth sole heiress and executrix of real and personal property. Witnesses J. Becker, alderman and Hend. van Dyck. Albany Co. Records, Wills, I., p. 9.

1978 1690 May 8 — Dutch

van SLYCK, Jacques Cornelissen, of Shennechtady. Wife Gerritie Ryckman, children Susanna, Grietie, Herman, Cornelius, Geertruyd, Marten, Helena, Fytie and Lidia. Real and personal property. The wife executrix, with Pieter-Schuyler, Dirck Wesselsen (ten Broeck) and Johannis Glenn as assistants and guardians of minor children. Witnesses A. Appel, Jacob Staets, surgeon, and Jan Becker. Albany Co. Records, Wills, I., p. 11.

1979 1697 Jany. 8 — Dutch

VEEDER, Symon Volkertsen, of Rensselaerswyck Colony. Wife Engeltie, sons Gerrit, Johannes and Volkert. Real and personal estate. Van Rensselaer Manor Records, No. 1196.

1980 March 8 1700-1 — Dutch

van VEGHTEN, Gerrit Teunissen, of Rensselaerswyck Colony. Wife Grietie Volkersen Dow. Sons Johannis, by first wife Antje Jans, Volkert, by present wife; Pieter, son of Jonas Dow. Real and personal estate. No executors named. Witnesses J. Abeel, Justice, David Schuyler, Justice, Johannis Cuyler, Justice, Wessel ten Brook. Albany Co. Records, Wills, I., p. 112.

1981 1703 April 10 1710 June 7 Dutch **van BEUREN, Marten Cornelissen,** of Rensselaerswyck Colony, farmer. Children Cornelia Martens, wife of Robert van Deusen, Peter Marten, Maria, wife of Cornelis Gerritsen, Catelina, wife of Johannis Jansen, Magdalena, grandson Tobyas Cornelisen van Beuren, son of dec'd eldest son. Land in Kinderhook, personal property. Executors sons Peter and Marten with Albert Ryckman and Dirk Wessels (ten Broeck). Witnesses Captain Gerrit Teunissen, Wessel ten Broeck and Dirck Wessels, Justice. Albany Co. Records, Wills, I., p. 131.

1982 1706 Novbr. 24 1707 April 18 **van den BERGH, Cornelis Williamsen,** of Albany City, carman. Wife Marike, children mentioned, but not by name. Real and personal estate. Executors Wynant Williamsen van den Bergh and Francis Winne. Witnesses Hend. Hansen, Abrm. Staets and John Collins. Albany Co. Records, Wills, I., p. 125.

1983 1709 Decbr. 10 1710 June 7 Dutch **van BRAKEL, Gysbert Gerritsen,** of Schonhechtade, Albany Co., farmer. Wife Elizabeth, sons Gerrit Gysbertsen, Gysbert and other children not named. Real and personal estate. Executors son Gerrit and Volkert Symonsen. Witnesses Philipp Schuyler, Johannis Mynderts and Arent Danielsen. Albany Co. Records, Wills, I., p. 129.

1984 1714 March 3 1717 July 6 **van den BERGH, Cornelis Gysbertsen,** of Rensselaerswyck Manor. Wife Cornelia, children Gysbert, Gerrit, Tryntie, wife of Peter Waldron, Marritie, wife of Cornelis van Alstyn, Cornelia, wife of Martin van Alstyn, Mathyas, Geertie, Wynant and Goose. Real property in Albany City and N. Y. City, homefarm on E. side of Hudson R., 1 mile back into the woods. The wife sole executrix. Witnesses Goose van Schaick, Anthony Coster and Volkert van Veghte. Albany Co. Records, Wills, I., p. 171.

1985 6th Ann Decbr. 6 1714 Recorded Septbr. 18 **van NESS, Gerrit,** and wife Maria, "late by the name of Maria Lokermans"; have made marriage contract Febry 14, 167$\frac{6}{7}$. William van Ale, of Albany City, mariner, whose mother was the first wife of Gerrit van Ness, the testator, Jannetie Oothout, wife of Lawrence van Schaack sole heirs and executors of real and personal estate. Witnesses Albert Ryckman, Myndert Schuyler and Robt. Livingston jun. Albany Co. Records, Wills, I., p. 140.

1986 1715 Aug. 1 1716 Decbr. 27 **van OLINDA, Peter,** of Rensselaerswyck Manor, tailor. Sons Daniel, Jacob, Mathys. Land above Schinectade on Mohawk R., do. in the Boght of the Kahoos, personal property. Executors Col. Peter Schuyler, Col. Kiliaen van Rensselaer and Mr. Johannis Cuyler. Witnesses Abrm. Cuyler, Justice, Dirk ten Broeck and Hend. Cuyler jun. Albany Co. Records, Wills, I., p. 148.

1987 1720 Novbr. 5 1725 March 31 **van BENTHUYSEN, Baltus,** of Albany City, merchant. Wife Liedia, children Johannis, Catrena, Jacobus Perreker, and Elizabeth. House and lot in Albany City, do. in Kingston, Ulster Co., personal estate. The wife sole executrix, brothers Marten and Barent van Benthuysen and Mr. Barent Sanders tutors and trustees. Witnesses Barent Sanders, Justice, Augustinus Turck and Marten van Benthuysen. Albany Co. Records, Wills, I., p. 211.

1988 1733 April 7 June 1 **van BUREN, Maas,** of Albany Co., yeoman. Wife Magdalena, children Hendrick, Johannis, Callyntie. Real and personal estate. Executors the two sons. Witnesses Niecalaes Gaerdenier, Hendr. Beckman, Ja. Stevenson and Barent Hebun. Albany Co. Records, Wills, I., p. 202.

1989 1739 Aug. 17 1752 Octbr. 17 Dutch

van VECHTEN, Dirck, of Schagtekoek, Albany Co., farmer. Wife Maragrieta, sons Theunis, Harmen, Philipp, Benjamin, da. Anna, wife of Hendrick Fonda. Real and personal estate. Brother Leendert van Vechten mentioned. The wife sole executrix, Livynes Lewissen and Dirck ten Brock guardians the children. Witnesses Barent Egberten, Harmen Knickerbacker and Dirck ten Broeck. Albany Co. Records, Wills, I., p. 233.

1990 1740 May 24 1742 Octbr. 8

van DUESEN, Isaac, of Kinderhook, Albany Co., yeoman. Wife Bertha, children Mathewis, Cornelia, Batha, Cornelis, Isaac, Marytie, Tryntie, Elizabeth, Annatie, Sarah, Johannis and Helena. Real and personal estate. Executors the wife, son Mathewis and bro.-in-law Davidys Alsteen. Witnesses John van Rensselaer, Kielyan van Rensselaer and Rutger Bleecker. Albany Co. Records, Wills, I., p. 246.

1991 1743 Octbr. 14 Decbr. 6

van LOON, Jan, of Loonenburgh, Albany Co., yeoman. Wife Rebecca, children Johanis, Peterus, Rachel, Elsie, Elizabeth, Lenora, Susanna, Mary and Catrina. Real and personal property. Executors the wife, Barent Staats and Johannis Provoost. Witnesses Willem Waelderon, Jacob Kidney and Arent van Duese. Albany Co. Records, Wills, I., p. 278.

1992 1746 Aug. 10 1755 March 1 Dutch

VEDDER, Arent, of Schonectendy Village, Albany Co., farmer. Wife Sarah, children Harmen, Seymon, Albert, Antje, Rebecca, Angenietje, Maria, Susanna, Sarah and Eliezabeth. Real and personal estate. Executors son-in-law William Brower and Major Jacob Glen. Witnesses Albert Vedder, Vredrheh (Frederick) van Petten and John Sanders. Albany Co. Records, Wills, I., p. 290.

1993 1746-7 March 2 1755 July 8 Dutch

VEEDER, Gerrit Seymonsen, and wife Catriena, of Schonechtendy Village, Albany Co. Children Helmer, Nickes, Henderickes, Seymon, Cornelis, Aryantie, widow of Daniel Daniels, Engeltie, wife of Johans. Alb. Veeder, Annatje, wife of William Bancker, Magdelena, wife of Johannes Bancker, grandchildren Catriena, da. of Engeltie Vedder, Catriena, Maria, Elizabeth and Aryantie, daughters of son Cornelis by his first wife, Gerrit van Antwerpe, Engeltie van Antwerpe, da. of Daniel Danielse dec'd, Catriena, da. of Wm. Banker. Real and personal estate. Executors sons Helmer and Hendericks. Witnesses Joseph R. Yates, Abraham Meebie and John Sanders. In Index of Court of Appeals misplaced under S. 36.

1994 1747 May 6 1779 Octbr. 21 **VIELE, Teunis,** of Rensselaerswyck Manor, carpenter. Wife Maritie, children Lewis, John, Maria, Rebecca, Jannetie and Catherina. Real and personal estate. The wife sole executrix. Witnesses Jan Maesen whose signature is proved by his son Moses Bloomendale of said Manor, farmer, Adam Yetss, proved by his son Christopher A. Yates of said Manor, shoemaker, and James Stenhouse, proved by Peter Bradt, also of the Manor, merchant. Albany Co. Records, Wills, I., part 2, p. 25.

1995 1749 May 8 1759 Aug. 7 **van den BERGH, Wynant,** of Albany City, brickmaker. Children Volkert, Volkie, Catalina, widow of Hendrick van Hoese, Maria, William. Real and personal estate. Executors brothers Gysbert and Wilhelmus van den Bergh and daughters Catalina and Valkie. Witnesses William G. van den Bergh, Dirck B. van Schoonhoven, and Johannis van der Heyden. Albany Co. Records, Wills, I., p. 251.

1996 1756 Novbr. 24 1761 July 1 **van SCHAICK, Catherine,** of Albany City, widow. Sons Sybrant Goose van Schaick, Jacob C., Abraham, da. Debora, widow of Johannis Beeckman, heirs and executors of real and personal estate. Witnesses Volckert P. Douw, Henry van Dyck and Per. Silvester. Albany Co. Records, Wills, I., p. 255.

1997 1759 Jany. 19 1761 July 1 **van SCHAICK, Abraham,** son of preceding—of Albany City, bachelor. Brothers Jacob and Sybrant, sister Debora. Share in a house and lot at Amsterdam, Holland, derived from grandmother Elizabeth van Corlaer, do. in Loonenburgh Patent, personal estate (a silver-hilted sword, silverplate). Executors the two brothers. Witnesses Volckert P. Douw, Ino. R. Bleecker and Peter Lansingh, Albany Co. Records, Wills, I., p. 258.

1998 1760 Septbr. 8 1767 July 8 **van der WERKEN, Johannis,** of the Half Moon, Albany Co., farmer. Sons Hendrick and Johannis, heirs and executors of real and personal estate. Witnesses John Wandel, Jacob van Woert and John H. Lydius. Albany Co. Records, Wills, I., p. 312.

1999 1761 Febry. 3 July 1 **van SCHAICK, Jacob,** of Albany City, esquire. Cousins (nephews) Goose, son of bro. Sybrant van Schaick, and Goose van Schaick, son of sister Debora Beeckman. Real and personal estate. Executors bro. Sybrant and sister Debora. Witnesses Henry van Dyck, Gerrit van Sante jun., and Jno. R. Bleecker. Albany Co. Records, Wills, I., p. 261.

2000 1761 March 9 1763 Decbr. 8 **van SCHAICK, Anna Margreta,** da. of Anthony of Albany City. Sisters Catrena Coeman and Gerretje ten Eyck, Goose van Schaick jun., son of bro. Goose, daughters of bro. Anthony van Schaick, namely Maria, Anna, wife of Henry ten Broeck and Christina, wife of Anthony van Schaick jun., son of bro. Goose, Tobias, son of Coenraet ten Eyck, Anna Margreta ten Eyck. Real and personal estate. Executors sisters Gerretie ten Eyck and Catriena Coeman, with Anthony van Schaick jun. Witnesses Isaac Staats, Willem Staats, yeomen, and Abrm. Yates jun. Albany Co. Records, Wills, I., p. 286.

2001
1763
March 26
1766
Novbr. 17
Dutch

van WOORT, Pieter, of Rensselaerswyck Manor. Wife Ariantie, cousins (nephews) Jacob and Lewis, sons of bro. Jacob van Woort. Real and personal estate. Executors Casparus Pruyn and Cornelis C. van den Bergh, son of bro.-in-law Claas van den Bergh. Witnesses Ryckert van Vranken, Theunis van Waert and Ino. de Peyster. Albany Co. Records, Wills, I., p. 320.

2002
1764
May 10
1782
Febry. 8
Dutch

van Veghten, Dirck, of the Flats, Loonenburgh District, Albany Co. Wife Helena, children Teunis, Hubartis, Jannetie, Sara, wife of Isaac Kalier, Eva, wife of Abraham van Valkenburg, Maria, wife of Nicolas Spoor, Catriena, wife of Lambert van Valkenburg. Real and personal estate. Executors son Hubartis and sons-in-law Lambert van Valkenburg and Nicolas Spoor. Witnesses John ten Brouck, Martin Lydious, Jacob Roseboom and John H. Lydious. Albany Co. Records, Wills, I., p. 2.

2003
1764
Novbr. 15
1765
Septbr. 7
Dutch

van ALSTYN, Thomas, of Kinderhook Township, Albany Co. Wife Maria, children William, Cathariena, widow of Petrus Hoffman, Lambarth, Peter, Maria. Farms at Claverack, in Kinderhook Township, homefarm, personal property (silver things). Executors the wife, son William and Casparis Conyn jun. Witnesses Petrus Cool jun., Seybout Krankheyt and Gerrit van den Bergh. Albany Co. Records, Wills, I., p. 298.

2004
1769
March 30
1770
March 9

van ALEN, Jacobus, of Claverack, Albany Co., yeoman. Johannis, son of dec'd bro. Adam van Alen, Mayeke Witbeek, da. of Peter Koeyeman, children of dec'd bro. Evert van Alen and wife Margrieta, vizt. Johannis E., Abraham E., Lourens E., Jacobus E., Dirck, Adam E. and Maria E. Real and personal estate. Executors nephews Johannis E., Abraham E., and Lowrans E. van Alen. Witnesses Lourens L. van Alen, Cornelius van Dyck, both of Kinderhook, and Margrieta van Alen. Albany Co. Records, Wills, I., p. 338. Supra No. 1883.

2005
1769
Febry. 11
1770
Febry. 7

van SLYK, Andries, of Coxsaghe Precinct, Albany Co., yeoman. Wife Mary, children Baltus, Teunis, Jannitie, Lyedia, Mary, Catrina, Geertruy, Alida. Real and personal estate. Executors the two sons. Witnesses Rykert Hoghteeling, Mattys van den Bergh and David McCarty. Albany Co. Records, Wills, I., p. 341.

2006
1772
June 6
1774
June 30

van SCHAICK, Sybrant G., of Koxsaghie, Albany Co. Children Goosen, Myndert, Maria, Ryckje. House and lot in Albany City, land in Kinderhook, homefarm, share in house and lot in Amsterdam, Holland, personal property. Executors sons Goosen and Myndert. Witnesses Dejrk Vosburgh, Henry van Bergen and Peter Connyne. Albany Co. Records, Wills, I., part 2, p. 11.

2007
1770
Febry. 7
Aug. 13

van der HEYDEN, David, of Albany City, merchant. Wife Geertruy, children Dirck, David, Alida, wife of Rev. Baran Vrooman, Jacob and Rachel, wife of Dr. Samuel Stringer. Real and personal estate. Executors the wife and son-in-law Samuel Stringer. Witnesses Jno. N. Bleecker, Robert Yates, attorney-at-law, and Jacob Lansing, gentleman. Albany Co. Records, Wills, I., p. 345. Supra, No. 1887.

2008
1771
March 12
———

van der HEYDEN, Johannis, of Albany City, esquire. Children John, Jane, Mary and Rachel. Real and personal estate (a large Dutch bible). Executors da. Jane, Herme Gansevoort, Volckert Douw and Gerrit van Sante. Witnesses Martin Mynderse, blacksmith, Peter Waldron, bricklayer, and John Bay, schoolmaster, all of Albany City. Albany Co. Records, Wills, I., p. 356. Supra, No. 1889.

2009
1774
June 9
1775
March 31

van den BERGH, Mattys, of Albany Co., farmer. Wife Rebecca, sons Rykert, Mattys, John, Peter, daughters Rachel and Catrina. Real and personal estate. Executors sons Rykert and Mattys. Witnesses Philipp Connyne, Cornelius Connine and Reitsert Bronck. Albany Co. Records, Wills, I., part 2, p. 16.

2010 1785 March 19 1786 Decbr. 20 **VEEDER, Simon Johs.,** of the Normanskil, Albany Co., gentleman. Children Wyngart, Volkert and Catrena. Real and personal estate. Executors the two sons and son-in-law John Glen. Witnesses John van Neste, Hendrick van Neste and Volkert Veeder. Albany Co. Records, Wills, I., part 2, p. 51.

2011 1800 Jany. 20 Aug. 27 **van der ZEE, Cornelius,** jun., of Bethlehem, Albany Co. Wife Annautey, children Easter, Elizebeth, Affte, Rauchel, Anny, Storm, Walter, John, Garret. Real and personal estate. Executors bro. Teunis van der Zee, John Nelden Legransus, and Storm van der Zee. Witnesses Evert Wynkoop, P. D. Winne, Storm I. van der Zee. Albany Co. Records, Wills, I., part 2, p. 72.

2012 1813 March 19 1822 Decbr. 14 **van der ZEE, Albert,** of Bethlehem, Albany Co. Children Henry, Harman, Cornelius, Eva, wife of Henry Slingerland, Hester, wife of Jacobus La Grange. Home-farm, farm in Coeymans Town, purchased from Coenrad ten Eyck and David I. ver Planck, farms in Bethlehem, purchased from Nicholas Jeroleman and Garret A. Becker, the Stoner farm in Bethlehem, personal property. Executors the three sons. Witnesses Peter W. Hilton, Addison Mandell and E. Willett. Albany Co. Records, Wills, I., part 2, p. 87.

2013 (W 1) 1718 Decbr. 15 **WICK, John,** of Southampton, Suffolk Co., yeoman. Wife Temperance, sons Job, John, Henry, Daniel, James, daughters Temperance, Edith, Ann, Phebe. Real and personal estate. Executors Matthias Burnet, cordwinder, Thomas Cooper, yeoman, and Alexander Wilmut, joiner. Witnesses Saml. Gelston, Theophilus Howell and Nathan Sayze. Copy.

2014 (W 2) 1720 May 5 1745 Aug. 18 **WHITTAKER, Edward,** of Kingston, Ulster Co. Wife Hillitie, sons Edward, John, Henry, daughters Hannah, Eleoner, Theodosia, Hillitie. Real and personal estate. Executors the wife, and Major Johannis Hardenbergh. Witnesses Hendrick Schoonmaker, Samuel Burhans and Davidt Burhans.

2015 (W 3) 1725-6 Jany. 25 1727 April 10 Dutch

WESTBROECK, Johannis, of Knightsfield, Ulster Co. Wife Magdalena, sons Anthony, Johannes, Cornelius, Dirck, daughters Sarah, wife of Cornelius van Aken, Antie, wife of Jacob van Etten, grandson Benjamin, son of dec'd da. Ursulla. "My whole estate." Executors sons Anthony and Johannis. Witnesses Capt. Jacob Rutsen jun., Major Johannis Hardenbergh, Nicolaes Roosa and W. Nottingham.

2016 (W 4) 1732 April 6 1733 June 7 Dutch

WANBOMER, Pieter, of Kingston Corporation, Ulster Co., farmer. Wife Deborah, children Marcus, Christoffel, Margriet, wife of Hendrick Dojo, Marytje, wife of Simon Frere, Elizabeth, wife of Hendrick Oostrander, Antje Wanbome, Debora, wife of David Burhans, Debora, da. of stepson Nicolaas Schoonhoven. Real and personal estate. Executors sons Marcus and Christoffel. Witnesses Pieter van Aken, Mariniss van Aken and Ger. van Wagenen.

2017 (W 5) 1733 July 6 1744 May 19

WEESNER, Johannis, of Florida, near Goshen, Orange Co., yeoman. Wife Elizabeth, children Hendrick, Adam, Katherine, wife of Thomas Blain, Ann, wife of Philipp King, Mary. Real and personal estate. Executors the wife, Michael Dunning and Daniel Denton, both of Goshen. Witnesses John Smith, Joseph Sotherland and Josiah Reeder.

2018 (W 6) 1731 May 20 1735-6 March 24 Dutch

WINKLER, Herman, of N. Y. City, Captain, formerly of Curaçao. Annuls last will, made with his wife, at Curaçao March 2, 1720 at 5 p.m. Wife ——, and children, not named. Real and personal estate. Executors Joh. Cruger and Christoffel Bancker, both of N. Y. City, merchants. Witnesses Abraham Boelen, Abram Abramsen and Andries Abramsen junior. Codicil of March 15, 1734-5 appoints Charles La Roux and the wife executors. Witnesses Isabella Ashfield, John Spratt and Christopher Gildemeester. Winkler Seal.

2019 (W 7) 1735-6 Jany. 7 1749 May 27 **WULFFEN, Godfrid de,** of Albany Co. Wife Johanna, sons John and Godfried. "Whole estate" (land on Hudson R.). No executor named, but son Godfried qualifies as executor. Witnesses George William Mancius, Hiskia Dubois and Jeremia Dubois.

2020 (W 8) 1737 Aug. 31 1737-8 Jany. 30 Dutch **WALDRON, Gerardus,** of Horlie, Ulster Co. Wife Elisabeth, sister Marie Waldron. "Whole estate." Executors the wife, father John Waldron and cousin Gerardus Waldron. Witnesses Cornelis Wynkoop, Johannis Crespel and Johannis Wynkoop.

2021 (W 9) 1738 May 28 — **WEST, William,** of Kingston, Ulster Co. Mary, da. of John Davenport; freed negro slaves receive most of the real and personal estate. Executors Mattys Blanchan and John Davenport, who, refusing to act, Robert Beaver, yeoman, "the only friend or relation, that I know of," writes Edw. Whittaker, is appointed administrator July 28, 1738. Witnesses Aerri van Slit, Gisbert Krom, and Charles Brodhead.

2022 (W 10) 1739 Septbr. 19 1747 April 3 Dutch **WYNKOOP, Cornelis,** of Horlie, Ulster Co. Wife Hendrica, children Judickje, Elisabeth, Cornelia, Johannis, Catharina, Lea, Adriaan, Cornelis, Petrus and Maria. Real and personal estate (a large bible). Executors the wife and five eldest children, to wit Judickje, Elisabeth, Cornelia, Johannis and Cathariena with bro. Johannis Wynkoop. Witnesses Antony Créspel, Johannis Suylandt and Dirck Wynkoop.

2023 (W 11) 1744 June 5 1758 June 10 **WAAREN, William,** of the Fisk Kils, Dutchess Co. Wife Mary, sole heiress and with Jacob de Peyster executrix of real and personal estate. Witnesses Johannes Willsey, Henry Lewis, of said Co., schoolmaster, and John Cuer. When the widow qualifies as executrix, June 6, 1671, she is called "widow of Francis Wilson, formerly Mary, widow of William Waaren."

2024 (W 12) 1746 April 2 1752 March 9

WILTSE, Martine, of Rombouts Prect., Dutchess Co., farmer. Wife Janetje, sons Jacob and Martynes, daughters Maria, Sytje, Margarett, Janetje and Hannah. Real and personal estate. Executors the wife, bro. Cornelius Wiltse and friends Cornelius van Wyck and Francis Brett. Witnesses Maretje, Phillip, Ab: van Wyck, of N. Y. City, merchant, and Theodorus van Wyck, son of Cs. The wife qualifies March 9, 1752, being then the wife of Thomas Cornell.

2025 (W 13) 1746 June 14 1760 May 27

WILEMAN, Rachel, of Ulster Co., widow. Son John Bayard, and da. Elizabeth Wileman, heirs and executors of real and personal estate. Witnesses Vinc. Matthews, Josias Welling of Goshen, Orange Co., and Benjamin Eakerley. Proved in Orange Co. Daughter Elizabeth qualifies as Elizabeth Matthews.

2026 (W 14) 1747 Novbr. 25 1771 July 19

WOERTENDYCK, Frederick, of Tappan, Orange Co. Wife Dievertje, sons Rynier, Jacob and Frederick, daughters Aeltje, wife of Jan Vliereboom and Claesje. Homefarm, land on Paskack Brook, personal property (a great Byble) The wife sole executrix. Witnesses Teunis Blauvelt, of Tappan, farmer, Ysack Ab. Blauvelt and Johannes fferdon. Codicil of June 16, 1752, makes no change. Witnesses Lucas Cornel of Bergen Co., N. J., farmer, Albert Cornell and Abraham Haring.

2027 (W 15 & 16) 1748 June 29 1750 Septbr. 25 Dutch

WITBEECK, Johannes Luykassen, of Rensselaerswyck Manor, Albany Co. Mother Catharina Witbeeck, brother Abraham, children of dec'd sister Geertruy van Veghten, to wit, Catherine, wife of Hermanus H. Wendell, Cornelis, Luykas, Engeltie, Philipp, Marytje and Johannes van Veghten. Real and personal estate. Executors friends Andries Jansen Witbeeck and his brother Johannis Jansen Witbeeck. Witnesses Petrus Douw, Gerrit Lansingh and Johannis Glen.

2028 (W 17) 1748-9 March 3 1751 May 6 **WATKINS, Ephraim,** of Ulster Co., carpenter. Wife Joanna, sons Joseph, Abel, Samuel, Ephraim and Hezekiah, daughters Eunice, Tabitha, Joanna and Bridget. Real and personal property. Executors the wife and bro. Hezekiah Watkins. Witnesses Ino. Yalverton, Mary Yalverton and Amy Carman.

2029 (W 18) 1749 July 29 1750 June 20 **WENDELL, Evert,** of Albany City, attorney-at-law. Wife ——, children Johannis, Abraham, Philipp, Arjantie, Elizabeth and Engeltie. Real and personal estate. Executors son Abraham and daughter Engeltie. Witnesses John H. Lydius, Tieleman van Schelluyne and Peter Lansingh.

2030 (W 19) 1750 Decbr. 14 1751 May 1 **WOOD, John,** of Little Worth, Ulster Co. Wife Hannah, daughters Abigail, Deborah, Mary and Hannah, sons Daniel, John and Jonas. Real and personal estate. Executors bro. Timothy Wood and Abimal Youngs. Witnesses Daniel Wood, Jonathan Smith and Danl. Everett.

2031 (W 20) 1750 Septbr. 9 Octbr. 4 **WATTS, Robert,** of N. Y. City, merchant. Grandsons Robert Watts, John Watts, grandda. Anne Watts, kinsman John Riddle, nephew John Watts of Edinburgh, North Britain, niece Margaret Watts, da.-in-law Ann Watts, son-in-law Richard Riggs, and son John Watts. Real and personal estate. Son John Watts executor. Witnesses Jos. Robinson, W. Hamersley and Jos. Murray. Copy.

2032 (W 21) 1751 Aug. 12 Aug. 30 **WYTT, John,** of N. Y. City, carpenter. Wife Sarah, small children, not named. Real and personal estate. The wife sole executrix. Witnesses Peter Kirby, Isaac Lardant and Chas. Johnston. Copy.

2033 (W 22) 1753 Decbr. 10 1754 Septbr. 28 **WEBER, Alexander,** of Orange Co. Wife Maria, children of first and second marriage Susanna, Marritie, Geertruy, Cathreana, Hendrick and John. Real and personal estate. Executors Hendrick Snider and Jehenes

Frees. Witnesses Andries Onderdonck jun., farmer, Cornelus Eckesen, boatman, and Abrm. Onderdonck, shopkeeper.

2034 (W 23) 1753 Aug. 28 1759 Octbr. 11 **WINNE, Peter,** of Albany City, gentn. Bro.-in-law Abraham Dow, sisters Maritie, wife of Barent van Bura, Anna, wife of Johannis Hun, Elizabeth, widow of Abraham Vosburgh, nephews Peter Winne Dow, Volcart Dow, nieces Elsie and Margret Dow. Real and personal estate. Executors brothers-in-law Barent van Beure, Johannis Hun and Abraham Dow. Witnesses Jacob van Schaick, Harme Gansevoort, both of Albany City, merchants, and Harmanis Wendell. Codicil of Septbr. 26, 1757, devises land at Anthonys Nose, Albany Co. and a large silver tankard. Witnesses Gs. D. Bois, John van Cortlandt, both of N. Y. City, gentlemen, and Philipp v. Cortlandt.

2035 (W 24) 1754 22d Day 9th Month 1758 Aug. 21 **WINTER, John,** of the Out Ward, N. Y. City, taverner. Wife Hannah, children Joseph, Benjamin, Gabriel, John, Hannah and Mary. Real and personal estate. Executors the wife with sons Joseph and Gabriel. Witnesses Stephen Carpenter, Paul Roome and Nathaniel Hutchins of N. Y. City, schoolmaster. Copy.

2036 (W 25) 1754 June 26 1763 April 5 **WENDELL, Hermanus,** of Albany City, shoemaker. Nephew Philipp, son of dec'd bro. Evert Wendell, sister Arryantie Wendell, brothers Jeronimus and Tjerck Wendell. Real and personal estate. Executors Jacob Glen of Scotia, Schenectady Township, gent., and Evert Wendell of Albany City, merchant. Witnesses Ja. Stevenson, attorney-at-law, Isaac Kip, merchant, and Neicholas Cuyler, merchant, all of Albany City. Sister Aryantie Wendell enters a caveat against granting letters of administration Decbr. 20, 1762, but is officially declared insane, by Volckert P. Douw, Mayor of Albany. The executors named being dead letters testamentary are granted to nephew Philipp Wendell, cordwainer, and cousin John Beekman, trader.

2037 (W 26) 1755 Aug. 18 Novbr. 11 **WHITLOW, John,** of Goshen Prect., Orange Co. Wife Pheby, sons of bro. Alexander Whitlow. Real and personal estate. Executors Jeremiah Smith and Bazalel Seely, both of Orange Co. Witnesses Michael Jackson, Daniel Gale and Isaac Smith of said Prect., weaver.

2038 (W 27) 1756 31st Day 12th Month 1764 Febry. 7 **WHITE, Benjamin,** of Crum Elbow Prect., Dutchess Co. Sons Peter, William and Andrew. Real and personal estate. Executors sons William and Andrew. Witnesses William Palmer, John Hustead of said Co., yeoman, and Jacob Watson.

2039 (W 28) 1756 Decbr. 22 1761 June 1 **WALDRON, Resolvert,** of Haverstraw, Orange Co. Wife Matcha, sons John, Addriaen, Jacob, daughters Anne, Elizabeth, Pegge, Cate. Real and personal property. Executors the wife and Thomas Osborn. Witnesses James Lamb of said Co., farmer, and John Kreun.

2040 (W 29) 1758 Decbr. 22 1759 May 1 **WERTH, Johannis,** of Albany City, yeoman. Friends Johannis Frickhever and wife Catharina of said City, innkeepers, sole heirs and executors of real and personal estate. Witnesses Georg Habacher, Johannis van Santen and Johs. van der Heyden.

2041 (W 30) —— 1759 Septbr. 10 **WRAXALL, Peter,** at present of N. Y. City. Wife Elizabeth, father John Wraxall of Bristol, England, sisters Mrs. Ann Wraxall, Mrs. Mary Wraxall, niece Elizabeth, da. of bro. Richard W., Sir William Johnson, Bart. Real and personal estate. The wife sole executrix. Not signed nor witnessed, but proved by the testimony of Ann Devisme, wife of Philipp Devisme of N. Y. City, merchant, and sister of Mrs. Elizabeth Wraxall, who says P. W. died July 11 last and that the paper was found in his travelling bag. John Watts and Beverly Robinson testify as to handwriting. Copy.

2042 (W 31) 1759 June 2 June 18 **WHITMAN, Zebulon,** of Huntington, Suffolk Co. Wife Phebe, da. Margaret, sons Isaiah and Jarvis. Real and personal estate. Executors John Whitman and Joshua Wood. Witnesses Isaac Powell, Eliphelet Whitman, Nathaniel Whitman of said Co., carpenter, and Robart Jarvis. Copy.

2043 (W 32) 1759 Febry. 9 1761 Febry. 14 **WESBROEK, Jonathan,** of Rochester, Ulster Co. Wife Jannetie, children Dyrck, Frederick, Jonathan, Helena and Annatje. Real and personal estate. Executors the wife, bro.-in-law Fredrick van de Merken, and cousins Benjamin, Jacob and Hendriekus Hoornbeek. Witnesses Jacob de Witt, yeoman, Philipp Swartwout and Jacobus Wynkoop.

2044 (W 33) 1759 May 19 1785 March 8 **WING, Jedediah,** of Beekmans Prect., Dutchess Co. Wife Elizabeth, sons Elihu, Garshom, Elisha, Prime, daughters Abigail, Mehetabel, Deborah, Elizabeth, and Dorcas. Real and personal estate. Executors the wife and son Elihu. Witnesses Philipp Allen of said Co., farmer, Weston Allen and Elisha Allen.

2045 (W 34) 1760 April 6 1761 April 18 **WINSLOW, Joseph,** senior, of the Fishkils, Dutchess Co., yeoman. Children not named, grandchildren by da. Sarah. "Worldly estate." Executors sons Samuel and Joseph Winslow. Witnesses John Griffin and Cornelious Teatchout.

2046 (W 35) 1761 May 26 Septbr. 24 **WALL, Elisabeth,** of N. Y. City. Son James Quig, da. Mary Clark, who has son Thomas. Real and personal estate. Executors son James Quig and Richard Bidden. Witnesses Edward Man, Patrick Flynn and Henry Peckwell of N. Y. City, schoolmaster. Copy.

2047 (W 36) 1761 Octbr. 17 1771 Octbr. 8 **WITBEEK, Jonas,** of the Neutenhoek, Albany Co., yeoman. Wife Dorotha, son Volckert, daughter Engeltie heirs and with bro.-in-law Abraham Douw executors of real and personal estate. Witnesses Peter W. Douw of Albany City, schipper, Myndert Vosburgh, tailor, and Robert Yates.

2048 (W 37) 1763 May 2 1764 Octbr. 6 **WENDELL, Evert Io.,** of Albany City, trader. Mother Annatie E. Wendell, sisters Geesie, Cathaline, wife of Gysbert Marselis, son of sister Catharine, children of dec'd. sister Elizabeth. Real and personal estate. The mother sole executrix. Witnesses Gerrit van Sante junior, Robert Yates and Cornelius Wendell, all of Albany City.

2049 (W 38) 1763 Decbr. 18 1764 June 15 **WOOD, Alexander,** of New Windsor Prect., Ulster Co., millwright. Wife Ruth, sons Reuben, Stephen, George. Real and personal estate. Executors the wife, Silas Wood and Joseph Belknap. Witnesses Charles Clinton, Isaac Belknap of said Co., yeoman, and Cornelius Wood.

2050 (W 39) 1763 Jany. 12 1778 Octbr. 7 **WYGANT, Jury,** of Newburgh Prect., Ulster Co., yeoman. Wife Jane, children William, Catharine, Susanna, Mary, Sarah, Nancy West (a girl) and Michael. Real and personal estate. Executors Lieutenant Lewis du Boise, Humphrey Merrit and son Michael. Witnesses William Mitchel, of said Prect. yeoman, George Hallett and Thomas Palmer.

2051 (W 40) 1764 Septbr. 25 1765 Aug. 5 **WHITE, Joseph,** of Albany City, merchant. Mother Mary Tucker of Studley, Wilts Co., Great Britain, sisters Abigail Smith, Mary Deacon, Ann Afternoon, bro. Adam White of Trowbridge, Wilts Co., "my lad John Cole." Real and personal estate. Executors Volkert P. Douw, esquire, Martin Gerse van Bergen and George Wray, all of Albany City. Witnesses Wm. Benson, merchant, John Roorback, schoolmaster, both of Albany and Johannes Yates.

2052 (W 41) 1765 Octbr. 22 1784 May 17 **WITBEEK, Abraham,** of Rensselaerswyck Manor, Albany Co. Wife Annatie, sons Harpert, Johannis, and Abraham, daughters Marretje, Cathariena and Geertruy. Real and personal estate. Executors sons Harpert and Johannis. Witnesses Abraham Witbeek, Gerrit van den Bergh, of said Co. farmers, and Jacobus Cool.

2053 (W 42) 1765 March 22 June 1 **WATKINS, Hezekiah,** of the Parish of New Windsor, Ulster Co., minister of the Church of England. Cousins Tabitha Tuthill, Eunis Reeve and Bridget Goldsmith, nephews Edward Wooster, Joseph Watkins, Samuel Watkins, Ephraim Watkins and Hezekiah Watkins. Real and personal estate. Executors nephews Joseph, Samuel and Ephraim Watkins. Witnesses Silas Peirson of said Co., yeoman, Rachel Colman and Flet[r] Mathews.

2054 (W 43) 1765 Novbr. 7 1767 April 15 **WESTERVELT, Roelif,** of Poughkeepsie Prect., Dutchess Co., yeoman. Children Casparus, Aultie and Albert. Real and personal estate. Executors brothers John Westervelt of Bergen Co., N. J., Cornelius Westervelt of Poughkeepsie Prect., Gulian Ackerman of Dutchess Co. and Christian Demorrie of N. Y. Witnesses Johannis van Stenbergen, Benyamen Westervelt and Peter Dubois of Dutchess Co., yeoman.

2055 (W 44) 1765 Octbr. 20 1768 Septbr. 5 **WHITAKER, Edward,** of Kingston, Ulster Co. Children James, Edward, Abraham, Nelly, Elizabeth, Rachel, Hillitje and Margaret. Real and personal estate. Executors the three sons and son-in-law Jacobus Swart. Witnesses Sampson Davis, blacksmith, James Hamilton, yeoman, both of Kingston Corporation and Samuel Legg.

2056 (W 45) 1766 6th Day 2d Month Aug. 28 **WING, John,** of Batemans Prect., Dutchess Co. Wife Hannah, sons John and William, daughters Dinah, Martha and Hannah. Home farm, land in Newtownships on Otter Creek, personal property. Executors the wife, Benjamin Duvel and Edward Shove. Witnesses Daniel Hoag, yeoman, Judah Hoag and Dobson Wheeler of New Milford, Connt.

2057 (W 46) 1768 March 4 1774 Octbr. 19 **WAELDERON, (Waldron), William,** of Albany City, "*measoner*." Children Peter, Cornelia, wife of Patrick Clark, Neeltie, wife of Volkert van den Bergh, Anna, children of da. Tryntje vizt. Elizabeth and Engeltie. Real and personal estate (a large Bible). Executors

Jacob C. ten Eyck, Hendrick Isaac Bogert and Peter Yates. Witnesses Adam Yates of said City, cordwainer, Peter W. Yates and Ann Mary Yates.

2058 (W 47) 1768 Jany. 12 Febry. 10 **WHARREY, John,** of Wallkil Prect., Ulster Co. Wife Mary, sons David, Evins, Robert, John, James, Daniel, Grahames, Charles, daughters Jain, Nancy, Sarah. Real and personal estate. Executors the wife and Hugh Umphrey. Witnesses James McClaghry of said Co. esquire, Thomas Peacock and Alexander Graham.

2059 (W 48) 1769 May 31 1771 April 27 **WENDELL, Harmanis,** of Albany City. Wife Catharine, sons Harmanis, Cornelius, Johannis and Jacob, daughters mentioned, but not by name. Land at Canejoharrie between the two Canada Creeks, do at Schenectady, personal property. Brothers-in-law Lucas and Philipp van Vechten with son Cornelius, executors. Witnesses Abrm Yates jun., Matthew Visscher and Christr. P. Yates.

2060 (W 49) 1769 Octbr. 11 1785 March 3 **WITTBECK, Leendert,** of Hagtekock, Albany Co., yeoman. Wife Catalyna, sons Johannis and Isaac, heirs and executors of real and personal estate. Witnesses Dirck van Veghten, Nicolas Spoor and Henry Knoll of Coxhacky District, surgeon.

2061 (W 50) 1770 Jany. 30 1774 May — **WILLETT, Isaac,** late Sheriff of the Borough of Westchester, Westchester Co., gentleman. Wife Margaret, nephews Isaac Willett, Lewis Graham, Gilbert Colden Willet, grandson of Lt.-Gov. Colden, brothers William and Cornelius Willett, Ann McElworth. Homefarm on Cornwells Neck, lands in the Mohawk Country, personal estate. Incomplete copy.

2062 (W 51) 1770 March 10 May 28 **WILLIAMS, Gilbert,** of Orange Co. Brothers John and William, sisters Mary and Sarah Williams. Real and personal estate. Executor bro. William Williams. Witnesses Henry Wisner junior, of said Co., esquire, Joseph Wood and Joseph Clark.

2063 (W 52) 1771 April 10 June 3 **WARD, John,** of Charlotte Prect., Dutchess Co., yeoman. Son Daniel. Real and personal estate. Executors brothers Daniel and Anthony Ward. Witnesses Wheeler Case, Daniel Carpenter of said Prect., yeoman, and Mary Ward.

2064 (W 53) 1771 March 11 Septbr. 5 **WHEELER, Samuel,** of Kinderhook, Albany Co., farmer. Wife Margeret, daughters Hillitie, wife of William Fitch, Syna, wife of Tobias van Slyck, stepson Peter Hendr. Gardenier, granddaughters Margaret and Abigail Fitch. Real and personal estate. Executors son-in-law Wm. Fitch, Robert van Dusen and Peter Abrm. Vosburgh. Witnesses Johs. Schrom, John E. Wheeler and Catrena van Duesen.

2065 (W 54) 1771 Jany. — Febry. 12 **WILSON, Alexander,** of N. Y. City, shopkeeper. Wife Jane, children Alexander and Jane. "Worldly estate." Executors the wife, Samuel Lowdon and Jonathan Blake. Witnesses John Willson, Alexander Robertson of said City, shopkeeper, and James Gourlay. Copy.

2066 (W 55) 1772 June 20 1773 Jany. 23 **WINCKEL, Lydia,** of the North East Prect., Dutchess Co., widow. Children Lydia, wife of William Smith, Sarah, wife of David Benton, of Salisbury, Litchfield Co., Connt., Stephen, Timothy, Anna, Justus, heirs of dec'd son Robert. "Worldly estate." Executors son Timothy Winckel and James Winckel of said Prect. Witnesses Whealer Robinson, Benjn. Crosby and Elisha Calver.

2067 (W 56) 1772 — — **WITBEEK, Luycas,** of the Nuttenhook, Albany Co., farmer. Nephew John Witbeek of Wolvenhook, Doratha P., da. of Peter I. van Valkenburgh, Volkert V. Witbeek, nephews John and Volkert, sons of bro. Jan Witbeek, Andries A., Albert and John A., sons of bro. Andries Witbeek. Land at Hosick and in Albany Co., personal property. Executors Andries A. Witbeek, Peter

Winne Douw and John A. Witbeek. Witnesses Jacob v. Valkenborgh, Pieter J. v. Valckenburgh, and Mataewes v. Valckenburgh. Endorsed "filed Novbr. 24, 1774."

2068 (W 57) 1773 Octbr. 1 Novbr. 16 **WOOD, Daniel,** of Florida, Goshen Prect., Orange Co. Wife Mary, children John, Jonas, Andrew, Daniel, Mary Hutron, Elizabeth Papinoe and Deborah Baylie. Real and personal estate. Executors Ananias Whiteman and John McCamly. Witnesses Jonas Roe of said Co., farmer, Joshua Whitman and Ruth Jayne.

2069 (W 58) 1773 March 6 1779 Jany. 6 **WICKHAM, Samuel,** of Goshen Prect., Orange Co. Wife Hannah, children Samuel, Israel, Jerushe, Mathew, Elizabeth Jackson, Abigail Smith, Julianah, Margaret and Mary. "Worldly estate." Executors Benjamin Gale and Samuel Denton. Witnesses John Gaery, weaver, John Case, saddler, and Samuel Wilkeson.

2070 (W 59) 1773 April 3 1779 April 9 **WELLS, Abel,** of Wallkil Prect., Ulster Co. Wife Mary sole heiress and executrix. Witnesses William Denn, Phebe Denn and Daniel Denn.

2071 (W 60) 1773 Febry. 23 1783 Novbr. 11 **WOHLEBEN, Nicolaus,** of Burnetsfield, yeoman. Wife Maria Elisabeth, children Henry, Dieterick, Johannis, Abraham, Jacob, Sophia, Catharina, Elisabeth, Magdalena, Anna and Anna Maria. Real and personal estate (a bible). Executors da. Anna Maria, Jacob Boeshorn and Dietrich Staehl. Witnesses Lorentz Herter, John Nikass Herden and Wm. Petry. Proved in Tryon Co.

2072 (W 61) 1774 July 16 Novbr. 30 **WHITE, John,** of Rockingham, Cumberland Co., N. Y. (now in Vermont), yeoman. Wife Jemima, children John, Jonathan, Jemima Wheeler, Samuel, Joas, Moley, Colego (a son), Lydia, Anna, Ruth, Lucy. Real and personal estate. Executor Oliver Covell of Rockingham. Witnesses Joseph Wood, Simon Baker, both of the same place, yeomen, and Patience Barker.

2073 (W 62) 1773 Novbr. 10 1775 Jany. 17 **WATKINS, Joseph,** of Wallkil Prect., Ulster Co. Wife Sarah, children Sarah, Debora, Dolle, Thomas, Joseph, Abel. Real and personal estate. Executors bro. Samuel Watkins and Stephen Harlow. Witnesses Joshua Brown jun., of Orange Co., yeoman, Joanna Brown and Dolle Watkins. Codicil of Decbr. 7, 1774, disposes of land in Connecticut. Witnesses Abimail Youngs of Ulster Co., yeoman, and Silas Peirson.

2074 (W 63) 1774 Septbr. 2 Septbr. 22 **WHEELER, Elijah,** of Amenia, Dutchess Co. Wife Sarah, children Nathan A., Robert K., Joanna, Elizabeth, Elijah, Cyrus M. and William. Real and personal estate. Executors the wife and bro. Eliphalet Wheeler. Witnesses Peter Mills, Martin Delamatter and Oliver Fuller.

2075 (W 64) 1775 May 10 1780 July 17 **WELLS, Joshua,** of Goshen Precinct, Orange Co., blacksmith. Wife Joana, sons Goshum, Samuel and Joshua, daughters Bathia, Joana, Debora, Deliverance, Mahitable and Hulda. Real and personal estate. Executors the wife, bro. Samuel Wells of Long Island, and Thomas Moffat of Bloomingrove. Witnesses Hugh Dobbin, George Howell of said Prect., yeoman, and David Howell.

2076 (W 65) 1775 May 26 1784 Decbr. 28 **WILTSE, James,** of Beekman Prect., Dutchess Co., weaver. Wife Sarah, da. Elizabeth, wife of Wm. McNeil, grandson James Wiltse McNeil. Real and personal estate. Executors son-in-law William McNeil and John A. Brinckerhoff. Witnesses Joseph Balding of said Co., farmer, William Shearer and William Humfrey.

2077 (W 66) 1775 April 8 1784 Decbr. 13 **WESTFAEL, Jacob,** of Goshen Prect., Orange Co., yeoman. Grandchildren Jacob Cole, Jacob Schoonhoven, Jacob Westfael jun., Margaret Cole, wife of Haremanus Vanimwegen, Margaret Westfael, wife of Hezekiah Rosekranse, Margaret, da. of George Kimber, Margaret and Dievertje, das. of son Cornelius dec'd, heirs of daughters Marya and Johanna, dec'd daughters Leonora, Elizabeth and Sarah. Real and personal estate. Executors grandsons Josias Cole of Wantage, Sussex Co., N. J. and Jacob Cole of Goshen Precinct. Witnesses Joseph Drake, Jacob Schoonhoven of said Prect., farmer, and Thomas Kyte.

2078 (W 67) 1776 Aug. 15 1781 June 18 **WACHTEL, George L.,** of Rhinebeek Prect., Dutchess Co., physician. Wife Catharine, da. Elizabeth; Dorothy, da. of George Stevers, Polly, da. of stepda. Anna Maria Hessin, stepchildren Catharina Riegler, Susannah Fischer and David Riegler. Real and personal estate. Executors the wife, John Ketteman, John William Tillman and Conraat Baumes. Witnesses John Michael Fridrich, John Schultzs of said Prect., miller, and Christian Schultz.

2079 (W 68) 1776 May 30 1783 May 5 **WELLS, John,** of Orange Co. Wife Abigil, sons Israel, Joshua, daughters Abbigil, who has son David (Swese ?) Mary, and other children, and nephew Richard, son of bro. Samuel Wells. Homefarm, land bo't from Henry Wisner, tract in Orange Co. along the Jersey line, do. in Pochuck Seder swamp, do. in Town of Battle Burrow, 12 miles from Connecticut R., do. on Shongum Kil near Minnesink Mts., personal property. Executors sons Israel and Joshua Wells, and Henry Wesiner jun., son of Henry Wesiner, esquire. Witnesses John van Tuyl, Jacob Eichhorn and Arthor van Tuyl.

2080 (W 69) 1777 April 10 1782 June 28 **WILLBUR, Benjamin,** of Little Nine Partners, Dutchess Co. Wife Maribah, sons William, Robert, Benjamin, daughters Sarah and Ruth. Real and personal estate. Executors Brittain Tallman and Clark Willbur. Witnesses Stephen Atwater, Benjamin Atwater and Bette Willbur, at date of proof wife of George Brownenn of Charlotte Prect.

2081 (W 70) 1778 Febry. 1 1786 Febry. 21 **WINCHELL, James,** of Little Nine Partners, Dutchess Co. Wife Mary, sons James, Martinezer, Philo Mills, John and Aaron Ely. Real and personal property. Executors the wife and bro. Nathaniel Winchell. Witnesses Simon Lewis of said Co., farmer, Hopson Bebee and George Morehouse.

2082 (W 71) 1778 Septbr. 15 Decbr. 30 **WISNER, John,** of Orange Co. Wife Anne, sons John, Henry, William and Asa. Real and personal estate. Executors bro. Henry Wisner esquire and son Henry Wisner esquire. Witnesses James Butler, shop-joiner, Sarah Wisener and Thomas Waters, labourer.

2083 (W 72) 1779 Novbr. 2 1790 Octbr. 26 **WEIR, Alexander,** bookseller in Paisley. Wife Sarah Collins, children John, Smith, Edward, Susan, Richard. Real and personal property. Executor son John Weir. Witnesses Nath. Gibson, John Gibson. Proved at Paisley.

2084 (W 73) 1779 April 20 1781 April 21 **WEYGANT, William,** of New Marlborough. Wife Mary, son John, daughters Jane and others not named, William Silkworth. "Fast and moveable estate." Executors the wife, Rick Bush and Thomas Silkworth. Witnesses John Bont, blacksmith, Matthew Wygant, yeoman, both of Ulster Co. and Robert Harford.

2085 (W 74) 1779 April 13 1782 June 28 **WILLBOR, Robert,** of Charlotte Prect., Dutchess Co., yeoman. Wife Freelove, sons Samuel, Clark, Brownen, Obediah, Car, daughters Phebe Crandel, Freelove Hod, Elisabeth, grandsons William, Robert and Benjamin, sons of dec'd son Benjamin, Britton and John, sons of dec'd son Robert. Farm, bought of tailor John Mott, personal property (a silver spoon, marked M. W.). Executors sons Clark and Brownen. Witnesses Job Taber, Thomas Tripp and Stephen Pratt of said Prect., yeoman.

2086 (W 75) 1779 July 6 1784 Octbr. 26

WERTH, Johann Jacob, of Shoharry, Albany Co., Doctor. Wife Maria Elisabeth, sons Henrich, Johannes, da. Maria, wife of Johs. Snyder, "*nevphews*" Johann Jacob and Johannes Werth, sons of son Johannes, Maria, da. of son Johannes, High Dutch Reformed Church. Real and personal estate (a pitcher or seal ring of gold, silver shoe and knee buckles, a great bible). Executors Johannes Rickert and Johannes Becker. Witnesses George Hilts, farmer, Christoph Hilts and George F. Reinhard, schoolmaster.

2087 (W 76) 1779 Jany. 9 1783 May 22

WILLIAMS, Christian, daughter of Thomas Applin, heretofore of Shepton Mattet, Sumerset Co., England, clother, dec'd, and now wife of Henry Williams of London, draper, but at this time of the Oblong, Paulings Prect., Dutchess Co. Leader Cox of Brixton Causeway, Surrey Co., England, esquire, his sister Mary Cox, Lionel Watts, schoolmaster, son of Mary, wife of Thomas Humpkins of Shepton Mattet, "wyer drawer." Real estate in Europe and America, personal property. Executor the husband Henry Williams. Witnesses Catharine McConnal, wife of Hugh McConnal of Rumbouts Prect., saddler, Isaac Talman and John Keating.

2088 (W 77) 1780 Febry. 14 1787 Novbr. 12

WHITE, Anthony, of Middlesex Co., N. J. Children Anthony Walton, Isabella, Johanna and Euphemia. Real and personal estate. Executors all the children. Witnesses Ann Kearny, Ravaud Kearny and Edward McShane. Proved at New Brunswick, N. J. Copy.

2089 (W 78) 1780 April 25 1784 Decbr. 23

WHITNEY, Daniel, of Worriek, Orring Co. Wife Martha, sons Thomas and Aaron, daughters mentioned, but not named. Real and personal estate. Executors the wife and her bro. Daniel Burt. Witnesses Daniel Burt jun. and James Burt of Goshen, said Co., yeoman.

2090 (W 79) 1780 Jany. 18 1784 May 10 **WIDDERWAX, Andreas,** of Tamhanick, Albany Co., farmer. Children "of my former wife Barbara," vizt. Bastian, Henry, Andreas, Anna Margreth, Anna Maria, Dorothea, Elisabeth and Catharina, other children by wife Anna are Hannes, Martin, Alexander, David, Peter, Jacob, Barbara Tincle. Real and personal estate. Executors Henry Grauberger and George Wetzel. Witnesses Wendell Overacker, Hannes Kebler, farmer, and John Clints, schoolmaster.

2091 (W 80) 1780 Octbr. 6 1782 Novbr. 4 **WICKHAM, Daniel Hull,** of Orange Co. Sisters Abigail, Sarah, Elizebeth, Jerusha, brothers Paker, Thomas, John, heirs of dec'd bro. Joseph. Farm at Warwitch, personal property (gold sleeve buttons and brooch, silver shoe and kneebuckles). Executors bro. John, Benjamin Pain (?) son of sister Abigail and John Sickels. Witnesses Samuel Denton of Goshen Prect., hatter, Thomas Swafford and Thomas Wickham. Codicil of May 28, 1782, adds name of John, son of bro. Doctor Thomas Wickham and is witnessed by Coe Gale, Benjamin Gale and Joseph Denton of Goshen Prect., yeoman.

2092 (W 81) 1781 April 10 May 18 **WILLSON, Justus,** of Amenia Prect., Dutchess Co., yeoman. Wife Elisabeth, brothers Samuel, Andrew and Thomas. Real and personal estate. Executors the wife and bro. Thomas. Witnesses Saml. Thompson, James Reynolds and Stephen Herrick of said Prect., carpenter.

2093 (W 82) 1781 March 9 1783 Jany. 7 **WELLS, Abigal,** of Orange Co., widow. Granddaughters Abigal, Dorothy and Julia Sweezy, daughters Abigal Sweezy and Mary Carpenter, son Israel. Personal estate (a large and two small silver table spoons, two do. teaspoons). Executor Henry Wisner jun. of Ulster Co. Witnesses Isaac Parish of Goshen Prect., cooper, James Dunning and Sarah Dunning. See No. 2079.

2094 (W 83) April 9 1782 April 26 Dutch **WENDEL, Maria,** widow of Evert, of Schonectady, Albany Co. Bro. Isaac Truex, Johannes and Simon Arientsen Vedder, Maria Arents, da. of Arent S. Vedder, Maria Rosa, Geertruyd Lambert, sisters Susanna, Elisabeth, wife of Caleb Beck, Sara, wife of Claas van der Volgen and Catalyntie, wife of Claas de Graaf. House and lot, derived from grandfather Andries Nahis (?), personal property (gold necklace, do. rings). Executors Claas van der Volgen and Andries van Petten. Witnesses John Henry, hatter, Dirk van Ingen, Doctor, both of said Township and John P. Truax.

2095 (W 84) 1782 Aug. 24 1784 Septbr. 20 **WILLIS, Richard,** of Rumbouts Prect., Dutchess Co. Wife Elizebeth, son James, grandsons Charles and Richard Willis, grandda. Elizibeth Willis. Land in New Rochelle, Westchester Co., personal property. Executors son James and Benjamin Smith senior of North Castle. Witnesses John Schut, James Schutt and Benjamin Smith, yeoman.

2096 (W 85) 1782 Aug. 10 Septbr. 18 **WHEELER, Valentine,** of Pawlings Prect., Dutchess Co., Captain. Wife Sarah, sons Josiah, Ephraim, John, da. Catherene, children of son Ephraim vizt. Catherene and a son, not named. Witnesses Edward Wheeler, George Wheeler, yeomen, and Jno. Chamberlain, physician, all of Dutchess Co. Nuncupative will, made the next day, asks John Chamberlain to assist the widow in settling the estate. Witnesses Jno. Chamberlain, Catharine Wheeler and Anna Conant.

2097 (W 86) 1784 April 20 July 6 **WARNER, John,** of Kings District, Albany Co. Wife Abigail, children Cloe and John. Real and personal estate. Executors brothers Jonathan Warner and Elijah Bostwick. Witnesses John Camp, Asa Douglass and Daniel Warner.

2098 (W 87) 1784 Aug. 8 Septbr. 3 **WHITE, Henry,** of Goshen Prect., Orange Co. Wife Sarah, children Hamilton, Samuel, Anna, Sarah and Susannah, bro. John White. Real and personal estate. Executors the wife, father Ebenezer White and Captain Abner Wells. Witnesses Jonathan Swezy of said Prect., physician, Mary Marshall and Rhoda Cossman.

2099 (W 88) 1784 July 15 Aug. 21 **WICKES, Daniel,** of Charlotte Prect., Dutchess Co. Wife Rebecca, daughters Rebecca, Elisabeth, Johanna, sons Jacob, Zopher, Silas, Joel and David. Real and personal estate. Executors the wife, sons Jacob and Silas and Isaac Bloom. Witnesses Isaac Bloom of Dutchess Co., merchant, Samuel Smith and John Stilwill.

2100 (W 89) 1785 Decbr. 17 1786 Febry. 8 **WATKINS, Ephraim,** of Wallkil Prect., Ulster Co. Wife Phebe, sons Able, Ephraim, George, Joseph and Birdseye, daughters Phebe Watkins, Jean Fairchild. Real and personal estate. Executors bro. Captain Samuel Watkins and Stephen Harlow. Witnesses James Martin, schoolmaster, George Houston, yeoman, and Samuel Pouley, labourer.

2101 (W 90) 1785 Novbr. 10 1786 Septbr. 8 **WYNKOOP, Tobias,** of the Blumountains, Ulster Co. Wife Leah, sons Hezekiah, William, Tobias, Petrus, daughters Lea and Annatie. Real and personal estate. Executors sons Hezekiah, Tobias and Petrus. Witnesses William Davenport, Adam Baer, farmer, and John York, farmer.

2102 (W 91) 1786 April 6 May 19 **WILLBOUR, Abishai,** of Washington Prect., Dutchess Co. Wife Ruth, children Oen, David, Jonathan, Daniel, Ruth, Sarah, Rachel and Mary. Real and personal estate. Executors sons David and Jonathan. Witnesses Jabez Smith, John Blayney, farmer, and Tripp Mosher, farmer.

2103 (W 92) 1786 July 2 Septbr. 12 **WAUGH, John,** of New Windsor Prect., Ulster Co. Daughters Mary, Sarah, Elizabeth and Jane, bro. Robert Waugh; dec'd bro. James Waugh mentioned.

Real and personal estate. Executors Robert Waugh of Newburgh Prect., farmer and Thomas McDowell of New Windsor Prect., farmer. Witnesses Andrew Walker of Montgomery Prect., yeoman, John Deales and David Stout.

2104 (W 93) 1793 April 13 1800 Febry. 18 **WENDELL, Abraham H.,** of Albany City, merchant. Sons Harmanus, John and Jacob, daughter Susannah or Sanneke, son of dec'd da. Annatie, vizt. John van Veghten. House and lot in Albany, land back of the Fort on the hill, Albany, do. in Sacondaga Patent, pasture lot at Schonectady, personal property. Executors the three sons and the daughter. Witnesses John Stevenson, Cornelius Wendell and John I. Pruyn.

2105 (W 94) 1775 Aug. 17 1780 May 6 **WOOD, Timothy,** of Goshen, Orange Co., cordwiner. Sons Timothy, Richard, Joseph, daughters Sarah Little, Deborah Duning, Mary Brewster, Kezeiah Oldfield, Abigail Oakley and Susannah Corrington. Real and personal estate. Executors sons Richard and Joseph Wood. Witnesses Rogr. Townsend of said Prect., merchant, his wife Keziah and Danll. Everett. Codicil of Aug. 21, 1779 adds grandda. Abigail Coleman and is witnessed by John Gale, Daniel Everett and Rogr. Townsend.

2106 (W 95) 1836 12th Day 7th Month 1837 July 15 **WRIGHT, Jordan,** of Flushing, Queens Co., farmer. Children John D., Charles, Jane, wife of John White, Susan W., widow of Abraham Cook, Margery Franklin, Mary Gulager, Catherine Rogers, Daniel D., grandsons Benjamin Cox and Jordan Wright Cox. Real and personal estate. Executors son John D. Wright, George Seaman of N. Y. City and Silas Hicks of Flushing with grandson Benjamin Cox. Witnesses Stephen Leonard, Cornell Peck and James D. Scott, all of Flushing. Copy.

2107 (W 96) 1775 Janry. 12 **WILLIAMS, Margaret,** of N. Y. City, spinster, letters of administration on the estate of, granted to John Taylor, one of the City Marshals, as creditor.

2108 (W 97) 1758 June 13 **WRIGHT, Thomas,** of Orange Co., weaver, letters of administration on the estate of, granted to Robert Thompson of said Co., yeoman, as principal creditor.

2109 (W 98) 1676 April 3 July 25 **WINTHROP, John,** of Connecticut Colony, now in Boston. Sons Fitz John and Wait Still, daughters Elizabeth, Lucy, Margaret, Martha and Anne heirs and executors of real and personal estate, with Captain John Allyn, William Joanes, and Major Robert Treat, all of Connecticut, Humphrey Davie, James Allyn and bro. John Richards, all of Boston, as overseers. Witnesses Thomas Thacher sen. and John Blake. Copy.

2110 (W 98a) 1701-2 March 14 1707-8 Jany. 13 **WINTHROP, Fitz John,** Governour of Connecticut. Wife Elizabeth, daughter Mrs. Mary Livingston, bro. Major Wait Still Winthrop; Trustees of Connecticut Collegiate School (Yale College). Homestead, land at Massapeage, at Mistick Mill, in New London, in the Naraganset country, on Fishers Island, personal property. Executors bro. Major Wait Still Winthrop, the da. Mary and her husband John Livingston, James Noyes, Gurdon Saltonstall and Richard Christophers. The wife spoken of only as the daughters mother. Witnesses Tho. Buckingham, Capt. John Prentts, Lieut. Jonathan Prentts and Samuel Rogers jun. Copy.

2111 1780 Septbr. 29 1786 Decbr. 29 **WHALY, Thomas,** of New York City, yeoman. Wife Sarah, sons Thomas and Hercules, da. Margaret; William Buxton of N. Y. City, baker, nephew John, son of Hercules Mulligan. Real and personal estate. Executors the wife, bro.-in-law Hercules Mulligan and Cornelius Bogert, attorney-at-law. Witnesses John Breath of said City, gentleman, Ino. Watson and Thomas Longley. Recorded in Wills and Probates, Vol. I., p. 14.

2112 1781 Jany. 15 1787 April 25 **WITTER, Thomas,** of N. Y. City, gentleman. Daughter Frances Nicholson. Real and personal estate. Trustees and executors Honble. Hugh Wallace and Alexander Wallace, merchant, both of N. Y. City. Witnesses

Dan. Gautier, Samuel Deall and James McEvers, merchant. Recorded ut supra, p. 126.

2113 1787 Febry. 11 May 10 **WOODGER, Thomas,** master of the sloop *Liberty* from New York, bound to St. Croix. Wife Mary, children Mary, Robert and William, all living at Whitby, Yorkshire Co., England. "The whole I may be found Possest of." Executor John Anderson. Witnesses James Brownbill, Frederick N. Lander and Christian Hamler (Stamler ?). Recorded ut supra, p. 143.

2114 1772 March 4 1787 Novbr. 5 **WAUGH, Thomas,** from Legerwood near Kelso in the Shire of Merse, Scotland, at present master of the schooner *St. George*. Brothers George, William and John Waugh, Rev. John Mason of N. Y. for his church. Real and personal estate. Executors Rev. John Mason and Gerret Roorback, gauger, both of N. Y. City. Witnesses John Barrea and Frederick Stymes. Recorded ut supra, p. 184.

2115 1780 March 13 1781 April 7 **WEEKS, John,** senior, of Oysterbay. Wife Rebecca, da. Jane, son Augustin, granddaughters Anne, Elizabeth, Judah, Ruth and Charlotte Weeks, grandsons William, John and Rasine Weeks, da.-in-law Elizabeth Weeks (wife or widow of son John ?). Real and personal estate. Son Augustin Weeks of Oysterbay executor. Witnesses Samuel Townsend, esquire, Michael Butler and Thomas Wright. Recorded ut supra, p. 328.

2116 1793 Octbr. 10 Octbr. 21 **WEIR, Edward,** of Philadelphia, Penna., bookbinder. Wife Margaret, sole heiress and executrix of "all the estate." Witnesses Jacob Bankson and George Judge. Recorded ut supra, p. 402.

2117 1795 Aug. 15 Aug. 31 French **WACHER, Catherine,** born at Treves, 45 yrs. old, widow of Chevalier Reser of St. Domingo. Children mentioned, but not by name. Property in Europe and at New York. Executor Duboys de la Barnarde, natif of Angoumois, 37 years old, living at Aux Cayes, Island of

St. Domingo. Witnesses Marianne Geoffrey, wife of Mr. Collier of Jeremie, and Doctor Sculle, physician to Hospital of the French Republic on Bedlo's Island, N. Y. Recorded ut supra, p. 493.

2118 1795 Octbr. 10 Octbr. 26 **WAYLAND, Levi.** Children Charles and Mary; Sarah Woollet, bro. Seth Wayland and his wife Elizabeth, children of Job David of Tromein, Somerset Co., England and Ann, bro. Job Wayland. Personal property, real estate (Tennessee Company, Georgia—Mississippi Company). Executors William Allum, Francis Wayland and Alexander Cuthill. Witness John Segar of N. Y. City, labourer. Recorded ut supra, p. 514.

2119 1808 Aug. 28 Novbr. 29 **WATERMAN, Asa** junior, of Ballston, Saratoga Co. Wife Abigail, children David, Frederic, Betsey, John, Belinda and Zelpha. Real and personal estate. Executors the wife, son David and Beriah Palmer. Witnesses Adam Comstock, David Rogers and Beriah P. Rogers. Recorded ut supra, Vol. II., p. 293.

2120 1776 Aug. 31 1784 May 28 **WILLETT, Margaret,** of Westchester Borough, Westchester Co., widow. Nephew Lewis Graham, Mary, Anna, Euphemia, and Gilbert, children of brother-in-law Thomas Willett, Gilbert Colden, Alice and Anna, children of bro.-in-law William Willett, nephew Isaac Willett, Augustin, Morris, Charles, John, Isabella Landon and Arabella, children of sister Graham, Ann McIlworth. Personal estate (a silver tankard and soupspoon). Executors nephew Lewis Graham and Dr. Daniel White. Witnesses Anthony Glean of said Co., farmer, Elizabeth Ashfield and Jane Glean. Recorded ut supra, Vol. III., p. 26.

2121 —— 1781 Aug. 15 **WHITE, Thomas,** of N. Y. City. Wife Ann, sons Thomas, Matthew, Daniel, daughters Charlotte and Amelia. Land at Elizabeth Town, N. J., personal estate. Executors the wife, son Thomas White, Alexander Wallace, Robert Ross Waddell, John Thurman and John Kelly. Witnesses Honble. Hugh Wallace of N. Y. City, esquire, John Marston and John Miller, merchants. Recorded ut supra, p. 62.

2122 1811 June 1 1813 Jany. 7 **WHITE, Hugh,** of Whitestown, Oneida Co., esquire. Wife Lois, children of dec'd son Daniel C., vizt. Fortune C., Andrew and Esther Stoers (late White), sons Joseph, Hugh, Ansel, Philo, daughters Aurilia Wetmore, Mary S. Young, Rachel Allen. Homestead, farm on Whitesborough—Utica road, land in Scriba's Patent, do. in Coxe's Patent, do. in Town of Leyden on the Black river, personal property. Executors sons Joseph, Hugh and Ansel. Witnesses Elizur Moseley, William G. Tracy of Whitestown and Lodewick Miner. Recorded ut supra, Vol. IV., p. 53.

2123 1806 March 3 1828 March 4 **WILLIAMS, John,** of Salem, Washington Co. Wife Mary, daughters Mary Blanchard, Susannah Proudfit and Elizabeth Proudfit, son John. Real and personal estate. Executor son John. Witnesses Mary Townsend (dead at date of proof), Robert Proudfit and William Proudfit. From proceedings in Supreme Court it appears that Mary was the wife of Anthony I. Blanchard, Susannah, wife of Alexander Proudfit and Elizabeth, wife of Ebenezer Proudfit, also that Mary Blanchard died on or about March 16, 1813 leaving children Maria, late wife of John McLean, John, Anthony, Susannah, wife of Henry H. Ross, Hamilton, Williams; Ann Eliza, wife of Frederick L. C. Sailly, Ellen-Jane and James-Francis; and that Maria McLean dying March 21, 1827, left Mary Blanchard, Catherine and Susannah Ross. Recorded ut supra, p. 250.

2124 1829 April 19 Novbr. 2 **WARREN, Esaias,** of the City of Troy. Trustees of St. Paul's Church, Troy. Wife ——, children George B., Phebe, Eliza Ann, wife of John Paine and Lydia. Real and personal estate. Executors bro. Stephen Warren, son George B. Warren and son-in-law John Paine. Witnesses David Buel jun., Lewis Lyman, and Elisha Sheldon. Recorded ut supra, p. 263.

2125 1818 Jany. 11 1720 Octbr. 28 **WALKER, Benjamin,** of Utica, Colonel. Daughter Eliza L. de Villehant, sisters Sarah, wife of William Salter, Deborah Morris. Real and personal estate. Executors Morris S. Miller, Abraham Varick and Nathan Williams. Recorded ut supra, Vol. V., p. 1.

2126 1652 June 20 — Dutch **WOUTERSEN, Egbert,** from Isselsteyn, and wife Engeltie Jans from Brested, living on Manhatans Island. The survivor, brothers and sisters living in the Netherlands. Witnesses Vincent Pikes and Jan M. de Lamontagne jun. N. Y. Coll. MSS., III., 109.

2127 1664 June 12 — Dutch **WEMP, Maritie Mynders,** widow of Jan Barentsen, about to become the wife of Sweer Theunissen van Westbroeck, secures to the children by her first husband vizt. Myndert Jansen Wemp, 15 yrs old, Grietie, 13 yrs, Anna, 11 yrs and Barent 8 yrs, their patrimony. Her eldest da. Aeltie Jans Wemp is wife of Jan Cornelissen van der Heyden. Albany Co. Records, Notarial Papers, I., p. 435.

2128 1677 June 1 — Dutch **WINNE, Pieter,** of New Albany, born in the City of Ghent, Flanders, and wife Jannetie Adams, born in the City of Leuwaerden, Friesland. Son by first wife Aechie Jans, vizt. Pieter, other children mentioned, but not by name. Real and personal estate. The survivor executor. Witnesses Jan Verbeeck, Mr. Cornelis van Dyck and Adriaen van Ilpendam, Notary Public. Albany Co. Records, Notarial Papers, II., p. 11.

2129 1677 Novbr. 28 — Dutch **WILLEMSEN, Heyndrick,** of New Albany. Children of Jan van Eeckelen dec'd. and wife Gysseltie Alberts, whose guardians are Albert Andriessen Brat and Storm van der Zee. Personal estate. No executor named. Witnesses Jan Andriesen Dou, Jacob Kaspersen and Adriaen van Ilpendam, Not. Public. Albany Co. Records, Notarial Papers, II., p. 21.

2130 1684 July 6 Dutch **WINNE, Peter,** Commissary or Magistrate, of Bethlehem, Albany Co., born at Ghent. Wife Jannetje Adams, children Peter, living at Esopus, Adam, Livinus, Frans, Allette, wife of Casper Leendersten Tenyn, Killiaen, Tomas, Lyntje, Marten, Jacobus, Eva, Daniel, and Rachell. Real and personal estate. Witnesses Marten Gerritsen (van Bergen) and Cornelis van Dyck. Letters testamentary granted to son Livinus van Schaik Winne and son-in-law Caspar Leendertsen Febr. 22, 169$\frac{5}{6}$. Albany Co. Records, Wills, I., p. 44.

2131 1690 July 23 Dutch **(WYNGAARD), Jan Lucassen,** who has been obliged to flee from his farm near Schanechtede and is now going on an expedition against the French and their Indians to Canada. Wife Catharyna sole heiress and executrix of real and personal estste. Witnesses Johannis' Becker jun., and J. Becker. Albany Co. Records, Notarial Papers, II., p. 560.

2132 1690 Novbr. 24 1703 Decbr. 27 Dutch **WENDEL, Evert,** of Albany City, merchant. Wife Elizabeth Sanders, children Susanna, Robert, Ephraim. Real and personal estate. Guardians of children bro. Johannis Wendel and Jan Herberdingh of N. Y. The wife sole executrix. Witnesses Evert Wendel senior and Robert Sandersen. Albany Co. Records, Wills, I., p. 97.

2133 1691 Novbr. 23 1691-2 Febry. 25 **WENDELL, Johannes,** of Albany City, merchant. Wife (second) Elisabeth, children by first wife Maritie Sillis, vizt. Elsie and Maritie, by second Abraham, Susanna, Catalyntie, Elisabeth, Johannes, Ephraim, Isaac, Sarah and Jacob. Share in Saratoga Patent, land at Steenarabia (now Rensselaer Co.), do at Klinckenbergh (South part of Albany Co.), house and lot in Albany. The wife sole executrix. Witnesses Bernardus Lewis and Gerrit Lansing, Albany Co. Records, Wills, I., p. 2.

2134 1747-8 March 5 1749 Decbr. 27 **WEMPLE, Jan,** of the Mohawks Country, Albany Co. Wife Arjaentie, children Ryer, Isaac, Ephraim, John, Maria, wife of Lieut. Walter Butler jun., Rebecca, wife of Peter Coneyn, grandchildren John, son of dec'd son Myndert, Arent, son, and Catelintje, da. of dec'd da. Aryantie, late wife of Captain Andries Bradt. Land in Schenectady Township, homefarm in the Mohawks Country and other land there, personal property. Executors brother Jacob Glen and Robert Sanders. Witnesses John Sanders, Jacobus Glen jun. and Sander Glen. Albany Co. Records, Wills, I., part 2, p. 4.

2135 1750-1 Jany. 18 1757 March 2 **WINNE, Daniel,** of Rensselaerswyck Manor, yeoman. Wife Dirkie, children Pieter, Killyan, Jan, Frans, William, Adam, Cornelis, Altie, wife of Hendrick van Buren, Maria, w. of Cornelis Schermerhoorn. Real and personal estate. Executors sons Pieter, Killyan and Jan. Witnesses Johannis Gansevoort, Pieter Gansevoort and Johs. R. Bleecker. Albany Co. Records, Wills, I., p. 264.

2136 1769 May 31 1771 April 27 **WENDELL, Harmanus,** of Albany City. Wife Catharine, sons Harmanus, Cornelius, Johannis, Jacob, daughters mentioned, but not named. Land at Canejoharrie, between the two Canada Creeks, personal estate. Executors brothers-in-law Lucas and Philipp van Veghten and son Cornelius Wendell. Witnesses Abrm. Yates jun., Mathew Visscher and Christr. Yates. Albany Co. Records, Wills, I., p. 350.

2137 1774 Octbr. 12 1775 Febry. 21 **WINNE, Douwe,** of Albany City. Brothers Daniel and Francis Winne, sister Dirickje, wife of Guy Young, nieces Rebecca, da. of bro. Francis, Rachel, da. of bro. Jellis. Real and personal estate (a large bible and a large picture). Executors sister Dirickje Young, Wouter Knickerbacker and Abrm. ten Broeck. Witnesses Leonard Gansevoort, Elbert Willett and John ten Broeck. Albany Co. Records, Wills, I., part 2, p. 15.

2138 1774 March 19 1783 Aug. 5 **WENDELL, Annatie J.,** widow of Johannis E., of Albany City. Daughters Geese, Cateline Merselis, children of dec'd da. Elizabeth Wendell, viz. Harmanis A. Wendell, Susan A. Wendell, John Wendell and Jacob Wendell, grandson John N. Visscher, John, son of Anna and Ephraim van Veghte. Real and personal estate. Executors da. Geese, sons-in-law Abm. Wendell, Gysbert Merselis and Nanning Visscher. Witnesses Ino. Ostrander, Henry Beasley and J. Roorbach. Albany Co. Rec., Wills, I., part 2, p. 37.

2139 1783 March 21 Aug. 5 **WENDELL, Geesje,** of Albany City, single woman. Nephew John N. Visscher, sisters Cathalina, widow of Gysbert Merselis, niece Susanna, nephews Harmanus A., John A. and Jacob A. sons of sister Elizabeth Wendell, John, son of Ephraim van Veghten. Pasture land in 1st Ward, Albany City, farm in Tryon Co., Sacandaga Patent, personal property (a silver tankard, a do, teapot, another do. tankard). Executors Cateline Merselis, John N. Visscher and Harmanis A. Wendell. Witnesses Henry Truax, Henry Beasley, cordwainer, and Isaac Truax. Albany Co. Records, Wills, I., part 2, p. 40.

2140 1815 May 6 May 30 **WILLETT, Edward,** Albany City. Wife Margaret, 2 children Ann Eliza and Edward. Real and personal estate. Executors the wife, bro.-in-law Isaac Hansen and John I. Ostrander. Witnesses John Lovett, Solomon Southwick and Andrew Cooper. Albany Co. Records, Wills, I., part 2, p. 122.

2141 1833 Decbr. 2 1834 Decbr. 31 **WEBB, Charles B.,** of Albany. Catherine L. Cogswell, sisters Elizabeth B., Francis C. and Amelia Webb, niece Levinia Morgan, nephew Henry C. Morgan, John Bloodgood, Mason F. Cogswell, brothers John H. and Henry L. Webb. Personal property (testators portrait). Executors the two brothers. Witnesses John H. Webb, merchant of Hartford, Conn., and Elizabeth B. Webb. Proved at Hartford, Conn. Albany Co. Records, Wills, I., part 2, p. 144.

2142 (Y 1) 1743 Septbr. 14 Decbr. 22 **YOUNGS, Henry,** of Goshen Prect., Orange Co. Wife Ruth, sons Henry and Birdsey, daughter Ruth. Real and personal estate. Executors brothers Abimal and Silas Youngs. Witnesses George Colman, David Dayton and Danll. Everett.

2143 (Y 2) 1747 Novbr. 12 1748 April 2 **YATES, Robbert,** of Schenectady, Albany Co., merchant. Children Joseph R., Abraham, Elizabeth, wife of Ephraim Smith, Sarah, wife of Jacobus Mynderse, grandchildren Robbert, son of Joseph R., Ariantie and Marya, daughters of dec'd. da. Marya, late wife of Gerret van Antwerpen. Farm on N. side of Mohawk R. below Schenectady, do. on S. side near Fort Hunter, do. on Schohary Creek called Cadarede, houses and lots in Schenectady, do. in Albany, personal property (a large Dutch bible, a silver tankard, 2 do. cups). Executors the two sons. Witnesses John Dellemont, Benjamin Allen and Abraham Dellemont.

2144 (Y 3) 1760 March 24 1767 Aug. 17 **YALVERTON, John,** of New Windsor, Ulster Co., merchant. Wife Mary, son Anthony, grandson Abijah Yelverton. Real and personal estate. Executors Anthony Yelverton and the wife. Witnesses James Jackson of Ulster Co., skipper, John Monell and Alexr. Steele.

2145 (Y 4) 1760 April 4 1761 Jany. 10 **YEOMANS, Nathaniel,** of Beekmans Prect., Dutchess Co. Wife Mary, son Elial, daughters Ruth, Sarah and Mary. Real and personal estate. Executors the wife and son. Witnesses John Haight of Crum Elbow Prect., yeoman, Sarah Haight and Joshua Haight. Copy.

2146 (Y 5) 1760 April 26 June 21 **YOURKSE, Johannes,** of the Fishkils, Dutchess Co., farmer. Wife Anne, children John, Catrena, Mary, Harmen. "My estate." Executors John Jewell, Peter Monfort and Johannes de Witt. Witnesses Stephen Thorn and Gerret Noortstand.

2147 (Y 6) 1767 Febry. 23 June 1 **YOUNGS, Henry,** of Orange Co. Wife Abigail, son Henry, da. Unis. Homefarm, land in "Chenecut Government, New England," personal estate. Executors father-in-law Barnabas Horton, uncle Silas Yongs and Abigail Youngs. Witnesses Jediah Fuller, Hugh Hughes, Isaiah Howell and Phineas Rumsey, farmer. Vide, No. 2142.

2148 (Y 7) 1769 26th Day 5th Month 1770 March 22 **YOUEN, Benjamin,** of Nine Partners, Charlotte Prect., Dutchess Co. The mother, cousins Charles and Mary Blowers. Real and personal estate. Executors cousins Charles and Mary Blowers. Witnesses Joseph Winslow of said Co., farmer, James Mott and James Mott junior.

2149 (Y 8) 1769 April 1 June 28 **YOUNGS, Abigail,** widow of Henry, of Goshen Prect., Orange Co. (supra, No. 2147). Children Unus and Henry, father Barnabas Horton, whose wife's name had been Abigail, bro. Barebas Horton, late husband's bro. Birdsey Youngs. Real and personal estate. Executors the father, uncle Silas Horton and Archibald Little. Witnesses Colvill Carpenter, Matthias Gilbert of said Co., farmer, and James Smith.

2150 (Y 9) 1773 Decbr. 13 1785 Decbr. 3 **YEOMANS, Jonathan,** of Haverstraw Prect., Orange Co., carpenter. Wife ——, son Jonathan and other children, not named. Real and personal estate. Executors the wife, bro.-in-law Jacobus Blauvelt and John Jersey. Witnesses James Waring, Elbert Onderdonck and James Anson.

2151 (Y 10) 1774 Aug. 15 1783 May 9 **YELVERTON, Anthony,** of Goshen, Orange Co., gentleman. Daughters Mary, Hannah and Phebe. Real and personal estate. Executors father-in-law Abimail Youngs, da. Mary Yelverton, John Everett and Birdsey Youngs. Witnesses Balthr. de Haert, esquire, Isaac Nicoll and Joseph Chilson.

2152 (Y 10a) 1774 May 1 1784 Aug. 24 **YELVERTON, Anthony,** of New Paltz Prect., Ulster Co. Wife Abigail, sons Gale and Anthony, daughters Mary and Abigail, grandchildren Mary, da. of dec'd son Andrew, Anthony Ostrom, son of da. Elizabeth, heirs of da. Hannah. Real and personal estate. Executors the wife, sons Gale and Anthony, sons-in-law Nathaniel Goodspeed and William Keech. Witnesses Peter Drew, of said Prect., farmer, Thomas Chambers and Simeon Crandell.

2153 (Y 11) 1775 Decbr. 27 1776 June 4 **YATES, Johannis,** of Rensselaerswyck Manor, Albany Co. Wife Rebecca, sons Christopher, Peter, daughters Tryntje, wife of Anthony Briess, Annatje, wife of William Staats, Engeltje, wife of Cornelius van Schaack jun. and Rebecca Yates. Real and personal estate. Executors the wife, da. Rebecca and son-in-law William Staats. Witnesses Jacob I. van Schayick, copper, Herman van Hosen, carpenter, both of said Manor, and Gerrit C. van den Bergh.

2154 (Y 12) 1782 June 26 Aug. 21 **YALE, Benjamin,** of Paulings Prect., Dutchess Co. Children Ozias, "if living," Job, Thomas, Enos, Stephen, Benjamin, Uriah, Lydia and Ruth Rice. Worldly estate. Executors sons Enos and Stephen. Witnesses Alexander Kidd, David Close, Saml. Mills and Jehieh Weed of Fredericksburgh Prect., said Co., yeoman.

2155 (Y 13) 1785 Aug. 23 Novbr. 14 **YATES, Christopher,** of Schnectady. Wife Jannetie, children, Elizabeth, Eva, Magdalen, Joseph, Hendricus, Agnes, Anna, Jelles and John. "My estate." Executors the wife, bro. Jelles Yates, son Jelles Fonda, brothers-in-law Cornelius van Dyck, Johannes Peck and Gerrit I. Veeder. Witnesses Hunloke Woodruff, William Mead and Abrm. Yates jun.

2156 (Y 14) 1786 Novbr. 22 Decbr. 15 **YOUNGS, Abimail,** of Wallkil Prect., Ulster Co., yeoman. Grandchildren Abimail Y. and Frances Nicoll, Mary Moffat, Hanah Denton, Phebe Yelverton, John and William Nicoll; Joseph Denton, John Moffat. Late wife's name was Phebe. Real and personal estate. Executors kinsman Birdsey Youngs, Silas Pierson and Ebenezer Woodhull, all of Orange Co., yeomen. Witnesses Fletcher Mathews, John McMullin and Joseph L. Conkling of said Co., farmers.

2157 1788 Febry. 1 May 21 **YEAMAN, George,** of Essex Co., N. J. Bro. Joseph Yeaman. Real and personal estate. Executor Capt. John Wiley of Essex Co. Witnesses John Mun, Cornelius Jones, both of N. J., farmers, and Nehemiah Wade. Recorded in Wills and Probates, Vol. I., p. 185.

2158 1755 Jany. 15 1783 July 4 **YORK, Nicholas,** of Schohary, Albany Co., farmer. Wife Elizabeth, bro.-in-law Philipp Bark. Real and personal estate. Executors the wife and John de Peyster. Witnesses John de Peyster, Gerard de Peyster jun., of Albany City, merchant, and Joh. Nich. Becker. Albany Co. Records, Wills, I., part 2, p. 44.

2159 1766 Jany. 11 Febry. 28 **YATES, Luickes,** of Albany City, blacksmith. Wife Sarah, bro. Abraham I. Yates. Homestead and personal property. The wife sole executrix. Witnesses Thomas Cooper, Obediah Cooper and Gerrit van Sante jun. Albany Co. Records, Wills, I., p. 315.

2160 (Z 1) 1781 April 26 1784 May 29 **ZUERICHER, Hans,** of Haverstraw Prect., Orange Co., stone cutter. Children Lodiwick, Magdalen, Elizabeth, Hannah, Nancy, Marrito, or Molly, wife of Fredrick Eckert. Lots in N. Y. City, personal estate. Executors da. Magdelan and son-in-law Frederick Eckert. Witnesses Jacob Brouwer and Abraham Brouwer, both of N. Y. City, hatters.

2161 1786 March 30 1787 Jany. 24 **ZABRISKI, Jacob,** of Hackensack, Bergen Co., N. J. Grandchildren Sarah Zabriski, John Lansing Zabriski and Catherine Zabriski, children of dec'd son John, and grandda. Sarah Lansing, living with her grandfather John Lansing at Albany. Real and personal estate. Executors bro. Peter Zabriski, Jacob Terhune and Albert C. Zabriski. Witnesses Yan van der Beek, James Bertholf and Ino. Zabrisky. Recorded in Wills and Probates, Vol. I., p. 171.

2162 1774 June 27 Octbr. 25 **ZABRISKIE, John,** of the New Bridge, Bergen Co., N. J. Wife Annatje, son John, grandchildren John, Benjamin and Edmund Seaman, children of dec'd da. Elizabeth and Edmund Seaman. Real and personal estate. Executors the wife, the son and son-in-law Edmund Seaman. Witnesses Peter Zabriskie, Hendrick Banta and Robert Morris. Recorded ut supra, p. 365.

INDEX OF PERSONS

(BY RUNNING NUMBER OF WILLS).

A

Adriansen, Jores, 12
Adriansen, Ram, 12
Aertsen, Aeltie, 1
Aertsen, Aleph, 1
Aertsen, Gebbeke, 1
Aertsen, Lambert, 1
Aertsen, Rutt, 1
Afternoon, Ann, 2051
Aigron, Claudius, 3
Aird, Mrs., 1373
Akely, Benjamin, 355
Aken, Aploniea Swyts, 1491
Akin, Abraham, 32
Akin, Elisha, 32
Akin, James, 32
Akin, Jonathan, 32, 183, 637
Akin, Margaret, 32
Akin, Murray, 32
Akin, Olive, 32
Akin, Sarah, 32
Akin, Timothy, 32
Akin, Thomas, 32
Akins, Benjamin, 1336
Alberts, Tunitje, 956
Albertse, Johannes, 1299
Albertsen, Barent, 1268
Albertsen, Susannah Dirckx, 1268
Albertsen, Wouter, 1957, 1972
Albertson, Deborah, 10
Albertson, Elizabeth, 10
Albertson, Mary, 10
Albertson, Richard, 10
Albertson, Sarah, 10
Albertson, Steven, 10
Albertson, Susannah, 10
Albertson, William, 10, 857
Alburtus, Elizabeth Bedell, 102
Alden, Major Robert, 1453
Aldrich, Enus, 28
Aldrich, Gershom, 29
Aldrich, Peter, 29
Aldrich, Phebe, 29
Aldrig, Bethiah, 1603
Alexander, Alexander, 45
Alexander, Ann, 45
Alexander, Catherine, 37
Alexander, Catherine Mary Porteous, 1354
Alexander, Harriet, 45
Alexander, James, 37
Alexander. Jenny, 37
Alexander, Joseph, 37
Alexander, Maria, 45
Alexander, Mary Porteous, 1354
Alexander, Robert, 1029
Alexander, Stephen, 45
Alexander, Wm., 45, 216, 1354
Algeo, David, 44
Algeo, John, 44
Algeo, Margaret, 44
Algeo, William, 44
Algeo, William, 145
Allainville, Chartier, 1097
Allanson, Richard, 656
Allen, Abraham, 31
Allen, Anna, 31
Allen, Asa, 31
Allen, Benjamin, 2143
Allen, Catren, 648
Allen, David, 1355
Allen, Ebenezer, 1445
Allen, Elisha, 2044
Allen, Elizabeth, 27
Allen, Ezra, 31
Allen, Hannah, 27, 1423
Allen, Hester, 27
Allen, Honble. Samuel, 254
Allen, James, 31
Allen, Jane, 254
Allen, John, 27, 1178
Allen, John W., 648
Allen, Jonas, 483
Allen, Joseph, 27, 895
Allen, Mary, 27
Allen, Philipp, 932, 2044
Allen, Rachel White, 2122
Allen, Rhoda, 31
Allen, Sarah Auryonche, 27
Allen, Timothy, 607
Allen, Weston, 2044
Allen, William, 27
Allenor, Martha Montagne, 1179
Allenor, Thomas, 1179
Allicocke, Joseph, 947
Allicocke, Martha Jandine, 947
Alliger, Benjamin, 146
Allin, Elisha, 1170
Alling, Isaac, 535
Allisan, Abigale, 28
Allison, Abigail Roe, 1420
Allison, Alice, 615a
Allison, Amey, 34
Allison, Ann, 19
Allison, Benjamin, 7, 9, 11, 34
Allison, Bridget, 18
Allison, Cornelius, 9, 19
Allison, Deborah, 28
Allison, Elizabeth, 9, 18, 25, 34
Allison, Edward, 11
Allison, George, 14
Allison, Henry, 18
Allison, Isaac, 9, 34
Allison, James, 19, 45a, 766
Allison, Jeremiah, 34
Allison, John, 7, 11, 15, 18, 25, 28, 34
Allison, Joseph, 7, 9, 11, 14, 19, 25, 28, 34, 1120

Arnold, David, 580
Arnold, Elisha, 1932
Arnold, Henry, 8
Arnold, Isaack, 47
Arnold, John, 8
Arnold, Sarah, 8
Arnout, Cornelius, 22
Arnout, Deborah, 22
Arnout, Hannah, 22
Arnout, Jacob, 22
Arnout, John, 22
Arnout, Lena, 22
Arnout, Lydia, 22
Arnout, Mary, 22
Arnout, Peter, 22
Arnout, William, 22
Arskin, Jonas, 760
Arthur, Samuel, 1187, 1334
Aryaensen, Leyntie, 252a
Ashe, Dudley, 17
Ashfield, Elizabeth, 2120
Ashfield, Isabella, 1121, 2018
Ashfield, Isabella, 1121
Ashfield, Isabella Morris, 1121
Ashfield, Lewis, 1121
Ashfield, Mary, 1121
Ashfield, Patience, 1121
Ashfield, Pearse, 1121
Ashfield, Richard, 1121
Ashley, Mrs., 1599
Ashmead, Peter, 1364
Ashton, William, 1538
Askew, John, 1095
Askin, Archange, 1373
Askin, John, 1373
Atkinson, Thomas, 888
Atwater, Benjamin, 2080
Atwater, Stephen, 2080
Auchmity, Rev. Samuel, 330
Aukes, Dowe, 1480
Aumermann, Elbert, 1179
Aumermann, Pelonch Montagne, 1179
Aurnold, Sarah Dekay, 457
Austen, Ann, 24
Austen, Isaac, 24
Austen, Job, 24
Austen, John, 24
Austen, Jonathan, 24
Austen, Phebe, 24
Austen, Rebecker, 24
Austen, Robert, 24
Austen, Silas, 24
Austen, Smith, 24
Austin, Eusebeus, 864
Austin, Ralph, 878
Avery, Alpheus, 838
Avery, Joseph, 838
Avery, Thaddeus, 838
Avignon, A., 394
Axtell, Hon'ble William, 334
Axtell, Margaret, 334
Axtell, Mary, 41
Axtell, William, 41
Ayres, Daniel, 21
Ayres, David, 21,
Ayres, Enos, 21, 352
Ayres, Martha, 21, 926
Ayres, Martin, 21
Ayres, Mary, 21
Ayres, Mary Cooper, 371
Ayres, Rev. Enos, 926

B

Bache, Ann Dorothy, 117
Bache, Theophilact, 117
Back, Elizabeth, 1743
Backer, Anna, 177
Backer, Christian, 177
Backer, Jan, 213
Backer, Jan Harmensen, 243
Backer, Margaretha Clara Berewout, 213
Backer, Peter, 653
Backer, Petrus, 177, 1177
Backer, Wilhelmus, 177
Bacon, Asahel, 223
Bacon, Daniel, 223
Bacon, Jabez, 223
Bacon, Jemima, 223
Bacon, John, 223
Bacon, Lidia, 223
Bacqué, Jean Baptiste, 1227
Badaux, John, 1487
Badeau, Isaac, 362
Badgelly, Elizabeth Tobias, 1734
Badgelly, Samuel, 1734
Badger, Ebenezer, 1428
Baer, Adam, 2101
Baerd, Willem, 1185
Bages, Samuel, 1056
Bagley, Josiah, 1219
Bailey, Abigail Pine, 1319
Bailey, James, 401, 1309
Bailey, John, 120, 359, 972, 1544, 1702
Bailey, Nathan, 1724
Bailey, Simeon, 1366
Bain, Alexander Mack, 1144
Bain, Casparus, 191
Bain, Hannah Lesher, 1058
Bain, James, 191
Bain, John, 191
Bain, Peter, 1058
Bain, Philipp, 191
Bain, William, 191
Baird, Francis, 1279

Baird, Robert, 658
Baker, Henry, 173
Baker, Samuel, 1086
Baker, Simon, 2072
Balding, George, 260
Balding, Joseph, 260, 2076
Baldwin, David, 1344
Baldwin, Ebenezer, 561
Baldwin, Thomas, 1344
Ball, Allen, 164
Ball, Daniel, 560
Ball, Hendrick, 527
Ball, James, 226
Ball, Jane, 205
Ball, John, 226
Ball, Katharine, 254
Ball, Marilis Dietz, 527
Ball, Samuel, 205
Ball, Sarah Mullender, 1169
Ballou, Marguerite, 1094
Balton, John, 1088
Baly, Asa, 138
Baly, Benjamin, 138
Baly, David, 1604
Baly, Elizabeth, 138
Baly, Jonathan, 138
Baly, Phebe, 1407
Baly, Richard, 138
Baly, Samuel, 1604
Bamfield, John, 1640
Ban, Kathren, 191
Bancker, Abraham, 215
Bancker, Adrian, 71, 215
Bancker, Annatje Veeder, 1993
Bancker, Catriena, 1993
Bancker, Christoffer, 71, 215, 2018
Bancker, Elisabeth, 71
Bancker, Evert, 71, 215, 352, 519, 664, 1018, 1234
Bancker, Gerard, 519, 1091
Bancker, Gerardus, 71
Bancker, Gerrit, 1968
Bancker, Jannetie, 71
Bancker, Johannis, 71, 1993
Bancker, Magdalena Veeder, 1993
Bancker, Thomas Brower, 1863
Bancker, Willem, 71
Bancker, William, 1993
Bancroft, Catherine Oothoudt, 1292
Bancroft, David, 1292
Bander, Maddalan Straight, 1611
Bangs, Abner, 192
Bangs, Bethia, 192
Bangs, Hannah, 192
Bangs, John, 192
Bangs, Lydia, 192
Bangs, Mary, 192
Bangs, Samuel, 1056
Banker, Adolph, 137
Banker, Annatie, 61, 137
Banker, Capt. Evert, 61, 1477
Banker, Elizabeth, 61, 137
Banker, Evert, 4, 244, 1378
Banker, Gerardus, 4106
Banker, Magdalen, 137
Banker, Nathaniel, 137
Banker, Sarah, 137
Banker, Stephen, 137
Banker, William, 61, 1725
Banks, Abraham, 68
Banks, Edward, 68
Banks, James, 68, 1796
Banks, John, 68
Banks, Josiah, 560
Banks, Mary Lowarear, 1065
Banks, William, 68
Bankson, Jacob, 2116
Banta, Hendricks, 2162
Banter, Daniel, 401
Banyar, G., 5
Banyar, Goldsborow, 286, 325, 503, 1215
Banyar, Hariot, 1215
Banyar, Martha, 1215
Banyar, Wm., 495
Banyer, Elizabeth Mortier, 1215
Barbarin, Noel John, 539, 1444, 1653
Barber, David F., 734
Barber, Marie Kast, 971
Barber, Patrick, 149, 988, 1257, 1759
Barberie, Elizabeth, 60
Barberie, Frances, 60
Barberie, John, 60
Barberie, Peter, 60, 948
Barbier, François, 741
Barbier, Henry, 741
Barbor, Arthur, 1063
Barclay, Andrew, 117, 174
Barclay, Ann, 117
Barclay, Catherine, 117
Barclay, Charlotte Amelia, 117
Barclay, Helena, 117
Barclay, Helena Roosevelt, 1446
Barclay, Henry, 117, 174
Barclay, James, 117, 350
Barclay, John, 174
Barclay, Margaret, 117, 174, 188
Barclay, Rev. Henry, 117
Barclay, Sarah, 117
Barclay, Thomas, 117
Barcley, Harriet, 889
Barcley, John, 889
Barcley, John Mortimer, 889
Barcley, Mary, 889
Barcley, Sophia, 889
Barheyt, Jeroon, 246

Boswell, Rachel, 779
Bouderick, John, 401
Boudinot, Elias, 762
Boulla, widow, 779
Boulyn, Maria, 412a
Bouquet, Jacob, 57
Bouquet, Margaret, 57
Bourdet, Samuel, 3, 1390
Bourdett, Lewis, 964
Bout, Evert, 915
Bout, Harmanus, 168
Bout, Jan Evertsen, 236, 910
Bower, Cornelius, 30
Bowers, Susannah, 658
Bowhanon, Charity, 1572
Bowie, John, 461, 1540
Bowland, William, 1123
Bowles, John, 495
Bowly, Cornelia, 1831
Bown, Caroline Rodman, 1434
Bown, James, 1434
Bowne, Andrew, 1232
Bowne, Benj., 1408
Bowne, Elizabeth Hartshorne, 1648
Bowne, Robert, 1648
Bowne, Sarah Rodman, 1408
Boyd, Agnes, 180
Boyd, James, 180
Boyd, Jennet, 180
Boyd, John, 180
Boyd, Robert, 180
Boyd, Samuel, 180, 1346
Brackett, James, 1463
Bradford, Catherine, 1430
Bradford, John M., 1101
Bradford, Mary Lush, 1101
Bradford, Will., 1242
Bradhurt, Samuel, 1358
Brading, James, 1475
Bradley, R., 58
Bradner, Benoni, 103
Bradner, Capt. Colvil, 517
Bradner, Christian, 103
Bradner, Colvil, 103
Bradner, Elizabeth, 103
Bradner, Gilbert, 103
Bradner, John, 103, 447
Bradner, Margret, 9, 103
Bradner, Mary, 103
Bradner, Mary Borland, 172
Bradner, Sarah, 103, 1617
Bradner, Susannah, 103
Bradnor, John, 377, 1583
Bradrick, Anthony, 1407
Bradstreet, Mary, 189
Bradt, Aaron H., 1946
Bradt, Abraham, 401
Bradt, Adrian, 203
Bradt, Albert, 203
Bradt, Arent, 401, 1863, 2134
Bradt, Aryæntie Wemple, 2134
Bradt, Capt. Andries, 2134
Bradt, Catarien van Geyseling, 1890
Bradt, Catelintje, 2134
Bradt, Claura, 203
Bradt, Cornelius, 401
Bradt, Edward, 203
Bradt, Elisabeth, 203, 281
Bradt, Eve, 401
Bradt, Francis, 203
Bradt, Frederick, 401
Bradt, Gerret, 281
Bradt, Hannah, 203
Bradt, Harmanis, 1863, 1928
Bradt, Helena, 401
Bradt, Hermanus, 351
Bradt, Jacobus, 401
Bradt, John, 401
Bradt, Magdaline, 203
Bradt, Peter, 203, 1994
Bradt, Samuel, 401
Bradt, Samuel Ar., 1890
Bradt, Storm, 203
Brady, Betty, 161
Braham, John, 893
Brainard, Rev. John, 1599
Braine, Thomas, 900
Braithwaite, James, 1076
Brakin, Jeames, 98
Brakin, Mathew, 98
Brando, Nicholas, 1847
Brandow, Arent, 202
Brandow, Elizabeth, 202
Brandow, Janatie, 202
Brandow, Johannis, 202, 1849
Brandow, Margaret, 202
Brandow, Maria, 202
Brandow, Nicolas, 23
Brandow, Wilhelmus, 202
Brandow, William, 202
Brant, Ann, 954
Brant, Elisabeth, 954
Brant, George, 954
Brant, Johnson, 954
Brant, Magdalene, 954
Brant, Margaret, 954
Brant, Mary, 954
Brant, Peter, 954
Brant, Susannah, 954
Brant, Young, 954
Bras, Adolph, 82
Bras, Catherine, 82
Bras, Gerrit, 82
Bras, Gertie, 82
Bras, Hendrick, 82
Bras, Jannetie, 82
Bras, Maritie,
Bras, Mary, 82

Brasher, Abraham, 893
Brasier, Lydia, 58
Brasier, Richard, 58
Brasier, Thomas, 58
Brasted, Hannah, 718
Brat, Albert Andriessen, 2129
Brat, Andres, 113
Brat, Anthony, 1385, 1818
Brat, Arent, 113, 250
Brat, Arent Andressen, 113
Brat, Barent, 1303, 1396
Brat, Barnardus, 801
Brat, Benj., 1395
Brat, Cornelia, 119
Brat, Daniel, 1688
Brat, Dirck, 119, 1688
Brat, Dirck Arentsen, 1017
Brat, Eghbert, 1402, 1830
Brat, Elizabeth, 1303
Brat, Engeltie, 119
Brat, Harjaentie, 113
Brat, Harmanus, 113, 250
Brat, Helena, 113
Brat, Jannetie, 113
Brat, John Andressen
Brat, Johannes Arentsen, 113
Brat, Maria, 113
Brat, Maria Ryckman, 1404
Brat, Peter Drs., 119
Brat, Samuel Art., 250
Brat, Trintie, 119
Bratt, Aarent, 238
Bratt, Andries, 238, 1785
Bratt, Annatje, 238
Bratt, Arent, 1785
Bratt, Arent And., 1848
Bratt, Arent Andriessen, 1785
Bratt, Baarent, 618
Bratt, Barent, 971
Bratt, Barent Albertsen, 913
Bratt, Barnardus, 800
Bratt, Catharine, 390
Bratt, Dirck, 238, 390, 1785
Bratt, Dirck Arentsen, 1785
Bratt, Elizabeth, 238, 1776
Bratt, Elisabeth van Dyck, 1848
Bratt, Gerrit, 800, 1776
Bratt, Haramanes, 1848
Bratt, Jannitie, 800
Bratt, Johannis, 238
Bratt, Johannes A., 1848
Bratt, John F., 390
Bratt, Maria, 238
Bratt, Marya, 1848
Bratt, Peter, 390, 1019
Bratt, Samuel, 1785
Bratt, Vroutye, 390
Breasted, Josiah, 718
Breath, John, 2111
Brede, William, 977
Breese, Samuel, 279
Breested, Andrs., 122
Breested, Christina, 1508
Breested, Gerrit, 1508
Breested, John, 1112
Bremer, Ludwig, 1207
Brenkerhof, George, 1400
Bresy, Jacob, 276
Brett, Catherine, 120, 140
Brett, Francis, 120, 2024
Brett, Matthew, 120, 140, 1724
Brett, Robert, 120, 140, 1836
Brett, Rombout, 120, 140
Brett, Sarah, 120
Brettell, Jos., 1457
Brevoort, Abraham, 40
Brevoort, Elias, 207
Brevoort, Henry, 207, 897
Brevoort, Jacomintie, 207.
Brevoort, John, 207
Brevoort, Lea, 207
Brewer, Adam, 517
Brewer, Cornelius, 1911
Brewer, William, 724
Brewster, Charity, 144
Brewster, Daniel, 154
Brewster, Edward, 144, 154, 1550
Brewster, Experience, 154
Brewster, Francis, 144, 154, 871
Brewster, Isaac, 144
Brewster, John, 144, 154, 1550
Brewster, Mary Wood, 2105
Brewster, Ruth, 144
Brez, ——, 220
Briant, John, 1891
Brickman, Catherine, 217
Brickman, Henry, 217
Bridge, David, 1456
Bridge, Samuel, 1522
Bridgen, Charles, 1368
Bridon, Francis, 50
Bridon, Susannah, 50
Bries, Anthony, 245, 2153
Bries, Catharine, 245
Bries, Cathrina Ryckman, 1404
Bries, Eva, 245
Bries, Hendrick, 245
Bries, Margrett, 245
Bries, Marritie, 245
Bries, Nellitie, 245
Briess, Tryntje Yates, 2153
Briggs, Amy, 183
Briggs, Anna Concklin, 337
Briggs, Edward, 32, 335
Briggs, Elizabeth, 183
Briggs, Elkana, 845
Briggs, John, 1005
Briggs, Nathaniel, 183

Burger, John, 251, 465
Burger, Maria, 251
Burger, Mary Hewson, 251
Burger, Nicholas, 465
Burger, Petrus, 477
Burger, William, 251
Burges, Jeremiah, 52, 192
Burges, John, 52
Burges, Mary, 52
Burges, Thomas, 52
Burgess, David Campbell, 401
Burgess, Mary, 375
Burgess, Samuel, 232
Burghert, John, 941
Burhans, Abraham, 67, 1021, 1305, 1692, 1736
Burhans, Barent, 67, 110, 1113
Burhans, Barnet, 167
Burhans, Cathrena, 110
Burhans, David, 67, 110, 462, 2014, 2016
Burhans, Debora Wanbomer, 2016
Burhans, Elizabeth, 67, 110
Burhans, Grietie ten Eyeck, 1693
Burhans, Helena, 67, 110
Burhans, Hilletje, 67, 167
Burhans, Isaac, 67
Burhans, Jacob, 110, 462, 1054
Burhans, Jan, 67, 415
Burhans, Jannetie, 67
Burhans, Jerrick, 167
Burhans, Johan, 67
Burhans, Johannis, 110
Burhans, John, 167
Burhans, John V. L., No 43
Burhans, Margrieta Mattysen, 1113
Burhans, Marytie, 110
Burhans, Samuel, 67, 1243, 1692, 2014
Burhans, Wilhelmus, 110, 167, 1054,
Burhans, Willem, 1693
Burhans, William, 67, 451
Burk, Mary Maudeline, 1010
Burk, Michael, 1010
Burling, Edward, 107, 1846
Burling, George, 176
Burling, Peter, 610
Burn, Andries, 1863
Burn, Batseba Vedder, 1863
Burn, Catoleyn, 1863
Burn, Jacomeyn, 1863
Burn, Samuel, 1863
Burnat, Matthias, 1475
Burne, Francis, 583
Burne, Francis, 583
Burne, George, 583
Burnet, Anne Reid, 1415
Burnet, Bavid, 738
Burnet, Dr., 738
Burnet, Fredrick, 999
Burnet, Gertruyda Gouverneur, 735
Burnet, Isaac, 735, 738
Burnet, Matthew, 999
Burnet, Matthias, 2013
Burnet, Patrick, 356
Burnet, Robert, 437
Burnet, Staats, 738
Burnet, Staats, G., 735
Burnet, William, 999
Burnett, James, 1415
Burns, James 1415
Burns, Jean, 1415
Burns, Jean Reid, 1415
Burns, Kathrine, 1415
Burns, Mary, 1415
Burns, Phoebe, 1639
Burns, William, 1415
Burnside, Mary, 132
Burnsides, Mary, 111
Burr, Aaron, 613
Burr, Major Peter, 1482
Burr, Oliver, 949
Burr, Sturgis, 949
Burris, Thomas, 1584
Burroughs, Benjamin, 126
Burroughs, Deborah, 126
Burroughs, Elizabeth, 126
Burroughs, James, 126
Burroughs, Joel, 672
Burroughs, Joseph, 126
Burroughs, Nathan, 126
Burroughs, Thomas, 126
Burroughs, William, 126
Burrowes, Fanny, 109
Burrowes, Jo., 632
Burt, Benjamin, 1558
Burt, Catharine, 401
Burt, Daniel, 2089
Burt, James, 2089
Burt, John, 1226
Burting, Lancaster, 1437
Burtis, Amy, 199
Burtis, David, 199
Burtis, Isaac, 199
Burtis, James, 102, 1328
Burtis, John, 199
Burtis, Stephen, 199
Burton, Isaac, 1532
Busch, Gratia Anna, 418
Busch, Heinerig, 1029
Busch, John Hendrick, 418
Bush, Catharina, 1172
Bush, Johannis, 1882
Bush, Hellegontie van Wagenen, 1882
Bush, Neeltie, 1717
Bush, Rick, 2084
Bush, Zachariah, 157

Bussing, Aaron, 186
Bussing, Abraham, 1151, 1710
Bussing, Arent, 1450
Bussing, Elizabeth Fort, 654
Bussing, Elezabeth, Mesier, 1151
Bussing, James, 654
Bussing, Sarah, 1699
Bussing, Susannah, 186
Bust, Amaziah, 1745
Butcher, Robert S., 1037
Butler, Anne, 104, 109
Butler, Captain, 1229
Butler, Catlintie, 113
Butler, Deborah, 104, 109
Butler, Elizabeth, 108
Butler, James, 108, 621, 2082
Butler, John, 104, 109, 113, 954
Butler, Lieut. Walter, 109, 965, 2134
Butler, Maria, 109
Butler, Maria Wemple, 2134
Butler, Martha Bishop, 107
Butler, Mary, 104, 108
Butler, Mathias, 108
Butler, Michael, 2115
Butler, Nelly, 108
Butler, Thomas, 104, 965
Butler, Walter, 104, 965
Butler, William, 1051
Butt, Aaron, 142
Butt, Else, 142
Butt, Gershom, 142
Butt, John, 142
Butt, Moses, 142
Butt, Samuel, 142
Butt, Thomas, 142
Butterfield, Daniel, 1123, 1208
Butterfield, Jane McNeall, 1123
Buttolph, Hezekiah, 1262
Buttolph, John, 1262
Butts, Mary Huestis, 877
Buxton, John, 1643
Buxton, William, 2116
Buys, Henry, 1319
Buys, Jacobus, 1707, 1712
Buys, Jan Cornelissen 564
Buys, Mary Teller, 1707
Byard, Samuel, 272
Byfield, Elizabeth, 77
Byfield, William, 77
Byrn, Barneby, 308
Byrn, Hugh, 1725
Byrne, John, 612
Byrne, William, 954
Byse, Catherine Storm, 1564
Byse, Jacob, 1564
Byvanck, Anthony, 111
Byvanck, Catherine, 111
Byvanck, Evert, 977, 1400, 1791
Byvanck, John, 111
Byvanck, Sally, 900

C

Caddell, Robert, 951
Cadmus, Andrew, 390
Cadmus, Deborah, 390
Cadmus, Richard, 390
Cadwalader, Elizabeth, 376
Cadwalader, Hannah, 376
Cadwalader, Lambert, 376
Cadwalader, Rebecca, 376
Cadwalader, Thomas, 376
Caldwall, James, 650
Caldwell, Abraham, 875
Caldwell, Dr. William, 1373
Caldwell, Joseph, 1290
Caldwell, Wm., 1946
Calier, Engeltie, 409
Calier, Magdalena, 409
Calier, Michiel, 409
Callaghan, Nabby, 383
Caln, East, 210
Calver, Elisha, 2066
Calvin, Catharine, 1904
Calwall, Robert, 1526
Cambell, John, 1838
Cameron, Charles, 401
Cameron, Donald, 1559
Cameron, Dugald, 402
Cameron, Elizabeth, 402
Cameron, Frances, 402
Camfield, Saml., 350
Cammel, Anateje Masten, 1205
Cammel, Barent, 577
Cammel, John, 1205
Cammer, William, 1551
Camp, John, 2097
Camp, Joseph D. 1183
Campbell, Alexander, 325, 397, 400, 702, 1439
Campbell, Angelica, 400, 401
Campbell, Ann, 325, 397
Campbell, Archibald, 315, 325, 397, 398
Campbell, Aury, 335, 337
Campbell, Captain Archibald, 378
Campbell, Catrin, 315
Campbell, Caty, 398
Campbell, Christena, 398
Campbell, Daniel, 273, 328, 400, 401, 954, 1051
Campbell, Daniel David, 401
Campbell, David, 400
Campbell, Donald, 1645
Campbell, Duncan, 325, 378, 396
Campbell, Edward, 400, 1349

Cornell, Susannah, 350
Cornell, Thomas, 1328, 2024
Corning, Erastus, 561
Cornu, Elisabeth, 1816
Cornu, Peter, 1816, 1859
Cornue, Peter, 1704
Cornwall, Amoz, 393
Cornwell, Aspinwall, 1434
Cornwell, Richard, 1301
Corrington, Susannah Wood, 2105
Corry, William, 104
Cortelyou, Jacques, 1022
Cortet, Cabaril, 385
Cortet, Jeanne, 385
Cortet, Perpignette, 385
Cortet, Tite, 385
Cortet, Valentin, 385
Cortie, Altye, 1585
Cortlandt, Col. Stephen, 1387
Cortrecht, Willem, 1393
Cortreght, Benjamin, 516
Cortreght, Lawrence, 1693
Cortreght, Sarah ten Eyck, 1693
Cortright, Christenah Rosenkrans, 1393
Cortright, Hendrick, 1393
Cortright, Lawrens, 459
Cortright, Mattheus, 1050
Cortur, Harmanus, 1585
Corvin, Elisabeth, 1492
Corvin, Thomas, 1492
Corwin, David, 598, 842
Cory, Abijah, 278
Cory, Bradick, 278
Cory, Dorothy, 278
Cory, Elnathan, 320
Cory, John, 278, 320
Cory, Jonathan, 320, 687, 1405
Cory, Patience, 320
Coryell, Emanuel, 402
Cosby, Grace, 262, 279
Cosby, Henry, 262, 279
Cosby, Philipp, 279
Cosby, William, 262, 1821
Cosine, Balm Johnson, 331, 340
Cosine, Catherine, 331, 340
Cosine, Cornelius, 331, 340
Cosine, Deborah, 331, 340
Cosine, Hannah, 331, 340
Cosine, John, 331, 340
Cosine, Nicholas, 331, 340
Cosine, Sarah, 331, 340
Cossié, Jean Pierre, 1094
Cossman, Rhoda, 2098
Costers, Antny, 1685
Costers, Elizabeth ten Broeck, 1685
Costigan, Fran., 279
Cottin, Daniel, 237
Cottin, Jean, 257
Cotton, Sarah, 612
Couch, John, 303
Couchendale, Mannes, 1439
Couenhoven, Adriaen, 531
Couenhoven, Barbara Dubois, 531
Counes, Elizabeth, 1441
Count, John Lay 431
Courteney, Laurence, 383
Cousen, Cornelius, 263
Couszens, Ino., 282
Couzens, Isabel, 282
Couzens, Samuel, 282
Coveleir, Colonel John, 619
Covell, Oliver, 2072
Coventry, William, 607
Covet, Elisha, 141
Cow, Isaac D., 196
Cowan, Michael, 546
Cowdin, James, 707
Cowe, John, 1454
Cowenover, Ann, 827
Cox, Benjamin, 2106
Cox, Catherine Beekman, 214
Cox, Charles, 379
Cox, Dorothy, 1492
Cox, Ebenezer, 343
Cox, Edward, 1492
Cox, Elizabeth, 343
Cox, Ino., 1121
Cox, Isaac, 214
Cox, John, 803, 1442
Cox, Jordan Wright, 2106
Cox, Leader, 2087
Cox, Ludwig, 217
Cox, Mary, 2087
Cox, Michael, 205
Cox, Robert, 343
Crabtree, John, 392
Crabtree, Mathew, 392
Crage, Adam, 347
Crage, Catalina, 271
Crage, David, 347
Crage, Isabel, 347
Crage, James, 347
Crage, Jane, 347
Crage, John, 347, 1252
Crage, Margaret, 347
Crage, Martha, 347
Craig, David Stewart, 221
Crain, Hannah Gregory, 743
Crain, John, 743
Cramer, Frederick, 1596
Cramer, William, 1596
Crandall, Azariah, 1758
Crandel, Phebe Willbor, 2085
Crandel, Samuel, 199
Crandell, Simeon, 2152
Crane, Dr. Joseph, 1344
Crane, John, 339

D

Dellemont, John, 2143
Delliend, A., 791
DLmontonje, John, 1046
Delong, Martin, 1609
de Long, *see* de Laenge, de Lang
Delvin, Frances Marion, 563
Delvin, James, 563
Delvin, John, 563
Demaree, David, 1941
Demarest, Caty, 1922
Demarest David, 65, 771, 1941
Demarest, David Benceman, 26
Demarest, Elenor, 481
Demarest, Grietie Haerring, 771
Demarest, Henry Oothoudt, 1292
Demarest, Jacobus, 771
Demarest, John, 1922
Demarest, Mary, 481
Demarest, Nelly, 1292
Demarest, Peter, 481
de Marest, Peter S., 1891
Demarest, Samuel, 724
de Metselaer, Anna, 1239
de Metselaer, Eghbert, 1239
de Metselaer, Eghbertie Eghberts, 1239
de Metselaer, Martin, 1239
de Metselaer, Teunis Teunissen, 1239
de Metselaer, Willemtie, 1239
D'Meyer, ——, 1012
de Meyer, Anneke, 421
de Meyer, Catrina, 421
de Meyer, Deborah, 421
Demeyer, H., 960, 1117
de Meyer, John I., 1309
de Meyer, Nicolas, 421
Demeyer, S., 263
D'Meyer, Wm., 414, 415
de Meyer, Wilhelmus, 421
de Mill, Peter, 1110, 1766
Demilt, Peter, 543
Deming, Abner, 223
Demler, Henry, 536
Demler, Susannah, 536
Demon, Walran, 1297
de Montarand, Couet, 1094
Demories, Margaret Haringh, 778d
Demorrie, Christian, 2054
Demot, Michal, 10
Demot, Sarah, 10
Demott, Catherine, 529
Demott, Elizabeth, 529
Demott, Isaac, 529
Demott, James, 529
Demott, Michael, 529
de Mott, Phebe Bedell, 102
Dempe, Jacob, 5
Demyer, Benjamin, 462
Demyer, Elsie, 462
Demyer, Jeremiah, 462
Demyer, Nicolas, 462, 1297
Demyer, Wilhelmus, 462
de Neufville, Mr., 385
Deniston, Hugh, 1048
Deniston, Jos., 1036
Deniston, Rachel, 1048
Denn, Daniel, 2070
Denn, Phebe, 1278, 1598, 2070
Denn, William, 14, 22, 96, 103, 116, 172, 285, 292, 299, 311, 509, 688, 699, 842, 928, 1278, 1579, 1598, 1605, 1755, 2070
Dennis, Jonathan, 1006, 1760
Dennison, Frances, 541
Denniston, Alexander, 1061
Denniston, Annie, 534
Denniston, Daniel, 478, 534
Denniston, Elizabeth, 638
Denniston, Geo., 844, 1061
Denniston, Hugh, 478, 534
Denniston, Isaac, 534
Denniston, Isabella, 534
Denniston, James, 534, 638
Denniston, John, 534
Denniston, Joseph, 478
Denniston, Lydia, 534
Denniston, Margaret, 534
Denniston, Sophia, 478
Dennius, Johannis, 1605
Dennius, Petrus, 1605
Denny, James, 556
de Normandie, Anthony, 471
de Normandie, Ensign Daniel, 471
de Normandie, Sarah, 471
de Noyelles, Charlotte, 503
de Noyelles, Edward, 503
de Noyelles, John, 403, 1717
de Noyelles, Peter, 503
de Noyelles, Rachel, 503
Denton, Abigail, 518
Denton, Ann, 494
Denton, Benjamin, 494
Denton, Daniel, 447, 474, 518, 819, 1271, 1416, 1541, 2017
Denton, Gilbert, 447, 474, 1040, 1516
Denton, Hanah, 2156
Denton, Isaac, 348, 1328
Denton, James, 166, 447, 518, 1040
Denton, John, 447, 474, 494
Denton, John Samuel, 447
Denton, Jonas, 447, 474, 518, 1416
Denton, Joseph, 447, 474, 624, 836, 2091, 2156
Denton, Mary, 261
Denton, Phebe, 518
Denton, Rachel, 494

E

Ellicott, Andrew, 615
Ellicott, Andrew A., 615
Ellicott, Benjamin, 615
Ellicott, John B., 615
Ellicott, Joseph, 615
Ellicott, Sarah, 615
Elliot, Ellinor, 210
Elliot, John, 814, 835
Elliot, Robert, 658
Elliott, James, 984
Ellis, Avis, 611
Ellis, Dolly, 611
Ellis, George, 608
Ellis, James, 608
Ellis, Mary, 608, 611
Ellis, Mercy, 611
Ellis, Samuel, 611
Ellis, William, 608
Ellisen, Teunis, 1791
Ellison, Gab., 136
Ellison, Colonel Thomas, 1711
Ellison, John, 1521, 1711
Ellison, Thomas, 898, 968
Ellison, William, 1711
Ellistone, John Francis, 530
Ellwell, Deborah, 594
Ellwell, Elizabeth, 594
Ellwell, Esther, 594
Ellwell, Grissel, 594
Ellwell, Isaac, 594
Ellwell, Jabez, 594
Ellwell, Mary, 594
Ellwell, Samuel, 594
Ellwell, Sarah, 594
Ellsworth, Jenny Dean, 526
Elmendorf, Peter Edm., 222
Elmendorpf, J., 1494
Elmendorph, Abraham, 1196
Elmendorph, Blandinah, 309
Elmendorph, Catharina, 309
Elmendorph, Catherine ten Broeck, 1727
Elmendorph, Coenradt, 125
Elmendorph, Coenradt Corns., 125
Elmendorph, Coenradt I., 1621
Elmendorph, Coernelius, 1494
Elmendorph, Cornelius, 106, 768, 872, 1529
Elmendorph, Counraedt Ja., 95
Elmendorph, Counrat Grs., 680
Elmendorph, Elizabeth, 309
Elmendorph, Engeltie Heermans, 768
Elmendorph, J., 1700
Elmendorph, Jaco, 1243
Elmendorph, John, 309
Elmendorph, Jonathan, 1727
Elmendorph, Lucas, 318
Elmendorph, Petrus Edmundus, 79, 309, 680
Elmendorph, Sarah, 309
Elmendorph, *see* van Elmendorp
Elmer, John, 742
Elmer, Nathan, 1407
Elmer, Nathaniel, 116, 320
Elmore, Nathaniel, 138
Elsefer, Lodewick, 860, 1441
Elsefer, Susannah Reichert, 1441
Elsworth, Hester, 1699
Elsworth, Nicolas, 422
Elsworth, Virdine, 176
Elsworth, William, 1647
Eltengh, Willem, 1791
Eltinge, Abraham, 576, 589, 592
Eltinge, Annatie, 575, 592
Eltinge, Catherintje, 589
Eltinge, Cornelius, 589
Eltinge, Elsie, 581
Eltinge, Elizabeth, 581
Eltinge, Elizabeth Depue, 456
Eltinge, Helena du Bois, 438
Eltinge, Hendericus, 575
Eltinge, Jacobus, 575, 592
Eltinge, Jacomyntje, 576, 592
Eltinge, Jacomyntje Eltinge, 575
Eltinge, James, 581, 973, 1888
Eltinge, Jan, 95, 97, 467, 575, 579, 581, 778b, 967, 973, 1305, 1403, 1701, 1839
Eltinge, Janitje Jansen, 927
Eltinge, Jannetje, 575, 579, 581
Eltinge, Jannetje de Lameter, 427
Eltinge, Jannetje Dubois, 499
Eltinge, Johannis, 579, 927
Eltinge, John, 438, 456, 576, 1632
Eltinge, Josiah, 438, 576, 589
Eltinge, Josias, 579
Eltinge, Magdalena, 589
Eltinge, Majeke, 579
Eltinge, Marytie van Steenbergen, 1888
Eltinge, Noah, 118, 438, 576, 579, 592
Eltinge, Noe, 575
Eltinge, Peter, 456
Eltinge, Petrus, 579, 581
Eltinge, Rachel, 579, 1839
Eltinge, Rachel Hasbrouck, 581
Eltinge, Rachel Whitaker, 581
Eltinge, R. Josias, 118
Eltinge, Roelof, 426, 576, 579, 589
Eltinge, Roelof J., 589
Eltinge, Sarah, 576, 579
Eltinge, Sara Dubois, 426
Eltinge, Solomon, 589
Eltinge, Thomas, 592
Eltinge, Willem, 95, 427, 575, 579, 581, 811, 933, 1165, 1321, 1403, 1690, 1888
Eltinge, William, 499, 592

F

Flagg, George, 1453
Flagler, Halanah, 640
Flagler, Hester, 640
Flagler, Jane, 640
Flagler, John, 640
Flagler, Peter, 640
Flagler, Sarah, 640
Flagler, Simon, 640
Flagler, Zacharias, 27, 640
Flake, Coenradt, 168
Flanagan, Margaret Hogg, 779
Flanagan, William, 779
Flanigan, Elizabeth, 308
Flansburgh, Bautche, 630
Flansburgh, David, 630
Flansburgh, Mary, 630
Fleerboom, John, 771
Fleming, Hannah, 1492
Fleming, Peter, 835, 1492
Fleming, Pierre E., 1657
Flensburgh, Anna, 618
Flensburgh, Daniel, 618
Flensburgh, Johanna, 618
Flensburgh, Johannis, 618
Flensburgh, Mathew, 618
Fletcher, John, 363
Fletcher, Thomas, 658
Flierboom, Jacob, 771
Flinn, David, 647
Florence, Gideon, 1575
Flynn, Patrick, 2046
Fogerty, Philipp, 305
Folbreght Marie, 257
Folk, Aaron, 641
Folk, Jacob, 641
Folk, Johannis, 641
Folk, Jonas, 641
Folk, Laurance, 641
Folk, Leah, 641
Folk, Mary, 641
Folk, Raenah, 641
Folk, Wilhelmus, 641
Folkertson, Broca, 627
Folkertson, Dina, 627
Folkertson, Folkert, 627
Folkertson, Nicholas, 627
Fonda, Abraham, 250, 628, 634, 1147, 1314, 1732, 1904
Fonda, Alexander, 1950
Fonda, Alida, 634, 1818
Fonda, Angenitje, 634
Fonda, Annatie van Vechten, 1818, 1989
Fonda, Cornelis, 628
Fonda, Dowe, 628, 700
Fonda, Elbertie van Alen, 628
Fonda, Hendrick, 1818, 1989
Fonda, Ino. W., 1080
Fonda, Jacob, 634
Fonda, Jannetje Muller, 628, 1147
Fonda, Jellis, 634, 954
Fonda, Jeremia, 628
Fonda, Johannis, 628
Fonda, Lawrence, 1314
Fonda, Lourens, 628
Fonda, Peter A., 1314
Fonda, Pieter, 628, 634
Fonda, Stephanis, 628
Fonday, Ino., 390
Fonseca, Abraham, 620
Fonseca, Isaac, 620
Fonseca, Esther, 620
Fonseca, Jacob, 620
Fonseca, Joseph, 620
Fonseca, Judith, 620
Fonseca, Moses Lapez de, 620
Fonseca, Rachel, 620
Fonseca, Rebecca, 620
Fonseca, Sarah, 620
Fontyn, Jaques, 252a
Foot, Brownson, 169
Foot, Hannah Brownson, 169
Foot, Mary Brownson, 169
Forbes, Charles, 17
Forbes, James, 1728
Ford, James, 1660
Fordam, Eliza Douglass, 555
Forguson, Ephraim, 635
Forguson, Hannah, 635
Forguson, Peter, 635
Forguson, Robert, 635
Forguson, Sarah, 635
Forman, Jos., 227
Forrest, Henry, 552
Forrest, James, 399
Fort, Abraham, 654
Fort, Aleda, 654
Fort, Elezibeth, 996
Fort, Johannis, 654, 1853, 1916
Fort, John, 996
Fort, John I., 654
Fort, Rebeccah, 654
Foster, Elizabeth, 210
Foster, Hannah Blair, 210
Foster, Hannah Susannah, 210
Foster, James, 192
Foster, John, 715
Foster, Mary Blair, 210
Foster, Mary van Hook, 210
Foster, Nathal, 164, 192
Foster, Sarah, 387
Foster, Thomas, 387
Fouetter, David, 791
Foulger, Benjamin, 651
Foulger, Thomas, 651
Fouquet, Baptiste, 1369
Fowler, Abigail, 631, 652
Fowler, Abigail Purdy, 1320

Gillespie, Robert, 1373
Gillespy, Daniel, 130
Gillett, Abner, 695
Gillett, Eli, 695
Gillett, Joel, 695
Gillett, Joseph, 930
Gillett, Mary, 695
Gillett, Moses, 665
Gillett, Sarah, 695
Gilliat, Mary, 257
Gilliat, Philipp, 257
Gilliland, William, 302
Gillmore, Robert, 707
Gilmore, Dorothy Gray, 707
Gilmore, Margaret, 1412
Gilmore, Robert, 803
Ginsalis, Hannah, 717
Ginsalis, Imanuel, 717
Ginsalis, John, 717
Ginsalis, Joseph, 717
Ginsalis, Peter, 717
Girard, Abraham, 673
Girard, Ann, 673
Giraut, Danl., 1487
Giveen (Given), John, 679, 681
Giveen (Given), Mary, 679, 681
Giveen (Given), Sarah, 679, 681
Given, Margaret, 681
Given, Robert, 681
Given, Thomas, 992
Glandorf, Johs., 1824
Glandorf, Maria, 1824
Glasford, Jane Little, 1051
Glasford, John, 1051
Glean, Anthony, 2120
Glean, Jane, 2120
Glean, Johannis, 1978
Gleason, Meriam, 952
Glen, Annetje, 666
Glen, Catharina, 666
Glen, Cornelius, 701, 1946
Glen, Elizabeth, 1946
Glen, Helena, 666
Glen, Hendrick, 701
Glen, Henry, 351, 1916
Glen, Ino., 307
Glen, Jacob, 666, 701, 1498, 2036, 2134
Glen, Jacob Sanders, 666, 669, 1103, 1607
Glen, Jacobus, 2134
Glen, Janneke, 669
Glen, Johannis, 701
Glen, Johannis, 666, 669, 2027
Glen, John, 701, 2010
Glen, John S., 1859
Glen, John Sandersen, 1017, 1388, 1607
Glen, Major Jacob, 1992
Glen, Maria, 388
Glen, Sander, 666, 669, 2134
Glen, Sarah, 1498
Glen, Sarah Saunders, 1607
Glenn, Antje, 747
Glenn, Captain Sander, 747
Glenn, Jacob, 747
Glenn, Johannes, 747
Glover, Hester, 739
Glover, John, 117
Glover, Robert, 546
Glover, William, 739
Goaldsmith, Benjamin, 790
Goaldsmith, Susannah, 790
Goaldsmith, Susannah Hains, 790
Godwin, Abraham Yates, 724
Godwin, Catelina, 724
Godwin, Catherine, 91
Godwin, Helena, 724
Godwin, Henrietta, 724
Godwin, Henry, 724
Godwin, Phebea, 724
Goebel, Johann Georg, 1609
Goecocks, Joseph, 441
Goelet, Catharine, 730
Goelet, Christopher Billopp, 730
Goelet, Elisabeth, 730
Goelet, Francis, 730
Goelet, Jacob, 1034, 1691
Goelet, James, 730
Goelett, Jennet, 730
Goelet, John, 730
Goelet, Peter, 730
Goelet, Rapel, 1401
Goelet, Robert Ratsey, 730
Goelet, Thomas Billopp, 730
Goes, Angenitje, 758
Goes, Anna Jans, 668
Goes, Christina van Alen, 710
Goes, Dirk, 668, 710, 749, 753
Goes, Elizabeth, 753
Goes, Ellibirtie, 100
Goes, Eitie, 758
Goes, Helena, 758
Goes, Jan, 668, 749
Goes, Jan Tysen, 668, 749, 753, 1706
Goes, Jannatie, 758
Goes, Johannis, 710, 753, 758, 1910,
Goes, John, 668
Goes, John D., 710
Goes, Judith, 668
Goes, Katharina, 758
Goes, Konelia, 758
Goes, Lowis, 121
Goes, Lowrens D,, 710
Goes, Luyckas, 753
Goes, Luykas I., 710
Goes, Matthew, 758, 823

H

Haas, Jurry, 1851
Haas, Zacharias, 1820
Haasbrock, Elsje Schoonmaker, 1485
Haasbrock, Joseph, 1485
Haasbrook, Benjamin, 802
Haasbrook, Daniel, 802
Haasbrook, Francis, 802
Haasbrook, Hettje, 802
Haasbrook, Jacob, 802
Haasbrook, Jonetje, 802
Haase, John, 229
Habacher, George, 2040
Habs, John, 1176
Hadaway, Thos., 950
Haddan, John, 1153
Hadden, Margarat Gardner, 671
Hadley, Bishop, 107
Hadley, Magdalen, 107
Haerring, Cozyn, 771
Haerring, John, 771
Haerring, Marytie, 771
Haes, Rd., 1792
Haff, Anna, 792
Haff, Anthony, 794
Haff, Catherine Shurrie, 1626
Haff, Elizabeth, 781, 792
Haff, Ellis, 781
Haff, Hannah, 781
Haff, Isaac, 781
Haff, Jacob 781, 792
Haff, Joseph, 300, 781, 792, 975
Haff, Lawrence, 781, 792, 794, 1626
Haff, Mary, 794
Haff, Mergit, 792
Haff, Peter, 794
Haff, Sarah, 794
Haff, Susannah, 781, 794
Haff, William, 781, 792
Haff, Winche, 794
Haffe, Susannah, 1310
Hagadorn, Cornelius, 906
Hagadorn, John, 906
Hagadorn, Jonathan, 906
Hagadorn, Leah, 906
Hagadorn, Margaret, 906
Hagadorn, Samuel, 906
Hagadorn, Sophia, 906
Hagaman, Elizabeth van Wagenen, 1882
Hagaman, Joseph, 1882
Hagaman, Mary, 1867
Hagedorn, Annatie, 869
Hagedorn, David, 869
Hagedorn, Elizabeth, 906
Hagedorn, Francis, 869
Hagedorn, Henry R., 906
Hagedorn, Jacob, 869
Hagedorn, Johannis, 869
Hagedorn, Jury, 869
Hagedorn, Laritie, 879
Hagedorn, Peter, 869
Hagel, Yan, 962
Hageman, Adrian, 814
Hageman, Heatrich, 814
Hagerman, John, 814
Hagerman, Francis, 777
Haggarty, Agnes, 210
Haight, Aaron, 520, 840
Haight, Abigail, 840
Haight, Ann, 563
Haight, Benjamin, 840, 856
Haight, Caleb, 840
Haight, Chas., 370
Haight, Cornelius, 856
Haight, Eborn, 815
Haight, Elanor, 840
Haight, Elizabeth, 840, 856
Haight, Jacob, 624, 781, 856
Haight, John, 2145
Haight, Jonathan, 856
Haight, Joshua, 142, 683, 694, 2145
Haight, Josiah, 840
Haight, Martha, 856
Haight, Nathanel, 840
Haight, Phebe, 142
Haight, Samuel, 24, 856
Haight, Sarah, 2145
Haight, Stephen, 1356
Haight, Susan, 856
Haines, Anna, 134
Haines, Casper Wister, 892
Haines, Catherine, 892
Haines, Charles, 134
Haines, John, 98
Haines, Josiah, 892
Haines, Margaret, 892
Haines, Mary, 134
Haines, Mary Booth, 134
Haines, Mehitebel, 134
Haines, Reuben, 892
Haines, Samuel, 702, 1122
Haines, Susanna, 134
Hains, Abigail, 790
Hains, Benjamin, 790, 1251
Hains, David, 790
Hains, Elizabeth, 1251
Hains, John, 1251
Hains, Martha Neely, 1251
Hains, Nathan, 790
Hains, Samuel, 790
Hains, Susannah, 790
Hains, William, 1251
Hait, Mary Green, 689
Hake, Helena, 1089
Hake, Samuel, 1089
Halenbeck, Casper, 784
Halenbeck, Casper Jansen, 784
Halenbeck, Jacob, 76

Halenbeck, Jan Caspersen, 76, 784
Halenbeck, Maddalena, 784
Halenbeck, Maria Schram, 1625
Halenbeck, Merten, 784
Halenbeck, Rachel Klauw, 998
Halenbeck, William, 76, 784, 1625
Halenbeek, Anthony, 917
Halenbeek, Barnardus, 917
Halenbeek, Catrine, 784
Halenbeek, Daniel, 917
Halenbeek, Dirk, 568
Halenbeek, Dorothy, 917
Halenbeek, Garret, 917
Halenbeek, Hendrick, 917
Halenbeek, Isaac, 917
Halenbeek, Jacob, 784, 917
Halenbeek, Nicolas, 917
Halenbeek, Rachel, 784
Halenbeek, Susannah, 917
Halenbeek, Willem, 568
Halenbick, Abraham, 1500
Halenbick, Elizabeth, 1500
Halfpenny, Thomas, 886
Halifax, Earl of, 1152
Hall, Anna, 1432
Hall, Benjamin, 861
Hall, Edward, 1010
Hall, George, 1478
Hall, Gideon, 349, 861
Hall, Hannah Bedell, 102
Hall, Hendrick, 1432
Hall, Jacob, 909
Hall, Jacob B., 909
Hall, James, 1185
Hall, Johanna, 1139
Hall, John, 861, 909, 1296, 1890
Hall, Joseph, 909
Hall, Keziah, 1185
Hall, Magdalen, 703
Hall, Magdalena Gouveneur, 738
Hall, Margaret Puiroe, 1295
Hall, Mary, 887
Hall, Moses, 909
Hall, Rachel Clements, 349
Hall, Rachel Hall, 909
Hall, Sarah, 909
Hall, Thomas, 404, 564
Hall, William, 349, 861
Hallenbake, Andrew, 1102
Hallenbake, Angelica Le Grange, 1102
Hallenbake, Ann Le Grange, 1102
Hallenbake, John, 1102
Hallenbeck, Casper M., 998
Hallenbeek, Capt. Jacob, 982
Hallenbeek, Casper, 982
Hallenbeek, Gertruy, 902
Hallenbeek, Hendrick, 902
Hallenbeek, Jacob, 902
Hallenbeek, Johanna, 902
Hallenbeek, Johannis, 902
Hallenbeek, Naning, 902
Hallenbeek, Maria, 902
Hallenbeek, William, 982
Hallett, George, 2050
Halloc, Joshua, 1335
Halloc, Molly Peters, 1335
Hallock, Clement, 862
Hallock, David, 778a
Hallock, Deborah, 862
Hallock, Dinah, 778a
Hallock, Elijah, 862
Hallock, Elizabeth, 778a
Hallock, Foster, 862
Hallock, James, 862
Hallock, Jesse, 778a
Hallock, John, 862
Hallock, Mehetable, 1603
Hallock, Obediah, 723
Hallock, Phebe, 862
Hallock, Richard, 778a
Hallock, Samuel, 862
Hallock, Sarah, 778a, 862
Hallock, Thomas, 862
Hallock, William, 778a
Halloran, John Brooke, 893
Hallsed, Jacob, 1130
Hallsted, Abigail, 833
Hallsted, Benjamin, 797, 833
Hallsted, Caleb, 797, 833
Hallsted, Cathrine, 833
Hallsted, Elisabeth, 832, 833
Hallsted, Hannah, 833
Hallsted, Henry, 797
Hallsted, Isaiah, 314
Hallsted, John, 797, 832, 833
Hallsted, Jonah, 33, 797, 832
Hallsted, Joseph, 1757
Hallsted, Margaret, 833
Hallsted, Martha, 797, 833
Hallsted, Mary, 832, 833
Hallsted, Phebey, 833
Hallsted, Rachel, 833
Hallsted, Sarah, 832
Hallsted, Serah, 833
Hallsted, Thomas, 797
Halsey, Henry, 885
Halsey, Syela, 337
Halstead, John, 173
Halstead, Jonis, 1332
Halstead, Mary, 1231
Halsted, Aberham, 876
Halsted, Caleb, 1280
Halsted, Isac, 876
Halsted, Jacob, 876
Halsted, John, 876
Halsted, Joseph, 377
Halsted, Riahel, 876

Halsted, Stphson, 876
Halsted, Thomas, 1556
Ham, Antho, 77
Ham, Casper, 1611
Ham, Christina Straight, 1611
Ham, Counradt, 1611
Ham, Frederick, 1611
Hamanond, Aaron, 882
Hambly, Joseph, 834
Hamersley, W., 2031
Hamersly, William, 428
Hamill, Daniel, 1734
Hamilton, Alexander, 1662
Hamilton, Alexander Mark Ker, 330
Hamilton, Alice Colden, 330
Hamilton, Alice Margaret Campbell, 330
Hamilton, Arch., 350
Hamilton, Archibald, 330
Hamilton, Elizabeth Schuyler, 1662
Hamilton, James, 110, 2055
Hamilton, Mary Elizabeth Jane Douglas, 330
Hamilton, Pat, 183
Hamler, Christian, 2113
Hamlin, John, 230
Hamm, Casper, 1432
Hammon, William, 1166
Hammond, Aaron, 858
Hammond, Meacey, 858
Hammond, Rebeccah, 858
Hamon, Jacobus, 441
Hamory, Mr., 1218
Hanbrough, Hobart, 692
Hancock, Margaret, 1599
Hancock, Robert, 422
Hanly, Mathias, 161
Hanna, Esther Tarepenning, 1703
Hanna, Robert, 1703
Hannagan, William, 656
Hannion, Catharine, 1741
Hannium, Cornelius, 994
Hansen, A., 392
Hansen, Andries, 1239
Hansen, Deborah, 767
Hansen, Dirck 880
Hansen, Elsie, 913
Hansen, Gerret, 761
Hansen, Gerritje, 1239
Hansen, Hans, 72, 767, 786, 1495
Hansen, Helena, 880
Hansen, Hendrick, 53, 255, 329, 567 767, 786, 913, 1018, 1688, 1785, 1790, 1982
Hansen, Isaac, 2140
Hansen, Johannis, 786, 913, 1116
Hansen, John, 68, 569, 893
Hansen, Maria, 767
Hansen, Nicolas, 767
Hansen, Peter, 767, 786, 1716
Hansen, Pieter, 761
Hansen, Rachel, 1091
Hansen, Richard, 767
Hanson, Sarah, 786
Hanson, Charles, 608
Hanson, Elizabeth, 893
Hanson, Hughes, 893
Hanson, James, 893
Hanson, Maria Seal, 1536
Hanson, Martha, 893
Hanson, Mary, 893
Hanson, Robert, 893
Hanson, Thomas, 893, 1536
Harbord, Capt. Alexander, 791
Harcourt, Esther, 820
Harcourt, John, 820
Harcourt, Nathaniel, 320
Harcourt, Richard, 320
Hardenberg, Abraham, 821, 1494
Hardenbergh, Benjamin, 863
Hardenbergh, Catherine, 796
Hardenbergh, Catie, 863
Hardenbergh, Charles, 796, 863
Hardenbergh, Corneleja du Bois, 459
Hardenbergh, Cornelius, 1440
Hardenbergh, Elesabet, 863
Hardenbergh, Elias, 821
Hardenbergh, Ellenger, 863
Hardenbergh, G., 1515
Hardenbergh, Gerrit, 911
Hardenbergh, Hermanus, 863
Hardenbergh, Jacob Rutsen, 863
Hardenbergh, Jaepie Schepmoes, 911
Hardenbergh, Johannes C., 863
Hardenbergh, Johannis, 440, 796, 821, 863, 1483
Hardenbergh, Johannis A., 532
Hardenbergh, Johannis G., 776, 507
Hardenbergh, Johannis Grad., 459
Hardenbergh, John, 863, 1216
Hardenbergh, Johs., 1180
Hardenbergh, Major Johannis, 424 426, 1494, 1684, 2014, 2015
Hardenbergh, Marritie, 821
Hardenbergh, Mary, 821
Hardenbergh, Mary Bruyn, 178
Hardenbergh, Nensie, 863
Hardenbergh, Nicholas, 178, 821 875
Hardenbergh, Pagie, 863
Hardenbergh, Pallie, 863
Hardenbergh, Racel, 863
Hardenbergh, Rachel, 821
Hardenbergh, Thomas, 863
Hardenbrock, Fommetje, 1406

Hart, Sarah, 615a
Hartgers, Jennetie, 237
Hartgers, Pieter, 237
Hartgers, Rachel, 237
Hartgers, Sytge Roeloffs, 237
Hartshorne, Richard, 1648
Hartshorne, Robert, 1648
Hartshorne, Sarah, 1648
Hartshorne, Thomas, 1648
Harvey, Obed, 38
Harwood, Robert, 1362
Hasbrook, Abraham, 106
Hasbrook, Antye, 522
Hasbrook, Elisabeth Swartwout, 1284
Hasbrook, Francis, 1584
Hasbrouck, A., 462, 468
Hasbrouck, Abraham, 476, 813, 844, 1165, 1494, 1529, 1703
Hasbrouck, Benjamin, 438, 778, 1595, 1900
Hasbrouck, Colonel Abrm., 639
Hasbrouck, Cornelius, 521, 844
Hasbrouck, David, 589
Hasbrouck, Elias, 491, 1552
Hasbrouck, Esterre, 778
Hasbrouck, Francis, 719
Hasbrouck, Isaac, 625, 778, 844
Hasbrouck, J., 85, 452
Hasbrouck, Jacob, 85, 118, 476, 502, 521, 589, 778, 804, 808, 850
Harbrouck, Jacobus, 813, 1632
Hasbrouck, Jan, 813
Hasbrouck, Jonathan, 438, 844, 1518
Hasbrouck, Joseph, 507, 581, 639
Hasbrouck, Josiah, 521
Hasbrouck, Lydia Schoonmaker, 1595
Hasbrouck, Mary, 844
Hasbrouck, Mary Hoornbeek, 804
Hasbrouck, Peter, 152
Hasbrouck, Petrus, 813
Hasbrouck, Rachel van Wagenen, 813
Hasbrouck, Tryntje, 844
Hasbroucq, Daniel, 778
Hase, Johannis, 1565
Hasenclever, Maria, 1221
Hasher, Catharina, 1118
Haslin, Margaret Nash, 1265
Haslin, Thomas, 1265
Hasslen, Thomas, 350
Hasting, Perez, 909
Haswell, John, 1950
Hatch, Asa, 903
Hatch, Charles, 903
Hatch, Jonathan, 903
Hatch, Lucy, 903
Hatch, Lydia, 903
Hatch, Simpson, 230
Hatch, Warner, 903
Hathaway, Abner, 878
Hathaway, Cornish, 878
Hathaway, Daniel, 878
Hathaway, Elisha, 878
Hathaway, Guilford, 878
Hathaway, Jacob, 878
Hathaway, Lydia, 878
Hathaway, Thankful, 878
Hathway, Abigail Cooper, 371
Hatton, Rev. George, 254
Hauck, Anna, 846
Hauck, Catrine, 846
Hauck, Christina, 846
Hauck, Elizabeth, 846
Hauck, Henrich, 846
Hauck, Jacob, 846
Hauck, Peter, 846
Hauden, Michael, 762
Haughwoort, Peter, 215
Hauk, John, 531
Haulenbake, Jerom, 1552
Haulenbake, Polly Schermerhorn, 1552
Hauser, Elisabeth, 457
Hauver, Frederick, 190
Hauver, Magdaline Bice, 190
Havens, Amy, 885
Havens, Clarissa, 885
Havens, John, 885
Havens, Phebe, 885
Havens, Robert, 727
Haver, Frederick, 1610
Haviland, Ebenezer, 291, 838
Hawes, Peter, 663
Hawey, Thomas, 890
Hawkings, Benjamin, 836
Hawkings, Desire, 836
Hawkings, Eleazar, 936
Hawkings, Martha, 836
Hawkings, Sarah, 836
Hawkings, William Havens, 836
Hawkins, Elinora, 1854
Hawley, Ebenezer R., 908
Hawley, John, 1663
Hawley, Olive Higby, 908
Hawley, Reuben, 1663
Hay, Mary, 2
Hay, Mrs., 1599
Hay, William, 764
Hayes, Nathaniel, 1635
Haynes, John, 886
Haynes, Joseph, 881
Hayns, Hendrick, 1035
Hays, John, 1173
Hays, Moses I., 893
Hazard, Jonathan, 77

Hazebroeck, Zeger, 1816
Hazen, Colonel Moses, 733
Hazerd, Meribe Taber, 1748
Heart, Jacob, 739
Heath, Sarah, 899
Heath, William, 899
Heathcote, Caleb, 763
Heathcote, Col. Caleb, 1387
Heathcote, George, 763
Heaton, Adna, 532
Hebard, Robert, 997
Heckeweller, Christ. Rens., 1943
Hedden, Morgred Low, 1055
Hedger, Hannah Gardner, 671
Hedger, Hannah Genoung, 672
Hedger, John, 671
Hedges, Stephen, 1288
Hedly, Sarah, 671
Hedon, Mary, 1031
Heegar, Doortie Kast, 971
Heegar, Hendrick, 971
Heegar, Marie, 971
Heeremanse, Abraham, 1250
Heeremanse, John, 1250
Heermance, Ryer, 171
Heersmans, Araham, 809, 1250
Heermans, Andries, 768, 778b, 809
Heermans, Catharina, 809
Heermans, Clara, 809
Heermans, Gerrit, 809, 1543
Heermans, Gerritje Schermerhoorn, 1543
Heermans, Goze, 809
Heermans, Hendricus, 768, 809
Heermans, Jacob, 768, 809
Heermans, Jacomyntie, 809
Heermans, Jan, 768, 809
Heermans, Jannetje, 809
Heermans, Margarieta, 768
Heermans, Nicholaas, 809
Heermans, Petrus, 809
Heermans, Philipp, 809
Heermans, Wilhelmus, 809, 1306
Heermanse, Ackamanchee, 843
Heermanse, Anderies, 778b
Heermanse, Andries P., 843
Heermanse, Antje, 7786
Heermanse, Elizabeth, 843
Heermanse, Evert, 843
Heermanse, Goze, 843
Heermanse, Hendrikus, 778b
Heermanse, Jacob, 863
Heermanse, Philippus, 778b
Heermanse, Wilhelmus, 778b
Heermansen, Henderickes, 996
Hegeman, Adrian, 1462
Hegeman, Dirck, 1564
Hegeman, Joseph, 1462
Hegemans, Denys, 1386
Height, Benjamin, 27
Height, Joshua, 1153
Height, Solomon, 1285
Heil, Christian Matthias, 369
Heint, Abrm., 376
Heisler, Pitter, 1417
Helling, Elizabeth Halenbeek, 917
Helling, Gretie, 65
Helling, Tunis, 65
Helling, William, 917
Helm, Elesebeth, 795
Helm, Finnias, 795
Helm, Vinsent, 795
Helm, William, 795
Helme, Anselem, 871
Helme, Benjamin, 313a, 1560, 1935
Helme, Jean, 91
Helmer, Anna Margaretha, 807
Helmer, Catherina, 807
Helmer, Christina, 807
Helmer, Elizabeth, 807
Helmer, Gottfried, 807
Helmer, Henry, 807
Helmer, Johannes, 807
Helmer, John, 807, 1351
Helmer, Joost, 807
Helmer, Leonhart, 807
Helmer, Margaretha, 807
Helmer, Philipp, 123, 798
Helms, Amos, 782
Helms, John, 782
Helst, Anthony, 1282
Hempsted, Abigail, 884
Hempsted, Elizabeth, 884
Hempsted, Experience, 884
Hempsted, John, 884
Hempsted, Joshua, 884
Hempsted, Mary, 884
Hempsted, Mehetable, 884
Hempsted, Robert, 884
Hempsted, Thomas, 884
Henderickson, Cornelius, 893
Henderson, Anne, 1454
Henderson, James, 45c
Henderson, Robert, 1252
Hendorff, Ensign Frederick Christopher, 901
Hendricks, Jacob, 1386
Hendrics, Hans, 910
Hendricksen, Adrian, 38a
Hendricksen, Eva, 913
Hendricksen, Hannes, 1306
Hendricksen, Hans, 913
Hendricksen, Jan, 1693
Hendricksen, Maeycken, 38a
Hendricksen, Wyntie ten Eyck, 1693
Hendrickson, Thomas, 1328
Henneon, Gerret, 65

Hoffmeyer, Willem, 409
Hofman, Anthonie, 95
Hofman, Crestena, 778c
Hofman, Gertruy, 778c
Hofman, Haramanus, 778c
Hofman, Jury, 778c
Hofman, Nicolas, 55
Hofman, Rachel, 778c
Hogan, Daniel, 62, 247, 770
Hogan, Gerrit, 918
Hogan, Isaac, 824
Hogan, John, 805
Hogan, Jurian, 72, 770, 805
Hogan, Maria, 805
Hogan, Marten, 805
Hogan, Martiena, 770
Hogan, Mary, 824
Hogan, Neeltie, 919
Hogan, Patt, 171, 1899
Hogan, Pietertie Douw, 444
Hogan, William, 244, 444, 770, 805
Hogeboom, Abram, 874
Hogeboom, Adam, 1934
Hogeboom, Albertge, 874
Hogeboom, Annatie, 859
Hogeboom, Bartholomeus, 1147
Hogeboom, Bartholomew, 866, 874
Hogeboom, Catrin, 866
Hogeboom, Cornelias, 874
Hogeboom, Cornelius, 1910
Hogeboom, Elizabeth, 866
Hogeboom, Hannah, 866
Hogeboom, Hendrickje Muller, 1147
Hogeboom, Jacob, 866
Hogeboom, Jacobus, 1197
Hogeboom, James, 859, 866, 874
Hogeboom, Janitje, 874
Hogeboom, Jenny, 1197
Hogeboom, Jeremiah, 859
Hogeboom, Jeremyas, 569, 578
Hogeboom, Johannes, 874, 1197
Hogeboom, John, 866
Hogeboom, Laurance, 874, 1147
Hogeboom, Margaret, 866
Hogeboom, Mary, 1197
Hogeboom, Peter, 859, 866
Hogeboom, Polly, 866
Hogeboom, Sarah, 866
Hogeboom, Stephen, 569, 1197
Hogeboom, Thomas, 874
Hogeland, Dirck, 1160
Hogeland, Polly Montross, 1160
Hogen, Wm., 1865
Hogenboom, Annatie, 916
Hogenboom, Bartholomeus, 916
Hogenboom, Cornelis, 916
Hogenboom, Jeremyas, 916
Hogenboom, Johannes, 916
Hogenboom, Peter, 916
Hogenboom, Rachel, 916
Hogencamp, Minder, 70, 774
Hogencomp, Catharina, 774
Hogencomp, Gerritje, 774
Hogencomp, Honnes, 774
Hogencomp, Jannetje, 774
Hogencomp, John, 774
Hogencomp, Martynes, 774
Hogencomp, Minard, 774
Hogenkamp, Jan Mynder, 1582
Hogenkamp, Johannis, 590
Hogenkamp, M., 1079
Hogenkamp, Myndert, 1276, 1582
Hogg, Rebecca, 779
Hogkins, Abigill Green, 727
Hogland, Abraham, 184
Hoghteeling, Rykert, 2005
Hoghteyling, Abraham, 810
Hoghteyling, Ariaentie, 810
Hoghteyling, Blandina, 810
Hoghteyling, Philipp, 810
Hoghteyling, Wilhelmus, 810
Hogteling, David, 918
Hogteling, Gerrit, 918
Hogteling, Hilmas, 918
Hogteling, Maria, 918
Hogteling, Peter, 918
Holbrook, Eunice, 825
Holbrook, Nathaniel, 825
Holbrook, Sarah, 825
Hole, Benj. Ayshford, 60
Hollahan, Thomas, 661
Holland, Captain Henry, 883
Holland, Ed., 1484
Holland, Edward, 785, 883
Holland, Elizabeth, 785
Holland, Frances, 785
Holland, Henry, 66, 785, 1395, 1580
Holland, Hitchen, 444, 801
Holland, Jane, 785
Holland, John Collins, 801
Holland, John C., 708
Holland, Lieut. Henry, 1468
Holland, Margarett, 801
Holland, Phillipp, 801
Hollenbeck, John W., 1763
Holliday, David, 642
Holling, Elisabeth, 800
Hollis, William, 524
Holloway, Joseph, 600
Holloway, Mary, 600
Hollowell, Elizabeth, 1457
Hollowell, Isabella, 1457
Holly, Ebenezer, 929
Holly, Ebn., 1405
Holly, Jean, 116
Holly, John, 275

Hunt, Gillead, 985
Hunt, Gilleath, 654
Hunt, John, 153, 422
Hunt, Joseph, 616, 734
Hunt, Lewis, 845
Hunt, Mary Miller, 1184
Hunt, Moses, 162, 338
Hunt, Sarah, 845
Hunt, Solomon, 838
Hunt, William, 1501
Hunter, Andrew, 204
Hunter, Anne Neelly, 839
Hunter, David, 839
Hunter, George, 422
Hunter, James, 799, 839, 1028
Hunter, John, 839
Hunter, Lilly, 839
Hunter, Mary Robinson, 663
Hunter, Matthews, 839
Hunter, Mathew, 502
Hunter, Polly, 204
Hunter, Robert, 502, 839, 844
Hunter, Samuel, 839
Hunter, Susannah, 801
Hunter, William, 663, 839, 844, 891
Huntington, Ozias M., 1681
Huntly, Elizabeth, 812
Huntly, John, 812
Huntly, Lowes, 812
Huntly, Raner, 812
Huntly, Williams, 812
Hurd, Pheba Paine, 1317
Hurdy, Robert, 888
Hurgronze, Jacoba Berewout, 213
Hurgronze, Paul, 213
Hurlbutt, Stephen, 1624
Hurry, Anna, 45
Hurry, William, 45
Hurst, Mary Brownejohn, 224
Hurst, Timothy, 224
Hurtin, Susannah, 168
Huson, Thomas, 815
Hussey, James, 551
Hustead, David, 1325
Hustead, John, 2038
Husted, David, 1323
Hustis, Charity Rogers, 1426
Hutchings, Dinah, 799
Hutchings, Elizabeth, 7
Hutchings, Isaac, 799
Hutchings, Jacob, 799
Hutchings, John, 799
Hutchings, Joshua, 1547
Hutchings, Pheby, 799
Hutchings, Richard, 799
Hutchings, Sarah, 799
Hutchins, John, 1683
Hutchins, John Nathan, 162, 857
Hutchins, Mary, 857
Hutchins, Nathaniel, 2035
Hutchinson, Jas., 1253
Hutchinson, Mary Lynott, 1048
Hutchinson, Ralph, 760
Hutchinson, Robbart, 760
Hutron, Mary Wood, 2068
Hutton, Elizabeth, 1079
Hutton, Isaac, 905
Hutton, John, 1079
Huyck, Aaron, 816
Huyck, Andries, 746a
Huyck, Andries B., 816
Huyck, Andries L., 816
Huyck, Arent, 816
Huyck, Bata 816, 823
Huyck, Burger, 816, 823
Huyck, Burger J., 896
Huyck, Casparus, 1909
Huyck, Dirk, 816, 823
Huyck, Elizabeth, 710, 816, 823
Huyck, Engeltije, 1909
Huyck, Jacobus, 816
Huyck, James, 896
Huyck, Johannes, 816, 823
Huyck, Lambert, 1802
Huyck, Majeke, 823
Huyck, Margaret, 896
Huyck, Moyaca, 816
Huyck, Rachel, 816, 823
Huyck, Sarah, 823
Huygh, Andrieje Hansen, 914
Huygh, Anna, 914
Huygh, Burger, 914
Huygh, Cate, 914
Huygh, Catherine, 914
Huygh, Cornelis, 914
Huygh, Jochem, 914
Huygh, Johannis, 914
Huygh, Lambert, 914
Huygh, Margaret, 914
Huygh, Maria, 914
Huyser, Adriana, 549
Huyser, Cornelis, 549
Hyatt, Abraham, 140
Hyatt, Jekiel, 150
Hyatt, Joshua, 141
Hyatt, Nathaniel, 150
Hyer, Abraham, 1112
Hyer, Jacob, 1092
Hyer, Johannis, 769
Hyer, Katerlyntye Mull, 1112
Hyer, Walter, 1112
Hyer, William, 945, 1112
Hylton, Ann, 900
Hylton, Daniel L., 900
Hylton, Jakobis, 16
Hylton, John, 900
Hylton, Mary, 900

K

L

la Borde, Emilie, 220
la Borde, Sophie, 220
la Borde, Susette, 220
Labouisse, Mr., 385
Laboyteaux, Gabriel, 1085
Laboyteaux, Hannah, 1085
Laboyteaux, John, 1085
Laboyteaux, Nancy, 1085
Laboyteaux, Peter, 1085
Laboyteaux, Samuel Smith, 1085
Laboyteaux, William, 1085
Lacey, Rev. Wm. B., 562
Lacoste, Jean Baptiste, 1368
Ladou, Stephen, 1502
Lafalze, Hendrick, 219
La Fevour, Andries, 475
La Fevour, Rachel Dubois, 475
Laffiteau, Mr., 385
Laffiteau, Pierre, 1096
Laford, Abraham, 1017
Laford, Anna, 1017
Laford, Daniel, 1017
Laford, Isaac, 1017
Laford, Jacob, 1017
Laford (Libertee), John, 1017
Laford, Maragrieta, 1017
Laford, Nicholae, 1017
Laforge, Charles, 108
Lagrange, Annatie, 1109
La Grange, Christian, 1102, 1109
Lagrange, Christientie, 1109
Lagrange, Christoyan, 604
La Grange, Elizabeth, 1102
Lagrange, Eytje, 1109
La Grange, Hester van der Zee, 2012
Lagrange, Isaac, 1105
Lagrange, Isaac Koonradt, 1105
Lagrange, Jacob, 604
La Grange, Jacobus, 2012
La Grange, James, 1952
La Grange, James D., 1102
Lagrange, Johannis, 1109
Lagrange, Margaret, 1109
Lagrange, Maria, 1105
Lagrange, Mary Evertsen, 604
Lagrange, Omey, 1105, 1108
la Grangie, Gerrit, 1009
Lagranse, Annatie, 1108
Lagranse, Arie, 1108
Lagranse, Barnardus, 1108
Lagranse, Christean, 1108
Lagranse, Deborah, 1108
Lagranse, Engeltie, 1108
Lagranse, Jacobus, 76, 1108
Lagranse, John, 1108
Lagranse, Myndert, 1108
Lagranse, Susanna, 1108
Lagransie, Antjie, 574
Lagransie, Isaac, 574
Lagransie, Omy, 574
Laidlie, Archibald, 1902
Laight, Edward, 900
Laino, Chs., 643
Lake, Daniel, 1835
Lake, Judah, 932
Lakeman, Abraham, 1022
Lakeman, Anje, 1022
Lakeman, Jacob, 1022
Lamarque, Jean, 1096
Lamater, David, 1530
Lamater, Jeremiah D., 1073
Lamb, Caleb, 333
Lamb, Cathrine Jandine, 947
Lamb, Colonel, 643, 1286
Lamb, James, 2039
Lamb, Joseph, 533
Lamb, Mary Jandine, 947
Lambert, Daniel Campbell, 401
Lambert, Geertruyd, 2094
Lamberts, Andries Juriaens, 1015
Lamberts, Catrina van Niewenhuysen, 1792
Lamberts, Elisabeth, 1015
Lamberts, Sarretie Jans, 1015
Lamberts, Thomas, 1015
Lametter, Cathalina, 577
Lammertsen, Jochem, 409
Lammertson, Gerrit I., 572
Lamon, Elisabeth, 1063
Lamon, William, 1063
Lamontagne, Jan M. de, 2126
Lamoureux, James, 562
Lampen, John, 80
Lampen, Mary, 80
Lancaster, Joseph, 1631
Lancaster, William, 1454
Lancey, P. D., 413a
Lander, Frederick N., 2113
Landon, Isabella Graham, 2120
Lane, Henry, 1024, 1406
Lane, Joseph, 1024
Lane, Richard, 580
Lane, Thomas, 1024
Langdon, Abraham, 1064
Langdon, Eleoner, 1064
Langdon, Femmetje, 1064
Langdon, Johannis, 1064
Langdon, John, 139
Langdon, Mary Montross, 1160
Langdon, Phemmetie, 133
Langdon, Thomas, 133, 1064
Langdon, Willemtie, 260
Langendyk, Catherina, 1059
Langendyk, Cornelius, 1059
Langendyk, Maria, 1059
Langendyk, Petrus, 1059
Lansing, Abraham, 72, 1794

Lansing, Abraham A., 188, 1055
Lansing, Annatie, 806
Lansing, Annautie, 1072
Lansing, C. Y., 1101
Lansing, Cornelius, 1047, 1859
Lansing, Elisabeth Dunn, 251
Lansing, Elizabeth, 1072
Lansing, Else Hun, 806
Lansing, Elsie, 1292
Lansing, Gerardus, 228
Lansing, Gerrit, 754, 1072, 1292, 2133
Lansing, Gerrit A., 250, 1126
Lansing, Helenah, 1072
Lansing, Hendrick, 1012
Lansing, Henry R., 174, 894
Lansing, Honble John, 1661
Lansing, J., junior, 43
Lansing, Jacob, 251, 767, 781, 1887
Lansing, Jacob Ja., 587, 1864
Lansing, Jannetie Hun, 894
Lansing, Jannetie Knickerbacker, 1012
Lansing, Johannis, 1810
Lansing, Johannis J., 411
Lansing, Johannis Jacobsen, 756
Lansing, John, 754, 800, 1820, 2161
Lansing, John Johannes, 16
Lansing, Maghdalena van der Poel, 1794
Lansing, Peter, 754
Lansing, Philipp, 754, 806
Lansing, Thomas, 894
Lansingh, Abrm. A., 905, 1937
Lansingh, Aeltie, 1963
Lansingh, Alexander, 1047
Lansingh, Catharine, 1025
Lansingh, Cornelius, 1047
Lansingh, Elizabeth, 1025
Lansingh, Franciskys, 1498
Lansingh, Gerrit, 1025, 1963, 2027
Lansingh, Gerrit A., 1816
Lansingh, Gerrit Gerritsen, 1818
Lansingh, Gerrit Ja., 1025
Lansingh, Gertruy Schuyler, 1512
Lansingh, Gysbertie, 1963
Lansingh, Harmanus, 1047
Lansingh, Helena, 1035
Lansingh, Hendrick, 1025
Lansingh, Henry, 1162
Lansingh, Heyndrick, 1963
Lansingh, Hilletie, 1963
Lansingh, Jan, 1391
Lansingh, Johannes, 1047, 1963
Lansingh, John, 754
Lansingh, John Ja.,1381
Lansingh, Maria Marselis, 1162
Lansingh, Neeltie, 1047
Lansingh, Peter, 1498, 1512, 1551, 1567, 1997, 2029
Lansingh, Thomas, 570
Lansink, Jan, 1378
Lantman, Catharina, 1625
Lantman, Frederick, 1625
Lapham, Benjamin, 1310
Lappeus, Domine Johan Kasper, 1545
Lardant, Isaac, 2032
Laroche, Madame, 553
Laroe, Mary Dean, 526
La Roux, Charles, 2018
Laroy, Elizabeth van Kleeck, 1892
La Roy, Jan, 1840
Laroy, John, 1633, 1892
Larreset, George, 1098
Larreset, Gracieuse, 1098
Larue, Samuel, 976
Larzelere, Nicholas, 1036
Lasher, Johannes, 1433
Lasher, John, 1644
Lashman, James, 1089
Lassing, Pr., 242
Lathem, Joseph, 1394
Lathem, Sarah Rousby, 1394
Latta, James, 1181
Lattimore, Abigail, 1078
Lattimore, Benoni, 1078
Lattimore, Hannah, 1078
Lattimore, Job, 1078
Lattimore, William Freeman, 1078
Lattin, Ambros, 1427
Latting, Ambrose, 1427
la Tourette, Ester, 1026
Laughton, John, 1431
Laumert, Anna Catherine, 1045
Launert, Johan George, 1045
Launert, Pitter, 1045
Laurance, John, 114
Laurence, François, 1225
Lavinus, Philipp, 1050
Lawes, Elesebeth Cory, 278
Lawrance, Catherine Kain, 995
Lawrance, David, 1262
Lawrance, John, 995
Lawrence, Abraham Riker, 1100
Lawrence, Daniel, 335, 1034, 1157
Lawrence, Hannah Jandine, 947
Lawrence, Henry, 1463
Lawrence, Hester, 1490
Lawrence, John, 196
Lawrence, John L., 1100
Lawrence, Jonathan, 1100, 1430, 1756
Lawrence, Joseph, 897, 1100, 1409
Lawrence, Major William, 616
Lawrence, Margaret, 1100
Lawrence, Mary, 1034

Legrettier, Marie Therese, 1218
Legros, Jos., 1086
le Mauguen, Matthieu, 1224
Lemay, Catherine, 1094
Lemay, Guilleaume, 1094
Lemay, William Theodorus, 1094
Leminton, Hannah Carle, 260
Leminton, John, 260
Lemsen, Joost, 1490
Lent, Abraham, 122, 133, 1172
Lent, Antie, 133
Lent, Isaac, 1590
Lenyne, Benj., 429
Leonard, Abigail, 1040
Leonard, Elisabeth Harris, 769
Leonard, Elizabeth, 1040
Leonard, Enoch, 1937
Leonard, George, 1040
Leonard, Jacob, 1296
Leonard, James, 1040
Leonard, Jane, 765
Leonard, John, 383, 740, 1040
Leonard, Mary, 765
Leonard, Mary Puiroe, 1296
Leonard, Rev. Silas, 765
Leonard, S., 275
Leonard, Silas, 678, 1040
Leonard, Stephen, 2106
Leonard, Temper, 1040
Leonard, William, 1040
Lereau, Hannah Bartholff, 179
Lereau, Jacobus, 179
Leroy, Annatje, 1074
Leroy, Deborah, 1074
Leroy, Francis, 1074
Leroy, Peter, 1074
Leroy, Petrus, 1074
Leroy, Simeon, 1074
Leroy, Simon, 501
Lertage, P., 220
Lesher, Bastiaen, 1058
Lesher, Coenrad, 653, 1058
Lesher, Elizabeth, 1058
Lesher, Lydia Fiero, 653
Lesher, Marks, 1058
Lesher, Samuel, 1058
Leslie, James, 608
Lespinard, Abeltie, 1104
Lespinard, Anthony, 1104
Lespinard, Cornelia, 1104
Lespinard, David, 1408
Lespinard, Johannis, 1104
Lespinard, Margarita, 1104
Lessley, Elizabeth, 1046
Lessley, John, 1046
Lessley, Mary, 1046
Lester, Elizabeth Flagler, 640
Lester, Enoch, 1882
Lester, Jacob, 640
Lester, Joseph, 1897
Lester, Murray, 32
Lester, Samuel, 1219
Lestrade, Louis, 1368
Letcher, Cornelius, 1947
Letcher, Elizabeth Vusburgh, 1947
le Tellier, David, 620
Letson, Ann, 1232
Lette, Johannis Arnold, 213
Letwoor, Aeltje Pieters, 243
Letwoor, Roeloff Pietersen, 243
Leverich, John, 1547
Leveridge, Susannah, 448
Levey, Jacob, 177
Levy, Abigael Israel, 1052
Levy, Abraham, 1052
Levy, Asher, 1062
Levy, Esther, 1062
Levy, Henrietta, 1062
Levy, Hiam, 1090
Levy, Isaac, 1062
Levy, Jabeca, 1052
Levy, Joseph Israel, 1052, 1086
Levy, Moses, 1062, 1090
Levy, Polly, 1086
Levy, Samson, 1062
Levy, Sarah, 1086
Levy, Simeon, 1090
Lewis, Anna, 1071
Lewis, Barent, 1029, 1970
Lewis, Bernardus, 2133
Lewis, Daniel, 1071
Lewis, Elijah, 820
Lewis, Elizabeth, 41, 1067
Lewis, Felix, 1437
Lewis, Francis, 214, 1139
Lewis, Gertrude, 1071
Lewis, Henry, 339, 2023
Lewis, Hestor van den Burgh, 1798
Lewis, Hillegond, 1083
Lewis, Isaac, 1067
Lewis, Jacob, 1067
Lewis, James, 1067
Lewis, Jehabad, 192
Lewis, Johanna, 1071
Lewis, Johanna van der Poel, 1970
Lewis, Johannis, 1798
Lewis, John, 1067, 1083, 1093
Lewis, Jonathan, 1071
Lewis, Joseph, 339, 1067, 1544
Lewis, Leonard, 1029, 1074, 1687, 1720
Lewis, Martha Gale, 729
Lewis, Meliora, 1406
Lewis, Mordecai, 214
Lewis, Piggy McLean, 1209
Lewis, Rachell, 1029, 1907
Lewis, Richard, 1029, 1132, 1573
Lewis, Saletje Leroy, 1074

Lewis, Samuel, 1067
Lewis, Sarah Carpenter, 339
Lewis, Simon, 2081
Lewis, Thomas, 1029, 1907, 1908
Lewis, William, 1036, 1067
Lewis, Zadick, 820
Lewissen, Livynes, 1989
Leydt, Jenneke, 1079
Leydecker, Albert, 1079
Leydecker, Sarah, 1079
L'Hommedieu, Ezra, 249a
L'Hommedieu, Martha, 1016
L'Hommedieu, Peter, 1016
Libot, Daniel, 257
Libot, Jacques, 257
Libot, Louis, 257
Libot, Susanna, 257
Lickly, John, 1912
Lievesen, Cathrintie van den Borgh, 1788
Lievesen, Harme, 1239
Lievesen, Livinus, 1788
Lievesen, Maritje, 1239
Light, Matthew, 151
Lightbody, Agnes, 1193
Lightbody, Elizabeth, 1193
Lightbody, Gabriel, 1193
Lilienthal, Hanninen, 1082
Lille, Thomas, 893
Lin, George, 1680
Lin, John, 1707
Lin, Rachel Teller, 1707
Lindsay, George, 44
Lindsay, James, 556
Lines, Abraham, 611
Lines, Thomas, 295
Linklaen, John, 1444
Linklon, Jeremiah, 1056
Linklon, Samuel, 1056
Linn, J. Blair, 384
Linn, James, 1087
Linn, Mary Livingston, 1087
Lipe, Adam, 1057
Lipe, Caspar, 1057
Lipe, Catharina, 1057
Lipe, John, 1057
Lipe, Jost, 1057
Lispanar, Elshe Rutgers, 1401
Lispanar, Leonard, 1401
Lispenard, Anthony, 1408
Lispenard, Elizabeth Rodman, 1408
Lissier, Catalyntje ten Broeck, 1685
Lissier, Johan, 1685
Liswell, John, 1947
Little, Archibald, 642, 1066, 1070, 1163, 2149
Little, Elisabeth, 1028
Little, Frances, 1008, 1031
Little, George, 817
Little, Hannah, 1070
Little, James, 306, 514, 817, 1051, 1066, 1070, 1275
Little, Jane, 1051
Little, John, 608, 1028, 1031, 1037, 1051, 1066, 1070
Little, Joseph, 1066, 1070
Little, Mary, 1070
Little, Sarah, 1051, 1066, 1070
Little, Sarah Wood, 2105
Little, Susanna, 1070
Little, Thomas, 1051
Little, Timothy, 1066, 1070
Little, William, 1051
Livingston, Abraham, 1068
Livingston, Alida Schuyler, 1473, 1641
Livingston, Angletie, 1020
Livingston, Brockholst, 1087
Livingston, Catharina ten Broeck, 1705, 1716
Livingston, Catherine, 334, 1068, 1076, 1089, 1091
Livingston, Catherine McPheadris, 1167
Livingston, Christina, 1068, 1076
Livingston, Christina ten Broeck, 1705, 1716
Livingston, Cornelia Beekman, 1392
Livingston, Edward, 1076
Livingston, Elizabeth, 1091
Livingston, George, 1076
Livingston, Gertruyd, 1886
Livingston, Gil., 430, 575
Livingston, Gilbert, 523, 615a, 920, 1089, 1392, 1483, 1693, 1698, 1930
Livingston, Gilbert R., 1089
Livingston, Hannah, 196
Livingston, Henry, 304, 1068, 1099, 1840
Livingston, Henry G., 1089, 1830
Livingston, James, 359, 1020, 1578, 1723
Livingston, James G., 454, 1707
Livingston, Jas., 188
Livingston, Jasper Hall, 1076
Livingston, John, 313a, 334, 364, 713, 1020, 1076, 1091, 1099, 1705, 1716, 2110
Livingston, Judge, 1599
Livingston, Margaret, 1020, 1068
Livingston, Margaret Beekman, 229
Livingston, Margrita Schuyler, 1512
Livingston, Mary, 1091
Livingston, Mary Winthrop, 2110
Livingston, Mrs., 1599
Livingston, Neel, 196

M

Mathews, Peter, 1390, 1694
Mathews, Vincent, 313a, 730, 1204, 1694
Mathieu, André, 1369
Matison, Mary Lakeman, 1022
Matison, Nicholas, 1022
Matlack, Josiah, 892
Matlack, Nathan, 892
Matthews, David, 176, 1247
Matthews, Elizabeth Wileman, 2025
Matthews, Henry, 41
Matthews, John, 1308
Matthews, Robert, 1133
Matthews, Samuel, 1133
Matthews, Vinc., 2025
Matthieson, Nicholas, 1212
Mattison, Aaron, 1022
Mattison, Joseph, 1212
Mattys, Elisabeth Kast, 971
Mattys, Niklas, 971
Mattysen, David, 1113
Mattysen, Hendrick, 1113
Mattysen, Jan, 1113
Mattysen, Madeleen, 1113
Mattysen, Mattys Jansen, 1113
Mattysen, Thomas, 1113
Mattyson, Jan, 920
Matys, Conraet, 1545
Mauerer, Paulus, 1038
Maul, Frederick, 1608
Maul, Gertoje Scherp, 1608
Maul, Jacop, 1150
Maunsell, Elizabeth, 550, 1213
Maunsell, General John, 550, 1213
Maurer, Jacob, 641
Maurer, Lenerd, 641
Maurer, Petrus, 602, 641
Maurin, P., 1227
Maurits, Jacob, 1792
Maurits, Paul, 1792
Maurius, Peter Jacobsen, 1472
Maus, Engeltie, 235
Maverick, Isabella, 762
Maverick, Jean, 762
Maxwell, William, 1217
Mayer, Dirck, 1268
Mayer, Dirck Dircksen, 1268
Mayle, Jacob, 416
McAllister, Mathew, 1358
McArthur, Catharine, 397
McArthur, Catharine Campbell, 325
McArthur, Duncan, 191
McArthur, John, 461
McBain, Farqhuer, 561
McCabe, John, 528
McCalaughan, Catharine, 1738
McCallum, John, 1195
McCamly, David, 457, 484, 923, 1279, 1695
McCamly, Ino., 361, 729, 1209, 1572
McCamly, John, 484, 2068
McCarthy, Cornelius, 1449
McCartney, James, 883a
McCarty, Charlotte, 174
McCarty, David, 174, 241, 1735, 1924, 2005
McCay, John, 1500
McCay, Mary, 1210
McCew, Mary, 1171
McCew, William, 1171
McClachry, Patrick, 1415
McClaghry, James, 321, 1169, 1181, 2058
McClaghry, Patrick, 321, 437, 1181
McClahry, Mary Reid, 1415
McClasky, James, 1102
McClasky, Janet La Grange, 1102
McClaughry, James, 1616
McClaughry, Jane, 289
McCleaf, Elizabeth, 1091
McClean, Catherine, 1872
McClean, John, 296, 1140
McClean, Margaret Christ, 296
McClellan, Hugh, 1215
McClellar, William, 1217
McCloud, Daniel, 1278
McClung, John, 707
McCobb, Elizabeth, 1181
McCobb, James, 1181, 1251
McCobb, Jane, 1181
McCobb, Mary, 1181
McCobb, William, 1181
McCollam, Samuel, 328
McConnal, Catharine, 2087
McConnal, Hugh, 2087
McConnell, John, 595
McConnick, Daniel, 1215
McCool, Margaret, 437
McCord, Andrew, 1740
McCormick, Danl., 224
McCornell, John, 1223
McCrea, John, 1561
McCree, J., 887
McCuchan, Robt., 1181
McCurdy, Archibald, 1208, 1598
McCurdy, James, 201
McCurdy, Margret, 1208
McCurdy, Robert, 1616
McDole, Arabella Ross, 1412
McDonald, James, 1372
McDonald, John, 330
McDonald, Patrick, 1574
McDonald, Susannah, 1167
McDonil, Sarah Edmonston, 595
McDonnell, Robert, 391
McDoual, John, 681
McDougall, Alexander, 709
McDougall, Andrew, 679

McDougall, John, 709
McDougall, Martha Giveen, 679
McDowel, Mary Norris, 328
McDowel, Mathew, 633
McDowel, Wm., 328, 353
McDowell, Thomas, 2103
McDowle, Hugh, 739
McDuff, Archibald, 378
McElcheran, George, 656
McElworth, Ann, 2061
McEuen, Danel, 1132
McEuen, John, 1132
McEuen, Mary, 1132
McEvers, James, 2112
McEvers, Jno., 70
McEvers, John, 84
McFall, Neal, 644
McFarland, Jane, 1183
McFarland, John, 1183
McFarland, Wm., 713, 870
McGarrah, Elinor Little, 1028
McGarrah, Elioner, 1031
McGarrah, John, 1028, 1412
McGee, Alice, 1412
McGinnis, Alexander, 1126
McGinnis, Capt. William, 1126
McGowen, John, 341
McGown, Daniel, 1450
McGown, Elizabeth Miller, 1190
McGown, Lydia, 1190
McGrah, Christopher, 954
McGrah, Mary, 954
McGuin, Daniel, 1348
McGusty, Daniel, 951
McHago, Samuel, 1336
McIlworth, Ann, 2120
McIntire, James, 1156
McIntosh, James, 381
McIntosh, Rachel Tanner, 1760
McIntyre, Neal, 542
McInvin, John, 1145
McKay, George, 1230
McKay, James, 1230, 1289
McKay, Jane, 1230
McKee, Therese, 1373
McKenzie, Alexander, 561
McKenzie, Hector, 1145
McKenzie, James, 1145
McKesson, John, 1066, 1152, 1256, 1710
McKinley, Elizabeth, 1206
McKinley, Jane, 1206
McKinley, Mary, 1206
McKinley, Nathaniel, 1206
McKinley, Rebecca, 1206
McKinley, Sarah, 1206
McKinley, William, 1206
McKinney, Elizabeth, 593
McKinney, John, 593, 700
McKinstry, Jenat, 1252
McKinstry, John, 358, 1252
McKnight, Charles, 1265
McKnight, John, 1415
McKown, James, 665
McKown, Wm., 665
McLachlin, Christian, 130
McLaren, Duncan, 1235
McLaren, John, 1235
McLauchlin, Archibald, 402
McLaughlin, Neal, 130
McLaughlin, Patience, 130
McLaughlin, Patience Borland, 172
McLaughry, Catherine, 289
McLaughry, James, 289
McLaughry, John, 289
McLean, Catherine, 2123
McLean, Charity, 1209
McLean, Cornelius, 1209
McLean, John, 1209, 2133
McLean, Jonas, 1209
McLean, Margrett, 1209
McLean, Mary Blanchard, 2123
McLean, Sarah, 1209
McLean, Susannah, Ross, 2123
McLeland, Colen, 1618
McLeod, Helena, 1167
McLeod, Margaret, 1228
McLeod, William, 1228
McMahone, Anna, 1090
McMahone, Margaret, 1090
McManus, William, 662
McMasters, Sarah Giveen, 679
McMaunis, John, 1223
McMaunis, Peter, 1223
McMennomy, Elizabeth, 1168
McMennomy, John, 1168
McMennomy, Margaret, 1168
McMennomy, Robert, 1168
McMichael, Daniel, 1612
McMichael, John, 1460
McMichael, Joseph, 149
McMichal, Walter, 437
McMillian, William, 721
McMullen, Alexander, 1262
McMullen, Ginnet, 1262
McMullen, John, 1198
McMullen, Richard, 1432
McMullin, John, 2156
McMunn, James, 1053
McMurray, John, 1639
McNachtane, Cornelia, 1233
McNachtane, John, 1233
McNaughton, James, 402
McNeal, Aner, 1122
McNeal, Archibald, 702
McNeal, Hannah, 1122
McNeal, James, 1122
McNeal, Janet, 679

McNeal, John, 172, 679
McNeal, Margarett, 1132
McNeal, Mary, 1122
McNeall, Ann, 1123
McNeall, Edward, 1123
McNeall, John, 1123
McNeall, Lydia, 1123
McNeall, Martha, 1123
McNeall, Mary, 1123
McNeall, Rebecca, 1123
McNeall, Susanna, 1123
McNeall, Thomas, 1123
McNeeley, Henry, 1053
McNeeley, Sarah, 1053
McNeil, Elizabeth Wiltse, 2076
McNeil, James Wiltsie, 2076
McNeil, John, 709
McNeil, Lieut. Donald, 1213
McNeil, Wm., 2076
McNeill, John, 191
McNelley, Henery, 681
McNiell, Daniel, 556
McPheadris, Helena, 1167, 1174
McPherson, Ann, 1174
McQueen, John, 381
McShane, Edward, 1088
McVicar, Annah, 1238
McVickar, Benjamin, 2238
McVickar, Edward Corp, 1238
McVickar, Henry, 1238
McWhorter, James, 37
McWhorter, Matthew, 37
Mead, Capt. Job, 1195
Mead, Enos, 1138
Mead, Gideon, 1634
Mead, Jonathan, 1138
Mead, Joseph, 1138
Mead, King, 1195
Mead, Nehemiah, 1138
Mead, Noah, 1138
Mead, Philipp, 1138
Mead, Sarah, 1138
Mead, William, 2155
Means, Johevit, 1118
Means, Judah, 1118
Mebie, Casparis, 778a
Mebie (see Mabie)
Meby, Peter, 1704
Meby, Sarah, 1704
Medeco, Rachel Cohen, 1086
Medeco, Sarah Cohen
Meebie, Abraham, 64, 1993
Meier, Abraham, 280
Meier, Domine, 863
Meier, Johannes H., 863
Meier, Rachel Hardenbergh, 863
Mekely, John, 1167
Melcher, Frederic, 782
Melcher, Jacob, 1221
Meldrum, Annatie, 1928
Meller, Philippus, 110, 680
Mellin, Noah, 387
Melrose, James, 1554
Melsbagh, Necolas, 1140
Melson, Charles, 1144
Melville, John, 1454
Menosa, David, 420
Menyin, Antide, 539, 1653
Mercadier, Jh., 553
Mercer, Alexander, 1946
Mercer, Dirck van Ingen, 1946
Mercer, Elizabeth van Ingen, 1946
Mercer, James van Ingen, 1946
Merckel, Catharine, 1207
Merckel, Hannes, 1001
Merckel, Henry, 1207
Merckel, Jacob, 1207
Merckel, Johannes, 1207
Merckel, Maria, 1207
Merckel, Nicolas, 1207
Merckel. Peter, 1207
Merit, Thomas, 616
Meritt, Caleb, 1136, 1137
Meritt, David, 1136
Meritt, Elizabeth, 1186
Meritt, Gabrill, 1136
Meritt, George, 1136
Meritt, Glorande, 1136, 1137
Meritt, Jen., 1136
Meritt, Josiah, 1136, 1137
Meritt, Samuel, 1136
Meritt, Umphere, 1136, 1137
Merkell, Benjamin, 850
Merkel, Lawrence, 554
Merkle, John, 203
Merrel, Morris, 1932
Merriam, Rev. Burragés, 1599
Merrit, Humphrey, 2050
Merrit, Thomas, 1136
Merritt, Caleb, 862, 1186, 1320
Merritt, David, 1186
Merritt, Gabriel, 1186
Merritt, John, 422
Merritt, Josiah, 1186
Merritt, Martha Purdy, 1320
Merritt, Mary, 631, 1186
Merry, John, 1475
Merselis, Ahashverus, 1948
Merselis, Barbara, 1154
Merselis, Cateline Wendell, 2138, 2139
Merselis, Eva, 1154
Merselis, Gerrit, 1154
Merselis, Gysbert, 1154, 2138, 2139
Merselis, Henry, 805, 1154
Merselis, Maria, 1154
Merten, Affie, 1135
Merten, Daniel, 1135

Miller, Jacomyntje Schoonmaker, 1485
Miller, James, 96, 153, 285, 1052, 1155, 1163, 1185, 1211
Miller, Jason, 1236
Miller, Jehannah, 1764
Miller, Jemima, 1211
Miller, Jenet, 1566
Miller, Jeremiah, 1189, 1288
Miller, Jesse, 1163
Miller, Johannes, 775, 1214, 1485
Miller, Johannis George, 229
Miller, John, 1155, 1163, 1190, 1236, 2121
Miller, Jones, 1590
Miller, Joseph, 1184
Miller, Joshua, 1189
Miller, Josiah, 1184
Miller, Lucretia, 1236
Miller, Magdalen Blattner, 197
Miller, Margret, 1163, 1236
Miller, Maria Sibilla, 197
Miller, Mary, 1163, 1189, 1211, 1236
Miller, Matths. B., 129
Miller, Moriah, 1236
Miller, Morris S., 2125
Miller, Moses, 479
Miller, Nathan, 1189
Miller, Nicolaes, 1281
Miller, Peter, 498, 1163
Miller, Phebe, 1256
Miller, Philipp, 1190
Miller, Ralph, 1171
Miller, Rebeckah, 1163
Miller, Richard, 1824
Miller, Ruth, 1236
Miller, Samuel, 197, 1063, 1084, 1189, 1793
Miller, Sarah, 1189, 1211
Miller, Sylvanus, 742
Miller, Thomas, 1236
Miller, Wm., 1067, 1155
Miller, Zephaniah, 1764
Millerd, Abiathar, 1158
Millerd, Abigal, 1158
Millerd, Bennajah, 1158
Millerd, Joshua, 1158
Millerd, Phebe, 1158
Millerd, Robert, 1158
Millerd, Temperance, 1158
Milliken, John, 1122, 1569
Mills, Alex., 1691
Mills, Amos, 1164, 1574
Mills, Bathiah, 1153
Mills, Catharina, 1172
Mills, Daniel, 1191
Mills, Ephraim, 1153
Mills, Hannah, 1153, 1231
Mills, Hezekiah, 647
Mills, Hope, 518
Mills, Isaac, 1134, 1231, 1256
Mills, Jacob, 647
Mills, Johanna, 1191
Mills, John, 282, 1153, 1191
Mills, John Reading, 1231
Mills, Jonas, 1231
Mills, Jonathan, 1134, 1191
Mills, Margaret, 1191
Mills, Mary, 1134, 1153
Mills, Nathan, 1533
Mills, Peter, 2074
Mills, Phebe, 1153
Mills, Rachel Holmes, 835
Mills, Rebecca, 835
Mills, Robert, 635
Mills, Ruth, 1134
Mills, Samuel, 288, 357, 1134, 1153, 1712, 1729, 2154
Mills, Sary, 1134
Mills, Stephen, 1153
Mills, Susannah, 1153
Mills, Thaddeus, 1231
Mills, Timothy, 1134, 1191
Mills, William, 1153, 1231
Mills, Zebadiah, 1066
Mills, Zebulon, 647
Miln, Mary, 160
Milner, James, 615
Milsbach, Jacob, 1161
Milsbach, Mathias, 1161
Milsbach, Peter, 1161
Milspah, Benjamin, 1140
Milspah, Jacob, 1140
Milspah, Peter, 1140
Milton, Altie, 1396
Milward, Elizabeth, 1490
Milward, Elizabeth Stillwell, 1490
Milward, James, 1490
Minard, Albert, 11
Minderse, Abraham, 570
Miner, Lodewick, 2122
Ming, Thomas, 1492
Mingael, Johannis, 567, 1018, 1116
Mingael, Mary, 1116
Mingael, (*see* Myngal)
Minkelaer, Jacob, 128
Minot, Saml., 1272
Minthorn, John, 787
Minthorn, Philipp, 207
Minthorne, Geertje, 1117
Minthorne, Hannah, 1117
Minthorne, Hillegonda, 1117
Minthorne, Johanna, 1117
Minthorne, John, 1117
Minthorne, Margaret, 1117
Minthorne, Philipp, 1117
Minthorne, Sarah, 1117

Minturn, Hester Robinson, 663
Minturn, Jonas, 663
Minvielle, David, 1478
Miserole, Elizabeth Praa, 1299
Mitchel, William, 2050
Mitchell, Allen, 1178
Mitchell, Hannah, 1035
Mitchell, Henry, 1178, 1642
Mitchell, John, 1178
Mitchell, Joseph, 557
Mitchell, Martha, 1178
Mitchell, Mary Dampier, 557
Mitchell, Phebe, 1178
Mitchell, Robert, 1178
Mitchell, Sarah, 1178
Mitchell, Susannah, 1178
Mitchell, William, 1178
Mix, Ebenezer, 615
Mix, Sally Johnston, 952
Mochie, Anna Eva, 1175
Mochie, Anna Maria, 1175
Mochie, Eva, 1175
Mochie, Harmanus, 1175
Mochie, Johannes, 1175
Mochie, Johann Michel, 1175
Mochie, Marcus, 1175
Moffat, George, 1373
Moffat, John, 1526, 2156
Moffat, John L., 1627
Moffat, Margaret, 1031
Moffat, Margaret Little, 1028
Moffat, Mary, 2156
Moffat, Rev. John, 1028
Moffat, Samuel, 144, 341, 684
Moffat, Susannah, 854
Moffat, Thomas, 144, 154, 180, 352, 506, 598, 854, 1190, 1204, 1601, 2075
Moffit, Hosea, 204
Mohr, Andries, 1214
Mohr, Ariel, 1214
Mohr, Catherine, 1214
Mohr, Christian, 1214
Mohr, Jacob, 1214
Mohr, Johannes, 1045
Mohr, John, 1214
Mohr, Nicholas, 1214
Mohr, Petrus, 1214
Mohr, Philipp, 1214
Mohr, Philipp Heinrich, 1045
Mohr, Philipp Hendricksen, 1214
Mohr, William, 1150
Mollard, Dame, 1369
Mollineux, John, 611
Molyn, Isaac, 1103
Molyn, Temperance Loveridge, 1103
Mompesson, Martha, 571
Monck, John, 478
Moncrieffe, Edward Cornwallis, 1203
Moncrieffe, Major Thomas, 1203
Moncrieffe, Richard, 1203
Moncrieffe, Thomas Barclay, 1203
Moncurr, Will, 1454
Monell, George, 1073, 1252
Monell, Hannah, 1173
Monell, James, 1252
Monell, John, 1173, 1246, 1259, 2144
Money, John, 1220
Monfoort, Albert, 1906
Monfoort, Dominicus, 999
Monfoort, Peter, 1172
Monfoort, Rem., 1273
Monfort, Antie, 450
Monfort, Catherine, 450
Monfort, Peter, 450, 794, 2146
Monfort, Peter I., 999
Monfort, Sarah, 450
Monier, Mary Sharpe, 1586
Monk, Christ., 1658
Monk, Christopher, 42
Monnel, Catherine, 535
Monnel, David, 836
Monnel, Gennet, 535
Monnel, Joseph, 535
Monnel, Robert, 836
Monnell, David, 1252
Monroe, John, 124
Monroe, Mary Brower, 124
Monrow, Samll., 445
Monson, Alex., 191
Monson, Mr., 378
Montagne, Abrm., 465
Montagne, Benjamin, 1179
Montagne, John, 1179
Montagne, Peter, 1179
Montagne, Rebecca, 1179
Montagne, Thomas, 1179
Montfort, Robert, 1358
Montgomery, Alexander, 273, 461
Montross, John, 1160
Montross, Margaret, 1160
Montross, Peter, 1160
Moody, James, 223
Mool, Stuffel, 1749
Moon, Daniel, 200
Moone, Robert, 525
Mooney, William, 308
Moor, A., 949
Moor, Cathrine McLean, 1209
Moor, David, 1198
Moor, Ebenezer, 1620
Moor, Eytje, 100
Moor, Eytje Borghart, 121
Moor, Geesje, 100
Moor, Hugh, 1198
Moor, Isabell, 1198
Moor, James, 1198

Moor, Jane, 1198
Moor, John, 121
Moor, Maddleen, 1611
Moor, Margaret, 1198
Moor, Mary McLean, 1209
Moor, Nancy, 1198
Moore, Alfred, 1265
Moore, Anna, 1120
Moore, Benjamin, 135, 974, 1120
Moore, Caty, 1216
Moore, Charles, 1646
Moore, David, 299, 842
Moore, Elizabeth, 1146
Moore, Elizabeth Diederick, 537
Moore, Enoch, 1183
Moore, Frances, 60, 1646
Moore, Frances Blair, 210
Moore, Hannah, 1238
Moore, Hope, 1183
Moore, I., 1846
Moore, Ino., 1036
Moore, Jacob, 1216
Moore, Johannes, 537
Moore, John, 60, 862, 1768
Moore, Lambt., 82, 313a, 1646, 1821
Moore, Margat, 1120
Moore, Martha, 1120
Moore, Mary, 842, 1146
Moore, Michael, 1216
Moore, Nathan, 1120
Moore, Samuel, 1216
Moore, Thos., 1148
Moore, W., 1212
Moore, William, 525, 1340, 1450
Moores, John, 1760
Moors, Elizabeth, 1188
Moors, Johannes, 1188
Moors, Philipp, 1188
Mor, Jacup, 1045
Moran, Isaac, 1086
More, Coonrod, 1161
More, Elizabeth Little, 1051
More, Henry, 1124
More, Jackman, 422
More, James, 1051
More, Lowis Cory, 320
More, Philipp Henrich, 1150
More, Robert, 1124
Morehouse, George, 2081
Morgan, Catharine Lakeman, 1022
Morgan, Henry C., 2141
Morgan, James, 610
Morgan, John, 1022
Morgan, Levinia, 2141
Morgan, Margaret Everson, 610
Morgan, Mary, 41
Morgan, Mary Ann, 41
Morgan, Sarah Emans, 572
Morgan, Thomas, 891
Morgane, Wm., 272
Morgen, Jeams, 483
Morgine, John, 1026
Morison, Don., 1535
Morison, James, 1526
Morison, Robert, 857
Morran, Jane, 583
Morrell, John, 1178
Morrell, Robert, 1409
Morres, John, 1044
Morris, Abraham, 1194
Morris, Anna, 256
Morris, Catharine, 1032, 1139
Morris, David, 1413
Morris, Deborah Walker, 2125
Morris, Euphemia, 1139
Morris, Fredk., 1484
Morris, Governeur, 738, 1068, 1139
Morris, Isaac, 1194
Morris, Isabella, 1121, 1139
Morris, Jacobus, 1194
Morris, Jenney Dekay, 457
Morris, John, 1194
Morris, Lewis, 1121, 1139, 1146, 1780
Morris, Margaret, 1121
Morris, Mary, 227
Morris, Rebeker, 272
Morris, Richard, 1032, 1073, 1139, 1640
Morris, Robert, 2162
Morris, Robert Hunter, 1121, 1139
Morris, Roger, 227
Morris, Sarah, 1139
Morris, Sarah Ludlow, 1073
Morris, Staats Long, 1139
Morris, William W., 1444
Morrison, John, 1346
Morrison, Marite, 1904
Morse, Charles, 1046, 1382
Mortier, Abraham, 1215
Mortier, Martha, 1215
Morton, Cornelia Schuyler, 1662
Morton, Washn., 1662
Mory, John, 820
Moseley, Elizur, 2122
Moser, Elizabeth Green, 689
Moser, James, 689
Moser, Rode, 689
Mosher, Caleb, 840
Mosher, Sarah Devel, 463
Mosher, Tripp, 142, 2102
Mosser, Jacob, 1176
Mosser, Jerry, 1176
Mosser, Thomas, 1176
Mosure, Mary, 686
Mott, Abigail, 861
Mott, Adam, 921, 1387

Murphy, Catherine, 563
Murray, Charles, 1148
Murray, Honble. Joseph, 279
Murray, John, 1148
Murray, Jos., 262, 1024, 2031
Murray, Lady Susan, 1357
Murray, Madeline, 1357
Murray, Major Gen. John, 1357
Murray, Mary, 1148
Murray, Mary Crosby, 279
Murray, Patrick, 1357
Murray, Rev. William, 1357
Murray, Sir Robert, 1357
Murray, Susan, 1357
Murray, William, 1148
Mushow, Paul, 921
Musier, Jacob, 602
Muter, Mrs. Robert, 1374
Muts, Cathereen, 1128
Muts, Johannes, 1128, 1399
Mutts, *see* Much
Muzelius, Frederic, 774, 1202
Myer, Andres, 49
Myer, Andrew, 1167
Myer, Annatje, 1177
Myer, Benjamin, 1177
Myer, Cattriena, 1177
Myer, Christiaen, 1177
Myer, Christina, 1177
Myer, Coenrat, 1080
Myer, Garret, 1316
Myer, Gilbert, 1167
Myer, Johannis, 1177
Myer, John, 1167, 1513
Myer, Petrus, 1177
Myer, Simon Johnson, 1167
Myer, Stophanis, 1177
Myer, Susanna McPheadris, 1167
Myer, Tobias, 1177
Myer, Willem, 1177
Myers, Adolf, 186
Myers, Fanny, 1086
Myers, John, 186
Mynders, Abraham, 1240
Mynders, Elizabeth, 1240
Mynders, Frederick, 1240
Mynders, Johs., 76, 1240
Mynders, Maria, 1240
Mynders, Marte, 1240
Mynders, Rachel, 1240
Mynderse, Barendt, 1127, 1291
Mynderse, Geertruyd, 1127
Mynderse, Harme, 1127
Mynderse, Jacobus, 250, 1125, 1127, 2143
Mynderse, Jannitte Person, 1304
Mynderse, Johannes, 1125, 1127
Mynderse, Joseph, 400
Mynderse, Margarieta, 1127
Mynderse, Maria, 1127
Mynderse, Marten, 1154, 1889
Mynderse, Myndert, 1125, 1127, 1304
Mynderse, Reynier, 1125, 1127, 1704
Mynderse, Sarah, 1127
Mynderse, Sarah Yates, 2143
Myndersen, Frederick, 618
Myndersen, Johannes, 1404
Myndersen, John, 634
Myndersen, Martin, 104
Myndersen, Myndert, 1504
Myndersen, Reynier, 1051
Mynderts, Johannis, 1983
Myndertse, Peter, 537
Myngaal, Johannis, 1675
Myngal, Joh., 1678
Myngall, Johs., 1775
Mysen, Tonis, 404

N

Nadaud, Jacques, 1225
Nagel, Barent, 1891
Nagel, Hendrick, 1276
Nagel, Jan, 1891
Nagels, Harmyntje, 1378
Nahis, Andries, 2094
Nahuys, Petrus Cornelis, 1945
Nase, Henry, 1501
Nash, Abner, 1265
Nash, Justina, 1265
Nathan, Simon, 1097
Navarre, Citizen, 1368
Nazareth, William, 48
Neate, Christiana, 1253
Neate, Jemima, 1253
Neate, Mary, 1253
Neate, Phyllis, 1253
Neate, William, 1253
Nebor, Powel, 950
Neeley, Thomas, 1191
Neelly, James, 839
Neely, Addam, 1246
Neely, Abener, 1259
Neely, Anna, 1262
Neely, Antje Bevier, 152
Neely, Capt. William, 1251
Neely, Daniel, 1259
Neely, David, 1246
Neely, Edward, 720, 839
Neely, Elexander, 1262
Neely, Ginnet, 1262
Neely, Henry, 1255
Neely, Isabell, 1246, 1559
Neely, Jean, 1259
Neely, John, 1246, 1257, 1259, 1262, 1526, 1566

Nicoll, John, 595, 1173, 1187, 1256, 1261, 1318, 1334, 2156
Nicoll, John Dowden, 1256, 1261
Nicoll, Leonard, 1318
Nicoll, Leonard D., 1187, 1210, 1261
Nicoll, Leonard William, 1256, 1261
Nicoll, Magdalen Mary Holland, 785
Nicoll, William, 885, 993, 1247, 1683, 2156
Nicolls, Captain, 760
Nicols, Caty, 1263
Nicols, Elizabeth Salisbury, 1514
Nicols, Mary, 1263
Nicols, Renselaer, 1514, 1530
Nicols, William, 1263
Niefus, Willempee, 1358
Niev, Joseph, 1315
Nightingale, John, 604
Nights, Samuel, 367
Nihell, Edmund, 1062
Niker, Cornelis, 69
Niles, Jonathan, 365
Niles, Nathl., 1342
Nisbit, Joseph, 1847
Nitschman, Emanuel, 1943
Nitschman, Mary van Vleck, 1943
Niven, D., 541
Nixon, Agnitie, 1904
Nixon, Margriet, 1904
Nize, Daniel, 219
Noble, Isaac, 397
Noble, Jabez, 524
Noble, James, 1252
Noble, John, 959
Noble, Lois, 524
Noble, Margaret, 1252
Noble, Mary, 1252
Nocus, Stephen, 1367
Noel, John Y., 379
Noell, Hannah, 1241
Noell, Noah, 1241
Noell, Richard Hall, 1241
Noell, Thomas, 416, 1241
Noortstrant, Gerret, 794, 999, 2146
Noozman, Jan Jansen, 1268
Norris, Alexander, 1217
Norris, Charles, 545
Norris, Euphemia Morris, 1121
Norris, John, 1765
Norris, Mary, 328, 1217
Norris, Matthew, 1121
Norris, Richard, 1780
North, Benjamin, 190
North, Catherine Bice, 190
North, Clarissa, 1434
North, Rachel, 1434
North, William, 1655
Northrop, Benjamin, 1861
Northrup, Dinah, 143
Northrup, Stephen, 1635
Northup, Abigail, 1245
Northup, Amos, 1245
Northup, Benjamin, 1245
Northup, Cornwall, 1245
Northup, John 1267
Northup, Joseph, 1245
Northup, Moses, 1245
Northup, Remington, 1267
Northup, Sarah, 1245
Northup, Stephen, 1267
Northup, William, 1267
Norton, Abigail, 1702
Norton, Ashbel, 1266
Norton, George, 1242
Norton, Lewis M., 1266
Norton, Margaret, 1242
Norton, Miranda, 1266
Norton, Phebe, 1266
Norton, Samuel, 1266
Norwood, Cornelia, 1406
Norwood, Deborah Dennison, 541
Norwood, Richard, 541
Norwood, van der Clif, 1406
Nottingham, Ann, 1244
Nottingham, Bridget, 1244
Nottingham, Capt. William, 1795
Nottingham, Catharine, 1244
Nottingham, Margaret 1244
Nottingham, Nealtie, 1254
Nottingham, Stephen, 674, 1244, 1254
Nottingham, Thomas, 1244
Nottingham, William, 59, 421, 768, 1113, 1244, 1389, 1666, 2015
Noxon, Bartholomew, 367, 866, 1043, 1060, 1813, 1814
Noxon, Elcebeth, 1813, 1814
Noxon, Robert, 1923
Noxon, Thomas, 421, 792
Noyes, James, 2110
Nugent, Arthur B., 708
Nukerk, Gerrit, 1243
Nutter, Valentine, 1089

O

Oakley, Abigail Wood, 2105
Oakley, Augustus, 1286
Oakley, Jeremiah, 1286
Oakley, Jesse, 349, 1077
Oakley, John, 1008, 1286
Oakley, Julianah, 1286
Oakley, Marthar, 1286
Oakley, Mery Gardner, 671
Oakley, Phebe, 1286

Outwater, Thomas, 1166
Overacker, Wendell, 2090
Overbagh, Catherine, 473
Overbagh, Christian, 473
Overbagh, Johan Jury, 473
Overbagh, Sarah Dubois, 473
Overocker, Martin, 367
Overton, James, 1277
Overton, Mary, 1277
Ovirton, Benjamin, 208
Owen, Abbe, 1287
Owen, Anning, 1275
Owen, Benjamin, 1287
Owen, Ebenezer, 1275
Owen, Elizabeth, 1275
Owen, Girshom, 1275
Owen, Israel, 1275, 1287
Owen, Jain, 1287
Owen, Jesse, 1287
Owen, John, 1275
Owen, Jonathan, 1287
Owen, Mary, 1287
Owen, Mowbery, 1275
Owen, Nathaniel, 1275
Owen, Salomon, 1287
Owen, Samuel, 1287
Owen, Sarah, 1275
Owen, Timothy, 25, 1275
Owens, Elizabeth, 1279
Owens, George, 1279
Oxnard, Edward, 422

P

Pacaud, Gabriel, 1368
Pacaud, Jean, 1368
Pacaud, Mary Jacoby, 1368
Paddack, Deliverance, 1344
Paddack, Judah, 1344
Paddack, Ruth, 1344
Paddack, Seth, 1344
Paddack, Stephen, 1344
Paddack, Zachariah, 1344
Paddock, Benjamin, 936
Paddock, John, 445
Page, Elizabeth, 1310
Page, Johanna, 1310
Page, John, 1310
Page, Lemuel I., 907
Page, Margot, 1310
Page, Patience, 1310
Page, Sarah, 907, 1310
Pain, Amos, 82
Pain, Benjamin, 2091
Pain, Ephman, 997
Pain, Thomas, 689
Paine, Abijah, 1350
Paine, Barnabas, 155, 1317, 1327, 1350
Paine, Brinton, 711
Paine, Chloe, 1350
Paine, Elisha, 1327
Paine, Eliza Ann Warren, 2124
Paine, Elizabeth, 1350
Paine, Ephraim, 143, 793, 1317, 1327, 1350
Paine, Ichabod, 1629
Paine, Ichabod Sparrow, 1317, 1327
Paine, John, 2124
Paine, Joshua, 1317, 1327
Paine, Lucy, 1350
Paine, Martha, 155
Paine, Mary, 1350
Paine, Rebecca, 1327
Paine, Sarah, 1350
Palding, Catherine, 1360
Palding, John, 1360
Palding, Joseph, 1360
Palding, Levi, 1524
Palding, Peter, 1360
Palding, William, 1360
Palen, Hendrick, 1307
Paling, Albert, 436
Palmer, Abigail, 1325
Palmer, Abraham, 1323
Palmer, Ame, 1323
Palmer, Ann, 114, 1301, 1329
Palmer, Beriah, 633, 2119
Palmer, Charity, 1301
Palmer, Colonel Thomas, 715, 1191
Palmer, Darkis, 1325
Palmer, David, 1747
Palmer, Deborah, 1329
Palmer, Edward, 1301, 1323, 1325
Palmer, Elizabeth Seaman, 1511
Palmer, Ephraim, 115, 1325
Palmer, Esther, 1323
Palmer, Ezekiel, 1323
Palmer, Gehannah, 1325
Palmer, Gilburt, 1323
Palmer, Henry, 364, 990
Palmer, Herry, 1329
Palmer, Jacomiah, 1323
Palmer, James, 1323, 1329
Palmer, Jeremiah, 1323
Palmer, John, 11, 573, 1301, 1442, 1511
Palmer, Marmaduke, 1301
Palmer, Mary, 1301, 1323
Palmer, Obadiah, 443, 1387
Palmer, Phebe, 1323
Palmer, Philipp, 838
Palmer, Rachel, 1323, 1325
Palmer, Rebeckah, 1325
Palmer, Reuben, 1323, 1325
Palmer, Richard, 1329
Palmer, Robert, 1301
Palmer, Ruben, 694

Peacock, John, 1169
Peacock, Thomas, 2058
Peacock, William, 615
Peak, Daniel, 401
Peak, Eve, 401
Peak, Susanna, 401
Pearce, Charles, 1338
Pearce, Daniel, 1338
Pearce, Elizabeth, 1338
Pearce, Hannah, 1338
Pearce, Robert, 1456
Pearce, Robert Gilbert, 1338
Pearce, Sarah, 1338
Pearce, Susanna, 1338
Pearce, William, 1338
Pearsall, Daniel, 1328
Pearsall, Henry, 1328
Pearsall, Hezekiah, 1328
Pearsall, James, 1328
Pearsall, John, 1328
Pearsall, Joseph, 1328
Pearsall, Martha, 1328
Pearsall, Thomas, 1085
Pearsall, William, 1328
Pearse, Mary Morris, 1121
Pearson, Thomas, 1265
Pearss, John P., 1639
Peck, Cornell, 2106
Peck, Harmans, 283
Peck, Jacobus, 1855
Peck, Jacobus Harmanus, 1928
Peck, James, 126
Peck, Johannis, 1114, 2155
Peck, John Ja., 1928
Peck, Ruth, 494
Peckam, Reuben, 1322
Peckam, Samuel, 1322
Peckwell, Henry, 2046
Peebles, Elizabeth, 188, 411b
Peebles, Thomas, 188, 411b
Peeck, Antje Vedder, 1863
Peeck, Harmanis, 1863
Peeck, Jacob, 1826
Peeck, Jan, 1474
Peeck, John, 634
Peeck, John J., 1890
Peeck, Margaret van Slyck, 1826
Peeck, Yacobus, 1125
Peelen, Cathrine, 1305
Peelen, Elisabeth, 1305
Peelen, Ezechiel, 1305
Peelen, Gysbert, 1305
Peelen, Paulus, 1305
Peelen, Petrus, 1305
Peers, Deborah van Bergen, 1847
Peers, John, 1847
Peet, Gilbert, 1318
Peet, Hannah, 1318
Peet, Sary, 1318
Peet, Stephen, 1318
Peet, William, 1318
Peirce, Lieut. John, 1212
Peirson, Abraham, 1359
Peirson, Elizabeth, 1359
Peirson, Henry, 1431
Peirson, John, 1645
Peirson, Matthew, 1359
Peirson, Nathan, 1359
Peirson, Samuel, 1359
Peirson, Silas, 2053, 2073
Peirson, Silvanus, 1359
Peirson, Timothy, 371
Peirson, William, 1359
Peirson, Zebulon, 1359
Pele, Hendrick, 1882
Pelen, Poules, 1307
Pell, Charles, 1341
Pell, David, 1341
Pell, Elijah, 838
Pell, Jonathan A., 1766
Pell, Joseph, 838
Pell, Mary, 1424
Pell, Mary Honeywell, 838
Pell, Philipp, 1341
Pell, Samuel T., 1341
Pelletreau, Elias, 257
Pelletreau, Elie, 1242
Pelletreau, John, 613
Pells, Samoon, 263
Pells, Simon, 1840
Pels, Johannis, 1074
Pels, Rachel Leroy, 1074
Pelton, Philipp, 1039
Pelts, Abraham, 770
Pelts, Jude Hogan, 770
Pemberton, Catherine Harris, 772
Pemberton, Rev. Ebenezer, 765, 769, 772
Pendleton, Daniel, 1358
Pendleton, David, 1358
Pendleton, Edmund, 1358
Pendleton, Nathl., 221
Pendleton, Solomon, 1358
Pendleton, Susanna Bard, 221
Pendleton, William, 1358
Peniston, Elizabeth, 52
Peniston, Jeremiah, 52
Peniston, John, 52
Peniston, Richard, 52
Peniston, Samuel, 52
Peniston, William, 52
Pennant, Edward, 1242, 1298
Pennear, Betsey, 1210
Pennear, Martha, 1210
Pennock, Geo., 892
Penny, Timothy P., 1355
Pepperell, Sir Wm., 282
Perger, John, 1536

Potter, Nathaniel, 1336
Potter, Riscom, 1336
Potter, Sims, 1336
Pouley, Samuel, 2100
Poulhameus, Johannes, 1730
Poulus, Martin, 1891
Powell, Isaac, 2042
Powell, Jacob, 1375
Powell, Jonah, 1008
Powell, Joseph, 1532, 1546
Powell, Moses, 1205
Powell, Thomas, 1008, 1375
Powell, Wm., 399
Poyer, Hannah, 1332
Poyer, Jacobmies, 1332
Poyer, Joseph, 1332
Poyer, Maregriet, 1332
Poyer, Sarah, 1332
Poyer, Thomas, 1332
Praa, Peter, 1299
Pratel, Jeurian, 404
Pratt, Azariah, 940
Pratt, Jacob, 1340
Pratt, John, 1340
Pratt, Nancy, 1340
Pratt, Noah, 940
Pratt, Stephen, 1340, 2085
Pray, Ephraim, 845
Preissac, Catharine Livingston, 1367
Preissac, Henry, 1367
Preissac, Pierre Joseph, 1367
Prentts, Capt. John, 2110
Prentts, Lieut. Jonathan, 2110
Preston, Abial, 1333
Preston, Anne, 1333
Preston, David, 1333
Preston, Ebenezer, 845
Preston, Joseph, 1333
Preston, Sibbel, 1333
Pretty, Richard, 1103
Prevoost, Augustin, 399
Prevoost, Susannah Croghan, 399
Prevost, Lieut. Augustin, 954
Price, Frances, 612
Price, John, 68, 224, 1780
Price, Mary, 68
Price, Rachel Brownejohn, 224
Price, Thomas, 1531
Price, Wm., 1212, 1363
Prime, Benjamin Youngs, 884
Prince, Benjamin, 884
Prince, Joseph, 884
Prince, Philipp Jacob, 1935
Prince, Thomas, 249a
Proctor, James, 1370
Proctor, John, 1370
Prosser, Benjamin, 1758
Prosser, Jonathan, 1751
Prothero, John, 1253
Proudfit, Alexander, 2123
Proudfit, Ebenezer, 2123
Proudfit, Elizabeth Williams, 2123
Proudfit, Robert, 2123
Proudfit, Susannah Williams, 2123
Proudfit, William, 2123
Provost, Catarina, 1356, 1380
Provost, Henderick, 1380
Provost, Isaac, 1380
Provost, Jacob, 1380
Provost, Johannis, 1356, 1380
Provost, Samuel, 1380
Provoost, Abraham, 1300, 1679
Provoost, Christiana Praa, 1299
Provoost, David, 1376, 1691, 1791
Provoost, Elias, 412a
Provoost, Hendrick, 1300
Provoost, Isaac, 1300
Provoost, Jacob, 1300
Provoost, Johannes, 1, 1300, 1679, 1804, 1965, 1991
Provoost, Samuel, 1300
Provoost, Willem, 1791
Provoost, William, 1691
Pruin, Chrystina, 1901
Pruin, John, 1901
Prujen, Samuel, 1788
Prune, Caty, 1901
Pruyn, Ann Dunn, 251
Pruyn, Arendt, 1116, 1775
Pruyn, Casparus, 228, 2001
Pruyn, Casparus F., 251
Pruyn, Frans, 913, 1858
Pruyn, Frans S., 1381
Pruyn, Frans Sa., 1858
Pruyn, Hendrick, 55, 106, 1483
Pruyn, Jacob S., 1381
Pruyn, Johannes, 767, 970, 1688
Pruyn, Johannis S., 1381
Pruyn, John I., 2104
Pruyn, Maritie, 1381
Pruyn, Samuel, 1381
Pryor, Mary, 1223
Pudney, Hannah, 1584
Pudney, Susannah, 691
Pue, Elizabeth, 1062
Pugsly, James, 1320
Puiroe, John, 1296
Puiroe, Martha, 1296
Puiroe, Peter, 1296
Pulffer, Michel, 1182
Pulteney, Henrietta Laura, 1357
Pulteney, Sir James, 1357
Purcardy, Henry, 741
Purdy, Abigail, 1320
Purdy, Abraham, 209
Purdy, Amos, 209
Purdy, David, 327
Purdy, Deliverance, 209

Purdy, Francis, 295, 1132
Purdy, Hannah, 494
Purdy, Phebe Ketcham, 1008
Purdy, Samuel, 1137
Purdy, Stephen, 1137, 1320
Pye, David, 181, 985, 990, 1005, 1275, 1585, 1588, 1754

Q

Qakenbos, Adryeyen, 88
Quackenbass, Johannis S., 996
Quackenbos, Anth., 1837
Quackenbos, Cornelia, 1382
Quackenbos, Johannes, 253, 496, 983, 1382, 1384
Quackenbos, John, 1382, 1384
Quackenbos, John P., 1384
Quackenbos, Margaret, 1382, 1384
Quackenbos, Nicholas, 1382, 1384
Quackenbos, Petrus, 1382, 1384
Quackenbos, Walter, 1382, 1384
Quackenbos, Wouter, 1688
Quackenboss, Adriaen, 1824
Quackenboss, Annatie Outhout, 1269
Quackenboss, Anthony, 1105, 1824
Quackenboss, Antje, 1105
Quackenboss, Catarina, 1824
Quackenboss, I. A., 1102
Quackenboss, Johannis, 1824
Quackenboss, Magtel, 1824
Quackenboss, Pieter Wouters, 1269
Quackenboss, Ragel Gardenir, 757
Quackenboss, Sybrant, 1824
Quackenboss, Wouter, 1788
Quackenbous, John Schot, 757
Quackenbush, Ann de Witt, 523
Quackenbush, Harme, 996
Quackenbush, John, 523
Quackenbush, Neeltie, 996
Quakenbouss, Anth., 1854
Quereau, Philipp I., 556
Quick, Abraham, 696
Quick, Cornelius, 1699
Quick, Elizabeth, 1383
Quick, Jacobus, 1383
Quick, Johanna, 1383
Quick, Jurean, 1687
Quick, Magery, 1383
Quick, Petrus, 1383
Quick, Rebecca Titsoor, 1687
Quig, James, 2046
Quinby, Josiah, 838
Quinten, Duncan, 1051
Quinten, Unice Little, 1051
Quockenbos, Elizabeth Knickerbocker, 983

R

Racket, Samuel, 1070
Radcliff, Hilletie Hogenboom, 916
Radcliff, Jochem, 916
Radcliff, William, 160
Radclift, Johannes, 1552
Radclift, Neeltie Schermerhorn, 1552
Radclift, Peter, 1552
Radel, Margaret Tanner, 1760
Ragon, Thomas, 594
Rakkefeller, Philipp, 1347
Raleigh, Edmund, 1445
Raleigh, Hannah, 1445
Raleigh, James, 1445
Raleigh, John, 1445
Raleigh, Abigail, 1445
Raleigh, John N., 1445
Raleigh, Polly, 1445
Raleigh, Walter, 1445
Ralyea, Denie, 521
Ralyea, William, 1751
Ramsay, Allen, 612
Ramsden, Grace, 387
Ramsden, John, 387
Ramsen, Cornelia Blauvelt, 151
Ramsen, George, 151
Ramser, Adam, 976
Randall, Marianne, 1438
Randall, Thomas, 1638
Randle, Stephen, 1422
Randolph, Robert, 900
Range, John, 382
Rank, Mary Masten, 1180
Rank, Philipp, 1180
Rankin, George, 606
Rapalje, Antje, 1462
Rapalje, Dina, 1462
Rapalje, Garret, 44, 1462
Rapalje, Jeromus, 1459
Rapalje, Jeronimus, 1462
Rapalje, John, 1462
Rapelye, Danl., 1100
Rapalje, Joris, 1462
Raveau, Daniel, 1411
Ray, John, 1301
Ray, Richard, 703, 772
Ray, Samuel, 703,
Ray, Stephen, 1429
Raymond, Eliakim, 1645
Raynolds, William, 557
Raynor, Elizabeth, 1431
Raynor, Hannah, 1431
Raynor, Isaac, 1431
Raynor, Jacob, 1427
Raynor, John, 1427, 1431
Raynor, Joseph, 1431

Raynor, Josiah, 1431
Raynor, Margaret, 1427
Raynor, Martha, 1427
Raynor, Mary, 1431
Raynor, Thirston, 1431
Raynor, William, 1427
Rea, Matthew, 839
Rea, Richard, 1042
Reach, Israel, 535
Read, Capt. Lawrence, 1241
Read, Israel, 712
Read, Joseph, 1897
Read, Mary, 1455
Read, Peter, 354
Read, Thomas, 1455
Read, Wm., 1744
Reade, Ann, 1418
Reade, Catharine Livingston, 1089
Reade, John, 1089, 1418
Reade, Joseph, 1418
Reade, Lawrence, 1418
Reading, Samuel, 738
Reading, Sarah, 738
Reardon, Yelvered, 1651
Reber, Andries, 798, 807
Rechtmayer, Jurreje, 971
Rechtmayer, Mary Kast, 971
Rechtmeyer, Hermanus, 653
Reckert, Elizabeth Lawyer, 1035
Reckert, Marcus, 1035
Redding, Jeremiah, 1397
Redliff, Jannetie, 1303
Redliff, Jochem, 1303
Reeder, Jacob, 1416
Reeder, Josiah, 1416, 2017
Reeder, Peter, 1416
Reeder, Philipp, 1416
Reeder, Samuel, 1416
Reeder, Sarah, 1416
Reeder, Stepen, 1416
Reeder, W. R., 955
Rees, Jonathan, 915
Rees, Sarah Hardik, 915
Reeve, Daniel, 1571
Reeve, Elijah, 689
Reeve, Eunis, 2053
Reeves, Edward, 1478
Reeves, John, 557
Regan, Elenor, 1425
Regan, Hulda, 1425
Regan, Thomas, 1425
Reghtmyer, Coen-Raet, 1800
Regnier, Jacob, 1447
Reichert, Barent, 1441
Reichert, David, 1441
Reichert, Henry, 1441
Reichert, Jacob, 1441
Reichert, Johannes, 1441
Reichert, Joseph, 530, 1441
Reichert, Mary, 1441
Reichert, Philipp, 1441
Reichert, Zacharia, 1441
Reid, John, 1415
Reid, Robert, 1415
Reid, Thomas, 1415
Reid, William, 739
Reims, Edward, 1468
Reims, Elisabeth, 1468
Reinhard, George F., 1001, 2086
Reinhard, George T., 846, 1207
Reitser, Conrad, 1432
Remoussin, Fanny, 386
Remsen, Ann, 1399
Remsen, Ariete, 1399
Remsen, Aris, 1448
Remsen, Catalina, 1448
Remsen, Cornelia, 1508
Remsen, Cornelius, 1386
Remsen, Dority, 1448
Remsen, Elisabeth, 1398
Remsen, George, 1398, 1399, 1654
Remsen, Henry, 224, 1448
Remsen, Jacob, 211, 1462
Remsen, Janneye, 1386
Remsen, Jeronimus A., 1448
Remsen, Johannes, 1352, 1799
Remsen, John, 1386, 1508
Remsen, John H., 1224
Remsen, Joris, 1386, 1448
Remsen, Lambatie, 1399
Remsen, Martha, 1386
Remsen, Phebe, 1448
Remsen, Rebecca, 1508
Remsen, Rem, 271, 1248, 1386, 1399, 1462, 1508, 1585
Remsen, Sarah, 1399
Remsen, Sophia, 1386
Remsen, Theodorus, 1398, 1399
Remsen, Tunis, 1398
Remson, Henry, 1580
Renaudet, Adrian, 1451
Renaudet, Ann, 1451
Renaudet, Peter, 279, 1451
Renne, Elizabeth, 1423
Renne, Hannah, 1409
Renne, James, 1409
Renne, John, 1423
Renne, Marget, 1409
Renne, Mary, 1409, 1423
Renne, Peter, 1423
Renne, Samuel, 1409
Renne, Sarah, 1423
Renullard, Marie Catherine, 1094
Renwick and Hudswell, 546
Rerson, George, 1822
Reser, Catherine Wacher, 2117
Reser, Chevalier, 2117
Reyers, Anatie, 1391

Rodman, Samuel, 1408
Rodman, Thomas, 1408, 1434
Rodman, William, 1408
Roe, Charles, 1410
Roe, Eleanor, 1410
Roe, James, 872, 1410, 1632
Roe, John, 1555
Roe, Jonas, 1420, 2068
Roe, Margaret, 1410
Roe, Mary, 1420
Roe, Nathaniel, 28, 1420
Roe, Silas, 38, 1262
Roe, William, 287, 794, 1410
Roeger, Hester Verveelen, 1840
Roeger, Johannes, 1840
Roehl, Maria Catherine, 1400
Roehl, Martin, 1400
Roelantsen, Adam, 910
Roeloffs, Jan, 237
Roeloffse, Sarah, 1707
Roeloffsen, Roeloff, 1464
Roerback, John, 1400
Roerback, Sophia, 1400
Roessell, Ludwigh, 653, 1752
Roff, John S., 230
Rogers, Benjamin, 861, 1426
Rogers, Beriah P., 2119
Rogers, Catherine Wright, 2106
Rogers, Charles, 1100
Rogers, Daniel, 1414
Rogers, Daniel G., 1349
Rogers, David, 2119
Rogers, Elizabeth, 1414
Rogers, Henry, 1642
Rogers, Israel, 1414
Rogers, James, 1414
Rogers, Jannetie, 1840
Rogers, John, 1426
Rogers, Marry, 1414
Rogers, Matthew, 371
Rogers, Platt, 1594
Rogers, Rachel, 1414
Rogers, Richerd, 1426
Rogers Samuel, 2110
Rogers, Serrah, 1414
Rogers, Stephen, 371
Rogers, Susanna, 1840
Rogers, Will., 1303, 1471
Rokeby, Elizabeth, 1390
Rokeby, Joseph, 1390
Rokeby, Philipp, 1390
Roles, Myndert, 1460
Roll, John, 1117
Roll, John H., 1445
Rolland, I., 3
Romeyn, Dirck, 146
Romeyn, Elizabeth Brodhead, 146
Romeyn, Symon Janssen, 413
Romyn, Claes Danielsen, 977
Romyn, Elizabeth Kip, 977
Romyn, Margita Frelinghuysen, 625
Romyn, Rev. Thomas, 625
Roome, John, 893
Roome, Luke, 1831
Roome, Paul, 2035
Roome, William, 1699
Roomer, Angenelia, 1450
Roomer, John, 1450
Roomer, Margaret, 1450
Roorbach, J., 1240, 2138
Roorbach, John, 165, 1055
Roorbach, John, 249, 1142, 2051
Roorbach, Johs., 1885
Roorback, Johs., 917
Roorback, Gerret, 2114
Roos, Elizabeth Masten, 1180
Roos, Johannes, 565, 1180
Roosa, Allert, 1389, 1483
Roosa, Andries, 1595
Roosa, Annatje, 1435
Roosa, Benjamen, 333
Roosa, Dirck, 318
Roosa, Egbert, 333, 1524
Roosa, Gysbert, 1389
Roosa, Heyman, 318, 1389
Roosa, Isaac, 1435, 1524
Roosa, Jacob, 460, 1520
Roosa, Jacobus, 1435
Roosa, Jan, 1389
Roosa, Johannes, 1435
Roosa, Lea, 1389
Roosa, Maas van Franken, 1435
Roosa, Magtildie, 1435
Roosa, Maria, 1435
Roosa, Maria Schoonmaker, 1595
Roosa, Neeltie Crispell, 318
Roosa, Nicholas, 821, 1389, 2015
Roosa, Petrus, 333, 1524
Roosa, Ragel, 1389
Roosa, Reikert, 1435
Roosa, Sarah, 821
Roosbom, Abraham, 981
Roosbom, Hendrik M., 981
Rooseboom, Barent, 1422
Rooseboom, Henderich Yansen, 1956
Rooseboom, Henry 113
Rooseboom, Jacob, 1396
Rooseboom, Johannes, 752
Rooseboom, John Jas., 1705
Roosenkrans, Ester, 776
Roosenkrans, Janneke Hoffman, 776
Roosenkrans, William, 776
Roosevelt, Adolphus, 1446
Roosevelt, Christopher, 1446
Roosevelt, Cornelius C., 1202
Roosevelt, Elisabeth, 1710
Roosevelt, Isaac, 1446
Roosevelt, Ino., 117

Roosevelt, Jacobus, 117, 1446
Roosevelt, Jas. N., 542
Roosevelt, John, 1401
Roosevelt, Nicholas, 1446, 1710
Roosevelt, Peter, 1446
Rosa, Benjamin, 933
Rosa, Isaac, 634
Rosa, Maria, 2094
Rosa, Nicholas, 927
Rose, Abigail, 1457
Rose, Anna, 1357
Rose, Arien, 1295
Rose, Carolina, 1896
Rose, David, 200, 1896
Rose, Gershom, 797, 1130, 1141
Rose, John Ja., 1404
Rose, Jonathan, 1398
Rose, Martha, 1457
Rose, Sarah, 1457
Rose, Thomas, 1457
Rose, William, 1457
Roseboom, Abraham, 504, 1463
Roseboom, Ahasverus, 1419, 1471, 1818
Roseboom, Deborah Staats, 1488
Roseboom, Dirck, 1419
Roseboom, Elsje, 1417
Roseboom, Eva Marselis, 1162
Roseboom, Gerrit, 1419
Roseboom, Geysbert, 1471
Roseboom, Hendr., 266, 587, 1471, 1488
Roseboom, Hendrich Minderse, 62, 247
Roseboom, Hendrick M., 582
Roseboom, Jacob, 1020, 1488, 1678, 1871, 2002
Roseboom, Johs., 307, 1497, 1862
Roseboom, Johannes, M., 1162
Roseboom, John, 1463, 1471
Roseboom, John J., 1463
Roseboom, John Jac., 1380
Roseboom, John Jas., 1356, 1402
Roseboom, Myndert, 1614
Roseboom, Robert, 1471
Roseboom, Ryckje, 1471
Rosecrants, Catrein, 1439
Rosecrants, Daniel, 1439
Rosecrants, Nicholas, 849
Rosecrants, Rev. Abraham, 849
Rosekrans, Antje, 1440
Rosekrans, Antje Schoonmaker, 1595
Rosekrans, Elijah, 1440
Rosekrans, Hannah, 1440
Rosekrans, Harmanus, 1595
Rosekrans, Johannis, 477, 1595
Rosekrans, Maria, 1440
Rosekrans, Peternella, 1440
Rosekrans, Sarah, 1440
Rosekrans, Sarah Schoonmaker 1595
Rosekrans, Thomas, 1626
Rosekrans, Zachariah, 1440
Rosekranse, Hezekiah, 2077
Rosekranse, Margaret Westfael 2077
Rosekranz, Elisabeth, 163
Rosekranz, Frederick, 146
Rosenkrans, Alexander, 1393
Rosenkrans, Ariaentie Oosterhout, 1270
Rosenkrans, Derrick, 1393
Rosenkrans, Harama, 1393
Rosenkrans, Harmen, 1270
Rosenkrans, Helenah, 1393
Rosenkrans, Hendrick, 1393
Rosenkrans, Hermanus, 1393
Rosenkrans, Johannes, 1393
Rosenkrans, Magdalena, 1393
Rosenkrans, Sarah, 1393
Rosie, Jan, 255
Rosie, Jean, 1469
Rosie, John, 1396
Rosman, Helena Lesher, 1058
Rosman, Jurry, 1058
Ross, Arabella Brown, 1412
Ross, Capt. Josiah, 1313
Ross, Catherine 1412
Ross, Henry, 1764
Ross, Henry H., 2123
Ross, James, 1412
Ross, James Isaiah, 1412
Ross, Jane, 1412
Ross, John, 906
Ross, Margaret, 1412
Ross, Maria Hagadorn, 906
Ross, Mary, 1412
Ross, Robert, 876, 1412
Ross, Sarah, 1412
Ross, Susannah Blanchard, 2123
Ross, Thomas, 1456
Ross, William, 875, 1076
Rosset, Antoine Auguste Theophile, 1444
Rosset, Antoinette, 1444
Rosset, Antoinette Marie Sophie, 1444
Rosset, Cecile Caroline Cazenove, 1444
Rosset, Cecile Henriette, 1444
Rosset, Ernest Emile, 1444
Rosset, Ferd. Ant. Henry, 1444
Rosset, Henry Nicholas Quirin, 1444
Rosset, Richd. Fred. Theophile, 1444
Rostine, John, 801
Rottenbourg, Ernest Guillaume, Baron de, 1443

Schermerhorn, Martin, 1552
Schermerhorn, Reyer, 1517
Schermerhorn, Simon, 1647
Schermerhorn, Symon, 1517
Schermerhorn, Tunis, 1552
Schermerhorn, William, 283, 1552, 1612
Scherp, Andries, 1824
Scherp, Elisabeth, 1824
Scherp, George, 1608
Scherp, Magrita, 1608
Scherp, Michael, 1563
Scherp, Peter, 1347, 1608
Scherp, Petrus, 1608
Schertz, Anna, 1590
Schertz, Catrina, 1590
Schertz, Johannis D., 1590
Scheutz, John H., 518
Scheutz, Sarah Denton, 518
Schifer, Philipp, 1793
Schmit, Auiustinus, 1175
Schneider, Adam, 1549
Schneider, Catryn, 1549
Schneider, Elsie, 1549
Schneider, Eva, 1549
Schneider, Geertruy, 1549
Schneider, George, 1045
Schneider, Harme, 1549
Schneider, Johannes Pieter, 1549
Schneider, Marya, 1549
Schneider, Wilhelm, 195
Schneider, William, 1549
Schneyder, Jacob, 1595
Schoeffer, Henrich, 1590
Schoenmaker, Thomas, 971
Schoennig, Frederich, 1383
Schofield, Alexander, 969
Scholefield, James, 443
Scholten, Jan, 1
Schoolcraft, John, 1291
Schoolcraft, Lawrence, 1207
Schoolcraft, Maria, 1551
Schoolcraft, William, 1551
Schoomaker, Deborah, 1504
Schoomaker, Doostie, 1504
Schoomaker, Edward, 1504
Schoomaker, Geertruy, 1504
Schoomaker, Hendrick, 1504
Schoomaker, Hiltir., 1504
Schoomaker, John, 1504
Schoomaker, Margereth, 1504
Schoomaker, Tyrick, 1504
Schoonaker, Hendr., 1054
Schoonhoven, Catherine, 182
Schoonhoven, Debora, 2016
Schoonhoven, Geertruy, 1672
Schoonhoven, Geurt Hendricksen, 1672
Schoonhoven, Hendrick, 1672
Schoonhoven, Hendrickie, 1672
Schoonhoven, Jacob, 2077
Schoonhoven, Jacobus, 1672, 1788
Schoonhoven, Jacomyntie, 1672
Schoonhoven, Margriet, 1672
Schoonhoven, Maritje Cornelissen, 1672
Schoonhoven, Nicholaas, 59, 2016
Schoonmaker, Abraham, 804
Schoonmaker, Annamaria, 1609
Schoonmaker, Antje, 1537
Schoonmaker, Antie Depue, 456
Schoonmaker, Antje Hussey, 1485
Schoonmaker, Ariaentie Hoornbeek, 804
Schoonmaker, Benjamin, 456, 1485, 1537, 1589
Schoonmaker, Catharina, 1537, 1609
Schoonmaker, Cornelius, 434, 532, 776, 804, 1485, 1589
Schoonmaker, Cornelius C., 163, 508, 510, 852, 1731
Schoonmaker, Daniel, 1485
Schoonmaker, Edward, 1284
Schoonmaker, Egbert, 458, 468, 1284
Schoonmaker, Elisabeth, 1537, 1609
Schoonmaker, Fredrick, 1595
Schoonmaker, Geertruy, 1606
Schoonmaker, Geertruy Brodhead, 146
Schoonmaker, Godfrey, 1609
Schoonmaker, Hannah, 1609
Schoonmaker, Helena, 1606
Schoonmaker, Hendrick, 1485
Schoonmaker, Henricus, 667
Schoonmaker, Henry, 967, 1609
Schoonmaker, Isaac, 804
Schoonmaker, Jacob D. Witt, 1595
Schoonmaker, Jacobus, 1485, 1606
Schoonmaker, Jan, 1485
Schoonmaker, Jenneke, 1589
Schoonmaker, Joachim, 1485
Schoonmaker, Jochem, 158, 1591, 1595
Schoonmaker, Jochem D., 1591
Schoonmaker, Johannis, 146, 344, 1392, 1606, 1609
Schoonmaker, John, 477, 1270, 1591
Schoonmaker, John Matthias, 1609
Schoonmaker, Joseph, 1537
Schoonmaker, Lodowyck, 1591
Schoonmaker, Margaret, 1609
Schoonmaker, Maria, 1606
Schoonmaker, Martinus, 827
Schoonmaker, Mary, 804
Schoonmaker, Petrus, 507, 1591
Schoonmaker, Samuel, 1284

1388, 1473, 1495, 1496, 1498, 1512, 1538, 1545, 1554, 1614, 1641, 1657, 1662, 1868, 1886, 1906, 1983
Schuyler, Philipp I., 1371
Schuyler, Philipp Jeremiah, 1662
Schuyler, Philipp Johannissen, 1495
Schuyler, Philipp Pietersen, 1959
Schuyler, Pieter, 1498, 1975, 1978
Schuyler, Rachel, 1496
Schuyler, Ranslaer, 1554, 1662
Schuyler, Samuel, 1902
Schuyler, Stephen, 1538, 1843
Schuyler, Stephen I., 1614, 1681
Schuyler, Swan, 1554
Schuyler, Swans, 1657
Schuyler, William, 826
Scidmore, Abner, 861
Sciner, Elisabeth Green, 727
Scot, Derrick, 89
Scot, Elizabeth, 1494
Scot, James, 1494
Scot, Jannetie, 1494
Scot, John, 189
Scot, John M., 104
Scot, Majory, 1494
Scot, Walter, 1626
Scot, William, 1494
Scott, Adam, 1569
Scott, Alexander, 1569
Scott, Anganista, 297
Scott, Anna Barlow, 233
Scott, Henry, 645
Scott, Isaac H., 233
Scott, James, 286, 1335, 1524
Scott, James D., 2106
Scott, John, 1569, 1599
Scott, John Morin, 632, 1152
Scott, Peter, 1044
Scott, Sarah, 1569
Scott, William, 180, 305, 970, 1685
Scranton, Charity, 183
Scrom, Gysbert, 101
Sculle, Doctor, 2117
Scudder, Nathaniel, 1068
Scudder, Sarah, 382
Seabury, John, 1720
Seacor, Isaac, 362
Seal, Anthony, 1536
Sealy, Israel, 127
Seaman, Benjamin, 108, 2162
Seaman, Caleb, 1130
Seaman, Cornelius, 11
Seaman, Edmund, 2162
Seaman, Elizabeth Zabriskie, 2162
Seaman, George, 2106
Seaman, Jacomiah, 1511
Seaman, John, 832, 1511, 2162
Seaman, Jonas, 1511
Seaman, Jonathan, 1511
Seaman, Joseph, 1130
Seaman, Joshua, 11
Seaman, Stephen, 724
Seaman, William, 1708
Seaman, Zebulon, 1708
Seamon, Jeremiah, 267
Seamour, Joseph W., 1263
Seamour, Zebulon, 1263
Searing, James, 829
Searles, Wm., 1024
Sears, Abigail, 1630
Sears, Abigail Drake, 1645
Sears, Benjamin, 1616, 1630
Sears, Isaac, 1645
Sears, Jasper, 1645
Sears, John, 1249
Sears, Lydia, 1630
Sears, Mary, 1645
Sears, Mercy, 1630
Sears, Rebecca, 1645
Sears, Sarah, 1645, 1770
Sears, Seth, 1630
Sears, Stephen, 1630
Sears, Sunderlin, 1630
Searse, Charles, 1536
Sebring, Catharine, 1592
Sebring, Cornelius, 1602, 1831
Sebring, Cornelis J., 710, 1592
Sebring, Femetie, 1592
Sebring, Isaac, 1592, 1602
Sebring, Isaac I., 1926
Sebring, Jacob, 1592
Sebring, Jane Goes, 710
Sebring, John, 1592
Sebring, John B., 185
Sebring, Joseph, 1592
Sebring, Katherine, 1602
Sebring, Margaret, 1602
Seckel, Lawrence, 892
Seckerly, Wellem, 1476
Secord, Isaac, 1408
Seeber, Jacob, 1057
Seeber, William, 1057
Seely, Bazalel, 2037
Seely, Bethia, 718
Seely, Bezael, 1562
Seely, Busul, 928
Seely, Ebener, 1709
Seely, Ebenezer, 834, 968, 1562
Seely, Eunis, 1575
Seely, Gilbert, 718
Seely, Israel, 1562
Seely, James Davisson, 718
Seely, John, 1562
Seely, Jonas, 718
Seely, Josiah, 1562
Seely, Nathaniel, 324, 1189, 1562
Seely, Samuel, 324, 1486

Smit, Johannis, 1509
Smit, Jurje Adam, 1509
Smit, Petrus, 1509
Smit, Teunis, 1509
Smith, Aaron, 312
Smith, Abigail, 524, 1534, 1627, 2051
Smith, Abigail Wickham, 2069
Smith, Abraham, 81
Smith, Aimy, 1555
Smith, Alexander, 1120, 1702
Smith, Ama, 1604
Smith, Ann, 1476, 1579, 1629
Smith, Anna Mary, 1671
Smith, Anne Anderson, 1616
Smith, Anning, 346
Smith, Arthur, 327, 1320, 1533
Smith, Asa, 1604, 1617
Smith, Aury, 1329, 1565
Smith, Azariah, 1629
Smith, Barent, 1513
Smith, Benjamin, 231, 377, 1210, 1510, 1547, 1555, 2095
Smith, Benjamin Bates, 1637
Smith, Caleb, 524, 1333, 1489, 1534, 1617, 1627
Smith, Carsten Fredericksen, 1671
Smith, Cateran Leonard, 1040
Smith, Catherine, 1210, 1513
Smith, Cattrain, 1633
Smith, Charity, 1516
Smith, Charles, 738, 1248, 1779
Smith, Charles Lyman, 1616
Smith, Colonel Robert, 1357
Smith, Cornel, 1594
Smith, Cornelius, 833
Smith, Cornelius Cor., 151
Smith, Daniel, 704, 1513, 1576, 1579, 1633
Smith, David, 1533, 1629
Smith, Deborah, 1330, 1576
Smith, Delilah, 1556
Smith, Derrick, 1571, 1725
Smith, Ebenezer, 42
Smith, Edward, 1556
Smith, Elias, 1489
Smith, Elihu, 1556
Smith, Elijah, 1629
Smith, Elizabeth, 361, 1513, 1516, 1518, 1534, 1565, 1573, 1598, 1599, 1636
Smith, Elizabeth Finger, 644
Smith, Elizabeth Leonard, 1040
Smith, Elizabeth Mott, 1143
Smith, Elizabeth Purdy, 1320
Smith, Elizabeth Snedeker, 1585
Smith, Elizabeth Yates, 2143
Smith, Ellethea, 1623
Smith, Elnathan, 469
Smith, Enos, 855, 1617
Smith, Ephraim, 1510, 2143
Smith, Ezekiah, 1629
Smith, Frederick, 1616
Smith, Gabriel, 500
Smith, George, 508, 1209, 1579, 1617, 1633
Smith, Gerret, 185, 1572
Smith, Gesey Upham, 1779
Smith, Granville, 612
Smith, Hanna Coe, 354
Smith, Hanna Gale, 729
Smith, Hannah, 336, 1534, 1579, 1636
Smith, Harriet Lucretia, 1236
Smith, Hendrick B., 644
Smith, Henry, 684, 857, 1132, 1271, 1489, 1518, 1534, 1541, 1573, 1696
Smith, Henry Conkling, 1627
Smith, Honble. William, 897, 1097, 1599
Smith, Hopkins, 1163
Smith, Irene, 1576
Smith, Isaac, 129, 517, 688, 1071, 1157, 1442, 1489, 1546, 2037
Smith, Isabel, 1526
Smith, Israel, 829, 1636
Smith, J., 672
Smith, Jabez, 2102
Smith, Jacob, 153, 640, 1335, 1594
Smith, James, 277, 1163, 1510, 1516, 1518, 1526, 1546, 1566, 1594, 1616, 1617, 1660, 1726, 2149
Smith, James S., 1652
Smith, Jane Mott, 1143
Smith, Jeremiah, 1489, 1534, 1598, 1696, 1779, 2037
Smith, Jesse, 1534, 1535
Smith, Joanna, 1579, 1604
Smith, Jobe, 895
Smith, Joel, 533, 1598
Smith, John, 21, 145, 303, 336, 760, 948, 1314, 1329, 1331, 1486, 1489, 1526, 1556, 1565, 1566, 1573, 1585, 1594, 1599, 1604, 1617, 1623, 1627, 1639, 1779, 2017
Smith, John Carpenter, 314, 1604
Smith, John Conraat, 1513
Smith, John d'Harriette, 435
Smith, John Peaterson, 11
Smith, John Robert, 1566
Smith, Jonas, 1598
Smith, Jonathan, 855, 1344, 1617, 2030
Smith, Joseph, 546, 1476, 1510, 1541, 1555, 1594, 1599, 1623
Smith, Joshua, 1489, 1516, 1555, 1579, 1617, 1627

Sutton, Abegell, 1547
Sutton, Benjamin, 1547
Sutton, Caleb, 1547
Sutton, Charles, 1547
Sutton, Elenor, 1547
Sutton, John, 18, 1547
Sutton, Josuah, 1547
Sutton, Mary, 1547
Sutton, Phebe, Huestis, 877
Sutton, Rachel, 1547
Sutton, Rubin, 1547
Sutton, Samuel, 954
Suydam, Altie Sebring, 1592
Suydam, John, 1592
Suylandt, Catharina, 1520
Suylandt, Elizabeth, 1520
Suylandt, Eva, 1520
Suylandt, Huybert, 1521
Suylandt, Johannes, 1520, 1521, 2022
Suylandt, Lena, 1520
Suylandt, Maria, 1520
Suylandt, Sarah, 1521
Swafford, Thomas, 834, 2091
Swaim, Hannah, 1897
Swan, Jacob, 619
Swanser, Sarah, 1540
Swanser, Sarah Cosine, 331
Swanser, William, 331
Swart, Adam, 453, 937
Swart, Antonia van Ryswyck, 1665
Swart, Bartholomaus, 1612
Swart, Catherine Plogh, 1307
Swart, Cornelius, 97, 811, 957, 1307
Swart, Cornelius L., 167
Swart, Dirck, 996
Swart, Engel, 1612
Swart, Eva, 1612
Swart, Evert W., 1072
Swart, Geerdreuy, 1612
Swart, Gerard, 1377, 1665
Swart, Jacobus, 2055
Swart, Jannetje Persen, 1321
Swart, Josaias, 1612
Swart, Mally, 97
Swart, Maria, 1612
Swart, Petrus, 937, 1321
Swart, Sarah, 1612
Swart, Steynge, 1612
Swart, Susannah, 1612
Swart, Tenes, 1612
Swart, Teunis, 456
Swart, Wilhelms, 937
Swart, Willem, 768
Swartt, G., 1958, 1963, 1967
Swartt, Gerard, 1968
Swartwoudt, Gerardus, 1523
Swartwoudt, Jacobus, 1523
Swartwoudt, Onake, 1523
Swartwoudt, Philipp, 1523
Swartwoudt, Yonake, 1523
Swartwout, Abraham, 1029
Swartwout, Adolphus, 1502
Swartwout, Aeltie, 133
Swartwout, Anna Guimard, 674
Swartwout, Barnados, 1483, 1884
Swartwout, Catherine, 1502
Swartwout, Cornelius, 1502
Swartwout, Dinah, 133
Swartwout, Elizabeth, 1502
Swartwout, Jacobus, 133, 145, 194, 674, 822, 1172, 1502, 1584
Swartwout, Jacomyntje, 1502
Swartwout, Jennetie, 1502
Swartwout, Johannis, 1584, 1825
Swartwout, Mindert, 1884
Swartwout, Philipp, 2043
Swartwout, Rudolphus, 133, 1584
Swartwout, Samuel, 1502
Swartwout, Sarah, 1584
Swartwout, Simon, 1226
Swartwout, Thomas, 1502
Swayze, Jonathan, 1416
Swazy, Dr. Jonathan, 348
Sweem, Matus, 1897,
Sweet, Elnathan, 1636
Sweet, Robert, 731,
Sweetzer, Annis Bassett, 232
Sweetzer, Osiah, 232
Sweezey, Dr. Jonathan, 361
Sweezy, Abigal, 2093
Sweezy, Abigal, Wells, 2093
Sweezy, Dorothy, 2093
Sweezy, Julia, 2093
Swezy, David, 1603
Swezy, Elisabeth, 1603
Swezy, Jonathan, 864, 1603, 1761, 2098
Swift, Elija, 1663
Swift Jarvis, 1663
Swits, Abraham, 1477
Swits, Aryantie, 1477
Swits, Claes, 1477
Swits, Cornelis, 1477, 1902
Swits, Debora, van Geyseling, 1890
Swits, Gertruy, 1864
Swits, Hester Visscher, 1864
Swits, Isaac, 250, 582, 800, 1477, 1853, 1864
Swits, Isaac Jacobus, 1853
Swits, Isaac S., 250, 1890
Swits, Jacob, 250, 1477
Swits, Major Isaac, 1864
Swits, Rebecca, 1477
Swits, Susanna Groot, 1477
Swits, Symon, 1477
Switts, Cornelis, 617
Switts, Hester ffisker, 617

ten Broeck, Wessel, 1674, 1685, 1693, 1698, 1775, 1981
ten Broeck, Zamuel, 1674
ten Broecke, Jenny Persen, 1339
ten Broecke, Wessel, 1339
ten Broek, Catharina, 1701
ten Broek, Cornelis, 1701, 1722, 1775
ten Broek, Dirck Wesselsen, 666
ten Broek, Elisabeth, 1701
ten Broek, Herman, 534
ten Broek, Jacob, 1701, 1727, 1775
ten Broek, Johannis, 1701
ten Broek, Wessel, 1701
ten Brook, Benjamin, 106
ten Brook, Capt. Petrus, 1306
ten Brook, Catherine Pawling, 1306
ten Brook, Dorothy, 1492
ten Brook, John, 1492
ten Brook, Mary, 1492
ten Brook, Nancy, 363
ten Brook, Petrus, 106
ten Brook, Wessel, 363, 1980
ten Brouck, John, 2002
Tenbruck, Hannah, 1700, 1923
Tenbruck, Hendricus, 1700
Tenbruck, John, 1700
Tenbruck, Mary, 1700
Tenbruck, Sarah, 1700
Teneur, Hend., 290
Teneur, Maritie Cuyper, 290
ten Eyck, Abraham, 1693, 1699
ten Eyck, Abraham R., 904
ten Eyck, Aldert, 1693
ten Eyck, Andries, 174, 188, 281, 411b, 935, 1693, 1776
ten Eyck, Andryes, 1117
ten Eyck, Ann, 401
ten Eyck, Anna Margreta, 2000
ten Eyck, Annetie, 1686
ten Eyck, Anthony, 188, 241, 281, 411b, 603, 1735
ten Eyck, Barent, 188, 281, 411b, 706, 1506, 1686, 1732, 1776
ten Eyck, Barent H., 297, 1812
ten Eyck, Barent John, 1543
ten Eyck, Barentje, 1686
ten Eyck, Catharina Cuyler, 268
ten Eyck, Cathereen, 1735
ten Eyck, Caty, 603
ten Eyck, Charlotte, 174
ten Eyck, Coenraedt, 174, 281, 411b, 1686, 1693, 1735, 2000, 2012
ten Eyck, Egbert, 603
ten Eyck, Elsje Cuyler, 701
ten Eyck, Elsje Sanders, 1607
ten Eyck, Geertie, 1686
ten Eyck, Gerritie, 281, 411b, 1735, 2000
ten Eyck, Gerritie van Schaick, 1776
ten Eyck, Hannah, 418
ten Eyck, Harmanus, 555, 1429
ten Eyck, Hendrick, 233, 418, 1686
ten Eyck, Henry, 1732
ten Eyck, Henry B., 1561
ten Eyck, Jacob, 411c, 603, 1102, 1686, 1693, 1732
ten Eyck, Jacob C., 93, 188, 281, 1776, 2057
ten Eyck, Jacob Coenraets, 268
ten Eyck, Jenneke, 1686, 1693
ten Eyck, Joannes, 1686
ten Eyck, Johannes, 916
ten Eyck, Johannis B., 1543
ten Eyck, John, 1496, 1706, 1886
ten Eyck, John Depyster, 1732
ten Eyck, John Sanders, 1607
ten Eyck, Koenradt, 53, 1776
ten Eyck, Maragrieta, 1776
ten Eyck, Margarittie, 281
ten Eyck, Margritia, 411b
ten Eyck, Maria, 1686
ten Eyck, Mary, 603
ten Eyck, Mathys, 1693
ten Eyck, Myndert Schuyler, 1607, 1732
ten Eyck, Peter, 174
ten Eyck, Philipp, 1213
ten Eyck, Rachel, 1732
ten Eyck, Richard, 1699
ten Eyck, Sarah, 1735
ten Eyck, Sara ten Broeck, 1705, 1716
ten Eyck, Susan, 1735
ten Eyck, Susanna, 1705
ten Eyck, Tobias, 188, 250, 281, 411b, 1732, 1776, 1833, 2000
ten Eycke, Barent T., 538
ten Eycke, Catherine Hoffman, 538
ten Eycke, John de Peyster, 538
ten Eycke, Mary Douw, 538
ten Hout, Geertruy, 1684
ten Hout, Severyn, 1684
Tenny, Elijah, 31
Tenyn, Allette Winne, 2130
Tenyn, Casper Leendertsen, 2130
ter Boosh, Elizabeth, 722
ter Boosh, John, 722
ter Boosh, Sarah, 722
ter Bos, Benjamin, 1712
ter Bos, Catharine van Wyck, 1845
ter Bos, Catharyna, 1712
ter Bos, Chaharyna, 1733
ter Bos, Daniel, 1926
ter Bos, Eleyas, 1733
ter Bos, Eleysahet, 1733
ter Bos, Elisabeth, 1712

ter Bos, Freer, 1712
ter Bos, Henry, 1707, 1712
ter Bos, Isack, 1712
ter Bos, Jacobus, 1733
ter Bos, Jeames, 1733
ter Bos, Johannis, 1845
ter Bos, John, 1845
ter Bos, Jonas, 1712
ter Bos, Lukas, 1712
ter Bos, Marya, 1712
ter Bos, Pieter, 1712
ter Bos, Sary, 1733
ter Bos, Seymon, 1712
ter Bos, Susana, 1733
ter Bos, William, 1733
ter Boss, Capt. Henry, 83
ter Boss, Daniel, 731
ter Boss, Henry, 1078
ter Boss, Jacobus, 83
Terbush, Abigail, 1320
ter Bush, Anne, 1172
ter Bush, Benjamin, 1724
ter Bush, Cornelis, 1717
ter Bush, Frayer, 1724
ter Bush, Henry, 652, 1724
ter Bush, Isaac, 1172, 1250, 1568, 1724
ter Bush, John, 1717, 1724
ter Bush, Jonas, 1724
ter Bush, Luke, 1724
ter Bush, Neeltie, 1717
ter Bush, Peter, 1724
ter Bush, Sarah, 1172
ter Bush, Simon, 1250, 1724
Terepenning, Dirck, 1703
Terhane, Stephen, 39
ter Hune, Catherine, 977
Terhune, Jacob, 2161
Terhune, Stephen, 1382
Terneur, David, 1730
Terneur, Hendrick, 1721
Terneur, Hendrick Jacobus, 1721
Terneur, Henry, 1730
Terneur, Jacamyntye, 1730
Terneur, Jacob, 151
Terneur, Jacobus, 1721, 1730
Terneur, Jane, 1721
Terneur, Jannitje, 1721
Terneur, John, 1721
Terneur, Lowrence, 1721
Terneur, Margaret, 1730
Terneur, Marritye, 1721
Terneur, Mary, 1721
Terneur, Michael, 1721
Terneur, Rachal, 1730
Terneur, Ranshye Blauvelt, 151
Terneur, Sarah, 1721
Terpenning, Boudewyn, 1751
Terry, David, 29
Terry, Edmond, 1723
Terry, Ellenor, 1723
Terry James, 1723
Terry, Ketcham, 1008
Terry, Wm., 355, 359, 1723
Terwelger, Evert, 440
Terwellege, Abraham, 1731
ter Wellgen, Hermanis, 1517
Terwilger, John, 821
ter Willgen, Cornelis, 1180
Tetwilligen, Abraham, 1731
Terwilligen, Arie, 1311
Terwilligen, Catharine, 1731
Terwilligen, Griete Phenix, 1311
Terwilligen, Isaac, 1311
Terwilligen, James Phenix, 1311
Terwilligen, Rebecca Phenix, 1311
Terwilligen, Sarah, 1731
Terwilligen, Teunis, 508, 1731
Terwilliger, Abraham, 938
Terwilliger, Annatie Oosterhout, 1270
Terwilliger, Matheus, 1270
Tetord, Frs., 1873
Teunisen, Egbert, 1385, 1688
Teunissen, Barent, 1688
Teunissen, Benjamin, 1688
Teunissen, Capt. Gerrit, 1981
Teunissen, Catrine Groesbeeck, 750
Teunissen, Dirck, 1688
Teunissen, Gerrit, 1972
Teunissen, Jacob, 750
Teunissen, Johannis, 750
Teunissen, Juriaen, 1771
Teunissen, Marritie Brad, 1688
Teunissen, Stephanus, 750
Teunissen, Susannah, 1688
Teunissen, Teunis, 1688
Teunissen, Wybrecht Jacobsen, 1771
Thacher, Thomas, 2109
Theal, Joseph, 30
Theall, Charles, 1033
Thew, Abraham, 985, 1754
Thew, Abram, 1585, 1588
Thew, Elizabeth, 1754
Thew, Jacobus, 1754
Thew, John, 1600, 1754
Thew, Thunis, 1585, 1754
Thirkell, Thos., 1654
Thirstan, Joseph, 1160
Thirstan, Rachael Montrass, 1160
Thirsten, Joseph, 794
Thirston, Samuel, 1032
Thomas, Abraham, 1748
Thomas, Benj., 428
Thomas, Catherina, 1529, 1743
Thomas, Elizabeth, 1743
Thomas, Greitie, 1743
Thomas, Hama, 1769

Trumport, Valentine, 860
Trumpover, Andres, 1749
Trumpover, Cathren, 1749
Trumpover, Cristen, 1749
Trumpover, Elizabeth, 1749
Trumpover, Margrit, 1749
Trumpover, Mary, 1749
Trumpover, Nicolas, 1749
Trumpover, Peter, 1749
Trumpover, Susannah, 1749
Tubbs, Amos, 1323
Tubbs, Benajah, 164
Tucker, Caroline, 1766
Tucker, Cornelius Wortendyke, 1766
Tucker, Fanning Cobham, 1766
Tucker, Hannah, 946, 1766
Tucker, James, 1766
Tucker, Mary, 2051
Tucker, Rachel, 946
Tucker, Robert, 1766
Tucker, Susanna Maria, 1766
Tuder, John, 615a, 779
Tudle, Eunice, 870
Tudle, John, 870
Turck, Augustinus, 1543, 1987
Turck, Jacobus, 651
Turck, Willem, 236
Turcke, Augustinus, 1876
Turk, Chasverus, 1639
Turk, Anthony, 1529
Turk, Cathrina Sleght, 1529
Turk, James, 1639
Turk, Sarah, 1639
Turnbull, Lieut. George, 791
Turnaar, Jacobus, 808
Turner, Hugh, 180
Turner, Jacobus, 1721
Turner, James, 1822
Turneux, Odle, 422
Turnpenny, John, 891
Turrettin, Mme. Grimes, 1458
Tusten, Benjamin, 991
Tusten, Col. Benj., 1725
Tuston, Joseph, 1332
Tuthill, Abigail, 1711
Tuthill, Barzilai, 595
Tuthill, Daniel, 1375, 1550, 1714, 1761
Tuthill, Fanny, 1761
Tuthill, Freegift, 1711
Tuthill, James, 795, 1601, 1702, 1709
Tuthill, Jamima, 1709
Tuthill, Jane de Key, 419
Tuthill, Joel, 1709
Tuthill, John, 47, 1702, 1714, 1725, 1761
Tuthill, John W., 598
Tuthill, Jonathan, 1702, 1725
Tuthill, Joshua, 1711
Tuthill, Mary, 1702, 1709, 1725, 1761
Tuthill, Nancy, 1761
Tuthill, Nathan, 1761
Tuthill, Nathaniel, 1711
Tuthill, Phenias, 1714
Tuthill, Samuel, 1714
Tuthill, Solomon, 1702, 1725
Tuthill, Susanna, 1714
Tuthill, Tabitha, 2053
Tuthill, Thomas, 1702, 1709
Tuthill, William, 1702,
Tuttle, Daniel, 548
Tye, John, 1095
Tye, Joseph, 1095
Tygart, Suphrines, 593
Tygert, John, 849
Tygert, Magdalene, 849
Tygert, Maria, 849
Tygert, Mary Catherine, 849
Tygert, Nicholas, 849
Tygert, Peter, 849
Tygert, Peter S., 849
Tygert, Werner, 849
Tyler, Jonathan, 1764
Tyler, Margaret, 1764
Tyler, Mary, 1272
Tyler, Miriam, 1272
Tyme, Michel, 1931
Tyrrell, Ann, 160
Tyrrell, William, 160

U

Ule, Margaret Straight, 1611
Umbrat, Stephen, 630
Umphrey, Agnis, 1579
Umphrey, Hugh, 1169, 2058
Umphrey, John, 1510
Underhill, Benjamin, 395
Underhill, Edmund, 395
Underhill, John, 1370
Underhill, Umfree, 1136
Upham, Barta, 1779, 1780
Upham, Elizabeth, 1779, 1780
Upham, Eme, 1780
Upham, Emelia, 1779
Upham, Gesey, 1779, 1780
Upham, Helene, 1779
Upham, John, 1779, 1780
Upham, Magdalena, 1780
Upham, Mary, 1779, 1780
Upham, Susanna, 1779, 1780
Upham, Wintie, 1780
Upton, Clotworthy, 1781
Upton, Joanna, 1781
Upton, Lieut. Francis, 1781
Ure, Masterton, 955

van Bergen, Petrus, 444
van Bergen, Wilhelmus, 23, 1847
van Bergen, William, 23, 1847
van Beure, Barent, 2034
van Beuren, Anna Goes, 753
van Beuren, Magdalena, 1981
van Beuren, Marten Cornelissen, 1981
van Beuren, Pieter Marten, 1981
van Beuren, Tobias, 499, 753
van Beuren, Tobyas Cornelissen, 1981
van Beuren, Sarah Dubois, 499
van Bockhoven, Claes Jansen, 1785
van Bonwell, Hendrick, 1112
van Boskerk, Lourens, 400, 1849
van Brackel, Catryntie van der Volgen, 1797
van Brackel, Gysbert, 1797
van Brakel, Elizabeth, 1983
van Brakel, Gerret, 429
van Brakel, Gerrit Gysbertsen, 1983
van Brakel, Gysbert, 1983
van Brakel, Gysbert Gerritsen, 1983
van Brakell, Martha, 921
van Brakell, Mary, 921
van Brakell, Matthew, 921
van Brakell, Rachel, 921
van Brakell, Rachel Johnson, 921
van Bramer, Hendrick, 827
van Brough, Peter, 417
van Brugh, Annatie, 237
van Brugh, Catrina Roeloffs, 237
van Brugh, Johannes, 237
van Brugh, Pieter, 1674
van Brunt, Angenitie, 1819
van Brunt, Cornelis, 1819
van Brunt, Marragreet, 1819
van Brunt, Marrytie, 1819
van Brunt, Nicolas, 1819
van Brunt, Rutger, 1819
van Brunt, Tryntje, 1819
van Bueren, Tobias, 768
van Bunschooten, Elias, 1687, 1798
van Bunschoten, Annatje, 1903
van Bunschoten, Catherine, 1925
van Bunschoten, Egbert, 1903
van Bunschoten, Egenas, 1903
van Bunschoten, Elias, 667, 1840, 1925
van Bunschoten, Elsje, 1903
van Bunschoten, Elizabeth, 1903
van Bunschoten, Harmanis, 1903
van Bunschoten, Jacobus, 1903
van Bunschoten, Jacomyntje, 1925
van Bunschoten, Johannis, 810, 1874
van Bunschoten, John, 1903, 1925
van Bunschoten, Nelly van Vliet, 1884
van Bunschoten, Rachel, 1925
van Buuschoten, Salomon, 1903
van Bunschoten, Tunis, 1798, 1842, 1903, 1925
van Bunscoten, Tunis, 1815
van Bura, Barent, 2034
van Bura, Maritie Winne, 2034
van Buren, Aaryaentie, 1924
van Buren, Altie Winne, 2135
van Buren, Callyntie, 1988
van Buren, Catalina, 1924
van Buren, Catherine, 1924
van Buren, Cornelius, 894
van Buren, Eva van Slyck, 1581
van Buren, Eyche, 1924
van Buren, Francis, 1581
van Buren, Gerrit, 682
van Buren, Hannah van Slyck, 1581
van Buren, Harme, 1581
van Buren, Hendrick, 1988, 2135
van Buren, Itie, 1924
van Buren, Johannis, 1924, 1988
van Buren, Maas, 1924, 1988
van Buren, Magdalena, 1988
van Buren, Maycka Hun, 894
van Buren, Peter, 1706
van Buren, Piter, 1302
van Buren, Yan, 1014
van Buskirk, Col. Abraham, 901
van Buuren, Pieter, 668
van Campen, Elsie Eltinge, 575
van Campen, Isaak, 575
Vance, Samuel, 1558
van Cleek, Baltus, 980
van Cleek, Chatarina, 980
van Cleek, Elizabeth, 980
van Cleek, Franz, 980
van Cleek, Grietje, 980
van Cleek, Peter, 980
van Cleek, Sarah, 980
van Cleek, Sarah Kip, 980
van Cleff, Gerrit, 1149
van Corlaer, Benoni, 252, 1970
van Corlaer, Elisabeth, 252, 410, 1824
van Corlaer, Elizabeth van der Poel, 1970
van Cortland, Col. Philipp, 945
van Cortland, Jacobus, 422
van Cortlandt, Augt., 1560, 1644, 1821
van Cortlandt, Augustus, 313a, 1203
van Cortlandt, Elizabeth, 1614
van Cortlandt, Elizabeth Cuyler, 316
van Cortlandt, Eva, 1938
van Cortlandt, Frederick, 313a
van Cortlandt, Geertruy Schuyler, 1473

van Schaick, Mary van der Poel, 1970
van Schaick, Myndert, 2006
van Schaick, Ryckje, 2006
van Schaick, Sybrant, 1339, 1997, 1999
van Schaick, Sybrant G., 1380, 1519, 1551, 2006
van Schaick, Sybrant Goose, 1996
van Schaick, Wissel, 677, 756, 1919
van Schaik, Catherine Staats, 1488
van Schaik, Catreentie Cuyler, 307
van Schaik, Elizabeth van der Poel, 1388
van Schaik, Gose, 1488
van Schaik, Jacob, 307
van Schaik, Jacobus, 1488
van Schaik, L., 1975
van Schaik, Sybrant, 1378
van Schajck, Abraham, 1824
van Schajck, Anthony, 1824
van Schajck, Arent, 1824
van Schajck, Gerret, 1824
van Schajck, Gose, 1824
van Schajck, Jacob, 1824, 1854
van Schajck, Sybrant, 1824
van Schajck, Sybrant Gosensen, 1824
van Schayck, Alida van Slichtenhorst, 1965
van Schayck, Annetje Lievens, 1959
van Schayck, Anthony, 1959
van Schayck, Arent, 76
van Schayck, Barent, 1959
van Schayck, Cornelis, 1959
van Schayck, Engeltie, 1959
van Schayck, Geertje Brants, 1959
van Schayck, Gerrit, 1965
van Schayck, Gerritie, 1959
van Schayck, Goosen Gerritsen, 1959
van Schayck, Jacob, 104
van Schayck, Livinus, 1959
van Schayck, Margarytje, 1959
van Schayck, Sybrant, 1959
van Schayick, Jacob I., 2153
van Schayk, Sybrant, 1545
van Schelluyne, Cornelis, 958, 1958
van Schelluyne, Dirck, 237, 405, 1467, 1667, 1771, 1772, 1956, 1957, 1958, 1959.
van Schelluyne, Harmanus, 1807
van Schelluyne, Hester, 1807
van Schelluyne, Johannis, 1807
van Schelluyne, Tieleman, 1807, 2029
van Schelluyne, Wellem, 1807
van Schoonhoven, Dirk B., 1419, 1995
van Scoy, Cornelius, 209
van Sellea, Abraham, 1799
van Sellea, Anna Mary, 1799
van Sellea, Casper Prime, 1799
van Sellea, France, 1799
van Sellea, France Abrahamsen, 1799
van Sellea, Isabala, 1799
van Sellea, Jan Prime, 1799
van Shaick, Jacob, 868
van Shaick, Maritie, 411c
van Sice, John, 1863
van Sice, Joseph, 1797
van Sise, John, 109, 1308
van Sleyck, Lydia Vedder, 1863
van Sleyck, Margariet, 1863
van Slichtenhorst, Bata, 408
van Slichtenhorst, Gerrit, 1377
van Slit, Aerri, 2021
van Slyck, Abraham, 1948
van Slyck, Adreejan, 1826
van Slyck, Albert, 1826
van Slyck, Alida, 1808, 2005
van Slyck, Andries, 1808
van Slyck, Anthony, 1928
van Slyck, Antone, 1826
van Slyck, Barentje, 1802
van Slyck, Chatrina, 1808
van Slyck, Clara, 1826
van Slyck, Cornelis, 1826, 1978
van Slyck, Cornelis Antone, 1826
van Slyck, Cornelis Petrus, 1826
van Slyck, Cornelius A., 1753
van Slyck, Dirck, 1802
van Slyck, Dorothy, 1581
van Slyck, Elisabeth, 1826, 1948
van Slyck, Eybie, 1808
van Slyck, Fytie, 1978
van Slyck, Geertruyd, 1978
van Slyck, Gerrit Teunissen, 1808
van Slyck, Gerritie Ryckman, 1978
van Slyck, Gertruy, 1826, 2005
van Slyck, Grietie, 1978
van Slyck, Harme, 250, 1826, 1928
van Slyck, Helena, 1978
van Slyck, Hellen, 1948
van Slyck, Hendrick, 1808, 1826
van Slyck, Herman, 1978
van Slyck, Isaac, 1581
van Slyck, Jacobus, 250
van Slyck, Jacques Cornelissen, 1978
van Slyck, Jannetje, 1808
van Slyck, Jemima, 1948
van Slyck, Jesse, 1948
van Slyck, Jesse C., 1948
van Slyck, Jesse M., 1948
van Slyck, Joghem, 1581
van Slyck, Johannis, 697, 1826
van Slyck, Johs., 1581
van Slyck, Lena, 1826
van Slyck, Lidia, 1978
van Slyck, Margaret, 1826, 1948
van Slyck, Margaritha, 1928

van Valkenburgh, Mataewes, 2067
v. Valkenburgh, N., 665
van Valkenburgh, Peter I., 1779, 2067
van Valkenburgh, Peter J., 603
van Valkenburgh, Susanna, 1779
van Varick, Effee, 1942
van Varick, James, 1942
van Varick, Richard, 1944
van Vechten, Ab., 538, 1937
van Vechten, Abraham, 1921, 1972
van Vechten, Annatie, 1818, 1866, 1972
van Vechten, Anthony, 1818
van Vechten, Antje Jans, 1980
van Vechten, Benjamin, 1818, 1989
van Vechten, Derick, 1520, 1521, 1849, 1989
van Vechten, Derick Teunissen, 1972
van Vechten, Elizabeth, 1921
van Vechten, Ephraim, 1865
van Vechten, Fytie, 1972
van Vechten, Gerrit Teunissen, 1975, 1980
van Vechten, Grietie, 1818
van Vechten, Grietie Volkersen Dow, 1980
van Vechten, Harmen, 1818, 1871, 1989
van Vechten, Hendricus, 1865
van Vechten, Jacob, 1921
van Vechten, Jannetie, 1972
van Vechten, Jannetie Michiels, 1972
van Vechten, Johannis, 53, 1865, 1972, 1980
van Vechten, Judith, 1921
van Vechten, Lidia ten Broeck, 1685
van Vechten, Lucas, 2059
van Vechten, Maragrieta, 1989
van Vechten, Michael, 1972
van Vechten, Neeltie, 1865, 1972
van Vechten, Philipp, 1843, 1989, 2059
van Vechten, Sally van Orden, 1951
van Vechten, Samuel, 202, 473, 1921, 1922, 1951, 1972
van Vechten, Sarah, 1972
van Vechten, Theunys, 1514, 1818, 1871, 1921, 1972, 1989
van Vechten, Teunis Ts., 388
van Vechten, Volckert, 1685, 1865, 1980
van Vechten, Weyntie, 1972
van Veghte, Anna, 2138
van Veghte, Ephraim, 2138, 2139
van Veghte, John, 2138, 2139
van Veghte, Volkert, 1984
van Veghten, Annatie, 1866
van Veghten, Annatie Wendell, 2104
van Veghten, Cornelis, 2027
van Veghten, Dirck, 1871, 2002, 2060
van Veghten, Dirk T., 996
van Veghten, Engeltie, 2027
van Veghten, Geertruy, 2027
van Veghten, Helena, 1871, 2002
van Veghten, Hubartis, 1871, 2002
van Veghten, Jannetie, 1871, 2002
van Veghten, Johannes, 2027
van Veghten, John, 1866, 2104
van Veghten, Lucas, 1886, 2136
van Veghten, Luykas, 2027
van Veghten, Margrita, 996
van Veghten, Marytje, 2027
van Veghten, Philipp, 2027, 2136
van Veghten, Teunis, 996, 1871, 2002
van Vegten, Judickje ten Broek, 1701
van Vegten, Teunis, 1701
van Vlack, Hewark, 782
van Vlackeren, John, 802
van Vleck, Abraham, 428, 1914, 1943
van Vleck, Elizabeth, 1943
van Vleck, Henry, 1943
van Vleck, Isaac, 1901, 1943
van Vleck, Jacob, 1943
van Vleck, John, 1914
van Vleck, Judith, 1943
van Vleck, Lawrence, 1943
van Vleck, Lydia, 1901
van Vleck, Lydia van Schaack, 1901
van Vleck, Margaret, 1901
van Vleck, Maria Elizabeth, 1943
van Vleck, Samuel, 1914
van Vleck, Tunis, 124
van Vleeck, Henry, 132
van Vleecq, Abraham, 960
van Vleg, Paulus, 668
van Vliet, Abraham, 1898
van Vliet, Arie, 1840
van Vliet, Aury, 1884
van Vliet, Catharina van Aken, 1898
van Vliet, Christina Viele, 1918
van Vliet, Derick, 1803
van Vliet, Dirck, 1205
van Vliet, Frederick, 1884
van Vliet, Garret, 1884
van Vliet, Janatje, 1884
van Vliet, Petrus, 1884
van Vliet, Rachel van Keuren, 1803
van Vliet, Sarah van Keuren, 1803
van Vliet, Tjerck, 1918
van Vliet, Tunis, 1884
van Vliet, William, 1803

van Wormer, Hannah, 1830
van Wormer, Johannes, 1830
van Wormer, Mary, 1830
van Wormer, Michael, 1372
van Wyck, Ab., 1394, 2024
van Wyck, Abraham, 194, 1691, 1836, 1845, 1902
van Wyck, Aeltje, 126, 194
van Wyck, Altje Brinckerhoff, 194
van Wyck, Anna-Mary, 1902
van Wyck, Antie, 1836, 1845
van Wyck, Catalina, 1836, 1845
van Wyck, Cornelius, 15, 480, 802, 1319, 1836, 1845, 2024
van Wyck, David, 1902
van Wyck, Dirk, 194
van Wyck, Dr. Theodorus, 194, 802
van Wyck, Elizabeth, 194, 1900
van Wyck, Hannah, 1845
van Wyck, Helena, 1902
van Wyck, Helena Bogart, 1902
van Wyck, Janiche, 1900
van Wyck, John, 1846
van Wyck, John Brinckerhoff, 194
van Wyck, Latetia, 1900
van Wyck, Margaret, 1902
van Wyck, Phebe, 1846
van Wyck, Richard, 15, 157, 480, 1836, 1845
van Wyck, Sarah, 1729, 1836, 1845, 1846
van Wyck, Stephen, 1846
van Wyck, Theodorus, 126, 194, 785, 969, 1160, 1502, 1602, 1836, 1845, 1876, 1900, 1902, 2024
van Wyck, William, 126, 194, 322, 802, 856, 898, 1160, 1900
van Wyck, Yanetje, 194
van Wye, Jan, 752
van Zandt, Johannes, 1299
van Zandt, Major Viner, 711
van Zandt, Peter Pra, 1148, 1299
van Zandt, Tobias, 1363, 1535
van Zandt, Viner, 738
Varick, Abraham, 1944, 2115
Varick, Ann, 1941
Varick, Gilliam, 1941
Varick, Mary, 1941
Varick, Richard, 1944
Vaughan, Anthony, 1861
Vaughan, Benjamin, 1861
Vaughan, Daniel, 1861
Vaughan, David, 1861
Vaughan, Dinah, 1861
Vaughan, Henry, 1861
Vaughan, James, 1861
Vaughan, John, 1861
Vaughan, Mary, 1861
Vaughan, Obediah, 1861
Vaughton, Michael, 673
Veal, Dorothy, 1598
Veal, Elizabeth, 1598
Veal, Elizabeth Smith, 1598
Veal, Gilbert, 22
Veal, Isaiah, 514
Vedder, Albert, 1833, 1855, 1992
Vedder, Albert Johse., 1844
Vedder, Albert S., 1928
Vedder, Alexander, 1607, 1904
Vedder, Angenietje, 1992
Vedder, Anna, 1833
Vedder, Antje, 1992
Vedder, Arent, 1833, 1992
Vedder, Arent S., 2094
Vedder, Catrina, 401, 1833, 1993
Vedder, Corset, 1833
Vedder, Eliezabeth, 1992
Vedder, Engeltie, 1993
Vedder, Eve, 401
Vedder, Eve Bradt, 401
Vedder, Harmen, 1833, 1863, 1992
Vedder, Harme Haramanes, 1862
Vedder, Jacobus, 1862
Vedder, Johannes, 1833, 2094
Vedder, Johannes Haramanes, 1862, 1863
Vedder, John, 1017, 1848, 1928
Vedder, Lieut. Helmas, 64
Vedder, Maria, 1833, 1863, 1992
Vedder, Maria Arents, 2094
Vedder, Mary Laford, 1017
Vedder, Marytie, 1833
Vedder, Myndert, 401
Vedder, Rebecca, 1992
Vedder, Sander, 1833
Vedder, Sarah, 1992
Vedder, Seymon, 1992
Vedder, Simon, 401
Vedder, Simon Ariantsen, 2094
Vedder, Susanna, 1992
Vedder, Takareus, 401
Veder, Abraham, 981
Veder, Simon, 981
Veeder, Angeltie Vrooman, 1821
Veeder, Annitje, 1126
Veeder, Barent, 1855
Veeder, Catriena, 1993, 2010
Veeder, Cornelis, 61, 1821, 1993
Veeder, Deborah, 1810
Veeder, Elizabeth, 1993
Veeder, Engeltie, 61, 1810, 1979, 1993
Veeder, Gerrit, 1979
Veeder, Gerrit I., 2155
Veeder, Gerrit Symonsen, 61, 1993
Veeder, Helena, 61
Veeder, Helmer, 1993
Veeder, Henderickes, 1993

W

Watkins, Charles, 550, 1213
Watkins, Debora, 2073
Watkins, Dolle, 2073
Watkins, Ephraim, 2028, 2053, 2100
Watkins, Eunice, 2028
Watkins, George, 2100
Watkins, Hezekiah, 2028
Watkins, Joanna, 2028
Watkins, John, 1087
Watkins, Joseph, 2028, 2053, 2073, 2100
Watkins, Judith Livingston, 1087
Watkins, Phebe, 2100
Watkins, Rev. Hezekiah, 2023
Watkins, Samuel, 550, 2028, 2053
Watkins, Sarah, 2073
Watkins, Tabitha, 2028
Watkins, Thomas, 2073
Watson, Abraham, 404
Watson, Cecilia, 41
Watson, David, 632
Watson, E., 890
Watson, Ino., 2111
Watson, Jacob, 2038
Watson, Mathew, 706
Watson, Susannah, 41
Watson, Susannah Miller, 1211
Watson, W. W., 909
Watson, William, 41
Watts, Anne, 2031
Watts, Honble. John, 1644
Watts, John, 370, 1247, 2031, 2041
Watts, Lionel, 2087
Watts, Margaret, 160, 2031
Watts, Robert, 370, 2031
Wauchope, Jas , 608
Waugh, Elizabeth, 2103
Waugh, George, 2114
Waugh, James, 159, 2103
Waugh, Jane, 2103
Waugh, John, 159, 2103, 2114
Waugh, Mary, 2103
Waugh, Robert, 2103
Waugh, Sarah, 2103
Waugh, Thomas, 2114
Waugh, William, 2114
Way, Francis, 126
Way, James, 1159
Wayland, Charls, 2118
Wayland, Elizabeth, 2118
Wayland, Francis, 2118
Wayland, Job, 2118
Wayland, Levi, 2118
Wayland, Mary, 2118
Wayland, Seth, 2118
Weare, John, 1210
Weare, William, 1210
Weaver, John G., 1664
Weaver, Joseph, 368
Webb, Amelia, 2141
Webb, Anthony, 423
Webb, Charles B., 2141
Webb, Elizabeth B., 2141
Webb, Francis C., 2141
Webb, Henry L., 2141
Webb, John H., 2141
Webb, Jonathan, 277
Webb, Joseph, 239, 1798
Webb, Samuel, 277
Weber, Alexander, 2033
Weber, Cathreana, 2033
Weber, Geertruy, 2033
Weber, Hendrick, 2033
Weber, John, 2033
Weber, Maria, 2033
Weber, Marritie, 2033
Weber, Susanna, 2033
Weber, Jost, 1577
Weed, Frederick, 548
Weed, Jehieh, 2154
Weeks, Abel, 1764
Weeks, Abigail Tyler, 1764
Weeks, Anne, 2115
Weeks, Augustin, 2115
Weeks, Charlotte, 2115
Weeks, Elizabeth, 2115
Weeks, James, 647
Weeks, Jane, 2115
Weeks, John, 2115
Weeks, Judah, 2115
Weeks, Phebe, 1729
Weeks, Rasine, 2115
Weeks, Rebecca, 2115
Weeks, Robert, 815
Weeks, Ruth, 2115
Weeks, William, 2115
Weemes, Capt. James, 1468
Weesner, Adam, 2017
Weesner, Elizabeth, 2017
Weesner, Hendrick, 2017
Weesner, Henry, 923
Weesner, Johannis, 2017
Weesner, Mary, 2017
Weir, Alexander, 2083
Weir, Edward, 2083, 2116
Weir, John, 2083
Weir, Margaret, 2116
Weir, Richard, 2083
Weir, Sarah Collins, 2083
Weir, Smith, 2083
Weir, Susan, 2083
Weismer, George, 874
Weiss, Lewis, 399
Wellar, Susannah, 142
Weller, Jatie Masten, 1180
Weller, Johannis, 1180
Weller, William, 1372

Welling, Isabella, 1169
Welling, Josias, 2025
Welling, Mary, 1169
Welling, Peter, 156
Welling, Thomas, 698
Welling, William, 1813
Wellings, Mary Mullender, 1169
Wells, Abel, 2070
Wells, Abigil, 2070, 2093
Wells, Austin, 1445
Wells, Bathia, 2075
Wells, Capt. Abner, 2093
Walls, Catharine, 472
Wells, David, 29
Wells, Debora, 2075
Wells, Deliverance, 2075
Wells, Goshum, 2075
Wells, Henry, 1763
Wells, Hulda, 2075
Wells, Israel, 2079, 2093
Wells, James, 1309, 1348, 1445
Wells, Joana, 2075
Wells, John, 25, 869, 1194, 1264, 2079
Wells, Joshua, 2075, 2079
Wells, Mary, 2070, 2079
Wells, Mehitable, 2075
Wells, Rev. William, 1457
Wells, Richard, 2079
Wells, Samuel, 2075, 2079
Wells, William, 472
Wemp, Abraham, 1821
Wemp, Aeltie Jans, 2127
Wemp, Anna, 2127
Wemp, Arent, 1784
Wemp, Ariantie, 1480
Wemp, Barent, 2127
Wemp, Cataline Schermerhorn, 1480
Wemp, Grietie, 2127
Wemp, Jan Barentsen, 1956, 2127
Wemp, John, 1480
Wemp, Maritie Mynders, 2127
Wemp, Myndert, 1480
Wemp, Myndert Jansen, 2127
Wemp, Rachel Vrooman, 1821
Wemp, Ryert, 1480
Wemp, Volkje Volkertsen, 1784
Wempel, Abraham, 1841
Wemple, Andrew, 329
Wemple, Arjaentie, 2134
Wemple, Dr. W. T., 1073
Wemple, Ephraim, 2134
Wemple, Isaac, 2134
Wemple, Jan, 2134
Wemple, John, 329, 2134
Wemple, John, Js., 1931
Wemple, Mindert R., 1862
Wemple, Myndert, 329, 2134
Wemple, Ryer, 2134
Wendel, Elizabeth Sanders, 2132
Wendel, Ephraim, 268, 2132
Wendel, Evert, 2094
Wendel, Evert Jansen, 237, 1667
Wendel, Jacamintje van Dyck, 1848
Wendel, Johannis, 666, 1472, 2132
Wendel, John A., 1614
Wendel, John Baptist, 1848
Wendel, Maria, 2094
Wendel, Robert, 2132
Wendel, Susannah, 2132
Wendell, Abraham, 1471, 2029, 2133
Wendell, Abraham H., 1561, 2104
Wendell, Ann, 1816
Wendell, Annatie E., 2048
Wendell, Annatie J., 2138
Wendell, Arjantie, 2029, 2036
Wendell, Catalyntje, 2133
Wendell, Catharine, 2059, 2138
Wendell, Catharine de Key, 428
Wendell, Catherine van Veghten, 2027
Wendell, Cornelius, 2048, 2059, 2104, 2136
Wendell, Elizabeth, 2029, 2048, 2133, 2138, 2139
Wendell, Elsie, 2133
Wendell, Engeltie, 2029
Wendell, Ephraim, 1497, 2133
Wendell, Evert, 66, 912, 1796, 2029, 2036, 2132
Wendell, Evert Io., 2048
Wendell, Evert Jansen, 1671
Wendell, Evert John, 1551
Wendell, Geesje, 2048, 2138, 2139
Wendell, Gertrude Vusburgh, 1947
Wendell, Harmanis, 66, 1795, 2034, 2036, 2059, 2104, 2136
Wendell, Harmanis A., 2138, 2139
Wendell, Hermanus H., 2027
Wendell, Harms A., 848
Wendell, Isaac, 1495, 2133
Wendell, J. H., 1661
Wendell, Jacob, 2059, 2104, 2133, 2136, 2138
Wendell, Jacob A., 848, 2139
Wendell, Jeronimus, 2036
Wendell, Johannes, 2029, 2059, 2133, 2136
Wendell, Johannis E., 2138
Wendell, Johs., 1679
Wendell, John, 2104, 2138
Wendell, John A., 2139
Wendell, John I., 1952
Wendell, Lena, 1429
Wendell, Maritie, 2133
Wendell, Maritie Sillis, 2133

Willis, Samuel, 373, 1454, 1708
Willits, Jesse, 778a
Willits, Joseph, 1523
Wills, James, 30, 184, 724, 2076
Willsey, Johannes, 2023
Willson, Andrew, 1181, 2092
Willson, Elisabeth, 2092
Willson, Elizabeth Titsort, 1720
Willson, Hugh, 1161
Willson, James, 1824, 1836
Willson, John, 2065
Willson, Jona., 1090
Willson, Joseph, 1720
Willson, Justus, 2092
Willson, Samuel, 2092
Willson, Sarah, 1720
Willson, Thomas, 280, 1717, 2092
Wilmot, James, 212
Wilmut, Alexander, 2013
Wilsey, William, 945
Wilson, Abraham, 1219
Wilson, Agnes McCurdy, 1208
Wilson, Alexander, 988, 2065
Wilson, Andrew, 377, 1257, 1361
Wilson, Ann Mann, 1219
Wilson, Capt. Ebenezer, 1242
Wilson, Catherine, 1361
Wilson, Daniel, 1361
Wilson, Ebenezer, 231, 1683
Wilson, Edwd., 546
Wilson, Eunice Cooley, 377
Wilson, Ezra, 1184
Wilson, Francis, 2023
Wilson, Hannah Kidd, 988
Wilson, Henry, 1361
Wilson, Isabell, 1208
Wilson, Jane, 642, 1208, 2065
Wilson, John, 1361
Wilson, Joseph, 1361
Wilson, Margaret Perrine, 1361
Wilson, Margrit, 1208
Wilson, Mary Neely, 1257
Wilson, Patrick, 713
Wilson, Thomas, 1135
Wilson, Wm., 1208
Wilt, Abijah, 33
Wilt, George, 33
Wiltse, Cornelius, 145, 2024
Wiltse, Hannah, 2024
Wiltse, Henry, 12, 1857
Wiltse, Jacob, 12, 2024
Wiltse, Janetje, 2024
Wiltse, Johannas, 12, 480, 1857
Wiltse, Margaret, 2024
Wiltse, Maria, 2024
Wiltse, Martin, 1594
Wiltse, Martine, 2024
Wiltse, Martines, 781
Wiltse, Martynes, 2024
Wiltse, Mertin, 303
Wiltse, Sarah, 2076
Wiltse, Sytje, 2024
Wiltsie, Martin, 1750
Wily, Caleb, 321
Wimpel, Catrena, 113
Wimple, Abraham, 250
Wimple, Reyer, 250
Winant, Amelia, 970
Winant, Stephen, 970
Winchell, Aaron Ely, 2081
Winchell, James, 2081
Winchell, John, 2081
Winchell, Martinezer, 2081
Winchell, Mary, 2081
Winchell, Nathaniel, 2081
Winchell, Philo Mills, 2081
Winckel, Anna, 2066
Winckel, James, 2066
Winckel, Justus, 2066
Winckel, Lydia, 2066
Winckel, Robert, 2066
Winckel, Stephen, 2066
Winckel, Timothy, 2066
Windover, Peter, 1814
Winegaert, Luycas, 1019
Winfield, David, 938
Wing, Abigail, 2044
Wing, Dinah, 2056
Wing, Dorcas, 2044
Wing, Elihu, 2044
Wing, Elisha, 2044
Wing, Elizabeth, 2044
Wing, Garshom, 2044
Wing, Hannah, 2056
Wing, Jedediah, 2044
Wing, John, 2056
Wing, Martha, 2056
Wing, Mehetabel, 2044
Wing, Prime, 2044
Wing, William, 2056
Winkeler, David, 1045
Winkler, Capt. Herman, 2018
Winkler, Mrs., 735
Winne, Adam, 2130, 2135
Winne, Aechie Jans, 2128
Winne, Anthony, 586
Winne, Arent, 1059, 1177
Winne, Cornelis, 2135
Winne, Daniel, 2130, 2135, 2137
Winne, Dirkie, 2135
Winne, Douwe, 2137
Winne, Eva, 2130
Winne, Francis, 1790, 1982, 2137
Winne, Frans, 2130, 2135
Winne, Jacob L., 1947
Winne, Jacobus, 2130
Winne, Jan, 2135
Winne, Jannetie, Adams, 2128

Y

Yates, Sarah, 2159
Yaugher, Elizabeth, 1743
Yaugher, Jacob, 1743
Yeaman, George, 2157
Yeaman, Joseph, 2157
Yeates, High Sheriff Abraham, 1545
Yelverton, Abigail, 2152
Yelverton, Abijah, 2144
Yelverton, Andrew, 2152
Yelverton, Anthony, 2144, 2151, 2152
Yelverton, Cowdewine Lecounte, 1049
Yelverton, Gale, 2152
Yelverton, Hannah, 2151, 2152
Yelverton, Mary, 2151, 2152
Yelverton, Phebe, 2156
Yeomans, Elial, 2145
Yeomans, Jonathan, 2150
Yeomans, Mary, 2145
Yeomans, Nathaniel, 2145
Yeomans, Ruth, 2145
Yeomans, Sarah, 2145
Yetss, Adam, 1994
Yong, John, 820
Yongh, Abimal, 466
Yongs, Abimil, 1725
York, Elizabeth, 2158
York, John, 2101
York, Nicholas, 2158
Yorke, Mary, 1413
Youen, Benjamin, 2148
Youmans, William, 24
Young, Ann Elizabeth, 890
Young, Ann Hawey, 890
Young, Benjamin, 1051, 1904
Young, Brook, 890
Young, Chas., 1602
Young, Dirickje Winne, 2137
Young, Dr. Joseph, 1042
Young, Elizabeth Mosser, 1176
Young, George, 890
Young, Guy, 2137
Young, John, 39, 149, 182, 313, 425, 528, 671, 862, 1132, 1308
Young, Mary S. White, 2122
Young, Peter, 1176
Young, Phil., 580
Young, Richard, 601
Young, Seth, 1051
Young, Shaw, 1630
Young, William, 313, 992, 1076, 1251, 1309
Younglove, Jno., 1192
Youngs, Abigail, 2147, 2149
Youngs, Abimail, 1261, 2030, 2073, 2142, 2151, 2156
Youngs, Benjamin, 884
Youngs, Bimuel, 711
Youngs, Birdsey, 718, 2142, 2149, 2151, 2156
Youngs, Henry, 2142, 2147, 2149
Youngs, Ruth, 2142
Youngs, Silas, 21, 2142, 2147
Youngs, Unis, 2147, 2149
Yourkse, Anne, 2146
Yourkse, Catrena, 2146
Yourkse, Harmen, 2146
Yourkse, Johannes, 2146
Yourkse, John, 2146
Yourkse, Mary, 2146
Yundl, Leonard, 887

Z

Zabriski, Albert C., 2161
Zabriski, Catherine, 2161
Zabriski, Jacob, 2161
Zabriski, John, 2161
Zabriski, John Lansing, 2161
Zabriski, Peter, 2161
Zabriski, Sarah, 2161
Zabriskie, Annatje, 2162
Zabriskie, Ino. Jost, 511
Zabriskie, John, 2162
Zabriskie, Peter, 2162
Zabrisky, Jno., 2161
Zebriska, Jane Goelet, 730
Zebriska, John, 730
Zebe, Christian, 1035
Zenger, Peter, 772
Zeubel, Henrich, 847
Zielen, Adam, 329
Zielen, Ally Conyn, 329
Zielen, Ariaentie, 329
Zuericher, Elisabeth, 2160
Zuericher, Hannah, 2160
Zuericher, Hans, 2160
Zuericher, Lodiwick, 2160
Zuericher, Magdalen, 2160
Zuericher, Molly, 2160
Zuericher, Nancy, 2160
Zufeldt, Jerge Jan, 1869
Zufeldt, Jury Adam, 493
Zufelt, George, 1421
Zuile, Francis, 1365